# ABRAHAM
# KUYPER

*Collected Works in Public Theology*

GENERAL EDITORS

JORDAN J. BALLOR

MELVIN FLIKKEMA

AbrahamKuyper.com

# COMMON GRACE

## GOD'S GIFTS FOR A FALLEN WORLD

Volume 1: The Historical Section

## ABRAHAM KUYPER

Edited by Jordan J. Ballor and Stephen J. Grabill

Translated by Nelson D. Kloosterman
and Ed M. van der Maas

Introduction by Richard J. Mouw

**LEXHAM PRESS**

**ACTON INSTITUTE**
FOR THE STUDY OF RELIGION AND LIBERTY

*Common Grace: God's Gifts for a Fallen World*
Volume 1: The Historical Section

Abraham Kuyper Collected Works in Public Theology

Lexham Press, 1313 Commercial St., Bellingham, WA 98225
LexhamPress.com

Originally published as *De Gemeene Gratie. Eerste Deel. Het Geschiedkundig Gedeelte.*© Boekhandel voorheen Höveker & Wormser, 1902.

This translation previously published by Christian's Library Press, an imprint of the Acton Institute for the Study of Religion & Liberty, 98 E. Fulton Street, Grand Rapids, MI, 49503.

Print ISBN 978-1-57-799653-8
Digital ISBN 978-1-57-799694-1

Translators: Nelson D. Kloosterman, Ed M. van der Maas
Acton Editorial: Jordan J. Ballor, Stephen J. Grabill, Timothy J. Beals,
    Paul J. Brinkerhoff, Eduardo J. Echeverria, Andrew M. McGinnis, Dylan Pahman
Lexham Editorial: Brannon Ellis, Abigail Stocker, Joel Wilcox
Cover Design: Christine Gerhart
Back Cover Design: Brittany Schrock
Typesetting: ProjectLuz.com

# CONTENTS

# GENERAL EDITORS' INTRODUCTION

In times of great upheaval and uncertainty, it is necessary to look to the past for resources to help us recognize and address our own contemporary challenges. While Scripture is foremost among these foundations, the thoughts and reflections of Christians throughout history also provide us with important guidance. Because of his unique gifts, experiences, and writings, Abraham Kuyper is an exemplary guide in these endeavors.

Kuyper (1837–1920) is a significant figure both in the history of the Netherlands and modern Protestant theology. A prolific intellectual, Kuyper founded a political party and a university, led the formation of a Reformed denomination and the movement to create Reformed elementary schools, and served as the prime minister of the Netherlands from 1901 to 1905. In connection with his work as a builder of institutions, Kuyper was also a prolific author. He wrote theological treatises, biblical and confessional studies, historical works, social and political commentary, and devotional materials.

Believing that Kuyper's work is a significant and underappreciated resource for Christian public witness, in 2011 a group of scholars interested in Kuyper's life and work formed the Abraham Kuyper Translation Society. The shared conviction of the society, along with the Acton Institute, Kuyper College, and other Abraham Kuyper scholars, is that Kuyper's works hold great potential to build intellectual capacity within the church in North America, Europe, and around the world. It is our hope that translation of his works into English will make his insights accessible to those seeking to grow and revitalize communities in the developed world as well as to those in the global south and east who are facing unique challenges and opportunities.

The church today—both locally and globally—needs the tools to construct a compelling and responsible public theology. The aim of this translation project is to provide those tools—we believe that Kuyper's unique insights can catalyze the development of a winsome and constructive Christian social witness and cultural engagement the world over.

In consultation and collaboration with these institutions and individual scholars, the Abraham Kuyper Translation Society developed this 12-volume translation project, the Abraham Kuyper Collected Works in Public Theology. This multivolume series collects in English translation Kuyper's writings and speeches from a variety of genres and contexts in his work as a theologian and statesman. In almost all cases, this set contains original works that have never before been translated into English. The series contains multivolume works as well as other volumes, including thematic anthologies.

The series includes a translation of Kuyper's *Our Program* (*Ons Program*), which sets forth Kuyper's attempt to frame a Christian political vision distinguished from the programs of the nineteenth-century Modernists who took their cues from the French Revolution. It was this document that launched Kuyper's career as a pastor, theologian, and educator. As James Bratt writes, "This comprehensive Program, which Kuyper crafted in the process of forming the Netherlands' first mass political party, brought the theology, the political theory, and the organization vision together brilliantly in a coherent set of policies that spoke directly to the needs of his day. For us it sets out the challenge of envisioning what might be an equivalent witness in our own day."

Also included is Kuyper's seminal three-volume work *De Gemeene Gratie*, or *Common Grace*, which presents a constructive public theology of cultural engagement rooted in the humanity Christians share with the rest of the world. Kuyper's presentation of common grace addresses a gap he recognized in the development of Reformed teaching on divine grace. After addressing particular grace and covenant grace in other writings, Kuyper here develops his articulation of a Reformed understanding of God's gifts that are common to all people after the fall into sin.

The series also contains Kuyper's three-volume work on the lordship of Christ, *Pro Rege*. These three volumes apply Kuyper's principles in *Common Grace*, providing guidance for how to live in a fallen world under Christ the King. Here the focus is on developing cultural institutions in a way that is consistent with the ordinances of creation that have been maintained and preserved, even if imperfectly so, through common grace.

The remaining volumes are thematic anthologies of Kuyper's writings and speeches gathered from the course of his long career.

The anthology *On Charity and Justice* includes a fresh and complete translation of Kuyper's "The Problem of Poverty," the landmark speech Kuyper gave at the opening of the First Christian Social Congress in Amsterdam in 1891. This important work was first translated into English in 1950 by Dirk Jellema; in 1991, a new edition by James Skillen was issued. This volume also contains other writings and speeches on subjects including charity, justice, wealth, and poverty.

The anthology *On Islam* contains English translations of significant pieces that Abraham Kuyper wrote about Islam, gathered from his reflections on a lengthy tour of the Mediterranean world. Kuyper's insights illustrate an instructive model for observing another faith and its cultural ramifications from an informed Christian perspective.

The anthology *On the Church* includes selections from Kuyper's doctrinal dissertation on the theologies of Reformation theologians John Calvin and John a Lasco. It also includes various treatises and sermons, such as "Rooted and Grounded," "Twofold Fatherland," and "Address on Missions."

The anthology *On Business and Economics* contains various meditations Kuyper wrote about the evils of the love of money as well as pieces that provide Kuyper's thoughts on stewardship, human trafficking, free trade, tariffs, child labor, work on the Sabbath, and business.

Finally, the anthology *On Education* includes Kuyper's important essay "Bound to the Word," which discusses what it means to be ruled by the Word of God in the entire world of human thought. Numerous other pieces are also included, resulting in a substantial English volume of Kuyper's thoughts on Christian education.

Collectively, this 12-volume series will, as Richard Mouw puts it, "give us a much-needed opportunity to absorb the insights of Abraham Kuyper about God's marvelous designs for human cultural life."

The Abraham Kuyper Translation Society along with the Acton Institute and Kuyper College gratefully acknowledge the Andreas Center for Reformed Scholarship and Service at Dordt College; Calvin College; Calvin Theological Seminary; Fuller Theological Seminary; Mid-America Reformed Seminary; Redeemer University College; Princeton Theological Seminary; and Southeastern Baptist Theological Seminary. Their financial support and partnership made these translations possible. The society is also grateful for the generous financial support of Dr. Rimmer and Ruth DeVries and the J. C. Huizenga family, which has enabled the translation and publication of these volumes.

This series is dedicated to Dr. Rimmer DeVries in recognition of his life's pursuits and enduring legacy as a cultural leader, economist, visionary, and faithful follower of Christ who reflects well the Kuyperian vision of Christ's lordship over all spheres of society.

Jordan J. Ballor
Melvin Flikkema

Grand Rapids, MI
August 2015

# EDITORS' INTRODUCTION

There is often a temptation, particularly among evangelicals, to engage in social reform without first developing a coherent social philosophy to guide the agenda. To bridge this gap, Acton Institute and the Abraham Kuyper Translation Society have worked together with other institutions to translate Abraham Kuyper's seminal three-volume work on common grace (*De gemeene gratie*). *Common Grace* was chosen because it holds great potential to build intellectual capacity within evangelicalism and because a sound grasp of this doctrine is missing in evangelical cultural engagement. *Common Grace* is the capstone of Kuyper's constructive public theology and the best available platform to draw evangelicals back to first principles and to guide the development of a winsome and constructive social witness.

Common grace, as Kuyper conceived it, was a theology of public responsibility and cultural engagement rooted in Christians' shared humanity with the rest of the world. Kuyper did not intend these volumes to be academic tomes. They were popular works—collections of newspaper articles written over a six-year period—in which he equipped common people with the teaching they needed to effectively enter public life. Kuyper neither politicized the gospel to accommodate his agenda nor did he encourage his followers to develop a siege mentality in isolation from the rest of the world. As Kuyper writes in his foreword to volume 1, "If the believer's God is at work in this world, then in this world the believer's hand must take hold of the plow, and the name of the Lord must be glorified in that activity as well." This project involves the complete translation of Abraham Kuyper's three volumes, totaling more than 1,700 pages.

One challenge in editing this translation of Abraham Kuyper's volumes on common grace was to meet the twofold requirements of scholarly accuracy and completeness, while also rendering the text as useful as possible for a nonspecialist audience. These volumes are based on the published versions of Kuyper's collected essays rather than on some other critical edition with the addition of a large scholarly reference apparatus. As such, this translation is not a substitute for direct academic research into the original source material itself. A significant purpose of this translation project is to render into accessible English primary source material that has been foundational both for positive constructive theology as well as for doctrinal controversy throughout the twentieth century. But the original genre of this work should not be overlooked. These were neither written nor published primarily as exercises in academic theology. Although the task of translating and editing requires scholarly sensitivities, the goal of this project is to produce a translation that will be as accessible as possible not only to a specialized audience of researchers, but also to interested pastors and laypersons.

With all this in mind, the additional editorial apparatus in these volumes has been kept as minimal as possible. Where Kuyper references particular historical events or figures that are likely to be unfamiliar to an Anglophone audience, we have provided some necessary context for Kuyper's remarks. In places where Kuyper refers to other works, we have attempted to provide some more detail about those sources in order to facilitate further research on Kuyper's arguments and train of thought. Given the nature of the source material, which originally appeared serially as newspaper articles, there is an unavoidable redundancy in places where Kuyper recapitulates his position, summarizes the flow of argument, and reorients the reader to the larger contours of the work. We have resisted the temptation to abridge the translation at various points, and thus the resulting translation is as faithful and complete a representation of the original text as possible.

Kuyper's unique voice resonates on these pages, and in an attempt to provide a translation faithful to the author's original intentions, we have retained as much of his particular, and sometimes even idiosyncratic, renderings as possible. Where Kuyper emphasizes words or phrases through italics in direct references to Scripture, for instance, that emphasis has been retained where it was clearly meaningful. Similar emphasis also commonly occurs throughout the main text itself in the original, but that formatting has been maintained in the English text only where that emphasis is meaningful and not simply distracting or spurious. Editorial interventions in the main text, most often making explicit a reference to Scripture that remained implicit in the original direct quotation, are enclosed in square brackets. In some cases, there were errors or inconsistencies in biblical references, arising in many instances from the difference in versification between the Dutch Bible and English versions. These have been updated and corrected to conform to standard English conventions. Likewise we have adjusted paragraph breaks and broken up some of Kuyper's longer sentences to enhance the readability of the text in English. One difficulty relating to the accessibility and format of these volumes on common grace involved the decision to number sections of chapters in this modern edition that were originally unnumbered. The hope is that this will enhance accessibility of the text for today's audience.

A key issue facing those working on translations is how best to render gender-specific references in the original into a different language. Wherever Kuyper's original intent clearly included both men and women, the translation has preferred a gender-inclusive English rendering. But this practice was not extended in cases where the original reference was more specific or where the resulting English translation would have suffered in terms of style or readability. In some instances, this approach requires understanding *man* inclusively to refer both to men and women. We have thus not imposed gender-inclusive language on to Kuyper's text, but rather have sought to provide a gender-accurate and accessible translation.

This choice is part of our response to a great challenge related to translating the corpus of Abraham Kuyper involving his views on race, gender, and society. Although there is much of timeless value to be found in his life and work, Kuyper was a man of his times, and writing at the end of the nineteenth and beginning of the twentieth centuries Kuyper had opinions about non-Europeans that are variously unsophisticated, crude, or downright offensive. Kuyper traffics in stereotypes about other peoples and viewed Europeans as greater inheritors of God's civilizational gifts. As James Bratt puts it in his biography of Kuyper, "In *Common Grace* Kuyper bluntly set the white race over the yellow and yellow over black, with red doomed to extinction in the wilds of North America. It was in his commentary on common grace and art that he deployed some of the most offensive rhetoric in his entire corpus."[1] Vincent Bacote, a Kuyper scholar and himself an African-American, has struggled with these problematic aspects of Kuyper's thought even as he finds much to be praiseworthy in the Dutch polymath. Bacote's fine introduction to *Wisdom & Wonder: Common Grace in Science & Art* is worth quoting here at length:

> It is not necessary to have total agreement with a person in order to admire them or find their contributions to be of great value. Some of Kuyper's specific views on science and art may not be embraced by all readers; while incredibly prescient regarding some developments in society, Kuyper was not omniscient, and at times ventured opinions we might find surprising. This may be most apparent in the comments regarding Africans and "primitive peoples" that appear in these discussions of science and art. Like many of his era, Kuyper regarded Africans as far behind other civilized people groups. While his theology emphasized the creation of all humans in the divine image and while his emphasis on cultural diversity (multiformity) encourages humility about the extent of our knowledge, these emphases did not lead him to proper regard for all humans. While this reveals that Kuyper had feet of clay, this is no warrant for disregarding the tremendous contribution of works such as his volumes on common grace. Instead, this helps all of us to sharpen our critical thinking abilities; we can critique Kuyper on race and gender while also recognizing that such statements are in fact peripheral to his argument.[2]

As editors, we have done our best to try to provide context for Kuyper's remarks without airbrushing them or playing down their problematic aspects. Achieving a balance between charity toward the author and justice

---

1. James D. Bratt, *Abraham Kuyper: Modern Calvinist, Christian Democrat* (Grand Rapids: Eerdmans, 2013), 200.
2. Vincent E. Bacote, "Introduction," in *Wisdom & Wonder: Common Grace in Science & Art*, ed. Jordan J. Ballor and Stephen J. Grabill, trans. Nelson D. Kloosterman (Bellingham, WA: Lexham Press, 2015).

toward the subject matter and his audience today is a significant challenge. We hope that instances where we have failed to do justice to the material in the notes will not be a stumbling block to appropriately critical appreciation of Kuyper's merits and understanding of his demerits today.

The editorial apparatus has been updated to conform to the *Chicago Manual of Style*, 16th ed. Kuyper's original references have been maintained, but where these were incomplete or provided as in-text citations, they have been dropped to footnotes and wherever possible the publication details have been updated and corrected. The opening formula *Note by the author*: identifies Kuyper's original footnotes. Throughout the text Kuyper refers to the classic Dutch translation of the Bible, the *Statenvertaling* (SV). The standard translation of choice for this project is the English Standard Version (ESV), and references to other translations or Kuyper's own paraphrases are noted throughout the text. Kuyper's quotations to works that appear in published English translation, such as Calvin's commentaries, have been adapted to conform to the published version wherever doing so does not obscure or alter Kuyper's argument. Likewise the references to various doctrinal standards, such as the Heidelberg Catechism, are based on the versions appearing in *Reformed Confessions of the 16th and 17th Centuries in English Translation*.[3]

As Richard Mouw rightly notes in his introduction to volume 1, the task remains for this material "to be interpreted in terms that are accessible to 'ordinary' Christians, by teachers, pastors, and other leaders in the faith community." The publication of these volumes on common grace is only the beginning of a much larger endeavor to responsibly assess and apply Kuyper's deep insights into the significance of the Christian faith for the contemporary world. It is our hope and prayer that these volumes on common grace will be a fruitful source of revitalization and reformation for Christian social thought and engagement in the Anglophone world and beyond.

Jordan J. Ballor
Stephen J. Grabill

---

3.  4 vols., ed. James T. Dennison Jr. (Grand Rapids: Reformation Heritage Books, 2008–14).

# VOLUME INTRODUCTION

## A COMPREHENSIVE THEOLOGY OF "COMMONNESS"

What does God think about French Impressionism? Or about the ethical teachings of Confucius in ancient China? Or about the courage shown by a Muslim mother who risks her life to save her son from a burning building?

Furthermore, what does God want *us* to think about those things? How do we answer those questions in ways that honor what the Bible teaches about the pervasive reality of human sinfulness in our fallen world?

These important volumes address those kinds of questions. Abraham Kuyper's extensive treatment of the doctrine of common grace has been around for more than a century, but it is now being made available for the first time in its entirety in an English translation. Kuyper had thought long and hard about how we as Christians can look for positive things in the culture around us, even when those things come to us from people who do not worship the God of the Scriptures.

Abraham Kuyper was one of the great Calvinist theologians of the nineteenth century. Calvinists typically do not have a reputation for offering positive assessments of the intellectual, artistic, and moral achievements of unregenerate people. One of the things people think of when they hear the word "Calvinism" is "total depravity." Kuyper was a good Calvinist, but he did not believe that this prohibited him from looking for truth, beauty, and goodness beyond the boundaries of the Christian community. So he developed a comprehensive theology of "commonness," a perspective that could provide a helpful framework for encouraging and enabling Christians to benefit from the efforts of unbelievers.

Kuyper's efforts will surely be helpful to contemporary Christians who share his Reformed theological commitments. But they can also help others who struggle with these concerns from different theological traditions. After all, it can be illuminating to see how someone who operates out of a theological framework that places a strong emphasis on human depravity can nonetheless develop a vibrant theology of active cultural engagement.

It is important to mention, in that regard, that this first volume is one of the products of a partnership between the Abraham Kuyper Translation Society and Acton Institute—the latter being an exciting forum that has been focusing on being a "safe haven" for creative dialogue about Protestant and Catholic social thought. This is a much-needed engagement, and those of us who care deeply about such matters are grateful for this and other fruits of those partnerships.

~~~~~~~~~~~~~~~~

Again, Kuyper does not reject the Reformed tradition's strong emphasis on the devastating consequences that resulted from humankind's fall into sin. Our shared sinfulness has put human beings in a condition of what is often described in the Reformed tradition as "ethical rebellion." This means that the turning of our wills against God—the decision of our first parents to succumb to the Serpent's invitation to "be like gods"—resulted in a desperate state. To quote the old formula, "In Adam's Fall / We sinned All."[1] Created to exercise a God-honoring dominion over the affairs of the creation, we chose instead to serve purposes that defied the Creator's design for human flourishing. And this decision resulted in the corruption of the totality of our being. Our rebellion has affected our capacity to think clearly about the basic issues of life, which means that all of our efforts—moral, political, economic, interpersonal, plus our interactions with the nonhuman creation—all of it exhibits the effects of our fallen state.

Kuyper not only accepted all of that; he made a point of featuring it in his overall theology. There is an antithesis, he taught, that runs through the entirety of human life and thought in our present world. Once we

---

1. The *New-England Primer* (Boston: Kneeland, 1727 [1690]), 5r.

have been taken hold of by the salvation that can only come by God's sovereign grace, our lives are meant to take a very different direction than the ways of fallen humanity. Salvation is meant to impact the totality of our lives: Our moral dealings, political perspectives, economic practices, and the ways in which we farm and create art and shape the patterns of our family lives. In all areas of human interaction we are to honor God's revealed will for his creation.

Calvinists, then, with their doctrine of total depravity, are clearly disposed to distrust the ways of fallen humanity. These pessimistic expectations, however, often run up against realities that do not conform to what our theology of human sinfulness might lead us to anticipate. We often find the church acting worse than we had expected and the world acting better. In their theological formulations, then, Calvinists have frequently found it necessary to introduce some qualifications into their theological perspectives on the capacities of unredeemed human beings. Kuyper took up that challenge of spelling out those qualifications with great dedication.

In setting out to develop a detailed theology of common grace, Kuyper did not see himself as introducing something brand new into the Calvinist way of viewing things. John Calvin himself had already taken up the task. The reformer of Geneva had started in developing his theology at the point where we would expect any good Calvinist to start—with a low estimation of the capacities of the unregenerate mind. In his classic work, the *Institutes of the Christian Religion*, for example, Calvin tells us that while we may come across occasional "sparks" of the light of creation shining through an unredeemed person's "perverted and degenerate nature," that original light is so "choked with dense ignorance ... that it cannot come forth effectively." The efforts of sinful humanity to find the truth, says Calvin, amount to little more than a "groping in the darkness."[2]

Having set forth clearly his view of the implications of his teaching on the effects of the fall, however, Calvin was not content simply to leave it there without some modifications. He was motivated to take some further steps because of his experiences before his conversion as a student studying law. In those studies he had come to admire the writings of some of the

---

2. *Inst.* 2.2.12.

ancient Graeco-Roman thinkers, especially Seneca. He was not inclined, after he had come to an evangelical faith in Christ, simply to change his assessment. This meant that he had to account for the fact that some of these unregenerate thinkers seemed capable of producing a little more than simply the occasional "spark" of truth.

So in the *Institutes*, Calvin admits that things are not quite as bleak as his straightforward affirmations of human depravity would suggest. God has not completely given the unredeemed human mind over to darkness. There are, he says, some "natural gifts" that are "by nature implanted in men" by God, and these gifts are "bestowed indiscriminately upon pious and impious"—a bestowal, he argues, that should be seen as a "peculiar grace of God."[3]

Furthermore, this gift is so significant that when we come across a truth set forth by an unbeliever, "we shall neither reject the truth itself, nor despise it wherever it shall appear, unless we wish to dishonor the Spirit of God."[4]

Subsequent Reformed theology continued to deal with these matters. Calvin's followers devoted much attention to issues of natural theology, general revelation, the image of God, and similar ways of accounting for a more positive assessment of the deliverances of the unredeemed mind, in a way that did not simply abandon Calvin's emphasis on the serious effects of human rebellion for human life and thought. In exploring these options, these thinkers attempted to be faithful to what they had learned from Calvin himself, who had insisted that whatever good we can get from our studies of pagan thinkers is not due to some area of their being that is untouched by sin. Rather, the positive contributions they continue to make are the result of divine "gifts," offered by a kind of "peculiar grace of God."

The ideas of "gifts" and "grace" in that kind of formulation are meant to highlight the fact of divine sovereignty. While our radical sinfulness poses a threat to the unfolding of God's creating purposes, the Creator still loves his creation, and in his sovereign goodness he will not allow human rebellion to bring great harm to that which he loves. God has ways of exercising restraints on depravity—a fallenness that, if left unchecked, would lead to creation's ruin. John Calvin put it this way: God keeps our sinful

---

3. *Inst.* 2.2.14.
4. *Inst.* 2.2.15.

strivings in check "by throwing a bridle over them ... that they may not break loose," especially when the Lord deems doing so "to be expedient to preserve all that is."[5]

~~~~~~~~~~~~~~~~~~~~~~~~~~~~~~~~~~~~~

This picture of a God who continues to love the creation and who expedites the means to restrain and preserve in the midst of human fallenness—this is the picture that Abraham Kuyper fleshes out in this wonderful treatise. And again, what Kuyper has to offer us on this subject has relevance far beyond the Calvinist community that would share his explicitly Reformed convictions. To be sure, non-Calvinists will have to forgive some of the "Calvinism-above-all" tone that frequently shows up in his writing. That offensive tone is all over the place, for example, in his 1898 Stone Lectures, delivered at Princeton Seminary, where he rails against Anabaptists, Lutherans, Catholics, and others. That combative tone, though, is less evident in this series on common grace, where he offers more ecumenical observations, particularly in his quite creative comments about the blessings afforded by the "pluriformity" of the church. Indeed, it would have been odd for Kuyper to show much negativity toward other Christian traditions in a work in which he is exploring the ways in which Christians can learn good things from the unbelieving world!

Again, then, this is a book that can help all of us as we struggle with new twenty-first century versions of the challenges that Kuyper takes up. For one thing, the need for a theology of human "commonness" should be attractive to all believers who worry about the fragmented conceptions of human realities that are so prevalent in our postmodern (or, if you wish, our post-postmodern) world. We are surrounded today by voices that deny—in practice if not also in theory—the existence of any metanarratives. Claims of deep reaching diversities abound: racial, ethnic, sexual, national, religious, and generational. Ironically, as the technological capacity for communication increases, the ability to understand each other often seems to be decreasing. All of this poses important theological challenges about an underlying commonness for those of us who believe that God's ultimate intention for his human creatures is not the curse of Babel

5. *Inst.* 2.3.3.

but the blessings of Pentecost. Kuyper's common grace theology can help to cast light on these matters.

And while Kuyper clearly operates out of a Reformed framework, his theology of common grace is not tied in any necessary manner to, say, specific doctrines about predestination and election. Indeed, many of the theological themes that Kuyper saw in his nineteenth-century context as comprising the unique property of Calvinism—concepts like covenant, kingdom, people of God, cultural discipleship—loom large in the contemporary vocabularies of a variety of Protestant and Catholic traditions.

What *is* foundational to Kuyper's presentation of common grace theology is a deep devotion to the notions of God's sovereignty and our obligation to participate in the divine call to be obedient to the lordship of Jesus Christ in all areas of life. And it is clear that many Christians these days—Wesleyans, Baptists, Lutherans, Catholics, Mennonites, and others beyond the boundaries of Reformed/Presbyterian life and thought—are looking for resources for equipping Christians to find alternatives to the various world-fleeing spiritualities that have long afflicted the broader Christian community.

~~~~~~~~~~~~~~~~~~

To use a present-day label for assessing personality types, Abraham Kuyper was an amazing—even compulsive—multitasker. He not only wrote in much detail about a variety of areas of Christian cultural engagement, but actually did a lot of that engagement himself. He was a member of his country's parliament, heading up the political party that he had created, and even serving for a few years as the nation's prime minister. He taught and administered at the university he established. He wrote regularly for the newspaper he had founded. He spoke regularly to groups of farmers, at labor union conventions, and to artists' guilds.

And he was a churchman. This is important to emphasize in thinking about his career, because very often people who have attempted to carry out his vision in a variety of cultural spheres have not paid as much attention to the church as Kuyper would have insisted upon. If he sometimes in his writings seemed to treat the church as simply one among many spheres, it was because he took the realities of the church and its mission so seriously that it was always assumed in all that he said about God's plan for the creation.

More specifically, Kuyper saw the church as the area in which "particular grace" functioned in a very special way. Kuyper knew the transforming power of saving grace in an intensely personal way. He had been trained, in his theological studies at the great University of Leiden, in the emerging liberal theology of the day, and had begun his ministry as a proponent of that theological perspective. But through the testimony of some very ordinary folks in his first parish, laity who met in their own homes for prayer and Bible study, he came to experience what he later described as "a blessing for my heart, the rise of the morning star in my life."[6] After that, the church's proclamation that human beings are sinners desperately in need of God's gracious offer of salvation through the atoning work of Christ was a concept always central to his life and thought.

So for Kuyper, common grace always had to be seen in its vital relationship to God's sovereign and gracious workings both in the church and in the larger world. The church is where God's renewing purposes, both for individuals and the creation, are openly revealed and taught about in the light of biblical revelation. But God is also at work in the broader human community. Common grace is a key force for this larger renewing mission.

Thinkers who find much that is helpful in Kuyper's common grace theology have still wondered at times whether it is helpful to call this phenomenon a kind of grace. As we noted earlier, John Calvin himself employed that concept, in suggesting that the insights offered by pagan writers were the result of a "peculiar grace." Like Calvin, Kuyper did not limit the operations of divine grace to God's saving activity, using instead the broader understanding of grace as *unmerited favor*.[7] In that sense of grace, the very air we breathe is an undeserved gift from God, as is recognized in the hymn writer's prayerful confession: "I'll love thee ... and praise thee as long as thou lendest me breath."[8]

The good things that come forth from the unredeemed portion of humankind, then, are not to be attributed to a capacity of fallen human beings to produce meritorious works on their own. They flow from God's own sovereign choices to fulfill his purpose for the creation. This is why

---

6. Quoted in Louis Praamsma, *Let Christ Be King: Reflections on the Life and Times of Abraham Kuyper* (Jordan Station, ON: Paideia, 1985), 49.
7. For a statement from Kuyper about this terminology, see appendix, "Why the Term 'Common' Grace?"
8. "My Jesus, I Love Thee," words by William R. Featherstone (ca. 1862), music by Adoniram J. Gordon (1876). First published in the *London Hymn Book* (1864).

Kuyper's common grace has to be clearly distinguished from the notion of prevenient grace that shows up in a number of traditions, particularly Wesleyanism and Roman Catholicism. From Kuyper's perspective, prevenient grace is a way of downplaying the extent of human depravity by positing a kind of automatic universal upgrade of those dimensions of human nature that have been corrupted by sin. To put it much too simply, the goal of prevenient grace is the upgrade; it is to raise the deeply wounded human capacities to a level where some measure of freedom to choose or reject obedience to God is made possible. Common grace, on the other hand, is for Kuyper a divine strategy for bringing the cultural designs of God to completion. Common grace operates mysteriously in the life of, say, a Chinese government official or an unbelieving artist to harness their created talents to prepare the creation for the full coming of the kingdom. In this sense, the operations of common grace—unlike those of prevenient grace—always have a goal-directed ad hoc character.

In discussing various examples of common grace, Kuyper distinguishes between the ways in which God operates both internally and externally in the lives of unbelievers. The internal aspect of these operations is both a risky topic and an important one. It is risky because Kuyper does not want in any way to suggest that common grace transforms human hearts in the way that particular grace surely does. God works mysteriously in, for example, the artistic efforts of a Picasso, without doing anything to the painter's inner life that might approximate a kind of regeneration of his heart.

But the internal side of things is still an important feature of Kuyper's insights regarding common grace. Many in the Reformed tradition who have made use of his common grace theology have focused exclusively on matters that can easily be characterized as external workings of God in the lives of the unregenerate. A classic example is the 1924 statement issued by the Christian Reformed denomination, with its "three points of common grace." That church's synod, drawing directly on Kuyper's theology, affirmed that there is indeed a kind of nonsalvific attitude of divine favor toward all human beings that manifests itself in these three ways: (1) the bestowal of natural gifts, such as rain and sunshine, on creatures in general; (2) the restraining of sin in human affairs, so that the unredeemed do not produce all of the evil that their depraved natures might otherwise bring about; and (3) the ability of unbelievers to perform acts of civic good.[9]

Those points certainly fit clearly into Kuyper's common grace theology. They do, however, have the kind of purely external character that could lead us to attribute them, not necessarily to actions motivated by a divine favor toward unbelievers, but simply to a traditional understanding of divine providence, where God in his own mysterious manner uses the actions of sinful people to further his own unfolding plan for the creation without bestowing any real gifts on them in the process. And that is exactly the interpretation offered by the opponents of Kuyper's common grace theology within the Reformed tradition.[10]

The fact is, however, that Kuyper goes further than those examples of common grace that lend themselves easily to a more providential interpretation, and in doing so he does point to phenomena that have an internal character. In addition to the purely external operations, he says, common grace is at work "everywhere that civic righteousness, family loyalty, natural love, human virtue, the development of public conscience, integrity, fidelity among people, and an inclination toward piety permeates life."[11] These are precisely the features that point us to the internal lives of, say, the virtuous Confucian and the courageous Muslim mother.

~~~~~~~~~~~~~~~~~~~~~~~

Kuyper obviously has much to offer us in our attempts to engage the larger patterns and processes of cultural life. But here is a basic question: What is the real *point* of this engagement? If Kuyper is right that God wants us to take all of this seriously, why is this so important to God?

To answer these questions we need to pay attention to two aspects of his theology that do not often show up in other theological explorations of culture matters: his theological views about the original creation and about the end of time.

---

9. See the Christian Reformed Church's position statement on Common Grace, available at http://www.crcna.org/welcome/beliefs/position-statements/common-grace.

10. See Herman Hoeksema, *The Protestant Reformed Churches in America: Their Origin, Early History and Doctrine* (Grand Rapids: First Protestant Reformed Church, 1936). Hoeksema's book provides the texts of numerous documents dealing with debates about common grace in the Dutch Calvinist community, as well as his own extensive case against Kuyper's theology.

11. *CG* 1.61.6, p. 539–40.

Kuyper is arguably the most prominent proponent of the idea of a cultural mandate issued by God to human beings in the first chapter of Genesis. God programmed cultural formation into the original creation. When the Lord told the first human pair to "be fruitful and multiply," he was surely talking about procreation, but when he went on to instruct them to "fill the earth and subdue it, and have dominion" over it (Gen 1:28), he was referring to something more, the filling of the Garden with the products and processes of cultural activity. As they began to fashion tools, work schedules, and patterns of interaction, Adam and Eve would be adding to the original contents of the creation, and eventually, even without the appearance of sin, the Garden would become a city, an arena of complex spheres of cultural interaction. In that sense, not only the family, but also art, science, technology, politics (as the collective patterns of decision making), recreation, and the like were all programmed into the original creation in order to display different patterns of cultural flourishing. God wanted artists to bring aesthetic excellence to the creation and scholars to advance the cause of knowledge. Economic activity would foster stewardship, while politics would promote justice.

Needless to say, all of this was deeply affected by the fall into sin. But the capacity for cultural formation was not lost in fallen humanity. Scarred, yes, and even seriously distorted and corrupted. But the impulse toward cultural activity deeply implanted in human beings by God continues. And common grace sees to it that good things are produced, even where rebellious human spirits are in charge.

God *preserves*, then, the patterns of cultural formation that he desires for the creation. For Kuyper, though, it is not only about preservation. Common grace is a means by which God *prepares*. Common grace aims at that which is yet to come. To acknowledge, for Kuyper, that God cares about art, athletics, education, business, politics, and entertainment is to acknowledge also that God will not ever give up on these areas of human cultural achievement. All that has been accomplished in human history in promoting truth, beauty, goodness, justice, stewardship, even that which has flourished in contexts where the name of Jesus has not been lifted up—all of this will be revealed in the end time as counting toward the coming of his kingdom. To be sure, much of it will need a final cleansing, a purging of all that falls short of the full glorifying of God. But it will be gathered in.

Kuyper had a strong interest in eschatology. He was convinced that the works of culture would be gathered into the holy city when it descends from the heavens as the new Jerusalem. His younger colleague Herman Bavinck had argued that there is a collective sense of the divine image that "is not a static entity but extends and unfolds itself" in the rich diversity of cultures, and that this image will be revealed in the end time when redeemed people from many cultures will enter the holy city—and here Bavinck quotes from the book of Revelation's final vision—to "bring into [the city] the glory and the honor of the nations" (Rev 21:26).[12]

Kuyper held to the same perspective. He actually wrote a commentary on the book of Revelation, and as he focuses on that same final vision, he argues that in that city, "The whole reborn humanity stands before God as a holy unity that is athrob with life," and this fully redeemed humanity "does not remain on its knees in uninterrupted worship of God," but it also engages in "new callings, new life-tasks, new commissions." The life of the future age *will be a full human life* which will exhibit all the glory that God in the first creation had purposed and appointed for the same, but which by us was sinned away."[13]

This is a vision that, rightly understood, gives us hope in our daily efforts to serve the Lord, the kind of hope described so nicely in more recent years by the great twentieth-century missionary-theologian Lesslie Newbigin:

> We can commit ourselves without reserve to all the secular work our shared humanity requires of us, knowing that nothing we do in itself is good enough to form part of that [heavenly] city's building, knowing that everything—from our most secret prayers to our most public political acts—is part of that sin-stained human nature that must go down into the valley of death and judgment, and yet knowing that as we offer it up to the Father in the name of Christ and in the power of the Spirit, it is safe with him and—purged in fire—it will find its place in the holy city at the end.[14]

---

12. *RD* 2:577–78.
13. Abraham Kuyper, *The Revelation of St. John*, trans. John Hendrik De Vries (Grand Rapids: Eerdmans, 1935), 331–32.
14. Lesslie Newbigin, *Foolishness to the Greeks: The Gospel and Western Culture* (Grand Rapids: Eerdmans, 1986), 136.

Kuyper was an activist who often did his theology on the run, with an eye to the very real practical challenges that he faced as a Christian leader in public life. That is one of the strengths of this book. While Kuyper probes some theological issues quite deeply, it is always out of an urgent concern to promote the cause of Christ's kingdom.

If some Christians in the English-speaking world only know one thing about Kuyper, it is likely his oft-quoted manifesto: "There is not a square inch in the whole domain of our human existence over which Christ, who is Sovereign over *all*, does not cry: 'Mine!' "[15] That simple but profound affirmation of Christ's supreme lordship over all of creation—including what human beings are commissioned by God to add to the creation in their cultural engagements—has to be seen as what undergirds Kuyper's theology of common grace. Christ rules over all—that is basic. But we also need the theology of common grace as a practical fleshing out of how we can best understand the implications of our affirmation of Christ's lordship.

What Kuyper offers us in these volumes is a perspective that can equip present-day Christians to engage in our own on the run involvements in daily life, with an overall perspective that is solidly grounded in God's revealed Word. Not all Christians today, of course, will have the patience or the technical understanding to make their way through the pages of this book or the volumes that follow. It needs to be interpreted in terms that are accessible to ordinary Christians, by teachers, pastors, and other leaders in the faith community. The encouragement and inspiration for doing so can come from the example of Kuyper himself. He was well known in his day as a much-admired champion of "the little people" (in Dutch, *de kleine luyden*) in the Christian community. Those folks had not mastered the texts he had authored, but they did catch his vision, putting it into practice in farming, labor, business, politics, education, family life, and the arts.

That is the kind of putting into practice that is much needed in our own time. This will not happen effectively if we simply repeat Kuyper's strategies for practical implementations of the cultural mandate. There is much, of course, in his also well-known doctrine of sphere sovereignty

---

15. Abraham Kuyper, "Sphere Sovereignty" (inaugural address at the founding of the Free University of Amsterdam, October 20, 1880), in *AKCR*, 488.

that speaks clearly to the issues of our own day. But we need to look for new ways to breathe life into the idea that Christians are obliged to seek out uniquely God-honoring patterns of involvement in all of the spheres of cultural interaction.

All of this calls for the kind of discernment that is grounded not only in solid theological reflection, but also in a communal seeking of the guidance of the Holy Spirit through prayer, mutual correction, and the recovery of a variety of other spiritual practices that have strengthened God's people for kingdom service in the past.

And—to draw directly on an important element in common grace theology—this will mean openness to accepting truth, goodness, beauty, and justice wherever we find it. But this openness must always be accompanied by an awareness of the dreadful reality of the antithesis, the fundamental opposition between the ways of our shared rebellion and the sanctified desire to serve the Lord in all dimensions of our lives.

This book and its subsequent volumes in the series give us a much needed opportunity to absorb the insights of Abraham Kuyper about God's marvelous designs for human cultural life.

Richard J. Mouw

# ABBREVIATIONS

## GENERAL AND BIBLIOGRAPHIC

AKB      Kuipers, Tjitze. *Abraham Kuyper: An Annotated Bibliography 1857–2010*. Translated by Clifford Anderson and Dagmare Houniet. Brill's Series in Church History 55. Leiden: Brill, 2011.

AKCR      *Abraham Kuyper: A Centennial Reader*. Edited by James D. Bratt. Grand Rapids: Eerdmans, 1998.

CCS      Calvin, John. *Calvin's Commentaries Series*. 45 vols. Edinburgh: Calvin Translation Society, 1844–56.

CE      *The Catholic Encyclopedia*. Edited by Charles G. Herbermann, Edward A. Pace, Condé B. Pallen, Thomas J. Shahan, and John J. Wynne. 15 vols. New York: Robert Appleton, 1907–12.

CG      Kuyper, Abraham. *Common Grace*. Translated by Nelson D. Kloosterman and Ed M. van der Maas. Edited by Jordan J. Ballor and Stephen J. Grabill. 3 vols. Bellingham, WA: Lexham Press, 2015–.

CO      Calvin, John. *Ioannis Calvini Opera Quae Supersunt Omnia*. Edited by Guilielmus Baum, Eduardus Cunitz, and Eduardus Reuss. 59 vols. Corpus Reformatorum, 2nd ser., 29–87. Brunswick: Schwetschke, 1863–1900.

DLGTT      Muller, Richard A. *Dictionary of Latin and Greek Theological Terms*. Grand Rapids: Baker, 1996.

ESV      English Standard Version

| | |
|---|---|
| *Inst.* | Calvin, John. *Institutes of the Christian Religion* (1559). 2 vols. Edited by John T. McNeill. Translated by Ford Lewis Battles. Philadelphia: Westminster, 1960. |
| KJV | King James Version |
| *LW* | Luther, Martin. *Luther's Works.* 55 vols. American ed. Edited by Jaroslav Pelikan and Helmut T. Lehmann. Saint Louis: Concordia; Philadelphia: Fortress, 1955–86. |
| LXX | Septuagint (Greek translation of the OT) |
| NIV | New International Version |
| *NSHE* | *The New Schaff-Herzog Encyclopedia of Religious Knowledge.* 13 vols. Edited by Samuel Macauley Jackson. Grand Rapids: Baker, 1949–50. Originally published in 12 vols., 1908–12. |
| NT | New Testament |
| OT | Old Testament |
| *PRRD* | Muller, Richard A. *Post-Reformation Reformed Dogmatics.* 4 vols. Grand Rapids: Baker, 2003. |
| *RD* | Bavinck, Herman. *Reformed Dogmatics.* 4 vols. Translated by John Vriend. Edited by John Bolt. Grand Rapids: Baker, 2003–8. |
| SV | *Statenvertaling* ("States Translation" of the Dutch Bible, 1637) |

## OLD TESTAMENT

| | |
|---|---|
| Gen | Genesis |
| Exod | Exodus |
| Lev | Leviticus |
| Num | Numbers |
| Deut | Deuteronomy |
| Josh | Joshua |
| Judg | Judges |
| Ruth | Ruth |
| 1–2 Sam | 1–2 Samuel |
| 1–2 Kgs | 1–2 Kings |
| 1–2 Chr | 1–2 Chronicles |
| Ezra | Ezra |
| Neh | Nehemiah |
| Esth | Esther |
| Job | Job |
| Psa (Pss) | Psalm(s) |

| | |
|---|---|
| Prov | Proverbs |
| Eccl | Ecclesiastes |
| Song | Song of Songs |
| Isa | Isaiah |
| Jer | Jeremiah |
| Lam | Lamentations |
| Ezek | Ezekiel |
| Dan | Daniel |
| Hos | Hosea |
| Joel | Joel |
| Amos | Amos |
| Obad | Obadiah |
| Jonah | Jonah |
| Mic | Micah |
| Nah | Nahum |
| Hab | Habakkuk |
| Zeph | Zephaniah |
| Hag | Haggai |
| Zech | Zechariah |
| Mal | Malachi |

## NEW TESTAMENT

| | |
|---|---|
| Matt | Matthew |
| Mark | Mark |
| Luke | Luke |
| John | John |
| Acts | Acts |
| Rom | Romans |
| 1-2 Cor | 1-2 Corinthians |
| Gal | Galatians |
| Eph | Ephesians |
| Phil | Philippians |
| Col | Colossians |
| 1-2 Thess | 1-2 Thessalonians |
| 1-2 Tim | 1-2 Timothy |
| Titus | Titus |
| Phlm | Philemon |
| Heb | Hebrews |

| | |
|---|---|
| Jas | James |
| 1–2 Pet | 1–2 Peter |
| 1–3 John | 1–3 John |
| Jude | Jude |
| Rev | Revelation |

## OTHER ANCIENT WRITINGS

| | |
|---|---|
| *b. Sanh.* | *Babylonian Sanhedrin* (Talmudic Tractate) |

# PREFACE

The Reformed paradigm has suffered no damage greater than its deficient development of the doctrine of common grace.

The cause for this deficiency was the struggle to preserve its hard-won position, a tireless battle with pen and sword. Wrestling to dislodge the ecclesiastical monopoly of Rome required such incredible effort in France, the Netherlands, and Scotland. In addition, the Anabaptist movement arose in Western Europe, while Northern and Eastern Europe periodically faced the extremely hostile opposition of Lutheranism, as well as Arminian and Erastian agitation in our own land.[1]

---

1. In general, Kuyper uses the term "Anabaptism" to refer to a manner of dealing with the problem of the relation of the Christian and the world, a position that expresses an excessive spiritualization, a version of otherworldly Christianity that is aversive to the world or culture. Historically, "the name 'Anabaptists' (meaning 'Rebaptizers') was given by their opponents to a party among the Protestants in Reformation times whose distinguishing tenet was opposition to infant baptism, which they held to be unscriptural and therefore not true baptism." See "Anabaptist," in *NSHE* 1:161. The term "Arminianism" derives from the Dutch theologian Jacobus Arminius (1560–1609) and refers to his understanding of the relationship between predestination, grace, and atonement in salvation. Among other things, Arminius "taught conditional predestination," and "his followers expressed their convictions in the famous five articles which they laid before the States as their justification. Called Remonstrants from these *Remonstrantiæ*, they always refused to be called Arminians." See "Arminius, Jacobus and Arminianism," in *NSHE* 1:297. Among other things, Kuyper associates Arminianism with a more optimistic view of human capability after the fall than that of orthodox Reformed teaching. "Erastianism" refers to the conception of church-state relations associated with

This is how, already in its earliest decades, Reformed ecclesiastical, political, and intellectual life came under severe pressure after its remarkably quick blossoming. When finally, by their stout resistance, Reformed people in the Netherlands and in Scotland had secured their freedom of existence, their robust strength was exhausted. Along with their success came a sense of ease that enervated them and diluted any ardor for pursuing the ideal. This explains why all their doctrinal energy was initially concentrated on endless polemic, leading ultimately to endless repetition of doctrinal platitudes.

After 1650, little doctrinal development occurred, either in Switzerland, the Netherlands, or Scotland. After the earliest flowering of Reformed life, not one original talent blossomed in the doctrinal field. The stream of Reformed thinking that had once flowed so freshly across the plains of religious thought dried up. What had begun earlier with breadth and vastness withered into narrow-minded, truly byzantine investigation, the kind of inspection that lacks even the resilience to go back to the root of the Reformed idea. With their narrowness, people were simply repristinating their well-worn polemic against Arminianism, hardly noticing any of the new challenges that have arisen. In this way the connection with the past was lost, and people became isolated from the ethos of their own time. This explains why there has been hardly any influence on the present era. People have quarantined themselves within their own circle, positioning themselves beyond reach of the forces driving cultural life. All the while, the barrenness of hairsplitting within their own ranks has awakened a reaction within their hearts. In various quarters the opposition toward all such intellectualistic biblical learnedness could no longer be averted, and resulted in disjoining what, in the sixteenth century, had been unified.

At the present time a change has occurred in this regard, among us at least. Historical investigation into the Reformed foundation has been reawakened, with the result that people have discovered this memorable truth: initially Reformed people had emphasized various principles that they had developed broadly and logically, looking very much like an all-embracing worldview, one that possessed enough flexibility to

---

Swiss Reformed physician and theologian Thomas Erastus (1524–83): "Since that time the doctrine of state supremacy in ecclesiastical causes generally goes under the name of Erastianism; though in its broad sense and wide application this doctrine is by no means due to Erastus or in accord with his views." See "Erastus, Thomas, Erastianism," in *NSHE* 4:167.

determine our own internal attitude amid the contemporary generation in this century.[2]

What had seemed initially to offer merely historical value acquired significance as being intensely relevant for today. In addition, the pressing question arose concerning the relationship between the Christian life, as we understood it, and the life of the world in all of its manifestation and diversity. How could we restore our influence on this common life, an influence that at one time had extended so widely but regrettably had later been lost? The answer to that question would not arise from a process of give-and-take, but had to be derived from the Reformed paradigm itself. An investigation had to be launched regarding what creative idea had originally governed Reformed people in their relationship to the non-Christian world, a study every bit as practical as it was theoretical.

Every Anabaptist sect had systematically isolated itself from the world. In opposition to this, Reformed people had chosen as their guiding principle the apostolic notion that "all things are yours ... and you are Christ's" (1 Cor 3:21, 23), and had self-consciously invested themselves, with unusual talent and surpassing resilience, into the full range of human living amid the tumult of the nations. This defining character trait, standing out prominently in the history of all of Western Europe, could not have been accidental. The explanation for this character trait was to be found in its comprehensive and dominant foundational conviction. Accordingly, the identity of this governing foundational idea had to be investigated.

This investigation showed with immediate and indisputable clarity that this foundational idea consisted in the doctrine of common grace, an idea deduced directly from the sovereignty of the Lord, a doctrine that is and remains the root conviction for all Reformed people. If God is sovereign, then his lordship *must* extend over *all* of life, and it cannot be restricted to the walls of the church or within the Christian orbit. The non-Christian world has not been handed over to Satan, nor surrendered to fallen humanity, nor consigned to fate. God's sovereignty is great and all-dominating in the life of that unbaptized world as well. Therefore

---

2. The concept of worldview, or life- and worldview, and even "life-system," which is the term Kuyper favors in his 1898 Princeton Stone Lectures, refers to an all-embracing worldview that takes as its starting-point "the three fundamental relations of all human existence: namely, our relation to *God*, to *man*, and to the *world*." See "Calvinism a Life-System," in *Lectures on Calvinism* (Grand Rapids: Eerdmans, 1931), 31.

Christ's church on earth and God's children cannot simply retreat from this life. If the believer's God is at work in this world, then in this world the believer's hand must take hold of the plow, and the name of the Lord must be glorified in that activity as well.

Therefore everything came down to resuscitating the rich foundational idea embodied in the doctrine of common grace.

Precise formulation of this doctrine could occur only after all the historical and doctrinal material relevant to this doctrine had first been carefully assembled and organized in terms of the Reformed paradigm. I have tried to the best of my ability to perform such a task in this work on common grace, offered in these volumes to Reformed churches around the world. A comprehensive and well-ordered presentation of the material was most important in this regard. What needed to become apparent was just how extensive this Reformed foundational conviction is, extending across the whole of human living.

Therefore I have divided the material into three sections. In the first section, common grace in its origin and operation must be objectively demonstrated. In the second section, theological reflection must focus on this subject, so that what has earlier been identified in its substance needs now to be illuminated doctrinally. Finally, in the third or practical section, we must bring to light the significance of this doctrine for living.

Spiritual isolation and ecclesiastical isolation are equally anti-Reformed. This work will have achieved the goal I have envisioned only when it ends such isolation without, God forbid, tempting believers to lose themselves in that world, a world that may not hold dominion over us, but rather a world within which we in the power of God must exercise dominion.

Abraham Kuyper

August 1, 1902

# CHAPTER ONE

# INTRODUCTION

*When God's patience waited in the days of Noah.*

1 PETER 3:20A

With its appearance in 1878, the initial summons to duty that *De Heraut* §1
sounded throughout our country once again bore witness to our people
regarding the Calvinistic confession of our ancestors, namely, *that grace is
particular.*[1] From then on the struggle to restore Reformed truth has been
ongoing. We thank the Lord, to whom all glory belongs, that fifteen years
after engaging in this battle, our struggle has achieved its goal. The par-
ticularity of grace, this bastion of our defense, at one time so threatened,
is safe once again. In recapturing *the particular character of grace,* we re-
captured the heart of our Reformed confession, which finds its necessary
background in the *doctrine of the covenant,* and still further back, in the
doctrine of *common grace.*[2]

---

1.  The first issue of *De Heraut* appeared on December 7, 1877. For more on the estab-
    lishment of *De Heraut* by Kuyper as a paper focused on ecclesiastical, as opposed to
    political, matters, see *AKB,* 1877.05, p. 95.
2.  Kuyper writes that "two aspects must be distinguished in [the] manifestation of
    grace: (1) a *saving* grace that ultimately cancels sin and completely neutralizes its
    consequences; and (2) a *temporarily restraining* grace that stems and arrests the
    continued effect of sin. The former, saving grace, is by the nature of things *partic-
    ular* and is connected with the elect of God. The latter is *common* and covers the en-
    tire sphere of our human life. Here the question arises whether these two forms of
    grace, this *particular* grace and this *common* grace, stand disconnected side by side,

Particular grace deals with the *individual*, the *person* to be saved, with the *individual* entering glory. And with this individual, as child of God, we cannot wrap the golden chain of redemption around his soul unless that golden chain descends from personal, sovereign *election*.

For that reason, the almighty sovereignty of God, who elects whom he will and rejects those to whom he does not show mercy, remains the heart of the church, the *cor ecclesiae*, which the Reformed churches must hold firmly until the return of the Lord. The consequence of forsaking this truth would be their vanishing from the earth, even prior to the *Maranatha*.[3] This doctrine is and remains, therefore, the heart of our confession. This is the testimony that, on the authority of God's Word, sealed by our personal experience, we shout aloud for all to hear: *grace is particular.*

Nevertheless, that same child of God is something other than an isolated individual limited to himself. This individual is also part of a *community*, member of a *body*, participant in a *group identity*, enclosed within an *organism*. The *doctrine of the covenant* emphasizes and does justice to this truth.

Without the doctrine of the *covenant*, the doctrine of *election* is mutilated, and the frightening lack of the assurance of faith is the valid punishment resulting from this mutilation of the truth. If separated from the confession of the covenant, election in isolation attempts to take hold of the Holy Spirit without honoring God the Son. The Third Person in the Trinity does not allow that violation of the honor of the Second Person. Christ himself testified that the Holy Spirit "will take *what is mine* and declare it to you" [John 16:14]. Anyone who presumes to trample upon this divine ordinance will not escape the severe anguish with which this unshakeable ordinance wreaks its misery of soul.

Therefore, in Holy Scripture this sovereign, personal election never appears in any other manner but within the context of *covenant grace*. The *individual*, this *single soul*, must experience being incorporated into the *community* of the saints. We are elected personally, but together we are

---

or rather function in mutual connectedness and if so, how." *CG* 1.30.1. For a classic analysis of the relation between special and common grace in Kuyper's thought, see S. U. Zuidema, "Common Grace and Christian Action in Abraham Kuyper," in *Communication and Confrontation* (Kampen: Kok, 1972), 52–105.

3. *Maranatha* is a transliteration of an Aramaic expression that appears in 1 Cor 16:22, and which is usually rendered as a request, "Our Lord, come!" In Kuyper's usage the phrase often refers to the fulfillment of this plea, Christ's second coming.

branches of the one Vine, members of the same body. For that reason, the confession of particular, personal grace is untrue and unscriptural unless it arises within the context of the *covenant*.

However, this is not the end of the matter.

The divine *covenant* in the Mediator in turn has its background in the work of original *creation*, in the existence of the *world*, and in the life of our *human race*. As *individuals* God's children belong to the *community* of the saints. But that community of saints also consists of the children of *men*, born of a woman by the will of man. Consequently they are interwoven and interconnected with all of human living that originated in paradise and continues in its misshapen form even after humanity's fall from God.

Neither our election nor our attachment to the *community* of saints negates our common *humanity*, nor removes our participation in the life of family, homeland, or world.

Therefore, we need to consider not two, but three aspects: first, our *personal* life; second, our incorporation into the *body* of Christ; and third, our existence as *human beings* (that is, our origin by *human birth*, our membership in the *human race*).

These three aspects, which our Heidelberg Catechism distinguishes as radiating from God's triune being, are differentiated in the following way.[4]

First, concerning *God the Holy Spirit* and our sanctification, it refers to the powerfully personal aspect in God's dealing with his child. For the first time, in that sanctification one's personal election becomes a certainty.

Second, concerning *God the Son* and our redemption, we confess the *covenant of grace*, of the Head of the *body*, of the one and only blood through which we find *complete* reconciliation.

And then third, concerning *God the Father* and our creation, we confess that our origin is in paradise, our ascent from natural life, our interconnection as *human beings* in the life of our *human race*.

Naturally, here the Catechism takes the order, the sequence, in reverse, for it began with our creation, and in this way at the same time proceeds according to the sacred order within the divine Being: first the Father, then the Son, eternally begotten of the Father, and thereafter the Holy Spirit, eternally proceeding from the Father and the Son.

---

4. The Heidelberg Catechism (1563) is one of the Reformed confessions that belong to the Three Forms of Unity of various Reformed denominations, the other two confessions being the Belgic Confession of Faith (1561) and the Canons of Dort (1618–19).

Thus the Catechism treats first *our creation*, then our *redemption*, and finally our *sanctification*. But in the understanding of God's child, who looks within and reflects on the progress of the soul's life, and consequently calculates from that point where he now stands, the course presented by experience and recollection is just the opposite. The child of God acknowledges God the Holy Spirit, who assures the believer of his personal election, thereby acknowledging that *grace is particular*. In none but Christ alone, however, does the believer find that assurance of faith, realizing that he is a member of the body, in the community of the saints, and in this way the glory of *the covenant* rises up before him.

Even with this, the matter is not yet finished, however.

Regarding that covenant, God's child looks backward to his origin, to his birth, to his ancestry, to the world in which he walks about as a human being. In so doing, he arrives at that *third* confession, not only that grace is particular, and that this particular grace lies entwined in the bonds of the covenant, but also that God was present before and after his creation, such that by God's own hand he has been skillfully and wonderfully knit together in his mother's womb [see Psa 139:13–14]

This is what it means to confess *God the Father*; and with a voice louder than ever before, this boast of faith resonates from the lips of every believer: "I am elect, I am in Christ, and only for that reason do I believe deeply and fully in God the Father, the Almighty, Creator of heaven and earth, Creator of my being, both body and soul."

§ 2    Even so, something is still missing here.

Between the creation glory in paradise and one's own birth lies *the fall*, and thereby a shadow of death rests upon that world and on that human life in that world, and on one's interaction with that world estranged from God. The line of grace seems to be broken. In one's *personal* election, that *grace* is particular; that *grace* is working organically in the *covenant*; but in the third place, that *grace* encounters the broken and violated creation. The line does not seem to continue.

For that reason, *covenant grace* must come to expand into *particular grace*, but behind covenant grace there is yet a third phenomenon expanding into covenant grace, namely, *common grace*.

So we find three emanations of God's grace: a grace that applies to you *personally*, then a grace that you have in common with *all God's saints* in the covenant, but also thirdly, a grace of God that you as a human being have in common *with all people*.

There is nothing in this that does not glorify God. Your personal salvation is entirely the fruit of sovereign grace. Your blossoming as a branch, together with all the sacred branches of the Vine, is the result of nothing except sovereign grace bestowed upon you. But now also your progress in that redemption *as a human being*, by virtue of your ancestry, by your birth and your entire human life, is a gift, a kindness, an outworking *of the very same grace of God*.

Do not stop with your *assurance* of faith or with the *inculcation* of your faith, not even with the creation within your soul of the *capacity* for faith. Rather, keep on moving further back, beyond conversion and regeneration, to your *natural* birth, yes, in order to bemoan your own sin and guilt, and the fatal guilt of your race, but also in order to extol the grace of your God in that very same natural birth.

Here, then, are three touchstones of grace. One is entirely personal, a white stone, engraved with a name known only to God and to you. This is wholly *particular grace*. The second one is the touchstone of the *covenant grace*, a blessed gift you enjoy in *common with all God's children*. The third is the touchstone of a *general human grace*, coming to you because you are among the children of humanity, yours together with not only all God's children but *in common with all the children of humanity*.

This new series of articles will treat this third element, in order to supplement both of our earlier series that dealt with *particular grace* and the *doctrine of the covenants*.[5] Only when you comprehend *particular grace* and *covenant grace*, as well as *general grace*, in their essence, significance, and connection, will your thinking find rest in its quest for unity. §3

We have purposely avoided the expression *general grace*, and for our title we have chosen instead *common grace*, that is, *gratia communis*, to

---

5. Kuyper is referring here to two series originating as articles in *De Heraut* and subsequently published as devotional Bible studies under the title *Uit het Woord* [From the Word], on particular grace (*Dat de genade particulier is*) in 1884, and on the doctrine of the covenant (*De leer de verbonden*) in 1885. See *AKB*, 1884.09, p. 138; 1885.04, p. 142. For an in-depth discussion of the doctrine of the covenants in the Reformed tradition from a contemporary of Kuyper, see Geerhardus Vos, "The Doctrine of the Covenant in Reformed Theology," in *Redemptive History and Biblical Interpretation: The Shorter Writings of Geerhardus Vos*, ed. Richard B. Gaffin Jr. (Phillipsburg, NJ: Presbyterian and Reformed, 1980), 234–67.

prevent misunderstanding.[6] The assumption could so easily have slipped in that once again we meant [to suggest] that grace belonged to everyone and were thereby attempting again to dislodge the established foundation of *particular* grace. The notion of "general" grace is so easily misused, as if by it were meant *saving* grace, and that is absolutely *not* the case. The only grace that is saving in the absolute sense is particular, personal grace, and even covenant grace receives this title of honor only with certain qualifications. Nevertheless, even though covenant grace in certain instances is saving in terms of its nature and significance, this may never be ascribed to *general grace*.

In order to emphasize this strongly and forcefully, let it be noted immediately that in some measure *animals also* share in general grace (see Gen 9:9–10). To differing degrees, general grace is apportioned to *all* people, including the worst apostates whose consciences are completely seared and who are lost forever.

In itself general grace carries no saving seed within itself and is therefore of an *entirely different nature* from particular grace or covenant grace. Since this is often lost from view when speaking about general grace, to prevent misunderstanding and confusion it seemed more judicious to revive in our title the otherwise somewhat antiquated expression, and to render the phrase *communis gratia*, used formerly by Latin-speaking theologians, as *common grace*.

§ 4    The specialist knows that the discussion of this subject presents unique difficulties for reasons that are obvious. After all, in former times this subject never enjoyed separate treatment. Among the various main sections into which people usually divided academic theology, none bore this title. They treated the topics of Holy Scripture, God, the decrees, creation, sin, Christ, salvation, the church, the sacraments, the state, and the last things, but a separate main section treating *common grace* or *general grace* appeared nowhere.

When in the footsteps of Calvin, the attention primarily of Reformed theologians was specially directed to this extremely important subject, they managed to work out its main features, but without devoting a

---

6. Here Kuyper is contrasting two Dutch expressions, *algemeene genade* and *gemeene gratie*, which could each be rendered into English as "common grace." In this section, the former will be rendered as "general grace," while the latter, Kuyper's preferred expression, will appear as "common grace." For a statement from Kuyper about this terminology, see appendix: "Why the Term 'Common' Grace?"

separate chapter to it. The subject was treated mostly in connection with "the virtues of the heathen," "civic righteousness," "the natural knowledge of God," and so on, but without ever arranging all the various elements belonging to this subject into one ordered, coherent discussion. Nor does our Heidelberg Catechism treat it separately, and this in turn prevented us from completing a discussion of common grace in its own set of chapters in our commentary, *E Voto Dordraceno*.[7]

Although we have repeatedly drawn attention to this common grace since 1878, and even though we took note with gratitude and interest of the well-formulated address on "Common Grace" published by Dr. Herman Bavinck in 1894, this weighty subject has until now not yet been treated with any degree of *coherence* and *completeness*.[8] It remains for us then, with this work, to open our own path, with absolutely no pretense of finishing once and for all this section of dogmatics. Rather, since this subject reaches so deeply into life and into our present struggles, our goal is to offer an initial sample that could lead later to a more developed and polished doctrinal treatment.

Among the perfections of God, it is particularly his *forbearance* that is not exhausted in this common grace, but rather is magnified in a moving way. God's holiness and majesty respond against all sin, not merely in part, but completely, in the most absolute sense. If this outworking of God's holiness against sin were to proceed unimpeded in all of its dreadfulness, there would be no common grace. But the Lord our God is not merely *holy*, but also in his holiness he is at the same time *forbearing*, and it is from that forbearance, which yields the divine patience of the Almighty for bearing *temporarily* with sin, that common grace is born.

§ 5

In his *Institutes*, Calvin formulated the profound understanding of this *common grace* most clearly when he answered the question of how we can explain the fact that uprightness and nobility excelled among pagans and unbelievers so often to such a high degree. Most people who expressed

---

7. This is the title of Kuyper's extensive commentary on the Heidelberg Catechism, *E Voto Dordraceno: Toelichting op den Heidelbergschen Catechismus*, 4 vols. (Amsterdam: Wormser, 1892–95).

8. In 1879 Kuyper began a series in *De Heraut* focused on special or particular grace. See *AKB*, 1884.09, pp. 138–39, for information about original and subsequent publication. Kuyper also refers here to Herman Bavinck, *De Algemeene Genade, Rede bij de overdracht van het rectoraat aan de Theologische School te Kampen op 6 December 1894* (Kampen: Zalsman, 1894); ET: "Herman Bavinck's 'Common Grace,' " trans. R. C. van Leeuwen, *Calvin Theological Journal* 24, no. 1 (1989): 35–65.

their views always made it appear as though this fact provided proof against the deep and pervasive depravity to which our human nature had sunk through sin. "You slander our human nature," so they argued, "if you confess that through sin we are inclined to all evil and incapable of any good. Those many excellent pagans, who do not know Christ and who nevertheless often put us to shame, prove the opposite. And unbelievers as well who live among us often surpass many a child of God in quiet, sober devotion to duty."[9]

Calvin protested against this view. Their claim would indeed be valid if these people were like that in and of themselves. But precisely this must be refuted, and the explanation sought rather in the claim that "amid this corruption of nature there is some place for God's grace; not such grace as to cleanse it, but to restrain it inwardly."[10] Already in the first French edition of his *Institutes* Calvin formulated the matter this way: "When speaking of universal corruption, we need to consider that God's grace does somehow occur, not in the sense that he will alter the perverse nature, but bridle and restrain it from within."[11] The formulation in the Latin edition is shorter and stronger: "grace does not purge our sin, yet dwells within us,"[12] something he repeats even more pointedly at the end of that paragraph: "God by his providence bridles the perversity of nature, that it may not break forth into action; but he does not purge it within"[13] Here lies the root of the doctrine of common grace, together with the explanation of why it forms such an indispensable part of the Reformed confession. It arose not from philosophical invention, but from the confession of the deadly character of sin. Our Reformed ancestors have always insisted on sin's lethal character. They unanimously confessed, "Dead by nature through sin and trespasses."[14]

---

9. Kuyper here gives a summation of the position to which Calvin is responding in *Inst.* 2.3.3.
10. *Inst.* 2.3.3.
11. "Nous avons à considérer, qu'en la corruption universelle, dont nous avons parlé, la grace de Dieu a quelque lieu, non pas pour amender la perversité de la nature, mais pour le reprimer et restraindre au dedans."
12. "*Gratia non quae illam purget, sed intus cohibeat*"
13. *Inst.* 2.3.3.
14. See Eph 2:1. See also Wilhelmus à Brakel, *Logikē latreia, dat is Redelijke godsdienst*, vol. 1 (Leiden: D. Donner, 1893), 764; ET: *The Christian's Reasonable Service*, trans. Bartel Elshout, ed. Joel R. Beeke, vol. 2 (Grand Rapids: Reformation Heritage Books, 1992), 255.

However, this did not appear to fit with reality. There was in that sinful world, outside the church, so much that was beautiful, that was worthy of esteem, that provoked jealousy. This placed a choice before people: either deny all this good, contrary to better knowledge, and join the ranks of the Anabaptists, or suggest that fallen humanity had not fallen so deeply after all, and thereby succumb to the Arminian heresy. Placed before *this* choice, the Reformed confession refused to go with either one. We may not close our eyes to the good and the beautiful outside the church, among unbelievers, in the world. This good exists, and that had to be acknowledged. At the same time we may hardly minimize in any way the pervasive depravity of sinful [human] nature. So then the solution of this apparent contradiction lay in this, that outside the church grace operates among pagans in the midst of the world. This grace is neither an everlasting grace nor a saving grace, but a temporal grace *for the restraint of ruin that lurks within sin.*

# CHAPTER TWO

# THE STARTING POINT OF THE DOCTRINE OF COMMON GRACE

*This is like the days of Noah to me: as I swore that the waters of Noah should no more go over the earth, so I have sworn that I will not be angry with you, and will not rebuke you.*

ISAIAH 54:9

§ 1      The fixed historical starting point for the doctrine of *common grace* lies in *God's establishment of a covenant with Noah after the flood*. In the past, inadequate attention has been paid to this significant and decisive event. People move too quickly to Abraham and the patriarchs, with the result that the weighty significance of the Noahic covenant initially slipped into the background and then was almost forgotten.[1]

---

1. The Noahic covenant is highlighted by the reformer Wolfgang Musculus (1497–1563), an older contemporary of John Calvin, as a manifestation of the general covenant (*foedus generale*), made unconditionally with all of creation, including especially animals. This is distinguished from the special covenant (*foedus speciale*), manifested in the covenant with Abraham, which as an expression of special grace has its

Many people, including pious children of God, behold and admire the rainbow without being aware of the underlying covenant that is so powerfully addressing them. For that reason, we must begin with placing the lofty significance of that Noahic covenant in more radiant light once again. It must come alive for us once again, address us once again, become for us once again an essential component of the grace of God that sustains us.

What must then stand out in the foreground is that this covenant established by God with Noah appears in Holy Scripture not at all as a subordinate matter, and by no means does it appear incidentally as a matter of secondary importance. Rather, the establishment of the Noahic covenant is narrated to us more solemnly, more comprehensively, with greater detail than the establishment of either the covenant in paradise or the covenant with Abraham. The establishing of a covenant is not mentioned indirectly, but the establishment itself and the making of the covenant are included in the narrative as a historical event. What God the Lord spoke and testified about is communicated with meticulous details. The entire event is concluded with reference to a sign in the clouds that as a sacred covenant sign would remind people century after century of the steadfastness and truth of the Noahic covenant.

Thus it is obvious that when the Lord our God gave the Holy Scriptures to his church, he clearly wanted to confirm for the church of all ages the remembrance of this covenant agreement. He necessarily approved the detailed knowledge of this event for his church. And he desired that his church throughout the ages would take into account the significant and rich meaning of this covenant agreement. Our Heidelberg Catechism understood this as well, and its description of the providence of God, that "herbs and grass, rain and drought," and so much more, "comes to us not by chance, but by his fatherly hand," was apparently taken from Genesis 8:22: "While the earth remains, seedtime and harvest, cold and heat, summer and winter, day and night, shall not cease."[2]

---

focus on the elect. Attention to the general covenant remained present but of secondary importance in the development of covenant theology among the Reformed in the sixteenth and seventeenth centuries. See Vos, "Doctrine of the Covenant in Reformed Theology," 234–67. See also Heinrich Heppe, *Geschichte des Pietismus und der Mystik in der reformirten Kirche, namentlich der Niederlande* (Leiden: Brill, 1879), 205–40, esp. 208–9; and Jordan J. Ballor, *Covenant, Causality, and Law: A Study in the Theology of Wolfgang Musculus* (Göttingen: Vandenhoeck & Ruprecht, 2012), 46–57.

2.  *Heidelberg Catechism,* Lord's Day 10, Q&A 27. Compare Kuyper, *E Voto Dordraceno,* Zondags-afdeeling 10, 211–13.

§ 2    Noah became in fact the second progenitor of the human race; not that he replaced Adam, since Noah himself was the fruit of human procreation, as God had not directly formed Noah by his own hand. Noah inherited his nature and character from his parents and grandparents, which had not been the case with Adam. Adam was purely the product of God's creative imagination. Nor was Noah's wife taken from Noah's side, as Eve was taken from Adam's, but in Noah's wife we also find the outworking of the ancestral nature of her parents, grandparents, and great-grandparents. And what applies to Noah and his wife applies as well for the wives of his sons. They too were the descendants and spiritual heirs of previous generations, bringing the corruption of these previous generations into Noah's family.

So it is absurd to want to put Noah on a par with Adam. As far as the source and the originality of their existence are concerned, they are simply not comparable. In Adam we find the source, the original fountain of all the generations of our human race. In Noah's family we find the flowing together and intersection of the various streams that by now had become tributaries. From our human race the only person who can be compared to Adam is the second Adam, the Man from heaven, by whom and in whom we once again find an entirely renewed source. Noah is our second *progenitor*; he is not a second *head* of our race.

Although Noah occupies a more modest position, this much is certain, that the current of the different streams of humanity came to a standstill in him for one brief moment, and then came to divide from him again into diverse streams. You see such a phenomenon in higher elevations where the plateaus differentiate the higher mountain ranges from the lower bluffs, with all the little streams of those mountains flowing together into an azure lake that deepens into a basin, and from the other side of the lake water flowing out into two or three streams that seek their way to the plateau below.

With Noah there was just such an incision, one that was extremely severe, one that cut into the life of our human race. Nothing survived from what preceded it, except what was present in Noah and his wife and his daughters-in-law, and from this fivefold fruit of earlier human life there sprouted the entire subsequent development of our human life. Noah and those eight souls did not form a *new* humanity. Rather, they are merely the continuation of the original human race. But now, after this ancient race was radically pruned by the Lord and was cut down to the root, such that in fact nothing but these five shoots survived, represented by those eight souls, who would soon cause the life of our race to spread out in three main branches, through Shem, Ham, and Japheth.[3]

So the ancient church of God was not cut off with the flood, in order to have begun as a newly formed entity with Noah's family. But the church came forth out of paradise to Noah, borne by him in the ark, proceeding from the ark to dwell upon the earth once again, and in this way continued its original existence in Noah's generation. The only difference is that after the flood the church appeared *in a new condition*. Shem would expand its tents; Japheth would be the first to depart from the church and later return; and Ham would forego its blessing.

The establishment of the Noahic covenant is also properly related to the future of God's church, but this relationship is in terms of the alteration that our general human life underwent. In this Noahic covenant there is after all nothing that intentionally or primarily pertains to *saving* grace. It involves neither forgiveness of guilt and sin, nor promise of adoption and eternal life. Salvation is not being bestowed on some, but in this covenant God's promise extends to *all* the children of men. The covenant does indeed benefit the church, and does have as its goal, if you will, the future flourishing of the church. This covenant seeks to make the church possible and to secure a place of rest for the church, but it does not involve the church as such. This covenant involves man *as man*, man in his society on earth with other *men*, man in his relationship to the *animals*, and man in his relationship to the destructive elements of *nature*. §3

After Noah the situation of our entire earth was different than before; and on that earth the situation of our human race and of our human life is in many respects different than in the days before the flood came. We know very little of the situation that existed before the flood. We read of people with a life span of almost ten centuries. We read of the outbreak of violence, of a devout generation that maintained the fear of the Lord; and of the earliest development of human artistic capacity. But we also read of a frightening crisis that gave godless people supremacy and made unrighteousness and violence increase rapidly.

Finally all of human life appears to have degenerated into wantonness, sensuality, and bloodshed until, after Enoch's removal, only in Noah's

---

3.  Kuyper is apparently referring here to the entire family unit of Noah, his wife, and three daughters-in-law as the "fivefold fruit of earlier human life," totaling "eight souls" with the addition of Noah's three sons.

family did the sacred service of the Lord continue. But only those general features are mentioned. We are not given many details. There is no material at hand to fuel our imagination. What the opening chapters of Genesis offer you is not an interesting story for stimulating your curiosity, but a completely sober portrait sketched in outline, with broad strokes, in order to humble you as a member of the human race in your human understanding.

So gloriously had paradise been opened, so abundantly blessed by God, and look, that is what our human race brought forth from its own wicked root, until at last the judgment of the Almighty is issued, that "*every* intention of the thoughts of his heart was *only* evil *continually*" (Gen 6:5b).

You can see clearly that if the One who created us had not intervened and had not called into being a new order of things, that is, a new living situation, the church would have ceased to exist, and our entire race would have perished in its own pitiful ungodliness. Only in one family was the fear of the Lord still flourishing. How long would it have been until this particular family would also have been swallowed up by the universal stream?

Exactly *what* took place cannot be determined with precision. What Holy Scripture tells us about it is expressed with majesty and written down with ornate, impressive language, but it refrains from recording all the details.

The traditions of the ancient peoples tell us little more than the recollection of an awesome event. And what the investigation of this earth, of its surface, of its mountains and its core have taught us thus far indicates that colossal changes have taken place, but it still lacks the graphic detail and exactitude of history. Meanwhile, this much is certain, that even if Holy Scripture had been silent about the flood, and even if the traditions of the peoples had contained no recollection of an event like this, simply observing the earth in its mountainous regions, and exploring the earth's surface in almost every country, would provide us the certainty that a massive cataclysm had taken place on this earth, one that altered the entire form of the earth and completely altered even its climatic patterns.

§ 4     When God had completed his work in paradise, and had crowned humanity as lord of creation, God saw "that everything was *good*" and our entire earth, as it had come forth from God's hand, must originally have displayed the image of complete harmony and purity.

But that earth no longer exists; *that* world you will not find. Especially those who hike through the rugged and rough mountain regions become deeply aware of this fact. The devastation to which the mountains testify, particularly in their upper reaches, is startling and enormous. Of course, we can still admire the natural beauty and the majestic and delightful scenes of these high mountains, but then mostly from afar, and only in those elevated regions where the snow and ice fields conceal the destruction below the surface by the brilliance of its virgin snow and ice. Where there is no cover, and the naked rocks protrude, the mighty mountain monster displays its savagery. There we observe nothing but destruction, and sense an eerie wilderness, the ruin of what once existed, proclaimed in a most powerful language. Consider how terrible the ruptures and seismic activity involving the entire surface of the earth that must have occurred before this chaos emerged from the harmony of its original creation.

We leave the researchers of nature's phenomena to their own speculations and calculations, although we admire their perseverance and the ingenuity wherewith they pursue their investigations, extending as far as the earth's core. The only thing of interest for our subject is that the factual condition of our earth corresponds to what Holy Scripture tells us, namely, that *our earth is no longer* what it was originally, but that *colossal cataclysms* took place on the earth's surface.

Scripture records two such upheavals. In the first place, the original condition of the earth was changed immediately after *the fall*. Second, that condition underwent a colossal change through *the flood*. Scripture gives us no detailed account of the first change. Genesis 3 does not chronicle all the details of the fury of the elements that showed themselves so clearly in the flood. We are told only that (1) a curse had come upon the earth; (2) the plant world began to bring forth thorns and thistles; (3) the wild animals came to have a different nature; and (4) the beauty of paradise languished and then vanished.

Despite the brevity of this explanation, it supplies enough for us to surmise that an entire reversal of the condition of this earth must have occurred at that time. If the nature of the plant world had changed, if the nature of the animals had undergone such important alterations, if the original beauty of paradise had departed, and the curse was placed on the earth, then these brief indicators say enough for us to realize that entirely different relationships had entered life, and an entirely different, severely altered situation had come into being.

We simply cannot make a comparison with the earth *before* and *after* the curse. The world as God had originally created it at one time had perished under the curse, and an entirely different, sorrowful, and somber form of this same earth had now appeared. Only powerful processes within the elements could have brought this about, and the presumption is obvious that in the desolate scenes that nature still offers in many geographical regions to this day, we have before us the results of what occurred at that time.

§ 5    In that world thus ruptured and disheveled lived the race that had reproduced from Adam until Noah. But then followed a *second* powerful upheaval, one that in a violent manner again tore and fractured the earth that existed. This catastrophe wholly changed the earth's appearance, and it was upon that earth's surface, crushed and rearranged for a second time, that the current development of our race began after the flood.

The narrative of the flood makes clear that in this second cataclysm the element of *water* played the major role. That same account also tells us that the earth's surface itself ruptured again, for it says that "all the fountains of the great deep burst forth" [Gen 7:11]. Apparently this intends to tell us that enormous masses of water, hidden under the surface of the earth, forced through the fissures of earth's surface with great power and flooded the surface of the earth. To what degree this coincides with a sudden massive thaw of the ice fields covering the highlands, and whether this thaw caused the terrible and destructive downpour, can no longer be determined.

Enough is said for us simply to know that during the flood over this our earth, for the second time a comprehensively disruptive and comprehensively altering agitation of the elements occurred, and that from this point forward, this earth as we know it received this form and shape that we now encounter.

Whereas this earth became what it now is through those two upheavals, Holy Scripture testifies to us both times concerning something about which the natural scientists know nothing, namely *this*, that both the first and the second upheaval were effected by *the wrath of God* against the *sin of our human race*. Once more for a third time, so this same Holy Scripture testifies, such a tremendous upheaval is awaiting us, one that will surpass both of those previous ones in terror, when "the heavens will pass away with a roar, and the heavenly bodies will be burned up and dissolved" (2 Pet 3:10).

However, that third global catastrophe will not come until the hour has arrived when the *Maranatha* is ushered in and the sign of the Son of Man appears in the clouds. This third catastrophe will differ from the previous ones inasmuch as the former two disasters caused nothing but destruction, whereas the last catastrophe will actually serve to restore the harmony of creation and with it, the glory of paradise, indeed, causing a glory of a *still higher order* to radiate upon this earth (that is, the new earth under a new heaven).

Until then the current situation of this earth continues. Prior to that last hour no new catastrophe will occur. There will be some regional disasters and even local destructions, especially in the countries and regions with active volcanoes; but what has *not* occurred since the days of Noah, and will not occur before the Lord's return, is such a universal catastrophe like the entrance of the curse, and during the flood, when the entire face of the earth was changed.

The extent to which the other heavenly bodies affected the earth during those two powerful upheavals is not reported to us. But it is prophesied to us that this will occur with the final catastrophe that will come one day. Then sun, moon, and stars will also cooperate in this global destruction, as repeatedly attested in the prophecy of the old covenant, and again in the Revelation of the apostle John. But until that day, the relation of this earth to the sky will in general remain what it is now, which is clearly expressed in the promise that while the earth remains, seedtime and harvest, cold and heat, summer and winter, day and night, shall not cease (Gen 8:22).

Since the days of the flood, a *new condition of the earth* has come into being that pertains to the surface of this earth, as well as its atmospheric conditions. That new condition will not be disturbed, as it was twice before. Instead, it will remain unaltered until the final consummation and until the entrance of the new order of all things, when the glory of the Lord will fill his creation in undisturbed harmony.

And this fact, this permanence of the existing order, affecting our entire earth and human life on that earth, is now sealed for us in the *Noahic covenant*.

§ 6

Until the time of Noah, everything surged back and forth in continual unrest and was subjected to change. The curse continued its wrathful operation. But with Noah that turbulence was changed into rest through an omnipotent act of the Lord's mercy. After the flood God provided his covenant: his covenant given to this earth, to all who were called human beings, his covenant even to the animal world and to all of nature. It extends from Noah to the *Maranatha* for the external order of things, in undisturbed stability, rest, and order. It is the Lord's design. It is his sovereign good pleasure.

Moreover, so that we, the children of men, would taste and enjoy this rest, this peace and tranquility that had been prepared for us in this stability, the Lord God not only took counsel with himself to do this, but he also revealed his decision to Noah, and through Noah to us. And so that it would have a sure certainty for us, he anchored and sealed this decision in a covenant promise for us.

It is for that reason that we need to go back to Noah for the condition of our human life in all its aspects. There, at Noah's altar, erected after the flood and sanctified by the sacrificial blood, lies the mighty, majestic, predominant starting point for the entire developmental history of our human life. By means of that starting point with Noah, *common grace*, which began in paradise, acquired its more definite form.

# CHAPTER THREE

# THE NOAHIC COVENANT WAS NOT PARTICULAR

*I will remember my covenant that is between me and you and every living creature of all flesh. And the waters shall never again become a flood to destroy all flesh.*

GENESIS 9:15

The far-reaching significance of the Noahic covenant requires no further demonstration at this point. We have seen that this significance includes nothing less than the truth that the present condition of our earth and of our human life on that earth, from the flood until Christ's return, possesses the foundation for its certainty and permanence in this covenant of grace. The certainty that no further violent ruptures of the earth's surface will occur before the return of Christ, stands at the forefront of the Noahic covenant. § 1

This comes to forceful expression in Isaiah 54:9, where Israel's God powerfully declares: "This is like the days of Noah to me: as I swore that the waters of Noah should no more go over the earth, so I have sworn that I will not be angry with you, and will not rebuke you." That this is not referring exclusively to a flood upon this earth by means of water, but refers generally to a universal destruction, appears from what verse 10 says about the mountains departing and the hills being removed. The flood is in the foreground, and the fact must be accepted that ultimately the supremacy and the totally destructive force of the water that dragged everything with it was most terrifying and frightening. But throughout all Scripture the memory echoed just as clearly of mountains that were wrenched loose and moved, of mountain tops that trembled and shook, and similarly of valleys that rose up from the deep, and of flourishing fields that later became scorched and withered into a desert.

All of this is an allusion that returns in the portrait of the end of all things. With a view to that end, Jesus speaks of "mountains that fall on people" and of "hills that will cover them" [see Luke 23:30]. The apostolic word testifies that the earth will once again be shaken, and that "the elements of the earth will melt" [see 2 Pet 3:12]. Furthermore, when reading the Scriptures we encounter the shaking of the mountains, the collapse and elevation of the earth's surface, the transformation of fertile land into a barren wilderness, and the changes that can occur in the earth's elements. We find the language of Scripture corresponding entirely with the scenes of terrible destruction that testify of former catastrophes in numerous regions.

Those who advocated theories of water and fire, the Neptunists and Plutonists, might contend by an appeal to Scripture, and identify the Noahic covenant as unworthy of God, only because they read into it that even though there would not be another flood, nevertheless a catastrophe just as terrifying that would involve other elements or would proceed from another cause could overtake us at any moment.[1] The Noahic covenant gives rest, security, and confidence to the children of men only if you understand it in its wider and fuller sense to mean that such a violent cataclysm, like the one that occurred at that time and still awaits us at the

---

1. The Neptunian and Plutonian were two major theories of the eighteenth and nineteenth centuries regarding the formation of the earth. The Neptunists "believed that essentially all rocks had been formed in water," and that "volcanoes were late and largely inconsequent phenomena caused by the burning of plant remains." According to James Hutton, a leading Plutonist, "heat was responsible both for the consolidation of rocks at the bottom of the ocean and for their subsequent elevation to form land." See Rachel Laudan, "Neptunism and Plutonism," in *The Oxford Companion to the History of Modern Science*, ed. J. L. Heilbron (New York: Oxford University Press, 2003), 571.

final judgment, is by means of God's sure promise excluded during this interim period and thus does not await us again.

In the meantime, we need to consider a serious objection concerning §2 this Noahic covenant. Already in the time of our fathers, the question arose as to whether this covenant as well, since it bears the character of a covenant of *grace*, needs to be understood as established with believers only, such that it did not concern the world in general. In particular, Pareus, Perkins, and Mastricht[2] understood it in this more restricted sense, and Rivet also uses an expression that seems to indicate that he was of the same opinion.[3]

Since the view we have begun to present here does not agree with this analysis, but follows the older perspective of Calvin, we will defend our rejection of this narrower view as follows. Calvin says unambiguously, "There is no doubt that it was the design of God to provide for *all* his posterity. It was not therefore a *private* covenant ... but one which is *common* to all people, and which shall flourish in all ages to the end of the world."[4] His expression is *Foedus omnibus populis commune*, that is, "a covenant of grace common to all people." The choice of these words shows clearly that Calvin did not understand the Noahic covenant as "saving," but as pointing to God's mercy, for the benefit of every human being, among all nations, through every age, until Christ's return.

No more words need to be devoted to arguing that we are indeed following in Calvin's footsteps. The above quotation from his commentary should suffice and any doubts may be expelled by a close rereading of his entire exposition about the Noahic covenant.[5] The mistake of later divines consisted in failing to do justice to the clear formulations of Scripture,

---

2. David Pareus (1548–1622) was a German Reformed theologian who taught at Heidelberg. William Perkins (1558–1602) was a Cambridge theologian, clergyman, and one of the leaders of the Puritan movement in the Anglican Church. Petrus van Mastricht (1630–1706) was a German-Dutch theologian, pastor, professor at Frankfurt and Utrecht, and author of a widely-acclaimed work, *Theologia Theoretico-Practica* (1682–87), which is currently in the process of translation by the Dutch Reformed Translation Society.

3. *Note by the author*: The French Huguenot theologian, André Rivet [1572–1651], *Opera theologica*, 3 vols. (Rotterdam: Leers, 1651–1660), 1:218b, merely observes incidentally that this covenant had in view not only the present, but also the future, and referred not only to past but also to ongoing benefits. He does not express himself regarding the principal question.

4. See *CCS*, ad loc. Gen 9:8 (emphasis Kuyper's).

5. See *CO* 23:147–49.

seeing them as focused too exclusively on the church and too little on human life in general.

This becomes even more evident since the Lord's words in Genesis 9 are so understandable, so clear as to avoid any possible misunderstanding, and so plain, that even the possibility of another opinion is excluded for anyone who seriously examines these words. These are, after all, the words of God spoken in the first person. And God is speaking not only to Noah, but to Noah and his *three sons*—thus not only to Shem, but also to Japheth and Ham, including the *descendants* of Japheth and Ham: "Behold, I establish my covenant with you and your offspring after you" (Gen 9:9). Had this covenant been established only with Noah, one could still claim that the words "and with your offspring after you" referred only to Noah's *spiritual* descendants. But this interpretation is impossible. The Lord God is speaking here not only to Noah, but to four persons, namely, Noah, Shem, Ham, and Japheth.

Actually it should be rendered, "I myself hereby establish my covenant with all of you and with the seed of each one of you after all of you." In the original text we read *you* as well as *your seed*, not in the singular but in the *plural*, and so the entire notion that commonly prevails in Sunday school classes and catechism classes, suggesting that God was speaking only to Noah, is false. God stated explicitly and in plain language that he establishes his covenant not only with believers, nor even only with Shem's descendants, but also with Japheth and Ham, and with their descendants.

This is exactly what Calvin says: "A covenant of grace to *all* people and nations *in common*."[6] And as if God had foreseen that a misunderstanding could nonetheless easily creep in, he added as further specification the literal statement: "and with every living creature that is with you, the birds, the livestock, and every beast of the earth with you, as many as came out of the ark; it is for every beast of the earth" [Gen 9:10]. In [Genesis 9:]12 something along this line is repeated: "the covenant *that I make between me and you and every living creature that is with you, for all future generations*." Indeed, as if to express still more concretely and clearly that this covenant applies essentially to our human life on this earth, we read in verse 13 of "the covenant *between me and the earth*," and in verses 15, 16,

---

6. See Kuyper's rendering above of Calvin's reference to "a covenant of grace common to all people" (*foedus ... omnibus populis commune*) in CO 23:148.

and 17, it is repeated three more times: "my covenant that is *between me and you and every living creature of all flesh.*"

As often as *six times* in this brief span of verses it is explicitly stated that we are *not* dealing here with a covenant of *particular* grace, but a covenant of *common* grace.

It is almost inconceivable how people, in contradiction of this, not considering this explicitly repeated, sixfold statement, nevertheless have explained away and virtually denied the *common* character of this covenant. Only a *false spirituality* could have induced them to do this. Having failed to consider Jesus' statement that not even a sparrow falls to the ground without the will of the heavenly Father [Matt 10:29], they cannot comprehend what that caring for the birds in the sky and for all the animals on earth means here. Having neglected the testimony of John the Evangelist that *all things* are made by the Word, and therefore life is in that Word and this life is the light *of men* [John 1:4], people could not conceive of any other covenant of grace than one with a particular scope, and had no room in their limited conception for a covenant of grace with all the children of men.

The fact that we belong soul *and body* to Jesus with all its consequences did not penetrate their consciousness.[7] That godliness yields a fruit of grace not only for the future life but also *for the present life* was not understood in its fullest.

It is for this reason that we move to the foreground once again, with some emphasis, the full scriptural truth concerning the Noahic covenant, and show Calvin's excellence here as well. Without evading this pursuit of a one-sided spirituality, he openheartedly acknowledged the establishment of this covenant with *all* peoples and nations around the globe. §3

Even the use of the name with which the highest Being is named, who established the covenant, forbids us from viewing the matter any other way. When the redemptive covenant of particular grace is mentioned, in Genesis 3 the name LORD is used, and when Shem receives the blessing of the Messiah, we read in Genesis 9:26 the name LORD. By contrast, with the Noahic covenant, as well as with the blessing of Japheth in verse 27, that covenant name of LORD is understandably omitted, and we read in this

---

7. Heidelberg Catechism, Q 1: "What is your only comfort in life and death?" A: "That I, with body and soul, both in life and death (Rom. 14:7–8), am not my own (1 Cor. 6:19), but belong to my faithful Savior Jesus Christ (1 Cor. 3:23)."

context only the name God.[8] It is not the Lord, but the *God* of all flesh who enters covenant with all flesh, and in that covenant swears an oath that actually and simultaneously extends to *all* flesh, to "*all* that has breath."

Calvin's observation is therefore exactly right, when he says that for this reason the animals are also mentioned, because what is involved is *the breath of life* (*vitalis spiritus*) that we have in common with the animals. This covenant applies to the condition and the existence of the earth and the atmosphere that surrounds this earth, for both that earth and that atmosphere have been given not only to people, but along with them to the animals.

Therefore, where God extensively mentions and describes the animal world, and includes in the covenant both animals and people as the single party, precisely by that mention of the animals he demonstrates as clearly as possible that a promise is involved that affects not the *spiritual* life of our soul, but our *outward* existence in the world and on the earth.

That promise itself closes the door to further argument. The promise is described clearly and it includes nothing spiritual whatsoever. It includes nothing other than this one element: "the waters shall never again become a flood to destroy all flesh" [Gen 9:15]. Only this. Nothing else. Not another word is included.

Of course, the terrible mass of water that once swallowed up all life was not destroyed after the flood. That very same mass of water still exists, whether soaked into the surface of the earth as groundwater, or collected in the oceans, which together cover three-fourths of the world, and in some places have a depth of more than seven thousand meters. Large amounts of water lie frozen in the glaciers on the mountains and in the ice mass of the North and South Poles.

At any moment these waters could be released. *God* alone is the reason they remain in their place, and do not swallow up this world. He keeps that frightening mass bound together in the hand of his almighty power. He does this according to his decree of common grace, solemnly sworn and sealed in his covenant with Noah *and* his sons.

§ 4     After having placed this clearly in the foreground, we now need to direct our attention to a second point, one that grants relative validity to

---

8. The covenant name of God, represented by the tetragrammaton YHWH, is often rendered in English and Dutch Bibles with the word "Lord" (*Heere*) in small capital letters, to differentiate it from the more general Hebrew word indicating a liege or master.

the observation of Pareus, Rivet, Perkins, and Mastricht. We note that in Genesis 8, before the blessing of Noah and the establishment of the covenant, another action occurred that relates well to the covenant of *particular* grace.

In *this* narrative, the eternal Being is called as many as three times not by the creator name of *God*, but by the covenant name of *Lord*. This *earlier* account does not speak of establishing a *new* covenant. We read only that Noah brought thank offerings, that the Lord accepted this from his servant, and that he was speaking now to himself, *not* to Noah.

People usually overlook this, as if what follows were spoken to Noah and his sons. But clearly this was not the case. We read that the LORD "*said in his heart*" [Gen 8:21]. This speaks of the counsel God took with himself, which only then in chapter 9 is revealed to Noah and his sons with the blessing and the establishment of the covenant.

The communication of that *intention* of God agrees in large measure with what we read about the establishment of the covenant, but with one considerable difference. Something is added here, namely, the reason why henceforth no new flood would swallow the earth. That reason is contained in these words: "for the intention of man's heart is evil from his youth" [Gen 8:21].

Much has been written about these words, and people have wondered why God says in Genesis 6:5 that precisely because the intention of the thoughts of the human heart was only evil continually, he would *bring* the flood over the earth, whereas here in Genesis 8:21, and precisely *for this same reason* he would henceforth *ward off* such a flood from the earth. Nevertheless, the correct understanding of this declaration is not difficult.

First, observe that it is not true that the *same* reason is given both times. A similar reason, to be sure, but not the *same*. Before the flood it states that "the wickedness of man was *great* in the earth, and that *every* intention of the *thoughts* of his heart was *only* evil *continually*" [Gen 6:5]. Here it is not the condition of the heart of sinners that is being described in general, but that particular *situation* affecting our human race before the flood. This situation had reached an extremely terrible outburst of cruelty and unrighteousness, and the spirit dominating the life of our race was so brutalized and appalling that it suppressed every noble impulse, suffocated every voice of conscience, such that literally and constantly, in all conversation and life expressions, nothing except evil manifested itself. In short, it had become a *hellish* situation on earth. If the fear of God had not survived in Noah's family, there would no longer have been a church on earth.

For that reason the flood came. From the human race that had become so thoroughly sinful no continuation of humanity could occur, equipped to make God's church flourish. Therefore, the current human race was wiped from the earth, and from the single remaining family of Noah, in which the fear of God was still maintained, a renewed human race arose.

By contrast, *after* the flood it states the matter entirely differently: "the intention of man's heart is evil" [Gen 8:21]. Here we have a description not of human development during a particular period, but of *the orientation of the heart of the sinner* in general. Because sin takes refuge so deeply in the root of the human heart that from birth onward it poisons the soul—for that reason God will never again provide redemption by means of a flood. Rather, he will take an entirely different route for the salvation of his church.

Calvin expresses this most characteristically as follows: "As this is the condition of the human heart, floods would be a perpetual necessity and there would be no end to the global deluges and continual upheavals of life on earth."[9] Therefore, because man had reached such a condition, and a flood could at once wipe away a completely brutalized race, but could not arrest sin nor bring about salvation, for that reason God the Lord chooses another route now.

*There will never again be a flood!* The condition of life on earth will never again be violently disrupted. But through the increase of common grace, sin will be restrained with bridle and rein, so that sin will never again before the end of the world develop into such gruesome, hellish outburst and tyranny. If after the flood the earth had become *less* hellish than earlier, this is not because the sinner has essentially improved. Before and after the flood the sinner is just as evil in the core of his being. But the difference lies in this, that the restraining power proceeding from common grace against sin, has become *increased* from God's side after the flood. The beast within man remains just as evil and wild, but the bars around its cage were fortified, so that it cannot again escape like it used to.

9.  See *CCS*, ad loc. Gen 9:8: "And truly, since at the present time, impiety overflows not less than in the age of Noah, it is especially necessary that the waters should be restrained by this word of God, as by a thousand bolts and bars lest they should break forth to destroy us. Wherefore, relying on this promise, let us look forward to the last day, in which the consuming fire shall purify heaven and earth."

At a later time a similar situation will occur once more, when the "man of lawlessness" [2 Thess 2:3] is revealed, whereby God will then have withdrawn his common grace. But then that will be the end, and the judgment of this world will be executed not by another global deluge, but by the burning of the elements.

This is consequently the counsel that God the Lord took with himself. No flood ever again, but a superior grace for the binding and restraint of sin. And this counsel that he revealed *thereafter* for the first time (see Genesis 9) in blessing and covenant establishment with Noah and his sons, is intended in its depths not for our external life, nor for our temporal life. It is a counsel of God's good pleasure that is intended for the Son of his good pleasure, for the body of the elect, and for the honor of his holy name. This is what Mastricht's argument, despite its confused presentation, saw correctly.

CHAPTER FOUR

# THE SPIRITUAL AND PRACTICAL SIGNIFICANCE OF THE NOAHIC COVENANT

*By faith Noah, being warned by God concerning events as yet unseen, in reverent fear constructed an ark for the saving of his household. By this he condemned the world and became an heir of the righteousness that comes by faith.*

HEBREWS 11:7

§ 1     Without question, the Noahic covenant has a *spiritual* significance as well, and therefore occupies a place in the course of redemptive revelation. It certainly may not be assigned to a less holy domain, provided that you distinguish sharply between the *content* and the *purpose* of this covenant. That *content* of the Noahic covenant lies entirely within the sphere of *natural* life, envisions *temporal* and not *eternal* goods, and applies to unbelievers just as much as it does to those who fear God. Furthermore, it is not for humankind alone, but also for the animals. The content of this covenant is simply and plainly this: *that until the end of the world, the surface of our globe will not again be in a position to be disturbed, but will remain as it is now.* To identify this content in a *spiritual* manner and to wish to explain it in a redemptive way is therefore preposterous. That is just as impossible as it would be for you to identify creation itself as redemptive. When God creates light, demarcates the seas, and makes the herbs grow and the earth to swarm with animals, all these activities are related to *natural* things, which indeed may have a *connection* with something spiritual, but in themselves are not spiritual. Calvin rightly observed that the actual promise of the Noahic covenant does not extend further than reestablishing the result of the first creation, and securing *the normal course of nature.*

You reach the *spiritual* significance of the Noahic covenant only when you look past its content, its special promise, and its subjects (humankind and animals) to which that promise extends, and approach the subject from a completely different angle and ask: for *what purpose* was this covenant established? Then it will become obvious that the *purpose* of this work of God's grace can lie not with the *lost,* but with the *elect.* Consequently, this purpose is to be sought in Christ, in his people and their future, and through Christ in the glorification of the Lord's decree and name.

Beware of understanding this in a forced sense, as if this covenant were exclusively intended for maintaining access to a particular domain of ordered human life, so that the formation of local churches would be possible. This would be a mechanical concept, imaginable in the fantasy of human invention, but entirely inconceivable within the organic whole of a *history* directed by God. There is a connection, a life connection, organic connection between the elect and our human race, between soul and body, between us and Christ, and between Christ and his kingdom. Every redemptive work goes back as far as creation, and beyond creation to the eternal decree.

Here too we need to maintain a full and forthright confession of the Holy Trinity in the divine Being. The work of the Holy Spirit proceeds from the work of the Son, and the work of both may never be considered separately from the work of the Father in the creation. Therefore, Christ is also connected with the life of the peoples and with our natural life. You do not understand John's prologue if you disconnect the eternal Word in creation from the Mediator in the work of redemption.

So there does indeed exist a strong connection between the covenant of grace, established with the elect, and the Noahic covenant, established with "everything that has breath." That connection is guaranteed for us through the unity of God's decretive counsel and the unity of the work of the Mediator. It is guaranteed by the undeniable fact that God preserved his church in Noah's ark, and by the prophetic calling granted to Noah. In addition, it is guaranteed by the foreshadowing of the final judgment that was embodied by the flood, and which, in the waters of the flood, pointed to holy baptism. But above all, it is guaranteed by the all-determining circumstance that the fruit of the Noahic covenant, as *covenant*, could and still can be enjoyed only within the sphere of believers.

Of course, the fact itself that natural life on earth would not again be violently disturbed, is also beneficial for unbelievers and for animals. But the imperturbability, the certainty, the comfort that lay within what God promised us, sealed and sworn, that "never again shall there be a flood," [Gen 9:11] is shared only by believers. The animal does not know that God established his covenant with the animals also, and the unbeliever, even if he has heard of it, does not believe it, does not accept it, and either forgets the entire account of the history of Noah, or he makes it a target of unholy mockery.

This Noahic covenant applies to all peoples, and if only the native tribes in the heart of Africa and the Mongolian peoples of Asia realized this, they would also be able to savor the joy of knowing that the almighty God, Lord of heaven and earth, has entered into a permanent covenant with them also. Even though a certain memory of the flood still lives among these peoples, nevertheless every memory of God's covenant is lost, and they no longer know anything about God's covenant. Even if you were to speak to them about it, they would not understand it any longer or believe it. The memory of the Noahic covenant now lives on only among those nations where the banner of the cross has been raised. Wherever the church of Christ has appeared, it reacquainted these apostate nations with the Noahic covenant and inserted it once again into their confession of faith.

In fact, one could therefore say that no matter how much the Noahic covenant applies to all the nations, it lives within human consciousness only where the church of the Lord became manifest. Consequently, this covenant is similar to the promise of an inheritance made to *all* the children of the same family, but which can be enjoyed and appreciated only by those children who have reached the age of discretion. The promise indeed still *applies* to the others, and they received the benefit thereof, but *in their consciousness* that promise does not exist. They are oblivious to it.

Thus, you see that the *spiritual* significance of the Noahic covenant is hardly unappreciated, even where one strictly maintains that the covenant itself has only a *temporal* reach, promises nothing but a *natural* good, and is common to *all that has breath*. Exactly for this reason, however, the observation may not be omitted that the church of Christ in later ages has read somewhat quickly past that Noahic covenant, a practice which may be blamed for people not maintaining the memory, value, and significance of that covenant. Every child among us indeed still learns of Noah and the flood, that no flood will come again. But in the church's faith confessions, justice is hardly ever done to this former work of God, and it is remarkable how little attention is paid to the Noahic covenant in the manuals of theological dogmatics. Calvin grasped and emphasized the full significance of this covenant very well—something that is clear to everyone who reads his commentary on Genesis—but after him hardly any attention has been given to it. Perhaps this might have been prevented if Calvin had discussed this matter in his *Institutes* as well. Then as a matter of course this would have been carried over from the sourcebook of our Reformed dogmatics into later manuals.

Calvin's *Institutes* date, however, to his earlier years, when he understood the entirety less fully, and for good reasons not wanting to revise the original edition too much, he decided to treat this matter in his commentary, but then in detail, and thus it was omitted from virtually every subsequent manual of doctrine.

Only when Cocceius broke up the single revelation of God into the multiplicity of consecutive covenants, did the Noahic covenant come up for discussion again, and in this way especially Petrus van Mastricht discussed still more extensively the revelation that had occurred.[1] Already by that time, however, the work of redemption had come to the foreground in the doctrine of the covenants so one-sidedly, that people knew no better than to view the Noahic covenant merely from its *spiritual* side. This explains why ministers rarely preached about this covenant, taught it in

§ 2

---

1. Johannes Cocceius (1603–69) was an influential German-born theologian and professor in the Netherlands, first at Franeker and then at Leiden. Important modern studies of Cocceius in relation to covenantal theology include Willem J. van Asselt, *The Federal Theology of Johannes Cocceius (1603–1669)* (Leiden: Brill, 2001); and Brian J. Lee, *Johannes Cocceius and the Exegetical Roots of Federal Theology: Reformation Developments in the Interpretation of Hebrews 7–10* (Göttingen: Vandenhoeck & Ruprecht, 2009).

catechesis, or discussed it. One can safely say that virtually this entire period in divine revelation lay dormant, not only among the Lutherans and Methodists, but also among us Reformed.

We need to resist this. Anyone who is not an unbeliever, but who genuinely accepts and confesses that after the flood, God Almighty spoke in this way to Noah and his sons, and established a covenant with all people and all persons through all generations until the end of the world, including with *our* generation, with *our* family, and with *us* personally, indeed, with the animals of the field that surround us—such a person comes before his God with inadequate reverence and gratitude if he does not incorporate this divine covenant into his thought system, if he does not take it into account, if he does not factor it in.

This unbelief is particularly evident in connection with the appearance of the rainbow. With an abundance of words God said to Noah and his sons: "This is the sign of the covenant that I make between me and you and every living creature that is with you, for all future generations: I have set my bow in the cloud, and it shall be a sign of the covenant between me and the earth. When I bring clouds over the earth and the bow is seen in the clouds, I will remember my covenant that is between me and you and every living creature of all flesh. And the waters shall never again become a flood to destroy all flesh. When the bow is in the clouds, I will see it and remember the everlasting covenant between God and every living creature of all flesh that is on the earth" [Gen 9:12–16]. Thus reads God's testimony.

We cannot resolve the question as to whether the rainbow appeared for the first time then, or whether the already familiar rainbow was simply made into a sign at that time. Among the Lutherans the first view predominates; among us Reformed the latter view is more common. Calvin once stated that "it is pure audacity to imagine that the rainbow appeared then for the first time."[2] As a result, most people among us have rejected the first idea.

Even now, however, there are well-respected scientists who maintain the opposite, and defend the conviction that the rainbow appeared for the

---

2. See *CCS*, ad loc. Gen 9:13: "*I do set my bow in the cloud*. From these words certain eminent theologians have been induced to deny, that there was any rainbow before the deluge: which is frivolous. For the words of Moses do not signify, that a bow was then formed which did not previously exist; but that a mark was engraven upon it, which should give a sign of the divine favour towards men."

first time at that point. For this sentiment they appeal especially to what we read in Genesis 2:5–6, where it says: "When no bush of the field was yet in the land and no small plant of the field had yet sprung up—for the LORD God had *not caused it to rain on the land,* and there was no man to work the ground, and a mist was going up from the land and was watering the whole face of the ground … ." They fully accept that the rainbow *must* have existed before, because the atmospheric conditions were the same then as they are now. Furthermore, they do not deny that the rainbow colors can be reflected without rain, on a waterfall, for example, or as a circle around artificial light in the mist; and that the colors of the rainbow can be seen through a prism, thus without mist, or even by rubbing our eyes.

Nevertheless, they believe that with the release of heaven's floodgates, the atmosphere took on its current relationships, and from that time onward the atmospheric firmament has appeared in its current form. Thus, for the first time from that hour onward, when for the first time the waters were gathered into clouds and the sun's rays could play upon those clouds, the rainbow could be seen spanning the entire horizon. The refraction of light into colors would have been seen earlier, along with the tinting of those colors by the mist and by a waterfall, but that mighty bow *in the clouds,* spanning the entire heavens, would have been observed for the first time only at that point after the flood.

We will never be able to achieve certainty on this. The meteorologists can give us no solution, since they can only proceed from the assumption that the atmosphere worked in the same way before the flood as it does now, and on that basis everyone naturally admits that the rainbow must have been observed before the flood. But *whether* that is true, nobody can determine with certainty; and in that respect the message of Genesis 2:5–6 is particularly remarkable.

Meanwhile, in the arena of faith, the chief thing continues to be that we have to maintain that the rainbow—aside from the question whether it appeared then for the first time or earlier—from only that time forward was the *sign of the covenant.*

Every Christian shortchanges the honor of God when, as the rainbow appears in the clouds, he does not remember the faithfulness of his God, and does not recognize in that rainbow the sign of the covenant. He is acting like the pagans and unbelievers who observe nothing but a necessary phenomenon of nature, and a beautiful spectacle. Our God has emphatically testified that, as often as he displays the rainbow in the clouds, he is our God, and that he would "see it and remember the everlasting covenant between God and every living creature of all flesh that is on the earth" [Gen 9:16]. This now lays upon us, the children of men, the duty to do in such moments what God is doing, and from our side to view the rainbow in a way that remembers the faithfulness of his covenant.

This was done among our ancestors. They did this and taught their children to do this. And there are still pious people among us who do the same. But their number is dwindling. The younger generation thinks itself wiser, is less concerned about practicing intimacy with God, and the church of Christ, which hardly ever talks about these things, shares the blame or that decline in devotion.

This subject therefore required that we present this Noahic covenant somewhat more broadly, and focus attention once again on the *rainbow in the clouds*. Only in terms of its interrelatedness will we sense the high importance and the rich significance of such a portion of revelation. The Methodist will never view it rightly, but the person whose confession is Reformed needs only to have these things specified in order once again to see the seriousness of it.[3]

So we will not give up hope that in part through the reach of our word, as often as *the rainbow in the clouds* is seen, the memory of God's covenant will once again be quickened among every living soul, among everything that has breath.

§ 3    For that purpose one needs a clear understanding of the difference in the situation before and after the flood. Before the flood, God the Lord allowed humanity—not completely, but certainly partly—to indulge sin without restraint. But not entirely, because the bridle of grace had already made its entrance in paradise, right after the fall, but still only in a limited way. God wanted to show people by their own bitter experience how they would fare, were he to leave humanity to itself. At that point sin was unleashed in anarchy and vulgarity. It persisted and continued until, in just a few centuries, godlessness and cruelty had reached such a height that

---

3. Kuyper's criticism here is not directly of individuals or churches within the Methodist-Wesleyan traditions, but of what he describes as "an unhealthy fruit" of the revival movement at the beginning of the nineteenth century, which set up a false tension between the subjectivity and individuality of spiritual life and the organic unity of a Christian worldview that addresses social, economic, political, and cultural questions. See Kuyper's postscript for American readers in his *The Work of the Holy Spirit*, trans. Henri de Vries (Grand Rapids: Eerdmans, 1946), xii.

a *universal* violence had set in, not only in a few spheres, but stretching from the center to the circumference of human life, so that finally the *entirety* of human life displayed a *hellish* character.

This was the situation of which God spoke: "and that *every* intention of the thoughts of his heart was *only* evil *continually*" [Gen 6:5]. The situation had deteriorated to such an extent that the entire life of our race had sunk to such a degree of *general* madness, cruelty, and murder that it would ultimately have destroyed itself. Therefore, the judgment of God that came in the flood could not be averted. When the branches and stem of a bush are entirely diseased or withered, the expert horticulturalist cuts them off near the root. This is what God did with our human race in the flood.

Of course, God himself did not have to learn for the first time from this terrible degeneracy and corruption of our race where it would all end if this race were left to its own lusts, *but we needed to learn to understand it by experience*. In what happened here, there lies a terrible lesson for the church of all ages. From what happened at that time, we know, once and for all, where our race, where a people, where a family, and where a person will end up if God lets us go, leaves us to ourselves, and withholds his preserving and comforting grace. It also teaches us what it will be like at the end of the age, when the "man of lawlessness," or if you will, the Antichrist appears, when once again the mystery of iniquity will be unveiled. Indeed, in the terrifying outcome of the degeneration of our race before the flood, lies a pointer toward what the self-generated abomination will be in the place where "there will be eternal weeping and gnashing of teeth" [see Matt 8:12; 13:42; Luke 13:28].

If nothing in the state of affairs had changed after the flood, then in just as short a time as before the flood, the development of our race would again have reached the same gruesome point, and once more a flood would have had to destroy us. In that way, therefore, the development of our race would have been nothing but a permanent repetition of the hellish development of that time, each time followed by a universal destruction. Consequently, there would never have been a continuous human *history*. Development would never have gone forward. The mercies of God in his work of salvation would have had no arena for its manifestation. What people now call our humane, our Christian world, would never have existed.

For that reason, after the flood *another order of things*, another state of affairs, emerged. From that moment on, life itself was entirely different. §4

COMMON GRACE • VOLUME 1

It was different even in *nature* and in the *animal* world, but always according to the fixed regulation that connected this *nature* and this *animal* kingdom to the life of our human race. This was not through a connection that we lay down, but by virtue of a connection that God himself grounded in the creation of all things. When people are *righteous*, they live in *paradise*, when they *fall*, a curse comes upon the earth, and when they will be *holy* again, the glory of the Lord will shine once more on a new earth under a new heaven.

However mysterious this may be to us, it is true that after the flood, nature with its elements emerged in another manner, and that entire species of animals that formerly moved upon and across the earth disappeared. People still find their remains, but not the animals themselves.

There is a direct link between those changes in the form of the earth and in the atmospheric conditions, and the promise that there will never again be a flood. The fact that there will never be a flood reflects the decision of God's sovereign decree. He prevents it, but this prevention is worked out by the nature of things, which are now arranged in such a way that a flood no longer *can* occur.

When we speak of a human ruler we would say that he took measures to prevent a certain undesirable situation. Of course, we do not use this same expression when we talk about the Lord our God. But this does not obviate the fact that within God's providential order, the natural relationships on this earth were of such a form and shape that the execution of God's promise was hereby ensured. His revelation to Noah ran parallel with what he, as our God and our Creator, had wrought in the earth itself and in the atmosphere.

This was not the end of it. God's merciful saving hand extended not only to nature's elements, but to *people* themselves. Within the life itself of human beings, a remarkable change took place. One of the most significant changes was the shortening of life spans. Noah almost reached the age of ten centuries. Shem's life was reduced by half, that of Peleg to a fourth, while the length of Jacob's life was 147 years. Yet, this particular change did not stand alone, since that change in the human condition carried a much more universal character. After all, prior to the establishment of the covenant there was a blessing and the instituting of a *life ordinance*, a course which Shem, Ham, and Japheth were to follow by a *prophetic* appointment.

More about this in our next chapters.

# CHAPTER FIVE

# THE BLESSINGS OF THE NOAHIC COVENANT

*Because they formerly did not obey, when God's patience waited in the days of Noah, while the ark was being prepared, in which a few, that is, eight persons, were brought safely through water.*

1 PETER 3:20

The conviction has been established now that the world *after* the flood was arranged differently than the world *before* the flood, and that with the Noahic covenant an altered order of affairs emerged that still continues and will continue in the future until Christ returns on the clouds.

§ 1

From this fact it directly follows that no one can say, "Well, all these particulars applied to Noah and his sons, but they do not apply to us." Rather, each person has to take as his starting point in every domain of life precisely that situation that arose at that point, and calculate from that point. One must instill in himself and others that he as well as all others with him, including his pets and farm animals, stand within the Noahic covenant in exactly the same way as Shem stood with that covenant after leaving the ark.

It is precisely this situation that one senses less and less. It almost seemed as though the Noahic covenant belonged to the dispensation of shadows, as though what had been prophesied in this Noahic covenant had been fulfilled in Christ, and therefore, after the appearance of Christ, that entire Noahic covenant fell away, like circumcision and the unleavened bread of the Passover. Indeed, this estrangement from what had been given to Noah went so far that people, without putting it this way, nevertheless actually viewed this Noahic covenant as being included in the covenant with Abraham or in the covenant at Sinai. With Noah there had been merely an initial start, the first taste of such a covenant. That supposedly fell away when the much holier covenant with Abraham arrived. That covenant with Abraham was later included in the covenant with Israel. Finally all those ancient, earlier covenants were abrogated by Christ when at Golgotha he established the *new* covenant in his blood.

This is how people have become accustomed to viewing the series of covenants. The New Testament is in front, as the only one we need to maintain, and behind this, but having now become obsolete and pointless, were those covenants with Abraham and Israel. And then there is a third covenant, even *much farther back* beyond those two obsolete covenants, which in days long gone and forgotten was made with Noah and his sons. Precisely for this reason it has no other value for us except as a historical remembrance. And as a result of these notions, people want to know of no other covenant except one designed for saving the soul.

Naturally, when people went to register the spiritual quality of the Noahic covenant, they found so little in it that was saving that they soon let it drop. If they had recognized that the Noahic covenant is *not* redemptive, but that it applied to the life of every human being, indeed, even to the life of the animals, they would not have made the mistake of putting it on par with the other covenants. Instead, they would have treated it separately, as a covenant of an entirely different kind. Only then would they have realized that it *could* not have fallen away when those others passed away, but that by virtue of its character and no less in view of its clear formulation, the Noahic covenant *continues* and *continues in force to this day*. We must place heavy emphasis on this now.

Anyone who overlooks these words is not possibly competent to discern the implications of this series of articles and be able to evaluate their truth. It is a wrong, unsound interpretation that is being rejected here, and the scriptural presentation that is here being advocated.

In all of our subsequent analysis we will proceed from the truth, which for us is incontrovertible, that the covenant established by God with Noah and his sons was established with you and me as well, and with everything that has breath that is now living, and that therefore the situation that came about at that time still governs *our life*.

Did the establishment of this covenant depend on the agreement of people? Were there negotiations regarding this covenant? Were stipulations accepted or rejected, after which a deal was clinched? In other words, may we place the *establishment* of this covenant on par with a *contract* among people? Definitely not, and those devoted to covenant theology will do well to pay more attention to the fact that concerning such covenants it is repeatedly said, as it is here, that God *establishes* them.

§ 2

These are the precise words God employs in Genesis 9:9: "Behold, I *establish* my covenant with you." And in verse 11: "I *establish* my covenant with you," and again in verse 17: "this is the sign of the covenant that I have *established*." Only one time (in verse 12), another even stronger expression is used: "this is the covenant that I *make*," unless this "making" is interpreted as making the rainbow.

Nowhere do we read of an agreement; nowhere do we read of any approval or of any act on the part of people. It is God who acts. He does it. This covenant comes into existence not through people and God acting together, but through an act of God alone. It is not negotiated, but *established*—an expression which means that because of that act, the covenant does not lie dormant, but rather stands *upright* and *fixed*. It is therefore partially comparable to *an ordinance of God*. God does not ask whether people approve it, but he decides and it remains that way, even if people should resist it with all their might.

You might understand this best if you compared it with the course of the heavenly bodies. They also move and have their own places according to God's ordinance; nevertheless, the Lord says to Jeremiah that he has *a covenant* with sun and moon. We read in Jeremiah 33:20–21[a]: "Thus says the LORD: If you can break my covenant with the day and my covenant with the night, so that day and night will not come at their appointed time, then also my covenant with David my servant may be broken."

An *ordinance* given by God and established as a fixed appointment, an order of things that he has divinely and sovereignly prescribed and determined, can therefore receive the name of *covenant* if it applies to a subject with its own midpoint of motion. Hence this name of *covenant* is used already when it refers to sun, moon, and stars, but finds a much stronger application where it refers to people.

For that reason, and only for that reason, God's ordinance, which governs and rules the current arrangement of things after the flood, is called *a covenant*, but a covenant that is entirely unilateral, and not in the least dependent on people having to follow certain stipulations. It is not: "I will not send a flood if you *abide* in my covenant, but if you *break* my covenant, the floodwaters will once more destroy the earth." No, the promise is absolute, independent of every condition. There will never be another flood, and whether we observe the stipulations or do not observe them has no influence on the outcome.

In this covenant, God binds only himself, and the ordinances that he joins to his covenant are not stipulations or conditions, but commands and statutes that God in his omnipotence institutes and imposes on man as his *creation* and as his *subject*. Age after age, among every country and nation, there is a struggle with one or more of the ordinances that accompany this covenant, but never for one moment was there any suggestion that for that reason another flood would come. God's covenant remained and still remains. Similarly, his ordinances continue to this day, quite apart from the question of whether people act according to them.

And thus not the form of a bare promise or pledge is chosen, but the form of a covenant, since the entire revelation of God serves to arouse in man the religious sense. In every religion a bond, a connection, a covenant becomes operative between two persons, namely, between him whom we must worship, and between us from whom that worship must proceed to the eternal One. The covenant form is nothing else than the form of religion. Where it never gets beyond ordinances, you find a *legalistic*, or at most, an *ethical* relationship. But the manifestation of God's hidden concourse, of religious devotion, of a soul's relationship to the eternal One, comes only with *the covenant*.

§ 3    Therefore note well that the ordinances accompanying the Noahic covenant are *not* included in this covenant itself. Certainly they stand alongside it, but they precede it, and only after they have been treated— *fully* treated and concluded—does a new and independent subject follow, commencing in verse 8: "*Then God said to Noah* and to his sons with him, 'Behold, I establish my covenant with you and your offspring after you' " [Gen 9:8–9].

Of course, we should not infer from this that the preceding ordinances have nothing to do with the covenant, or that they are in no way related to it. The entire chapter shows otherwise. Nevertheless, the fact remains that these ordinances and commandments are not formally inserted into the covenant, but exist outside of it. Therefore, we need to distinguish among three subjects. First we are told of God's *intention*, in Genesis 8:21-22. There it says: "The LORD said *in his heart*." That is the first item. Following the first is the second in Genesis 9:1-8, where *God's address to rescued humanity* is set before us. And only then, in Genesis 9:9-17, do we have the third item: *the establishment of the Noahic covenant*, containing nothing other than God binding himself solemnly to everything that has breath, in order never again to bring a universal destruction upon this earth until the return of Christ, and sealing this promise with the sign of the rainbow.

Let us therefore put aside the Noahic covenant for a moment, and consider more closely *that address of God Almighty to rescued humanity*. That address, full of majesty, spoken not by the LORD to his own people but by the Creator of heaven and earth *to all of humanity*, reads as follows:

> And God blessed Noah and his sons and said to them, "Be fruitful and multiply and fill the earth. The fear of you and the dread of you shall be upon every beast of the earth and upon every bird of the heavens, upon everything that creeps on the ground and all the fish of the sea. Into your hand they are delivered. Every moving thing that lives shall be food for you. And as I gave you the green plants, I give you everything. But you shall not eat flesh with its life, that is, its blood. And for your lifeblood I will require a reckoning: from every beast I will require it and from man. From his fellow man I will require a reckoning for the life of man.
>
> > Whoever sheds the blood of man,
> >> by man shall his blood be shed,
> > for God made man in his own image.
>
> And you, be fruitful and multiply, increase greatly on the earth and multiply in it [Gen 9:1-7].

This divine discourse *begins* and *ends* with "pronouncing a blessing" and includes all the rest within this framework of blessings. It does not say: "And God spoke to Noah," but explicitly, "And God *blessed* Noah and his sons." For this reason people mangle the significance of the spoken narrative if they seek this character of a *blessing-granting* grace only in verses 1 and 7, and exclude it from what lies in between. This much may be admitted, that in verses 1 and 7 this character of blessing is more explicit. Note what is written here: "Be fruitful and multiply and fill the earth," and again in verse 7, "Be fruitful and multiply, increase greatly on the earth and multiply in it."

What lies included between both of these explicit blessings involves the following: First, man is given moral supremacy over all the animals. Second, man receives permission to eat the flesh of the animals. Third, man is prohibited from eating raw meat with its blood. Fourth, God provides the establishment of government and the institution of the death penalty. These four items are to be understood as expressions of *grace*, and only in that way can they be correctly understood.

Eight persons stood there around the altar, and they stood there as one, or if you like, as four families, with the question in their hearts: Has mankind been ruined now in one single family, or has the human race been saved, and will the human race expand again into a great multitude? And the answer was: With *a multitude* all the earth would be filled. God Almighty and he alone could create people, could make that restored humanity come forth from the loins of those four men, and in this way ensure the continued existence of our human race.

But a fear of the animal world had come over this small crowd. A wild, raw, destructive power against human beings had survived in that animal world. It remains one of the most surprising outcomes that this powerful animal kingdom did not succeed in eradicating what at that time was such a tiny human race. What could four men do against that multitude of animals, when one single lion or tiger was enough to overtake and destroy people who were as yet so poorly armed?

In Europe nowadays we hardly think of that fear any more, and in order to understand that fear with which the animal world terrified people in those earlier years, one needs to travel to Asia or Africa where each year thousands and tens of thousands of people are still being killed especially by tigers and snakes. Bears still live throughout Europe, and with bitter frost they become somewhat overconfident and descend from the mountain regions to the flatland, only to encounter immediately an entire host of experienced hunters armed with first-rate rifles, who shoot them.

And from their sleighs people shoot the wolves that still render especially Eastern Europe unsafe.

But it was not like that in earlier times, especially not in Noah's days. The greatest problem then was how *human society* could defend itself and be safe from the *animal kingdom*. This problem became the foremost issue, and it was primarily with a view to this fear and dread having entered the human heart that God reassured our human race immediately after the flood. The animal world would not overpower our human race, but the hand of mankind would be over the animal world.

That this would be the case was not due to man, but came to man from God, along a twofold route. The first route was that God endowed man with leadership and deliberation, and granted him ingenuity, in order to outwit the lion and to defend himself against the lion with the right weapons. And, secondly, it pleased God to instill *fear* of humans among the animal world.

The wild animal especially surpasses a human being in raw, destructive power, such that human resistance would be inconceivable. But you see most clearly in the mighty horse, that it adapts to a human being; it yields to a human being; it moves out of the way for a human being, and it bonds so intimately with its master that it seems to become nothing less than an extension of that human being. Now this is a universal phenomenon that manifests itself, albeit in a less evident manner though quite noticeably, among various kinds of animals. The lion of the forest will suddenly pounce on a buffalo, but hesitates to attack a human being. A wild animal will soon withdraw to places further afield when it notices a person entering a wild habitat.

So we are dealing here with the impression animals receive from people, and what that impression would be depends on the relationship between man and animal, ordered by the Creator, who brought both together on the earth. This was therefore a grace, a good favor of our God, that he laid "the fear and dread of man" upon the animal kingdom. Not that people had control over the animals, but "they were *given over* by God into the hand of man" [see Gen 9:2].

The fact that in this phenomenon it is *grace* that is speaking, is to be understood not only in the sense that for man it was a gracious arrangement, but also that by this act of grace God suppressed the evil consequences that man had brought upon himself through sin.

§ 4

COMMON GRACE • VOLUME 1

In paradise, fear of man did not exist in the animal kingdom. The animals came to Adam in quiet submission, and he observed them and understood them, and called them by their name. When the plant world did not yet produce thorns and thistles, there was no dangerous threat to man from the animals.

But when the curse burst forth on account of sin, and the divine harmony of paradise was broken, then indeed thorns and thistles sprouted, and a bloodthirsty appetite to kill men entered into the wild animal. If God had permitted this bloodthirstiness to operate unbridled, and humanity had been annihilated in this way, then what would have overcome us would only have been the righteous punishment for our apostasy from God.

But instead of leaving us as prey to the natural consequences of our own wickedness, God the Lord comes to us in his mercies, and in this wrestling between human society and the animal world he takes our side against the animals and fills the animals with fear and dread of man. Conversely, he has granted to man a capacity and alertness over against the animal that is more than a favorable arrangement, but consists of *grace*, because, our sin notwithstanding, it diverts from us the just punishment of sin. Even the fact that the birds of the heavens and the fish of the sea are mentioned in this context is hardly superfluous. People have discovered the remains of earlier species of birds that must have spread fear and dread wherever they roamed because they were terrifying monsters of gigantic proportions. There were animals whose hideous representations people have reconstructed and whose skeletons still make us shudder. For that reason, it was necessary for Noah and his sons, who were surely still acquainted with the tradition concerning these monsters, that the birds of the heavens would have been mentioned, and the animals from the watery depths also had to be mentioned, so that neither shark nor crocodile nor any other river monster or sea monster would fill man with deadly fear of sea and stream.

§ 5   Nevertheless, God's ordinance concerning the animal world was not yet complete. Not only did it please God to transfer the fear that man had for the animal to the animal itself, but he also gave the animal to man *for food*. "Every moving thing that lives shall be food for you. And as I gave you the green plants, I give you everything" [Gen 9:3].

This ordinance in the Noahic covenant is new. Originally in paradise this was not the case. At that point, food for humans consisted in what the plant world offered as its delectable fruit, but you will discover no trace of eating meat. We are inclined to doubt that this justifies the claim that before the flood people would not have consumed meat.

It is almost unbelievable that during such a wild situation as the one resulting from the development of our race before the flood that the only human nourishment would have continued to consist of herbs and fruit. But a more clear indication is that the division between clean and unclean animals had already become customary before the flood, and with the ordinance concerning the animals that had to be gathered into the ark, God himself accommodated this division. Nor may we forget, as our fathers already observed, that in paradise after the fall, God clothed Adam and Eve with the skins of sheep, something that presupposes the slaughter of these animals.

In addition, after the flood, eating raw meat with its blood was forbidden, a prohibition that makes sense only if this crude, barbaric practice had appeared widely before the flood. For that reason, we reject the supposition, advocated even now by some believers, that before the flood all people would have been vegetarians. Even though formerly the eating of meat was *common*, nevertheless the original creation ordinance that designated the plant world as man's food was never in that sense supplemented and expanded. Yet this is what happened *after* the flood. It is God himself who after the flood institutes the use of meat for people. It does not say, "If need be, you may eat it, but it is better to refrain from it." Rather, as generally as possible, it says, "It shall be food for you as I have given you the green plants"—a phrase that referred of course to paradise. Even though this ordinance certainly does not include the claim that people *must* eat meat, such that not to eat meat would be a sin, nevertheless it cannot be denied that in one and the same breath meat is here identified with the green plants as ordinary food for people. The result is that anyone who goes on to set up a different rule in opposition to this and *condemns* eating meat as illegitimate wants to be wiser than God, and violates his divine right to determine how things must be.

# CHAPTER SIX

# THE ORDINANCES OF THE NOAHIC COVENANT

*But you shall not eat flesh with its life, that is, its blood.*

GENESIS 9:4

§ 1    In the solemn word spoken by the almighty God to rescued humanity after the flood—that is, to the human race that had been spared—immediately after granting the right of man to kill an animal to take its meat for nourishment, there follows a twofold ordinance designed, in contrast to the forfeiting of the *life of the animal*, exactly for the opposite purpose, namely, for the preserving of the *life of man*. The significance of this ordinance must therefore be brought to light.

We begin with the observation that people often mistakenly confuse both of these ordinances with what the Jews call the Noahic commandments. According to the Jewish scholars there are seven "Noahic Commandments." These consist of prohibitions against (1) idolatry, (2) whoredom, (3) blasphemy, (4) murder, (5) theft, (6) eating blood, and (7) anarchy, or as they express it in the *explanation*, concerning the obligation to establish a government.[1] They imposed these seven commandments on the "prose-lytes of the gate," and even ascribed to the observing of these seven com-mandments a certain share in eternal salvation.[2]

That they called these seven commandments "Noahic" in no way im-plied that they held that these seven commandments were given first to Noah. They judged rather that six of these commandments had been laid down already for Adam in paradise, and that during the time of Noah only the prohibition against eating blood was added. To the extent, however, that in Noah's time the incomplete six commandments were completed by the addition of that seventh commandment, and in this way the complete set of "seven ordinances" applied for the first time to Noah's descendants, they called them the *Noahic* commandments. To prevent any misunder-standing we had to make this comment at this point; for the rest, however, we will not engage this Jewish invention.

Let us return immediately to both ordinances of God reported to us in Genesis 9:4–6, which the church usually reads past far too quickly. Both of those ordinances are (1) the prohibition given to the humanity that sprouted from Noah against "eating flesh with its life," and (2) the com-mandment given to this renewed human race to punish a murderer with death. Both ordinances are given in terms of their mutual connection in Genesis 9:5: "And for your lifeblood I will require a reckoning: from every beast I will require it and from man. From his fellow man I will require a reckoning for the life of man."

Let us pause to consider each of these two ordinances separately.

§ 2

The first ordinance concerning not eating *"flesh with its life"* has occa-sioned much misunderstanding, and even Calvin, and in his line our most Reformed expositors, have weakened the power and significance of this ordinance by a less correct observation.[3] With this commandment, the

---

1. "In the Talmud, it is taught that 'descendants of Noah'—that is, universal humani-ty—are obligated by seven commandments: (1) to establish courts of justice, (2) to refrain from blaspheming the God of Israel, as well as from (3) idolatry, (4) sexual perversion, (5) bloodshed, and (6) robbery, and (7) not to eat meat cut from a liv-ing animal (*b. Sanh.* 56a)." See *The Jewish Study Bible* (New York: Oxford University Press, 2004), ad loc. Gen 9:8–17, p. 25.

2. "Proselytes of the gate" refers to resident aliens or Gentiles who observe basic commandments but who are not circumcised members of the covenant communi-ty. The term is derived from texts such as Exodus 20:10 and is roughly equivalent to later terms such as "God-fearers."

3. Calvin observes that this commandment "is expressly declared, in order that men may have the greater horror of eating blood," but also "that this restriction was part of the old law." See *CCS*, ad loc. Gen 9:4.

Jewish scholars did not go about placing the general idea embedded in this ordinance in the foreground, but gave it a formalistic interpretation that descended into minutiae, and precisely in this way limited the moral scope of the commandment.

This ordinance, as some imagined, referred to the loathsome custom that had become ingrained especially among several nomadic shepherd tribes of cutting a piece of raw flesh from the body of a living animal and letting the mutilated area close by itself. The title of the seventh of their Noahic commandments, *Ever min Hachai*, literally means "the limb of the living" and it is probably still related to this interpretation. Expanding the formalistic meaning, the second ordinance was read as a prohibition against introducing any drop of blood in one's food. Finally, from this the rule was deduced that God was forbidding us to eat the flesh of any animal, since with its slaughter all of the blood had not drained out down to the last drop.

The custom, still maintained among the Jews, of slaughtering cattle or sheep in such way that all of the animal's blood is completely drained, is due in part to such understanding of the original ordinance. And since they derived this custom from a Noahic commandment, it was obvious that not only were they to follow this manner of slaughter, but they must place this requirement on others as well. According to these scholars, every other method of slaughter went against an *explicit* command of God.

When Calvin and others came to explain this prohibition, they did not adopt this rabbinic interpretation, but they nevertheless saw in this ordinance nothing other than a *ceremonial command* that as such bore a temporary and pedagogical character. This explains why, given their natural aversion toward all superstition and works righteousness, they did not concede the applicability of this ordinance of God in the Christian dispensation, and counted themselves bound to the universal command that condemns cruelty and brutality. Amid the tumultuous struggle then raging in ecclesiastical and civil arenas, there was no time for pressing the full significance of the Noahic covenant. And the suspicion that here as well people were on the path of a kind of works-holiness activism led imperceptibly to making the familiar distinction at this point between the *ceremonial* and the *moral* within the commandment—a distinction that certainly fits with the covenant of shadows but not with the Noahic covenant.

Neither in paradise nor with Noah, but with Israel the *ministry of shadows* arose for the first time, at that particular moment when the sacrament of circumcision was instituted. Consequently, with Israel the entire ministry was a foreshadowing in symbolic form of the spiritual truth that would arrive in Christ. You find nothing of this, however, with the Noahic covenant. This covenant refers not to an eternal, but to a temporal good. And the promise of this covenant was hardly abrogated by Christ, or hardly fell away with his coming. We still now, after eighteen centuries, boast in the certainty that no flood will again destroy the earth. You see this most clearly in the sign of the covenant. The signs of the Israelite covenant, namely, circumcision and Passover, are abrogated and have fallen away, but the sign of the Noahic covenant still shines in the sky. So then, we do not hesitate for a moment to leave this ceremonial view of Calvin for what it is, and to maintain the perpetual validity of this ordinance.

The position you need to have on this matter was indicated by a person §3 no more thorough than Calvin himself. Do you possess of yourself, that is, by nature, the right to put an animal to death and to eat it? Stated another way, does your right to kill an animal and use it for food proceed from creation, or not? Calvin denies this and is absolutely correct.[4] Killing an animal is an act of violence that goes against a sense that has been created within us. The initial instincts of our heart still protest against the cruelty of such a business. Throughout their entire lives, especially women, by virtue of this sense, continue to feel aversion toward all killing of animals. Many a butcher has suffered a nervous breakdown by constantly suppressing this aversion. Vegetarians find support in this protest that arises from our very nature. The more refined and nobler our development becomes, the more painful our experience when we ourselves are called to lead a sheep to slaughter. Many feel this aversion less with hunting, because killing occurs either after a chase or from a great distance. But taken in general, it cannot be doubted that by nature we recoil from shedding blood *also with animals*. Even the *sight* of blood in itself is gripping. The right to kill an animal can be inferred even less from property rights. Such has been argued, and on the same basis some have argued for the right of a slave owner to kill his slave and the right of a father to kill his child. But this pretense rests entirely on circular reasoning, of course. First one declares property rights to be absolute, a right *without limits*, and

---

4. Calvin emphasizes "that to eat the flesh of animals is granted to us by the kindness of God; that we do not seize upon what our appetite desires, as robbers do, nor yet tyrannically shed the innocent blood of cattle; but that we only take what is offered to us by the hand of the Lord." See *CCS*, ad loc. Gen 9:3.

then one classifies slave, child, and animal as property, over which the capriciousness of the owner has limitless power.

Since, however, in order for us to classify the animals, the primary Owner found and captured the animals for us, and in terms of the procreation of the animals, even though their number is limited or expanded by man, nevertheless *life* must be recognized never as coming from man but only from God, since as the one who created and gave life, only *he* has authority over that life, including the life of the animals. Without arguing the matter in broad detail, Calvin admits that man would have no right at all in this matter, if the Lord had not explicitly assigned him this right. The granting of the right to kill animals and to be fed with their flesh demands therefore the character not of a natural ordinance but of a *positive ordinance*. Exactly here lies the basic reason why the granting of this right was tied to a *restrictive* stipulation. You may kill an animal and you may eat it, but under one condition: that in your roughness and barbarity you do not lose sight of the honor you are obliged to show me as the Creator of the life of that animal.

So it does not say that you may not consume meat with blood; rather, *blood* is mentioned only in the second place, and what is placed in the foreground in the ordinance is that you shall *"not eat flesh with its life [soul]"* [Gen 9:4]. That "soul" [as older Bible translations render the word] certainly does not refer to a spiritual essence within the animal, but simply to its *life*, that which is in the animal as long as it is alive and disappears from the animal when it is dead. Therefore it is your God by whose power alone life is granted also to the animal, who by his ordinance requires from you—who can indeed *take away* the life of an animal but cannot *give life* to an animal—that when you eat of the slaughtered animal, you must wait until life has completely departed from the animal. You may slaughter the animal; but then you must wait until all life has departed from the animal, until the *soul* is no longer in the animal, and only when it has become flesh *without the soul* may you take it for your food. It is therefore a very serious question whether drinking warm animal blood, as some doctors in our day prescribe, does not go against this positive ordinance of God.

Concerning this life of the animal, or as Scripture calls it, the *soul* of the animal, we are told that it is in its blood. Of course, not as if this blood itself is this soul, for this blood later congeals and then disintegrates. It only means that within the body, blood is the chief conduit for keeping the body in motion. The life that is the soul is different in the entire body, and Scripture itself teaches us that even when all the blood remains in the body, nevertheless the soul leaves the dying by means of the last breath. So the blood is presented here as the preeminent and, from our vantage point, most expressive and tangible conduit of life. If that animal has just been killed and the warm blood is flowing from the wound, then man must keep his distance. That flesh can become food only when the animal is gone and nothing remains but stuff that is set to decay.

For this reason, the letter of this ordinance is observed but the spirit of it is killed if one loses sight of the soul, the life, and continues to be devoted fearfully to the blood, as though eating a piece of cooked or roasted flesh from which a few drops of blood escape when it is cut, renders us guilty before God. Anyone who comes to such a judgment loses sight altogether of respect for God the Creator of the life and of the soul of the animal, and continues hanging on to the material elements of the blood. Such a person reads Scripture as though it said, "But the flesh in which there is still one drop of blood you shall not eat," and forgets that it says something very different: "But you shall not eat flesh with its life, that is, its blood." Our translation does include the phrase "that is," but those words are not in the original text. With this we are keeping carefully in view that in Leviticus 17:14 and other passages, under the dispensation of shadows, not only the eating of *fat* but also of *blood* was forbidden (Lev 3:17; 7:26; etc.), but this was entirely in agreement with the ministry of the shadows among Israel, which in everything had to be specified formalistically and outwardly. Nevertheless, it is exactly that specification of Leviticus 3:17, "you [shall] eat neither fat nor blood," that shows in a convincing way, precisely through the addition of the word *fat*, that we are definitely not dealing here with the ordinance given to Noah but with a Levitical stipulation. This was valid for the Jews until Christ came, but has fallen away in the dispensation of the New Testament.

The occasion for this ordinance would likely have been that in Noah's preflood environment, raw meat containing the warm blood was frequently devoured. This practice is acceptable for a *beast of prey*, but not for a *human being*. A beast of prey attacks its prey and puts its claws and teeth into it. So too a beastly man who imagines that he has a right to the animal and thus attacks, downs, and devours it. And against this unholy and brutish situation God institutes a situation of order: An order in which man receives the right to the animal, the right to kill it and take its flesh for food, from the One to whom that animal belongs and who gave life to that animal. But that order is also an order in which man kills the animal in the name of his God, respecting the supremacy of his Creator over that animal, and therefore takes it for food only when its life has completely departed and the flesh that initially *contained the soul* became flesh *without the soul*. Since this fact was observed for the normal use, that as soon as the blood has been drained and as a result the life-warmth has departed, that prior draining of the warm life-blood is established as a requirement.

§ 4    With this enough has been said about the first ordinance, an ordinance that in its sacred significance naturally applies to us as well. It remains valid until the end of the world, and must be obeyed by everyone who honors God as Creator and fears him as the only Giver of all life.

We come now to [Genesis 9:]5, which constitutes a transition to the second ordinance. That verse reads as follows: "And for your lifeblood I will require a reckoning: from every beast I will require it and from man. From his fellow man I will require a reckoning for the life of man." These words oppose first of all what people call cannibalism; that is, they oppose the gruesome custom that unfortunately still exists among numerous peoples, of eating the flesh of a dead person. In three regions of the world, Africa, Australia, and on a few Asiatic islands, that dreadful custom is still maintained. Formerly it was even more common, and it must undoubtedly have been just as rampant before the flood, not to mention the number of human bodies that were cut up in a way resembling the carcasses of animals, and devoured by people either raw or roasted. The reports about this that have been circulated by travelers and missionaries make your hair stand on end. Even stores selling human flesh were not a rarity until recently.[5]

Well then, this cannibalism is an imitation of animal behavior, and therefore both are joined together in verse 5: "And for your lifeblood I will require a reckoning: from every *beast* I will require it and from *man*." The wild animal kills a man, not out of malice or rage, but to devour him as its prey. This is how one animal kills another, and this is how an animal

---

5.  Here Kuyper is passing along the conventional wisdom of his day regarding the extent to which cannibalism was practiced in various parts of the world. Cannibalism, along with other exotic practices, was a standard topic of travel narrative, speculation, and even literature in the eras of European exploration and colonization in the seventeenth and eighteenth centuries. See Cătălin Avramescu, *An Intellectual History of Cannibalism*, trans. Alistair Ian Blyth (Princeton: Princeton University Press, 2011).

kills humans, *as if humans were also animals*. On that devouring rage of the animal, man puts his seal, and *in so doing man becomes like an animal*, as often as he, like a cannibal, kills a human being to devour him as prey. In that manner the boundary line between animal and our human race is erased. Man is incorporated into the animal kingdom like a unique species of animal, and the same theory that the Darwinists preach philosophically today has been put into practice for centuries already by the cannibals with their hellish bacchanalia.[6]

So a dam needed to be erected here. The profound distinction between our *human* race and the *animal* world needed to be safeguarded against weakening and blurring, all the more now that man acquired the right to kill animals and take them for food. For that purpose the ordinance of "not eating flesh with its life" was initially given. Here, after all, lies exactly the distinction between a tiger or a man choosing an ox for food. The tiger devours the ox with its life; the man takes it for food only *when the life has departed*. The tiger steals its prey and does not know God; the man uses a right given him by God, but simultaneously honors the Creator and the Giver of life by waiting until life has departed.

But verse 5 erects a second dam. From the fact that man receives from God the right to kill the animal and after its life has departed, to take it for food, it hardly follows that the animal in turn receives the right to devour the man, or that a man may eat his fellow man. On the contrary, both of them are explicitly denied *that* right. No animal may devour a man, and no man may take a fellow man as food. Despite this having occurred, however, God will require an accounting for all this shed blood.

In what manner God executes his judgment in the animal world is not mentioned. Therefore, concerning the words, "from every beast I will require it [your lifeblood]," one can come up with nothing more than guesses, to which our next chapter will return. The subject of requiring payment for shed human blood from the hand of murderers will be discussed as part of the interpretation of Genesis 9:6. At this point we will suffice with the observation that, when viewed properly, the starting point for the arrangement that God instituted for Noah's posterity lies in the distinction between *human beings* and *animals*. This was actually the first distinction

---

6. Here Kuyper is connecting what he views to be a consequence of Darwinian evolutionary accounts with the animalistic nature of cannibalism. The bacchanalia are festivals of drunken revelry, named for Bacchus (Gk., Dionysius), the Roman god of wine, drunkenness, and ecstatic liberation.

confronting these *eight* "children of men" who came out of the ark. From that first and most natural distinction proceeds the entire divine instruction. The claim of Keil and others, that within this ordinance one can supposedly find an early pointer to Israel's peace offering, appears less acceptable for that reason.[7] Calvin's judgment is more attractive, that the goal and design of this ordinance are to ensure the *human* character of *human society*, even though we admit (but then in the *reverse* sense) that the sacrificial ministry under the dispensation of the shadows concentrated exactly for that reason on the "*shedding of blood*," because in the difference between *blood* and *blood* lies the basis of the entirely distinct value of *man* and *animal*.[8]

---

7. Johann Friedrich Karl Keil (1807-88) was a German Lutheran OT commentator best known for his contributions to the biblical commentaries with German Lutheran theologian and Hebraist Franz Delitzsch (1813-90). See Keil and Delitzsch, *Biblical Commentary on the Old Testament*, trans. James Martin, vol. 1 (Edinburgh: T&T Clark, 1866), 151-53.
8. According to Calvin, God provides this ordinance "because he accounts the life of men precious: and because the sole end of his law is, to promote the exercise of common humanity between them." See *CCS*, ad loc. Gen 9:5.

# CHAPTER SEVEN

# THE PROTECTION OF HUMAN LIFE

*If anyone is to be taken captive, to captivity he goes; if anyone is to be slain with the sword, with the sword must he be slain. Here is a call for the endurance and faith of the saints.*

REVELATION 13:10

The fact that the command given to Noah concerned the avenging of *murder*, not just primarily but almost exclusively, is in accordance with human nature and history. After all, history narrates how the situation with Cain and Abel almost immediately issued in murder, and human nature explains why in the protection against murder, the protection of all our human existence is provided simultaneously. The danger of being exterminated was for our human race at that time very great. After the flood our entire future depended on four men, and how easily an attack by a wild animal, or murder after a fraternal quarrel, or even death by disease could have taken that foursome. A fear that must have come over them early on, now that they had just stared at the appalling spectacle, how except for eight souls the entire human race had drowned in the flood. How easy it would have been for the lone family of Noah to have gone down under the waters, along with the thousands and ten thousands of families, and then our human race would have been *gone*.

§ 1

After a shipwreck where virtually everybody has drowned, the one person who survived senses, at least for the first little while, that life is a precarious and anxious possession. Even after a terrible epidemic, that fear for endangered life continues to lodge in the heart of survivors for months long afterward. The tension following a great war is similarly explicable as arising from a similar kind of fear. What, then, must it have been like in that one family of Noah, who had seen the whole world drown and now stood alone and solitary and abandoned in an almost crushed world, having soon to fear the worst from the quickly multiplying wild animals? An ordinance of God like the one promulgated here, coming like a shield to cover the life of people, as much against the wild animals as against human bloodthirstiness, was therefore entirely *relevant*, fully suited to the situation, and must have had a comprehensively encouraging and comforting effect.

It is sufficiently apparent how before the flood the life of people was often cut off by an attack of a predatory animal or by murder, and how necessary it was that the promise never again to bring universal death through a flood over the earth was supplemented by an ordinance of God, which assuaged death by predatory animals and by murder. Up to this point, three factors had been operative in causing people to disappear from the earth: predatory animals, murder, and the flood. People were terrified of those three factors, and it is over against those *three* factors that God places the contracted and diminished human race in safety. Against the flood by means of his *promise*, against the predatory animal by means of his *ordinance*, and against murder by means of his *commandment*.

§ 2    "For your lifeblood I will require a reckoning: from every beast I will require it," is God's ordinance that precedes even the command against murder [Gen 9:5]. Naturally in this connection the question is very weighty whether we have to imagine the flood as covering the entire globe or only the inhabited portion thereof. Of course nothing is to be deduced from Genesis 7:23, which says, "He blotted out every living thing that was on the face of the ground, man and animals and creeping things and birds of the heavens. They were blotted out from the earth." When in John 12:19 we learn of the complaint of the Jewish hierarchy, that "*the whole world has gone after him,*" no one takes this in the sense as though the members of the Sanhedrin had intended to say that the inhabitants of the entire globe were following Jesus. When it says in John 21:25 that the world would not contain the written books, no one takes this literally. The saying in Lamentations 4:12, "The kings of the earth did not believe, nor any of the inhabitants of the world, that foe or enemy could enter the gates of Jerusalem," hardly means that every living soul, head for head, in every region of the world, had an opinion about the strength of Jerusalem's fortress, but only that those who lived in the surrounding area and who had lived in Jerusalem held the view that Jerusalem was impregnable.

Already from these few examples, therefore, one sees that such formulations in Holy Scripture hardly need to be understood in the *broadest* possible sense, but very often must be taken in the *narrowest* sense. "The whole world has gone after him" means: the whole world *to the extent that it came into contact with him*. That "the world itself could not contain the books that would be written" intends to say that there would not have been room for them at the current book shops; and with "any of the inhabitants of the world" who saw Jerusalem as an impregnable fortress, Scripture is referring only to those who had heard the rumor of Jerusalem's strength.

So it could well be that in the narrative of the flood, such general expressions are referring only to that part of the world that counted for Noah or where people lived. Most likely at that time only the middle of Asia was inhabited, and that inhabited region was entirely covered with water. But this does not entail the conclusion that the other side of the globe, what we now call America, underwent the flood. It *could* have been that way but does not necessarily follow from the expression. This being the case, God's ordinance against the predatory animal presupposes that no universal extermination had occurred. If at that moment all the wild animals were extinct, except those few pairs rescued in the ark, it is not clear what kind of danger would have threatened humanity from the wild animals. At that point they would have been entirely under the control of Noah and his sons. They would have locked them in cages or stalls, and nothing would have compelled them to release them, and they could have dealt with the young newborn animals as they saw fit. So on the assumption that all the rest of the wild animals except the few specimens that were in the ark had become extinct because of the flood, it is difficult to explain how that definite feeling of dread for the predatory animal would have come to dominate people.

Just as we observe these animals in our zoos without fear, so Noah and his sons may have also viewed the enclosed lions and tigers, and the ark with its strong construction may have served as a repository for the beasts of prey. Nothing forced them to release those animals, thereby endangering the women and children. The ordinance against the predatory animals is explainable then only if one accepts the premise that the extermination affected only that portion of the earth where people were already living, and not the remaining portions of the earth. There the predatory animals continued to exist, and from those regions those animals could find entrance again into the region where Noah lived after the flood waters receded.[1]

§ 3    How we should understand those words, "and for your lifeblood I will require a reckoning: from every beast I will require it" [Gen 9:5], is not so easy to determine. Only this much can be said, that it does not mean one for one, as if each particular beast of prey that attacked a human being must be killed as punishment for that. The text itself opposes such

---

1.  *Note by the author*: An esteemed correspondent has objected to our position that the flood most probably did not cover the entire globe, and in connection with this, that predatory animals perhaps remained alive elsewhere in the world. Let it be stated immediately that we attach very little importance to this dispute. Our only interest was to emphasize the significance of the protection of humanity against predatory animals.

    For the rest, we note that Scripture itself says that "the waters prevailed so mightily on the earth that all the high mountains under the whole heaven were covered" [Gen 7:19], after which Scripture mentions the highest mountain, Mount Ararat. Nevertheless it is clear that numerous mountains were higher than Ararat. In the second place, that not *all* the animals were destroyed appears from the fact that since the flood consisted of water, the fish could not have been killed, but rather received a rare and rich prize of human and animal corpses. Third, numerous fossils have been found in the earth's depths, fossils of animals that did not belong to this time period. Fourth, it is indeed true that in Genesis 8:17 we read that all the animals had to leave the ark, but a literal interpretation of this presents us with insoluble difficulties. Suppose there were eight people, together with a small number of horses, cattle, camels, sheep, goats, and so on., and you let loose two lions, two tigers, two hyenas, two snakes, two wolves, two bears, and many more. How could people have defended themselves at this point? What did those animals live on? Would not the entire small stock have been killed within a short time? Were you to say that Noah and his sons might have been animal tamers, or that God might have restrained the predatory animals at that point so that they didn't attack people, we would certainly admit that these were possibilities, but precisely at that point justice is not being done to Genesis 9:5.

    In any case, we are facing difficulties here that arise from the brevity of the narrative. One person can posit this, while another can posit that, and those opinions should be permitted. But Genesis 8 and 9 are revealed to us not to have a dispute about them. The main point here involves God's ordinances given to the new human race. [Ed. note: The text of this note originally appeared at the conclusion of *CG* 1.8.]

interpretation. Concerning people the words are emphatic: "from his fellow man I will require a reckoning for the life of man" [9:5], and therefore, head for head. But with regard to the beasts of prey we do *not* read, "from the hand of *the same* animal," as if the meaning were one for one, but in general, from all animals. Consequently this permits the other interpretation, that each kind of animal that attacks a person would commit its own death.

By God's providential arrangement the course of things would be regulated in such a way that the animal species that respected and served men would gradually increase and gain in significance, and conversely, the animal species that shed people's blood would be wiped out. In fact, this has been the course of history, and even now, all the beasts of prey of the entire populated world have in a restricted sense been driven back, and they exist now only in some mountainous regions and in forests.

This goal has now been achieved by means of God's twofold action. First, he armed man with heroic courage, ingenuity, and weaponry, in order to overpower the beasts of prey; and secondly, he instilled fear into the predatory animal so that it would withdraw as soon as people approached it. We see this best when we observe a tamer of wild animals. Even those historians who do not acknowledge God recognize these facts. The beast of prey has withdrawn and extinction is its future.

And, although these facts are recognized, Scripture gives us more. Indeed, it reveals to us how behind and within these facts, a *divine administration of justice* is at work that exacts satisfaction from the beasts of prey for the human blood they shed. People who have been attacked by a tiger or a bear, recoiling in fearful desperation and being torn apart by their claws, while dying, have in that moment, when nobody was there to help, cried out to God to avenge the gruesome act that caused their death. And although an ordinary account senses nothing of what was happening within the victim at such a moment, and certifies only his death, Scripture reveals the mystery operating behind the veil of the visible, and hence tells us that God Almighty will exact payment from the predatory animal for its nefarious deed.

Predatory animals will not succeed in wiping out the human race, but § 4 people will drive out the predatory animals as revenge for the shed blood. But this does not ensure that the life of every person is now saved or protected. No less serious is the second danger, namely, that humanity might destroy itself by murdering *each other*.

Until recently it was the rule in the interior of Africa that in the autumn one tribe would attack another tribe, and the victorious tribe would then usually massacre the vanquished tribe or sell the prisoners as slaves. Time and again entire tribes were massacred in this way, and slaughters occurred on a scale that would make you shudder if you read about it. Even in devouring their victims people could match the predatory animal.

This is the reason why the second *command against murder* comes after the ordinance concerning the beasts of prey, and in this formulation: *"From his fellow man I will require a reckoning for the life of man."* Concerning the beasts of prey, we read that God will require a reckoning for human *blood* from the *animal species*, but here we read that he will require the *soul* of the victim from the hand of another *human being*.

Both differences deserve attention. Although we admit that the words *soul* and *blood* are very closely connected, and that the one word is often used instead of the other, nevertheless this does alter the fact that we need to note well the difference when both words appear in a different way in the same verse. It is remarkable that with the predatory animal mention is made only of *blood*, but with the murderer mention is made of *the soul*. The blood is the carrier of the soul, and the soul is the life that is found in the blood. Where only the *blood* is mentioned, this refers more to the outward, just as the predatory animal often licks up the blood. With the person who commits murder, by contrast, the matter is taken more seriously. The murderer makes himself wittingly and willfully guilty not only of shedding blood, but occasionally even apart from shedding blood, guilty also of killing life, that is, of extinguishing the life of a person, such as by means of poisoning, strangling, or causing death in a number of other ways. Predatory animals kill for food, and therefore feed on the blood, but people act far worse, for often their act involves the enjoyment of seeing their victim suffer and die, finally to take him from the land of the living, or only to kill him out of hatred and revenge.

As peculiar as it was to speak of *blood* in connection with *predatory animals*, it was as natural in the case of a *person* to mention not the *blood* but the *soul of a person*. The animal knows nothing of a soul, and thirsts only for *blood*. By contrast, blood is only the means to get to a person's *soul*, that is, his *life*. The root of murder lies not in hunting for prey, but in hatred and malice. He who hates his brother is a murderer [see 1 John 3:15].

Just as remarkable is the *second* stipulation: *from the hand of his neighbor,* that is, from the hand of the person's murderer, head for head, separately, because he is the brother of the one murdered, and thus *the murderer's brother*. Evidently this refers back to Cain and Abel. In that case they were two brothers, of which one murdered the other, and precisely in the fact that it was the murder of a brother, the abhorrent nature of this act is heightened in our human consciousness.

However, the Lord now declares that this same evil character attaches to all murder, because all who are called human are joined by one communal fraternal bond. Cain asked, "Am I my brother's keeper?" [Gen 4:9]. But God answers by issuing a command that declares that every person should guard the life of his neighbor, because he is *his brother*. Someone who murders his fellow man is therefore inhuman, who instead of preserving life extinguishes life, and squanders instead of protecting.

And since this is the reason that every murder comes to stand in the sober light of *fratricide*, the Lord therefore declares to Noah and his sons, *"From his fellow man I will require a reckoning for the life of man."*

The command for capital punishment is not included here per se. In these words exclusive mention is made of what God says *that he will do*. The parallel with what is declared about the predatory animal may therefore not be lost from view. God will require the *blood* of the one murdered from the predatory animal, and he will require the *soul* of the one murdered from each and every murderer. If in the case of a predatory animal there is no mention of a judicial inquiry by man, but of vengeance that God executes in his providential order, then the context requires that one apply the same to what is said about the murderer as well. Concerning him as well it is declared here *what God will do*. God will require of him the soul of his victim, and he will do this by means of his providential order. This verse says nothing more, and Calvin was absolutely correct when he spoke here of "God's hidden action."[2] Our Bible commentators also first mention the capital punishment executed by the government in connection with the following verse.[3] What is said here about "requiring from the hand of the murderer the soul of the one murdered" [see Gen 9:5]

§ 5

---

2. Calvin writes that "however magistrates may connive at the crime, God sends executioners from other quarters, who shall render unto sanguinary men their reward." See *CCS*, ad loc. Gen 9:6.

3. Kuyper is referring here to the marginal notes of the Dutch *Statenvertaling* (lit., "States Translation," hereafter cited in notes as SV). Published in 1637, the SV was the first Bible translation from the original biblical languages of Hebrew, Aramaic, and Greek into Dutch, commissioned by the States General of the Netherlands.

must be explained on its own, and refers to what we were told earlier, that "the voice of your brother's [Abel's] blood is crying to me from the ground" [Gen 4:10]. Likewise it refers to what we read elsewhere about the blood of the martyrs that cries out from the ruins of the cities accursed by God (Rev 6:10 and elsewhere). Not a single person was ever murdered whose blood God did not avenge or will avenge.

This occurs in various ways. Often this occurs simply by means of an immediate deadly fear cast into the murderer's soul, which from that moment on robs him of all rest and peace and joy of living. More than one murderer has finally surrendered to the authorities because he could not deal with the remorse of his conscience, and he literally *thirsted* for punishment in order to regain his peace of conscience. The identity of murderers who never reached this point and whose crimes were not discovered, who suffered the rest of their lives on account of that remorse of conscience, came to be known on more than one deathbed. They were tortured and tormented for their crime, sometimes for forty or more years, day and night. The murder they committed was punished with a *moral death*, with carrying around a living corpse for years afterward.

In the second place, God very often punishes the murderer whose crime remained undetected by overwhelming him in terms of his divine providential order with a very violent punishment, occasionally with a punishment equal to his crime. Someone who did not spare the child of another would occasionally be punished with the murder of his own child, more terrible than if he himself had been murdered.

Added to this, in the third place, is the eternal punishment. There is a prelude to God's justice here on earth, but the actual administration of his divine justice comes only in the last judgment. So when God says that he will require the soul of the one murdered from the hand of his murderer, and you are dealing with a villain whose conscience has been seared and whose life went on without unusual punishment, that does not in the least contradict the absolute truth of this declaration. God will require the soul of the murderer's victim from him, and the fact that he has not yet done so up to this point simply means that he will do it all the more terribly on the last day. This applies to *all* of God's judgments. Undergoing his punishment already here and now is indeed seen to be grace. The most fearful thing is if God spares us here and heaps up his vengeance for the day of his irrevocable judgment.

Apparently, there is only one exception to this. There are indeed many who, after having reached out their hand to take another person's life, came to accuse themselves and by God's grace were led to genuine conversion. Such is known about several whose crime of murder came to light, but also by the deathbed disclosure of several people whose manslaughter had remained hidden from the worldly judge. These people have passed away, whether on the scaffold, or on their deathbed, in the full assurance that their terrible sin had been forgiven, and that the soul of their victim would no longer be required from them. Only in this way did they die in peace.

§ 6

But does this remove the truth of God's ordinance? Obviously, not in the least, because every child of God confesses that the punishment that brought them peace was laid on the Lamb of God. In this way, such a converted murderer has found peace for his soul only when he believingly confesses that his Savior has borne also this his murderous guilt, and has atoned the guilt of the shed blood in the shedding of his own life blood.

Therefore, we must in no way—absolutely none at all—limit the complete validity and the full extent of the Lord's declaration. Even now, as in the days of Noah, the established regulation continues to operate with exactitude and strictness, namely, that God had required, does require, or will require the soul of every one who was slain from the hand of the one who has slain him.

Until now, however, the motive for God's never-abrogated judgment continued to consist simply in this: that God created men from one blood as brothers, and that therefore the extinguishing of the life of a person is for that reason a violation of the deepest awareness that God has imprinted in the heart of all humanity, and that this breaks the bond wherewith our God has bound one person to another. Whoever commits murder acts from the root of hatred, of malice, of sin in its divisive and socially-undermining form. It is egoism and self-interest that one employs in order to eliminate any competitor to his egoism. In murder, sin reveals its principally devilish character as it goes directly against the fraternal bond of love. The wretch who commits this crime in this way assaults God's fundamental ordinance for all of human society. He violates his inborn human instinct. For this reason, as the One who created people under the ordinance of fraternal solidarity, God must avenge this brutal violation of his divine order. Only in that way can his ordinance continue to be maintained. *Not* to avenge would at this point be to abandon his decree and order, to surrender his ordinance, and to hand over the entirety of our human life to the wild turbulence of sin and passion.

But even with this we have not yet said enough. There is more at stake among humanity than God's ordinance, even more than the fraternal bond. Man was also *created in the image of God*. This entails that whoever extinguishes the life of another person assaults not only God's ordinance but *God himself* in his image-bearer, and this explains why later in [Genesis 9:]6 God speaks of an entirely different vengeance. With this we come to our discussion of *capital punishment*.

# CHAPTER EIGHT

# THE INSTITUTION OF CAPITAL PUNISHMENT

*Then Jesus said to him, "Put your sword back into its place. For all who take the sword will perish by the sword."*

MATTHEW 26:52

We come now to an extremely important verse, *Genesis 9:6*, a scriptural statement to which we cannot pay enough attention, given its extraordinary significance. We read in this verse: *"Whoever sheds the blood of man, by man shall his blood be shed, for God made man in his own image."*

Very recently, Professor Mr. J. Domela Nieuwenhuis, who teaches Criminal Law at the National University in Groningen,[1] has discussed this statement of Holy Scripture once again, in the weekly journal of the *Nieuwe Sprokkelaar*, in the dispute about capital punishment, but in a manner that is entirely untenable, as will become apparent.[2]

§ 1

---

1. J. Domela Nieuwenhuis (1836–1924) taught at the Rijksuniversiteit Groningen from 1884 until 1906.
2. *Note by the author*: June 21, 1895.

Here is the professor's argument:

> Genesis 9:6 seems to point to the private vendetta practiced
> in ancient times by almost all known peoples. Nothing else is
> being said here other than that whoever sheds blood will for
> that reason receive from people a corresponding recompense,
> suited to the culture of that time. Here the Lord is permitting
> what in verse 5 he had identified as his right. There he had
> said, "I shall avenge," that is to say, "Vengeance belongs to me."
> From this, however, it hardly follows that God is issuing for
> all peoples and all times an obligation placed on the govern-
> ment to apply capital punishment. And if one does read that
> out of the verse, then let him be consistent and not distin-
> guish between murder, voluntary manslaughter, and invol-
> untary manslaughter. For it says, "Whoever sheds the blood
> of man, by man shall his blood be shed." The remaining pas-
> sages that you cite from the Old Testament contain no words
> directed to Noah but contain stipulations in the Mosaic leg-
> islation that applied to the Israelite people. Concerning this I
> simply want to ask you whether you seriously mean that the
> Israelite legislation possesses any binding authority for our
> nation and our time? In my opinion the Christian lives in the
> new dispensation and not in the old dispensation. Now it is
> surely known to you that our Savior and Lord repeatedly said,
> "It was said to those of old, but I tell you." Those words applied
> to, among other things, "eye for eye and tooth for tooth."

The twofold conclusion of this argument can be quickly refuted.
The claim that the legislation that was placed by God upon Israel would
be applicable still today in its full scope was never made, neither by the
aforementioned journal nor by any other person representing our side.
Therefore the professor is wasting his arrows when he shoots them at
that claim.

But the Reformed position has always maintained, and still maintains,
that within this legislation one must distinguish between the moral, the
ceremonial, and the political [civil] laws, and that as far as the latter [the
civil law] is concerned, a distinction must be made between the *general principle* that underlies such a legislative stipulation, and the *form* in
which this principle is applied to various times and situations. That form

has now passed away, but that principle has remained, and we continue to be bound only to those principles, since they have been established by God.

Already with Professor Junius, one of the first Reformed theologians who provided higher education in our country, Professor Domela Nieuwenhuis can find this position explained.[3]

The second comment can be dealt with just as quickly, since it proceeds from the assumption that our Savior, when he contended against what had been said "by those of old" would have meant by this the legislation of Moses. Not only by others but also in our magazine it has been shown with clear and extensive proof that this assumption conflicts entirely with what it says. "Those of old" are not Moses and Aaron, but the Jewish scribes who after the captivity severed the stipulations of the Mosaic law from their spiritual root, and formalistically restricted and falsified them. The requirement of "an eye for an eye" was a stipulation of a judicial nature in the Mosaic legislation. It was hardly intended that the individual citizen would act according to this rule, but only that the government would function in terms of recompense when it came to judicial punishment. "Those of old," by contrast, who were the scribes, falsified this regulation by deriving from it the right for personal revenge, and saw in this regulation a rule of conduct for personal living. So with an eye to that, Jesus now says as it were: The false scribes have taught you that you may live by "an eye for and eye" and "a tooth for a tooth," but I tell you—not as something new, but something that had already been taught in the Old Testament—love your enemies, and do good to those who hate you [see Luke 6:27].

The same is recorded in Proverbs 25:21: "If your enemy is hungry, give him bread to eat, and if he is thirsty, give him water to drink." Had the professor [J. Domela Nieuwenhuis] simply checked the annotations in our standard Dutch Bible, he could have avoided erring on this point.[4] The annotation accompanying Matthew 5:21 comments that here "the interpretations of the scribes" are refuted by Jesus; that the teachings mentioned

---

3.  *Note by the author*: See Franciscus Junius (1545–1602), *De Politae Mosis Observatione*, in *Opuscula Theologica Selecta*, ed. Abraham Kuyper (Amsterdam: Muller, 1882), 329–92. [Ed note: ET: *The Mosaic Polity*, trans. Todd M. Rester, ed. Andrew M. McGinnis (Grand Rapids: CLP Academic, 2015).]
4.  Kuyper is referring to the SV, which included marginal notes. The note for Prov 25:21 indicates that "bread and water" is to be understood as referring to all physical needs.

here are found not with Moses but only with them; and thus what Jesus posits over against that is not new *but appears this way already in the Old Testament*. Now the professor is of course free to oppose that explanation, if he sees an opportunity to overthrow it. But what he should not have done was to suppose that no other explanation of Jesus' discourse existed other than his own. In the meantime the professor can still catch up on the things he overlooked, and *if* there is a serious counterargument to be made, then the professor is welcome to make it.

§ 2    The important thing, however, continues to be the question whether it is true that in Genesis 9:6 nothing besides personal vengeance is intended, and whether this declaration has nothing to do with capital punishment. We must challenge this sentiment of the professor, and we want to defend that challenge.

We begin then by observing that Genesis 9:6 does not follow Genesis 9:5 as something new, but seeks to further specify the conclusion of verse 5. In verse 5 God Almighty had said, "From his fellow man I will require a reckoning for the life of man." Here in verse 6 the manner in which that would occur is instituted, namely, that God will judge the murderer *by another man*. The fact that this, and only this, is the correct and convincing interpretation appears from the omission in the sixth verse of any conjunction. If it had said, "And," or, "And furthermore, whoever sheds the blood of man, by man shall his blood be shed," then that *conjunction* of "*and*" or "*and furthermore*" could give us to understand that the preceding was finished and a new topic was being started here. But the fact that there is no *conjunction*, and verse 6 is joined to verse 5 without any connective particle except in the form of a participle,[5] requires the sound interpretation that verse 6 is to be understood as the further explanation of what was taught at the end of verse 5. There is no kind of contrast present. Such a contrast would need to have been expressed in the original language. Since there is none, one may understand verse 6 neither as treating a *new* subject nor as a *contrast*, but must understand it in an *explanatory* sense, that is, as further stipulating in what way and by what means God himself shall avenge the shedding of man's blood. Even the choice of the Hebrew words points to that by means of alliteration,[6] in order to imprint this judicial regula-

---

5.  *Note by the author*: In the original [Hebrew].
6.  *Note by the author*: By *alliteration* we understand that words beginning with the same letter or with a similar sound are intentionally chosen.

tion deep in the heart and firmly in the memory. The Hebrew *dam ha'adam ba'adam damo* exhibits an intentional choice and arrangement of words.

The first uncertainty that must be removed here concerns the question whether in verse 6 we are dealing with an explanation that it *will* happen this way, or with an institution that it *must* happen this way. When Jesus says to Peter, "all who take the sword will perish by the sword" [Matt 26:52], nothing is being commanded or stipulated or launched or instituted, but Jesus is simply pointing to the fact that anyone who draws the sword makes himself vulnerable. Likewise one could wish to understand Genesis 9:6 as though the words, "Whoever sheds the blood of man, by man *shall* his blood be shed," indicated nothing other than that this is how things ordinarily go, in part because the victim probably will have someone to avenge his blood with the blood of his murderer, or also because a certain mysterious justice often ensures sooner or later that one who murders another is himself murdered by another. If this were the intention of these words, then of course there would be nothing here about capital punishment, and the institution of capital punishment could never be deduced from this verse. So everything hinges on this point. If the idea is correct which claims that here it is simply being stated, "Ordinarily the murderer gets murdered in turn," then we must surrender our view. On the contrary, if this idea appears absolutely untenable, and that conversely verse 6 is to be understood as a *command* and an *institution*, then herewith the position of the professor is found to be untenable and the way has been paved for assessing our view.

That the latter view is indeed the case is apparent *in an absolutely certain manner* from the conclusion of the verse, where it says, *"for God made man in his own image."* Here of course all the emphasis falls on the conjunction *for*. This conjunction was not added to the translation, but it is also present in the Hebrew. *"For"* in the Hebrew is *ki*, and in the original this *ki* immediately precedes the last part of the sentence. So there is no point in resisting the fact that man's having been created according to God's image must be the reason, the fundamental ground, the motive for *why* one who sheds *a man's* blood shall by *man* be put to death.

§ 3

As long as one simply keeps *this* sharply in focus, the entire notion that here the verse is dealing with personal vengeance is hereby completely refuted.

You sense this immediately if you would reformulate verse 6 in line with that view [in favor of personal vengeance] this way: "Whoever kills a man will discover that a friend or blood relative of the victim will avenge his life; that appetite for vengeance therefore dwells in man, because man was created according to the image of God." But that is absurd, you say, since the avenger kills the murderer *not* because the avenger was created in God's image but because he is a *sinner*, and as sinner takes up the Lord's justice, giving free rein to the passion of anger that drives him. And that is indeed the case. It *is* absurd, but exactly that utter absurdity shows in an incontrovertible manner the absolute untenability of this entire idea.

The *lioness* that sees that you have killed her cubs will immediately attack you, though she is not hungry, simply out of anger about what you have done to her cubs. To the degree that a man allows himself to be driven by a similar impulse, he is manifesting neither a higher understanding nor a nobler lineage, but a *beastly* trait is operating within him. The fact that man was created in God's image would therefore have to result in exactly the opposite—in *not* being incited by vengeance but the reverse, *keeping the impulse for vengeance under control*.

For that reason we are not denying that a certain kind of *vendetta* can dominate, as still happens on [the island of] Corsica and in other regions. But this is completely different. The *vendetta* is in this respect on a continuum with the American *lynch law*, and aims *to render justice*.[7] Even anyone who was not at all driven by the passion of revenge was nevertheless held to be executing the *vendetta*. Even though the murdered blood relative was his personal enemy, such that his death was a relief for him, the assigned person is nevertheless held to carry out this verdict of punishment. Even if the murderer was his friend, the obligation for executing a *vendetta* or reprisal still rests on him. This means nothing else than that, with the absence of a sufficient, or sufficiently strict, administration of justice, maintaining justice is placed on part of the people.

We admit without reserve that very often, perhaps even as a rule, evil passions are *mixed in*, but this does not eliminate the fact that as soon as the retaliation occurs on the basis of the notion that one is appointed in a given case to maintain *justice*, then the retaliation itself becomes part of the procedure for corporal punishment and only then is permitted and justified. In the same way, capital punishment was introduced into the

---

7. Kuyper is not defending the vendetta, particularly in the form of Corsican blood feuds or the American vigilante practice of punishment administered by private citizens, but is simply intending to contrast such human retribution with the response of animals, such as the lioness referenced above.

justice procedure by the justice of God. With that, however, one has come to embrace precisely the position we have adopted, which is *that God instituted capital punishment*.

Nor can one say that *the compulsion for justice* would lie in our having been created in God's image, and that therefore one would be able to understand *verse 7* this way: "Because man was created according to God's image, and consequently a strong impulse for justice lies within man, the blood relative or friend of the victim shall avenge the one murdered." This is so for four reasons.

§ 4

*First*, we cannot take this view because after the fall it is impossible or impermissible to reason that way from having been created in God's image. In Genesis 6:5 it is explicitly observed that although man was created in God's image, now his heart is depraved—that the imagination of that heart has become totally wicked. The line of reasoning that man was created in God's image and for that reason certain good things are found in him was valid in paradise but became invalid as soon as man was chased out of paradise. Even assuming that such a *pure* impulse for justice already lay within man originally, after the fall that is no longer present within him in such a pure fashion, and therefore one cannot argue on the basis of such an impulse for justice. So too we can see how in our contemporary society this impulse for justice has so little vitality, such that rather refined people like Professor Domela Nieuwenhuis, although they have been created in God's image, hardly feel that impulse for justice leading to putting the murderer to death.

But also *in the second place*, this interpretation will not work because then it would need to have said, "*For man was created in God's image.*" That is not what it says, however. The active voice is used: "For *God created* man in his own image." The emphasis was placed not on the fact that man stood in this particular situation and therefore must sense this particular impulse within himself, but just the opposite, on the fact that *God* made it so that as a result justice must be enforced not according to what man himself would invent, but according to God's original order. These two reasons are joined by two more.

*First*, exactly the opposite [conclusion] would flow from the fact of having been created in God's image, namely, that a person should not avenge himself but leave vengeance to God. In his original rectitude man knew and honored the justice of his God and did not arrogate to himself what belonged to God. Now since Scripture clearly teaches us that, according to his original command, God did not place *vengeance* within man but reserved it for himself, then every retaliation born of passion or revenge constitutes a *violation* of the image of God and can never constitute *respect* for the image of God.

In the *second* place, one cannot say that the person who retaliates is therefore moderating his revenge because the murderer was so evil-natured as to murder "someone created in God's image." For the person retaliating is not thinking about that at all. A husband whose wife was murdered pursues the murderer not because his wife was created in God's image but because she was his wife. You find that passion most strongly among people who are completely godless, who consider neither God nor his commandment, and least strongly precisely among those who genuinely respect a human being as having been created in God's image. This cannot be otherwise. It would be absurd to say that such a husband killed the murderer of his wife because the murderer had assaulted a being who was made in God's image, since *that murderer himself is also just such a being*, and the husband deprived of his wife *may* not himself take the murderer's life precisely on that account.

From whatever angle one looks at it, it seems increasingly impossible to do justice to the words, *"For God created man in his image,"* as long as one reads in [Genesis 9:]6 nothing but a certain prophecy that things would occur this way, and refuses to interpret these words as a *prescription* or an *institution*. That entire notion conflicts irreconcilably with the end of the verse, and Professor Domela Nieuwenhuis will never succeed in giving an explanation of these words, in terms of *his* position, that does justice to the context and does not come into direct contradiction of the comprehensive fact of creation in God's image, of the fact of the shattering of that image through sin, and similarly of the practical facts of retaliation.

It is then remarkable that to be on the safe side, the professor *simply omits* these words that govern the entire argument, excising them from the verse and saying nothing about them. One hereby instinctively gets the impression that the professor, who has of course read these words in his Bible, did not know what to do with them, and sensing that they weighed in against his position, preferred to leave them untouched.

More than that, from what the professor writes it appears most clearly that he himself sensed how as a bare prophecy that this would be the course of things could not be persuasive. For that reason he admits that there really is something more in these words, and he seeks that more in the fact that the Lord here *permits* what in [Genesis 9:]5 he had reserved as *his* right. Of course this does not satisfy, but rather is self-contradictory. First he says, *"Nothing more is said* than that he who sheds man's blood will for that reason receive from man a recompense that corresponds to the current situation and is suited to [the present] society." Immediately thereafter, however, he says *that there is still something else* in these words, namely, an abdication to man by God of the right that had belonged only to God. That this is *not* the same but is something entirely different, requires no argument. But this *difference* encompasses an idea that cannot be permitted in Holy Scripture. Then one cannot speak of any instituting of government, nor even of any instituting of capital punishment as punishment, but only that the relative of the victim who before this time had killed the murderer, knowing that he was thereby sinning against God, from now on could say, "Now I may innocently stab the murderer to death. God himself has given me his eminent permission for doing so." That approach, however, is never God's order, ever. The judicial order was indeed adjusted at more than one point with a view to man's weakness, but then as a *judicial order*, and never as a license for sinful man to give free rein to his passion.

Should the professor reply to this that he did not intend to say this, but merely wanted to say that "retaliation by the nearest blood relative" is being instituted here as a *judicial institution*, fine, but then he has moved over to our position and acknowledges with us that here we are not dealing with a fact that is being communicated or prophesied, but a *prescription*, an *institution* is being provided that consists in this, that capital punishment is prescribed to be exercised by the nearest blood relative. Then he is surrendering his position and coming over to our position, and with us he must accept the consequence that in [Genesis 9:]6 properly speaking the institution of government is being sanctioned. Taken apart from an instituted judicial order, however, the rule that he who kills a man must himself be put to death because that victim was created in God's image, would lead to a complete annihilation of our race. That murderer was also created in God's image, and the shedding of *his* blood would then also have to entail identical consequences. As we will show in a subsequent chapter, this important verse [Genesis 9:6] is not interpreted properly unless one understands it to contain the institution of government and the command for that government, either itself or through others, to punish the murderer with death.

# CHAPTER NINE

# GOVERNMENT AND CAPITAL PUNISHMENT

*For we know him who said, "Vengeance is mine; I will repay." And again, "The Lord will judge his people."*

HEBREWS 10:30

§ 1     After having challenged and, we trust, sufficiently refuted those who find no *prescriptive ordinance* in Genesis 9:6, one that obligates the government to exercise corporal punishment, we come now to the Reformed interpretation of this crucial statement. As we see already from the annotations in the Dutch Bible, that interpretation consists essentially in the position that in this declaration God "establishes the government and ordains capital punishment because after the flood, something of God's image remained in man, and he does not permit his image being violated without that being punished." Literally they wrote, *"Here the office of government is established, and the sword is given to it for punishing evildoers, Rom. 13:1, etc."* At the conclusion of the verse, they make this note: "Although God's image was marred and broken through the fall, God has still left in man some remnant thereof, for various reasons, *which he does not wish to have violated, but here ordains punishment for such a violation."*

This brief explanation indeed expresses the general sentiment of the Reformed regarding this item, as can be seen in, among other places, the commentary of Professor Rivet of Leiden, who extensively refutes the sentiment being advocated now again by Professor Domela Nieuwenhuis, and clearly shows how completely untenable the opinion is that sees Genesis 9:6 as simply predicting, with the help of indeterminate prophecy, that the murderer shall sooner or later die an otherwise violent death by means of retaliation.[1] He says that this incorrect opinion was advocated by the Anabaptists and the Socinians, and posits the following over against them, as the result of his own investigation: "That which lies before us here is an *ordinance or institution of God*, proclaimed by his own word, according to which ordinance it is our duty that everyone who as a private individual has perpetrated the outrageous act of shedding the blood of a man, is to be put to death *by a man* lawfully appointed thereto, that is, by the government." Calvin expresses himself in a similar spirit, and this opinion has always been defended by the Reformed against the Socinians and others. It may even be added that the Reformed do not stand alone in this position, but the Lutherans together with various early Christian interpreters agree in the main with this opinion. Luther placed even more direct emphasis on this than we find in Calvin's commentary.

This last fact has a particular cause. Calvin focuses attention on the fact that occasionally the murderer escapes his deserved punishment from the side of the government. Thus, to remove from the murderer all illusion that anyone escaping the government's punishment goes scot-free, he intentionally points out that in addition to the government's punishment, there is still a "divine judgment" that occasionally brings about corporal punishment of the murderer already here on earth. This occurs, as Calvin puts it, "through a hidden order" of God, so that sooner or later the murderer nevertheless perishes at the hands of men, as often happens, as Calvin observes, in war. Of course Calvin is not wanting to say that a murderer *always* perishes, whether by the sword of the government or by the sword of a private individual. Some murderers die in their beds. This, however, invalidates neither the sentence nor the punishment, but simply

---

1. *Note by the author*: André Rivet, *Opera theologica*, 3 vols. (Rotterdam: Leers, 1651–1660), 1:236.

postpones it to the "final judgment," and to "eternal punishment."[2] What is certain is that God requires punishment for every murderer, though this occurs in one of three ways. Where his commands and ordinances are obeyed, *by the government*. If this is absent, *by individual persons whom God raised up for that purpose*. And in the third place, if neither the first nor the second has occurred, *on the last day*.

Following Calvin, Rivet also focused attention on this. That our official commentators on the Dutch Bible were also of this opinion appears clearly from their reference, in connection with Genesis 9:6, to Lamentations 4:13, Matthew 26:52, and Revelation 13:10. These are three declarations wherein precisely this is observed, that one who slays by the sword will perish by the sword, and that the blood of the murder victim that soaks into the earth is known by God and will be avenged by God.[3] In so doing, these commentators provide the explanation first that here capital punishment was being ordained, but point out simultaneously, as Calvin did, that *in addition to* capital punishment, still other methods of retribution occur. These hardly cancel the ordinance of capital punishment, but become applicable where capital punishment is not applied, whether because the murderer was not discovered, his guilt was not proven, or his life was spared through the disobedience of the government to God's ordinance.

As far as the history of interpretation is concerned, without fear of contradiction one can say that the mainstream Christian church has always understood Genesis 9:6 as Rivet did, and that only heretics rose up in opposition against this interpretation, whether it was the Anabaptists, because they wanted to apply the administration of *special* grace as the touchstone for the government and the civil administration, or whether it was the Methodists and others, because they were looking in the first place for the conversion *of the sinner* and only then for *the justice of God*. What Luther declared in his explanation of Genesis 9:6 is hardly an exaggeration: "Here we have the source from which stem all civil law and the law of nations. If God grants to man power over life and death, surely

---

2. Calvin writes, "And we see some die in highways, some in stews, and many in wars. Therefore, however magistrates may connive at the crime, God sends executioners from other quarters, who shall render unto sanguinary men their reward. God so threatens and denounces vengeance against the murderer, that he even arms the magistrate with the sword for the avenging of slaughter, in order that the blood of men may not be shed with impunity." See *CCS*, ad loc. Gen 9:6.

3. These verses appear as cross-references in the SV.

He also grants power over what is less, such as property, the home, wife, children, servants, and fields."[4]

We still have not finished the matter. The possibility is indeed very small but nevertheless conceivable that the great exegetes of the Christian church had erred, and that the true interpretation of Genesis 9:6 is to be found with the Socinians, the Anabaptists, and other sectarians. For that reason, we have to investigate the place itself and see if indeed this interpretation comports and agrees with what it says. We begin, then, by taking up the conclusion of this verse and paying close attention to the words: "for God *made* man in his own *image*." After all, the key to understanding the entire verse lies in these words.

§ 2

This conclusion is *explanatory*. It is introduced by the *explanatory* conjunction *for*. Therefore it is a requirement that what preceded must be explained in such a way that the reason for the preceding is to be found in the fact that God has created man according to his image.

At this point two possibilities exist. The first is that the fact that God created man in his image contains the reason why *man* must punish the murderer. The other is that this contains the reason why the murderer of *a man* must be punished in this way. In the first instance the reasoning would go like this: The right to punish a murderer is given *to a man* because by virtue of his creation in God's image, man is clothed with majesty. In the second instance, by contrast, the line of argument would come out this way: Because man was created in God's image, the murder of a man is equal to attacking God's majesty, and the murderer must be put to death on account of this abomination.

A third explanation is inconceivable. You cannot say that a murderer usually perishes in a violent way and encounters in *his* turn a man who murders him, *for* man was created in God's image. Such a murder of the murderer is, after all, the fruit of hatred, vengeance, or malice, and neither hatred nor vengeance nor malice can be explained as something flowing forth from the image of God. Nobody can ever show that he was created in God's own image by the fact that, as a private individual, he puts someone who has a murder on his conscience to death . *Quite the opposite*. From Genesis 1 it appears that "being created in God's image" in itself does not yet contain any *dominion*, not even over the animals. Had this been the

---

4.   See *LW* 2:140.

case, the *dominion* over the animals would not have been added as something intentional. And yet that is exactly what Genesis 1 tells us.

After man was created in God's image, and when he as yet stood before God in his original rectitude, dominion over the animals was mandated for him through a *separate divine ordinance*. And this ordinance was indeed a creation ordinance that fit man's righteous nature completely, and in this way corresponded with his creation in God's image, but nevertheless from this, *apart from* any mandate, no right for man has flowed forth at all. Our Reformed fathers emphasized this in order to keep God's sovereignty from being violated. All things belong to *God*. *To him* belongs *every created thing.*[5] Including the animal. For this reason the disposition regarding the life of the animal belongs to God alone, and can be laid upon man *only by him*. If this is valid with respect to animals, then it is valid *a fortiori* with respect to man, and it can never be said that any man, no matter who he is, possesses by nature or by virtue of his creation the right to take the life of one of his fellow men. Only God has authority over man, and God decides. He is the one who kills and makes alive. No man ever possesses the right to take the life of another man, unless God himself grants that right or imposes the obligation to do so upon him.

Suppose that someone saw a defenseless child being brutally murdered, and roused to fury instinctively attacked the murderer and killed him. Even then, in this most plausible instance we would never derive the slaying of the murderer from the image of God. The fact that someone murders another person does not in the least create for you the right to murder him. In the aforementioned vendetta this can occur, insofar as a portion of *the judicial procedure* is handed over to the citizens, but at that point such retaliation flows forth from *the ordinance*, and thus falls outside our purview.

In no way whatsoever, therefore, is the saying, "for God created man in his image," treated justly if one lets the murderer die under the exercise of intentional vengeance or as a result of accidental bloodthirstiness by a third party. This concluding part of the verse makes sense, especially explanatory sense, *only* with the assumption that here the reason is being supplied as to why the murderer may not remain unpunished but will

---

5. Calvin writes, "For it is of great importance that we touch nothing of God's bounty but what we know he has permitted us to do; since we cannot enjoy anything with a good conscience, except we receive it as from the hand of God." See *CCS*, ad loc. Gen 1:28.

have to be punished according to the statement of God's ordinance and upon his authority. That reason, that justification why the punishment may not be averted can be explained perfectly from the dignity possessed by the murdered victim. The murder of an ambassador is punished more severely because that ambassador was a bearer of the king's authority, and to a certain degree displayed the king's image. In the same way we can explain and understand perfectly that God said, "The murderer must be punished with death due to the dignity that lay in the murdered victim as bearer of my image. It is a requirement to punish the murderer, not because he overpowered a creature, which would not yet be the most serious, but because he stretched out his hand to strike a creature that stood in relationship *with me*, originally created *in my image*, and thus could not be assaulted without at the same time violating and attacking my royal majesty. In himself a sinner is certainly not always a respectable person, and there are many scoundrels of whom it may be said that it would be a blessing for us if they disappeared from the earth. The dignity itself that requires capital punishment for a violation does not lie in sinful man as such. But in everything that is called human, no matter how deeply a man has sunk, you are dealing always with a creaturely being possessing basic features belonging to the image of God, and for that reason you shall spare the life of a man, not for the sinner's sake but for the sake of my will, and if you do not spare his life that wicked deed will have to be paid for with your own life."

Therefore, everything here has to do with God and his majesty. This is so, not as many assume, because it pertains to the protection of human life in order to prevent murder. That is indeed the result, as well as the purpose, why God instituted this ordinance, but it is *not the basis* from which the ordinance arises. That basis actually lies in God's sovereignty. People are *his* people. They belong to him. He has jurisdiction over them. Since in those people he has deposited something of his divine honor, for that reason the honor of God is always attacked with murder. That may not happen. His ordinance opposes that. Precisely on that basis alone can *capital punishment* be ordained for the murderer.

§ 3

Do not read too quickly past that last sentence. For a long time the objection has been leveled against this single correct interpretation of Genesis 9:6 that if this is correct, then the executioner who shed the murderer's blood would also have to be put to death. He too has shed human blood and his blood must also be shed.

Indeed, this observation would be fully persuasive, as our previous chapter demonstrated, if one understood Genesis 9:6 to involve the private execution of the murderer. Anyone who kills a man without a mandate from God becomes liable for the shedding of that man's blood. For that reason his blood must also be shed. Thereafter again the blood of anyone who killed him. In this way the final point would be reached only when the last man remained, who then could do nothing other than shed his own blood.

But this entire absurd argument falls away immediately if, according to the requirement of the Reformed principle, you take into account the sovereign justice of God. Then it is he whose justice and honor are being violated through murder; the execution of the murderer occurs then in no other way than through the one to whom God gives the mandate to do so. For that reason the exercise of capital punishment never entails a second violating of God's honor and justice, because it is performed by virtue of God's ordinance and upon his authority.

Consequently, only the ancient established interpretation avoids the aforementioned absurd implication, to which every view automatically leads that interprets this as a private undertaking. Not the *life* of a human being, but the *honor of God* in the creature created in his image, becomes the judicial motive. This is something that becomes clear even from the choice of words. As we observed earlier in another context, it states *not* "for man was created in God's image," but with the active voice, with the name of the Lord at the beginning: "for *God* created man in his image." This means that God placed man in this creation as his representative and sent him out across this earth as his ambassador and as the bearer of his dignity.

If with this, the interpretation of the end of the verse has been established, then at the same time the meaning of the first sentence of the verse has thereby also been decided. The words, "Whoever sheds the blood of man, by man shall his blood be shed," *cannot* contain bare prophecy or a superfluous comment about what occurs naturally, but must be understood in terms of the full power of the word "*shall*." Here *shall* means *must*, a meaning that lies embedded in the Hebrew words. In Exodus 21:12 we read, "Whoever strikes a man so that he dies *shall* be put to death." Here too it says not *must*, but *shall*, though it is perfectly clear that here *shall* means *must*.

As an aside, we need to add here that with stipulations that must be imprinted deeply within the memory, the original text often uses *alliterative* formulations, a phrase in which words begin with the same letter or syllable. For example, in the Dutch metrical version of Psalm 2, we read the phrase "zijn ... *st*oel op *st*arren *st*icht," where the *st* is repeated three times, forming an alliterative manner of speaking, something that adds force and aids the memory.[6] As we indicated earlier, this is also how the ordinance in Genesis 9:6 sounds in Hebrew: **dam** ha'**adam** ba'**adam dam**o, with a fourfold repetition of the syllable *dam*, which means "blood." So it catches our attention when in Exodus 21:12, where similarly capital punishment was instituted, now specifically for Israel, we find such alliteration once again. In Hebrew we read, "*makkeh 'ish wamet mot yomat*." Four words that begin with the letter *m*. This ceremonious manner of expression fortifies the already clear sentiment that in Genesis 9:6 we are dealing with an *ordinance*, with a *command*, with a divine *institution*. Here the form agrees with the content.

Our conclusion can therefore be none other than that the Christian church has always justifiably read in these words not a prophecy, but a *command*, an *ordinance*. In this word God granted to man the *right* over the life of the murderer, and placed upon man the *duty* to apply corporal punishment to the murderer. This leads immediately to the question *to whom* this duty is assigned. Then the context shows convincingly that it cannot mean *everyone who wants this*, but the identity of the man in view here must be determined according to established rule and order. To this extent, Luther was entirely correct to say that *here lies the official institution of government*, as were the Dutch Bible commentators in observing that here *the legitimacy of government* is being established.

§ 4

Nevertheless, it is noteworthy that before the flood as well, an individual despot had assumed some kind of dominion over others, or occasionally many people had appointed a leader among themselves in order to defend themselves, although all such functioning of an authoritative person until now lacked *every higher sanction*. People cannot create *authority*. Only God can do that. Even though everybody wants to declare together,

---

6. Kuyper is referring to the metrical versification of Psa 2:2, which reads in part, "Maar d'Opperheer, die zijn' geduchten stoel / Op starren sticht, en grondvest op de wolken." See *Het Boek der Psalmen, nevens de Gezangen bij de Hervormde Kerk van Nederland*, ed. F. L. Rutgers, with assist. from H. Bavinck and A. Kuyper (Amsterdam: J. Brandt, 1865), 2.

"We appoint a leader over us and assign him the right, in the event of murder, to slay the murderer," this would be nothing but presumption. Only God, who is sovereign over all, can set one man over others and clothe him with authority, and in the same way only God, who created the lives of all of us, can give to one so clothed with authority the right to decide about the life of another person. So then, that is stated here as well.

Until now, by divine providence there existed on earth nothing but *paternal* authority, and *paternal* authority entailed no right to *slay* the child. From paternal authority nothing can be derived analogously in this regard for the government. But after the flood that mandate of authority was given, in assigning the right over life and death. God himself is speaking here. He commands and ordains. He it is who assigns such a right to people, and all those who as people shall exercise this right have to do this in God's name and in obedience to his command. Whoever reneges at this point thereby dislodges God's command concerning *capital punishment*, but at the same time thwarts the explicit declaration of almighty God who, after the flood, grants *his sanction* to the functioning of the government. Suppose that Ham had put Shem to death; at that point Noah would have had to punish Ham with death, not because he was Ham's father, but as the government appointed over Ham and Shem.

# CHAPTER TEN

# FURTHER OBJECTIONS TO CAPITAL PUNISHMENT

*Whoever strikes a man so that he dies shall be put to death.*

EXODUS 21:12

By means of the accurate interpretation of Genesis 9:6, the difference [of opinion] regarding capital punishment has been decided for us. The words, "Whoever sheds the blood of man, by man shall his blood be shed," permit no other sense than that here a judicial institution is being ordained and putting to death a murderer is being assigned as a duty. If one believes and confesses that these words were indeed spoken to Noah *by God*, then it is God from whom this institution proceeded, and nothing remains for us other than *to obey*. Since God himself has ordained it this way, it *must* be this way.

§ 1

That many do not find this conclusion convincing is generally because they do *not* believe that these words were actually spoken in this way by God: "The text says that God spoke these words, but you must not take that in a literal sense. What is intended is merely that this thought arose this way within Noah's spirit, that under the impulse of that thought he imagined that God had given it to him, and on that basis he said to his wife and children, 'God said it this way.' "

We are unable to reason in this context with anyone who thinks this way. What Noah thought about capital punishment is completely irrelevant to us. The issue involves not what Noah thought, but what God *ordained*. What is at issue is not a historical point of disagreement, but the fear, the respect, the obedience that we are obliged to render to God.

Nevertheless with this the issue has not yet been settled once and for all. The objection continues still further and clothes itself in this form: "It is indeed the case that *at that time* God ordained capital punishment, but this no longer applies to us for that reason. For those days of barbarity, indeed, but not in our age of elevated refinement, [which is the] fruit of the gospel of the New Testament. All of that is now abrogated, just like all sorts of laws of the old covenant." This comes down to saying that one agrees with us about the interpretation of Genesis 9:6, but opposes us because, as it is said, Genesis 9:6 *is now no longer applicable*.

Our reply to this objection can be brief.

First, where does it say that this divine ordinance is abolished? If you acknowledge that God ordained it this way at that time, then of course this ordinance remains valid until God himself retracts or suspends it. What God himself ordains can be abolished only by the very same God. As long as this has *not* happened, *it remains valid*. We read *nowhere* about such an abolition or retraction. If someone should claim, "Yes, but the entire Old Testament is to be examined through the gospel, and thus this command has expired," then we would dispute this. In the Old Testament one must distinguish between that which *preceded* Israel, and that which was ordained specifically for *Israel as a nation*. Everything relating to Israel *as a nation* constituted the "dispensation of shadows," and to the extent that these were *shadows*, they naturally expired when the Messiah appeared. By contrast, what belonged to the Israelite dispensation but was *not* a shadow, such as the moral law, did *not* expire. Even for the specific Israelite dispensation it was only *very partially* true that it expired in and through Christ. But even if this expiration applied to what was ordained *for Israel*, then for a remarkable portion there was hardly any expiration of what God had ordained *before that dispensation of shadows arrived*. In that pre-Israelite dispensation God ordained that man shall work in the sweat of his brow in order to eat bread, that the wife shall bear her children in pain, and so much more. Has all of this *expired* in the new covenant, or has it continued? If you reply, "*It has continued, of course,*" then what right do you have to say that the command for capital punishment *has indeed* expired?

Secondly, this command was given to Noah *and his children*. Do you, or do you not, belong to the children, the descendants, of Noah? Has our own nation not descended from Noah and his family? Is he not the second progenitor of us all? In this light, the command for capital punishment was not issued to one particular people, but to *all of humanity after the flood*. It is not a national but a universal-human ordinance, just like bestowing the right to eat meat. One can find, however, numerous people who eat meat but no longer want capital punishment. If you would ask them, "*By what right do you eat meat?,*" they refer you to Genesis 9:3. There God gave us this right. There are people who don't fear God who imagine that they have an inherent right to kill an animal and eat it. But anyone who fears God and has a deep understanding of justice does not talk that way. Such a person appeals to Genesis 9:3, where God bestowed upon us the right to use meat. But then the question arises at this point as to whether it is anything but pure arbitrariness to say, "What it says in Genesis 9:6 about capital punishment has expired, but what is ordained in Genesis 9:3 about using meat is still valid." In fact one can say that as often as a Christian who opposes capital punishment eats meat, he is caught in his own inconsistency.

Thirdly, the ordinance of capital punishment belongs to the Noahic covenant. Is this covenant now abolished, or does it still exist, so that we still live under it? In order to find a conclusive answer to that question, one needs only to ask a counter-question: What did this covenant contain, and what was its sign? And if you *can* answer only with *this*: "It meant that there would not be another flood, and the sign was the rainbow," then with this answer the matter has been decided. You also still rely on God's promise that there will not be another flood, and as often as the rainbow appears in the clouds, you also still see in it a sign of God's faithfulness.

On the basis of these three considerations the following has been established: first, the ordinance of capital punishment was given *for the entire human race* that lived on earth or will live on it after the flood. Second, this ordinance *cannot* be and was not abolished. And third, therefore no difference can arise concerning the permanent validity of this ordinance. These are firmly established, such that whoever raises doubt already by that fact shows that for him the authority of Holy Scripture is not completely valid.

To this we add the following comment. Far from suspending this ordinance, the New Testament far rather confirms this ordinance. What we read in Romans 13, that *"the government does not bear the sword in vain,"* means, according to the univocal testimony of all expert interpreters, that the government possesses jurisdiction over life and death, even as it explicitly states in verse 4 that the government *"is the servant of God, an avenger who carries out God's wrath on the wrongdoer."* This is something that agrees entirely with the fact that in the only national legislation that came from God himself, capital punishment was indeed ordained. In Exodus 21:12 the Lord said, "Whoever strikes a man so that he dies shall be put to death." Similarly in Leviticus 24:17, we read, "Whoever takes a human life *shall surely be put to death.*" Even if we concede that *this* legislation *no longer* applies for us, it nevertheless remains established that the *principles* from which this legislation proceeds have abiding significance. In addition, from this it appears to us that since man is created in God's image, murder is a crime against God involving [his] wounded majesty, and for this reason capital punishment must be applied to the murderer.

§ 2   In order to be thorough, we still need to examine here those *anemic* arguments against capital punishment that have been advanced on spiritual grounds, among them especially the objections that by applying capital punishment one *eliminates the possibility of someone's conversion*, that occasionally an *innocent* person could be executed, and that the execution of a murderer *debases people.*

By putting someone to death because he killed another person, so people claim, you eliminate time for conversion. Here we must deal differently with Reformed people, on the one hand, and with Pelagians and semi-Pelagians, on the other hand.[1] If you are a Reformed Christian, then

---

1.  Pelagianism refers to a doctrine associated with Pelagius, a monk in the early fifth century identified "as the author or promoter of a heresy which sought to undermine the ancient faith by assailing the doctrine of divine grace." Pelagianism is at odds with the orthodox understanding of grace (particularly as articulated and defended by Augustine) through its denial of original sin and its consequences, and in its emphasis on a rigorous moral code as foundational for realizing salvation through one's natural, unaided powers. See "Pelagius, Pelagian Controversies," in *NSHE* 8:438–39. Semi-Pelagianism refers to a "synergistic view raised in opposition to Augustinian monergism." This "synergistic view involved the decision on man's part, with reference to eternal life, whether by virtue of his freedom he assented, and therefore submitted to the operation of divine grace, or was indifferent to grace, therefore rejecting it." See "Semipelagianism," in *NSHE*, 10:347–49.

such an objection is of course absurd. A sound Reformed person confesses that the salvation of the soul is a work of God's grace that he himself, the Lord our God, initiates, continues, and completes according to his eternal counsel. So if a divinely elect person should face capital punishment, then no capital punishment *can* eliminate his salvation; for "those whom he predestined he also called, and those whom he called he also justified, and those whom he justified he also glorified," as you can read in Romans 8:30. In terms of the Reformed position this objection *cannot* even be raised. God's counsel cannot be resisted, and no judge, no matter who he may be, "can snatch someone from the hand of his Father" [see John 10:28–29]. Moreover, this objection *may not* be raised in the Reformed context because to do so is to place oneself above God's ordinance in order to approve the virtuousness of the ordinance. Since God has prescribed capital punishment for the murderer, to us belongs no further evaluation of its propriety. What God prescribes, I as a person simply need to obey. Consequently, anyone who instead of obeying proceeds to claim, "Yes, but then someone is robbed of time for conversion," shows thereby that he wants to be wiser than God and is finding fault with God's way.

By contrast, the matter is different if you are dealing with a Pelagian or semi-Pelagian, who acknowledges *no* personal election, who places the matter of coming to salvation partially in the hand *of man*, and teaches *no* perseverance of the saints. In opposition to such views you can respond in two ways.

The most persuasive is to prove to them from God's Word that they in their entire position are straying from the way of salvation, and that Holy Scripture truly teaches us that God elects persons, continues irresistibly the work of his grace with everyone who is elect, and that consequently every saint must persevere. Then you are making them Reformed, and as soon as they become Reformed, their objection disappears.

In the usual debate, however, it doesn't go that way, and therefore you can also answer them directly by saying that on this very same basis, war must be abolished. In war, after all, the government is the reason why sometimes thousands of people die in one day, people who had not yet come to conversion. As long as you maintain in your law the right of the king [government] to engage in war, but not the right to punish the murderer with death, then you are worried about the soul of one single criminal but not with the eternal salvation of thousands of innocent people, and you thus come to contradict yourself.

The question then also arises how the government can allow maritime trade, mining development, railway travel, and much more, since statistics show how these and other activities annually block the path toward conversion for an incomparably far greater number of people than would occur by means of the strictest enforcement of capital punishment in any country. Naturally one cannot advance the counterargument that without the shipping industry we would have no coffee and grain, that without mining development we would be sitting without coal, and without railroads we could not travel very far. From the *spiritual* point of view held by these objectors, neither coffee nor grain nor coal nor travel counts nearly as much as the awfulness of the loss of one soul.

In addition, we can reply that they have always neglected to compile any statistics about spared murderers who later came to conversion, whereas conversely there are cases ready at hand of murderers who precisely by means of the seriousness of capital punishment came to experience the crushing of their souls.

Finally, we can say that insofar as capital punishment restrains the murderer, it is nonetheless a curiosity that they always take a stand on behalf of the *soul* of the murderer and never talk about the fact that the murderer (at least given their [Pelagian or semi-Pelagian] position) cut off the possibility of conversion for his victim. From all of which it seems sufficiently clear that their objection is calculated much more for influencing piously disposed souls against capital punishment than for honestly defending the soul of the murderer.

§ 3    Judicial mistakes do happen. Undoubtedly. But what conclusion do you draw from that? The following: that every action of government must be abolished that can lead in any way to the injury of a citizen. One would then have to abolish *all* judiciaries. It should also be clear that judicial mistakes were just as often the reason that someone who was innocent sat imprisoned for years. As far as the general mistakes of the government are concerned, it seems increasingly evident that the outbreak of the Franco-Prussian War of 1870, which cost more than one hundred thousand human lives, was the result of an intentional *mistake* in a dispatch sent from

Berlin to Ems. It may also be said that our Achin War would never have broken out if a *mistake* had not occurred in the preliminary negotiations.[2]

So various *mistakes* are made by the government, mistakes also with promotions where someone is passed by and thereby held back for his entire career. All these government mistakes have painful consequences for the subject who becomes its innocent victim. Yet, those mistakes are simply the disastrous consequence of the limitation and sinfulness of civil servants, and also of judges in cases of judicial mistakes. Preventing them would occur by appointing to the judge's bench only *perfect* people (who do not exist), or since there are no such people, by abolishing every judiciary and all administration of justice. As long as no one dares to draw this conclusion, this argument holds no water.

People sense this themselves, and therefore say, "Not every judicial mistake can be prevented, but here we are dealing with someone's life." We too find this appalling; but no more appalling than the diplomatic mistake of Ems, resulting in a war that cost the lives of ten thousands of men.[3]

And if you should want at this point to argue that by this mistake someone can be cut off from eternal life in the absence of conversion, we would refer you to what we recently set forth. No, judicial mistakes can only spur us to exercise extreme care, can lead to prohibiting the sentence of capital punishment as long as sufficient proof has not been provided, and can prompt the requirement of stronger proof in cases involving capital offenses. But wanting to abolish capital punishment or to acquiesce to its abolition for that reason, is an option only for the person who does not believe in eternal life and judges that capital punishment destroys someone's existence.

---

2. This conflict, which lasted sporadically from 1873 to 1914, involved the Sultanate of Achin (Aceh, in what is today Indonesia) and the Netherlands, and resulted in the annexation of Achin to the Dutch East Indies. It was during Kuyper's time as prime minister that the main resistance to Dutch occupation of Achin was definitively overcome.

3. The mistake of Ems refers to the occasion for the outbreak of the Franco-Prussian War noted previously. The incident of the Ems Dispatch or Ems Telegram involves edits and mistakes of translation made in published accounts of a disputed exchange between the Prussian king and the French ambassador. The French are estimated to have lost more than 138,000 troops, whereas more than 28,000 are estimated to have died on Prussian side. The Achin War is estimated to have claimed between 50,000 and 60,000 lives on the Achin side over the course of the conflict.

The third objection to capital punishment, that executions debase the masses, is hardly worth pausing to answer. It is obvious that the government is free in the choice of the manner of implementing capital punishment. No one disputes the claim that that choice is often misguided, but the blame for this falls not on capital punishment, but on the imprudence of the government that acts so ineptly and inefficiently. There have been times when the government comprehended its calling in connection with such an execution to allow the populace to participate in a manner that evoked sobriety and made a powerful impression. People sensed that it was *God's justice* that was being executed, and there was no trace of debasement or excess to be found. We need say no more about this.

§ 4 We are intentionally silent concerning statistical data. It is impossible to show by means of numbers whether capital punishment is a deterrent against murder and whether abolishing capital punishment causes the number of murder cases to increase. With numbers the plea can be made *for* as well as against capital punishment. If someone shows that formerly, when capital punishment was practiced, the number of murders was no lower than now, then we reply, "This is true, but according to your own argument we have advanced so incredibly far in our culture since that time that even a learned man like Opzoomer[4] thinks we can empty the prisons, which would cost the public school more. Ask yourself how much higher the number of murders would have been in those formerly uncultured times if there had not been capital punishment." And conversely, were you to show by the numbers that after abolishing capital punishment, murders increased in number, then people will neutralize your numbers with the observation that the increased use of alcohol and cheaper firearms are responsible, and that if the use of alcohol had remained what it had been earlier, and the revolver had not been invented, the decrease in the number of murders would have surprised you. The number of murders committed is the result of such a *variety* of causes that it will always remain unfeasible to determine what influence maintaining or abolishing capital punishment has had on this. In general only this may be claimed, that the murderer was very fond of the discontinuation of capital punishment and this certainly does not argue for its abolition.

---

4. Cornelis Willem Opzoomer (1821–92) was a Dutch jurist, philosopher, and theologian. He was a professor at Utrecht University from 1846 to 1889, and among other things, Opzoomer advocated for universal public education and was a proponent of positivist philosophy.

Moreover, we will not enter into this entire line of reasoning. It proceeds from the assumption that one would have to introduce capital punishment if it appeared that without it the number of murders *increased*, and could forego capital punishment if it appeared that the number of murders *remained relatively stable*. In other words, introducing or abolishing capital punishment would then be decided on utilitarian grounds. From our perspective, since we are dealing with a specific command of God, this can never be permitted. God's Word is, for the one who believes and confesses, *the end of all argument*. Where a particular and certain ordinance of God *is absent*, you can, may, and must decide after having weighed the reasons for and against. But as soon as God has spoken, there remains nothing else for you than *to bow your head and obey*.

For that reason, we cannot stop for even one moment to consider a question like whether restoring capital punishment should not wait until the government itself again acknowledges that it is God's ordinance, or until the general public understanding of justice is again sympathetic to it. *Voluntas Dei suprema lex esto*, which means "let God's will be always and everywhere the highest law." And since that will of God is certainly and decisively revealed, not one single objection possesses even the slightest value for us.

If one should claim that a government that does not believe this on this basis cannot implement capital punishment, then our reply is that Romans 13:3 was written under a government that did not believe in Genesis 9:6 either. We would reply further, that we who may confess the authority of Holy Scripture are never discharged from the duty to stand up for the honor of God's ordinance because of the unbelief of the government.

Meanwhile, with this enough has been said and the issue of capital punishment in connection with Genesis 9:6, also in opposition to the objection of Professor Domela Nieuwenhuis, has been, in our opinion, sufficiently explained. We trust that after reading our critique, this professor will himself agree that his article in the *Nieuwe Sprokkelaar* was constructed too carelessly. We also trust that the *Nieuwe Sprokkelaar* will kindly inform its readers that we have provided a substantive response to the article by Mr. Prof. Domela Nieuwenhuis of Groningen.

The only thing still left for us in connection with Genesis 9:6 is to show how in this verse we find at the same time God's ordinance concerning *government*, that is, the establishment of civil authority as such.

More about that in the next chapter.

CHAPTER ELEVEN

# THE INSTITUTION OF GOVERNMENT AUTHORITY

*By me kings reign, and rulers decree what is just.*

PROVERBS 8:15

§ 1     We now need to return to consider the establishment of the government as that took place, according to Genesis 9:6, immediately after the flood. Anyone who removes from this verse the instituting of capital punishment may have to consider that they not only advocate a conviction entailing weakened justice in the area of criminal law, but at the same time they dislodge the authority of government. That authority is stable only if it rests in the grace of God. The basis underlying all authority that arises from human free will shifts like sand, and only when that authority expands broadly and unshakably from the irresistible will of the eternal Being does the authority of government possess a foundation on which people can build and by which one dwells safely.

In three ways people have repeatedly tried to ground government authority in voluntary human action. From ancient times people saw acts of violence and domination as creating a right for the conqueror to subject to himself the people of the country that he controlled. Indeed, an authority thus established stood on a solid foundation as long as the conqueror always had the requisite military power at his disposal to maintain his supremacy, but no longer than that. As soon as the power of his sword weakened and the first conquered land saw a chance to set against him a power of some significance, then rebellion broke out against his authority, the bloodstained tyranny was broken, and those who were once oppressed rose to power. This explains the constant turmoil and unrest in regions and times when the authority of the government arose most often from such acts of domination.

Already in ancient times people sought to establish as a just view the claim that the conqueror must be allowed, after some time had passed at least, to consider his possession as lawful. But it does catch one's eye how this conviction, which on account of sin *had* to be nurtured (as long as no orderly state of affairs could otherwise be born), has nonetheless falsified the notion of justice through such large-scale crowning of robbery after murder, while in the private sector no murder was punished as severely as murder for the purpose of stealing. We will refrain from going into more detail here.

With this issue, however, civil justice faces a most difficult problem. For example, a hostile army invades your country, and whether or not a battle rages, against which you are powerless, you will either be crowned with honor for your faithfulness to the dynasty of your fatherland, or punished with a bullet as a traitor. In fact at this point justice does not rest on any foundation but hangs from the tip of a sword. This suffices to clarify that the right of the conqueror for his authority has no solid foundation.

The second way in which people have attempted to find such a foundation for authority lay *in the free will of man*. Each person, it is thought, by nature had the right to determine his own fate. Nobody could exercise any jurisdiction over him. Authority over him did not exist. But that person himself can call such an authority into being by his own free will. Standing alongside him were other people who were equally free. Were all these people to remain standing loosely alongside each other, this could be dangerous for all of them together. So it became desirable that a kind of administrative government would arise to keep order. Those individual persons, by an exercise of their free will, called such a government into being.

This was the foundation of the entire system of the French Revolution, with its doctrine of "social contract."[1] But of course this foundation was far from solid. Historically it could nowhere be demonstrated where that agreement had been made, where this contract had been concluded. It rested on pure fiction. In the nature of the case, someone could arrange something like that only for his own person, but not for his children. A person who reached the age of majority needed to have freedom of choice all over again. The system also entailed that anyone who wanted to choose differently tomorrow had to have the right to do so. It also meant that in one and the same city or village, one person had to be able to choose *for* such a government and another person *against*. As a result, along this path no comprehensive and overarching administrative government ever arose.

Finally, a third way in which people imagined that such authority originated is what one can express most clearly by speaking of *spontaneous development*. People who advocate this view believe that a certain irresistible natural impulse operates throughout history. They believe that as a result of this impulse, certain events are interconnected, and that as a result of those events, one person ascends higher and another descends lower. In that way a certain power of the one group arises over the other group, which ultimately is consolidated in the supremacy of an individual person.

This system appears more stable than both earlier systems, since it fits the facts of history. It has indeed happened this way. Unfortunately, however, this system, which is not merely historical but at the same time pantheistic, had to lead to the loss of every moral quality of [historical] events.[2] In this system, the noblest deed of a hero that liberated his na-

---

1. Kuyper is referring here to the French Revolution of 1789 with its principles of equality, citizenship, and inalienable rights. He highlights here the French Revolution's understanding of freedom as autonomy, antiauthority, and its individualism as the basis of its social contract theory, meaning thereby the voluntary agreement among individuals by which organized society, government, and communities in general are brought into being. One of the intellectual inspirations of the revolutionary movements was Jean-Jacques Rousseau (1712–78), whose treatise on the "social contract" was published in 1762. The political party that Kuyper founded was called "antirevolutionary" in reference to its opposition to the philosophical foundations of the French Revolution.
2. Pantheism is a doctrine that identifies in an absolute sense the divine with the world. It is an ancient doctrine that takes on different forms and variations in different eras and is usually connected with a kind of fatalism or determinism. In his engagement with pantheism, Kuyper often has in mind the thought of G. W. F.

tion comes by right to stand on the same level as the basest cruelty that massacred a nation. William of Orange won authority by risking his blood for his countrymen, but the [House of] Bourbons won it by cruelly massacring their countrymen by the thousands on St. Bartholomew's eve.[3] In this way every moral quality departs, and history leads to authority resting on the *right of the strongest*, but then only to yield later to an arm that is still stronger.

For that reason, everything must be constructed for the dignity, the ethical character, and the security of authority in such a way that authority exists and is believed to exist *by the grace of God. Grace* here is understood in the sense of *common grace*, the subject we are currently discussing. However, "by the grace of God" does not mean that God bestowed a special *privilege* upon a certain person, house, or dynasty, as if he had delivered a country or nation to such a house as its private hunting ground. *Grace* in this expression means God's gracious arrangement whereby he created order amid the chaos of a sinful world and arrested the disruptive destruction of sin.

§ 2

In every given case this arrangement consists of two parts. In the first place, God institutes government authority as such, and secondly, he ordains in his providential administration the person who will exercise this government authority in a certain region or appointed country. If this sovereign or regent believes that this is how he received his authority, and if the subjects believe that this is how authority was invested in him, then this conviction is the bond that binds sovereign and subjects together, and this authority bears a holy character for both, and both are accountable

---

Hegel (1770–1831), a major German philosopher, whose Idealism took the form of a historicizing of the divine absolute spirit. Thus, writes Kuyper, "With Hegel every religious motive sank away in dialectics; and after him the spirit of our age captured for itself the magic formula of pantheism, in order that, being freed from God and from every tie established by him, it might melt the world as it found it and cast it into a new form for every man in accordance with the desires of his own heart." See Abraham Kuyper, "Pantheism's Destruction of Boundaries.—Part I," trans. J. Hendrik de Vries, *Methodist Review* 75 (July 1893): 521.

3. William I (1533–84) was Prince of Orange, a leader of the Dutch Revolt against Spain, which led to the independence of the Netherlands, and founder of the Royal House of Orange-Nassau. The Royal House of Bourbon came to rule France in 1589 during the struggle between Roman Catholics and Protestants, and ruled until the revolution overthrew the monarchy in 1792. Kuyper refers here to the mass killing of Huguenots (French Protestants) by Roman Catholics at the wedding of Henry of the House of Bourbon to Margaret of Valois on August 24, 1572.

to God for the things they know they have done for or against that authority. The rule, then, is that "by me kings reign," and the apostolic word becomes true, that "all authority that exists comes from God" [Prov 15:8; Rom 13:1]. This is according to Jesus' answer to Pilate: "You would have no authority over me at all unless it had been given you from above" [John 19:11]. Therein lies the solid foundation of authority, since God's will is exalted high above the changing character of our human ways of life, and is in itself absolute.

This "reigning by God's grace" has nothing to do with the so-called "divine right" of kings, as if a sovereign were a privileged person who had received an entire people as his possession and at his disposal. Even less does it contain the idea of a theocracy, since a nation is governed theocratically only if God himself *gives the law* to a nation *without* the intervention of people, as he did to Israel, a law that is then also fixed and unchangeable.

§ 3    This being the case, it is therefore of utmost importance to understand in what manner this instituting and establishing of government authority has occurred. What originates in creation develops and operates automatically, and therefore need not be initiated separately and intentionally. That happens, for example, with the authority that a father exercises with respect to his child, because this authority arises imperceptibly and automatically from the nature of their mutual relationship.

But this is entirely different with government authority. In a sinless situation there would have been no government authority proceeding from people, even as in the kingdom of glory there will be no more government *from* people *over* people. Not even with respect to Christ. At that point he will deliver the kingdom to God the Father so that everything leads again naturally to the creation ordinance, because then God will truly be *all* and *in all*. Such government authority arising *from* people *over* people must therefore be instituted and validated. The person who exercises this authority must be free to be able to show his title. It should be patently clear to [every] conscience that such authority is bound by God's will.

Do not forget that this authority may lead to the greatest sacrifices. Your money may be taken for taxes, or your children for the battlefield, and however innocent you may be, you can be robbed of your freedom and even undergo corporal punishment [see 1 Sam 8:10-18]. Where government authority can make such an enormous infringement upon your personal existence and personal freedom, it is of course necessary that you be deliberately bound *in conscience*. And in order to be so, it needs to be divinely revealed to you that indeed this God, in whom is your life, has ordered and ordained it to be this way. In such a case we submit; otherwise we do *not*.

How shall you know that? Surely Paul's statement is very valuable, that all authority that exists is from God [see Rom 13:1]. Also valuable is what Jesus said to Pilate: "You would have no authority over me at all unless it had been given you from above" [John 19:11]. Similar value comes from the Lord's declaration through the poet of Proverbs as the personification of Wisdom: "By me kings reign."

Still, by itself this does not satisfy you. Before Christ's birth and Paul's appearance, nations and peoples had lived for thousands of years under various governments. Government authority did not appear for the first time with Pilate, to whom Jesus spoke, or with Nero, under whom Paul wrote. Even when the poet of Proverbs compiled his wise sayings, governments had already existed for centuries, and among many people who lived outside the sphere of Israel, governments had existed under which the wisdom poet sang and lived.

This is how the matter stands, then: All of this explains in what way government authority arose from God's side, but it does not tell us how and where it was instituted and validated. Involved here is the *institution*, the *establishment*, an act or declaration of God whereby he ordained [government] to be that way. Such a human governmental authority is not natural, but *anti*natural. For that reason it is not automatically legitimate, but is legitimate only by virtue of an ordinance of God. *Where* will we find that ordinance? *Where* is the authority of government instituted and validated?

To this our fathers always answered by referring to Genesis 9:6. That this is clearly the case is apparent from the addition of the official comment in the Dutch Bible at Romans 13:4, which reads that in Genesis 9:6 the government "*received its authority* to employ capital punishment."[4] And this *receiving authority* is the point at issue. You people think you have authority over other people, but from whom did you receive that authority? You cannot have this authority from yourselves. Your fellow men cannot have given you this authority, for then they would have needed to possess it first themselves. None of us is his own master, for nobody lives

§ 4

---

4. The marginal notes in the SV understand the idea in Rom 13:4 that the civil magistrate "does not bear the sword in vain" to refer to capital punishment, and connects this explicitly with the text of Gen 9:6.

of himself and dies to himself, but together we belong to our God who *alone* has authority over us [see Rom 14:7–8]. And so the question still remains: how, from where, and when did we receive this authority?

We urgently request our readers to place all the requisite emphasis on this. The one true position that Scripture points out to us is that as people we by nature have authority over *nothing*. All authority belongs to God and God alone. All things belong to him and nothing to you. You have no authority over anything, no matter what it might be, unless God grants you this authority.

Just read the creation account. In Genesis 1:26 and 28 God *grants* humanity dominion, dominion over the fish of the sea, the birds of the sky and the cattle. In the second place, humanity is given dominion *over the earth* in Genesis 1:28. And in the third place, humanity received authority over "every plant yielding seed that is on the face of all the earth, and every tree with seed in its fruit" (Gen 1:29). Initially all of this belonged to God, *not* to people; but now God *gives* it to people, and only because God gave it to people do people obtain the authority, dominion, and jurisdiction over it. People were not even allowed to eat what was edible without God's permission. This explains why Genesis 2:16 says, "You may surely eat of every tree of the garden," but then note what follows: "but of the tree of the knowledge of good and evil you shall not eat." This would not have made any sense if by virtue of their nature people had everything at their disposal.

Indeed, on this one tree, the tree whose fruit God had forbidden people to eat, depended the principial,[5] all-determining question, whether God or a human being was lord and sovereign over this creation. If God had the right to permit or to forbid eating, then *he* was sovereign. By contrast, if humanity had the right and authority, contrary to God's command, over this tree as if it belonged to them, then God was *not* sovereign over the world, but the authority over the whole world belonged *to humanity*. And so it becomes clear at once why the entire issue of God's sovereignty and supremacy was involved in the prohibition against eating from this particular tree.

---

5. The Dutch word *principieele* has the meaning of foundational, basic, and primary. But since none of these words captures the richness of the Dutch term, it has become a commonplace to render *principieele* into English as *principial*, a practice which is followed here.

Now if this establishes that human beings have no authority, not even over an animal or tree, not even over a worm or an insect, unless God gives that authority to them, then even far less can someone set himself up as an authority in order to assume power and control over another *person*, let alone over millions of *people* at the same time. Such a power and such a control can exist only if God institutes and ordains that dominion of one *person* over other *people*.

Judicial experts, who should construct jurisprudence as before the face of Christ, surrender in an unusually thoughtless manner the entire foundation of jurisprudence if they do not show clearly where that *mandate for authority* of one person over another was introduced. And exactly for that reason the study of law itself causes such incalculable harm when it lets Genesis 9:6 slip from view or glosses over it as though it were an obsolete injunction. Actually, not only capital punishment but also the *institution of a government* itself is then being entirely abandoned.

If you should ask, then, where the first dominion of one *person* over another *person* was instituted by God, we would point to Genesis 3:16, where God speaks to the woman after the fall as follows: "Your desire shall be for your husband, and *he shall rule over you*." The commentators on the Dutch Bible add here: "This means, you shall be obliged to adapt yourself to your husband's will, and *he will have authority over you to command you*, which will be burdensome for you according to the flesh, whereas before the fall it was nothing but delightful." Here we have the *bestowing* of an authority, a jurisdiction, a right to command. The dependence [of the woman on the man] existed here by virtue of creation itself, but in such a way that the woman did not want it to be any different. It was natural for her to follow. At that point there was no commanding, and there was nothing like *authority*. But now that two wills have risen in opposition against each other, order had to be created amid chaos, and for that reason God instituted the authority of the man over the woman. §5

By nature a woman's influence on a man is much stronger than a man's influence on a woman, but when it concerns authority, decision, administration, and establishing rule and order, then God has clothed a husband with authority over his wife.

Actually in a certain sense this marital authority already carries within it the character of *government authority*, for it is the granting of authority of one *person* over another *person*, so that the one person must yield to the other, *since God commanded and ordained it in that way*. It is certainly true that usually the man is *stronger*, and as such actually possesses some supremacy; but this does not yet create any superior right. This superior right, however, is contained within the *authority* over the woman that God is here explicitly bestowing upon him.

§ 6     Meanwhile, there is still a certain distance between the institution of the authority of one person over another in the small family circle and the larger circle of human society in nations and lands. For a time this arrangement of family life was able to extend by means of patriarchal authority to the bond between generations, families, and tribes. But when humanity began to multiply and came to occupy too large a territory, generations and families began to lose touch as they began living too far from each another. Eventually this marital authority, which naturally extended to the children of the woman, was unable to extend to the entire society. This explains why there was a need for government authority that would no longer emerge from the family circle and would bear a *mechanical* character. Mechanical, because the head no longer existed organically with his subjects through kinship or marriage.

Already before the flood such authority must have emerged. Yet the question now arises whether *such authority*, which had not arisen organically from the family, could be legitimate as an authority *that God had bestowed*. Before the flood you find no trace of any revelation concerning this. Exactly for that reason, it is of paramount importance for the Lord God to validate (as our fathers used to put it) *this* specific authority after the flood.

How can such an authority be validated only in an absolute sense? The answer is, only by the Lord God making such authority, the authority *of* one person *over* another person, *absolute*. And the authority of one person over another person becomes absolute only by God granting the right to have jurisdiction over the life and death of another human being. Where that authority, where such power is granted, there we necessarily find the most absolute authority over people invested in one human being, and this therefore validates government authority in an absolute sense.

Well then, *this* is precisely what God did after the flood. When Cain killed Abel, Adam did not yet have the right to kill Cain on that account. Rather, God opposed this. But after the flood God instituted for Noah and all his descendants, including us, the ordinance that the blood of the one who sheds blood must and thus also may be shed *by another*.

The conclusion that therefore involuntary manslaughter should also be punished by death is obviously unfounded. God's ordinances do not work that way. When it says, "By the sweat of your face you shall eat bread" [Gen 3:19a], this hardly means that nobody may eat bread unless his work made him sweat first. Rather, all such explanations violate God's word. Such ordinances are not statutes from a penal code, but divine institutions with a rich germ that will develop by itself. That is also how it happened, namely, from this ordinance [in Genesis 9:6] there automatically developed both government authority and the right for putting a murderer to death, in good order and under further regulations.

All those who claim that people arranged it this way among themselves and that no ordinance, no institution from God was necessary, simply repeat the sin of paradise. Just like Adam was not allowed to eat from any tree without permission from God, so too no government may rule over us people apart from God's decree. And whoever ignores this is acting as Adam did when he ate from the forbidden tree, and together with Adam he is proceeding on the assumption that man himself can determine his own affairs without God granting him that right.

The conclusion, therefore, is that in Genesis 9:6 both government authority is validated and capital punishment is instituted, not only for that time *but for all times*, for all of Noah's descendants, and thus also for us and for our descendants, until the coming of the Lord on the clouds.

# CHAPTER TWELVE

# A NEW DISPENSATION

*"This is like the days of Noah to me: as I swore that the waters of Noah should no more go over the earth, so I have sworn that I will not be angry with you, and will not rebuke you. For the mountains may depart and the hills be removed, but my steadfast love shall not depart from you, and my covenant of peace shall not be removed," says the* LORD, *who has compassion on you.*

ISAIAH 54:9–10

§ 1    We are now ready to present the conclusion from what we have been considering thus far. Taken broadly, the result comes down to this: *after the flood, an altered order of affairs has entered upon our earth*, and it is this altered order of affairs under which we are still living. Before the flood the situation of the earth itself and of humanity dwelling on earth *was different*. The earth itself underwent a remarkable transformation during the flood. After the flood, life on earth displays a *different* character.

That altered order of affairs resulted from the Lord's lofty decree. The plan of God's counsel unfolded in what occurred at that time. In the chain of events that binds together paradise that was lost with paradise that will be regained, the flood and the alteration that this flood brought about in our existence constitute a very important link.

The Lord's holy wrath was manifested in the flood, but the dreadful verdict executed by this flood nevertheless pointed to *his grace*. According to the holy apostle Peter's formulation, the water of the flood corresponds to baptism, which now *saves* us through the resurrection of Jesus Christ (1 Peter 3:21).[1] The grace displayed in the flood was not *special* grace but *common* grace. The ark did not save unto eternal life but for temporal life on earth. This explains how in the ark not only the church of God was rescued, but also the reprobate Ham, together with the animals. For this reason a difference of opinion about this is impossible. The grace shown here is not particular, restricted to the elect and leading to eternal life, but *common*, extending to everything that *has breath*, for *this* dispensation. Precisely for this reason the Noahic covenant is of such paramount important to us, since it points to the situation that still continues and in which we still live. This situation will endure for our children and grandchildren until the Lord's return.

For that reason, the idea that we need to be concerned only with the New Testament, and with the Old Testament only insofar as the shadows of the new dispensation overlay the people of Israel, and that even further behind this lay the Noahic covenant that is entirely irrelevant for us, must be resisted to the utmost. It is precisely the other way around. The Israelite situations have lapsed, and for us they have no other significance than principial and prophetic significance. But what lay *back beyond* Israel in the Noahic dispensation has *not* lapsed, but existed before Israel, among Israel, after Israel, and still exists. It is the order of affairs in the midst of which we ourselves live, which was introduced during Noah's time.

For that reason we began our discussion of *common grace* by taking our point of departure in the Noahic covenant. From there we will return to paradise, and then trace the course of history up to our own time, so that ultimately the entire tableau of the general grace or common grace of our God may appear before us in clear portrait, and so that the significance of that common grace for our Reformed confession and Reformed practice may be illuminated clearly. With a view to this we saw the need of discussing the Noahic covenant in depth. Many who did not discern our purpose thought we went into *too* much depth; some even grumbled about verbosity. Yet a more concise discussion here would have been a mistake.

§ 2

---

1. Kuyper cites in quotation marks, but from a version requiring the reordering of the whole sentence; hence our paraphrase. The ESV reads, "Baptism, which corresponds to this, now saves you, not as a removal of dirt from the body but as an appeal to God for a good conscience, through the resurrection of Jesus Christ."

For the last century and a half, the entire Noahic history has been neglected, has been treated superficially in catechism instruction, and has disappeared almost entirely from sermons, so that we could not have obtained a firm basis unless we had started with an accurate exposition of Genesis 8 and 9. Especially the question regarding capital punishment had obscured the correct insight into these chapters in such a ludicrous manner that apart from honest and extensive interpretation at this point we could not have gone further. We may not rest content with placing one opinion over against another opinion, but it must be demonstrated in a *sure* manner why the vague opinion regarding these chapters is unconvincing.

The neglect of this Noahic account dates from the end of the disputes between Cocceius and Voetius.[2] This account played a major role in that conflict, but unfortunately it came to be included as only one of the many covenant accounts within a longer or shorter series of accounts. The result was that the entirely unique and principial significance of the Noahic covenant was gradually lost from view. The fact that it concerned common grace and not particular grace was not perceived. And when finally the battle-fatigued combatants put their swords in their sheaths, the congregation saw the Noahic covenant as nothing more than a judgment upon sin, a warning against a debauched life, and of little significance as a preparation for the covenant that later was to be established with Abraham. When we compare the [extensive] attention that Peter van Mastricht gave to the time of Noah with the sketchy discussions of later times, then we have to agree that we may legitimately complain about neglect and underestimation.[3] With a view to this, people will appreciate

---

2. Kuyper refers here to a debate between two Reformed theologians in the Netherlands, Gisbertus Voetius (1589-1676) and Johannes Cocceius (1603-69). As van Asselt writes, "The main issue was a different interpretation of the continuity and discontinuity of redemptive history in the Old and New Testaments. Whereas the Voetians stressed the substantial uniformity of salvation for believers in the Old and New Testament dispensations, Cocceius and his followers underlined the progression of salvation in history and, therefore, the different status of the Old and New Testament believers." The dispute between the Voetians and the Cocceians "continued long after the death of both great personalities in the history of Dutch Reformed Protestantism in the seventeenth century." See Willem van Asselt, "Cocceius, Johannes," in *Dictionary of Major Biblical Interpreters*, ed. Donald K. McKim (Downers Grove, IL: InterVarsity, 2007), 316–17.

3. Mastricht treats Noah and the Noahic covenant at various points in the context of his discussion of the dispensation of the covenant of grace under the patriarchs.

our attempt to revive once more the significance of the Noahic history by means of a somewhat broader treatment.

Allow us to summarize in the following main points the results we obtained. §3

*First*, what is rescued from the flood is the *human race*—not simply a few people, but the race itself, which God had created in Adam as the head of humanity. Thousands and tens of thousands were swallowed up by the flood and only *eight* people rescued, but those eight were related to each other. These were not eight men or eight women, not eight young people or eight old people, and not eight people gathered from far and near, but these eight people stood in an organic relation to one another. They constituted a family; they constituted a race. They were men and women, old and young, fathers, mothers, and children, and those children were married. However terribly the flood had ravaged the human race, so that almost all its branches were snapped off and the trunk itself was nearly cut down to the ground, yet the tree was still alive at its root and at its severed stump. Later that stump sprouted again with remarkable speed, its branches sent forth shoots on every side, and those branches blossomed with a rich show of foliage. So today our *human race* lives on the earth, having come forth from the ark, and as something rescued by the ark, it is the same *human race* that was once created in Adam.

In the *second* place, the earth on which we live is still the *same* earth that existed before the flood, but significantly *changed* in its nature by the catastrophe of the flood. The idea that nothing would have happened at that time except a temporary rising of the waters that, after having covered the earth, retreated for the earth to appear again in the same form, seems to rest on a misunderstanding. God himself speaks in Isaiah 54:9–10 of the waters of Noah, and of the oath of his covenant that he would never again bring another flood upon the earth, and then immediately states, "For *the mountains may depart and the hills be removed*, but my steadfast love shall not depart from you, and my covenant of peace shall not be removed, says the Lord, who has compassion on you." §4

We read in Genesis 7:11 that all the fountains of the great deep *burst forth*, and if the earth's surface teaches us that enormous ruptures, shifts, rifts, and eruptions had taken place, then it appears that in the *departure*

---

See Petrus van Mastricht, *Theoretico-practica Theologia* (Amsterdam: Societatis, 1715 [1655]), 8:863–92.

*of the mountains* and the *removal of the hills* something of the events during the flood still reverberates. It is therefore remarkable that Psalm 46:2 and elsewhere speak *of moving mountains "into the heart of the sea,"* and that in his instruction about faith, Jesus alludes once more *to mountains being moved into the sea* [see Matt 17:20; Mark 11:23]. Also the fact that in Genesis 8:4 Ararat is called the highest mountain, coupled with the fact that to-day *many* mountains of greater height have been discovered and scaled, tells us that a colossal change must have occurred in the earth's surface. Consequently, after the flood our earth must have displayed a different form and appearance than before the flood, and the *bursting forth* of the fountains of the great deep may not be interpreted as poetic language, but must be understood in a literal sense.

§ 5     In the *third* place, with this the likelihood is simultaneously provided that the relationship of the *atmosphere* to our earth also underwent change. It states that the *"windows of heaven were opened,"* which is definitely not the same as clouds being emptied. We must relate this to Genesis 2:5–6, where we read, "for the LORD God had not caused it to rain on the land, and there was no man to work the ground, and a mist was going up from the land and was watering the whole face of the ground." We must also relate this to the remarkable fact that *the rainbow* was appointed as sign of the covenant. Taken together, these supply ample warrant for supposing that certain alterations occurred at that time in the atmosphere.

We will not discuss to what extent these changes in the atmosphere were connected with any occurrence in the galaxies, although it deserves notice that when speaking of the final catastrophe that is still coming, all the prophets, including John on Patmos, specifically mention extreme changes that will occur in the position of sun, moon, and stars.

For our purpose it is enough if we pay attention to two things: (1) the flood was not a mere cloudburst or a tremendous torrential downpour, but a wholly extraordinary phenomenon in the atmosphere, and (2) the water that had descended was not destroyed, but was divided in a different way than before, whether at the North and South Poles, or across the earth's surface. However, before the flood the condition of the atmosphere was such that it caused the flood, and the condition of the current atmosphere possesses a safeguard against the return of such a flood.

What we can expect at the return of Christ is not a catastrophe by *water* but a catastrophe by *fire*. You can read this in 2 Peter 3:12: "The heavenly bodies will melt as they *burn*!" If a catastrophe by *fire* awaits us, which before came by *water*, then the general condition [of the earth], and particularly the relation of the earth to the atmosphere, must have undergone changes.

In the *fourth* place, the blessing of the new situation was intended not only for God's church, but for *everything that is human*, indeed even for the *animal kingdom*. It is not that the church was saved in order to abandon everything outside the church to general ruin. But the grace shown here extends to the entirety of human life. Most surely the purpose was so that God's church could find a place to set its foot, and also so that the church of the new covenant would gather together believers from all peoples and nations. But its purpose was also so that in a proper sense God the Lord would continue his work in that broad sphere of human life, not unto the saving of souls but no less unto the praise and glory of his great name.

§ 6

Later when Hiram built Solomon's temple, he was still a wanderer outside God's church. He had no share in the particular grace of Israel. Nevertheless, the gift that worked in him was a gift bestowed on him by God, and that gift was devoted to building Jerusalem's temple to the glory of the Lord's name.

In the *fifth* place, the relationship between the human world and the animal kingdom is regulated, and now for the first time introduced into the situation in which we are familiar with that relationship. The dominion over the animals, which according to Genesis 1:26 was given to Adam in his state of rectitude and which according to Genesis 2:19–20 Adam exercised in such a glorious way, had of course suffered injury through the fall. In paradise it was organic, that is, working automatically, but through sin it turned into a *struggle* against the animals, and now after the flood it took on the character of *fear and dread* (Gen 9:2) which overcomes an animal when it encounters a human being. In connection with this, all the animals were delivered into the hands of people. Indeed, even more strongly, human beings received the right to kill an animal and to take it for food. However, they must stay far away from using the fresh blood, so that eating the flesh of animals would not turn them into barbarians.

§ 7

In addition, God's righteousness functions to protect people against the wild animals. God will *require a reckoning from every animal* for the blood, the soul, of a human being. God's grace stands between humanity and the animals in order to protect people. This grace is expressed in the claim God placed upon the animals over against human beings, in a Nimrod-like heroism with which God inspires humans against animals, and in the vengeance of destruction and extermination that gradually extended to all the predatory animals wherever human life became more developed.

§ 8     In the *sixth* place, a remarkable change took place in the life of *humanity* itself. Apparently human strength diminished and the rate of human physical development quickened. Human strength decreased, for although Noah reached an age of *ten centuries*, Shem's age decreased to six centuries, Eber's to four, Serug to two centuries, and Abraham reached an age not too different from ours. The rate of human physical development was also increased, since although before the flood Methuselah's age was 187 when his son Lamech was born, [after the flood] Shem fathered his son Arphaxad at the age of 100, and Arphaxad was 35 years old when obtained his son Selah. In Abraham's time the situation had already changed to such an extent that Isaac's miraculous birth occurred at an age at which Methuselah still had to live almost a century before obtaining his first child.

To explain this as due to a gradual regression of our human race is absurd. In the two thousand years before the flood human longevity extended for centuries. Adam lived to the age of 930, and Noah, who lived [nearly] twenty centuries later, lived to 950 and thus twenty years longer. We do not find a trace of this gradual regression before the flood. The decrease in human longevity after the flood was *sudden*, occurring in steps of two centuries at one time. God intervened here and deliberately decreased human vitality and simultaneously increased the rate of human physical development. At 35 years old, Arphaxad was at the same point as Methuselah was at 187. Abraham died at the age when the earlier patriarchs had begun to have children.

Undoubtedly this previous longevity had contributed significantly to the development of wickedness and unrighteousness. Even now old sinners are the most dangerous. And how fierce this eruption of unrighteousness must have been when these old *sinners* had eight or more centuries in front of them in order to complete their wickedness. The explanation that "the wickedness of man was great in the earth, and that every intention of the thoughts of his heart was only evil continually," was definitely connected with the long life of the ungodly and unrighteous folk. Reducing this longevity would thwart unrighteousness. The reduced longevity is grace. Grace also for God's children, for how long must the pining for heaven have been for a child of God who had to live on this earth for eight centuries or more.

And in the *seventh* place, the Lord God institutes an *order for human life* §9
that was designed to thwart the outbreak of violence. The single former
existing order of paternal authority and patriarchal influence had seemed
to be insufficient. Hence *government* was instituted to make an orderly human society possible. That government was clothed with *majesty* because
to government was entrusted the right over life and death, so that it would
display not the tyranny of one person over another, but God's rule over his
creature. Murder, something certainly common before the flood, could be
restrained from now on by means of capital punishment, and in this way
the filling of the whole earth by our human race would be possible. *"And
you be fruitful,"* says the Lord, *"and multiply, increase greatly on the earth and
multiply in it"* [Gen 6:7], after having already said, *"be fruitful and multiply
and fill the earth"* [Gen 6:1]. And precisely to this blessing the institution
of capital punishment was added, so that the mutual massacring that began with Cain would be restrained, whereby populating the whole earth
would become possible.

In that way this *regulated and stable order of affairs* was established, §10
when for the first time the *history of our race* could get underway. Scripture
indicates this in two ways. First, the *stability of the new order of affairs* was
indicated by the promise, *"While the earth remains, seedtime and harvest,
cold and heat, summer and winter, day and night, shall not cease"* [Gen 8:22].
The fact that now for the first time the actual history of our human race
gets underway is expressed in the prophecy that the Holy Spirit placed on
Noah's lips. It led him to sketch out the lines along which the history of
the world would unfold, in his full blessing for Shem, his partial blessing
for Japheth, and his curse on Ham. Within that prophecy lay embedded
the concise program of all of world history; the disappointing experience
with blacks, the enduring significance of the Jews and Muslims as Shem's
offspring, and the great significance Japheth has currently achieved, provide us to this day with the key for explaining world history.[4]

---

4. It was not uncommon in the nineteenth century to find attempts to trace out the
   contours of human history as seminally present in Noah's blessings and curses
   of his progeny. Here Kuyper is pointing in part to his judgment of the historical
   primacy of Caucasians and European civilization (often linked to the descendants
   of Japheth) relative to that of Middle Eastern, Asian, and African peoples. Some
   exegetes also linked the so-called curse of Ham with the historical phenomenon of
   slavery, and in some cases this interpretation was ideologically driven as a defense
   of the practice of chattel slavery. Here Kuyper may simply be describing the age of
   European colonialism more broadly as that which is "disappointing" (*teleurstellend*).

So in the changed order of affairs that was introduced after the flood there is indeed revealed an act of *general grace* or of *common grace* that is all encompassing, governing all of history, decisive for our situation, and extending into the farthest future. This common grace must be gratefully accepted. Our confession must take account of common grace, and our perspective of life and of the entire situation of the world must be formed on the basis of common grace.

Whoever ignores or underestimates this powerful act of God's grace, and thereby also his *common grace*, distorts his view on life, ends up with a false dualism, and easily runs the risk of allowing his Christian religion to deviate from the *Reformed* track, that is, from the correct track.

# CHAPTER THIRTEEN

# FROM NOAH BACK TO PARADISE

*But the* Lord *God called to the man and said to him, "Where are you?"*

Genesis 3:9

The significance of the so-called Noahic covenant has now been sufficiently elucidated to show us in a convincing way how the entire *current order of affairs* essentially came into existence for the first time *through* and *after* this Noahic covenant. The situation, or if you like, the state of affairs in which we ourselves live, is not that of prefall paradise nor that of postfall paradise—even less like that of the earth at the time it was burdened with the curse—but it arose *after the flood*. The postflood situation is different from the preflood situation. The powerful event of the flood caused a considerable change in the life of humanity and in the relation of humanity both to the earth and to the animal world.

§ 1

Therefore it is not putting the matter too strongly to say that with the Noahic covenant a new dispensation, a new state of affairs, an altered order of affairs began. We judged that it was necessary to place this significant fact, all too often lost from view, prominently in the forefront of our treatment of common grace.

When reflecting on the past, believers usually jump straight from the present day back to paradise without ascribing any significance, either for themselves or for our present world, to what happened with Noah.

People take into account the state of innocence and paradise, along with the fall and the curse, but then they usually move directly to Abraham, the people of Israel, and Christ, without ascribing any intentional or unique significance within that salvation structure to the great and tremendous event of the flood. The fact that in those days humanity's personal and social life, along with the earth itself, underwent a comprehensive alteration is certainly not denied when you point to these texts, but in the nineteenth century at least, these realities have not been sufficiently taken into consideration. The various parts of this history were not adequately considered in terms of their coherence. The result was that everything that happened at that time slipped into the background and got lost in the mists. To be sure, at every baptism in Reformed churches the meaning of the flood for the covenant of grace was still mentioned, but often only by allusion rather than with appreciation for the full and rich significance this has for the church of Christ.

In order to be able to shed full light on the issue of common grace or general grace, we thought it would be most effective if at the outset we ended this glaring oversight by accentuating clearly the comprehensive alteration that this world underwent at that time. The issue of common grace comes down to discerning clearly that we are dealing here with an *act of God*. An act of God not for the benefit of those eight persons living at that time, but *an act of God* that extends to the entire earth and the entire human race—not in a *saving* but in a *preserving* sense, of course. The fact that the Lord God has performed such an act of *preserving* grace that extends to *all* of our human life comes to no clearer expression than with the Noahic covenant. Everyone senses and perceives that here a promise is being given for the benefit of the *whole* world, and people discern immediately that what was promised contained rescue and preservation not for eternity but for this *temporal* life.

§ 2    With this having been firmly established, we now return from Noah to paradise. Common grace did not appear for the first time with Noah but began operating much earlier. Preflood humanity shared in that grace. It first began not after the flood, but after the fall. But note well: this same common grace that appeared immediately after the fall and began when God called to Adam, "Where are you?" is now no longer the same as in the days of Enoch and Methuselah. It has become different because it underwent alteration with Noah. Nevertheless, what appears in changed form continues to exist in that changed form, such that this one and the same common grace that began in paradise still continues in the altered form it acquired with Noah. Its origin lies not initially with the ark but in paradise, and to understand common grace in its unique character and true nature, we must return to paradise.

In paradise this rather strange phenomenon appears, [namely,] that you read about [a threat] that subsequently did not occur. You read that in the state of innocence man was told [regarding the tree of the knowledge of good and evil], "the day that you eat of it you shall surely die" [Gen 2:17]. And when man nevertheless eats from that tree, *he does not die on that day*. On the contrary, Adam lives for a remarkably long time afterward—nine long, some would say endless, centuries.

Now we would not say that the Word of God was *not* fulfilled. We will return to this later. But it cannot be denied that it did *not* occur in the way that Adam and Eve *must* have understood it when it was told them. On the very day Adam sinned, Adam *did not* die. This fact is certain. Adam received, if we may put it this way, a remarkable stay of execution, not in answer to his own prayer but as a free act of God's will. And that act of God's will, which accounts for Adam *not* dying on that actual day but continuing *to live* that day and for *centuries* thereafter, is nothing other and nothing less than a very powerful act of common grace that affects all people, including us personally.

Imagine once what would have been the result of Adam dying on the day itself when he fell: The entire history of this world would have been cut off. No human race would have developed. According to the Bible, before the fall Adam and Eve had no children yet. Suppose that the Word of the Lord, "*In the day* that you eat of it you shall surely die," had been literally fulfilled, then with their death the entire root of our race would have died and none of us would ever have been born on earth. If common grace is the means whereby Adam's presence on this earth was unexpectedly extended, then it follows that your own life, your birth, your existence as a human being arises not merely from *creation,* but is an act that is rooted in *grace.* The total and direct outworking of sin, *had it not been arrested,* would have destroyed the entire human race with a single death sentence.

As we investigate the origin of this common grace, we will stay close to §3 the account of Scripture. If you deviate from this account in any way at all, you might as well save yourself and others the trouble of reflecting any further about the issue of common grace. Then all certitude will elude you, and the ground beneath your feet will disappear. Such a way of speaking is far from unusual today among Christians of other stripes. Especially among the Ethical theologians, people have gradually become accustomed to giving the appearance of defending the accounts of Genesis 1–5, whereas *in reality* they have surrendered and undermined them.[1] We do not doubt that originally this began with good intentions. At the end of the eighteenth and beginning of the nineteenth centuries, a mocking, superficial spirit gained the upper hand, having no understanding of the depth of these accounts, engaging in unholy sport with Adam and Eve, the apple, and the rest. The sacred was held up for contempt.

Then during and after the time of Schleiermacher, the Ethical theologians were moved by this sharp and chilling mockery to stand up and defend the profound significance of these opening chapters of Holy Scripture against this ridicule. We should not lose sight of this, since although the position of the Ethical theologians seems to us to be slippery and quite unsatisfactory, we must never forget that they were the first ones who, when a stream of contempt and abuse was poured out upon Scripture, were courageous enough to defend Holy Scripture.

Still less may we forget about the Bible-believing teachers of former times, because it was precisely their barren view of the Bible and their even more barren use of the Bible that in so many ways caused the disdain that came gradually to impact Holy Scripture. Especially at the end of the eighteenth century, Bible-believing theologians were making little more than a mechanical use of Holy Scripture. They no longer had an eye for its depth and its spiritual value. That was precisely how they prepared the coming generation to reject the Bible. Arresting this evil was the enduring gain registered by the school of Schleiermacher, and even though duty obligates us to oppose him in this respect as well, nevertheless we do not want to do so without first having acknowledged our gratitude for that achievement.

§ 4    The mistake they committed consisted in separating *form* and *content* from one another. Without doubt, so they reasoned, the course of events *can* be no different from what is portrayed in Genesis 1–5. In that sense, what lies before you there is indeed essential and sacred history. Everything transpired in this way, and only in this way, at the beginning

---

1. After his conversion in the early 1860s, Kuyper came to see the danger that theological modernism posed to vibrant Christian faith. In this respect, he was especially critical of the modernist Ethical theology associated with figures like Friedrich Schleiermacher (1768–1834) and Albrecht Ritschl (1822–89).

of our race. But such powerful things as happened at that time cannot be encompassed within the limits of language. What happened is far more rich and powerful than the account can communicate. So you must not imagine that all of this transpired literally only in this way. The story is merely an incidental form designed to evoke within you an imagination, a picture, of the course of things that yielded such a result.

People allowed themselves to be deceived by this perspective by acknowledging that the account was so profound and so full of information that an entire world of ideas was packed into almost every verse. They began to ponder those profound ideas. They found them so beautiful and so true. They corresponded so completely to the relation by which people felt connected to the origin of things. They explained so completely the present situation, the prevailing misery, the corruption of the human heart, and our nobler and better aspirations as well. Precisely here the deception emerged.

They felt so much at home in the thought world of these accounts that they imagined, "If I had to invent it from the experiences of my own heart, then I would have invented it precisely this way." That is why they ultimately imagined that the entire account could be a product of the invention of the human heart. Not of one person, but of many people. Not of the superficial folk among our race, but of the best and most profound. Already in ancient times these people must have undergone experiences similar to those that people undergo nowadays. From this a certain communal idea must have gradually taken shape; it was the result of this invention of the human heart that had eventually received this new narrative garment. Some traditions and recollections could have been included so that a historical background could be detected, but the spiritual development portrayed in the account was not an actual *tradition*, but had to have been an *invention* of the human heart. Precisely in this way it spoke most powerfully to us. Understood precisely in that way, our heart was most easily attracted to it. Truly, just as the human heart in earlier centuries had invented it for us, so too all the generations thereafter reinvented it for our heart. In this way every conflict disappeared, and people at once felt at home again in these beautiful, invented stories.

It was true, of course, that the common man who viewed all that inventing simply as a farce had to conclude that with such an approach the *value* of these stories was lost, but the more refined person did not judge that to be so. People knew all too well that genuine poetry arises from the heart and is therefore real. Precisely for that reason, turning back from the *dead* tradition to the *living* invention of the human heart represented not loss, but gain. Only along this route, what stood written there became for us nobler, holier history.

§ 5     We feel at once the seductive power of this idea, and we should not be surprised that so many theologians have gone along with it. Obviously no one was interested in the dry recitation of facts apart from their meaning, but in the sense and meaning of these facts. Well, in the manner explained above, people could continue accepting this profound meaning, talking about it with warmth and conviction, even with passion, without on that account having to understand it literally as it appeared in the Bible. The problem was, however, that these theologians unintentionally ignored some indisputable facts that overturned their entire position.

In the first place, there is the fact that the human heart in India, China, Babylon, among the Germanic people, and everywhere else *did not* come to this position about the origin of things, the fall, and the reestablishment of the human race. Even the deep-thinking Greeks had construed all of this completely differently. From this fact alone it is evident that the human heart by itself does *not* come to a presentation such as Genesis 1–5 provides, but construes the course of events *completely differently*.

In the second place, people ignored the fact that these theologians who declared that they find the experiences and conclusions of their own heart explained so accurately in these accounts, had come to these ideas and perspectives not apart from these accounts, but *after* having become acquainted with them and *after* having been nurtured in a Christian church that was nourished by the content of these accounts.

Combining these two facts, one obtains the result that the human heart does *not* fabricate in this manner when it did *not* know these accounts [beforehand], and conversely, where the human heart imagined it was inventing them, this invention began only *after* it had borrowed the content of its fabrication from these accounts.

§ 6     The comment that they did not really mean that the human heart naturally would discover all this, but that such a fabrication emerged only where the Holy Spirit had exercised his influence on the heart, does not remove our objection in the least. The Holy Spirit, understood now as the cultivator of the human heart, can indeed disclose to us our internal condition, but not inform us of *facts*. And the issue involves precisely the denial that we are dealing here with *facts*. These theologians believed that the idea that people in China, India, and so on, formed concerning primeval matters fit the human heart *more accurately*. Their hearts felt differently, sensed differently, contemplated differently, thereby coming up with an idea that was nothing but a mirrored reflection of what went on in their own hearts. Thus the human heart, to the extent that it lived with more or less depth, has fabricated various ideas about paradise and the fall, and our ideas would have no greater value beyond correctly reproducing what agreed with our inner perceptions. They had *their* ideas and we have *ours*, and both for them and for us that idea agrees with the perceptions and ponderings of our heart. But this is quite apart from any certainty that this idea corresponded with *reality*. At most one could say that our hearts perceived and pondered more deeply, and that therefore the assumption originated that our idea came closer to the truth.

However, something that comes close to the truth is not yet completely identical with the truth itself. The Muslim stands much closer to the truth than the servant of Baal or Molech, and yet Muhammad stood infinitely far from *the* truth.

What we need is *certainty*—certainty regarding the things that occurred at the origin and the emergence of our human life, and certainty regarding things that have governed life in all of its further development. Above all, we need certainty concerning what the Lord God did, ordained, and spoke at that time, as well as concerning the promises he gave regarding our future. And that certainty is *utterly* missing in the idea of the Ethical theologians. One of the elementary rules of logic is this: *ab posse ad esse non valere conclusionem*, that is, you can never say that because something *can* be so, therefore it *was* so.[2] These theologians violated this basic truth of all sound logic.

True, these theologians explained to us with absolute clarity how we could derive much from the experience of our hearts and from our inner life, and that these things could have taken place in that way. If it had happened the way we read in Genesis 1–5, then everything was fine. All of this

§ 7

---

2. The full formula in modal logic includes the positive as well as the negative principle: "The consequence follows from what is necessary to what is, from what is to what is possible. The consequence does not follow from what is possible to what is, from what is to what is necessary" (*ab oportere ad esse, ab esse ad posse valet consequentia: a posse ad esse, ab esse ad oportere non valet consequentia*). See Friedrich Ueberweg, *System of Logic and Logical Doctrines*, trans. Thomas M. Lindsay (London: Longmans, Green, and Co., 1871), §98, p. 333.

corresponded to our heart, and our heart agreed with what was narrated there. For that reason they were able to say that it *could* certainly have been so. But between this *could* and the certainty that it *had been so*, lies a deep chasm that no one can bridge without receiving a direct account from the past. Not a report or message that something *approximately* like this, or something of that nature, or something that along these broad lines must have occurred. *Broad* lines are useless here. All depends precisely on the *small*, fine, individual lines. Only when those are established, when you know what God created, spoke, and ordained, and what the head of our race did thereafter, and what judgment then fell upon us, and what promise was then given, and what grace was then bestowed, only then do you have solid ground under your feet and a solid base under your chiseled sculpture.

§ 8    It is on this basis that the community of believers always refused, and will continue to refuse, to go along with such half-baked ideas. All *origins* lie in obscurity. Just as someone who lacks information about his parents or relatives can know nothing from himself regarding his earthy origin, and would not even know who his mother is unless that mother herself or others had disclosed that to him, so too here. Regarding the origins of our human race we would know nothing, absolutely nothing, if God had not told us and revealed it to us. Even though a child might declare afterwards, "I feel in my heart that this is my mother," this is hardly any basis for certitude. Many a child who was switched soon after birth, or entrusted to a woman who was not his mother, nonetheless honored, adored, and loved that woman as his mother for his entire life. But the conclusion *that the woman was therefore his mother* would still be a fallacy. *Facts* cannot ever be constructed from the notions of the heart. The kind of facts that function here appear in the realm of the objective, and can come to us from objective history only by means of communication and by means of the record of that communication.

This is a truth we must therefore discuss somewhat more broadly, because before turning to the history of paradise, we must maintain and prove our right to take the words as *literally* as they stand in Genesis 1–5, to depend on the *facts* told us in those words, to draw our *inferences* from those facts and words, and thus to come to the *conclusion* that not simply for our imagination and not merely in appearance, but in reality and in truth, the origin of things transpired precisely in the way we are told in these opening chapters of Holy Scripture.

# CHAPTER FOURTEEN

# THE PARADISE STORY AS HISTORICAL NARRATIVE

*And God saw everything that he had made, and behold, it was very good.*

Genesis 1:31a

We had to recall explicitly that the first chapters of Genesis must be understood as history. Only if the paradise narrative is history do we have the right to draw conclusions from the events that are recorded in those chapters and to rely on what is reported to us as having been spoken by God or man or Satan. Those who deny that we have history here before us still appeal with a measure of ostentation to the so-called paradise gospel, which states that the seed of the woman will crush the head of the serpent, or also to the ordinance that a sinner will eat bread in the sweat of his brow. But this is simply *impermissible* on *their own* perspective. Whoever does not believe that God actually spoke in this way in paradise has no right to appeal to such expressions as if they were clothed with divine authority. Appealing to such statements is legitimate only if we acknowledge wholeheartedly that we have in these first chapters a narrative of events *that have really taken place in this way,* and in which the same words were actually used that are reported to us as having been spoken. Therefore

§ 1

not only what is *narrated* must be real history, but also the *report* of it that has come to us must be such that we can rely on it. What is narrated in these first chapters of Genesis is of such extreme importance and governs our entire view of the world to such an extent that literally every word, indeed, *every* letter is crucial. Thus it is of no use to us if we are told that approximately such-and-such may have happened. No, we must know accurately and with certainty. Only then can we rely on it, draw conclusions from it, and build our worldview on it.

The question whether the words we read as having been spoken back then have actually been uttered in that sequence and with the same phrases that now lie before us does not need to deter us here. For as long as the Holy Spirit gives us the guarantee that the *meaning* and *significance* of those words—even if they were *expressed* differently—are entirely the same, then any uncertainty is precluded for us. Even if it is stated that the serpent spoke, we must have certainty that this and no other thought came from Satan to humanity. And also when it is continually said that God spoke, we must not take this as meaning that God did *not* speak and that man merely felt the thought come up in him. Also, and especially when it comes to God's speaking, we must understand without doubt both the fact *that* God really spoke and the *content* of what was said.

This speaking by God is the great fact that is placed in the foreground throughout Holy Scripture, ceaselessly and with stress and emphasis. It is that which makes Scripture [to be] Scripture. The crucial point in Scripture is not what man thought or contemplated, but precisely that which God spoke. Today God no longer speaks to us. He has spoken at many times and in many ways by the prophets and, after prophecy came to an end, by his Son [Heb 1:1–2]. But now this speaking of God has ceased, and that is precisely why this past speaking is of such all-decisive value to us. When we close our ear to this, we have only ourselves to blame if, without the light of revelation, we grope in the darkness for the wall. Whoever listens to what God has said walks in the light, and that which God spoke is a lamp for our feet on the path of life [Psa 119:105]. We can still say that God speaks in nature, that there is a voice of God in the thunder and the lightning, in the howling of the hurricane and in the whispering of the soft coolness, and also a voice of God in the moving of the Spirit in the heart and in the language of conscience, but all of this is *metaphorical*. It is not speaking in the proper sense of the word. True, all these voices engender a feeling of reverence and worship, or stimulate an urge in us, or keep our foot from the wrong path. But all such speaking reveals nothing to us, communicates nothing to us, and does not let us know God's will.

In the proper sense of the word, speaking takes place only when from the *consciousness* of the speaker *conscious* thoughts are transferred into the *consciousness* of the hearer. This is the sense in which we must understand God's speaking in paradise and after the fall. If we do not do this, we are playing with words if we continue to derive our notions from such sayings. Thus when it states, for example, that God said, "Let us make man in our image, after our likeness," [Gen 1:26] and we do *not* believe that this was spoken in this way, then we lack any right to build our system about humanity on the creation of man in the image of God. Yet that is precisely what people do today. They cling to a notion as beautiful as the creation of man in the image of God, they build systems and theories on it, but when asked, "Do you really believe that Genesis 1:26–27 must be taken literally in this way?" people shrug at your naïveté. Surely people don't believe *that*. But equally naturally, all further reasoning on the basis of this standpoint about the creation of man in the image of God has no solid foundation whatsoever on which their edifice could rest. All that people write down then is nothing but their own concoction, ideas that one expresses, beautiful thoughts by which one lets oneself be attracted. But that it would contain reality is an assertion without proof. One does not have a *foundation*, a firm foundation for saying all this.

This speaking by God must therefore be emphasized [today] more than in the past. It is perfectly true that God is a spirit and consequently does not have a mouth or power of speech. But the same applies to the *eye*. A spirit has no body and therefore also no eye, yet no one hesitates to acknowledge that God can nevertheless *see* without an eye, indeed, can see everything, much better than we do with our eye. Exactly the same is true of the *ear*. Because he has no body, God has no ear. That goes without saying. And yet everyone agrees that even without an ear, God hears everything very well, with a sensitivity that far transcends all our hearing. We show that we believe it ourselves when we pray. Why else would we pray, if we were not firmly convinced that God hears us, even when we whisper almost inaudibly.

This is what the psalmist sings: "He who planted the ear, does he not hear? He who formed the eye, does he not see?" (Psa 94:9). The difference between God and the idols is precisely that the idols have ear and eye, but neither hear nor see, and that God, by contrast, sees and hears everything

§ 2

*without* eye and ear. And this *must* be so because before he created the eye and the ear, God within himself *thought up* the eye and the ear. It must first have been in his thought before it came into being. The act of seeing and hearing must thus have existed for God before he created eyes and ears in humans and animals, and the whole functioning of seeing and hearing must have been known to God in order to create ear and eye, also in relation to the vibrations of the sound and light waves[1] and the effect on our nerves, and the working of the nerves on the soul. Seeing and hearing thus were to God antecedent to his calling ear and eye into being. Thus [it follows that] for God seeing and hearing must therefore be independent of these instruments that are indispensable for us.

And this is also how it is with God's speaking. It is explicitly stated about the idols, "They have mouths, *but do not speak*" [Psa 115:5]. Not speaking is therefore the mark of an idol; by contrast, the activity of speaking much and speaking well characterizes the living God. Here also the question applies: Would he who formed the mouth and gave speech to man not speak? Did the mouth then come first and did God at that point give speech to humankind on the basis of that mouth? Or has that mouth been created by God exactly as it had to be in order to be capable of bringing forth speech? If the latter, then must not speech have been in God before he made the specifications, the plan for the mouth and all kinds of speech organs? And are these organs of speech anything other than an aid, an instrument that is indispensable for us creatures to be able to speak, but that God, who is not in need of anything, does not need?

If the living God wants to work by means of your ear by letting sounds play on your auditory nerves, what would prevent him from doing so? Or even when he wants to bypass your hearing to excite directly within your soul the same sensations a human being excites in you by speaking, what would hinder him? Are not all languages his, given by him to the nations? Would there be a single language that is unknown to God? And what, indeed, would prevent him from transmitting his thoughts into our lucid and clear consciousness by means of a language that is clear and precisely understandable? Let us therefore allow that speaking of God [to stand] in the unimpaired, full sense of the word. Adam, Eve, Cain, Noah, Abraham— they all have plainly and clearly heard the same thing we become aware of when a human being speaks to us. No vague ideas arose within them, but

---

1. Dutch: *luchtgolven en aethergolven*, lit., "air waves and ether waves."

*language* went out to them, words were caught by them, *sayings, expressions, proofs, declarations, promises* came through to them, which they could repeat literally. They were not floating feelings affecting the soul, which they themselves interpreted, but clear, firm, well-formulated thoughts that they received in their consciousness.

Let no one think it superfluous that we have insisted here in somewhat greater detail on the reality of this speaking of God. Especially in more sophisticated circles the firm belief in such a real speaking of God has been weakened to such an extent by a theology that has lost its way, that the only way to make the weak knees firm again is by means of a deliberate argument. People *say* they believe, but they *don't*. Well, yes, approximately, more or less, provided that it is not firmly and on all points ... and in this way the overwhelming impression of what it means when God has spoken is totally lost. People do not bow before the Word because they cannot cling to the Word as an actual *word of God*. If this is how you view the matter, then the reading and rereading of Genesis 1–5 does not give you anything. Yes, it is beautiful and lovely as things are presented there, but whether it all was like that and whether its truth still holds, then people shrug their shoulders. This is why by way of introduction to what follows, the reality of God's speaking had to be insisted on with some emphasis. Only those among our readers who with us heartily believe in such an actual speaking by God can be convinced by that which we will unfold hereafter. Others may take note with a measure of goodwill, but it gives them no ground under their feet, no standpoint from which they can view the life of the world. And yet this is precisely the point of this series of articles about common grace.[2] We must move away from floating notions back to the *firmness* of *conviction*. As people who confess the Lord we must once again adopt an unshakeable position. We must know how things really are, and in order to know that, we must *first know where we stand*.

§ 3

No matter how hard we try to set aside the all-dominant questions of life, they always come back. The questions about where we come from, how this universe and this world came into being, and how we came into existence in this world, will simply not be repressed. The unbeliever who, in his confusion, in order to cede nothing to faith in the end forbids

§ 4

---

2. Recall that the original form of the contents of these volumes on common grace was a series of newspaper articles published in *De Heraut* between 1895 and 1901. See *AKB*, 1902.13, pp. 339–40.

himself to reflect on these questions, dulls his own mind, and darkens his consciousness. We can cut off the question about *the origin* of things as little as we can suppress the questions about where we go when we die, and how this whole world will one day end up, and what the purpose of this whole creation is. And it is precisely the rich book of Genesis that gives us a fully satisfying answer to this question of *the origin* of things.

Indeed, we do not understand this book as long as we fail to realize that it has in fact been given to us for the specific purpose of informing us about *those origins*. It is called *Genesis*, and *Genesis* means *birth*. Hence we read in Genesis 2:4 in the *Statenvertaling* [the standard Dutch Bible], *"These are the births* of the heavens and of the earth."[3] The same expression "these are the births" is repeated in Genesis 6:9, 10:1, 11:10, 25:12, 25:19, 36:1, and 36:9. And because this word *birth* was rendered *genesis* in the Septuagint, this word has come to be used as the title for the whole book.[4] The Jews called it not Genesis but *Bereshith*, that is, *in the beginning*, which are the opening words of Genesis 1:1. Yet "in the beginning" also pointed already to the origin of things, to their birth, to their beginning, to their appearance. And indeed, the book of Genesis presents us with the *origin* of all things: The origin of the universe; the origin of the angels; the origin of all creatures; the origin of humanity; the origin of marriage; the origin of sin; the origin of grace; the origin of suffering; the origin of the present state of the earth; the disruption of the order of human society; the origin of all justice and all dominion. The *origins* of all that still stirs your interest, of all that surrounds you in your own personal life, and of all that goes on within your heart, are unfolded before us in this book of Genesis.

For this reason that book of Genesis is extremely important for the church, for the nations, for the government, for our living together in home and society, and no less for our whole thought world. We must always, again and again, immerse ourselves in the wealth of treasure that lies before us in this book. The church must ceaselessly try to firmly establish

---

3. The annotations in the SV denote *geboorten* ("births") as *oorsprong of beginselen* ("origin or foundations"). The ESV and many other English versions render the Hebrew *toledoth* as "generations," such as in this case, "These are *the generations* of the heavens and the earth."
4. The Septuagint (here in the Dutch, lit., "translation of the Seventy") is the ancient Greek translation of the OT dating from the third century BC, and is thus named because of the seventy translators traditionally held to have contributed to the work. It is abbreviated LXX for the same reason.

the congregation in the certainties of this book that dominates our entire life, and in Sunday school and catechism classes everyone's efforts must be aimed at firmly establishing in the consciousness of the upcoming generation the basic principles of our whole being, life, and existence.

It would, of course, take us much too far afield to even consider unraveling the entire content of this book in all its details. We will stick to our purpose and therefore limit ourselves to our subject, which is common grace. But precisely in order that the doctrine of common grace, which has so sadly sunk into obscurity, would regain acceptance and again exert its influence on our thought and life, it is of such vital importance that also the remaining aspects of this revelation that has been given to us in Genesis reenter our thinking. The mind must live in it, must be at home in it, must stand firm in it. §5

The world outside of Christ is in search of all manner of life philosophies and worldviews. In this search it repeatedly slips and falls and repeatedly hopes to regain a sure footing, that is, to find again a position that can serve as a vantage point from which to view things. And those worldviews and philosophies of life change daily. Time and again the one replaces the other. And in the end people are desperate and do not know anymore what they must cling to; they often end up with the despondent exclamation that certainty has not been granted us human beings, so we must retreat into our ignorance. But it is precisely the great privilege of the church of Christ that it does *not* need to search and does *not* need to ask, but that things have been revealed to us by God. A well-grounded Christian always has his answer ready. He no longer doubts and hesitates, but rests in the revelation given to him. The philosopher *seeks* a philosophy, but a Christian who knows God's Word *has* his philosophy, has his view of reality, has his standpoint, and from that standpoint has an unfaltering view on what lies behind, around, and before him.

Here, then, lies the mystery as to why simple Christian people among farmers and laborers often have as clear a perception as those who are wealthy and educated. Even opponents have often commented that no book equals our Bible in its suitability to provide people with a well-rounded development. Those who have been raised in the light of the Scriptures have their philosophy, know their world history, and have a firm and correct outlook on the great world events. For them, there is a perspective in things. Christ and his cross constitute the center, and all that lies before it leads up to that center. All that happens now is explained by that cross, and all that will happen hereafter has been prophesied in that cross. But precisely for that reason it is so essential that Christians stand firm on Scripture as their point of departure. That is also why it causes such incalculable harm to the church of God if the narratives of Genesis 1–5 are declared *not* to be authentic.

§ 6    But even with all of this not enough has yet been said. The fact that Christians are so divergent in their confession of the truth, and that they stand over against one another with such variant ideas, can be ascribed in no small degree to the fact that they do not all understand these important chapters in the same way. The differences that keep Christians divided find their birth, their origin, in these first chapters of Genesis. Especially the contrast that emerged between the Roman Catholic Church and the Protestant churches finds its origin in the different way in which each side understands the creation of man in the image of God, the disruption caused in humanity by sin, and the relationship between nature and grace. And when subsequently a new opposition arose between the Anabaptist and the Calvinist aspirations, then the origin of that contrast lay again in the different ways in which the narrative of paradise and the fall and the restoration of the sinner were understood. Indeed, the fact that Reformed life flourished in many respects so richly in the days of our forefathers, and after 1650 declined so sadly until ultimately the stream silted up completely, can be explained to no small degree from the fact that our forefathers stood firm on these first chapters, read them lucidly, and understood their content and significance, whereas the rich meaning of these chapters was later lost sight of, neglected, and not taken into account.

The latter is true especially of common grace, which our forefathers discovered, honored, and confessed, and which was later entirely neglected and disregarded in Reformed circles. It is not going too far to assert that the future of the Reformed churches and the renewed flourishing of Calvinism hangs on the question as to whether this doctrine of common grace will revive again with the force it once had. If this doctrine remains neglected as it has been thus far, then the Reformed churches are doomed to locking themselves into a preaching of salvation without background and without foundation, and they will be unable to find their way to reaching once again a firm starting point and a firm position in the midst of the war of the minds and the turbulences of this world. They then bob to and fro and lack a firm rudder. On the other hand, if we succeed in once again finding acceptance for this rich, beautiful doctrine and allow it again to take the place it deserves in our convictions, then the awareness *that we know where we stand* will once again become common, and we will be able to determine once again, with a firm hand, the relationship in which we find ourselves placed vis-à-vis the life of the world. The Twelve Articles of Faith[5] not only deal with the Redeemer and with the Holy Spirit, but begin by bringing us face to face with *God the Father, the Almighty, the Creator of heaven and earth.* And even our confession of God's Holy Trinity even its foundation if we do not trace our whole confession of the Son and the Holy Spirit back to God the Father. Our whole preaching of salvation and the preaching of sanctification in the church must therefore be brought back again to the preaching of God the Father, and with it back to creation and to the re-creation of all things. Only in this way do we acquire *unity* in our confession, *firmness* in our standpoint, *determination* in our conviction. And because *sin* breached this and restoration followed, and because common grace is the doctrine that shows us *the situation that resulted from this*, we cannot but stand weakly and hesitatingly as long as the doctrine of common grace has not been brought to clarity again before us. No matter how much we enclose ourselves within our church, we cannot escape the necessity of living also in the midst of the world. And we cannot perceive clearly the relationship between those two, namely, between *church* and *world*, as long as we have not been grounded in the doctrine of common grace.

---

5. That is, the Apostles' Creed.

# CHAPTER FIFTEEN

# THE STATE OF RIGHTEOUSNESS

*And the* Lord *God planted a garden in Eden, in the east, and there he put the man whom he had formed.*

Genesis 2:8

§ 1    The starting point for a correct understanding of what sin has wrought lies in the correct knowledge of the state of righteousness. This has been recognized by all who have reflected on the sacred things. Three kinds of states must be considered: (1) the state of righteousness; (2) the state of sin; and (3) the state of grace. Or, as it has also been expressed, humanity as *created, fallen,* and *restored.* However, the approach was one-sided in that the emphasis was too exclusively on the *spiritual state* and too little attention was paid to the *external condition* associated with these three states.

The Heidelberg Catechism avoided this one-sidedness by speaking not only of the knowledge of *sin,* but also of the knowledge of *misery;*[1] if sin is the poison, misery points to the consequences that flow from the destruction brought about by this poison. In line with this train of thought we will therefore take *state* and *condition* together and consider them both in their interconnectedness. Each *state* has a corresponding *situation* or *condition.* Humanity in the state of righteousness befits a *paradise* as in

---

1.   See Heidelberg Catechism, Lord's Day 2, Q&A 3.

the Garden of Eden. Fallen humanity befits an earth on which the *curse* rests. Humanity utterly fallen for all eternity befits *hell*. The redeemed who have been made perfectly righteous befit a *glory* like that of heaven.

This also applies to the body. To human beings in the state *without* sin belongs a body *without* pain or illness. To *fallen* human beings belongs a body subject to pain and affliction. To the *utterly fallen* human being belongs a body of damnation. And to human beings in the state of perfected holiness belongs a glorified body. We can extend this list also as it applies to our senses, our capacities of knowledge and will, and so much more. But for the time being we can leave this, as long as we realize clearly that according to God's ordinance, perfect consonance and pure harmony must exist in all things. One thing must fit in with the other. Whatever does not fit *clashes* and does not spring from the ordinance of creation.

When we ask on the basis of this perspective how we should imagine the *condition* of humanity before sin, then it should be noted that the name "paradise" does not occur in the oldest record of Scripture. The word occurs three times in the New Testament: in Luke 23:43, "today you will be with me in paradise"; in 2 Corinthians 12:3–4, where Paul relates how in an ecstatic experience he was drawn up in paradise; and in Revelation 2:7, where Christ writes to the church of Ephesus that to "the one who conquers I will grant to eat of the tree of life, which is in the paradise of God."

§ 2

The Old Testament, on the other hand, uses the word only of Solomon's pleasure garden in Song of Solomon 4:13. The word gained currency in its present sense through the Septuagint translation of the Old Testament. They wrote in Genesis 2:8, "God planted a garden [*paradeison*, literally, "paradise"] in Eden," because *paradise* was at that time the common word for *pleasure garden*. From this Septuagint translation the word came to the Greek-speaking Jews of Jesus' day, and thus it crept into the New Testament. And because the Roman Catholic Vulgate[2] read in Genesis 2:8, *Plantaverat Dominus* paradisum *volputatis*, that is, "God had planted a paradise of pleasure" [Douay-Rheims version[3]], the word *paradise* has

---

2. The Vulgate is a Latin translation of the Bible that was largely the work of biblical scholar Jerome (347–420).

3. The Douay-Rheims Bible is a translation of the Bible into English from the Vulgate. The English college at Rheims completed the NT in 1582, and the English college at Douay published the OT in 1609–10. These translation efforts from Roman Catholic strongholds in northern France were intended to provide vernacular alternatives in the face of theological challenges from Protestants.

gradually come to be used in the whole Christian church as the fixed, standard term, so that now the *Garden of Eden*, which is exactly the same thing, makes an entirely different impression. *Paradise*, after all, has become the euphonic word to express the ideal state of happiness that once existed, then went away, and will be brought back in even richer glory.

But let it be noted here immediately that not the whole earth was paradise. The "Garden of Eden" is sharply and clearly distinguished from the rest of the world, in two ways. First, because it says, "the LORD God planted [that is, on the earth] a garden in Eden, *in the east*." That addition "in the east" shows that the garden extended in only one direction. Not to the south or north or west, but only *in the east*. And second, it follows from the fact that after the fall, Adam and Eve could be expelled from paradise to another part of the earth. Thus we must not imagine that after creation the earth was one paradise. The whole earth was indeed *good*, so that it far exceeded in lushness and splendor what we can still see of the beauty of nature, but nevertheless paradise was something different. It was a garden, a pleasure garden, a deliberately appointed location. Not a garden in the sense in which we speak of it, let alone a kind of orchard. The additional statement that the sources of the four great, mighty rivers let their waters roar through this paradise proves that we have to do here with a pleasure garden of immense vastness. Yet, no matter how vast, it was a *garden*, that is, an expanse of terrain that was appointed with a certain purpose in mind, that was laid out for this purpose and that immediately gave the impression that this was not merely a valley or an immense forest, but a *planned* region.

Whenever human beings penetrate wild regions, the first thing they do is *develop* it to make it suitable for them. Where there is development there is a center, there are roads and paths that connect the parts with the center, and a design to give the whole a certain unity by means of the arrangement of hills and meadows and parks. Wild animals do not need any design. Cows and horses already need a measure of design. But this applies much more to the place where *human beings* shall live. Human beings have special needs, and human life makes certain demands. And when we read that God planted a garden or paradise in Eden, it *cannot* mean anything else, therefore, than that God arranged a certain place on earth in such a way that man could live there, could feel at home there, and received the impression that this garden suited his situation. This surmise is fully confirmed by the statement that this garden certainly had a center, for it speaks of "the midst of the garden" [Gen 2:9]. And also by the fact that two special trees had been placed there, the tree of *life* and the tree of *conscience*, if we may state it succinctly. This garden or this paradise must also have had a certain evident boundary, for it says that Adam was instructed to *work* it and *keep* it.

This entire garden or that paradise was thus a creation of God's all-providing love for humankind. Nothing that could in any way hinder or distress humanity is compatible with the thought of paradise. There was neither cold nor heat. It did not rain, because Genesis 2:5-6 states that "the LORD God had not caused it to rain on the land, and there was no man to work the ground, and a mist was going up from the land and was watering the whole face of the ground." Harmful changes in atmospheric conditions were thus entirely precluded. There was no thunder and lightning. Adam experienced nothing in the whole outside world that surrounded him as unpleasant. Rather to the contrary, his whole environment provided him with a luscious, refreshing, invigorating experience. The whole flora smiled on him and offered him food abundantly and generously. There was neither thorn nor thistle that could scratch. No weeds grew. There was no fear of poisonous fruit. No worm could enter the abundant fruit that had grown perfectly.

§ 3

We still see occasionally a few marvelously beautiful specimens of fruit at an agricultural show, but such and even much more beautiful and refined was the wealth of the plant world with which God had surrounded his human children. Flowers so delightfully beautiful as we no longer know them. Foliage that by shape and variegated colors enticed the eye. Trees that far exceeded the cedar and the palm tree in splendor. Inexpressible gloriousness all around. And in addition to all this there was also the animal world. Paradise was not funereal and quiet, but the whole Garden of Eden throbbed with life, not only through the wind in the daytime, and through the water that splashed and gurgled from all sides, but also through the songbirds in the branches and the noble, pure-blooded animals that populated paradise, newly created by God in undamaged perfection. And also in the animal world peace reigned. No tormenting insect, and no prowling tiger that raised its paw. Everything was, of course, still *much* more beautiful and glorious than our words can sketch it. Paradise is gone, and only the imagination can to some extent conjure it back for us. But none of us who have been conceived and born in sin can get a full, profound impression of what that heavenly paradise must have been for Adam. Only when one day we rise from the dead will we have the receptive capability to perceive such inexpressible beauty and glory.

This is sufficient, as long as paradise ceases to be a hollow sound for us, and as long as we once again realize that the glory of paradise was something exquisite, intentionally so ordered by God's love for mankind, which saw to it that mankind, newly created, did not experience any suffering or was in any way exposed to it, but on the contrary felt his whole being vibrate with a glorious happiness. Not only were suffering and misery absent in paradise, and every need was met, but there was an overwhelming splendor of overabundance and magnificence, as the name "Eden" itself clearly expresses: "all-round delight." It was not enough for our God that humanity did not experience any harm nor lacked anything; from the golden cornucopia of his abundant power he poured over humanity also the overabundance of his divine love. The *fountain of all good*[4] flowed, neither hindered nor hampered by anything.

§ 4    This must be placed clearly in the foreground, lest the true resilience of our faith be broken in us. In our present condition we are used to pain and sorrow. There is a cross that must be borne daily. Therefore, the highest that we can imagine is living in a state in which sorrow spares us for a while, in which we lack nothing, and in which a measure of joy refreshes our heart. For anyone who may enjoy life in this way, "the lines have fallen ... in pleasant places" [Psa 16:6]. The heart virtually never strives after a higher ideal. But the heart *should* do that. We *must* not put the condition of our highest desire lower than God has ordained it for us. When we do that, we demean our life and surrender that which God has destined for us and has by grace ordained for us once again. It dulls us when we settle for less. We then *miss* less because we *desire* less. We make ourselves less sensitive, and therefore have less pain. But that impassivity then also brings us into a false situation, falsifies the standard whereby we measure things, and distorts our view of the past and of the future. And what we also must not forget is that our sense of guilt suffers from this, because when we do not clearly recognize from how high a state of bliss and heavenly overabundance we have fallen, we cannot gauge the depth into which sin has thrown us. It is therefore not an indifferent, incidental matter to clearly perceive in what state of bliss God had originally placed humankind. Only when we form the correct conception of this state of bliss do

---

4.   See Heidelberg Catechism, Lord's Day 50, A 125.

we understand what has been thrown away through sin and has been lost, and also what the ideal is toward which we reach in Christ.

In this paradise the first human felt only *one* lacuna and void. He felt §5 *alone*. Not in the least in the manner in which we would feel alone if we stood all alone, as the only one in the whole world. In loneliness *we* miss the presence of others, because we have been accustomed to their presence our whole life long. Also, sin makes loneliness so much more terrible. Those who are holy endure loneliness so much more easily. Furthermore, the fellowship of the newly created human being with his God was a perfect one, and to that extent "lonely am I, not alone"[5] was applicable to him in a much higher sense than for us. When it is recorded of Enoch and Noah that they walked with God, then this walking with God was a memory of the condition in paradise. After his creation, Adam not only walked with God, but was not without God's fellowship for a moment. Even as the life of a child in the first days of his life is at one with that of the mother, so also immediately after creation, the life of the first man was one with the life of his God. He had just come from God's hand, and he still lived from moment to moment out of and through that hand, the hand that had let him go in the act of creation and yet still held him caringly. Yet there was something about being alone that became burdensome as soon as it was felt, and it ultimately had to be felt because the duality of the sexes and the unity of human being with human being [man and woman] were included in the ordinances of God's creation.[6]

We read, then, that the social life of the animals evoked this feeling of lack in Adam. Not as if human beings had evolved from the animals. Exactly the opposite is apparent from this narrative. The animals already had a social life. If humanity had evolved from the animals and had been the most highly developed species of the animal kingdom, then the social

---

5. This quote, "eenzaam ben ik niet alleen," is an allusion to a line from a play by Pius Alexander Wolff (1782–1828), a German actor and writer. In his *Preciosa* (1821) with music by Carl Maria von Weber (1786–1826), the text appears as the first line of the title character's singing, "Einsam bin ich, nicht alleine" (Lonely am I, not alone). See Taco H. de Beer and Eliza Laurillard, eds., *Woordenschat, verklaring van woorden en uitdrukkingen* (The Hague: Haagsche Boekhandel, 1899), 240.

6. Kuyper is referring here to Gen 1:27, "So God created man in his own image, in the image of God he created him; male and female he created them," and Gen 2:24, "Therefore a man shall leave his father and his mother and hold fast to his wife, and they shall become one flesh." He is making the point that the "two-in-one-flesh" unity of man and woman is grounded in the order of the original creation.

impulse would have manifested itself to a rather high degree in humankind. But this is not so. The animals were created in pairs, but the man in his singularity. For man, the female being would be taken *from himself*, in order to give expression to that highest unity that comes into existence not when the one is added to the other, but only when both are one at the very root of their being.

The woman should not be something that came to man from the outside, but something that came *out of him*. Not man's creation—the woman also had to be God's creation—yet taken from man, in order to express in this way the highest, most intimate, most perfect unity in that wondrous creation.

§ 6    Man, therefore, did not come from the animals, but the animal world is intended for man and was created with man in view. When God created the animals, he already knew within himself the human being he would create, and he knew that human being in soul *and body*. And in order that that animal world would be suited to man and would not be too alien to man, but as it were, a part of his own life, God created the animal world in such a way that, in increasing measure, the bodies of the animals contained a clear foreshadowing of the body he had intended and ordained for man. We can also express this succinctly: *God created the animals in the image and likeness of humankind.*

If we view it in this manner, we understand immediately the peculiar relationship that exists between man and animal. We do not find anything strange in all the discoveries that have, since Darwin, brought to light such a strong physical correspondence between man and animal. We sense immediately why the conclusion, which many in our day have drawn from Darwin's discovery, that man evolved from the animals lacks all compelling power. No one will say that God has his origin in man because man has been created in God's image. And in the same way, we now lack any right to deduce from the undeniable fact *that God created the animals in the image of man* that man would have come from the animals. There is unity, equality, relatedness. This is a fact we must never deny. But this unity, equality, correspondence, and relatedness have their origin in the mind of God. In God's thought, man was first, and then the animals; but from that thought of God came forth, first the animals, and then man. Whoever perceives this clearly is not for a moment at a loss vis-à-vis the Darwinist.

§ 7    Thus when it says that the social life of the animals evoked in Adam a certain sense of lack, we must not for a moment think of a certain animal trait that surfaced in Adam. It is simply absurd to think of an animal trait in man apart from sin. The matter was quite different. In the thought of God's ordaining, man was ordained not to be lonely but to be in company with people. Because man had been thus ordained, God foreshadows that trait of sociability also in the life of the animals. So when that social life of the animals drew Adam's attention, it did not awaken something of the animal nature in him, but that life trait was awakened within him that had been ordained of God, that belonged to man and was only foreshadowed in the life of the animals.

The awakening of that feeling preceded the creation of Eve. And then came the woman. She found the man from whom she had been taken, and Adam saw in her not so much a second individual but rather a part of himself. *Isha* would be her name or, as it has been translated, *wo-man* [Gen 2:23].[7] She was not yet Eve; that name she received only after the fall. "Counterhalf" or "counterpart" would be too strong a word. "*Other self*" is too philosophical an expression. But both her wondrous creation and the first name she was given express that she was not an addition to the man but was part of his life, which became complete only through her. A *wedding* in our sense was inconceivable at that point. At our *weddings* people are brought together who were strangers to each other and first lived separately; such a ceremony is therefore conceivable only after the fall. It is a weak effort to restore and redress what was lost through sin. In paradise there was no wedding but a creation *in* marriage, a being one together through the origin of life itself.

Byzantine argumentations have been advanced about the rib of Adam from which the woman was taken, and it has even been calculated whether from that moment on Adam lived with one fewer rib. The text prohibits such vain pedantry. When Adam sees his wife he does not say, "This is one of my ribs," but something quite different: "This at last is bone of my bones and flesh of my flesh" [Gen 2:23]. The further explanation that follows immediately, given by Adam himself, must not be overlooked. Granted that it reads "one of his ribs," but this must not be construed as if this expresses the *whole* matter. The full sense of the phrase is that the bone and the flesh

---

7. In Hebrew, *isha*, "woman," is the feminine form of *ish*, "man." The SV uses *Manninne*, an otherwise nonexistent word, consisting of "man" with a feminine ending. The English word *woman* was in Old English *wifmon*, a combination of *wife* ("woman") and *man*. The rendering *wo-man* (with hyphen) seeks to show likewise that *Isha* is a derivative of *man*.

of Eve, that is, her whole physical presence, was not taken from the *dust from the ground* but of his bone and flesh, and was built into a complete body by creative power alone.

We do not read anything about children born before the fall. But Genesis 2:24 shows that procreation was most definitely not a consequence of sin, as if, in the absence of sin, each new human being would have been created individually. This has been suggested, but wrongly so.[8] After all, after the creation of Eve it is stated explicitly, "Therefore a man shall leave his *father* and his *mother* and hold fast to his wife, and they shall become one flesh" [Gen 2:24]. The designations *father* and *mother*, which are unthinkable apart from procreation, are thus discussed already before the fall and are associated directly with the creation ordinance of God. This is also apparent from the formation beforehand of the animals in the image of man. Reproduction exists in the animal world as well, and that trait in the life of animals was also a foreshadowing of what would be revealed perfectly only in man.

In that high, holy unity, therefore, man and woman stood in a paradise that was bathed in divine overabundance. It was a divine masterpiece. The masterpiece that was the ultimate goal of all of creation. The whole world existed for the sake of that paradise, and that paradise existed for the sake of humanity that had been called by God and blessed by God. Man was the center in that creation, and the crown of God's entire creation.

---

8.  This seems to have been the early view of Augustine, for instance, in his *The Literal Meaning of Genesis*, perhaps exhibiting the vestigial influence of Manicheism. See Peter Lombard, *The Sentences*, trans. Giulio Silano (Toronto: Pontifical Institute for Mediaeval Studies, 2008), 2:20.1.2, p. 86: "Some hold that the first humans in paradise would not have been able to join sexually for the procreation of children, except after sin, since they say that sexual intercourse cannot occur without corruption or stain. But there could be neither corruption nor stain in humankind before sin because these things were the consequence of sin." But see also, referring to Augustine's later view in *The City of God*, David G. Hunter, "Sexual Ethics," in *Augustine through the Ages: An Encyclopedia*, ed. Allan D. Fitzgerald (Grand Rapids: Eerdmans, 1999), 327: "In his mature thought Augustine held that God had originally created human beings to propagate children through sexual intercourse (*civ. Dei* 14.22)."

# CHAPTER SIXTEEN

# THE ORIGINAL LIFE SPAN

*Blessed are they that do his commandments, that they may have right to the tree of life, and may enter in through the gates into the city.*[1]

REVELATION 22:14 KJV

We degenerate sinners simply cannot compare Adam to ourselves, with his original perfection and fullness of strength. We wear the autumnal robe of fadedness and decay, whereas Adam blossomed in the springtime luster of a strength not yet injured by anything. We know this from what we are told about the age of the early patriarchs. The report that the oldest patriarchs lived to be almost a thousand years of age must not in any way be discounted. There can certainly be differences of opinion as to the extent and duration of a year, and history shows that such differences of opinion did indeed exist for a long time. The manner of calculating time could develop only gradually to the level of accuracy and precision that we have today. In ancient times, people as a rule had to make do with inadequate data.

§ 1

---

1. Ed. note: The SV and the KJV follow the Stephanus (1550) text, which reads "that do his commandments" instead of "those who wash their robes" (ESV et al.). Kuyper uses the phrase "that do his commandments" implicitly (and explicitly) in his argument. Therefore the KJV is used here.

This resulted in a degree of difference between the results of their measuring time and the changes of seasons in the course of nature. Attempts were made to smooth out those differences. One group of people did this more roughly, others with more refinement. As a result, divergent chronologies developed, especially as a result of the difference between the so-called *solar year*, based on the course of the sun, and the *lunar year*, based on twelve months of four weeks each, and thus having only 336 days. Yet it is absurd to appeal to this difference in calculating time in seeking an explanation for the high age of the early patriarchs. After all, nature itself indicates unfailingly the passing of a year through the cycle of the seasons. Life in nature, in the field, and in the orchard knows a beginning of the resurgence of life, a going on to blossoming and to a ripening to the full harvest, followed by a waning and finally a hibernation, and awakening again only after this hibernation.

This cycle is what constitutes a year, and in demarcating the limit of that cycle no people would have been able to make any significant mistake. One year the cycle may differ somewhat from the next. But no matter the extent of that difference, there is no year inserted between the two and no year can drop out from between them. Even in regions where two harvests are gathered within a year, the farmer knows very well how to distinguish between the late harvest of the preceding year and the early harvest of the new year.

When the first chapters of Genesis speak of *years*, therefore, we must think of natural years, in which nature completes its life cycle; and it is absurd to say, as has been done, that those years should be viewed as months. Mahalalel fathered Jared when he was 65 years of age [Gen 5:15]. If we take this to be months, then Mahalalel would have begotten this son when he was *five years old*. Furthermore, if years did indeed mean months, then the change in the meaning of the word should be indicated. But we do not find any indication of this. Gradually the life expectancy drops, and already with Abraham we find a life span that corresponds more or less to the life span that is reached still today in Russia and other countries.[2]

---

2. *Note by the author*: Not long ago reports surfaced about an old man of 137 who had traveled the road from Moscow to Petersburg largely on foot, and about a married couple that celebrated their hundredth wedding anniversary. [Ed. note: Such claims were not uncommon in the nineteenth century. See, for instance, Charles Hulbert, "Instances of Human Longevity in Europe," in *Museum Europæum; or, Select Antiquities, Curiosities, Beauties, and Varieties, of Nature and Art in Europe*

We must therefore abandon any attempt to make the life span of the early patriarchs equal to ours. We are told that they lived *ten times* as long as we, and we must accept this report. *Ten times as long as we* is the clear indication given to us in these ages: Adam, 930; Seth, 912; Enosh, 905; and so on. These numbers divided by 10 give the still very respectable ages of 93, 91, and 90 years, respectively. If it is incontrovertible that a person's life *force* is related to his life *span* and vice versa, then we can draw the conclusion that the early patriarchs surpassed us nine times in natural vitality. This is true also of the ancient patriarchs after the fall, when their strength had already been partially injured and was maintained only through grace. Thus the life force that was in them then already was *no longer* what that life force must have been immediately *after creation*. And although we lack any criterion to calculate the difference in vitality immediately before and after the fall, it is in the nature of things that that vitality must have been even greater before the fall.

This is relevant also when we come to the incarnation of the Word. When we hear that the Son of God took upon himself human nature, not in its original but in its *later, feeble* state, we generally fail to understand this properly, because Jesus was, after all, neither deformed nor sick, and his entire appearance undoubtedly made a blindingly noble impression. This then easily leads to the thought, what then did Jesus still lack? But if we take into account the difference between us and the early patriarchs, then we know that they possessed a vitality *ten times* stronger than ours, and when furthermore we take into account that Adam before the fall must have shone in a still nobler light, then it becomes clear to us what [it means that] the Son of God "took upon himself our lowly nature." Had he not assumed our "lowly nature" but our original one, then with respect to his body he would have had to have been like Adam.

Already this difference in life span is significant for the entire position §2
of original man. After all, we must not say, "*After the fall* Adam reached the age of 930 years; without the fall he might have reached *one thousand*," because no matter how much truth this may contain, this idea is incorrect. It presupposes that without sin, Adam's vitality would have become exhausted and that he would ultimately still have died. And this is precisely

---

(Shrewsbury: C. Hulbert, 1825), 451–57, which calculates that "according to a list published officially in Russia, of the number of deaths in 1815, there were 1,068 instances of people who died at upwards of one hundred years of age" (456–57)].

the wrong way of thinking. Apart from sin, the life force does *not* diminish at all. All decrease in vitality is a consequence of the fall. Human life was not designed to decline, to diminish, and to finally dissolve in death. The life that God created in human beings was designed for *living*, for living *eternally*. Death is not part of God's creation. Death entered God's creation through, and as a result of, sin. And if sin had *not* entered the human race, humanity would never have experienced death.

The slow decline and depletion of the life span comes to light, therefore, in the presence of a slow work of destruction. In the beginning, the supremacy of life over death was still great. The life of humankind, then as now, was borne by two factors: first, by the hereditary strength inherent in the *race* and, second, by the strength inherent more specifically in the *individual*. This is still true. In one family we find people who often reach eighty or ninety years, in another family they generally die between sixty and seventy years. This depends on the strength inherent in the lineage. But within the families themselves there are still differences. In a family whose members generally reach a high age, one person will reach ninety-five or ninety-six while another passes away at eighty-six or eighty-seven years of age. That then depends on the strength of the individual. And so too in the earliest times, when death had just begun to break [down] our vitality. Death's destructive influence had to work on both factors. First the strength of the *race* had to be broken, then the *personal* strength of the individual. We see this breaking [down] of the strength of the *race* in the decline of the life span from more than 900 to less than 100, and the breaking [down] of the *individual* strength we see happening immediately in the decline from 930 to 912 in Adam and Seth, respectively.

§ 3    In Adam and Eve before the fall, on the other hand, both the strength of the race and the strength of individual life were entirely intact and unimpaired, and there was no question of a decline in vitality. Without sin they *could not have died*. Scripture teaches us clearly that *death came into the world through sin* (Rom 5:12). On this point there can be no doubt among Christians. This is true for us, and in our view we must not tamper with this. Life in paradise was a life without even the *shadow* of death. If we understand this in something more than the superficial sense, then what is expressed here differs entirely from saying that Adam would not have died apart from sin. That too, of course, but much more. Dying, after all, is absolutely not merely breaking the thread of life, but also the result of a protracted process that takes place in us. It is said that already at birth a child brings into the world the seed of its death. And even though this is manifestly true for us in the case of hereditary illnesses such as cancer, it is nevertheless true in principle for each child. We do not *become* mortal at a later point in time; we are *born* mortal.

Thus death does not arrive first at the moment when we breathe our last, but is at work in us throughout our life. The pangs of death precede death itself, in part through illness and sickness, but also apart from sickness through the diminishing of our strength, the withering of our face, the dulling of our eye, the graying of our hair. Yes, we even see these signs of decline manifest themselves in all kinds of pain and discomfort, in all kinds of susceptibilities and disorders, in nervous exhaustion and fatigue. Thus, if we want to imagine a human being at the point of creation, we must completely eliminate from that image not only death, but also all sickness, all aging, all pain, all breakdowns, all weariness and nervous exhaustion. It must have been a life in perfectly unbroken strength, in profound harmony, moving along in continuous balance. Even the dread or fear of the possibility that something *might* go wrong with them was entirely alien to their state of bliss.

Holy Scripture does not give us a direct answer to the question of what the outcome, the course, the end of man's existence on earth would have been if sin had not entered. We are taught *negatively* that man would then *not* have died, but what *would* have happened to man is not stated *positively*. Nevertheless, we cannot suppress this question, and throughout the ages believers have considered themselves justified in thinking that had sin not entered, then after having completed God's counsel on earth, the first man would have been taken up into glory without dying. This notion was based especially on what the apostle [Paul] teaches us will happen to those who confess the Lord and will be living on the earth when he returns on the clouds. He says that they will, without dying, be *transformed*, that is, will change into a more glorious form and appearance in order to thus be forever with the Savior [1 Thess 4:17].

§ 4

One is justified in using that reference to the extent that it shows that also without dying it is possible to change from one condition to another, from one shape to another, from one form to another. For this reason the transfiguration on Mount Tabor can also be considered in this context, since the event on Tabor also speaks of such a transition prior to death intervening [Matt 17:1–13].[3] We cannot doubt this possibility, therefore, and to that extent there is no objection to considering the possibility of such a transition from a lower to a higher state, form, and shape without death taking place also in the case of Adam in paradise.

§ 5    All the same, we must add that neither what Paul prophesies nor what is reported to us about Tabor is directly applicable here. The children of God who on the day of Jesus' return will not die but be "changed," will have been conceived and born in sin and are therefore subject to all manner of misery and therefore also to the abasement of their nature. When Jesus returns they will stand here on earth in their weakened and degraded body, and what Jesus will do to them is that he "will transform our lowly body to be like his glorious body, by the power that enables him even to subject all things to himself" (Phil 3:21). Also, on Tabor Jesus still bore that "humiliated nature" that he had put on for our sake. Both cases thus involve a human nature that had been *humiliated* and now changes over into a state of glory. But this self-evidently could *not* have been applicable to Adam. In Adam, human nature had *not* yet been humiliated, and without sin it would not have been humiliated. In a sinless development, his leaving this state of being would consequently neither have been parallel to the "change" of which the holy apostle Paul speaks, nor to the glorification on Tabor—indeed, not even to the glorification of the Christ in his resurrection and ascension.

But even this does not yet show the distinction completely. For us who live on an earth that has come under the curse, no ultimate escape is possible without the perishing of this earth in its present form and the appearing of the new earth under the new heaven from the hand of God's omnipotence. Then the redeemed first go from the earth to heaven, and only when at the return of the Lord the contrast between heaven and earth shall have fallen away through the destruction of *this* earth and the appearance of the *new* earth, shall the children of the kingdom inherit the earth and live in glory with their Lord. But in a development of humanity without sin, this would not have been so. Without *sin* in humanity, no *curse* would have come on the earth, and no destruction of an earth apart from a curse is conceivable. To some extent we might even say: glory

---

3.  Mount Tabor is held to be the site of the transfiguration by ancient Christian tradition, but for various reasons modern scholars are dubious and suggest alternatives, such as Mount Hermon or Mount Meron.

would not have had to come, for glory was already present. The whole of paradise was bathed in the glory of the Lord.

We might incorrectly conclude that if no sin had come at all, and Satan had not invaded our human life, the paradisal condition would simply have remained what it was originally. Our forefathers expressed this by saying that *eternal life* had been promised as reward in the covenant of works, and our Catechism also gives as the ultimate goal of the service of God that we might "live with him in eternal happiness."[4] It cannot be denied that a distinction is clearly drawn between the paradisal condition and the coming kingdom of glory. Doctrinally this is expressed by saying that in paradise Adam could fall, whereas in the kingdom of glory any sin would be utterly inconceivable. In paradise there *was* no sin, but sin *could* enter. In the kingdom of glory, on the other hand, not only *is* there no sin, but any entering of sin is utterly inconceivable.

This spiritual difference is, of course, also linked with a difference in the external aspect. Paradise could perish, as indeed it has perished, and in its place could come the curse. Conversely, in the kingdom of glory, any thought of perishability is incongruous. The same is also true of humanity's external existence. In paradise, Adam existed in such a way that his vitality remained unimpaired, but he *could* lose it, he *could* be humiliated in his nature; he was not yet a *mortal*, but he *could* become subject to death. And this is precisely what will no longer be true in the kingdom of glory. On the new earth under the new heaven, death will no longer rule over us. Death will have been eradicated. The glorified nature will no longer be *capable* of being humiliated. Vitality will not be possible to lose there.

Herein, and only herein, lies the transition that Adam would have had to make, apart from sin, if he were to attain his enduring, permanent condition. We will speak later about his spiritual state and position. Here we confine ourselves to saying that in the first place he had to acquire spiritual incorruptibility; secondly, that the world had to become *curse*-proof, if we may express it so; and thirdly, that his human nature had to become *insusceptible* to humiliation.

In our language we use the word *fireproof* to describe what cannot be affected by fire. Something is fireproof if fire cannot get at it. And so we could also put it succinctly this way, namely, that by virtue of his creation Adam was susceptible to sin, death, and curse, such that he had to make

§ 6

§ 7

---

4.  Heidelberg Catechism, Lord's Day 3, A 6.

a transition to a state that was sin-*proof*, death-*proof*, and curse-*proof*. Perseverance of the saints was not enough. The perseverance of the saints does not preclude sin or even a temporary falling away. What is meant here is that neither sin nor death nor curse can penetrate his being and his world.

This condition Scripture calls *eternal life*, and the Catechism calls *eternal happiness*.[5] Adam most definitely was not yet in that condition by virtue of his creation. He had to *go over* to that condition. And it is that transition from one condition to the other that would have brought an end to his first existence.

§ 8　　In paradise itself, this transition was denoted sacramentally by the *tree of life*. This *tree of life*, we read in Genesis 2:9, stood in the midst of paradise. It constituted its center. This phrase "tree of life" is found again in Proverbs 3:18, where it says, "*[Wisdom] is a tree of life* to those who lay hold of her," which is then explained further: "those who hold her fast *are called blessed*." So here this tree of life is something by means of which one enters into blessedness. In Proverbs 11:30 the same is said about righteousness, in Proverbs 13:12 about a desire fulfilled, that is, of the reaching of our ideal, and in Proverbs 15:4 words of love, compassion, and comfort are the "medicine of the tongue."[6] And then, after the rest of the books of Holy Scripture have been silent about the *tree of life*, it returns in the book of Revelation, where Christ says to the church of Ephesus, "To the one who conquers I will grant to eat of the *tree of life*, which is in the paradise of God" (Rev 2:7). And in the depiction of the kingdom of glory the tree of life is shown, not as one tree but as a row of trees on both sides of the river of crystal that flower and yield fruit twelve times in a single year, that bring about the healing of the nations (Rev 22:2), and whose fruit may be eaten by those who "have the right to the tree of life," that is, those who are blessed because they do the commandments of him who is the Alpha and the Omega (Rev 22:14).

Thus all these references to the tree of life point to a tree of God whose fruit gives or maintains life, and whose leaves even bring healing. The same is confirmed by what we read in Genesis 3:22, where God expresses the fear that fallen man in his audacity might "take also of the tree

---

5. Heidelberg Catechism, Lord's Day 3, A 6.
6. At Prov 15:4 the SV reads, "The medicine of the tongue" (*De medicijn der tong*), and the marginal note offers a gloss of "The health of the tongue" (*De gezondheid der tong*). The ESV refers in this verse to "a gentle tongue."

of life and eat, and *live forever,*" which is why God decides to expel man from paradise. "Then the LORD God said, 'Behold, the man has become like one of us in knowing good and evil. Now, lest he reach out his hand and take also of the tree of life and eat, and live forever.'"

From of old, two interpretations have been prevalent here. The one maintained that this tree of life contained a divine power, so that whoever ate from that tree added divine, eternal power to his life by the eating as such. The other view rejected such a notion and saw in the *tree of life* nothing but a *sign*. Eating from this tree was, on this view, nothing but an act of obedience, the obedience of faith, and whoever demonstrated this obedience of faith received from God a heavenly strength. People preferred to compare this to the sacrament. At the Lord's Supper we use *bread* and *wine*. This bread and wine do not possess the power of grace in and of themselves, but whoever takes, eats, and drinks these sacramental signs in the obedience of faith receives from Christ from heaven, through the Holy Spirit, the grace that the sacrament promises and seals. In the same manner, it is then said, this tree of life was placed there as a sacramental sign, whose fruit which man was given to eat, simply as the fruit of a tree, and this eating was linked with the promise of higher grace. It was not as if this grace came from the tree; rather, in this case the obedience of faith was followed by the giving of higher grace. Others, finally, do not even want to go this far and are of the opinion that in fact the first human was *not* allowed to eat the fruit of this tree but simply had to *look* at it, even as the Jews in the wilderness had to look at the serpent, and to this sacramental act of looking at this sign was attached the promise of higher grace.

The battle over the sacraments that our forefathers waged against the Roman Catholics and Lutherans has undoubtedly not remained without influence on their choice in the interpretation of this mystery. Even as they still tried to maintain the truth over against the Roman Catholics and Lutherans that the water in baptism was and remained simply water, and thus also the bread and wine at the Lord's Supper were nothing but common bread and common wine, they also maintained that this *tree of life* was nothing but a common tree, and that only the *promise* was the source of inflowing grace.

# CHAPTER SEVENTEEN

# THE TREE OF LIFE

*Then the* LORD *God said, "Behold, the man has become like one of us in knowing good and evil. Now, lest he reach out his hand and take also of the tree of life and eat, and live forever—"*

GENESIS 3:22

§ 1     As we stated briefly in the preceding chapter, currently the most common interpretation of the *tree of life* as if it were nothing but a sacramental sign in the covenant of works is not adequate.[1] This interpretation does not satisfy. One feels that something of this nature may be involved, but the notion that this marvelous tree in paradise served only this purpose does not resolve the difficulty facing us.

This tree is assumed to have been nothing but a common tree. Adam then would occasionally have looked at that tree. And looking at that tree would have had a sacramental effect on his faith that strengthened his inner life. What else would this be but transporting a means of grace from the covenant of grace back to the period of the covenant of works? Under the covenant of grace the Lord most certainly commands us to take

---

1.  See M. Eugene Osterhaven, "Covenant," in *Encyclopedia of the Reformed Faith*, ed. Donald K. McKim (Louisville: Westminster John Knox, 1992), 85: "In elaborating the theology of the covenants, some Reformed theologians taught a covenant of works as God's first covenant in history. This consisted of the promise of eternal life and confirmation in righteousness for Adam if he would be obedient throughout a probationary period and death if he were disobedient."

common water and equally common bread with wine and to see in these common elements a sign that is a seal of his solemn promise. And he, our God, graciously grants us under the sacramental use of these signs a spiritual grace that strengthens either the implanted capacity for faith or the faith that has budded. But this whole view of the sacrament is geared to *fallen man*, not to man in the state of righteousness. In fallen man that original faith has been damaged and disrupted, and has in part even changed over into *unbelief*. In him, therefore, *faith* cannot be restored other than by a spiritual, miraculous act of God in the heart, and only in the form of faith in Christ. This *restored* faith, then, is opposed in the child of God in all manner of ways. This is why it must be strengthened. And for that strengthening of saving faith in its continual oscillations, the sacrament is serviceable.

In that sacrament, therefore, nothing is required of, nor presupposed in, the sinner other than that, first, restored faith be present (whether as yet only potentially or already in its budding out); second, this faith be threatened; and third, the strengthening of this faith be sought with God and not with man. All the rest then comes from God the Lord, by virtue of the Word of promise, by the mystical inworking of the Holy Spirit. Precisely for this reason the signs have to be so completely common: water, bread, wine. It is then sufficient that these simple, quite common signs point symbolically to the substance: the water to cleansing, the bread to sustaining, and the wine to the exhilarating and enhancing of life; that the action in the sacrament likewise have a symbolic interpretation; and that all this has not been devised or invented by man but has been ordained by God.

But *can* this apply equally in the covenant of works? Definitely not. In the covenant of works what matters is not *believing*, but *doing*. The ground rule of that covenant is not "Believe and you will live," but quite otherwise: "If you *do* these things, you will live forever." At this point we cannot elaborate further on this contrast. Let it only be said that all *doing* presupposes faith. But the faith that Adam possessed in paradise was not faith in the Mediator and Surety, but faith in God. Even as Christ himself, of course, also did not have faith in the Lord Jesus Christ but rather, and exclusively, general faith in God. This general faith does not mean, as it is often understood, admitting readily and wholeheartedly that there exists a provident God who holds our breath in his hand. Faith as Adam possessed it in the state of righteousness and as Christ possessed it according to his human nature has nothing to do with that kind of rationalistic bleating, but is the immediate connection, without any interference or obstacle, of the conscious life of the soul with the living God.

This is the faith presupposed in the whole covenant of works. Whoever does not live in original or restored conscious fellowship with the living God does not bow before his law, does not have his law written on his heart, does not know the impulse to fulfill the law, and does not seek to grasp eternal life through fulfilling the law. This general faith as Adam possessed it in the state of righteousness is always the foundation and presupposition of fulfilling the law. It is inseparable from it. And as soon as this faith allows even a sliver to be split off, it is damaged, its power is broken, it is turned into unbelief, and it can no longer lead to the fulfillment of the law.

For this reason, any strengthening of this faith is inconceivable. As long as it is sound, it does not need strengthening; and as soon as it becomes unsound, it would not benefit by it. A human being who has turned from faith to unbelief cannot be saved by a *strengthening* of damaged faith; in him the capacity for faith must be restored and renewed in another form. He needs to be born again, and only after that rebirth does the sacramental strengthening of the newly implanted faith, which is now faith in Jesus Christ, become possible. For that reason it was not adequately and sufficiently thought through when people spoke of a strengthening of faith before the fall. Theirs was a failure to adequately distinguish between the very different natures of the two covenants. The tree of life was therefore certainly not a sacrament in the sense of a means of grace as we receive and enjoy it.

§ 2          In order to arrive at a more correct insight into the significance of the tree of life, it is safest to start with what is *known* and what is *certain* in order to ascend from there to the *unknown*. These firm particulars we have in Genesis 2:9 and in Genesis 3:22. About the *institution* of a sacrament we read nothing—not a single word. But we are told that there was a garden in paradise, and that in this lush garden there were two trees that had a distinct significance. Not in the sense that the rest of the trees were unsightly and of a lesser sort and that only those two trees were splendid specimens. On the contrary, it says that *all* trees were beautiful to the eye and yielded noble fruit. We read, "And out of the ground the Lord God made to spring up every tree that is pleasant to the sight and good for food" [Gen 2:9]. But two trees are set apart from all the rest, and of those two it is said that the one has to do with our *being*, the other with our *consciousness*. The one is called the tree of *life*, that is, of *being*, the other is the tree of moral *knowledge*, that is, of consciousness.

It strikes us immediately that the number *two* here dominates. Not one tree, not three trees, but *two*, and these two trees are placed in relationship to man, even as man himself has been created as a duality: as *soul* and *body*. The human being for whom these two trees are intended, for whom they have been planted, and for whom they stand there, has two aspects to his existence; and corresponding to these two parts, sides, or aspects of his existence, two trees are pointed out to him. Of those two trees he is told that the one has to do with his *intellectual consciousness*, with his *moral knowledge*, hence therefore with his inner, spiritual existence, with the existence of his soul. Of the other tree, by contrast, is said that this one involves not his moral insight but his *life* in general. If we take this contrast as it stands, then we may surmise that this tree of life points more to natural life, whereas the second tree relates more to our spiritual existence. No one will be able to maintain that the moral knowledge of good and evil lies outside our spiritual life. Only, we must not misunderstand the expression "natural life" here.

Today, "natural life" constitutes a contrast with the supernatural power that Christ generates in us, but originally natural life was life itself, life as it was intended to pass over into eternal existence, in short, what we now call our *existence*. And over against that *existence* then stands the spiritual *consciousness*, which arises from our *moral* knowledge. And even as that tree of knowledge stood in relation to our consciousness, so also the tree of life stood in relationship to our existence as such. Or to express it more simply (though not entirely accurately), the tree of life related to our *body*, the tree of knowledge to our *soul*.

What we read in Genesis 3:22 dovetails and fits completely with the preceding. [By now] man has fallen and stands unregenerate in his sin, in the midst of paradise. Both trees still stand within his reach. He has eaten from the fruit of the one tree, and it became his fall. And now the Lord says: We must be on guard that *(fallen) man does not "reach out his hand and take also of the tree of life and eat, and live forever."* In our circles these words have generally been interpreted in an ironic sense, as if God the Lord said mockingly, "Look, there stands man in his conceit, as if he had become one of us and as if, by eating from the tree of life, he now could also make his life and his existence eternal." Even Calvin takes this same

§ 3

ironic approach in his explanation of this verse. But we cannot agree with this, because irony can never induce one to implement a serious measure. And yet a very serious measure is indicated here. Fallen man is expelled from paradise. A heavenly guard of cherubim is placed at the entrance to the garden to guard it. And man wanders off, his heart still holding the memory of paradise lost, now to dwell upon the curse-laden earth. Would it make sense for God to say, "That foolish man fancies that by eating from the tree of life he can make himself immortal, and therefore I will execute this radical turnabout in the existing order of things. Indeed, what he fancies is not true, but just because he imagines it in his pride, I will take away paradise from him and leave him with only the cursed earth." Who does not sense that this interpretation is unsatisfactory?

The matter lies very differently, however, when we view, according to the interpretation we found in Genesis 2:9, the *tree of life* as a tree whose fruit has to do only with our *physical* existence and not with our *spiritual* existence. Calvin's claim, and that of all theologians before and after him who took refuge in an ironic reading of Genesis 3:22, was implicit in the fact that they thought of spiritual life in relation to the *tree of life*, and then, of course, they *could* not admit that fallen man could have acquired *spiritual life* by eating of that tree. This was self-evident, and as long as we continue to think of *spiritual life* in connection with the *tree of life*, Genesis 3:22 is simply unintelligible and incongruous. If, on the other hand, we abandon this unproven thesis and attach the *spiritual* significance to the *tree of knowledge* only, but a physical significance to the *tree of life* as pointing to only *natural* life, then the matter appears in a very different light. We could very well think that fallen man, who was utterly powerless to grasp *spiritual* life, nevertheless reached for what could strengthen his *natural* life. Today the extravagant sinner still grasps for all that nature offers him to strengthen his body weakened by sin, so that he can all the more freely indulge his appetite for sin. The urge to do this springs up of its own accord. Sin gives a feeling of weakness, also in relation to the body. And the first thing the sinner does is to seek not the welfare of his wounded soul, but the renewal of strength for his weakened body. And what then was more natural than that fallen man, feeling God's wrath upon him and threatened in his existence, was in the first place intent on taking from the *tree of life* and seeking in its fruit the strengthening of his life?

§ 4      To see the significance of this, we have only to remember the undeniable truth that our *physical* life does not maintain itself spontaneously, but lasts only by continually taking in nourishment. Our body continually digests, and that loss must be compensated for by the steady intake of new nourishment. This is true not only now, as a result of sin, but was also true in paradise: "You may surely eat of every tree of the garden" [Gen 2:16]. And so it will also be one day on the new earth under the new heaven. The heavenly Bridegroom awaits us at a wedding banquet full of fat and marrow, and along the river of life stand, as delightful fruit trees, the same *trees of life* from which all those are empowered to eat who have fallen asleep in Christ [1 Cor 15:18; Rev 22:2].

We are therefore mistaken if we imagine that in paradise the maintenance of the body was of secondary importance. On the contrary, the body had to be fed in paradise as well. Add to this, secondly, that in paradise this body was only in a *provisional* state. If Adam had kept God's law, then he would also have gone physically from a condition of mortality to a condition of immortality, *without dying*, even as he would have progressed from being *able* to fall to being *unable* to fall.[2] This then assumes both a spiritual and a physical transition. The soul that is able no longer to fall is different from the soul that is still able to fall. And thus also the body that is still *able to die* is different from the body that is *no longer able to die*. And now we venture to ask whether it is so unlikely that the *tree of life* bore precisely that fruit that man had to eat to bring about this momentous change in his physical condition? The purpose of all the other trees in the garden was to maintain man's physical life in the state in which it had been created, but this one tree had the purpose of taking his *physical* body into the state of glory. After all, in paradise the *tree of life* is an exception, but on the new earth it is a common fruit tree.

In this connection we must indeed remember that the cursed earth still bears the tree of life, but it has turned into its opposite, or its purpose has been changed. The opposite of the tree *of life* is, of course, the tree *of death*, and what is that other than the *poison tree* whose fruit brings death to man, be it slowly, be it suddenly. The *belladonna*, the *upas* tree in Java,

§ 5

---

2. Here Kuyper describes the primal condition of Adam somewhat differently than earlier, although by "condition of mortality" (*toestand der sterfelijkheid*) he should be understood as pointing to the provisional nature of Adam's original state. He was not "mortal" in the sense of already being subject to death, but he was mortal in the sense of being subject to death if he would sin.

the *strychnine*,[3] and so many more are all plants that were inconceivable in paradise but that sprouted from the cursed earth. Related to the *tree of life* are, on the other hand, the quina tree[4] and so many others that offer beneficial sap or medicinal fruits that do not kill life, but save it when sick. These facts therefore show that at present, God the Lord has substances in his plant kingdom that either threaten or save natural human life and can do this with such intensity that a single drop of a particular poison is sufficient to destroy life, and that one thousandth and one ten-thousandth part of belladonna or another plant can save a life from certain death. Poison and life are thus linked most closely. Does not the practice of homeopathy have this indisputable merit, that it has discovered how the same botanical substances that usually bring death can by contrast sustain life when taken in very small doses?

So the poisonous tree and the life-giving tree have in common one underlying principle, and for this reason we have every right to maintain that the poisonous and the medicinal trees that we now find on the cursed earth take us back directly to the *tree of life* that stood in paradise, and that one day will bloom on the new earth that is to come in the kingdom of glory with a splendor that was unknown even in paradise. All these trees have a very different character than the common trees that provide nourishment. Their nature and character are that they do not nourish life but affect our existence directly at the root, whether to destroy that root or to strengthen that root of life within us. And this agrees fully with the view that the *tree of life* in paradise, unlike the common fruit tree, was intended not to feed and sustain human life, but to bring it to a state of higher strength.

---

3. These are all toxic plants. Some, like the belladonna, also have medicinal uses. The belladonna (*Atropa belladonna*) is also known as Deadly Nightshade and is native to Europe, northern Africa, and western Asia. *Antiaris toxicaria*, or upas, is a tropical tree that produces poisons called *antiarins*. Strychnine is a highly poisonous chemical commonly derived from the seeds of the *Strychnos nux-vomica* tree, native to India and southeast Asia.

4. The *cinchona* or *quinine* is a genus of flowering plants famed for their medicinal uses, including the production of quinine, a natural painkiller, antimalarial, and anti-inflammatory.

Think what would have happened if after his fall, Adam had partaken §6
of this "elixir of life" as it is called in theosophy[5]—what would have been
the consequence? This, that his natural life, which now served sin, would
have developed to a higher level of strength and that he would have physically fortified himself against physical death. This is what is referred to
in Genesis 3:22: "Lest he reach out his hand and take also of the tree of life
and eat, and live forever." This would have had the same effect as what we
see on a smaller scale in the villain who, in order to intensify the enjoyment of his crime, first raises his life spirit through strong drink, or, as so
often happens in case of a riot, that the lower class of people is first plied
with drink to inflame the populace and make them more reckless.

And thus the argument runs progressively, and erases all the difficulties. We then understand why there stood, in addition to the *tree of
knowledge*, which pointed to the life of the soul, another *tree of life*, which
pointed to the physical or natural life. We understand why that *tree of life
will be the rule* on the new earth, when the spiritual salvation will be fully
accomplished. We understand why Adam after his fall had to be intent on
eating precisely from that *tree of life* and thus fortify himself against death.
We understand the connection between the tree of life and the *poison tree*
on the cursed earth. We understand the profound connection discovered
by homeopathy between the life-threatening and the life-saving power
of poisonous plants such as belladonna. And finally, we understand why
Adam's intention had to be cut off and the cherub had to descend to ward
off such a sacrilegious abuse of the tree *of life*.

The main point is, therefore, that the *tree of life* will be the rule on the
new earth and was an exception in paradise, serving to physically prepare the transition to the state of perfect glory. An interpretation that we
offer herewith to our fellow theologians for reflection and consideration—
not without the quiet hope that the correct understanding of this mysterious tree may have been advanced somewhat through our comments.
We would add only two points. First, that eating from the tree of life in

---

5. The term "theosophy" is a combination of two Greek terms, *theos* (god) + *sophia*
   (wisdom): "Generally restricted to systems, such as that of [Emanuel] Swedenborg
   [1688–1772], of a pantheistic and mystical nature, and in particular that associated
   with Madame Blavatsky (1831–91), which includes the transmigration of souls, the
   brotherhood of man, the denial of a personal God and personal immortality, and
   belief in the fourth dimension [time]." See Simon Blackburn, *The Oxford Dictionary
   of Philosophy*, 2nd rev. ed. (New York: Oxford University Press, 2008), 362.

paradise was nevertheless most definitely sacramental, provided that we do not limit "sacramental" to the entirely unique meaning of baptism and Lord's Supper, but understand it in the sense in which also the rainbow in the Noahic covenant bears a sacramental character. Nourishment of the *body* and nourishment of the *spirit* are two acts that are generally viewed as having nothing in common. That this is a mistaken notion is sufficiently apparent from how frequently sumptuous food and drink are the cause of all kinds of sinful and excessive consequences. But in any case this much is certain, that eating from the tree of life was connected with Adam's faith in the salvation that was promised him, even as our partaking of the sacrament of the Lord's Supper is connected now for us with the hope of eternal life. And to that extent this *tree of life*, as the commentators on the authorized Dutch Bible say, was most definitely a sign. It stood there in the midst of paradise as a sign that life in paradise was not the highest good, but that Adam's striving and desire had to consist of wanting to leave the provisional paradisal condition and to reach for eternal life and perfect bliss, in the glory of God.

Our second comment concerns the other tree, the tree of *knowledge*. Of the tree of life man could eat, but he was not allowed to eat from the tree of knowledge. A directly opposite ordinance, thus, but in this context entirely natural. Body and spirit are distinguished in us in such a way that for our *physical* life we must *want* to be dependent on nature and its food. *Not* wanting this is to resist God's ordinance. But for the life of the spirit, conversely, that other law applies, that this higher life in us must be elevated above nature, and that we *must not* expect its sustenance from nature, but *must* expect it from God. Wanting to expect moral knowledge and the maturation of our spiritual life from the eating from the fruit of a tree would be a total reversal of God's instituted order. In that order, instituted by God, the command to *eat* applied to the *tree of life* and concerned the physical life. But for the *tree of knowledge* the command to *not eat* concerned the spiritual life. For the *tree of life*: You *must* eat; but for the *tree of knowledge*: You *may not* eat. The fact that Adam nevertheless did the latter, is really what constituted his fall.

# CHAPTER EIGHTEEN

# NATURAL OR SUPERNATURAL?

*And God saw everything that he had made, and behold, it was very good.*

From Adam's outward position we now move to his *inner existence*. We must also have a clear sense about this inner existence if we are to understand the consequences of the fall, the condition it brought about, and the common grace that ameliorated this condition. In this we merely follow the good example of all Christian authors who, in order to get a good perspective on the present, always began by rendering account of the influence of *sin* and *grace* on that which presently exists. In order to arrive at their conclusions they asked themselves in what state and position man stood before sin, and what changes sin brought about in these. Not only the Reformed, but also the Lutheran, Roman Catholic, and Greek Orthodox authors did this. This good habit was abandoned only when rationalism had undermined any faith in the state of righteousness and the fall. And it is pitiful to see how today even Christian writers are led from the right path by this evil example and deny this wisdom of our forefathers. It is as clear as can be that a physician called to attend to a sick person must first be aware of the human being in a healthy condition, as well as the cause of the illness that turns him from a healthy into a *sick* person. In the field of medicine or surgery, no one thinks differently on this point. And even

§ 1

architects and master shipbuilders entrusted with restoring or patching a damaged building or a damaged ship will always begin by asking for the plans and specifications according to which the building or ship was initially built. It is therefore a distinct error to consider a discussion of the state of righteousness to be superfluous here. The doctrine of common grace cannot be known nor understood without having a clear perception of the scriptural truth, especially with regard to the state of righteousness.

The Reformed understanding on this point was formed in antithesis to what the hierarchy under the influence of Rome had developed as the truth to be confessed long before the Reformation. From the Roman Catholic side, the notion had been accepted that man's original righteousness did not belong to our human nature by virtue of creation, but was added as a supernatural gift of grace to our natural gifts. In man as such, as he existed by nature, not righteousness but conflict ruled. In him the flesh stood by nature in opposition to the spirit. On this view, "concupiscence" or desire did not come into the world through sin and is in itself not sin; rather, it has been created in man by God. But precisely because this desiring of the flesh against the spirit made the possibility so great that the flesh would gain the upper hand over the spirit, God the Lord added a safety measure to this dangerous situation, which consisted in bestowing on man, by supernatural grace, something that was added to his nature. And what *was added to his nature* was original righteousness. Even as the horseman, in order to be sure of his horse, puts a bridle on it, so also God bestowed on Adam a bridle, in order to be able to control the flesh more firmly through the spirit. Even without that bridle it would not have been impossible that the spirit would have continued to reign over the flesh within Adam, but then such rule would have hung as it were by a thread. The balance would then have very easily swung to the wrong side. God therefore wanted to give man more safety. Man was not simply set on the horse, but first a bridle was placed on the horse. This bridle does not belong to nature, but it is added to nature. The bridle is not organic but instrumental. Where his organic, natural life was concerned, man had, properly speaking, nothing but the spirit to rule the flesh with its desires. But in order that it might be easier for him to keep that control, God now bestowed on him, over and above the spirit which he had by nature, in addition to this gift of his nature also a second means of control that did not belong to his nature but was added to it and was to that extent supernatural. This gift that was added to his nature was the original righteousness.

This Roman Catholic dogma about mankind's original condition does, §2 of course, have far-reaching influence on the whole view of man and on our human life as that has come to be as a consequence of sin. If we think that original righteousness was lost through sin, but that this righteousness as such was something that was added to our nature, then what was lost through sin was what had been given to us as a bridle for holding the flesh in check, but nature itself has not been affected. That nature may be in a somewhat languishing condition, but in itself it remains what it was before the fall. Now, as then, flesh and spirit stand over against one another in our nature, and the first impulse of desire is in itself not sinful. Grace must now come to our aid, it is true, to make redemption and salvation possible, since otherwise the horse would run away with its rider, that is, the *flesh* would run away with the *spirit*. But the capacity to choose by one's free will nevertheless continued in the sinful part of the human spirit, and today free will remains the starting point of moving toward spiritual perfection, if not in the Pelagian sense then at least in the manner of the semi-Pelagians.[1]

The import of this system is best understood if the human being is compared to the spider or the bee, or to any other animal that by instinct executes masterpieces. Such a small creature not only has the *capacity* of creating such a work of art, but it also *does* it. The question is, are *doing* as well as the *ability for doing* both part of its nature? Or does the creature's nature entail merely the *ability* to do something, whereas that the creature actually *does* something is effected by an internal divine operation added to its nature? We may answer by saying that for a bee, merely its *ability* to gather honey, to make a honeycomb, and to fill that honeycomb belongs to the bee's nature. But the fact that, instead of spilling the honey as many species of wasps do, the bee delivers the honey to the comb is a mysterious function that is *added* to the nature of this insect. In this answer we then have a depiction of the view of Rome concerning original righteousness. On the other hand, if our answer is, no, God created the bee not only with

---

1. Kuyper assumes that in the Roman Catholic theology of nature and grace, the order of grace is a mere *addition* to the order of nature, and thus when the former is lost because of the fall, according to Kuyper, "nature itself," which includes man's will, "has not been affected." Hence, we find here the reason Kuyper suggests that Roman Catholicism, even if not Pelagian in its view of the relationship between the will and saving grace, may be semi-Pelagian. For a brief discussion of Pelagianism and semi-Pelagianism, see *CG*, 1.10.2n1.

the *ability* to do it but also with the impulse and the instinct to actually *do* it, so that both the ability to do it and the doing itself belong to the nature of the bee, then we have the Reformed system.

Of course, the comparison does not in the least constitute proof here, but serves solely to clarify the two confessional positions. Otherwise the immediate answer from the Roman Catholic side would be, and correctly so, "We grant this in terms of the bee, but the bee lacks moral life, and it is precisely for the redemption of the moral life in man's nature that we have established our dogma in this manner concerning 'original righteousness.'" Only with that purpose in mind Bellarmine argues that within a human being there is by nature "a conflict between his flesh and his spirit, between his reason and his desire; that from this conflict certain sickness and weakness have ensued, resulting from a certain condition of the material; and that God therefore has added 'original righteousness' to [human] nature as a *golden bridle* to temper that conflict; or as a *robe* to cover his nakedness; or as a *medicine* to come to the aid of his weakness."[2] This image of the *robe* is in turn linked to the expression of being *in puris naturalibus*, that is, in his bare nature, apart from the added covering of original righteousness. And from this whole conception also follows the well-known statement that what man possessed by nature also remained after the fall, but that what he had received over and above his nature was lost. We must keep clearly in mind that in this context the word "supernatural" does not mean, as it usually does, something that belongs to a different world order. When it is said that original righteousness was a supernatural gift, this indicates merely that it was something that *was added to nature*.

§ 3        Our Reformed churches have resisted this view and taught that "from the fall and disobedience of our first parents, Adam and Eve, in paradise (Gen 3; Rom 5:12, 18–19), whereby *our nature became so corrupt* that we are all conceived and born in sin (Psa 51:5)."[3] Our confession is, therefore, that through the fall we did not lose anything that had been *added* to our nature, but something that *belonged* to our nature itself. Let there be no

---

2. Robert Bellarmine, SJ (1542–1621), was perhaps the foremost apologist, controversialist, and polemicist of the Roman Catholic (or Counter-) Reformation era. He was canonized in 1930 and named a "Doctor of the Church" (*doctor ecclesiae*) in 1931. Here Kuyper is referring to Bellarmine, *Opera omnia*, vol. 4, *De gratia primi hominis* (Naples: Josephum Guiliano, 1858), pt. 1, bk. 1, ch. 5, p. 7.

3. Heidelberg Catechism, Lord's Day 3, A 7 (emphasis Kuyper's).

misunderstanding here. Our Reformed churches have never gone along with those who taught that through the fall humanity's *essence* was affected, so that a sinner would no longer be a human being. This is what Flacius Illyricus, a Lutheran theologian, asserted in his conflict with Strigel, and has also been taught by Spangenberg.[4] But the Reformed have never wanted to have anything to do with this view. They even protested repeatedly against the incautious expression of Luther as though the sinner would be little else than a "stone and block."[5] *Essence* and *nature*, so they maintained, must be distinguished.[6] The essence is the *abiding*, while nature is the *changeable*, such that sin did change the functioning of

---

4. Matthias Flacius Illyricus (1520–75) was a Lutheran reformer who held an extreme position regarding the effects of the fall on human nature: total depravity damaged not merely the actual functioning of human nature but also its essence, rendering man's nature a completely corrupt vessel. Victorinus Strigel (1524–69) was a Lutheran theologian who was a follower of Philipp Melanchthon (1497–1560): "In making his statement concerning the substantiality of original sin, the purpose of Flacius was to wipe out the last vestige of spiritual powers ascribed to natural man by Strigel, and to emphasize the doctrine of total corruption, which Strigel denied." See Friedrich Bente, *Historical Introductions to the Symbolical Books of the Evangelical Lutheran Church* (St. Louis: Concordia, 1921), 145. Cyriacus Spangenberg (1528–1604) was a Lutheran theologian who sided with Flacius over the question of whether the fall into sin affected humanity essentially or only accidentally.

5. The Formula of Concord (1577), a Lutheran confessional statement, reads, "But before man is illuminated, converted, reborn, renewed, and drawn by the Holy Spirit, he can do nothing in spiritual things of himself and by his own powers. In his own conversion or regeneration he can as little begin, effect, or cooperate in anything as a stone, a block, or a lump of clay could." See *The Book of Concord: the Confessions of the Evangelical Lutheran Church*, ed. Theodore G. Tappert (Philadelphia: Muhlenberg, 1959), 525–26. Similar phrases with somewhat different emphasis are found in Reformed confessions, including the Canons of Dort (1618–19), Third and Fourth Heads of Doctrine, Article 16, where it is stated that the "grace of regeneration does not treat men as senseless stocks and blocks, nor take away their will and its properties, or do violence thereto," and in the Second Helvetic Confession (1566) in ch. 9, no. 2: "Secondly, we are to consider what man was after his fall. His understanding indeed was not taken from him, neither was he deprived of his will and altogether changed into a stone or stock."

6. Kuyper applies the distinction between essence and nature to clarify the distinction between that which makes man what he is by virtue of the order of creation and that which he now is as a consequence of the fall. See Francis Aveling, "Essence and Existence," in *CE* 5:544: "Essence and nature express the same reality envisaged in the two points of view as being or acting. As the essence is that whereby any given thing is that which it is, the ground of its characteristics and the principle of its being, so its nature is that whereby it acts as it does, the essence considered as the foundation and principle of its operation. Hence again St. Thomas: 'Nature is seen

the *nature* of man, but the essence of man has remained what it was, and will remain so, even if it descends forever into the place of damnation. In Satan as well, the essence of the angel remains unchangeably the same; only his nature has, with regard to its function, changed completely into its opposite. The same is equally true of mankind. All that belongs to the essence of man, and what makes him human as such, is present as equally in the sinner as it was in Adam before the fall. What has changed is not his essence but the functioning of his nature. *Undamaged* in his essence, he has become *depraved* in his nature.

This distinction returns when we discuss the image of God. If we understand having been created in the image of God as involving two things—(1) that the essence of man is created according to the image of God, and (2) that man stood in the likeness of God in the perfection of his nature—then we must say that the sinner, that fallen man, bears the *image of God* in his essence even as Adam did before the fall. Thus it also appears in Genesis 9:6, where it speaks of sinful people and yet states in so many words that the human being that is killed was made in God's image. But if we look at the second aspect, namely, the likeness of God in the perfection of *our nature*, then we must say that through sin man lost [that aspect of] the image of God, that only through common grace small remnants of it have been rescued, and that it can be restored in the sinner in and through Christ, already here on earth in principle and only above in its fullness.

§ 4    When God had created all things, he looked down upon his created world and "behold, it was *very good*" [Gen 1:31]. That verdict of God related to the natural condition of things, to the elements and the various kingdoms of nature and the ordinances under which they existed. Without anything supernatural intervening, this creation was *very good* in the eyes of the Lord, which of course means without defect and capable of answering to the purpose for which God had called it all into being. How then can we assume that only man was an exception, that only man was created deficient, that something was lacking in man, and that only in man a safety valve, if we may put it this way, had to be installed mechanically, as it were? If the response is that man was distinguished from all other creatures by the fact that in him a rational nature had been created, that

---

to signify the essence of a thing according as it has relation to its proper operation' (*De ente et essentia*, cap. i)."

precisely herein the danger lurked, and that precisely for this reason a means of prevention had to be installed within him, such a response does not bring us any further. This might have some validity if this "addition to original righteousness" would have prevented the fall. But this was not the case.

Despite the fact that man had been handed this "golden bridle," the evil animal was nevertheless beaten to death and man has come to grief. We grant that being *able* to fall is inseparable from the original nature of the moral life, and to that extent it is not a proof of the imperfection of God's creation. This would be the case if in God's counsel there would have been no provision to nevertheless save man if he became a sinner. Because the fall, by virtue of the nature of the moral life, had to be considered possible, a perfectly sufficient justification for the original creation lies therefore in the power of grace, which irresistibly restores the sinner and leads to imperishability. But that theodicy is lost, even when the possibility of the fall remains, if with Rome we conceive of the creation of human nature as being so defective *that something had to be added*. Human work is like this, but not the work of God. It is this way with our work because what we build, construct, or accomplish is dependent on all kinds of things beyond our control. We cannot increase steam pressure beyond a certain point or the danger exists that the boiler will explode, and *we* are therefore obliged to install a safety valve. If, on the contrary, the steam and the pressure of the boiler were under our control to such an extent that such an explosion would be impossible, then the addition of a safety valve would be absurd.

God, on the other hand, is Creator. When he creates, he is not dependent on anything. He speaks and it is. And it is as he has willed it. And if we say that in creating human nature, God ordained that nature to be so insufficient, so imperfect, so inadequate that at an incalculable moment after creation, something had to be added, affixed to it, coupled to it, dripped in, or whatever you want to call it, but nevertheless always in such a way that this human nature as created constituted a danger, and that in order to avert this danger a safety valve had to be installed—does not such a view detract from God's honor? What else is this than a mechanistic concept precisely at that point where only the organic is appropriate? And what then must we think of the perfection of a Creator who first creates imperfectly and later adds a safety device to that imperfect creation, when immediately thereafter the safety valve nonetheless fails and the fall shows that God's precaution was in vain? We admit, of course, without hesitation that the nature of the moral life makes a breach possible, and that such a breach requires mechanical restoration afterward. But even apart from this, how can it ever be explained away that in creation itself, before the fall and without preventing or averting that fall, a mechanical aid intervenes that is added to what has been created and yet fails to achieve its goal?

§ 5     The only position that allows for any support of this view is the position of those who are of the opinion that our human nature could not have been created other than at the very beginning of its development. If we posit that at its creation our nature could not have had a trace of moral strength because moral strength develops only gradually through practice, then yes, we could indeed say that original man was indeed morally so indescribably weak that he needed external support, just as we put a stake next to newly sprouted plant to support the stem. Viewed in this way, looking at it superficially, we might think that God the Lord created man with such an insignificant beginning of moral life that this moral life needed the support of a reed or a stick in order to be able to grow; this then would be the mechanical *addition*.

But this is incorrect for two reasons. In the first place, the entire notion that what God created could develop only gradually from a small kernel is contrary to the entire doctrine of creation. Adam's body was a complete, mature body. Every plant and animal was created in its mature state. And in full agreement with this is the claim that man's spiritual nature as well did not stand at the beginning of its development but was created in its normal strength. Adam was not mentally deficient when he began, but was supplied with normal human wisdom. And in the same way Adam was not a total novice in the moral realm, but was created with normal moral strength, and therefore stood in *original righteousness*, and because he was free from any abnormal development, was *holy*. This in no way means that his rich, normal moral life could not unfold even more richly, but rather that it was normal from the first and contained everything it needed for that richer unfolding. More about this later.

Our second objection is this: If Adam's moral life had needed an external support, then that support would have had to consist of something of a *different kind*. Then an angel would have had to be added to him to protect him against Satan, or something similar. But original righteousness is not external support, nor is it something of a different kind, but is precisely that to which he had to come via normal development. The nature of original righteousness itself therefore prohibits us from viewing it as something that is added to our nature. Righteousness is required of our nature—it is that for which our nature contains the data, it is the target placed before our nature, and it is the goal God's children still pursue even now. How then would we want to add something that must mature from within man's nature as something external? Would it make sense to say: Here is a small and tender child, but God has added the mature person to it, as something additional to that childlike nature?

# CHAPTER NINETEEN

# THE CROWN OF CREATION

*And to put on the new self, created after the likeness of God in true righteousness and holiness.*

EPHESIANS 4:24

§ 1   The important question whether the original righteousness in Adam was natural or supernatural—that is, belonged to his nature or was added to his nature—is ultimately linked to our confession concerning the essence of sin. Bellarmine, the skillful Roman Catholic polemicist, who has argued the case for the Roman Catholic side of this doctrine most thoroughly, returns time and again to the point that the temptation to sin lies in the makeup of *our nature*. Thus he says among other things, "The desire of the flesh is at present a punishment for sin, but for man in his natural state this condition would undoubtedly have been *natural*, not as a given *positive aspect* of his nature, but as a *deficiency*, yes, even as a certain *sickness* of his nature, *that flowed from the constitution of matter*."[1] This is not to say that God brought Adam to life imperfectly. To the contrary, Adam received original righteousness additionally, precisely in order that this imperfection would be prevented. And taken in that sense, Bellarmine himself

---

1. Bellarmine, *De gratia primi hominis*, ch. 7.

acknowledges that that original righteousness can be called *natural*.[2] But if we remove this additional gift from the picture and view man as he would have been if God had placed him in paradise with only that which his nature gave him, then, according to the constitution of all that is material, the flesh in him would have desired against the spirit, with a certain tendency toward following the inclination of the flesh. This implies that God was not free vis-à-vis matter; that the material has by nature a measure of power over God; and that once he decided to compose man from matter and spirit, or, if you will, from body and soul, God could do it only in a manner that incorporated the seed of sin in his nature.

If God the Lord would have been able to create human nature in such a way that it needed *no* further provision, then his perfection as Creator would have demanded this. A creature that is fully complete and perfect in itself, so that nothing needs to be added, stands of course on a higher level than a creature that is still in need of a bandage. In Bellarmine's view, God in fact created man's nature such that his nature had a defect, a defect that had to be rendered harmless by means of an added remedy. But this could not have been arbitrariness on God's part. Was he able to create man with a nature *without* defect, to which therefore nothing had to be added? That he did not do this can only be explained from the fact that God could not do it. And that God could not do it was not due to a lack of will or of intent, but to *matter*. There was something within the material from which man's body was formed that prevented this. Bellarmine states this himself: "It would not have been *because of* but *against* the intent of the Creator."[3] But now God triumphs anyway. If the constitution of matter and therefore of the flesh prevents the creation of a human nature *without defect* or *without sickness* (*defectus et morbus naturae*), then God overcomes that defect by adding to this defective nature something supernatural, namely, original righteousness, and by this means the evil *is* arrested. But the fact still remains that in matter, and thus also in the flesh, the spirit is being opposed by a power that makes it impossible for God the Creator to create a nature in man without defect or disease. The nature of man per se would stumble; now it gets a crutch and does not stumble. But that such a crutch was necessary, and that man's natural legs did not enable him to walk, was

---

2. Bellarmine, *De gratia primi hominis*, ch. 5.
3. Bellarmine, *De gratia primi hominis*, ch. 7.

caused by God's powerlessness to create a being from matter and spirit in which matter did not perform its contrary activity.

§ 2

Thus we see how profoundly this contrast makes deep inroads in the confession of the truth. A force within matter comes to stand over against God, and because of the inevitable contest against the spirit that lies raging within the flesh, the fountain of sin opens up within matter. As concerns his nature, man is therefore an imperfect being, as yet without sin, it is true, but nevertheless with the temptation and a certain tendency toward sin. And it is only through an additional expedient, through something that is added, by means of a crutch placed under his arms, that he is protected against this danger. It does not matter whether we say that man thus possessed this original righteousness as something of his own, as something that belonged to him. The fact remains that it stands outside his nature, and the very images of a bridle and a robe that Bellarmine uses give sufficient indication that he himself views original righteousness not as an organic part of man's being, but as something added mechanically. Thus it is the nature of sin and the omnipotence of God that are at issue here. Not sin itself, but the fountain of sin is sought here, not in a despoliation of the good but in a quality inherent within *matter*, and it is over against this inherent quality of *matter* that God is powerless. Not powerless in the sense that he would not be able to overcome evil, but powerless as regards creating a human nature without defect. Doubt is here impossible, since Bellarmine states it clearly: "Taken strictly in his nature, the desire of the flesh would have been for Adam a certain defect, a certain sickness that resulted from the constitution of matter."[4] To avoid misunderstanding, let us add that Rome does not consider the first stirrings of desire to be sin, but sees concupiscence becoming sin only when man in any way consents to it.

However much the Reformed churches rejoice in the agreement with the Roman Catholic Church in the confession of the mysteries of the Trinity and of the incarnation of the Word, as soon as we come to the doctrine of man and the doctrine of sin, they stand diametrically over against

---

4. *Note by the author:* Or, to add his words in Latin, "Concupiscentia carnis homini in puris naturalibus fuisset conditio, naturalis, non quidem ut bonum aliquid naturae, sed ut defectus, et quasi morbus naturae, ex conditione materiae consequens." Bellarmine, *De gratia primi hominis*, ch. 7, 29b–30a. [Ed. note: The text of this note originally appeared in the text proper and referred to the 1840 Rome edition of Bellarmine's works.]

Rome, and it is in the divergent confession concerning the state of righteousness that this difference emerges and finds its origin. We deny that the contrast between flesh and spirit, between soul and body, exists by nature. We deny that in this contrast a power stood opposed to God that prevented him from creating human nature other than with an inherent defect that had to be remedied mechanically. We deny that desire, as a first stirring, would be a defect but not a sin. Over against this we maintain that the nature of sin is spiritual and not fleshly or material, that sin finds its origin neither in God nor in man, but in Satan, who lacks a body and any material form, and who existed and still exists only as a spiritual being. We consequently confess that neither in substance nor in matter, neither in the body nor in the flesh, did a power ever stand over against God that constrained God to create human nature with a defect and to remedy this defect by means of something additional. We confess rather that God created our human nature in noble perfection, without any defect, and that our present misery does not consist in the fact that we have lost something that was added to our nature, but herein: that our nature itself is corrupt, robbed of its original excellence, and depraved. We maintain that this excellent nature was not created independent but dependent and therefore could not persist in its excellence for a moment without its bond with the grace of God (something Rome denies). In all spiritual creatures, be they humans or angels, in whatever state, now and forever, this belongs to their nature and is inseparable from that nature. And this we sum up in the acknowledgment that man was created in the image of God, and that by virtue of this creation he possessed a nature whose original perfection included standing before God in righteousness.

When we come, after this introductory remark, to the question of how then we must conceive of the original human being in paradise, we are not sidetracked by the opinion, current in various circles today, that man only gradually climbed up from animal wildness to a degree of human consciousness. Those who posit this do not believe in any paradise, do not believe in the creation of the first human, and even less delve into the delicate, tender issues connected with the doctrine of original righteousness. They simply have no eye for this. With such people one can enter into dispute, but that has to occur in an entirely different sphere: the sphere that deals rather with the question of languages, classification of races, historical tradition, zoology, and so much more. This set of issues does not belong in the present context. In general then, we suffice with

§ 3

the observation that from our perspective we do not deny a certain preformation of the human in the animal world. But we must keep in mind that because man was created in the image of God, God did not come forth from man. And so too, even if it became more and more apparent that God created the animals according to the image of man, from this it would not follow at all that man would have come forth from the animals. The only conclusion would be that since he knew how he would create man, God formed the animals with a measure of correspondence with what later would be seen in man. But what occupies us here is not the creation of the animals in the image of man, but the creation of man in the image of God.

In all this, let it be emphasized that God also created man *for his own sake*. This obligates us to take man from the outset, not as a being who stands independently vis-à-vis God, but as an instrument that he created for his glory. Man does not only stand *under* God, but in his creation he exists only *for* God and *for God's sake*. The objective of man's being and the purpose of man's existence do not lie within man himself, but man is, if we may express ourselves so, created for God's use. God uses man and has created him for that use, and in man's creation God equipped him for that use. This must not be toned down in any way, because any feebler statement elevates man at the expense of his Creator.

It is therefore necessary to cut off at the outset any notion of human greatness, to reduce to nothing every conceit of the pride that is inborn in us sinners, and not to imagine man, even for a moment, even in his original excellence in paradise, as anything other than a creature that exists *because of* the Creator and *only* because of the Creator. Not even a dual purpose must be admitted here. We must not say, for the glory of God *and* for his [man's] own blessedness. Even in that, there sounds an echo of Pelagianism, which is always intent on assigning to man, in any way possible, a certain independent position, if not *over against* God, then at least *alongside* God. God and man then become, if we may put it this way, the two great forces in the creation, and power must be negotiated between these two. All semi-Pelagian[5] schools of thought—Socinians, Arminians, and Methodists, as well as Roman Catholics and Greek Orthodox—lean more or less toward that thoroughly unhealthy conception, as if to some extent

---

5. For a brief discussion of the standard Reformed charge that Roman Catholicism embraces semi-Pelagianism, see CG 1.18.2n1; for Pelagianism and semi-Pelagianism, see also 1.10.2n1.

and in some way man possesses his purpose within himself. The reason this is so impious is that to the extent that man finds his purpose within himself, God himself becomes the means toward that purpose. Man then *begins to use God*, in general to improve his lot in life, and more specifically to effectuate his salvation; what man no longer wants is *to be used by God*.

When we therefore speak of our having been created in God's image, we must immediately emphasize that what is intended here is not *our* excellence, but our *suitability* for God. A teacher who educates a talented student will be delighted if he succeeds in shaping, even in a limited way, the mind of that young person in his own image, and when that talented young man later achieves a much higher and more influential position than he himself, and far surpasses him in learning, the notion that this young man was once his pupil and that he was able to help educate him will still invigorate him. But then the young man of exceptional genius becomes the central figure, and as teacher he has served him. But this is not the case here. God creates man in his image, not in order that in paradise this excellent being would be honored and worshipped and then would praise God because God had so outstandingly created that excellent human being. Rather, God creates man so excellently because as God he needed such an excellent instrument for himself. Not as if he needed anything, but because it had pleased him to glorify himself in this way. This is precisely why the Reformed steadfastly maintained over against Rome that also in the state of righteousness Adam lived by grace. Not, of course, by merciful grace, but by sustaining grace, so that it would be utterly out of the question that Adam could take up an independent position vis-à-vis God. He was a creature and had to remain a creature.

Now it is always extremely difficult to account for what God desired for himself in the creation of his creatures. Holy Scripture nevertheless gives us some indications when it comes to the creation of man. In Proverbs 8:31, Wisdom is "delighting in the children of man." Is it not being implied here that God wanted to see something of himself in his creature? All other creatures did bear a divine imprint, and all paths of creation showed the imprint of God's footstep, but what he could not see in the rest of his creatures was the image of himself. Therefore, the relationship referred to here does not apply to man as such, but to the divine in man. It is God who glorifies himself in the divine that he created within man. The world outside of man remains foreign to God. It lacks consonance with his spiritual nature. It displays shades of color and glimmerings, forms and lines,

§ 4

§ 5

powers and skills, effects and beauties, but no heart speaks in it, no inspired, conscious life directed toward higher things. And now God wants to draw this alien world toward himself by epitomizing it in man and reflecting his image in that human being; he desires to bring the world that went forth from him by the word of creation back to his divine heart. Only when the song of the worship from man's lips ascends to him is the word of creation interpreted before God in a spirit-animated word, and only then does it return to him. Apart from man the world stands at a distance from God; in man it comes near to him. Now for the first time something of God's own life beats and sparkles in this world. Mute before God as long as man was still absent, the whole creation now speaks to God through man. Even as for us a piece of nature remains dull and somber and dead as long as it is wrapped in darkness, but comes to life and speaks to us as soon as the sun rises upon it, so too without man, creation was cold and uninspired before God, and only now that the light of the human spirit shines upon this world and from that world shines back to God, only now is the creation alive for God and breathes thanksgiving toward him. Our Confession expresses this by saying that all creatures may serve mankind "to the end that man may serve his God."[6] And Adam was in fact placed in this creation as high priest in order that he would encapsulate that whole creation within himself and then, bearing that creation as an offering, he would bow down before his God in worship and thanksgiving.

§ 6    We can understand Adam's unique position in paradise only in this way. That creation and that paradise do not exist for his sake. Everything exists for God's sake, and also Adam himself exists only for God's sake. Without Adam creation was not finished. He is its crown, not that he might take creation for himself but in order that he might bring it to God. No altar stands in paradise, but all of paradise is an altar on which Adam as priest of God offers God the glory of his handiwork. Adam must not exist for himself, nor for Eve, nor for any animal. He must busy himself for God alone, continually serve God, untiringly devote to God the glory of his creation. And that he might be able to do this and might be suitable for and capable of doing this—for this purpose and this purpose alone was he created in the image of God. It is not as if God is in need of anything; from eternity, even without the creation, he was self-sufficient, bearing the creation in his eternal counsel. But having called the world into being

---

6. Belgic Confession, Art. 12.

in accordance with and through his sovereign will, he now also had to create man, because only through man could he receive the worship and the glorification of his name, and thus the fruit of his entire work of creation. Man's nature thus had to be prepared for this purpose, and he had to be qualified and equipped with the capability for it. And this would be unthinkable and impossible if man himself were not God's offspring [Acts 17:29], unless he were created in relation to the divine nature and could act as the bearer of his image. It goes without saying that in that elevated position lurked the danger of a deep fall, but that high position itself was not given to Adam for the sake of man himself, but only and solely because of the will of our God.[7]

---

7. *Note by the author*: In connection with 1 Corinthians 6:13, one of our *Kerkboden* ["Church Messenger," a Reformed periodical] asked whether it is possible to take nourishment "when the belly has been undone." Everything hinges here on the question whether one believes in Jesus' return on the clouds, in the coming of the kingdom of glory, and the resurrection of the flesh. If yes, then the blessed will forever be in glorified *bodies*, thus also somewhere on a glorified earth. Whether or not a metabolism is part of those glorified bodies—and on this depends of course in turn the question of nourishment—we cannot decide as such. This depends on all kinds of contingencies we do not know. This is why we pointed out (1) that the images Scripture gives us of that glory speak again and again of a meal, a wedding supper, of "rich food full of marrow" [Isa 25:6]; (2) that in the new Jerusalem are lush plantings of the "trees of life" on both sides of the river that ceaselessly bear fruit that is intended to be eaten (Rev 2:7[; 22:2]); and (3) that Jesus spoke of the cup that he would *drink* again with his disciples in the kingdom of his Father. In view of this it seems probable to us that a metabolism and thus also the taking of nourishment will continue, albeit in such a way that exclusively substances will be partaken of that completely, and without any excretion will be absorbed into the body. With this the objection based on 1 Corinthians 6:13 falls away. Also, what is said there about food does in fact not say anything. Most definitely all foods of the present will perish to make way for food of a higher order. Think of the "bread of the angels" in Psalm 78:25 [SV: "bread of the Mighty"].

# CHAPTER TWENTY

# PERFECT INTEGRITY

*See, this alone I found, that God made man upright, but they have sought out many schemes.*

ECCLESIASTES 7:29

§ 1  If we keep clearly in view the central Reformed position that our creation in the image of God took place, not because of man but *because of God*, then this automatically sheds light on original righteousness. One who must deliver a mirror must deliver it in unclouded purity, so that the owner can see his image reflected perfectly, to the maximum extent that glass covered with mercury can do this.[1] Later, for whatever reason, the glass may crack or the mercury may get tarnished, but this must not be the case when it is delivered. At delivery the mirror must be in good condition and must have no defects. This first of all. But the delivered mirror must also be flawless in a second respect. A corrected flaw remains a flaw. And whoever received a mirror that reflected perfectly but part of which had once been flawed, and over that unclear portion a thin, finely polished piece of glass had been very skillfully laid, would, as soon as he noticed it, refuse to accept the mirror. Whether the mirror maker had made the mirror on

---

1. See Per Hadsund, "The Tin-Mercury Mirror: Its Manufacturing Technique and Deterioration Process," *Studies in Conservation* 38, no. 1 (Feb 1993): 3: "Mirrors made of glass backed with a reflective coating of tin amalgam first came into general use in the sixteenth century. Production ceased around 1900. The mirrors were made by sliding glass over tin foil flooded with mercury."

order for someone else, or for himself, does not change anything. An honorable mirror maker would, even if the mirror were for his own use, have the double requirement (1) that he could see his image as clearly as the kind and nature of the glass allowed, and (2) that as a result of pure workmanship, the mirror would reflect without any modification, in order (to use a manufacturing term) to pass inspection.

Exactly the same applies here. In creating man, God makes for himself a mirror in which he wants to see his own image as clearly as the nature of the creaturely makes this possible. In this case it does not depend, as it does for the mirror maker, on glass and mercury that already exist, but he forms that glass and mercury himself as he needs it for this his creation. And this is why this creation would have been unworthy of God and a failure if, as soon as Adam was completed, God had not seen in Adam, as in a mirror, the clear reflection of his own image. The churches express that purity and perfection of this reflection by speaking of Adam's creation in original righteousness. The fact that this reflection could *later* become, and has become, tainted, touches on an entirely different issue and has nothing to do with the perfection of the work of the Creator as such. What we must hold fast is only that at the moment man came from God's creating hand, man possessed that for which God had created him, namely, that God clearly saw his image in him. In creaturely fashion, of course, yet with all the clarity that can exist in something that has been created.

Now the other point: The product of God's creation in man must function in a pure fashion, not thanks to repairs and modification—such that man originally did not really present this reflection, but God remedied the defect by means of an expedient, as Bellarmine teaches. It must function perfectly without anything affixed or added to it. If any creature had attempted to achieve such a result, and had it remained defective, then we could imagine that God might supplement and improve it; but it is contrary to the perfection of the Creator and the flawlessness of the work of creation to imagine God as delivering a creature that was in fact flawed, to whom he supplies a covering or remedy. And this is why our churches not only confessed Adam's original righteousness, but over against Rome, additionally maintained that this original righteousness was not added to his nature but was organically bound up with his nature. To use another image, Adam in his original state was not a rosebush without rosebuds to which a bouquet of roses was fastened, but a bush with buds that belonged to the bush. Thus the conclusion remains with regard to the newly created man that God saw that "it was very good" (Gen 1:31) and also that "God made man upright" (Eccl 7:29).

§ 2      God thus wanted to see an image of himself in his creation, and for this reason he created man in original righteousness, and that original righteousness he created *in* and not *in addition to* his nature. Here a question arises that, even though we cannot answer it with certainty, must nevertheless be considered. Let us go back to the rosebush with the buds. For us, no buds are thinkable on that bush unless we imagine that first the bush grew up and the buds sprouted from the branches of that bush. It is fully understandable that in terms of creation, we prefer to view it in such a way that God created the seed for the rosebush in the soil, that from this seed grew the bush, and that on this bush the buds sprouted. Thus far such a view does *not* contradict the story of creation, for Genesis 1:11 says, "And God said, '*Let the earth sprout vegetation*, plants yielding seed, and fruit trees bearing fruit in which is their seed, each according to its kind, on the earth.' And it was so."

But the matter becomes quite different if we were to explain this in such a way that the first palm tree needed many years to grow tall, and therefore the plant kingdom would not have stood in its full strength until fifty or more years later. Then we come directly into conflict with verse 13: "And there was evening and there was morning, the third day." Without entering into the question whether we must think here of 24-hour days, from the description of evening and morning it follows that only one light change is meant, not a long series of *light changes*. Apparently for that reason we must not understand it in such a way that God created only the seeds, so that they might sprout naturally and would need approximately as much time for this process as they do now; rather, the intent is apparently that through his miraculous creative power God brought forth from the earth at once the mature plant, the fruit tree already bearing its ripe fruit. In the meantime it remains clear that they were not planted in the earth from the outside but sprouted from the earth, in an accelerated process, so that on this one occasion, through God's omnipotence, there came into being in one moment of time what today, thanks to his sustaining omnipotence, takes sometimes fifty years or more to achieve the same result.

If we move from plants to animals, we find something similar, but already with a change. In verse 24 we read on the one hand, "God said, '*Let the earth bring forth* living creatures according to their kinds—livestock and creeping things and beasts of the earth according to their kinds," but in verse 25 it is stated very differently: "*And God made* the beasts of the earth," and so on. The substance from which the animals are made is thus drawn from earth, but here there is nothing like sprouting or accelerated growth. *God made the animals.* Every intermediate link falls away. The question of the *chicken* or the *egg* has hereby been decided, in the sense that first the chicken was created full-grown, and this created bird laid the first egg, from which then came the next generation.

With man, the difference is even greater. Here, unlike with the animals, it is *not* said, "Let the earth bring forth man ... and God made man." *Nothing* is said here to the earth. The earth does not do anything here; it remains altogether passive. Not to the earth, but to the persons of the Triune Being the voice goes out: "Let us make man," and from the dust of the earth Adam's body is fashioned, and in that body a soul is created until the spirit of life causes him to breathe.

Nevertheless, we can also raise the question at this point whether we must think of an accelerated growth process or of a direct creation in full dimensions. One senses what is meant by this. Even now a human being is constructed from a small, inner kernel. That kernel contains the data for his whole body. God had stipulated that during nine months this kernel, that first, unformed lump, would miraculously develop like a skillful embroidery. Then the child is born, and that child needs about three times seven, or twenty-one years, to grow into adulthood. What happened at Adam's creation? Was there also first an embryo, and did God arrange things, through an accelerated process, so that in a single moment the complete man would mature? Or did he place man at once in paradise in his full stature? It is not proper for us to conclude more here than Scripture reveals to us, and we cannot make a definite judgment. But let us note that the scriptural narrative *does not* support the former, but *does* support the second idea, for it says (1) that God formed man from the dust of the ground; (2) that God then breathed into his nostrils the breath of life; and (3) that man only then "became a living creature" [Gen 2:7]. With us it is different. When the body is ready, the breath of life is also breathed into our nostrils, but the child lives and moves already in the mother's body even before it can breathe.

Now the question certainly remains whether we have the right to draw conclusions from such minor indications, but this does not detract from the fact that we definitely stay closer to Scripture if we do not conceive of Adam's creation as an accelerated growth process but as an immediate, direct formation in the dimensions of the adult human being. This does not mean, of course, that Adam's body could not undergo any changes thereafter. After all, we ourselves distinguish three periods: (1) our life in the mother; (2) our life from birth to adulthood; and (3) our life after we have reached adulthood, as an adult and elderly person. The creation narrative, understood in the sense we have, says only that Adam stood all at once at the end of the second period, that is, as an adult man, but in such a way that the *third* period, with the changes belonging to it, still had to follow.

§ 3    We needed to explain this in detail with respect to the human body, because only now can we get to the question that occupies us at present, namely, Adam's *spiritual existence* at the moment of his creation. This question is of course much more difficult, because we know so much less about our soul than about our body. We speak of "soul science," but what does the most learned man know about the actual essence of the soul beyond what Scripture reveals about it?[2] We can observe manifestations of the life of the soul, and also determine the relationship between soul and body from the perspective of the body, but we know so extremely little of what is going on inside us. We have no conception, no notion of it, we have no language and no words for it, and everything we say about the soul is in fact couched in metaphorical language. We must therefore remain clearly aware of our ignorance in this area.

When we come to the soul we touch on a mystery, and we may be grateful if we can allow a single ray of light from the Word of God to fall on this puzzling mystery. This does not prevent the same questions from coming up that arose earlier in connection with the plants, the animals, and the human body. This much is certain: at present, our inner invisible being goes through a certain developmental process. We remember very well how there was a time when we understood less, grasped less, knew less, were less conscious of things, and felt less consciously. Back behind the

---

2. By "soul science" (Dutch, *zielkunde*), Kuyper here means psychology, although in reference to a comprehensive Christian view of the "soul" rather than something potentially more limited, such as "mind." See, for instance, the definition of psychology as the "science of mind" in D. Hack Tuke, *A Dictionary of Psychological Medicine* (Philadelphia: P. Blakiston, 1892), 2:1014. The term "psychology," in fact, is a combination of two Greek terms: *psychē*, meaning "soul," and *logos*, meaning "word" or "reason," but in modern usage meaning "study" or "science."

adult lies a period during which he was mentally trained and gradually matured, a process of maturation that still continues in adulthood. Thus when we retrace our life, we ultimately come to a period about which we have *no* memory, and we actually do not know who and how we were back then. In order to fill this gap we then observe other little children and assume that we must have been like what we now see in these children. In those children we see a slow development from the small bundle of humanity, without a will of its own, lying in the nurse's lap, to the little rascal who for the first time lets go of the chair and totters away. But beneath and within all of this, we always observe that such development involves *two* components. All kinds of things are added to the child *from the outside*; but the child also has all kinds of things *on the inside* through which it absorbs the things that are brought to it from outside.

There is therefore much similarity between *nurture* and *nutrition*. In the case of nutrition, there are two components: (1) the food that comes from the outside, and (2) the child's internal organs for eating and digestion. And so too with raising a child, all kinds of knowledge are offered to and instilled in the child; this is possible with a child, however, but not with a young dog, because the child has mental organs by means of which it absorbs the knowledge. This we call aptitude, ability, disposition, and so much more; and that ability, aptitude, and disposition have not entered the child for the first time in the cradle or after the cradle, but the child has entered the world with these things. All of this was present and dormant in the little infant, and manifested itself as the child grew up. Here, therefore, we see once again a three-stage process: (1) the period when all of this is inside but still dormant; (2) the period when it emerges and develops to adult dimensions; and (3) the subsequent period when the adult person increasingly matures and bears fruit.

§ 4

When we apply this to Adam, the question therefore arises: Was this inner aspect of Adam created in the condition of the first, second, or third period? When Adam opened his eyes to the light of life, was he a mature child? Physically mature, but mentally undeveloped and ignorant like a newborn infant? Or was he created in the second period of development, so that at most he could grasp something in, say, the manner of a seven-year-old child? Or, was Adam created at once with the mental capacity of an adult? By analogy with what we found earlier with plants, animals, and the human body, we answer: Certainly in the adult state of mental development. We are certain of this, in the first place, because an adult person who is mentally undeveloped like a child impresses us as something foolish and contradictory, and makes us laugh. An old man who becomes senile is an inept being. God could not have said concerning such a being that it was very good. Secondly, because such a silly figure would not have been suitable for God as the mirror in which he beheld his image. And we are certain of this, thirdly, since what is stated about Adam immediately thereafter does not even remotely remind us of a mentally undeveloped child but definitely of a mature, fully developed man.

The question now remains whether we must suppose that Adam came to this state through an accelerated process of development or through a direct act of creation. To this we answer: through a direct act of creation, and not through an accelerated process. Such a process of development happens with us through upbringing, that is, because something from outside comes to our aid. Never out of ourselves. A child left to its own devices remains, even if it grows up, still entirely foolish and naïve when it is twenty. Experiments have proven this.[3] So too here, where one of the factors needed for the process was entirely absent, an accelerated process is out of the question. Hence our definite conclusion that the adult state of mental existence in which Adam was created was the fruit of immediate, direct creation.

§ 5 And now we finally arrive at the most difficult question, that of his religious and moral state, and it is self-evident that also here our conclusion *cannot* be different. Not only his intellectual but also his moral and religious state had to be that of an adult, and in Adam this had to be the result not of development nor of an accelerated process, but of immediate and direct creation. God, who today makes the rose come from the bud and the bud from the branch and the branch from the seed, created the first rosebush with roses on it; so too that same God, who today makes first the seed appear, and from the seed the child and from the child the man, created Adam *as man*, with male *maturity* in body and soul. As for his intellectual life, this means that he was created in original *wisdom*; as for his moral life,

---

3. Kuyper is presumably referring here to the occasional discovery of so-called feral or wild children, who have survived apart from human community, sometimes into adolescence, and who, when studied and nurtured, often display long-term difficulties with socialization and language development. These realities belie the popular nineteenth-century Romantic conception of the "noble savage." See Michael Newton, *Savage Girls and Wild Boys: A History of Feral Children* (New York: St. Martin's, 2003).

that he was created in original *holiness*; and as for his *religious* life, that he was created in original *righteousness*. Does this preclude that he could still enrich his wise mind in all kinds of ways and make it fruitful? Ask yourself whether the mature scholar no longer improves himself and brings forth intellectual fruits until he dies. And in the same way it does not in the least preclude that Adam could also morally enrich himself and bear fruit; and could also in the religious realm develop and improve and bear fruit. This was the purpose of the probationary command of the covenant of works. The state of original wisdom, holiness, and righteousness was as yet not in the least the state of *absolute consummation*. This would come later, and would form the transition into eternal blessedness.

What the Christian church means by the *state of righteousness* will also have become clear at this point. With this term it expresses that the first human was created as an *adult*, in body as well as soul, and that in that soul he was intellectually, morally, and religiously an adult: *wise*, *holy*, and *righteous* before God. This denies that there was any foolishness or lie in Adam's mind that detracted from this *wisdom*. There was no darkness in him. No veil covered his intellect. He clearly and lucidly perceived the creation around him. There was nothing between him and the truth of things. This is why he was *wise*. Likewise there was neither defect nor weakness in him in the moral realm; his inclinations and expressions were in perfect conformity to the law of life that stood written in his heart. This is why he was *holy*. And finally, there was in him no mind nor will to be other than the image of God; there was no duality in his heart vis-à-vis God, but he felt himself to be wholly a creature before God as God, created for God's glory. This was his *correct position* before God, his *original righteousness*.

So in paradise he stood under God, before the face of God, existing only for God, and thus he had dominion over all of creation. Dominion is the Lord's, and therefore this trait of dominion could not be absent in his image. But dominion in Adam was nothing but a reflection, a shadow, and it served to let God see his image in man. It was not Adam who took the world for himself and gave a tenth of it to God, keeping the other nine-tenths for himself; he was the image-bearer of God who took the whole world into himself, to bring it to God. He was king because he was priest—an anointed one, a servant of the Lord. Thus in paradise there was spiritual *perfection*, though not yet the *final consummation*, in the three spheres of intellect, morality, and religious life. From that *perfection* it would have progressed, apart from sin, through maturation, development, and fruit-bearing to the *final consummation*. The shape of the image in his *being*, the traits of the image in his *capacities*, the radiance of the image in his *virtues*, [these were present] until the breach came and, though the basic shape remained, the radiance faded and the traits were distorted into impurity.

# CHAPTER TWENTY-ONE

# ORIGINAL RIGHTEOUSNESS

*And we all, with unveiled face, beholding the glory of the Lord, are being transformed into the same image from one degree of glory to another. For this comes from the Lord who is the Spirit.*

2 CORINTHIANS 3:18

Notwithstanding the confession that the first man was three things, namely, *wise, holy,* and *righteous* (wise in his *intellectual* life, holy *before the law,* and righteous *before God*), we nevertheless hardly ever speak of anything but Adam's original *righteousness.* There is no objection to this, as long as we are clear about our justification for doing so. This justification then includes that in terms of what is called "image" or what the image represents, the question of the relationship between *image* and *original* is always in the foreground. The original here is *God,* the image is *man.* The fact that man is created in the image of God makes everything here dependent on the pure or impure relationship in which man, as product of creation, stands to his God. For the purity of that relationship, Holy Scripture uses the word *righteous* or *righteous before God,* and for that relationship itself, if it is pure, the name *righteousness.* We only have to recall the whole doctrine of justification to make this immediately apparent. The sinner knows himself to be justified at the very moment that his faith breaks through. But this being justified is still something quite different

§ 1

COMMON GRACE • VOLUME 1

from his *sanctification*, which comes only afterward and is completed only in death.

According to the Reformed point of view, therefore, *righteousness can* mean nothing other than *being in the right position before God*. Only then, when man stands directly and immediately before God with the mirror of his essence, does the image of God reflect perfectly in him. Had Adam been created neutral, and had it been left up to him to take his position there where the image of God *could* reflect perfectly in him, he might conceivably have taken up a wrong position. But this was not the case. It was not imposed on Adam, nor was it left up to him, to *take* his position vis-à-vis God, but he was *placed* in his position by God.

For him, then, the question would arise whether he wanted to *remain* by a choice of will in that position where he had been placed passively; and this he did not do. But this does not detract in any way from the fact that the first man was not placed somewhere outside of God so that he might search for his God; rather, he began by finding himself in the right position vis-à-vis his God. That he began by thus standing in the right position was not the fruit of his choice or action, but the fruit of God's act of creation. God created him in that right position, and that is why, when he first became aware of himself, he stood in that state of righteousness. This is what the doctrine expresses by speaking with some emphasis of *original* righteousness. "Original" here means that this righteousness was not acquired nor later allotted to him, but was a fruit of creation itself. When Adam opened his eyes to the light he thus found himself in the right position before his God. Of course, the mirror of which we spoke in this connection is only an analogy, but it is an analogy that nevertheless clarifies the matter, and which we the more readily dared to make because in 2 Corinthians 3:18 the same comparison occurs in a similar context: "And we all, with unveiled face, beholding [as in a mirror] the glory of the Lord, are being transformed into the same image from one degree of glory to another. For this comes from the Lord who is the Spirit."[1]

§ 2 Upon reflection, the surprise is not that we speak of original *righteousness*, but that generally we do not speak separately of our original *holiness* and *wisdom*. After all, the least impurity in the moral arena would have

---

1. The Greek verb *katoptrizō* means "to look at (as in a mirror), to contemplate." The SV and the KJV make "as in a mirror" explicit; most modern versions, including the ESV, omit "as in a mirror" and translate simply "beholding."

removed the first man from his right position before God and destroyed his original righteousness. It is different with the imputed righteousness that the ungodly possess in the Mediator. The ungodly person is not holy, but he is nevertheless counted as being righteous, since he is not viewed as he is in himself, but as he is in Christ Jesus through regeneration and faith. But man in his [original] creation is not in Christ, but stands on his own account. And precisely for this reason the least defect in holiness would have been cause for his not standing before God as *righteous*. At creation, the moral life (that of holiness) and the religious life (that of righteousness) are inseparable from one another. They both stand and fall together. Original righteousness, therefore, includes original *holiness*.

It is no different with original *wisdom*. If Christ is given to us for "righteousness, sanctification and redemption," then he is given to us in the first place for *wisdom* [1 Cor 1:30]. Therein lies the starting point. Saving faith can therefore not be based on a mystical feeling, but must begin with choosing the wisdom of the cross over against the foolishness of the world. Unlike Buddhism in India, Holy Scripture knows nothing of truth driven merely by sentiment. Life with and for God is not shrouded in mists but shines in clarity and must be a conscious life. We do not *feel* or *guess*, but we *know* that we have passed from death into life. The moral life is not an unconscious life of the will, but our will follows and obeys our consciousness. This is why the fall into sin rapidly darkens the intellect, why the sinner is called a *fool*, and why the regenerated person has "the eyes of [his] heart enlightened" [Eph 1:18]. This is why Satan first attacked original wisdom. Satan did not mesmerize Eve, but he *persuaded with reasons*. In this way she departed for the first time from the law of God, and consequently from her right position before God. Righteousness, holiness, and wisdom are thus three pearls of the same strand, and it is in terms of the greatest of the three that man's state is named the state of original righteousness, since this one automatically encompasses the other two.

The objection often raised against this original righteousness actually touches more on the holiness than the righteousness. [Those who raise this objection] still grant, and can still accept, that Adam had not yet committed any wrong. But what they neither grasp nor understand is how Adam can be said to be holy. The cause here is misunderstanding. Man will be holy, so they say, only after death, in heaven. We are holy only when we are lifted above all sin. The stimulus of sin can no longer have an effect on the holy person. Only those can claim the label "holy" who have

§3

first known temptation, overcome and conquered it, and stand once again free over against it. Holy is God and holy are the good angels and holy are the beatified around the throne. But how can we speak of "holy" in the case of Adam, who had not yet known struggle and who failed in the first temptation? Our answer here is unequivocal. If taken in that sense, the first human *was not* and *could not* be holy, and Adam was thus definitely not holy in that sense. On this point no dispute can arise and we don't have to waste words on it.

But does it follow then that Adam's original state was *unholy*? Yet that is the choice facing us. Every rational being (which includes man) must be pronounced either holy or unholy. There is no *tertium quid* [third thing] between holy and unholy. You cannot be half holy or one-third holy. Whoever is not unholy is holy. Whoever is not holy is unholy. A sinful man, incorporated in Christ through regeneration and faith, is holy. Not half, but entirely. And the apostle attests this: one who is "born of God ... cannot keep on sinning because he has been born of God" [1 John 3:9]. But apart from Christ, this person in and of himself is still entirely unholy, a miserable human being, crying out "who will deliver me from this body of death?" [Rom 7:24]. Certainly, we can also speak of degrees in this context, so that even our Catechism speaks of "the holiest men, while in this life."[2] But this is an entirely different realm of concepts. One man can be more manly than another, one woman can show the feminine in her character more beautifully than the other, but this does not take away from the fact that the difference between what a man is and what a woman is, is fixed. And in the same way, we can speak among the "saints," that is, among believers, of less holy, holier, and holiest personalities, but this does not touch on the *principle* and points only to the lesser or greater virtuosity with which the principle is at work in them.

Given this contrast, the reason we have a measure of difficulty in thinking of Adam as holy is that we can never come *to* holiness other than *from* sin, whereas the holiness in Adam still existed entirely outside the contrast with sin. This distinction is best felt when it is transferred to an entirely different realm. Take, for example, the contrast between dry and damp. If someone has fallen into the water and gone under, then after you have pulled him to the shore, he is still wet through and through. And then you cannot say, of course, that he is *dry* until the last damp spot on him has

---

2.  Heidelberg Catechism, Lord's Day 44, A 114.

dried. For someone who has been in the water, being dry is the result of removing all dampness, something not achieved until this drying process has been entirely completed. On the other hand, for someone who has not fallen into the water being dry is not the result of such a process, but it is the original, natural condition, which is not disturbed until moisture is added. And so too here. Adam, and with him all of us, have been submerged into the stream of sin, and also when our Redeemer[3] pulls us out of that stream of unrighteousness again and puts us safely on the rock in Christ, sin still drips from us on all sides. This is what makes it impossible for us to imagine "being dry," that is, "holy," other than as the result of a struggle through which we gradually get rid of sin and of all that is sinful. And as long as a single drop from that stream of unrighteousness remains splattered on us, holiness has not been achieved.

Taken in this way, holiness lies only at the end of the long road and is inconceivable in this life. How then could we justify applying this to Adam before the fall, to Adam for whom as yet there could be no shaking off of sin that did not yet cling to him? To the newly created human in whose person there was nothing but that which God had created in him? In the case of Adam before the fall we must therefore take holy in a *positive* sense, not as an overcoming of and struggling free from sin, but as a state of *standing as yet completely outside of any communion with sin*. The angels who did not fall did not become gradually holy, but remained holy without ever slipping into sin. Had Adam not fallen, he would also have remained holy, as he was created holy, without ever having felt the grip of the bonds of sin. More than that: the fallen angels were also created holy, after all, and fell from holiness. And just like the fallen angels, Adam stood originally in holiness and fell away from that holiness by his yielding to Satan.

In the meantime, we are mistaken if we think that the image of God consists only of this innate wisdom, holiness, and righteousness, and if we think that therefore through the fall the image of God disappeared altogether from man. This would be the case if man's essence stood outside this image. Man then would have existed in his essence separate from that image, and only then the traits of the image of God would have been engraved in this already existing human being. The engraved traits of wisdom, holiness and righteousness then would have constituted in and of

§ 4

---

3.  Lit., "Goel," from Hebrew *go'el for* "redeemer" or "kinsman redeemer" (see, e.g., Ruth 3–4).

themselves the image of God, and when man became a sinner, he would by losing these three traits also have lost the image of God itself. In this view, there would first have been a man *without the image*, then man with this image *engraved in him*, and then man in whom this image had been *worn away* and *disappeared*. This entire notion must be rejected, and even Rome has not dared to teach this. Rather, the Roman Catholic Church is inclined to take the escape route of making a certain distinction between the *image* and the *likeness* of God. The *image* then points to man's essence and nature, the *likeness* to the supernatural righteousness that was added to human nature by way of a bridle. We will not dwell on this entirely arbitrary distinction.[4] Those making this distinction have to prove its validity, and until now no one has done so.

Close and careful consulting of Holy Scripture as to what can be found about the image separately, both with Christ as well as with man, or also about image and likeness together, and finally in the parallelism of the prophets about *likening* and *comparing*[5] rather supports the conclusion our forefathers reached from the outset, that we must understand image and likeness as the same thing being expressed in two ways. But there is an element of truth in this Roman Catholic notion to the extent that we must seek the image of God not only in the *quality* of man's nature, but definitely also in his *essence*. It was not true that a man who already existed was only later modeled into the image of God, but man as a whole, as created, was designed to manifest the image of God. There is nothing in man nor about him that was not created for the purpose of manifesting the image of God the better, the more perfectly, and the more gloriously. Just like the entire camera is devised, designed, and constructed to capture and record images accurately, and the camera is the more excellent to the degree that

---

4. For an example of what Kuyper thinks is an acceptable distinction between the ideas of *image* and *likeness* related to the distinction between essence and nature/quality, see the following discussion as well as that in *CG* 1.18. For an in-depth discussion of the image/likeness distinction as it pertains to the meaning of man as the image of God, see G. C. Berkouwer, *De Mens het Beeld Gods* (Kampen: Kok, 1957); ET: *Man: The Image of God*, trans. Dirk W. Jellema (Grand Rapids: Eerdmans, 1962), 67–117.

5. Kuyper refers here to the phenomenon in Hebrew poetry described since the eighteenth century as *parallelismus membrorum* ("parallelism of the members"). The Dutch phrase *ge-lijk-mak-en en vergelijken* has been rendered as "*likening* and *comparing*" in the above translation, and has textual similarities with Isaiah 40:18: "To whom then will you liken God, / or what likeness compare with him?"

everything *not* serving this purpose has been omitted, so too the whole human being is, if we may put it this way, an apparatus invented and designed to be capable of displaying the image of God. If you want to call this man's *essence* in contradistinction to his nonessential *qualities*, then we must indeed acknowledge that man has been created in the image of God in two respects: (1) in his essence to be *able* to reflect the image of God, and (2) in the qualities of his nature to actually do this.

Traditionally the more orthodox dogmatic theologians correctly applied this also to man's body. Not as if the body itself, as such, could be the image of a body of God, which is entirely foreign to God, who is a spirit. It would be absurd to even think this. We must nevertheless also maintain this application of the image of God to our body, by virtue of the correspondence that exists between soul and body. Our body belongs with our soul. It is not an envelope in which the soul has been inserted, but an artful instrument that is prepared by God to serve the soul, and that for each soul individually. Soul and body are organically one, and even though they are pulled asunder in death, they will nevertheless be reunited in the resurrection of the dead. The body also has abiding, enduring, eternal significance. One day the body will inherit immortality.

§ 5

Since this is the case, it is inconceivable that the soul of man would be designed for the image of God and that our body would have nothing to do with it. Yet these similarities cannot, of course, be sought in the *members* of our body as such, but must be sought in the *functions* of those members and senses. With our body we see, we speak, we walk, we descend, we climb, and so much more. And in Holy Scripture, all these functions, and so many more, are ascribed not only to our God, but they are ascribed in terms of the same senses and members of the body that we use for them. God also hears with his ear, sees with his eye, walks with his feet, strikes with his hand, saves with his arm, points with his finger, feels with his heart, moans in his inner parts, shows wrath with his face, and so much more. Of all these expressions and manifestations of life in God, an imprint has been put in man, and this imprint expresses itself through the members and senses of the body. And for this reason it won't do to say that our body as such has nothing to do with the image of God.

Nevertheless, our body is only the form of our being through which we manifest ourselves in the visible [world] and through which we have fellowship with the world outside us; our actual human essence lies deeper within us and exists spiritually. In the essence of the soul, therefore, the image of God radiates much more unmistakably. Even though we can also discover sensations and outwardly directed operations in animals with more highly developed organs, discoveries that certainly elicit our admiration, even in the most highly developed animal the faintest notion of the image of God is so completely absent that it seems as if these animals have been created for the express purpose of showing us the vast distinction between some animal traits possessed by these animals, and the complex of these higher phenomena as manifested only in man.

That consciousness and self-awareness, that having communion with the world of the beautiful, the good, and the true, that lighting up in passion and being inspired to pursue higher ideals, that all-round observing and discovering, that conceiving of and thinking through of things, that taking hold of the past in the present and that prophesying of the future out of the present, that warm and tender sentiment, that empathy with the suffering of others, that loving and devoting oneself, that strongly willing and persevering, that unlimited aiming all means toward a single chosen goal, and so much more—all of this teaches us to know all these capacities and powers as a disposition and capacity in man as human being that transcend the bounds of the lower creaturely life, and can be explained only on the basis of the reflection of the things of God in our human being. In that sense we are truly God's offspring, and in him we live and move and have our being [Acts 17:28–29], and even in the midst of the most horrible self-degradation, the foundation of our human being still remains lofty, so that the self-deification of the human being, created in the image of God, is well-nigh unavoidable on the part of those who have fallen away from that God.

§ 6    Thus the image of God dominates the whole creation, the whole manifestation, the whole presence, the whole existence, of man as human being. And only because he exists in *this* way as human being, he was able originally not only to capture, but also to reflect the image in his qualities and in the manifestations [of these qualities]. Thus God saw his own image in the human being he had created, and he saw that it was very good. But precisely because man bore the image of God, it belonged to his nature to be imperishable in soul and body. Plants come and go so that although the species remains, the specimens disappear. And in the same way animals are only transient bearers of the species to which they belong. But man *cannot* be thus.

Because God is enduring, the bearer of his image must also have permanence, not only the race but also the individuals. Our immortality is not for our sake, but for God's sake. A human being *cannot* cease to exist. His existence continues even if it goes through death. He is not a wave that materializes on the surface of the sea, reflects the light for a short while, and submerges again, but he is something distinctive, not only as species but also as person and as individual human being. Plants and animals perish, but the human being is imperishable, because he has been created in God's image. The image-bearer of the One who alone possesses immortality within himself must, by virtue of the image he shows, bear within himself the indestructibility and eternal permanence of the only immortal God. It scarcely requires reminding that this indestructibility does not preclude being *able to die*.

# CHAPTER TWENTY-TWO

# CONSCIENCE AND THE COVENANT OF WORKS

*And the* LORD *God commanded the man, saying, "You may surely eat of every tree of the garden, but of the tree of the knowledge of good and evil you shall not eat, for in the day that you eat of it you shall surely die."*

GENESIS 2:16–17

§ 1    The conclusion reached thus far was that God created man in such a way that he saw his image reflected in man for the purpose of being able to use him as an instrument for his glory, and that he created him for that purpose: *wise*, *holy*, and *righteous*, that is, not only without any defect, but also definitely at that normal point in the adult human life when that life just begins its richer unfolding. But this does not yet say nearly enough about the spiritual condition of man in paradise. We need only mention the tree of the knowledge of good and evil to immediately open up a new, and certainly not limited, field of inquiry. But if we are to feel at home in this new field, we must get it firmly in our mind beforehand that what we call "conscience" did *not* exist in the newly created human being.

At first glance this may appear strange, yet it is quickly and clearly grasped if we do not take conscience to mean what the unbelieving world has turned it into, but rather as our forefathers always understood it. As the people of the world want to delude us into believing, conscience would be a kind of Urim and Thummim [Exod 28:30] within us, a divine oracle. We would need only to inquire from that oracle to know what God wants from us. And also when we go against the will of God, the oracle rebukes us inwardly. So anyone who did what his conscience dictated and refrained from doing what his conscience forbade was on this basis a man after God's heart. And armed with that conscience-religion, people allowed themselves to push aside Scripture, the law of God, and the gospel. People could do without all of these as long as they went by their conscience and acted in accordance with it. With that compass one [presumably] always proceeded safely. Dangerous precipices left undisclosed by this compass did not exist.

It is striking, therefore, how this boasting in *conscience* arose at precisely the time when rationalism was busy trampling *faith*, and how even now people are most busily occupied with the conscience in [those] circles where faith in God has in fact been lost. This would not be the proper place to denounce the worship of conscience and its implicit self-deification of the man whose conscience it is. We limit ourselves here to a reminder that Holy Scripture does not know anything of such a *Urim* and *Thummim* in our heart, and that our Reformed forefathers had a wholly different view of the conscience. They actually denied that the conscience is something distinct in man; they refused to say that man has feelings, and will, and intellect, and inclinations, and so much more, and then, in addition, also a conscience.

Conscience is not a *capacity*; it is not an inner habit; rather, it is a continually recurring activity within us, an expression or activity of our *consciousness*. Our consciousness is compelled to be engaged *with ourselves*, to reflect on our moral situation, our thoughts, our words, our deeds, our omissions and commissions, and reflect on them with a measure of evaluation and choice. This requires [firstly] a certain moral awareness or knowledge of good and evil according to the law of God. For this it is necessary [secondly] that we know ourselves and that we objectify for ourselves our own person and our actions. And this requires, thirdly, a higher impulse that forces us again and again to condemn or acquit ourselves according to that yardstick of our moral awareness. Thus in the moral realm it is precisely the same as what must happen in the realm of the intellect, of beauty, and of so much more. We discover that in the realm of truth, fixed laws of thought apply. So we must investigate for ourselves whether we have respected those laws in our thinking. If we have not, then we must think differently and better. If we have, then we stand firm in our conviction.

We also affirm this sound doctrine concerning the conscience, but precisely for this reason it is inconceivable that there was in Adam immediately after his creation what we call "conscience." Indeed, Adam possessed consciousness, self-awareness, moral self-awareness, but as long as the first experience of guilt was missing, he could not act as judge vis-à-vis himself and render judgment. Had sin failed to appear, no government would have arisen, and no tribunal would ever have been held. And even as there would have been no external judge, so too there would have been no *internal judge*. Or, if you will, the person who had to act as judge when necessary did exist, but as long as no one appeared in court, the judicial function could not be exercised. That *judicial* role is inseparable from the function of our consciousness if we are to speak of a judgment of conscience, and therefore the conscience-function could come into existence only when there was guilt or at least an accusation. But it could *not* exist, and is unimaginable, as long as there is not the remotest hint of guilt, nor even of any self-accusation.

Therefore we *cannot* speak of conscience in the proper sense in paradise, *nor* in the case of him whom we worship in the image of the spotless Lamb, nor among the beatified. Conscience is the functional form of our rational awareness as soon and as long as sin has divided the unity of our inner life; and as such within this functioning of conscience there lies a piece of common grace of no little significance, even as Paul testifies that the Gentiles are morally accountable in terms of the acquittal or indictment of their conscience [Rom 2:15]. Precisely because of the breach that sin caused in our being, and the resulting permanent dividedness of our inner life, the image of our person in the mirror of our conscience takes on a form that differs from our ordinary self-awareness. And this explains why we begin to discern something distinct in this curious function of our consciousness, and why we are almost incapable of looking at it in any other way than that our conscience is a separate capacity.

§ 2 Therefore, with respect to Adam, although we could not yet speak of a *conscience*, he certainly did have *faith*—not, of course, the same faith whereby a sinner is justified. The faith that saves from perdition could not yet be present in the first human being who had not yet fallen. The faith that saves sinners is thus faith of a *special* nature, which came because of sin and it will, after sin will have been destroyed, once again show its *general* primary character. After all, faith as such is a foundational feature of human nature. Faith is the conscious rapport between the divine image and the human being who has been created in that image. Where that image goes into hiding, this faith darkens. Where the image turns into its opposite, this faith becomes deliberate *unbelief*. Christ was the perfecter of this faith [Heb 12:2]. And according to the apostolic testimony this faith, which makes the soul dwell with God and brings about a conscious rapport, abides, together with *love* and *hope* [1 Cor 13:13]. That faith is therefore a piece of creation. It belongs to the nature of man, as soon as we think of this nature as being in rapport with God. And this is why in Adam such faith, as the breath of life of the soul, was part of original righteousness. Adam's original righteousness is inconceivable apart from that faith.

The *covenant* in which God stood with Adam falls within the same line of thought. The word *covenant* for the relationship between God and Adam is derived from Hosea 6:7, where the Israelites of that time are reproached that "*like Adam they transgressed the covenant*," because "they dealt faithlessly with [their God]." Attempts have been made to omit Adam's name from Hosea 6:7 by means of a different translation, but this attempt was *bound* to fail.[1] It is very well known that the name Adam means man or human being in our language [Dutch: *mensch*]. Based on this, it has been suggested that Hosea 6:7 should be translated, "They have transgressed the covenant *as human beings*." But this rendering runs afoul of its own illogic. How in the world would the Israelites have wanted to transgress the covenant with their God other than as human beings? They simply were nothing other than human beings, and there simply *could* be no transgression of the covenant other than by humans. If this had referred in a special sense to the kings or the priests, who were held to a more scrupulous faithfulness than the common people, then it might be translated as "They, though being kings and priests, have transgressed the covenant as if they were *common people*." But this cannot be, because those who are being reproached *are* the common people. The rendering "They have

§ 3

---

1. See *PRRD* 2:436–441 for a discussion of the diversity of early modern understandings of this verse, including the identification of the Septuagint by the Jesuit Cornelius à Lapide (1567–1637) as representing a textual tradition that "understood *adam* as a universal rather than a proper name" (437).

transgressed the covenant like Adam" therefore encounters increasingly less opposition. For us it is the only option.

We attach importance to this statement because in Genesis 1–3 no explicit mention is made of a covenant of God with the first man, and also elsewhere in Scripture the name, but not the substance, occurs in connection with Adam. Furthermore, such an unexpected reference to Adam is also found elsewhere in Scripture. Thus we read in Job 31:33, "If I have concealed my transgressions as Adam by hiding my iniquity in my bosom."[2] And in Psalm 82:7 our preferred rendering is "Nevertheless, *like Adam* you shall die, and fall like any prince."[3]

Especially the Reformed have therefore correctly insisted that establishing the covenant of works with the newly created Adam must be fully taken into account. The silence of Genesis 2 and 3 must certainly not be disguised and must be explained, but it does not in the least refute the fact that a covenant was being established. This fact is certain on the basis of the whole contrast that runs through Holy Scripture between the covenant of grace that is based on *faith* and the covenant of works that is based on *doing*. Nobody denies this contrast, and it simply *cannot* be ignored.

It might be objected that the covenant that is based on the rule "Do this and you shall live" is generally found in the form in which it was proclaimed to the Israelites. But it is self-evident that a covenant based on this rule has not been made with *sinners* (and the Israelites were sinners). Or what sense would it make if God the Lord, knowing how fallen man was incapable of any good, would have presented a covenant, not to Adam in the state of righteousness, but after Adam was fallen, on the condition that he would do perfectly what is good and through this would live, but otherwise would forever be under the curse? Among humans such a consolation would be called repulsive deceit; how then can we ascribe it to

---

2. SV and KJV read "as Adam"; ESV primary text reads "as others do," with "as Adam did" as an alternative translation in a textual footnote.

3. *Note by the Author*: The rendering "nevertheless, like men you shall die" fits with what precedes, but not with what follows. Verse 7 is preceded by "You are *gods, sons of the Most High*, all of you," and then "nevertheless, *like men* you shall die" fits. But it does not fit with what follows: "and fall like any prince," for the princes were, like the judges, bearers of the majesty of God. The rendering "like Adam," on the other hand fits with both what precedes it *and* what follows. Adam was by virtue of creation "the son of God." Well then, they, even though they were children of the Most High, would die exactly like this "son of God." And even if they were judges, it would not save them. Princes who stood *above* the judges, also died.

God? Furthermore, according to Genesis 3:17 the curse already rested on this fallen world, and how then could it be that not until Horeb was the curse threatened for those who did not continue in all that was written in the Book of the Law? On that interpretation of Scripture, no guilty verdict against Adam would even have been possible. We categorically reject the entire notion that the covenant of works was revealed for the first time at Sinai, and there [at Sinai] was intended to be a covenant of works. This might be true in a symbolic and nationalistic sense, but it could *not* be true in relation to individual humans with respect to their soul before God; and yet this latter is how it is understood repeatedly in the New Testament (Rom 10:5).[4]

All of this can be explained very well if we accept that (1) the covenant of works was already established and broken in paradise; (2) that in this covenant the absolute bond between inner existence and external condition is expressed, which nevertheless continues forever; (3) that God in his covenant of grace with Israel has refreshed the memory of this covenant of works; and (4) that it was indeed valid for Israel in a symbolic and nationalistic sense. Abundance and delight as long and insofar as they served God, hunger and pestilence when they burned incense for the queen of heaven.

But as strictly as we maintain this, just as readily do we admit that especially since the rise of *covenant theology* the former restraint has been abandoned in far too large a degree. Everything was worked out precisely in terms of the tiniest particulars: who the parties were, where the covenant between them had been made, when the covenant was made, what the parties to the covenant were like, what the stipulations and conditions were, what promise was held out as enticement, and what threatened punishment struck terror. We would almost say that they were able to present these details with the scrupulosity of a notary. But Calvin and the best Reformed theologians did *not* do it this way. They remained more restrained and were therefore more in harmony with the paradise narrative itself.

§ 4

---

4. This conclusion comes at the end of Kuyper's chain of reasoning: the connection between the rule "do this and you shall live" and the Sinai covenant shows that a covenant of works could not have first been introduced in the Sinai covenant; it had to be a reiteration or a "refreshing," as he calls it, of the covenant of works in a nationalistic or symbolic sense. When the New Testament describes this aspect of the Sinai covenant in individualistic terms, it therefore proves this conclusion.

Nevertheless we do acknowledge the relative right with which people have approached the issue in this manner, (insofar as [their approach] can have a positive side) by drawing out into the spotlight everything that can be found on the issue and investigating it down to the details. Indeed, there certainly were parties, and obligations, and the obligations rested on conditions, and those conditions held beyond Adam for all his descendants. But we must guard against one thing: let us not describe *how* God presented this covenant to Adam nor what Adam presumably answered, for then we arrive at factual assertions that we must be able to substantiate from Scripture. In Scripture we find virtually nothing mentioned about this. Scripture tells us clearly that Adam was placed under the covenant of works, and we with him, and what the stipulations and promises and threats of that covenant were, and still are, but the entire paradise narrative tells us nothing about the way it came into being.

This silence in a matter of such importance can be explained only if we understand the covenant of works in its first revelation not as having been put together mechanically but as functioning organically. Two parties who at first did not belong together, but who negotiate to reach an agreement are establishing their covenant, if they reach it, perfunctorily. But this is not how it *can* have been here, because God had created man in his image and for himself, so that man was his and belonged to him. In such a relationship there is no *coming* together but a *being* together, and the form of the covenant can only function *organically*, that is, as a matter of course and as a natural expression of a mutual relationship. Because man was created in God's image, the mutual relationship between God and newly created man could be no other than that of a covenant, with all the emphasis this word implies and all the consequences it entails.

*Covenant* expresses a bond between two [parties] who are distinguished by relative independence. Where that independence is absent, there is a bond but no covenant. What is called *"covenant"* in human discourse therefore comes closest to what this original relationship of man to his God is. Here the stipulations are natural as well. There is no capriciousness or whim, but life, living completely according to God's holy ordinances. And the stipulations also emerge organically from the relationship. Living in terms of God's ordinances leads to a natural and complete flourishing of our existence as eternal life. Resisting that ordinance injures life and brings death. Nor could Adam separate himself, in his individuality, from his offspring. For God, the [covenant] bond encompasses us and all that is ours, now and forever. Adam could be no other than simultaneously the first man and the covenant head of us all.

This is the first point. But secondly, the link between *doing* and *living*, between *not doing* and *death,* was not a mechanical one either. This relationship is also definite and will not be shunted aside; it would not satisfy us if, in the wake of a few new philosophers, that bond were either made incidental or severed. The outcome shows that that bond could *temporarily* be severed, and precisely then the covenant of grace must intervene mechanistically to restore the breach. But even though the cross saves the world, the cross remains *unnatural*, and we are not back on the path of righteousness until our Savior receives a name above every name, and when we hear that every knee shall bow before him. But no matter how seriously this relationship may be disrupted temporarily, Scripture nevertheless prophesies and faith speaks into your soul that in the end the original relationship will be restored again, and the turbulence of chaos cannot come to rest before the internal and external states are once again reintegrated.

But if we turn this into a covenant made *perfunctorily*, then we start §5 from the false assumption that it was not fixed *in* creation but only formulated *after* creation. If, on the other hand, we follow the thought that the covenant of works is an *organically* determined covenant, fixed in the conditions of life itself, then creation and covenant firmly interlock, and we can understand why the law of the covenant of works that was not supposed to be broken, continues all the way to Golgotha, both in reconciliation and satisfaction. This is all the more emphatically so because in the case of a perfunctory establishing of the covenant, the entire covenant would depend on the probationary command. That command is stated. It is mentioned. The narrative tells us about it. But of course, a covenant made solely on the basis of a probationary command would definitely not be the covenant of works. The covenant of works must rest on *the whole of God's law*, and the whole of that law of God would then have had to be read aloud and written down, just like at Sinai, if it had come to an external making of the covenant in the literal sense. But no one supports this [notion]. Although some, following à Marck's[5] example, have calculated how

---

5. Johannes à Marck or Marckius (1656–1731) was a Dutch Reformed theologian at Franeker, Groningen, and Leiden. His major work is the *Christianæ theologiæ medulla didactico-elenctica* (Amsterdam: Borstius, 1690).

many commandments applied to Adam and how many did not—a calculation whereby in a true pharisaical manner they inevitably lost sight of the root of the commandments. But that approach has not found a following. When we speak of the law of God in connection with Adam, we speak of that law as created in Adam's heart and as belonging to and being part of that original wisdom with which the first human was adorned. It therefore convincingly appears that the stipulation of the covenant of works was *organically* woven into Adam's nature; how then would a covenant based on that stipulation have taken place *perfunctorily*?

But let us not exaggerate in the other direction either, as if the making of this covenant had taken place outside Adam's consciousness. To the contrary, in the first moments of his existence, when the newly created man awoke in the newly created world and for the first time entered into the relationships in which he stood, also in relation to his God, the fact of this bond *must* have crossed his consciousness in such a way that it also felt to him like a covenant. This is why God himself came to Adam's aid, for what we read about the probationary command did indeed take place perfunctorily. At that point God has revealed himself to Adam, has spoken to him, has said certain things to him that were easily understood, and has focused the whole relationship of Adam to his God into a single point, on which, as on the point of a needle, the entire future development of humanity would rest. In this we definitely encounter an *external* covenant making, and it is in the making of the covenant on this one point that Adam had to become conscious of the *whole* of his relationship to his God, and in which the whole meaning of the covenant of works was drawn together as in a single grasp.

# CHAPTER TWENTY-THREE

# THE BASIS
# FOR FURTHER
# DEVELOPMENT

*So when the woman saw that the tree was good for food, and that it was a delight to the eyes, and that the tree was to be desired to make one wise, she took of its fruit and ate, and she also gave some to her husband who was with her, and he ate.*

Genesis 3:6

Man stood in paradise, created in the image of God, in an original righteousness belonging to his nature, but without a functioning of conscience, in genuine faith, being wise, holy, and righteous—wise in mind, holy before the moral law, righteous before God. At the beginning there was therefore perfect flawlessness. Not a single defect, not a single weakness. A creature in the image of God, about whom it could truly be said, "And God saw that human being, and behold, it was very good."

With this the starting point had been determined for man, but as yet nothing about the end of the road, as was the case with the plants and the animals. A spider weaves its web century after century with uniformly impeccable accuracy. Crows and swallows migrate. The ant lives marvelously in its ant colony from generation to generation. The thunder with

§ 1

which God has clothed the neck of the horse continues to instill dread.[1] The bee gathers honey then as now. But it is not so with man. In his case two things stood at the door. In the first place, there was the development of that which had only been imagined. And second, within that development there was the choice between two possibilities: a development in accordance with God's ordinance, or a development that went against that ordinance. Choice in any event, but a choice that would correspond to the *requirement implicit in the position of image-bearer* or that would go against *being that image.*

Anyone called to resemble another's image should, in order to keep bearing that image, want to turn toward him. By turning away from him the image is lost. We can call such freedom of choice the manifestation, the characteristic feature of the moral life. But it was in fact nothing other than the fruit of having been created in God's image. God possesses sovereignty, and no natural necessity. He is a God above all things, because all things are his creation. In that sovereignty lies the mark of his divinity, and only by confessing that sovereignty can we escape the grip of pantheism, and only this confession elevates our entire human life.

Well then, man had to bear the *image* of this *sovereign* God, and this caused the contradictory problem both that this trait of *sovereignty* had to exist in man and yet this trait could exist in him only as a reflection, that is, as something *dependent*. In that contradictory notion of a *dependent* trait of *sovereignty* lies the whole mystery of our religious moral being: created in the image of God, consequently possessing the *moral choice of our will.* This moral choice of will as a trait of the image of God, and therefore *dependent*. A choice of will that was not exercised at every point along the way, for even God, once he created a world such as this, was bound to what he had created. Consequently, further along the way, man would similarly be bound by what lay behind him. Unconditioned power lies only in *the first choice of the will.* It involves not only unconditioned freedom, because at that point nothing binds man as yet, but also power, because it binds everything that follows.

---

1. This is an allusion to Job 39:22 in the SV, which like the KJV renders the Hebrew *ra'mah*, typically understood as related to waving or quivering, as a reference to thunder: "Hast thou given the horse strength? Hast thou clothed his neck with thunder?" (Job 39:19 KJV). Most other English versions translate the Hebrew in reference to the horse's "mane" (ESV) or "flowing mane" (NIV).

Those who in the distant past defined our concepts praised God as an eternal Being who is *omnia determinans, determinatus ab nihilo*: determining everything, determined by nothing. And the shadowed marker of this lay precisely in that first choice of man's will. In that choice of will, and in it alone, two things were implicit: being bound by nothing, and the dreadful reality that it determined all of existence forever. Thus we notice that we have here a shadowed marker of God's image. Everything of God that is reflected in us is so incomparably glorious, but also so fearfully terrible. We make a choice without fully thinking it through and that choice determines our whole existence. And yet, we cannot do otherwise. It must be so. God made a choice at one time, and it determined the existence of all things, for then and for now and forever. The most frightening thing is that man had to accomplish this act of sovereignty with derivative, with received, with dependent powers. Adam was indeed *wise*, but with received wisdom; he was indeed holy, but with a holiness that was instilled in him; and so too he was righteous, but in a state of righteousness because God had placed him in that state.

That decision was made when Adam had to move forward. The curious §2 thing about his position was that he had to develop. With animals there is certainly a process of development, partially also with plants, to the extent that both go from small to full-grown and bear fruit; but in the case of a human being something entirely different comes into play. He not only possesses the [feature] of developing from child to adult, but having reached adulthood, of continually growing in insight and skill, and even beyond that, of progressing through the centuries as a species, as humankind, to a higher state. Jacob is more mature when he blesses his sons on his deathbed than when as a deceitful character he stole the blessing from his father. But Isaiah stands on a higher [plane] than Jacob. In John a much richer world opens up than in Jeremiah. The life of humanity at the present is much more richly developed in every way than it was in the centuries before the Reformation.

Therefore Adam could not simply confine himself to being conservative, even though the notion would not be so strange: "Having been created so exquisitely by God, remain who you are, and don't change." Yet that option was cut off. That conservatism would have been sinful in itself. If God creates man with the burden that he move forward even at the risk of stumbling, then it is not proper for man to say, "I will stay where I am so that I won't stumble." Adam had to move forward. The state of simply being a product of creation could not continue. He had to move from that state to go on to that second state, which would be the product of creation together with a choice of will. Man himself working *in* God's work and *as* his work. Or, if he chose *against* God, working against God's work and therefore immediately locked in punishment and curse by the reaction of God's sovereignty.

So you cannot say, "Oh, if only that tree, and what is recorded about that tree, had stayed out of paradise, and if only Satan had never been let loose against Eve!" This would not have helped Adam at all. He *had* to go through the test, in this manner or another. Man, who until then was nothing but a passive product, had to be brought into *action*. He had to come to a choice. The road before him was long, but precisely for that reason the first step on that road had to be taken as soon as possible. A life stretched out for many years in the luxuriousness of paradise without man coming to his first moral act, is an incongruous notion. Even if you measure the course of things not in hours and seconds, the popular notion is still the most likely one: the fall does not wait; it comes immediately. No sooner was man seen in paradise than Satan immediately approached him.

§ 3 We therefore repeat what we said in the opening of this chapter: original righteousness was the *starting point*. It was nothing more, and from that starting point it had to progress through a rich development to a still higher existence. Involuntarily the question arises here *why* it had been ordained in this way, and why God did not much rather create man all at once in finished form, on the highest plane of perfection, so that no battle or struggle would be necessary, and eternal life would be his inalienable portion as a matter of course.

But that question doesn't get us very far, though on first hearing it sounds plausible. People ask: if it was God's purpose to have a gathering of perfectly righteous humans rejoice around his throne in eternal bliss, why then not have that large multitude of saints created all at once in that perfect degree of holiness, in the state of perfect sinlessness, in that state of inalienable righteousness? Then the same goal would have been reached, all the misery of sin would not have occurred, and all the bitter suffering that is concentrated in Golgotha would have stayed away forever.

Isn't it understandable that such a notion arises, that it arises from the same train of thought that now causes us to question why not all humans will ultimately come to eternal life? If God can save the most stubborn sinner, then why not also the less stubborn? And why then not all, either here or in the hereafter? Who keeps him from doing this? And in this way all human creatures would be saved!

Such questions are understandable. But both are questions that inexorably collapse as soon as we have insight into the creation of man *in the image of God*. This is why *sovereign power* must be reflected in the *choice of the will*, and therefore the goal cannot be reached unless man himself walks toward it. He can be *placed* at the starting line, but he cannot be *placed* at the finish line. Man must *walk* the road between these two. This is implicit in the fact that man was not created in such a way that he was unable to sin. That was the point he had to reach, but only in the second stage. First he had to be in a position where he could forfeit what he had in order that it might thereafter become inalienable. Perseverance of the saints is an excellence that *could* not be created in man. Perseverance is not an *original* gift. It comes only later. Having been created, man therefore stands immediately under an inexorable creation ordinance. He must stand the test. Only then can the gate open for him through which he shall enter into eternal life, that is, to that high existence that no longer knows change or development but *perseveres in what it is*. That is, after all, the hallmark of the eternal. Divine *conservatism*, because it is *absolutely complete*.

In connection with this, the Lord God plants in the midst of the Garden of Eden the tree of the knowledge of good and evil. It is difficult to know whether this was a single tree or a kind of tree. Both options have been defended over and over. But even though we must admit that the literal words also allow for thinking of a *kind* of tree with many specimens, we think we are safe in maintaining the standard notion of only a single tree. In no case could it have been a kind of tree that was found throughout the garden, for we are told in Genesis 3:3 that this tree stood only *in the midst* of the garden. So even if it was a kind of tree, it could have stood only in a small area in which a group of such trees perhaps stood close together, and this multiplicity might have had no other purpose than to draw all the more attention to this tree through its frequent fruit bearing. Such a deliberate exacerbation of the temptation does not seem to be very plausible to us, and the story itself teaches us that at first Adam did not ask about the tree but was induced by Eve to look at it. We therefore stay with the notion of one tree.

§ 4

We would prefer to give this tree the name *tree of conscience* because, as we saw, the functioning of conscience in newly created man was still inconceivable and, as we shall see later, was generated precisely by that tree.

In any case, it is impossible to maintain that the fixed and actual name of the tree was "the tree of the knowledge of good and evil." Holy Scripture teaches us in fact that the name "tree of life" was indeed the name of [the other] tree, because that name is found as the name of a tree not only in the paradise narrative but in a number of other places, including at the end of Revelation. But such is definitely *not* the case with this tree. It is not mentioned again anywhere else in Scripture, and even in the paradise narrative the phrase "the tree of the knowledge of good and evil" occurs only [in a single context], in Genesis 2:9 [and] 17. Already in Genesis 3:3 there is mention only of "the tree that is in the midst of the garden," and in verse 6 only of "the tree." In 3:11 God says, "Have you eaten of the tree of which I commanded you not to eat?" and also in verse 12 Adam speaks simply of "the tree." On this basis most theologians expressed as their opinion that the words "knowledge of good and evil" in Genesis 2:9, 17 indicate the evil to which this tree has led, but did not represent a name that would belong to the tree as such.

§ 5     In an earlier chapter[2] we have already combined this *tree of conscience* with the *tree of life* in such a way that their duality was related to the duality of *body* and *soul* in man. The *tree of life* was intended for the glorification of the *body*, the *tree of conscience* related to the life of our *soul*. This duality is neither arbitrary nor uncertain. There are, after all, the *visible* and the *invisible*, and there is no *tertium quid* [third thing] between these two. There is *mind* and *matter*, but not a third something that would as "mental-material" constitute the link between the two. Since God the Lord created man, not as an angel, exclusively from *spirit* in the *invisible*, but at the same time as *matter* in the visible [world], it is self-evident that man cannot consist of anything but *soul* and *body*, and all twaddle about man being constituted of *body*, *soul*, and *spirit* is simply absurd.

Attempts have been made to introduce this [trichotomy] also in our circles. Especially Delitzsch's *A System of Biblical Psychology* has promoted this view.[3] But the Reformed churches remained sober under all this and did not for a moment let themselves be diverted from the old, tried way, and implacably maintained the duality or, as it was called, the *dichotomy* of man. Especially the statement that in man's tripartite being the

---

2. See *CG* 1.17, "The Tree of Life."
3. See Franz Delitzsch, *System der biblischen Psychologie*, 2nd ed. (Leipzig: Dörffling und Franke, 1861); ET: *A System of Biblical Psychology*, trans. Robert Ernest Wallis (1869; repr., Grand Rapids: Baker, 1966).

Holy Trinity was mirrored was objectionable to us Reformed [Christians]. The spirit in us then would correspond to the Holy Spirit, the soul to the Son, and therefore ... the *body* would correspond to the Father. Do you sense the sacrilege implied in the latter? Your body the image of the Father!

We cannot enter into more detail here, although it will be good to expose the invention of the *trichotomy* that divides man into body, soul, and spirit once and for all for what it is, in all its futility, also in the interest of our pedagogy. For the time being it is sufficient for us to leave it at this, as long as the *duality* of our existence is understood to be a necessary [doctrine]. This duality persists also in death. Then the soul is separated from the body, yet the body is not gone—it is in God's keeping. That separation of the body from the soul is a state of privation. And when glory comes, the body immediately returns, then to be heavenly, and to abide forever, even as the soul.

If this is the relationship between *body* and *soul*, then it is entirely fitting that for man's transition from his original to his permanent state, *two* trees stood next to each other in paradise, in the midst of the garden. Both were real trees, but trees that did *not* belong to the order of paradise. To the order of paradise belonged that which did not yet *sink down* and did not yet *advance upward*. Both are possible for something that has been created. It can *sink below* its original state, when the curse descends upon it. But it can also *gain* [and rise] above its original state, when it is drenched in glory.

§ 6

Concerning the three orders, we now read with respect to the world of trees: (1) the trees as God created them; (2) the trees that produce thorns and thistles; and (3) the tree of life in the new Jerusalem or in the kingdom of glory. Neither a tree with *thorns* nor a tree of *life* thus belonged to the order of paradise. Since one specimen of the latter nevertheless stood there indicates that it was a tree of a higher order that pointed to a higher order of life, and was thus as such already a sign. This was apparently also the case with the *tree of conscience*, which was evidently also a tree of a higher order. The woman looked at that tree and saw that it was "good for food, and a delight to the eyes, and to be desired to make one wise," [Gen 3:6] a description that clearly points to something exceptional. We are told that the tree was not like the other, ordinary trees, but that to the woman it surpassed those ordinary trees in beauty and luster and appeal. On that basis we therefore argue that this *tree of conscience*, like the *tree of life*, was also a tree of a higher order, which as such was already a sign of the higher order of life man would occupy one day. Taken in this way, the two therefore belong together, and together they belong with man. Man must not remain who he was, but develop into a *higher* order of life, to an inalienable condition.

Well then, both of these trees stand in the midst of the garden as a prefiguration of what it would be in the kingdom of glory. As something that transcended the glory of paradise, they pointed man toward the destination and calling that beckoned him, not to sink below paradise, nor to stay forever in this paradise, but to ascend higher than paradise. And they also showed him that this transition from the good that could be lost to the good that could not be lost applied to him in his *totality*, that is, to both aspects of his being. That was the message given him by the tree of life concerning his *body*, and by the tree of conscience concerning the life of his *soul*.

§ 7     As natural as it is for a tree that points to the *body* to offer food to eat, it is just as natural that with a tree that points to the *soul*, *eating* is not the means to achieve its purpose. The body consists of matter, exchanges that matter, and takes in new matter. This is *eating*. Thus once we rightly understand that the tree of life points to the *body*, we understand automatically that eating from the tree was the means to bestow a higher existence on the human body. But conversely, it is then also entirely understandable that the *tree of conscience*, which has nothing to do with the *body* but relates only to the *soul*, does *not* accomplish its work by material means at all, but *must* do it by *spiritual* means.

This has also been understood differently, by imagining that there were certain powers in these trees that worked on the mind and could either strengthen or poison the mind, but this is not very plausible. Although in fairness it must be conceded that the fruit of a tree can very well influence our mental state. From of old, people pointed to the grapevine, and the question was raised whether the *tree of conscience* was not simply a grapevine. After all, it was sufficiently known that wine could stimulate or cloud the mind. Also, all kinds of plants that stimulate the sexual drive and thus degrade the mind have been pointed to as proof that through its fruits a tree can very easily have a direct impact on our brain. And this is true. Especially various poisons have a swift and strong impact on the life of the mind. This is the result of the connection between body and soul and is experienced by every individual, sometimes in a pleasurable way, sometimes in an unpleasant way.

We may concede all of this without this proving in any way that the fruit of the *tree of conscience* has a natural impact on the life of our soul. Wine may overstimulate the mind, but later, when the intoxication of the wine has fully run its course, the mind *remains* what it was before, and the quality of the life of the soul has not undergone any *change*. There may have been a *moral* weakness involved with indulging in the wine, and that has aftereffects, but the wine as such does not touch the state of the soul. We must therefore decidedly reject the notion that by means of a bite of the fruit of the tree Adam and Eve experienced a transition within their soul from good to evil, such that a food they ate caused a direct poisoning of the moral life. This is seeking sin in the material and takes us along the path of the Manicheans[4] and befits the pantheist who lets the functioning of matter and mind merge together; but it does not befit the confessor of God's triune being, who accepts matter and mind in their absolute contradistinction. Apart from the question, therefore, whether the fruit of this tree of conscience was, as said, entirely innocent, and even granting the possibility that a certain stimulating effect on the mind emanated from the fruit of this tree, all of this could in no way have had anything other than a secondary [effect]. The actual working of this "tree of conscience" consisted not in the stimulating effect its fruit might have had on the blood or on the nervous system, but rather in its exceptional attraction, coupled with God's command to stay away from it. A tree as such does not have rapport with the soul. Rapport can emerge only when either the beauty of that tree has a hypnotic effect on us, or when an ordinance of God, through a word or command, establishes a deliberate and mechanical connection between our soul and that tree. And in this way, the contrast here is completely transparent. The *tree of life* for the *body*, and therefore its fruit *must* be eaten; but the *tree of conscience* for the *soul*, and therefore a strict *prohibition* against any notion of "eating" from it.

---

4. Manicheism is identified with the doctrines of Mani, a third-century religious teacher. See K. Kessler, "Mani, Manicheans," in *NSHE* 7:153–61. "The fundamental part" of Mani's system "is the theory of the origin of the world, which is rooted in Persian dualism. The world began in a mixing of two opposing elements, light and darkness, one essentially good, the other essentially evil" (155). These opposing elements are identified with spiritual and material realities, respectively, and in the human person with the soul (good) and the body (evil).

# CHAPTER TWENTY-FOUR

# THE LANGUAGE
# IN PARADISE

*You shall not eat of the fruit of the tree that is in the midst of the garden, neither shall you touch it, lest you die.*

Genesis 3:3

§ 1    We left the question undecided whether the *tree of conscience* bore a fruit that could effectively stimulate man's blood or nervous system. We are not told anything definite on this point. And when it says that after Adam and Eve had eaten of the tree "the eyes of both were opened, and they knew that they were naked," this can be understood entirely in a *moral sense*. The only reason why we are not averse to the notion that a certain effect on man emanated from this fruit is because nothing neutral or indifferent was found anywhere in the work of God. If this *tree of conscience*, just like the *tree of life*, was of a higher order, then a power of a higher order must also have been at work in its fruit, although we do not know how it worked or what its properties were. It was certainly not a grapevine, as many surmise, since that fruit does not cloud the senses except after the fermentation of the grape juice. Rather, we would have to think of a tree along the lines of the grapevine, but of such a nature that the effect of this tree on the blood and nerves emanated directly from the fruit, without fermentation. We leave this question undecided, however.

There is no question of any kind of intoxication caused by the eating of this fruit. The whole narrative shows this. To the contrary, their shame sought covering for their shame. But what settles the matter for us, even if the forbidden fruit had a stimulating effect, is that it was in any case entirely secondary. The declaration *"You will die"* was definitely not intended to convey physical poisoning. Then they would not have felt *shame*, but they would have become *unwell* and together they would have fallen down, deathly ill. The natural effect of the fruit of the tree, which we do not deny in the least, is therefore certainly not the main issue, that which matters most. That this tree was a *tree of conscience* did not depend on its physical properties but on the word of God that had been pronounced over that tree. As Eve told Satan, God had commanded them that they should not even *touch* that tree. Even touching the tree of conscience would have fatal consequences, which amounts to this, that neither the touching nor the desiring of the fruit, but the *deliberate disobedience* that expressed itself in the eating of the tree, would be the cause of death.

This is the place to say something about *the language*. This would not be necessary if the poisoning of the soul had been the consequence of the poisoning of the blood. Everything that occurs physically can be accomplished without using the instrument of language. Motioning our finger toward our open mouth indicates clearly enough that we mean *eating*. But it is different, of course, now that we have come to the conclusion that the *tree of conscience* was merely an instrument, not a second cause, and that the effect proper emanated from the word of God to which they had to be obedient but had become disobedient.

§ 2

Now what really matters are the *words* that are used, and we must face the fact that Adam and Eve were capable of grasping the meaning of these words. Generally no attention is paid to this point. The words we refer to are so overly familiar to us since our youth, and all the concepts expressed here so common, that the thought doesn't even arise within us how Adam and Eve could understand these words. But this question is definitely legitimate. The single concept "die," "surely die," is so difficult and complex that we cannot escape the question how Adam, who had never heard or seen anything [connected with] dying, could form any conception of it when he heard the word. Even more strongly does the question press itself upon us when we take into account the temptation of the serpent. That temptation also occurred with *words*, by means of a fine web of words, by giving words a slightly modified meaning. [Because] this temptation [came in words,] it could either have no effect on Eve, or it could be too inhumanly difficult, since she was incapable of fully grasping with any of our clarity the snare in which Satan was trying to entrap her. So the question of *language* indeed comes to the foreground. And before proceeding it is therefore necessary to ask ourselves what meaning *language* had for Adam and Eve in paradise.

We who have been born later learn our language gradually. When we want to make clear to a very young child that a glass or cup contains deadly poison, we would not say, "By tasting this you will die," but we would try to give the impression of something horrible by means of strong gestures or vigorous sounds of *yuck* and again *yuck*! And so it is with our entire language. When we stand at the beginning of life, our language already exists outside of us, in the thoughts, conversations, and writings of older people, and only very gradually do we grow into that existing language. The great majority of people grow into their mother tongue so extremely imperfectly that for a normally educated woman to employ one tenth of the vocabulary of our language is already a significant feat. For many young men, who are less in touch with real life, the available vocabulary is generally even much more limited. Languages also differ among themselves. Languages such as those of our civilized peoples in Western Europe have a [level of] development that many indigenous African languages cannot come close to. As rich as our languages are, so poor are the languages of those primitive peoples, not at every point but in general.

Judging by this, when we think back to paradise, we might perhaps arrive at the notion that Adam and Eve's speech must have been very defective: an initial stammering or the uttering of some sounds that only in the course of the generations developed from those stammering sounds into something that resembled language. But this notion is completely incompatible with what the paradise narrative tells us. After all, from the very first moment God the Lord reveals himself to Adam not by means of signs or gestures, but in extensive speeches, in concepts, through words.

In a statement like "Be fruitful and multiply and fill the earth," we even see a certain luxuriance due to a multiplicity of words, a certain style, a certain nuancing of concepts. Stated crudely it would have been sufficient to say, "You must fill the earth with people." But now we find *three* concepts: first, *being fruitful*, then the *multiplying* that flows from it, and only then *filling the earth*. Similarly, when it says, "You shall surely die," and not simply, "You will die," the former displays a refined form of speaking,

a strengthening of the notion by repeating the word itself, something unthinkable if their language had been like that of infants.[1] Therefore it is
undeniable that Adam and Eve appear in this narrative as people who, immediately after their creation, are already capable of *fully understanding* a
rich, finely developed language.

If we nevertheless assume the contrary, and say that they probably understood something close to this, getting more or less the main point, but
that they were rather obtuse in their grasp of the language as language,
then an abhorrence creeps into the story. Then you assume that God,
knowing how Adam and Eve did not really understand him, or understood
him at best in a very limited way, nevertheless hung *their* future and the
future of their *entire* offspring on such an imperfectly understood command. This would assume injustice in God and is therefore unacceptable.

In addition, however, the notion that Adam understood language still
only imperfectly cannot be reconciled with the rest of the narrative. In the
first part of the story, Adam listens more than he speaks, but it is entirely
different in the continuation of the narrative. There, with astuteness and
nuance Eve argues with Satan, and Satan with her. Then she reasons with
Adam. And after the fall we hear Adam and Eve both plead their case with
God, and God rendering judgment, and all this in a manner that would
have no meaning if language were not understandable. Indeed, the data
the narrative provides go even further. It appears from the narrative that
at the outset Adam and Eve even had the capacity to create language and
were fully conscious of this. When Adam sees Eve he calls her *Isha*, that is,
wo-man, and later *Chawwah*, or Eve, that is, life. Later Eve in turn calls her
eldest son *Cain*, referring to the fact that she had *received* this child [Gen
4:1], and later another child *Seth*, because, she said "God has appointed for
me another offspring instead of Abel" [Gen 4:25]. The Hebrew word *Seth*
means "to set, to appoint." This shows a strong linguistic awareness. That
this was instilled in Adam is clearly apparent from the fact that God also
brought the animals to Adam to see what he would *call* them, and [Adam]
gave each a name according to how he perceived their nature and character. Thus once again [we see] a marvelously strong manifestation of linguistic formative power.

---

1. The Hebrew (an infinitive absolute) reads literally, "Dying you shall die." The repetition usually is rendered into English with the intensifier "surely."

§ 3    Let us here in passing remove an objection that easily arises. The names of Eve, Cain, Seth, and so on, are derived from Hebrew roots. Does this mean that Hebrew was spoken in paradise? This has indeed been thought for many years, and we would not claim that the generation that thinks this way has by this time died out entirely. Meanwhile, further research and comparative linguistics give us certainty that the Hebrew language as we know it from Holy Scripture was formed at a much later date and harks back to a language with much simpler roots. Hebrew is one of those languages that belong to the descendants of Shem and that as a group differ greatly from the languages belonging to the sons of Japheth and Ham's descendants. Hebrew arose after, and has therefore undergone the consequences of, the confusion of tongues at Babel.

Although it may be reasonable to think that the descendants of Seth lived near the paradise region, and thus spoke a language most closely related to the language of the first humans, there is nevertheless such an immeasurable distance between that oldest language and our Hebrew that even if they are related, the two languages still differed no less than, for example, Russian and our rural Frisian.[2] If we accept this, then the difficulty arises how the names Eve, *Isha*, Cain, and Seth can occur here as having been derived from Hebrew roots, since Hebrew did not yet exist then. But this objection can easily be eliminated. Already the word *Isha*, or woman, indicates how such names can be *translated* to make the motivation behind the name evident. If our translators had wanted to be consistent, they should have written, "she shall be called *Isha*," rather than "she shall be called woman." Or they should later also have written, "The man called his wife's name Life-giver, because she was the mother of all living." If instead of using the names Adam, Eve, and Cain, Genesis would speak of *Man*, *Life-giver*, *Received*, and *Substitute*, then the allusions would have been transferred to our own language, without anyone concluding from this that our language was spoken in paradise. Everything fits well, therefore, if we assume that the language of paradise was a much more original language, and that only later, when the paradise narrative was written down, this allusion to the derivation of the words was transferred from that paradise language to Hebrew.

---

2. Friesland is one of the provinces of the Netherlands, and Frisian is a Germanic language.

We now return to the main point, namely, that not only Adam but also §4
Eve were immediately after their creation capable of both understanding
and speaking a living, richly developed language. How did they come to
this [capability]? It is of course out of the question that they would have
memorized this language. How in the world would this have been conceivable? Where then was this language? And where were the aids for learning
this language? The only answer therefore can be that this language was in
fact created within them, not by means of a language or speech *capacity*,
but as a language they were fully conversant with and that belonged, as
part of the original righteousness, to the image of God. God speaks. It belongs to his divine majesty to utter the Eternal Word. With God, speaking
is creating, and creating is speaking. And thus it could not be otherwise
than that man also, having been created in the image of God, had to possess both the capability of speech *and* the language, in order to manifest
the image of God in this way, by means of this language.

As we saw, in his creation Adam was perfectly *wise*, *holy*, and *righteous*. But this *wisdom*, this *being wise*, is inconceivable without *language*.
Speaking and thinking belong inseparably together. Thinking is the basis
for speaking, and in language the thoughts and the deliberations of the
heart issue forth. So there is nothing inherently incongruous in the fact
that Adam understands a language and speaks a language. To the contrary,
if Adam were capable only of stammering, his creation in the image of
God would not have been properly reflected, nor would Adam's original
wisdom have shone forth.

The clearer we grasp the nature and origin of language, the less strange
this is. People have argued almost endlessly about the origin of language,
and two main notions have competed for dominance. On the one hand it
was maintained that language was an *agreed-upon patchwork*. People had
agreed among themselves that a creature with two legs would be called
a *bird* and a creature with four legs a *beast*. In this way the language had
become increasingly richer and ever more comprehensive. And humans
newly come [into the world] merely memorized what had in the past been
agreed upon by mutual consent. All kinds of attempts have been made to
make this view plausible; and all of these involved *conventional* language
systems, that is, systems that explain the origin of languages on the basis
of correspondence, derivation, or convention.

But over against this, a quite different paradigm emerged already
among the Greeks that explained language on the basis of human aptitude.

Humans, said the representatives of this paradigm, were created in such a way that [a given] thing made a fixed impression on them, and they represented that fixed impression not arbitrarily but necessarily in a fixed sound that God had intended for it. This paradigm has always been advocated by the theologians who took Holy Scripture into account. Human language, they said, is not a human invention but of divine origin. God first devised how this human language would be before it came across our lips. That language was created by God in man. Man therefore *had* to speak in that language. And it also explains how God himself could speak in that language to man. Later linguistic study, which was much more in-depth than the earlier study and was carried out much more systematically, came to confirm this to the extent that it led increasingly to a demonstration of a measure of fixed kinship among all languages and a confirmation of the hypothesis that all languages gradually developed from a single parent language.[3]

Except, however, that linguists again and again encountered the equally undeniable fact that *all kinds of confusion* are noticeable in the languages, that peoples who barely differ from one another in outlook nevertheless speak entirely different languages, and that in all languages today there is a whole series of phenomena that can be explained almost in no other way than on the basis of chance or arbitrariness. Apart from Holy Scripture this objection is indeed very difficult to eliminate. But if we take into account not only the paradise narrative but also the narrative about the confusion of languages at the building of the tower at Babel, as well as the event on the day of Pentecost, then all mystery is lifted.

The paradise narrative then explains the unity of the origin of languages; what happened in the plain of Shinar [at Babel] then clarifies how nevertheless there could and had to be such a boundless confusion within each language and among languages; and finally the story of Pentecost tells us how in the midst of that virtually boundless confusion, the unity

---

3. Sir William Jones (1746–94), in an address to the Royal Asiatic Society of Calcutta in 1786, asserted of Latin, Greek, and Sanskrit that "no philologer could examine all three, without believing them to have sprung from some common source, which, perhaps, no longer exists." See William Jones, "Discourse III. Delivered February 2, 1786," in *Discourses Delivered before the Asiatic Society: And Miscellaneous Papers, on the Religion, Poetry, Literature, etc. of the Nations of India*, 2 vols. (London: Charles S. Arnold, 1824), 1:28. Later comparative linguistic study hypothesized a language called "Proto-Indo-European" as this common source.

of our human language still persists. The languages of the Parthians and Medes and Elamites and so forth converge there once again in the basic unity they jointly possess, and thus all languages appear to be nothing but the rich multiplicity of forms in which the *one human language* has spread among the nations.

That one human language, then, was the *original*, the pure, the hitherto unconfused and unspoiled mother tongue among the languages from which all individual languages have come. And it is that one, original human language that flowed of necessity from the nature of man's creation, [the language] that God had prepared for man, and that Adam and Eve understood and spoke as soon as they attained consciousness as human beings.

This attaining consciousness was not a process they went through. They were suddenly awake with clear lucidity, and it was in this lucidity that they could think and speak and understand, as if they possessed the fullness of their instinct. It is exactly instinct that possesses the curious [quality] of manifesting life without any training school, suddenly with perfect clarity. Measure the angles and lines of the honeycomb in the beehive and you will see that they never deviate, that they are always accurate, as accurate as the angles and curves of the spider web, without the bee or spider ever having had to weary their budding little brains with learning angles and lines or with acquiring technical skills. God *causes* the small animals to *do* all this accurately and precisely, guided only by instinct.

Man has no capacity on this instinctive level. Granted, man has instinctive traits, and we see that this instinctive aspect is sometimes very prominent in people with artistic talent, but in humans all this has a very different basis. Our *nature* is not instinctive. Rather, it is our nature to come from nothing to something by learning, by copying, by imitating, by experience, and by force of habit. But in Adam at his creation, on the other hand, there was not the tottering and unsure appearance of a gradually emerging life, but rather the instinctive [use] of what was immediately available. He spoke and understood without learning and without repeating, which we can do only as the fruit of practice and habituation. Had we been able to converse with Adam, we would definitely have used many concepts and words that were foreign to him, but apart from that, we would have received not the least impression of a defective development. Rather, a certain feeling of inferiority would have overtaken us such as we sometimes experience when, having shaken off the dust of our bookish learning, we come to speak with a truly wise and sensible man from among ordinary folk.

We even emphasize "wise and sensible." There are people whose mouth resembles a fountain of words and who, without very much thinking, sometimes even with almost no thought at all, let whole series of well-turned phrases fall from their lips without any effort. The French call these kinds of people *moulins à parole*, "word mills" [or "chatterboxes"]. But this is not how we must conceive of Adam's use of language. The thought, if it is sound, must be the soul of the word, and the word is the incarnation of the thought. Words without thought are like the dead, shriveled snake skin from which the living snake has crawled. That such hollowness can be found in people is at present a consequence of sin, even as it reflects a lack of harmony when someone who thinks profoundly cannot find words for his thoughts.

Neither the one nor the other is conceivable in Adam, who had come from the hand of the Creator as a flawless product without spot or wrinkle, entirely unblemished. Harmony prevailed in him. The word was there to incarnate the thought, and the thought to animate the word. And in the words that came to him he grasped the spirit of the thought that sought expression in them. It is self-evident that at this point, there was no elaborate, fully developed treasury of thoughts [expressed] in words. Again and again thoughts had to arise for the first time and be expressed in words that had never yet come across his lips. But that which had not yet been worked out [in specifics] was nevertheless definitely present, present at any given moment to render precisely the service needed.

At this point we are not settling the matter as to whether the *images* rather than the *concepts* operated within his consciousness. Much is certainly to be said for the former. But we must never imagine that Adam had no comprehension and could only gradually form his first naïve concepts. Whoever holds this simply cannot accept the paradise narrative, for in this narrative numerous concepts appear, used in a very precise manner. There are certainly concepts of simple things and of composite things that Adam could not have, because these things would present themselves to him only later. It would have been ballast for him to have possessed them already then. What truly mattered here was that he had at his disposal those notions and concepts that were indispensable in his world at that point, and these he undoubtedly possessed. This should not surprise anyone.

If God created in us the marvelous capability to gradually form concepts, to combine those concepts, and to reach conclusions based on those
combined concepts, then both that capacity and the functioning of that
capacity within us have come from him, and there is no conceivable reason why that same God who achieves this result in us by more gradual
practice, cannot have put that same result in Adam solely by virtue of the
divine act of creation. Only in this way do we maintain the full reality of
what is reported to us from paradise. And we do not properly understand
the ordinance of God that lends the *tree of conscience* its significance if we
construe it as having been formulated later for the first time by Moses or
by whomever, but we must view it as actually having come from God in
paradise, in language audible to and eminently understood by Adam.

# CHAPTER TWENTY-FIVE

# THE PROBATIONARY COMMAND

*He said, "Who told you that you were naked? Have you eaten of the tree of which I commanded you not to eat?"*

GENESIS 3:11

§ 1    Our brief excursus about *language* in paradise served to restore faith in what was spoken by Adam and Eve in paradise. In the days of our forefathers all this was accepted as real in the full sense, but without reflecting on the way in which this speaking in paradise should be understood. Later, people came to think that the language ostensibly spoken in paradise was actually more an embodiment of later thoughts, thus in fact destroying the credibility of this narrative. Now for the first time, the church of Christ comes to this higher view that she fully realizes both what language in paradise was, and that this does not undermine the narrative but rather confirms it and accepts its truth.

If from this perspective we now take a closer look at what was discussed in paradise, then it immediately follows that the first human, when he heard the words addressed to him, must have thought something distinct and specific. That one tree was set apart for him from all trees in paradise as a tree that was linked with the knowledge of good and evil. He was forbidden to eat from that tree. And he was told that transgression of this command would mean that "in the day that you eat of it you shall surely die" [Gen 2:17]. Such an ordinance would, of course, have no meaning for a half-wit man-child or child-man, as many people imagine Adam to have been. A parent may tell an eighteen-month-old child about a plate with beautiful and tempting sweets, "Don't taste this marzipan, because eating it will bring you death," but it would have no effect. The innocent toddler would not understand it. And if the sweets did indeed contain strong poison, and the child ate of it anyway and died, then the child would not have committed *suicide*, but that reckless father or mother would be guilty of *infanticide* and could even be prosecuted by the civil judge.

Along the same lines, we falsify the portrait of the fall if we assume that Adam and Eve did not have a clear understanding of the probationary command and the threat connected with it. If they did not clearly understand the content of the probationary command, nor rightly understand what God meant by "dying," then guilt for the fall largely disappears, and this guilt is then to no small extent placed on God for jeopardizing his creatures by subjecting them to a test to which they morally should not be subjected. Then this whole portrait becomes a fantasy game. It is not fraught with any seriousness. And for a human being who has learned to think and to penetrate to the core of things, at least, it then becomes utterly *impossible* to deduce the guilt of his own heart and the eternal doom of his loved ones from what happened with the eating from the tree of conscience. The gravity returns, and the reality of what happened back then grips our heart, only when we know and realize that Adam and Eve understood the language that was spoken at least as clearly as we understand it, and we realize that when they heard the probationary command and the warning attached to it, they fully understood the Spirit's meaning and the meaning of God's ordinance.

We thus start from the notion that by virtue of his natural contact with the moral world order, Adam knew what was good and what was evil, and similarly by virtue of the life created in him, he knew what death was and what dying was—not as a memorized lesson but through the natural functioning of his consciousness. What happened with the animals and the creation of Eve sheds light on this for us.

§ 2

God placed nothing in the hands of Adam that even remotely resembled an academic text on zoology. He received no instruction either about their division into species, or about their nature and propensities, or about their mutual relationships and way of life. Nor did he know them from the past, because they appeared before him for the first time, and only then did he see them. And yet, no matter how unfamiliar he seemed to be with respect to these creatures, it appeared immediately that they were *not* unfamiliar to him, that he knew them much better than any zoology professor today, and that he grasped the nature of their being in its totality so excellently that naming their names was for him a matter of course. This can be explained only on the basis of *life contact*, that is, by the direct impact of life on the consciousness.

The same phenomenon manifests itself in the appearance of Eve. God brings Eve to Adam, and without further instruction, Adam immediately understands what this new being in paradise means. This is flesh of his own flesh, bone of his own bone. *Not* a man, and yet *from* the man and *for* the man and therefore he called her wo-man. And then he immediately perceives the whole matter of marriage and family, as yet without shame, in clear and innocent holiness before God.

For this reason we must not simply gloss over such facts; rather, we must look at them with intense concentration, and in this way clearly understand how differently human consciousness worked then compared with today. Now everything in and around us is darkened, but back then our human consciousness shone in the full, clear light. Man had been created in God's image, and thus in human measure and human form, God mirrored his own knowledge in man's consciousness. Man knew nothing by way of study, and even less from within himself. Neither did nature as such teach him. All his knowledge in which he had been created was light from God that glowed in the mirror of his consciousness.

§ 3    It must have been this way with his knowledge of good and evil as well, and with his knowledge of dying. If we had wanted to give Adam an examination about morality, he would have failed it. Or if we had asked him questions about biology or life skills, he would not have answered us. But in both respects his immediate awareness nevertheless functioned impeccably. So too it happens that we occasionally encounter among children who are shabbily clothed and neglected in almost every respect a boy or a girl with such perfect pitch that they immediately detect every wrong note and even experience that with a degree of pain. But when you ask that same boy or girl the names of notes or scales, they would look at you in surprise and not understand you.

In this sense Adam and Eve were also aware that there was something beautiful, good, and marvelous toward which their whole soul pressed them, and that conversely there was a pull, a tow, a force and energy they had to stay far from. The law of their God was written in their heart, not as a tacked-on list of commandments but as a fine-tuned, moral hearing of the notes vibrating in God's world order. An urge toward the holy and good is unthinkable apart from fleeing from what opposes it. There is no pole of goodness without a pole of evil opposed to it. To imagine the first humans as still being color blind in the moral realm cannot be squared with their having been created in the image of God. It is impossible to exist as a moral being and as an adult with clear awareness without knowing the contrast between good and evil, that is, between what must be sought and what must be shunned. A magnetic attraction emanates from the moral world order itself, which attracts and moves every moral creature.

It is less easy to imagine what Adam and Eve must have thought when they heard the words *death* and *die*. Nevertheless, not every trace is absent here either. But keep in mind that Adam came into existence suddenly from nothing, and that he consciously experienced this coming into being. This is something that happens to none of us. We come into being without knowing it. And only after we have been around for months and exist for more than a year, those very first, very faint impressions later take hold in us that, when we think back to the past, make us realize at most that we existed already back then. For us, therefore, there is no transition, no moment concerning which we know: at that moment I was, and before that moment I was not. In Adam, by contrast, this took place suddenly, completely and with full clarity. One moment he *was* not and did not yet think, and behold, the next moment he *is*, and he feels and knows that he is, with his whole being and with all that goes on inside him.

Adam therefore experienced the transition from *not being* to *being*, he experienced becoming aware of coming into existence, he experienced the first transition from *not-living* to *living*, and he did so neither as someone dreaming or drowsy, but in clear, perfect sober-mindedness. He felt how he came from God's hand. He *felt*, if we may express it so, himself being created, *felt* how he came to life. The contrast between first *not being* and then *being* was therefore not alien to him, but permeated his whole awareness and his whole being. And in this way it is not at all incomprehensible that the idea about how this life could be undone rose clearly before him. We lack any awareness of dying until now and then, through observation or stories of others, we come into contact with the deathbed and the grave, but for Adam this was entirely different. He knew death from the other side, because he had consciously entered *life* out of nonbeing.

We therefore totally reject the notion that Adam would have awakened to a moral self-awareness only through eating from the fruit of the tree, and that up to that evil moment he would have been a moral simpleton or dreamer. It is not so that there was darkness before the fall and clarity only after the fall. Rather the reverse: sin brought darkness, whereas *before* the fall there was clarity of insight. We therefore do not dispute that sin brought an "opening of the eyes" and that therefore something was known of sin that they did *not* know before. This is clearly stated, and we do not tamper with it, but we will return to this point later. What we must understand beforehand is that, when God gave him the probationary command, Adam was in no way a moral dimwit, but to the contrary, clearly bore the law of God in his heart, and bore in his soul the awareness of the contrast between what corresponded with that law and what deviated from that law.

§ 4    What does the probationary command do? Does it place before Adam the choice of keeping or not keeping one of the commandments God's law imposed on him? Certainly not. The probationary command did not embody a demand that flowed from the moral world order, but was rather an entirely arbitrary ordinance based on nothing but the sovereign determination of God's will. We cannot deduce from any one of the Ten Commandments that there must in the literal sense be a tree somewhere in our environment from which we must not eat. The law written in the heart could never have revealed this probationary command. Had this probationary command not been given to Adam in so many words, entirely mechanically, then he would never have known it nor known of it.

This probationary command as such therefore stands entirely *outside* the moral world order, falls *outside* the law of God, and the eating or not eating of the tree was as such morally indifferent. We must never lose sight of this entirely unique character of the probationary command, else we will fail to see its significance. Then we would not understand how its *strict* binding nature lies precisely in the *triviality* of the command. What mattered was not that tree, nor that fruit, but only that God presses upon man his absolutely sovereign will and forbids him something *by virtue of that sovereignty*.

What then is the great issue lying behind this? You can do what is good *for the sake of the good*, or you can do what is good *for the sake of God*. Everything you do because it agrees with the better instincts of your heart, you do *not* do because of God, but because you yourself feel and confess that it is good and in accord with the moral world order. You then follow the call of your own ideal, the urging of your own heart, the involvement of the moral law of life within your own heart. This position is the position of the unbelieving world, not the position of faith. We reach the position of faith only when, apart from any judgment of our own, we do what we do *because God wants it thus*. Only then does the *religious* life intertwine with the *moral* life, and does the worship of God through his image on earth celebrate its complete triumph. Doing what is good *for the sake of the good*, without taking God into consideration, is moral self-sufficiency, something not only able to be coupled with a very unbelieving heart, but also something that in fact ultimately murders all faith within the soul. So if Adam had continued entirely to follow the good *for the sake of the good*, because that good drew him and comported with the inner exhortation and sense of his heart, then he would have been a lover of virtue but of such a kind that he would have denied the God of his life in whose image he had been created.

And yet there was something in his being created in God's image that engendered precisely that danger of such a self-sufficient development. Because he had been created in God's image, it *could* not be otherwise than that he *had* to feel himself in conformity with God's law in his heart, he *had* to agree with that law, he *could* do nothing else than want that law, and he *had* to incline himself completely toward accomplishing the good of that law because it captivated him and appealed to him.

Leaving God out of consideration, we would even have to say that there was a certain recipe for disaster here. If Adam had brought into the world a measure of disinclination toward God's law in his heart, even if only on one point, then it could have appeared from this one point whether he would nevertheless obey God's will, even if the inclination of his own heart went against it. But that is precisely what could *not* be. His heart agreed on *all* points with the law of God. And it was therefore impossible and inconceivable that it could appear from any single component or element of the law whether he fulfilled it *for the sake of God's will* or because of the *good* it contained. To reach a moral decision there had to come one moment of contradiction between *God* and the *good*, and it had to appear from that whether Adam chose the good for God's sake or for the good itself. But this contradiction *could* not exist in the moral law and *could* not arise from within Adam himself by virtue of the original righteousness—*that* contradiction is implicit in the probationary command.

A command whose content does *not* speak to Adam's heart, that as commandment found *no* point of attraction with his inner awareness, and to whose fulfillment nothing could force or move him other than the sober, clear, unconditional obedience to the word of his God *because of that word*.

The struggle here was the same we encounter again and again in the small child or the soldier. You command or prohibit something for your small child, and the child wants to obey, provided that you first explain *why* it has to be this way and no other. If you do that, and you convince the child, then the child will act according to your command, but not because you commanded the child but because the child himself now views the matter in this way. At that point, in fact, both your command and the child's obedience are set aside, and what remains is your child acting according to his own moral insight. This is considered to be very good, but you have in fact undermined the foundation of all child-rearing.

Ask the great generals where the strength resides to which they owed their victories: They commanded, their soldiers obeyed. Even as the centurion in the Gospels says, "I say to one, 'Go,' and he goes; and to another, 'Come,' and he comes" [Matt 8:9]. On that principle rests all military discipline and military strength. But if the soldier says, "I will follow, but show me first that this will lead to good results," then the discipline is gone and the strength of the army is broken. And this is precisely how it stands with us vis-à-vis God. *We* are those children and *we* are those soldiers, and not our insight into the good, but the fact *that God commands* must be the impulse that moves us to devotion to our duty. *God wills it*, and that will of God is the end of all contradiction, without a *why* being tolerated.

§ 5     *Two* things had to be united in man, therefore. *First*, because he was created in God's image, his own moral awareness had to be in perfect and complete agreement with the law of God, and he had to do the good from a delight in the good. But *second*, this whole moral development had to be made dependent on the motivation *for God's sake*, and thus receive the stamp of obedience and display the nobility of *faith*. *This* then is what the probationary command had in view and what it was wholly designed for. Whether to eat from the tree or not was as such a matter of complete *indifference* to Adam. Morally there was nothing against eating from the tree, and conversely a certain stimulus could be exerted on him by the tree in order to make eating of the tree *desirable*. Here is therefore a command, an ordinance of God, not supported by any moral insight and therefore based solely on the fact *that God instituted it thus*. This moves the battle immediately from the *moral* to the *religious* sphere, from God's *law* to *faith*, from personal *insight* to *submission* to him in whose image Adam was created. Had Adam triumphed in this, then he would forthwith have come to the decision in his heart that his bond with the good was not about that good as such but *about God's will*. But now that he had gone against this probationary command, it had become clear that he sought the good *not* because of God but because of the good itself, and thereby had denied God in his heart and had elevated his own concept of virtue to his god. This is why the fall was absolute. It was a cutting through of only one link, but that link could not be cut without the whole chain collapsing. The right, perfect standing before God had been surrendered, and therefore the image could not but become warped. It was like the sundial that is removed from its place. Once removed from that location, it no longer shows the time.

We now also sense why the probationary command had to be so *insignificant* as to its content. It has been called recklessness, a mocking of man, to make a world and an eternity dependent on a peach or an apple. Wrongly so. If the probationary command had imposed a heavy, difficult task on Adam, his own moral awareness would have entered into it and he would have acted on the basis of his own moral insight and not in the blind obedience of faith. It was precisely to render Adam's moral insight inoperative this once, and to concentrate the whole focus of the soul on the obedience of faith, that the matter had to be so trivial, so insignificant, so trifling. A military leader who wants to test his soldier whether he obeys *strictly* has to test him on the basis of an order that has no material content, an order that in fact seems to him to be a mockery. At issue was the battle that thereafter continued through all the ages and still continues, whether God is who he is *because of the law* or the law is what it is *because of God*. If we say, "There is an eternal law, and God was bound to that law, and that is therefore why he gave us his moral law"—then God has in fact been denied, virtue is placed above God as an independent ideal, and your devotion to duty becomes self-sufficiency, a satisfying of your own insight, instead of a childlike submission to God. If, on the other hand, the law is binding solely *because God gave it to us*, and if our inner sympathy for that law is solely the inward fruit of the Holy Spirit, then it wouldn't matter *what* was commanded in the probationary command. The more insignificant the matter, the more decisively and certainly it would be clear whether obedience was because of God's will.

# CHAPTER TWENTY-SIX

# BEING LIKE GOD

*You are of your father the devil, and your will is to do your father's desires. He was a murderer from the beginning, and does not stand in the truth, because there is no truth in him. When he lies, he speaks out of his own character, for he is a liar and the father of lies.*

JOHN 8:44

§ 1     Before we come to the temptation in paradise itself, it is good to summarize the conclusions of what we have found up to this point. The first man was called into being on this earth through a single, direct act of God's omnipotence, in a single moment in time, in fully adult dimensions. He stood midway between God and the world. In that world the animals were created with man in mind, before man yet existed, prefiguring man's external form and manner of existence. Similarly, plants were created with the animals in mind, and untilled nature with the plants in mind. And thus there was a chain that linked all parts of creation and culminated in man. And while man thus epitomized the whole world, what made him essentially human was that in this human being God could and did mirror himself. Thus man stood in the Garden of Eden simultaneously as the epitome of creation and as the image-bearer of the Creator. As such his body was unimpaired and whole, and in terms of his spiritual existence, he was perfectly *wise* in mind, perfectly holy in moral nature, and perfectly righteous in his standing before God. This was his "state of righteousness" or "original righteousness," which was not added as a new component to his nature but was inherent in his nature.[1] Nevertheless, the flawlessness of this adult physical and spiritual existence did not in the least preclude the progression toward the ultimate goal that could be reached only through moral battle and would have brought him to eternal life, in the radiance of perfected glory. This placed him in the relationship that we call the covenant of works. If in this further development he also maintained the pure state in which he was placed at his creation, his life would have been elevated to eternal life. But if he fell away from this right state before God, then his life, no matter how indestructible it might be in terms of existence, would sink down to the depth of death.

And this could not be decided without the probationary command of the temptation. As holy as Adam was, he could not accomplish a small piece of the law that was imprinted on his heart without his heart addressing that law and leading to a doing of the good because it was good; whereas the true good is not accomplished until it is done because God wills it. Whether Adam would choose in this God-pleasing manner could become apparent only on the basis of a command that was not imprinted on his heart but came to him unwittingly as an apparently arbitrary command. This command and its correct meaning he could understand because in him language was not an initial stammering of sounds, but a sufficient composition of words adequate for the expression of his thoughts. And thus he stood in paradise, with God, by faith, as a man in companionship with his friend, not yet knowing the terror of conscience and therefore not yet knowing shame.

Briefly summarized, this is the result of our inquiry up to this point. Now we come to the temptation that led first Eve, and through her Adam, to transgressing the probationary command. Reading and rereading of the first three chapters of Genesis leaves no other impression than that the transgression would never have occurred without that temptation. This flowed directly from the original righteousness. In the state of rectitude matters would not have reached a struggle apart from temptation, and therefore would have resulted no more in a fall than a victory. Jesus

§ 2

---

1. Kuyper is alluding here to a Roman Catholic theology of the relationship between nature and grace in an effort to distinguish his own Reformed position from that theology. Kuyper assumes that in the Catholic theology of nature and grace, as he understands it, the order of grace is a mere *addition* to the order of nature. See *CG* 1.18.1–2, for the context of Kuyper's claim here about the relationship of nature and grace.

states this emphatically: Adam did not kill himself, but Satan was a murderer from the beginning [John 8:44].

In the meantime we read nothing about Satan in Genesis 2. The temptation comes by means of an animal. This really catches our attention. In paradise man and animal formed the only direct contrast between two forces, and man was explicitly given power and rule over the animals. And what is even more striking is that in his linguistic world, man had exercised his supremacy over the animals for the first time by assigning a place to each animal by giving as speaking ruler a name to the mute beast. The one who gives the name rules, and the animal that could only low or roar or neigh bore in this the mark of its lower, lesser position.

But listen, now suddenly language is coming to Eve, speech, an expression of thoughts in words, coming to her from an animal. The serpent addresses Eve. This speaking of the serpent fell outside the order of creation. According to that order God speaks and man speaks, but animals, including the serpent, do not have this gift of speech. Everyone knows that it is not therefore impossible for animals to mechanically utter understandable sounds. This can be heard in some birds, sometimes shrill and loud. The Mosaic narrative tells us this with regard to Balaam's donkey. This is not at all surprising if breath, throat, teeth, and lips are all present. But an animal cannot speak for a very different reason, namely, that it does not have a consciousness with which to be able to form thoughts, so it cannot acquire language. True, the animal does have expression of will or sensation, and it has been pointed out entirely correctly that through these sounds animals do communicate among themselves or even to humans, but because the thought is not linked to a word, no language in the proper sense is born. The ridiculous experiments of Professor Garner[2] who, while locked in a cage, wanted to study the language of apes has not refuted but confirmed this fact. But the matter changes drastically when the animal can be used as an instrument by a higher being, and when this

---

2. The source text here refers to "Professor Gordner," but it is likely that Kuyper is referring instead to Richard Lynch Garner (1848–1920), a self-taught American zoologist who studied the behavior and sounds of primates and theorized about the evolutionary development of language. An account in 1892 of his plans "to live in a cage" identify him as "Prof. R. L. Gardner, of Virginia." See "Notes," *Nature* 46, no. 1193 (September 8, 1892): 451. Kuyper is probably referring to experiments later recounted in R. L. Garner, *Apes and Monkeys: Their Life and Language* (London: Ginn & Co., 1900).

higher being makes use of the breathing, the throat, the tongue, the lips, the teeth, in short, of the animal's organs to accomplish through that animal what the animal itself cannot do.

Hypnotism has brought to light surprising phenomena in this area, even among humans. Until now we assumed that our speech organs could serve only ourselves, and that our language could be the vehicle for only our own thoughts. But now we know also practically that one individual can acquire such power over another that the strong one forces the weak one to serve him with his mouth and to speak, not what the weak one himself wills, but what the stronger one thinks, intends, and wills. Here someone penetrates the soul of another human being to the point where the nerves of the speech organs are activated, such that he is now speaking through someone else's mouth. Since humans can do this, it does not surprise us in the least that God could also seize a prophet in such a way that the prophet spoke, not what he, but what God thought. But what keeps amazing us is that also in the case of animals a similar phenomenon occurs, especially where power over the animal is exercised not by another animal, nor by a human, but in the case of Balaam's donkey, by God, and in the case of the serpent in paradise, by Satan.

The surprising element in that phenomenon must therefore also have stirred Eve['s curiosity]. She knew that animals did not speak—to the contrary, the sign of man's dominion over the animals lay in speech. The fact that a speaking animal made itself heard must have gotten her attention. It was immediately apparent to her that it was not God who thus used the animal, for what the serpent said went against God. She also knew that another, alien power was addressing her in these serpent sounds, and she discerned also that this power was inimical to God and connected with the animal side of creation. God had given man the duty not only to work but also to keep the garden (Gen 2:15). *Keeping* assumes that there was a power against which paradise had to be protected. Man also knew that there was a power of destruction. Until now he had not discerned anything of that power. But now that alien, mysterious, hitherto unknown power manifested itself. It spoke through the animal. It used the serpent as instrument. And there is therefore no doubt that Eve immediately realized that she was not dealing here with that serpent as an ordinary animal, but with that serpent as a possessed animal.

We will not busy ourselves with the question as to which demonic power it was, how it came into being, and how it functions. This has been covered adequately in the series of articles on the angels.[3] Nor do we have to argue about the question whether it was truly Satan who used the serpent like a phonograph; the clear statement of Jesus in John 8:44 places this beyond doubt. The choice of the serpent rather than another animal must be explained symbolically. The only thing remaining is to note how the serpent in paradise was the instrumental animal through which Satan persuaded the woman, and how people today, especially in India but also elsewhere, can, merely by means of the sound of tones, put a spell on the mightiest of snakes, charm them, coax them, and render them utterly powerless. The real snake charmer still makes the most enraged snake totally defenseless merely by means of sounds, and winds them like a cable around his body.

But even if [in this phenomenon] there is no connection with what happened in paradise, what happened [in paradise] must be understood, not allegorically, not as an inner experience in Eve's soul, but literally, as it stands written. Eve encountered language expressed in words. That language came from Satan and went through the serpent. That language was animated, it was used in an argument and distinct words were used in the dispute. It was a real temptation, as Jesus experienced near the Jordan and through which Jesus struggled victoriously. Only there was this difference: Satan attacked Jesus without an animal as intermediary, whereas Eve was tempted by Satan not directly but indirectly, with the animal standing between them as the only force that the newly created humans knew as yet in contradistinction to themselves.

§ 3 We come now to the temptation itself, and here we must first consider a question that hitherto has been neglected far too much, namely, what would have happened if Eve had *not* succumbed. In that case, would the knowledge of good and evil for the first human couple have remained as it was before the probationary command? Would no change have taken place in man's inner existence? And would man therefore, assuming that he had not succumbed, have remained who he was and have lived on as if he had never received a probationary command? Superficially this would indeed seem to be the case. The voice that came to Eve said, "*When* you eat of it your eyes will be opened, and you will be like God, knowing good and

---

3. Published in book form as Abraham Kuyper, *De Engelen Gods* (Amsterdam: Höveker & Wormser, 1902).

evil" [Gen 3:5]. Consequently, for this seems to follow from it, if they did not eat from it they would forgo this knowledge.

It is difficult to deny that this statement of the serpent contains a measure of truth, if we pay attention to two things. In the first place, it says that when they had sinned, their eyes were opened, which implies again that otherwise their eyes would have remained closed. And secondly, that after the fall God in his triune being says, "The man has become like one of us in knowing good and evil" [Gen 3:22], words that have been interpreted by Calvin and many after him in a mocking sense: "That foolish man imagines that he is like one of us and knows good and evil."[4] But as we noted earlier, this interpretation is untenable, for such a mocking statement would not have contained the grounds for expelling man from paradise, let alone for placing a cherub with a flaming sword at the entrance to paradise.[5] We must therefore definitely pay attention to what Satan says: "Then you will know good and evil"; to what Scripture says: "Then their eyes were opened"; and to what the Lord says: "Man has come to know good and evil." We must not view it as a dishonest fabrication on Satan's part that the fall disclosed a new world of knowledge to Adam and that such knowledge was a knowledge of good and evil. The results show that it contained truth. And the word of the Lord has confirmed it. From which, then, it also follows directly that, had he not fallen, man would have remained a stranger to that world of knowledge that opened up to him because of sin, and would not have come to know good and evil in this way.

But it definitely does not follow that he would have had less knowledge if he had not transgressed the probationary command. To the contrary, at that point a higher knowledge of good and evil would have come to him, but in a different manner, in a different form, in a way that did not lead to death, but to life. The difference between these two forms of the knowledge of good and evil, that is, between the sinful, deadly form in which it now came to Adam and the holy form that elevates life, the form that would otherwise have become his portion, can be explained only on the basis of the two statements of the Lord: (1) that this sinful form brought death, and (2) that now it was a knowledge as it existed in God and to which only God was entitled. What then is the fundamental difference between the

---

4. See CCS, ad loc. Gen 3:22, in which Calvin identifies this statement as "an ironical reproof, by which God would not only prick the heart of man, but pierce it through and through."

5. See the discussion of the tree of life in CG 1.16.8, and in 1.17, "The Tree of Life."

knowledge of good and evil as it exists in God and that derived knowledge of good and evil that belongs to man? This: that God himself creates light and darkness, God himself determines what is good and what is consequently evil, and therefore God has the moral criterion for good and evil within himself, he determines it himself, and he maintains it vis-à-vis all creatures. This is one side, whereas conversely for man, as a creature, the knowledge of good and evil neither can nor must be other than that he himself does not set the boundaries of the distinction between light and darkness, between good and evil, but accepts the boundary from God, as established by God as Creator.

From this follows, therefore, that for man all knowledge of good and evil which he does not accept as having been established by God but establishes himself, is sinful and godless, and that conversely, only such knowledge of good and evil befits man, and is true and holy, which he derives from God, accepts from God, and lets himself be given by God. If man does not want the latter kind of knowledge, but wants a knowledge of good and evil as can exist only in God, then precisely that is what constitutes his rebellion, his abandoning his position as creature, and placing himself in God's seat. The latter, of course, is not true in essence but only in his imagination. In his mind, in his false reality, it is so. He then feels as if he knows good and evil as God knows it. His eyes are opened upon a world that, as the world of lies, should have remained closed to him forever. The outcome is that he fantasizes that he has become like God, and now God has to say, "Man has become like one of us."

§ 4     The more closely we analyze the paradise narrative, the more clearly we see that we must take everything literally as it stands written. Eve and Adam, after her, did not eat from the tree because they judged that this was evil, but because they placed their *own judgment* over against that of God and deluded themselves and imagined that eating from the tree would open up their way to higher well-being. God had told them, "That is good and that is evil," but instead of accepting this stipulation from God in faith and obedience, and judging for themselves that it was so because God had said it, they now dared to place another opinion, another judgment, over against it, thus determining themselves what was good and what was evil, and to do this in a directly opposite sense.

Thus they robbed the Creator of heaven and earth of the right that belongs to God alone to determine what is good and what is evil, and appropriated it for themselves. They made so bold as to do themselves what is only God's to do, to appoint themselves, and to behave as if they were invested with a power that belongs to God alone. Doing this and acting accordingly: that was their sin. Had they, on the other hand, not done this, and faced with the temptation to draw the line between good and evil themselves, had they refused to do this with clear consciousness, rejected this, and not have willed and not done this, then they would have attained a higher insight from that moment on, in order now to do everything not only according to the instinct of their creation, but also knowingly honoring God as King, Lawgiver, and Judge. In this way they would also have entered into the highest fellowship with the truly moral life. They then would have done the good, not only because it was thus imprinted on their heart, but now also knowing that it was so, and why. Their moral existence would have fused with their religious existence into a higher harmony, and eternal life would have been bestowed precisely in this.

But now, instead of that blessed experience of high, holy harmony, the breach of conscience entered into them. For what is conscience in us other than the manifestation of the majesty of the Lord with which he, as God Almighty, maintains the true moral world order over against the dishonest conceit of the sinner? It is a manifestation that could not exist as long as, before the fall, the moral life was still only instinctive and emerged spontaneously from the participation of the human heart. [This manifestation] will fall silent again when the breach has been removed from our heart forever. But it had to come as soon as, and must continue as long as, the lie that exists in the moral realm persists in our heart, and when God reacts within us in a holy manner against us with his truth. §5

We cannot develop in further detail how the sinner tries to weaken the expression of conscience and silence it, and finally hardens and stifles his conscience. It would take us too far afield. We are satisfied if it is understood and conceded that the conscience does not function as long as no breach has been struck in our heart, as long as no two judgments struggle with one another at the base of our being and two worlds stand in opposition to one another for us. This first manifestation of conscience is clearly indicated by what Scripture reports, that immediately "the eyes of both were opened, and they knew that they were naked" [Gen 3:7]. Someone who has gotten over sin and has silenced his conscience does not feel shame. Look at the impudent woman who has shaken off all shame and who is neither bothered by nor takes offence at nakedness. For the sinner it is a holy sensation to feel shame arise with regard to his nakedness, a manifestation of conscience, a working of God in the heart. They did not discern their nakedness before their fall, even though they stood just as naked before one another. At this point this shaming goad of their conscience could not yet have an effect on them.

We will explain later how we must understand this; for now, let us point out merely that this manifestation of conscience immediately proceeded still further. It is the conscience that accuses one before God, and accordingly we see Adam and Eve not only covering their loins, but also fleeing into the heaviest stand of trees as God approaches. This shows most clearly that the first shame that arose in Adam and Eve was definitely not some prudish feeling about standing before one another as man and woman, but much more strongly, a shame about their whole being and their whole appearance. They felt themselves judged even before the judgment was pronounced, languishing in their wrong even as before they had stood proudly and royally in their right status before God. And that same Adam who, naked as he was, had come from the hand of his Creator and had communed with his God and had spoken with his God, now flees—flees and hides himself from this same God because he now feels naked and uncovered in his shame and disgrace. They cover themselves from one another with vine leaves sewn together, but their conscience declares that this covering and protection does not help before God. His eye penetrates through the vine leaf to their dismay. And therefore, with their aprons on, they flee from his searching eye. That was the goad of conscience before God.

# CHAPTER TWENTY-SEVEN

# KNOWING AS MAKING ONE'S OWN ASSESSMENT

*Let us choose what is right; let us know among ourselves what is good.*

JOB 34:4

Now the question must be answered regarding the actual meaning of the words that are in many respects so mysterious: "In the day that you eat of [the tree of the knowledge of good and evil] you shall surely die" [Gen 2:17]. It is our firm conviction that the common interpretation of these words is *not* the correct one, and we therefore ask our readers to pay special attention to what will be said about this.

§ 1

Let us begin with the words "knowledge of good and evil." This expression is commonly interpreted in the sense that by sinning, Adam and Eve acquired for the first time an experiential knowledge of evil. The commentators on the authorized Dutch Bible also interpret it in this way. In the Latin of those days, in which the theologians back then discussed all questions of this nature, this was called *cognitio experimentalis*.[1] They did not deny, therefore, that even before the fall, Adam knew the distinction between good and evil. Only, they maintained, it is something quite different to have heard about drunkenness than to have been drunk oneself. The first knowledge is derived knowledge, only the latter is experiential knowledge. The infantile notion that before the fall, Adam would have been morally naïve and was awakened to *moral* awareness for the first time through the fall, is a later invention. The great theologians of the church never recommended such an absurdity. To them, the new dimension that Adam would receive was the *experiential* aspect. An unmarried woman knows about the joys of motherhood, but only someone who has become a mother herself knows that joy in the deep sense of the word. This explanation as such had great appeal, and this author also went along with it for many years, since it is fitting that one not begin by rejecting the work of one's predecessors but by associating oneself with it. But gradually objections arose that were too strong and that finally led to abandoning this interpretation as inadequate.

Two objections were primary. After the fall, God the Lord says, "The man has become *like one of us* in knowing good and evil" [Gen 3:22]. Here it is clearly stated that the new knowledge of good and evil that accrued to man by eating from the tree is a knowledge of the same kind as the knowledge of good and evil which *God himself* possesses. No matter how you look at these words, you cannot eliminate that meaning from them. Meanwhile it is certain that God himself cannot have experiential knowledge of good and evil. If anything is certain, it is this. Indeed, God cannot even have experiential knowledge of the good in that sense, for God gives the law but does not fulfill it. Yet let this be for the moment, and let us focus on the evil. Then all doubt is precluded and everyone agrees that it would not make sense to say, "The man has become like one of us, for now he has experiential knowledge of good and evil." This would be nothing less than sacrilege.

Besides this first objection there is another one that similarly cannot be eliminated. The old interpretation can explain—in its own way—how man gained experiential knowledge of evil, but not how he acquired

---

1. See *CCS*, ad loc. Psalm 66:5, where Calvin writes that "experimental or practical kind of knowledge, if I might so call it, is that which makes the deepest impression." See also the definition in *DLGTT*, s.v. "scientia experimentalis": "*experimental knowledge; knowledge gained inductively from sense experience.*"

experiential knowledge of the good. The fall makes man in his unregenerate nature incapable of all good, whereas conversely before the fall he already possessed experiential knowledge of the good. Even if Adam lived only half a day before the fall, then during that half day he lived in complete conformity with the law of God and therefore did the good and therefore possessed experiential knowledge of the good. This was a knowledge of the good, therefore, that through the fall he did not acquire, but rather lost.

How then could we say, "By eating from the tree you will come to an experiential knowledge of good and evil," if the fact were, to the contrary, that he rather lost this kind of knowledge of the good and only acquired that of evil? The commentators on the authorized Dutch Bible sensed this latter difficulty and therefore said that the knowledge of evil must be understood here in the moral sense, but the knowledge of the good in the sense of eternal good. Adam would experience, so they wrote, "what good he would thereby acquire."[2] But such a bifurcation is not very plausible. No one reading [the text] would think of this possibility. To which we must add that this entire interpretation does not do justice to the tree. After all, Adam would have acquired this experiential knowledge of evil in the case of any sin. Indeed, the first thought of a sinful nature would have given him this. Every sinful thought defiles the heart.

On the basis of these objections, which to us are paramount, we consider that the notion of knowledge as experiential knowledge misses the target, and in order to give constructive rather than destructive criticism, we want to identify another interpretation that appeals more to us and would seem to remove all difficulties much better. Let not those who do not immediately agree with us ring the alarm right away to cry throughout the church that we are setting fire to the church. Let him not shout "Fire!" but let him refute. This is what Reformed theologians always did. §2

Well then, the interpretation we recommend with a measure of confidence starts with the observation that the word *knowledge* occurs in Holy Scripture with a meaning that we lack in our language, one that is the exact opposite of experiential knowledge. Our commentators on the authorized Dutch Bible have noted this themselves at Genesis 18:19. There God says to Abraham, "For I have *known* him, that he may command his

---

2. See SV, ad loc. Gen 2:9, note at *des levens* ("of life").

children and his household after him."[3] The commentators observe here, "I have chosen, prepared, and cared for him as my possession. In this way the word *knowledge* is used in various places." They then refer to Psalm 1:6; Jeremiah 1:5; 24:5; Hosea 13:5; Amos 3:2; John 10:27; and 2 Timothy 2:19. What we note here is therefore nothing new. As we see, the word *knowledge* occurs repeatedly in that sense, even in far more places than the Dutch Bible commentators indicated here.

We especially point to Job 34:4, which reads, "Let us *choose* what is right; let us *know* among ourselves what is good." This verse is so noteworthy for this reason, that here we find two parts of a single verse that both say the same thing but in somewhat different words, as we find frequently in Hebrew poetry. When verse 21 reads, first, "His eyes are on the ways of a man," followed by "he sees all his steps," then exactly the same thing is said twice in different words, which is called parallelism, that is, the running parallel of two series of words. And so it is here. First we read, "Let us *choose* what is *right*," and then "let us *know* among ourselves what is *good*." These two phrases both say the same thing. "Right" is here the same as "good," and also the word "know" is explained here by "choose" or select after evaluation. This is entirely the sense in which the commentators on the authorized Dutch Bible explain at Genesis 18:19 that "I have known him" means "I have chosen him." The Hebrew word does not leave any doubt. *Bachar* is "choose," "select," "elect," and is the same word that is used of the sovereign election of God.

We will not look at the many other places where "knowing" has this meaning [of "choosing"], however instructive this might be. This would detain us too long and would be more suited to a scholarly discourse. But let us be allowed to direct attention to one text, namely, Psalm 1:6. There we read, "The Lord *knows* the way of the righteous." The creators of the rhymed version of the Psalms, who did not grasp these profound words, turned them into "For the Lord *watches* the way of the righteous," and thus took these words in the sense of experiential knowledge, of the

---

3. The SV here uses *gekend* ("known"), which is analogous to the KJV (quoted in the main text here). Later English versions reflect the meaning as rendered by the SV commentators ("I have chosen him," as in the ESV, which includes a footnote that the Hebrew means "known").

knowledge of experience, thereby making Psalm 1:4[4] brutally Remonstrant in their rhymed version. But anyone who understands Scripture, on the other hand, knows very well that these words do not refer to what God experiences and sees of man, but to what he has foreseen of man according to his sovereign pleasure. Furthermore, the verse from Job is so remarkable for our purpose because, similar to the paradise narrative, Job speaks of the knowledge of the good, a reason why it is rather surprising that this verse has been referred to so infrequently in connection with the tree of the knowledge of good and evil. The reader will grant us that this must prompt us to pay attention all the more to the connection between the two passages, and when we do so, it appears that in Job 34:4 knowing good and evil is understood in the sense—quite unusual to us but quite common in Scripture—of choosing what is good and what is evil: determining, deciding, establishing what for me shall be good and what for me shall be evil.

Let us now look at whether or not this entirely different meaning fits with the interpretation of Genesis 2:9 and following. Let us keep clearly in mind that we do not give the word *knowing* a meaning here that is found in Scripture only once, but to the contrary, a meaning that is quite common in Scripture and is not disputed by anyone. God says in Genesis 3:22, after the fall, "The man has become like one of us in knowing good and evil." If we substitute here, "The man has become like one of us, himself *choosing*"—that is, assessing, determining—"what is good and evil," then the sentence flows very well, and is indeed for the first time correctly understood. The distinction between God as Creator and man as moral creature consists precisely therein, that God assesses and determines what is good and what is evil and that man must not do this but must accept it from God. It is therefore a turning away from God and turning to sin when man moves toward becoming like God, wanting to assess and determine like God what shall be good and what shall be evil. That is competing with God himself, doing as man what belongs only to God as God. In Genesis 3:5 Satan says to Eve, "God knows that when you eat of it your eyes will be opened, and you will be like God, knowing"—that is, assessing—"the good and the evil." And thus it was. God knew that man was capable of

---

4.   See *Het Boek der Psalmen, nevens de Gezangen bij de Hervormde Kerk van Nederland in Gebruik* (The Hague: Hendrik Christoffel Gutteling, 1773), 2: "De Heer toch slaat der menschen wegen gade." Psalm 1:6 in the SV is rendered as Psalm 1:4 according to the rhymed version's versification.

trying to rob him of his divine honor. But Satan concluded from this that "out of jealousy God does not want this and thus he keeps you from your happiness," whereas God kept man from doing this precisely because this autonomous morality, that is, such assessing and determining for themselves what is good and evil, would plunge man into ruin.

In Genesis 2:9 we read that God placed that tree of knowledge in the garden, and in verse 17 that he forbade Adam to eat from that tree. In the preceding chapter we have shown how man, as yet without sin, who had God's law written in his heart, assented to all of God's commandments, and thus did all this *good* because it was *good*.[5] And we also showed that, in order to reach the point that he did something not because he himself was in agreement with it but exclusively because God had commanded it to him, he had to have a commandment that fell outside the moral law, a commandment that he had to follow in blind obedience, only because God had imposed it on him. The probationary command of the tree of knowledge confronted Adam with the question that matters here: "Will you want to know"—that is, assess for yourself—"what is good or evil, or will you leave that evaluation to God and obey blindly?" Adam did not follow blindly but decided to evaluate for himself, and came to a conclusion opposite God's conclusion, and as independent evaluator of good and evil, he placed himself over against God and through this he fell away from God. He wanted to stand beside God as a second god, just as Satan had suggested. God and man thus would both independently and sovereignly evaluate what was good and what was evil, and this unlocked all depths of sin. Thus we see exactly how it was this arbitrary probationary command of the tree of knowledge that became the effective means to bring man to the decision whether he wanted to leave to God the knowledge, that is, the assessment of good and evil, or to take it to himself.[6]

---

5. See *CG* 1.26, "Being like God."

6. *Note by the author*: A kind correspondent brought to our attention that the interpretation we offered in a previous article of the words *knowing good and evil* is also indicated in the *Summa Theologica* of Thomas [Aquinas] in these words: "Namely that by his own natural power he might decide what was good, and what was evil for him to do" ("*ut scilicet per virtutem [propriae naturae] determinaret sibi, quid esset bonum, quid malum ad agendum*"; II-II, Q. 163, Art. 2), linking this, as we did, with a false *desire to be like God*. Inordinately. The statement is not exegetically elaborated there, but the notion is being expressed purely and clearly. [Ed. note: The text of this note originally appeared at the end of ch. 28, given this chapter's original

If this view is the correct one, then it fully confirms what we wrote about the tree as the tree of conscience.[7] The conscience begins to function only when two judgments about good and evil come into conflict. One who no longer heeds God's judgment no longer has a functioning conscience. He is left with only his own judgment. Someone who, like Adam before his fall, like Christ on earth, or like the saints in heaven, knows inwardly no other judgment than the judgment of God, also does not know a functioning of conscience. But conversely, that functioning of conscience begins as soon as, and continues as long as, one's own judgment comes into conflict with the judgment of God and must ultimately yield to it. Let us stand firm here.

§ 3

Also among us ever since Amesius[8] there have always been those who advocated the primacy of the will; think only of Cocceius and Lampe.[9] But our sound and pure theologians have always maintained in the past that the will only follows the evaluating mind.[10] However quickly this may happen in us, each sin involves a decision of our intellect that, taking everything into consideration, it is best for us to commit that sin, and we do it because the will follows our intellect. Each sin, therefore, starts from

---

publication in the author's weekly paper *De Heraut* and subsequent interaction with readers. See *CG* 1.14.3n2.]

7. See previous chapter as well as *CG* 1.23.7.

8. William Ames (Latin: Guilielmus Amesius) (1576–1633) was an English Puritan pastor, theologian, and controversialist who later in life served as professor of theology at Leiden. He was especially active as a Reformed opponent of Arminianism and is here identified as a leading advocate of anthropological voluntarism, a view that posits the primacy of the human will over the intellect and is expressed in his *Medulla Sacrae Theologiae* (Franeker: Balk, 1623), or in English translation, *The Marrow of Sacred Divinity* (London: Griffin, 1639).

9. Friedrich Adolf Lampe (1683–1729) was an eminent German theologian of the Reformed Church who introduced into the German church the principles of Johannes Cocceius' covenantal theology. See the entry on Lampe in Robert Benedetto and Donald K. McKim, eds., *Historical Dictionary of the Reformed Churches*, 2nd ed. (Lanham, MD: Scarecrow Press, 2010), 256.

10. This position, which emphasizes the primacy of the intellect rather than the will, is often called *intellectualism*. See *DLGTT*, s.v. "voluntas": "Will is distinct from intellect (*intellectus*, q.v.) in scholastic faculty psychology. The intellect is that which knows objects, the will is that which has an appetite or desire for them. Will and intellect are the two highest spiritual powers. The question immediately arises as to which of the faculties stands prior to the other." As Muller concludes, "The Protestant orthodox frequently state the problem of priority without solving it definitively; they recognize the interrelationship of intellect and will, but focus on the problem of fallen man."

and is based on a judgment in which we evaluate, determine, and decide what is advisable and desirable. At the same time, or [perhaps] afterward, another judgment comes into play, however: the judgment of God. This judgment either approves our own judgment or disapproves it. This is the functioning of conscience in us, precisely as it happened in paradise. No sooner does man sin than the judgment of conscience awakens for the first time, condemning and shaming him, forcing him to hide and conceal himself.

With this we have established a firm foundation for the doctrine of conscience. Conscience is a conflict between two judgments: the judgment of man himself and that of God. And this conflict exists not only where conscience disapproves what God approved, but in a sense also where it approves [what God approved]. For where man, outside of God's determination, begins to decide what is good or what is evil, he already shows through this that he stands in apostasy and sin. Whoever stands in the state of righteousness, or once again is cut off from all sin, does not evaluate first by himself, only then to ask whether his choice agrees with God's choice. But he asks first what God's choice is and knowing that, follows it. This conflict, that expresses itself as a manifestation of conscience, therefore calls forth the shaming of oneself at every difference with God's choice. In that experience or acknowledgement lies the confession of one's own foolishness. We should have started with God's choice, have leaned on it alone, and used it alone as the starting point. The Lord is our Lawgiver, our King, and our Judge. He alone.

§ 4   The preceding shows clearly, in our opinion, how all difficulty disappears with this perspective, and the profound meaning is grasped both of the event and of the words with which it is told us. Knowledge of good and evil means that man himself sovereignly evaluates, determines, and decides what is good and what is evil for him. The test he faces is having to decide once and for all whether he submits blindly to God's evaluation, or wants to exercise a choice of his own over against God, so that thereby he himself may be lawgiver and judge, just like God. Satan urges him to exercise his own evaluation, just like God. After the fall, God sees that man has come to this sin, that he has set himself up as god, knowing for himself, that is, evaluating for himself what was good and what was evil for him. That decision could not have been made with respect to any part of the moral law, but only with regard to a probationary command that required blind obedience. And finally, by wanting to assess for himself, his own judgment came to stand over against the judgment of God, and out of the struggle between those two judgments the activity of conscience emerged.

Thus everything falls into a well-ordered whole, every fact and every word in which the facts are reported to us are explained, and literally no difficulty remains. We must simply keep in mind that when we speak of this independent knowing, that is, assessing independently what is good and evil, we must not think of the discipline of ethics, as if this refers exclusively to an independent assessment of moral good and evil. Even for the conscience, and in the practical judgment of our moral consciousness, that distinction cannot be drawn so sharply. Good and evil mean in the general sense what is good for us and what is evil for us, morally and in its consequences. As the Dutch Bible commentators say about the good: "what good he *lost* through this."[11]

We have only to explain yet the enigmatic words, "*In the day* that you eat of it you shall *surely die*" [Gen 2:17]. This prophecy of judgment was not fulfilled in Adam [in the literal sense], for a reason that will become clear later. In the day of his fall Adam did not die in the sense he was told. Death did indeed creep into him immediately. Not later, but on the day itself. But death is not [fully] fulfilled in him, and if we may assume that Adam was regenerated, converted, enlightened, and glorified, we must similarly acknowledge that Adam himself never suffered, nor will ever suffer, eternal death. We cannot enter into this here but will discuss it later. Now we note only that the expression "You shall surely die" points to the completion of death in the absolute sense. The Hebrew expression is "dying you will die." This [emphatic] construction is used to indicate that an action or function takes place as powerfully as possible, as completely as possible, as drastically as possible, even to its [ultimate] completion.

§ 5

The Dutch Bible commentators also take it in this sense when they say that here a threefold death is in view: (1) physical death with all its antecedent misery; (2) the spiritual death of the soul; and (3) eternal death, which is at once physical and spiritual.[12] Thus they also teach us that "surely die" here means undergoing death in all its breadth, length, and depth, comprehensively and fully, inclusive of everything that is implicit in the notion of death. But precisely for this reason it is important not to allow a wrong notion of death to creep in. As we have seen, it belonged to the

---

11. See SV, ad loc. Gen 2:9, note at *boom der kennis* ("tree of knowledge").
12. See SV, ad loc. Gen 2:17, note at *den dood* ("death").

state of righteousness, not that man could fall into sin and thus be subjected to death, but that man was imperishable, indestructible, ineradicable, which is something entirely different from suffering death. Had man been able to maintain himself in the state of rectitude, he would never have tasted death. Not tasting death belonged to his nature. That he now does die belongs to the depravity of his nature. But the matter is quite different when we ask about his being rather than his nature.

Man's creation cannot be undone when it comes to his being.[13] Now that he exists, he cannot cease to exist. A rational, moral being, once it exists, is imperishable. In Satan there is not a trace of life. In Satan there exists nothing but death. But nevertheless he exists, and his existence cannot be destroyed. Yes, eternal death is eternal only because [the doomed] must eternally bear death without ever perishing. This is denied today in the doctrine of so-called conditional immortality, a doctrine that Scripture does not tolerate. We would [indeed] like for Satan and the doomed angels and the doomed people to be destroyed in a single stroke. Then their suffering would be over. But Scripture testifies that this is not possible. Plants and animals are metabolically destroyed, but a rational, moral being cannot perish precisely because it is and has an *I*. And this is why we do not understand death if we seek it in terms of destruction. Death in us is something quite different: death is a separating, a tearing apart, a pulling asunder of what according to God's creation must be harmoniously united in our person. Think only of our temporal death. Body and soul belong together; but in death they are torn asunder.

---

13. See *CG* 1.18.3n6, and Kuyper's discussion in the text.

# CHAPTER TWENTY-EIGHT

# "YOU SHALL SURELY DIE"

*And when Jeremiah had finished speaking all that the* Lord *had commanded him to speak to all the people, then the priests and the prophets and all the people laid hold of him, saying, "You shall die!"*

Jeremiah 26:8

With Holy Scripture before us, it needs no further proof that "to die" does not mean "to be annihilated." As we already mentioned briefly, the essential meaning of dying lies rather in the tearing loose or dissolving of the bonds that should be joined by virtue of our creation.[1] Tearing loose, dissolution, that is the actual essence of death, and when death is presented as a personal force, it is the dissolver of what God bound together, the one who tears asunder what God united. Until we observe signs of decomposition we cannot be sure that we are dealing not with someone who merely seems to be dead, but with a real corpse. This is why death will go away someday. It is an enemy that will be vanquished. Therefore Revelation clearly says, "And death shall be no more" [Rev 21:4], which in that context certainly does not mean, of course, that all the damned will have eternal life, but rather that there is nothing left to tear loose, nothing to dissolve.

§ 1

---

1.  See conclusion of the previous chapter, CG 1.27.5, "Knowing as Making One's Own Assessment."

Damnation certainly remains, even when death is no more. An undeniable truth that proves that "eternal death" does not mean a death that will persist throughout the ages and into all eternity but rather, as we would say, a death that is absolute, complete, and has penetrated into everything within us. A death as profound and as all-encompassing as death can be. The consequences of death may persist and continue, but death itself, as a decomposing force, will one day no longer exist.

This essence of death finds its origin herein, that God the Lord has established all kinds of bonds in creation, bonds that by virtue of creation brought about a marvelous unity. Those bonds were necessary because when man was created, a composite being came into existence, which was connected with other beings. Man was something different from the world around him; in that world he was thus something different from the other creatures. Within man, his soul was something other than his body. In the world of humans the man was something other than the woman, one person something different from the next. In the human heart diverse capacities and forces were operative. Man possessed a natural life, a moral life, a religious life, a life of beauty. And in addition to this, there were also the angels. And above all creatures was God. If all this were not to result in chaos, then all those parts had to be mutually related and collectively related to God. And this is precisely what happened in the creation ordinance, and life manifests itself in this. In creation God has created all this in such a way that there was automatically a bond that bound all this together. And thus emerged one holy, organically coherent whole from what otherwise would have been chaos.

We can best sense this when we focus in the first place on our soul and our body. Those two are actually distinct. Our soul is something other than our body, and our body is something quite different from our soul. In paradise, the Lord first creates man from the dust of the ground, and then he breathes the breath of life into him, and thus man becomes a living soul. Therefore those two dissimilar parts of our being were united at creation into one whole; they were created in a fixed relationship and designed for one another, like two shells that enclose the same pearl. There is nothing in the body that has not been created to serve as instrument for the soul. And by virtue of that unity they have been mystically riveted together in creation, if we may express it in this way. Yet we do not think here of two things that only later become one. Even as the three parts of our leg are joined together by tendons that have not been tied on from outside but have grown from the inside, so too the bond that ties together soul and body is not mechanically attached but organically created. This is why, when this bond becomes detached it is not an untying but a tearing away, even as the foot can be removed from the leg only by tearing the tendon that keeps both together. As for soul and body, it is therefore not in the least difficult to form a clear conception of dying or of death. We live as long as the bond that ties soul and body together is maintained, and we *die* as soon as that bond is violently torn asunder. In older Dutch this was even called *aflijvigheid*, that is, the state of being away (*af*) from the body (*lijf*). In death, soul and body are separated. And only when both will be reunited in the resurrection, death will have been undone for us.

Nothing is more clear.

But death is not limited to this, simply because the bond between soul and body is not the only bond that governs our existence by virtue of creation. The Dutch Bible commentators correctly note that the warning "you will surely die" refers, in addition to temporal death, also to spiritual death, and for anyone who knows Scripture it requires no further elaboration to show that again and again the word "death" is used in this sense.[2] "We were by nature dead through sin and offenses" [see Eph 2:1] and "We know that we have passed out of death into life" [1 John 3:14]—these are affirmations of persons whose soul and body are still joined together and who have not yet tasted temporal death. Yet, notwithstanding the fact that they still live among us, it says that they *were dead* or *are still dead*. This refers therefore to spiritual death.

§ 2

What then is spiritual death? Of course it entails severing the bond that God created in us at creation, but which bond? The answer is: the spiritual bond that connects our soul with God. Not only our body is tied to our soul with a bond, but [at creation] our soul was also tied with a bond to God. That bond is automatically unraveled through sin, and thus immediately at this point death enters simultaneously with sin. Instead of drinking in life with God, the soul is thrown back upon itself, even as a pipe unscrewed from the water supply empties out and dries up. It is thus entirely understandable that there is a dying, a death, in two respects. One involves the tearing asunder of the bond between body and soul in us, the other is a dying in which the bond between the soul and God is torn apart. And so the threat "in the day that you eat of it you shall surely die" meant

---

2. See SV, ad loc. Gen 2:17, and note at *den dood*.

two things: (1) in that day the bond that binds your soul to your God will be severed by sin and thus you will be spiritually dead; and (2) in that day the bond that keeps your soul and body together will let go and thus you will die temporal death.

Yet even this does not exhaust the meaning of dying. By virtue of creation there was not only a bond of the body with the soul and of the soul with God, but there was also a bond of man as such with the world. He was not simply placed in this world as an alien being, as we place a peach on a golden plate in such a way that that noble fruit and the valuable plate have nothing to do with one another. When an angel appears on earth, the angel is unrelated to this earth, since it has no organic bond with this world. But with man it is different. Man is a microcosm, a world in miniature. His body has been taken from the earth. In the animal kingdom his image was already prefigured. He is connected with all realms of nature. Light has been created with his eye in view, the air with his organs of hearing and breathing. In short, there is an organic bond that ties man to the world just as there is a bond that ties his body and soul together. Precisely for this reason we can say that man is a being who is inclusive of the world, who comprises the world in himself and offers it, as priest, to God. Death also destroys this bond, and the [consequence is] the painful realization that he no longer possesses his world—temporarily in the state of separateness and permanently in hell. What has already come over the world in the curse is at present not a complete severing but a partial tearing asunder of that bond. When sunstroke kills a man instead of the [sun's] warmth filling him with life and cherishing him, when the wind sends death into his breast instead of refreshing his blood, then we have a partial disruption of the bond that once tied man and world together. The same is also true when a wild animal, instead of coming to man at his request, as it was with Adam in paradise, kills a human being. In short, in every case where the world brings us harm or injury instead of serving us harmoniously, it becomes apparent how the bond that tied us to the world has already been disturbed, only to be completely severed later. For being torn loose from that world with which we are connected is part of our dying, a dying that will be undone only when in the resurrection we will receive that same world back, but then renewed and glorified.

We can continue this analysis. Man does not stand alone but is tied to his fellow humans by an organic bond. In that bond all of society originates. Its driving force is the love that binds together. But when sin enters, this love turns into selfishness, and the drawing together becomes an arrogant rejection of one another. This harms society and injects a lethal poison into the social fabric. And when the hour of dying arrives, then this dying also entails a tearing asunder of the sometimes tender ties with persons. Our death severs not only our soul from our body, but also our person from this world, and our heart from our nearest and dearest. Death is always separation and tearing asunder—tearing asunder of what God had joined together. "What God has joined together, let not man separate" [see Matt 19:6] is therefore in its general meaning applicable to the essence of death. Man has separated what God has united: he has separated his soul from his God, and now the consequence is that his soul must also be separated from his body, his person from his world, his heart from his loved ones. And all this is the natural, dreadful death.

In the sundering of this fourfold bond the essence of death is complete. §3 There is a bond of God to the soul, of the soul to the body, of the body to the world, and in that world between person and person; and where sin comes, and death along with it, these four bonds are torn asunder. Nevertheless death continues working also in the [various] parts. It is like an evil that eats through everything. We see this most clearly in the corpse. When body and soul are torn apart, the body does not remain what it was but soon undergoes a tremendous change that leads to decomposition. And wherein does this decomposition consist but the fact that the various substances and gases that compose the body break loose from their bond and each go their own way and in that mutual struggle demolish that once so beautiful body? And just as in the decomposition of the body, so it also happens in the soul, not only after our temporal death but immediately after spiritual death occurs. Even as various substances and gases make up one body, so also do we distinguish within the soul all kinds of functions, forces, and capacities that by virtue of the creation ordinance are in close harmonious connection with one another, thereby ensuring our inner balance, peace of mind, and full energy. No strength was lost in the state of righteousness, but from the very depths of our soul it was one holy chord [harmonizing] all the tones ascending from the life of the soul.

But when sin enters, then this is also done with. The organic and harmonious bond that kept all this together in the soul is ruptured; the one begins to act against the other; the desires of the heart come to rule the heart, and thus passion enters; inner battle, friction, and struggle become the normal condition; all balance of the soul is disrupted; and the spiritual death of the soul consists of nothing but one continuous, actual decomposition. Granted, we don't always notice this. Just like in an embalmed corpse the complete draining of all the separated fluids and the infusion of strong herbs mask the decomposition of the corpse inside the mummy, so too the masked sinner hides his inner decomposition and disguises his inner death behind a conventional life. But this does not take away one whit from the fact of decomposition. Sin loosens the inner bond of our soul and thereby brings death into the inner chambers of our being.

This is why the Form for the Celebration of the Lord's Supper confesses that apart from Christ, in ourselves we "lie in the midst of death."[3] Death surrounds us. Death inside and outside. All around a fraying and tearing asunder of bonds. One great chaos of what God had organically ordered and bound together in his creation.

§ 4   Thus every notion of annihilation disappears. Not a single particle of a corpse is annihilated. Of the corpse, nothing perishes. Its substance merely decomposes. And this is how death operates in everything it affects. It never annihilates. All it does is *separate what God had united*. Once we clearly realize this, we will also see the necessity of why sin had to bring forth death. As the holy apostle says, when it is completed, sin brings forth death [see Jas 1:15]. And when God says in paradise, "In the day that you eat of it you shall surely die," this most definitely does not mean "Then I will impose death on you from the outside, as a mechanistic punishment," but something quite, quite different: Sin is a poison, and as soon as this poison begins to work in you, you will feel death coming. Death does not come as a second component added to sin, but death arises from sin and belongs to sin, just like decomposition belongs to the corpse and automatically begins to work in it.

If man takes it upon himself to place himself over against God and begins to assess good and evil as if he himself were God, instead of accepting from God in silent submission the determination that God had established

---

3. Kuyper refers here to the Liturgy of the Reformed Churches in the Netherlands. See "The Form for the Administration of the Lord's Supper," in "The Liturgy of the Reformed Dutch Church, or the Forms Used Therein," in *The Psalms and Hymns: With the Catechism, Confession of Faith, and Canons, of the Synod of Dort, and Liturgy of the Reformed Protestant Dutch Church in North America* (Philadelphia: Mentz & Rouvoudt, 1847), 64: "For we do not come to this supper, to testify thereby that we are perfect and righteous in ourselves; but on the contrary, considering that we seek our life out of ourselves in Jesus Christ, we acknowledge that we lie in the midst of death."

with respect to good and evil, then this act automatically severs the bond that bound his soul to God, and immediately spiritual death sets in. Once the bond between God and the soul was torn loose, then as a consequence, also the bond between man and world, the bond between human beings, the bond between soul and body, the bond between the parts of the body, and the bond that wove together the powers and capacities of the soul, would all be torn asunder, and in this process death would find its completion. All this would be what God predicted: In the day that man would dare to have this audacity, he would not only make contact with death, but die death in the absolute sense. Not merely later, but *that very day*. Not gradually and progressively, but *all at once*.

The fact that the essence of death lies in separating what God had joined is confirmed by the death of Christ as Mediator, for us, in our place. It needs no further elaboration that in Jesus' case it came to a separation of soul and body. John mentions the spear that pierced his side and described how in his blood even the water was separated from the blood, as the incontrovertible testimony that lets us know for certain that the separation between soul and body had truly occurred within Jesus. But that was not all. In this connection we must also note the word spoken on the cross, "My God, my God, why have you forsaken me?" [Matt 27:46]. This also points to a separation, to the most fearful separation, to the separation between God and the soul. And although it is completely beyond our comprehension how and in what manner the Mediator in his humanity could be separated from God for even one moment, the fact is nevertheless irrefutable. Jesus' own word in his dying is our guarantee. He also struggled through that separation between his soul and his God when he sunk into the fearful realization that he was also being *abandoned* by God.

We may even add a third point here. Jesus also struggled through the abandonment, the separation, the being torn away, from his friends. What is reported to us about Gethsemane, especially after his moving farewell discourses, at least with respect to John and James and Peter, is so puzzling that anyone reading this senses how a mysterious force was at work here on the disciples. They slept and could not resist sleep while their Jesus wrestled in his agony. They flee when he is dragged away. Peter denies him while he is standing before the judge. But no matter how we try to explain this, the fact remains that Jesus was also abandoned by those nearest him before he was abandoned by his God. And also this abandonment by people, this tearing asunder of the most tender ties he possessed

§ 5

as a human being, was the draining of a bitter draught from the chalice of death that was handed him.

At the end of our last chapter already, we pointed out how in paradise, immediately after sin entered, the separation, the tearing apart of the natural bonds becomes manifest.[4] They flee from God and hide. And the unity, the harmony between soul and body is broken as well. The body has become something separate for them. In that separateness the body has become a force over against them, which is discerned immediately in the highest that God has given the body, the sexual life. This is why the blush of shame comes over them. Those parts of the body become an impediment for them, and therefore they sew fig leaves together so that they do not have to see those parts of the body and can act as if they were not there. There is nothing mysterious in all of this. It all proceeds very naturally and automatically. Once we understand the essence of death as the tearing asunder of what God had united in creation, we have the key in hand to understand all of this in its natural progress.

§ 6    But precisely with this we come to the important moment where *common grace* enters and begins to function. For it is clear as day that what God had said was not being implemented in this manner. What God, entirely rightfully, had indicated as the natural and immediate consequence of sin, *does not come to pass*. What was predicted was that in the day, that is, on that very day, when they ate of it, they would die in the absolute sense, but they did not die on that day. It is beneath the truthfulness of the Word of God to want to gloss this over. If human prophecy is only partially fulfilled, we may find some way to extenuate what is missing in the fulfilment, but where God has spoken it is neither fitting nor proper to do so. What God speaks is spoken with exhaustive and full knowledge of the course of things, and for that reason we lack any right to explain away the words "in that day" or to take anything away from the absoluteness of the death in the words "you shall surely die."

Had it happened as God had announced it, then the corpse of Adam and the corpse of Eve would have had to lie before the tree of life before sunset that evening, and decomposition would have begun its work of disintegration. Excuses are of no use here. For whether we say that they did die spiritually, and also that the seed of physical death was implanted in them,

---

4. See conclusion of the previous chapter, CG 1.27.5, "Knowing as Making One's Own Assessment."

we have not in the least provided an explanation of the definite and absolute "you will surely die." Someone who dies at age seventy of hereditary cancer is born with that cancer of death inside him and carries the seed of his death around with him for seventy years. But who would say that this man has always been dead, had died already when he was born, and has never lived? No one would claim this. And even if someone has carried the seed of death around with him for seventy years, we still say that he has lived seventy years and only then died. We don't achieve anything with all such playing with words.

In Hebrew the expression *surely die* is the strongest and most absolute expression for complete and final death, and we must therefore take it in no other way than in its full, absolute sense.[5] We must not limit it to a spiritual death that set in, nor explain it in the sense of taking the seed of death into oneself. It would have happened in accordance with the word God spoke only if, in that very day, things had ended for Adam and Eve, the curse had destroyed everything on earth, and full chaos had returned. But this is not what happened, and precisely in the fact that it did not happen in this way, we see that general grace or common grace enters and begins to function. And when we ask how we can square this with the word of God, then the answer is that every difficulty here would indeed disappear if we take the statement "In the day that you eat of it you shall surely die" not as a threat but purely in the sense of a prediction. Thus, in this sense: The eating of this tree will lead you into sin, and the necessary consequence of sin is death, death immediately, death continuing until the end, but then adding tacitly, *unless I, your God, in my mercy, arrest the continuing consequences of sin.*

---

5.   See *CG* 1.24.2n1, and Kuyper's discussion in the text.

# CHAPTER TWENTY-NINE

# IN THAT DAY

*We know that the judgment of God rightly falls on those who practice such things.*

ROMANS 2:2

§ 1      *Death*, considered in connection with the eating from the tree of knowledge, can be understood in one of two ways: either as a punishment that was threatened, or as a consequence that would result from it. If the punishment for treason is death, then death is a threatened punishment since one does not die of treason as such. But when I say, "Don't take any of that Prussic acid, otherwise you will die," then it is not a question of punishment; rather, what is stated is that this poison is lethal and that whoever ingests it will die.[1] If against my advice someone nevertheless were to take of it, I can even make an attempt to avert the lethal consequences by administering a strong emetic. Then I have said in full truth, "if you take of this you will surely die," but I do not in any way contradict myself if afterward I try the save the reckless poison-taker. If this is clear, then we must concede that the words "If you eat of the tree of knowledge you will surely die" are also done full justice if I take them to mean nothing other than the affirmation, the warning, "Know well that if you let yourself be enticed into eating from that tree, you will see that death will be the result." And if these words had this meaning, then there is nothing contradictory in the

---

1.   "Prussic acid" is a poison and industrial compound also known by its chemical name, hydrogen cyanide.

fact that death did not immediately come and [that the sentence] was not executed against Adam on that day, for the same God who had warned them rushed in immediately after their transgression to mitigate the consequences of the evil. We are therefore very much inclined to conceive of the intent of these words in this sense.

For reasons explicated earlier, the eating of the tree of knowledge broke the bond of life between God and their soul.[2] Through the breaking of this bond, the other bond, which kept together soul and body, also had to give way. And when these two bonds gave way, the bond that bound them to their being also had to tear, and thus at the same time and suddenly—in that day—spiritual, physical, temporal, and eternal death set in. God had told them this and warned them. And it would have happened this way, and death would have totally overpowered them immediately, unless *grace* had intervened, and unless mercy had averted this horrible result.

We must decidedly reject the notion that spiritual, temporal, and eternal death are not a *punishment* but must be viewed exclusively as a *consequence* of sin, since this involves an ordinance of God. In God's creation ordinance, and thus also in his providential order, everything is interrelated by causal connections. If we use strong drink excessively, we experience the sad results in the loss of health, good name, and living circumstances. But even though this loss flows automatically from the sin, it is also a punishment for the sin. The terrible illness, whose contagious poison so many take in through lasciviousness, is most certainly a result of the evil committed, but is it therefore any less of a punishment, experienced as such by the transgressor in his conscience? Conversely, the beneficial consequences in terms of health, good name, and living conditions brought about by a life of honor and virtue are not only a consequence of such honorable conduct but also a gracious reward that is experienced in the soul as an expression of God's favor. In the original divine order, as it existed by virtue of creation, neither a mechanical punishment nor a mechanical reward were even conceivable. Everything hung together in an organic coherence. Life in accordance with God's ordinance automatically led to happiness and to eternal blessedness. And conversely, resisting the ordinances of God would automatically mean deprivation of happiness and bring doom.

---

2. See previous chapter, *CG* 1.28, "You Shall Surely Die."

For that reason, consequence and punishment, outcome and judgment were one. Neither the punishment nor the reward was added externally, but both flowed automatically from faith or unbelief. But even if this was the case, it did not in any way alter the fact that this outcome of the good deed or of the guilty deed was also intended as reward or punishment and was experienced as favor or judgment. It wouldn't even occur to us, therefore, to remove the punishment character here; our intent is only to bring out sharply and clearly that the words "in that day you will surely die" were not fulfilled for Adam and Eve on that very day. We do this also to keep open the way of grace, without making God's definite statement untruthful. "In the day that you eat of it you will surely die" must not be toned down but must be maintained in its full, drastic meaning: "In that day you will sink down into spiritual, physical, and eternal death." And this has *not* happened in this manner.

§ 2    Having arrived at this point in our argument, the question cannot be suppressed as to *why* it did not happen in this manner. Upon some reflection we must agree, after all, that there would have been exceptional benefits to ending it in this manner with Adam and Eve, simply and to the point, and in no other way. Imagine that on that day Adam and Eve had not only been killed spiritually but had also died physically and both had sunk into eternal death—they personally would not have received grace, but on the other hand, the number of doomed would have been restricted to two, the curse would have remained away from the earth, and all that nameless misery that now, because of sin and as a consequence of sin, has been poured out as a flood, century after century, would have been prevented. If after this a new human pair would have been created on the same earth and in that same paradise, while the corpses of Adam and Eve were still lying there, and God had placed this new human pair, with the terrible experience of Adam and Eve before their eyes, before the same test, then it might have been possible that this new human pair would not have yielded to Satan and that a life of eternal jubilation would have filled this earth. We must concede that this notion is far from absurd and that it is good to entertain it, because only then do we fully understand what it meant that Adam and Eve were not immediately destroyed but received grace. It certainly was grace, but a fearful grace, an anxious grace, a grace whereby the soul trembles if it reflects on the ocean of human misery that opened up simultaneously.

Yet it is not difficult to understand why such a seemingly simple path could not be taken, at least if we do not get hung up on the ill-considered notion that our human race as such is going to be lost and that only a few individuals of our race are saved.[3] If we still hold on to this rather superficial notion, then there is no reason why those few individuals could not just as well have been bred by a new human pair, without sin intervening. This notion focuses only on the salvation of these few persons and fails to take into account the work and the glory of God. In this perspective it was of course not in the least necessary for the salvation of those individuals that they had specifically this fallen Adam as their primogenitor. A new progenitor, created immediately after Adam's bitter death in the same way in which Adam had been created, could just as well have brought these individuals into being, and then *without* all that nameless misery that was now poured out century after century.

But the matter becomes quite different, of course, if we abandon this one-sided perspective on individuals and focus on the work of God and pay attention to the upholding of the glory of God over against Satan. The very idea of redoing the creation of the first human pair after they fell and to start over with the creation of a second human pair then automatically becomes absurd. When humans have to do something over, it shows ipso facto that they have produced inadequate and defective work, something that should have been different. If this is impossible with God, and if his pronouncement is unassailable that what he had created was very good in an absolute sense, then the notion of redoing the creation of man is incompatible with the perfection of God.

In Adam God had created not just a solitary individual, but a man in whom lay the seed of our entire human race. He was not just a single, stand-alone individual, but in paradise his person and the human race were one. He carried us all, to speak with Scripture, in his loins. To put it distinctly yet not too daringly, the seed from which Enoch and Noah, Abraham and Jacob, David and Isaiah, yes, all the elect would be born was not added to but organically given in the creation of the first human pair. Nothing here is isolated or solitary. Everything exists in organic coherence. And precisely for that reason it was inconceivable and impossible that those same

---

3. Kuyper may be referring here to a particular construal of the Reformed doctrine of election as including only a small group of persons considered as individuals and apart from any organic relationship with humanity.

elect whose seed was already given in Adam would, through a new act of creation, now be made descendants of another human pair. If we consider each human being an isolated individual, we can think this way, but not if we confess with Holy Scripture that the descendants are already in the loins of the primogenitor (Acts 2:30; Heb 7:5; and also Gen 35:11 and 1 Kgs 8:19). On this scriptural basis there are not all kinds of human races that God will create at his own discretion, but in his counsel there can be only one human race, the one he has in fact created. That single human race is a notion consisting of two parts, and not, as the superficial person thinks, of only one part.

The superficial person has the notion that our human race is nothing but the sum total of its individuals. But this is wrong. Our race consists of two things: (1) the individuals, manifested in ordered groupings; and (2) what is common to this group of individuals, what is given them as the treasure of life, and what constitutes their bond as race. An army most certainly does not consist solely of a few recruits who have been incorporated into it; rather, those individual soldiers are unified into an army first by the uniform common to all, by the one banner to which they swore loyalty, by the training they have undergone, by the discipline under which they are kept, and by the leadership they receive from their superiors. And in this same way, both with each family[4] and with our human race, we must pay attention on the one hand to the individuals in the context of family and relatives, but on the other hand also to all that constitutes the common fund of humanity as a whole in terms of external and internal good that serves our happiness.

Take poetry, for example, and the power of song, and the appeal of harp strings plucked and organs playing, and you understand immediately that this certainly is not characteristic of all people individually. And you understand also that this power of song is not some private possession belonging to and intended only for a David or an Asaph, a Bilderdijk or da Costa,[5] but that the treasure of song belongs to all of us jointly, to our human race. And it is the same with every art form, with every talent, with all forms of excellence. Not everyone possesses them; it belongs to

4. The word *geslacht* as used by Kuyper has a range of meanings, from smaller groupings, such as a single generation, to the broadest group, the human race. There is of necessity some subjectivity in the choices made in translating it, based on the context. In this sentence, "family" and "race" are both renderings of *geslacht*.
5. Willem Bilderdijk (1756–1831) and Isaäc da Costa (1798–1860) were Dutch poets.

some individuals, but those individuals do not possess such excellence for themselves, nor do they have themselves to thank for it. Rather it is part of the human treasure that manifests itself in them and which they enhance through their talent on behalf of our human race.

For another example, look at language. Human language is absolutely not merely the sum total of the sounds that each individual utters. Rather, human language is a treasure of people as a group and of the human race as a whole; it exists outside of the individual human beings and does not disappear when everybody sleeps or is silent. It continues from age to age and belongs therefore to our humanness and must not be hijacked by an individual for himself or herself alone, for it is the common heritage belonging to everybody.

Only when we cease in that manner to bob on the surface of the water in our little boat but have the courage to dive into the depths and to descend to the bottom of things will we be able to understand fully what it meant for God to let go of fallen humanity in Adam and Eve and to summarily let them sink into absolute doom and death. Had it happened in this way, then all of humankind, with that entire hidden treasure of excellences that God had embedded within Adam, would suddenly have disappeared. Never, never would all the hidden glory have become manifest that God the Lord had ordained and implanted in its essence within humankind. Even as one cold night's frost in spring sometimes causes all fruit blossoms to wither so that in summer nothing can thrive and in the autumn not a single fruit can be picked, to the chagrin of the owner of the orchard, so too would that one sin of Adam and Eve suddenly have caused all the blossoms of glory that God had ordained for humankind to wither for all eternity, so that not even a single bloom would ever have opened up and not even a single fruit of the human race could ever have been picked to the praise of his holy name.

God the Lord had resolved to reflect his divine virtues in a world that he was going to create. Not for our sake did he create the world. He created all things for his own sake, so that the majesty of the glory of his eternal Being would be reflected in it, to the praise of his name. That creation, though organically one, progressed in segments, from the lowly creature in the mineral kingdom to the highest creature in the human race. Only in humankind would the pinnacle of this wonderful structure shine. But humankind would develop only gradually, over the centuries, from a small beginning. The magnificence of the firmament, of the plant kingdom, and

§ 3

of the animal kingdom were *immediately* manifest and visible, but not so with the human race.

The glory of the human race was enclosed like the pearl in its shell, like the grain of wheat that sprouts from the stalk as the head of grain. So what was visible and manifest did not correspond to *all* that God's plan had ordained. Only when the human race would have budded, would have blossomed, would have ripened and stood in its full strength, only then would heaven and earth be able to glorify God for the excellence of this his work. God saw in paradise that it was very good, because he saw the head of grain within the seed of wheat, but outwardly the creation showed as yet nothing but Adam and Eve, undoubtedly glorious in form and majestic in appearance, who nevertheless did not yet manifest anything but the closed flower bud and the first sprouting that did not betray even a hint of the treasures God had embedded in the human race. So if the matter had ended with them, then God's actions would have remained without justification; his divine arrangement and plan would have been thwarted. Not only the creation of our race but also the creation of the whole world, which reached its pinnacle only in our human race, would have been publicly displayed as one gigantic failure and as a manifestation of the power of Satan.

§ 4    Nothing less than *God's honor* was therefore at stake. God's honor, not on a single point but in the majestic whole of his work of creation. For that honor could not become evident unless what he had in essence ordained and decided for our human race was made manifest before all eyes. And this could not have happened, this would forever have been impossible and cut off, if it had been fulfilled in Adam and Eve that they would sink into spiritual, temporal, and eternal death that very day. "In that day" therefore carries a force that makes our heart shudder at what a violation of God's honor would have occurred and what thwarting of his plan of creation would have occurred if this had happened. But on the other hand, how momentous it is for the honor of God, for the entire theodicy, and for the entire history of the world that God's wondrous grace, both particular grace as well as common grace, has prevented this terrible outcome.

No, it did not happen this way. Adam and Eve did not die that day. Certainly, the cold breath of death has gone over their soul, has come between their soul and their God, and has brought spiritual death over their inner life. And that same breath of death has intruded between their soul and their body, has undermined their original life force, exposed them to illness and accident, and centuries later caused their body and soul to be torn asunder in temporal death. Yes, even eternal death has entered and has in the end hauled away into eternal doom as prey and plunder, not Adam and Eve personally but many of their descendants. Death truly has come. But it has *not* come to full fruition in that day. As eternal death it has *not* become a power that in fact overwhelmed Adam and Eve for eternity. Death has reigned as king of terror and still rules, but he has not prevented the human race as a whole from budding, from developing, from burgeoning, from manifesting its hidden treasure. Rather, the redeemed and all who believe shout with joy in death's face: "O death, where is your victory? O death, where is your sting?" [1 Cor 15:55].

If it is certain that death has indeed come but that it has not come to bring about that sudden and immediate end contained in the words "In the day that you eat of it you shall surely die," then it is clear that (1) immediately after the fall into sin the revelation of grace sets in; (2) it is this grace that has restrained the power and victory of death; and (3) this restraining of the otherwise necessary and inevitable consequences of sin had the goal, in the first place, to maintain God's honor over against Satan; in the second place, to maintain God's order in his whole work of creation, and specifically in the human race; and in the third place, to implement the decree of his eternal election. The first of these goals concerns theodicy, which is what Paul expresses in this way: "It was to show his righteousness at the present time, so that [God] might be just" [Rom 3:26]. The second discloses the broad sphere of common grace. The third reaches its realization through particular grace.

In the meantime, even if we distinguish these three goals in this manner, they must not be torn from their interconnectedness. Particular grace requires and presupposes common grace, because without that common grace, the Zion of God would not have had a place to stand. Conversely, the glory of common grace would never have sparkled in its springtime if particular grace had not brought it fully into bloom. Also God's rectitude over against Satan would not have been felt so absolutely and emphatically in heaven and earth, yes, even by Satan himself, if both the decree of creation and the decree of election had not been implemented and had in that implementation justified God. Although in this series of chapters we survey only the middle area, that of common grace, and therefore can mention particular grace only obliquely, let no one who reads what follows forget that particular grace always remains the highest grace, the

§ 5

core and center around which also common grace revolves, and that the diadem of God's sovereign counsel shines most perfectly in his bringing the elect to salvation.

It already became clear that there is a danger of forgetting this. As soon as it was pointed out that God the Lord does not give up on the creation of the human race in order to save at most a few stones of the fallen wall of his holy temple, but that one day he will bring to glory his creation, the human race with all the treasure he has embedded within it, then misunderstanding and superficiality led to the question whether this did not smell of universalism.[6] This question was entirely understandable for those who understood the term "our human race" exclusively to mean the sum total of individuals; but the question does not make sense, nor is it seemly, when we realize that the human race was saved in the ark although merely eight souls were left, even though tens of thousands perished; that David's family was saved even though one ruler after another was cut off from his house and even though in the end the only thing that sprouted was a shoot from a stump. Indeed, we must realize that this is the pattern of God's dealings: allow only a tenth portion to return, let that tenth portion be decimated again, and then, just like with the oak and the holm oak after the leaves have been shed, still allow a support to remain that, as the holy seed, maintains the life of the whole trunk, of the whole plant, of the whole tree. In this context such an explanation also provides a meaningful interpretation of what Jesus portrayed for us in the parable in which the evil ones are taken out from the midst of the righteous ones [see Matt 13:24–30]. All that spoils, wilts, withers, and discolors falls from the trunk; only that which has either remained healthy or was restored to wholeness by the grace of God adheres to the trunk.

---

6. Soteriological universalism holds that nothing in creation is excluded or lost, and hence all people from the beginning of time are saved by God in Jesus Christ.

# CHAPTER THIRTY

# FORMS OF GRACE

*And the free gift is not like the result of that one man's sin. For the judgment following one trespass brought condemnation, but the free gift following many trespasses brought justification.*

Romans 5:16

There is neither doubt nor uncertainty about the situation that began im- § 1
mediately after the fall. On the one hand this is because Scripture draws
that situation for us so sharply, and on the other hand because this situation still continues in part and we can therefore observe it for ourselves
from the living model. We already noted that this new situation did not
correspond to what had been announced as the consequence of sin. Death
in its absolute effect did not come that day, and the Reformed theologians
have continually pointed out how in this not coming of what had been
prophesied for ill lies the first manifestation of God's saving and long-
suffering grace. It is not as if grace appeared now for the first time, for it is
impossible to imagine man even for a moment in paradise without grace
hovering around him and permeating him. For every rational creature,
grace is the air of life he breathes. But now for the first time this divine
grace acquired the character of *saving* grace, which, since we are sinners,
is the form in which we understand grace primarily and most naturally.

But let no one understand this saving grace as a certain indulgence, as
a certain weakness in God, as if God should have continued with the full
extent of his justice but, being moved by compassion, merely let himself

be deterred. Such shrinking from what justice requires, such indulging out of pity, is utterly unthinkable in the Holy One and would be transferring to God what might adorn humans but would dishonor God. We must therefore never depict this divine display of grace as if his helping and saving us would in fact be at the expense of the perfection of the Lord's majesty. One of our objections to the perspective of the infralapsarians (though we gladly acknowledge its relative merit) lies precisely herein, that it cannot escape this inverse representation of the matter.[1] Without going into more detail here, we conclude that the purpose of this manifestation of grace ultimately served not to save us, but to disclose the glory of the eternal Being, and only secondarily, as result and consequence, to snatch us out of our self-chosen perdition.

This display of grace consisted herein, that the consequences that otherwise would have flowed from sin were thereby resisted, arrested, or changed in their operation. It is this display of grace that preempts the natural effect of the poison of sin, and deflects and changes it, or opposes and destroys it. This is why two aspects must be distinguished in this manifestation of grace: (1) a *saving* grace that ultimately cancels sin and completely neutralizes its consequences; and (2) a *temporarily restraining* grace that stems and arrests the continued effect of sin. The former, saving grace, is by the nature of things *particular* and is connected with the elect of God. The latter is *common* and covers the entire sphere of our human life. Here the question arises whether these two forms of grace, this particular grace and this common grace, stand disconnected side by side, or rather function in mutual connectedness and if so, how.

There is no doubt that a certain connection indeed exists between the saving grace that is particular and the restraining grace that is common.

---

1. On infralapsarianism and supralapsarianism, see *DLGTT*, s.v. "supra lapsum": "Two basic views of predestination emerged from the development of Reformed doctrine in the late sixteenth and early seventeenth centuries: the supralapsarian view, sometimes referred to as full double predestination, and the infralapsarian view, frequently termed single predestination. Both views arise out of consideration of an eternal, logical 'order of the things of the decree,' or *ordo rerum decretarum*, in the mind of God. According to the supralapsarian view, the election and reprobation of individuals are logically prior to the divine decree of creation and the divine ordination to permit the fall." By contrast, "The infralapsarian view, which is the confessional position of the Reformed churches, places the divine will to create human beings with free will and the decree to permit the fall prior to the election of some to salvation."

This is immediately evident in the undeniable fact that apart from common grace, the elect would not have been born and would not have seen the light of life. If Adam and Eve had died immediately on the day they sinned, then Seth would not have been born from them, nor Enosh from Seth, and there would never have come into being upon this earth a sprawling race of peoples and nations. For this reason alone, all particular grace already presupposes *common grace*. But there is more.

Even if we assume that their temporal death had been postponed so that the race could be born, but that for the rest sin had broken out, unrestrained and in all its dreadfulness, the problem would not yet have been solved. Then the earth would immediately have turned into a hell, and under such hellish conditions the church of God would nowhere have found a place to stand. We speak sometimes, though entirely erroneously, of a hell on earth, and then point to some terrible paroxysm of human depravity, which in some families and circles can take on such a devilish character that it results in general brutality, manslaughter, and insanity. But such conditions are so profoundly scandalous and heinous, indeed atrocious, that in a world consisting of nothing but these conditions the continued existence of a church of God would simply be unthinkable. It would not be able to live in the midst of such conditions and would be exterminated in no time. Thus no matter how we look at the data, particular grace presupposes common grace. Without the latter, the former cannot do its work.

A connection is thus undeniable, but how must we understand it? §2 Not uncommonly, and this does not need to be swept under the rug, the connection has been presented as if common grace served only to make it possible for the elect to attain salvation. This is a thesis that undoubtedly contains a partial truth but that is exaggerated in a manner that makes one shudder and evokes annoyance. For it is not a fabrication when we say that also in our country a man or woman has occasionally risen up who, believing in their own election, saw in their father and mother nothing more than outcasts, and who did not shrink from saying harshly and forthrightly, "My parents, oh, they stand outside of everything, and they have come only to make my existence possible." Fortunately such statements are very rare, though not unheard of. For this reason we must draw attention here to the correct connection between general and common grace. The horrible example we pointed to shows what misunderstanding on this point can lead to. The error lies solely in the fact that in determining the connection, the focus has shifted from God's honor to one's own salvation; and this is precisely the criterion that always allows us to discern whether we are dealing with the thoroughly sound Reformed confession or with a defective imitation of Reformed doctrine.

There is certainly nothing against saying that all things happen because of Christ, that therefore the body of Christ is the all-dominant element in history, and that on this basis we may confess that the church of Christ is the pivot around which the life of humanity does in fact revolve. Those who overlook or deny this will never discover unity in the flow of history; for them, century follows century, development follows decline, decline is followed again by progress, but the stream of life leads nowhere; it has no purpose. Life lacks a core; it has no pivot. If this is to continue for all eternity, then it results in endless boredom. And if it has to be cut short somewhere because the elements of fire or water overwhelm our earth, then such shortening is entirely arbitrary, without any goal being reached or any fruit obtained. The Reformed confession maintains that all things also in this world have Christ as their aim, and that his body is the chief element, so that in this sense we can say that the church of Christ constitutes the center of world history. Thereby the Reformed confession provides a principle for looking at history that is far elevated above the ordinary view of history. We will therefore strenuously guard against taking away anything whatsoever. Not *common* grace, but the ordained arrangement of *particular* grace dominates.

But this has validity and leads to a pure confession only if we let it stand in that order. Because of the Christ, and only as a consequence of this, because of his body and for the sake of the church. Thus not for our sake, and then consequently for the sake of the church, and thus also of the body of Christ, and then finally, as a consequence of this, also for the sake of Christ. No, Christ takes first position here. He through whom all things are, and we through him. He, the reflection of God's glory and the express image of his substance, of whom we confess that all things have been created through him, whether visible or invisible, in heaven and on earth, in whom even now all things hold together [see Col 1:16–17]. Everything revolves around this Christ because in him the fullness of God dwells bodily [see Col 2:9], and before him every knee must bow and he must be confessed by every tongue as Christ the Lord, to the glory of God the Father [see Phil 2:10–11]. And then his body certainly does also share in his glory, and something of his radiance will shine upon his church on earth, and in the glow of that radiance each elect individual will share.

This is something quite different from starting with myself as elect, pushing myself into the foreground, and from there coming at last, in the end, to Christ.

In this, as the only correct system, everything else follows while Christ stands in first place and is placed at the center, not insofar as he became our brother but because he is the Son of God, the Son of the Father, and because the Father loves the Son and glorifies him with eternal glory. When the focus is on Christ, the focus is on God himself, and our soul finds rest only when it surveys and summarizes the whole course of history from paradise to the return of the Lord under one perspective. In that sense we must therefore acknowledge that common grace is only an emanation of particular grace, and that all its fruit flows into particular grace, provided we understand that particular grace itself is not in the least exhausted in the salvation of the elect, but finds its ultimate goal in the glorification of the Son of love, and through this, in the extolling of the virtues of our God.

We must explain in yet another way that this is the only correct perspective of common grace by focusing on an extremely important point: the relationship in which nature and grace stand to one another. Later in our argument we will discuss this very important point in greater detail, but already here we must point out one aspect for consideration. §3

Is the Christ only the Expiator of guilt? With respect to many otherwise warm Christians, we should almost say yes, but certainly not with respect to Holy Scripture. The notion that the Christ had no other significance than that he died for our sin as the Lamb of God cannot be sustained when we consult Scripture. Let us be understood clearly. At this point we will not go into the question that has been raised as to whether the Word would have become flesh even if Adam had not fallen into sin; we answer this question, as often as it is raised, in the negative.[2] No, what we discuss now can be summarized this way: Shall we say that Christ is given only for our justification and sanctification, or shall we continue to confess with the apostle in 1 Corinthians 1:30 that Christ is given to us from God also

---

2. In another work, Kuyper writes that the incarnation of Christ "is by no means the necessary complement of the normal human development, but was demanded only and alone by sin," and that "without sin, this self-revelation of the Divine Ego to my personal ego would never have been, even in part, the fruit of Theophany, or of incarnation, but would have taken place normally in my personal being." See Abraham Kuyper, *Encyclopedia of Sacred Theology: Its Principles*, trans. J. Hendrik de Vries (New York: Scribner's, 1898), 280, 343–44.

for *wisdom* and *perfect redemption*? Shall we say that we have in him only atonement for our sin, or shall we continue to acknowledge that it is he who will one day transform our lowly bodies to be like his glorified body "by the power that enables him even to subject all things to himself" [Phil 3:21]? Shall we consider the work of the Christ on Golgotha as finished, or shall we with Scripture and with the whole church of the first centuries continue to expect our Lord from heaven in order to bring the present situation to an end and lead it to a new heaven and a new earth? To put it succinctly, shall we imagine that the Redeemer of our soul is enough for us, or shall we continue to confess a Christ of God as the Savior of both soul and body and as re-creator, not only of the things that are invisible but also of the things that are visible and apparent to our eyes? Does Christ have significance only for the spiritual, or also for the natural and visible? Does the fact that he overcame the world mean that one day he will cast the world back into nothingness in order to be left with only the souls of the elect, or does it mean that the world will also be his prize, the trophy of his glory?

We do not wish to exaggerate, nor close our eyes to the danger that lies in relegating the forgiveness of our sins to the background. It cannot be denied that this danger exists. There are indeed circles in which people so restlessly occupy themselves with issues concerning the return of the Lord that the much deeper issues that touch on the knowledge of our sin and the justification of the sinner are barely allowed to have their say. Over these past eighteen centuries the church of Christ has, with wise caution, always placed the issues concerning the soul in the foreground and issues relating to the last things somewhat in the shadow. The sects, on the other hand, have continually tried to shift this proper balance and have thus tried to divert attention from the deeper doctrines of justification by pushing us toward the issues of chiliasm or the millennial kingdom; toward talking a lot about how our body will be resurrected; about a first or second return of the Lord; about whether according to Paul the Jews will return to Jerusalem; and about so much more. They then had a pleasant religious conversation, a conversation that was stimulating and one could participate in without being personally affected in conscience or becoming convinced of one's own miserable state before God.

For that reason, we cannot warn enough against the danger within Christian circles of diverting attention away from the salvation of the soul to such external, piquant topics. In genuinely Reformed circles this danger is avoided, where the main content of conversation is not the issue of chiliasm, nor the matter of the Jews, but the issue of how God achieves his honor and how our soul is justified.

We are therefore not in the least blind to the danger that lurks here, and we certainly don't want to reinforce the evil whereby the soul's attention is diverted too much from the cross of Golgotha to the resurrection of the flesh. But from this it does not follow in the least that therefore we may understand the image of the Mediator differently from how Scripture presents it to us. And for that reason people go too far and fall into a wrong one-sidedness if, on the other hand, when they think of Christ, they think exclusively of the sprinkling with the blood of atonement and refuse to take into account the significance of Christ also for the body, and for visible things, and for the outcome of world history.

Consider well that thereby you run the serious risk of receiving Christ exclusively for your soul and of viewing your life in the world and for the world as something standing alongside your Christian religion and not as being governed by it. Then the "Christian" aspect is relevant to you only when it concerns a specific matter of faith, or things directly related to faith, such as your church, your school, missions, and the like, but all other areas of life then fall outside Christ. In the world you do as others do. The world is a less holy, almost unholy area that should take care of itself as best it can. And with but one more small step you arrive imperceptibly at the Anabaptist point of view, which ultimately focused everything holy in the soul, and dug an unbridgeable chasm between this inner, spiritual life of the soul and the life around you. Then science becomes unholy, the development of the arts, commerce, and business become unholy, as well as holding office in government—in short, everything becomes unholy that is not directly spiritual and focused on the soul. The result is that you end up living in two spheres of thought. On the one hand the very narrow, reduced line of thought involving your soul's salvation, and on the other hand the broad, spacious, life-encompassing sphere of thought involving the world. Your Christ then belongs comfortably in that first, reduced sphere of thinking, but not in the broad one. And then from that antithesis and false proportionality proceed all narrow-mindedness, inner untruthfulness, not to mention pious insincerity and impotence.

For this reason we must point out as decisively and earnestly as we can that for us sinners, the question "What must I do to be saved?" [Acts 16:30] must remain central and must govern our thinking. On the other hand,

§ 4

however, we must confess with equal clarity and explicitness how this same Christ who has been given to us for justification and sanctification is also given to us for wisdom and complete redemption, that is to say, for the re-creation of our whole being, soul and body, and all of this together with the inclusion of the whole world we live in, the world that belongs to and is inseparably linked to our existence.

Scripture demands the restoration of this balance in our confession. Scripture shows us Christ as Savior of the soul and also as Healer of the sick, as Expiator of our sins but also as the generous Savior who feeds the five thousand and the four thousand, and who turns water into wine at Cana. This Scripture not only focuses all the earnestness of our soul on the doctrine of justification, but also continually places before us in clear contours the resurrection of the flesh. Yes, in pointing continually to the primacy of God's honor and only then to the salvation of the elect, Scripture cannot unfold before us the final act of the mighty drama without showing us Christ who is also outwardly triumphant over all his enemies, and who celebrates his triumph on a new earth under a new heaven.

And with this clearly in view, you immediately encounter the connection between *nature* and *grace*. If grace were exclusively the atonement for sin and the salvation of the soul, then grace could be viewed as something standing outside nature, as something circumventing nature. Grace could be viewed like a jar of oil poured on turbulent waters, separate from those waters, floating on those waters merely so that the drowning person could save himself in the lifeboat quickly rushing toward him.

If, on the other hand, it is definitely true that Christ our Savior is dealing not only with our soul but also with our body; that all things in the world are Christ's and are claimed by him; that he will one day triumph over all enemies in that world; and that the culmination will be not that Christ will gather around himself some individual souls, as is presently the case, but that he will reign as King upon a new earth under a new heaven—then of course all this becomes entirely different and it becomes immediately apparent that grace is inseparably linked to nature, that grace and nature belong together. We cannot grasp grace in all its richness if we do not notice that the fibers of its roots penetrate into the joints and cracks of the life of nature.

And we cannot substantiate this coherence if with grace we focus first on the salvation of our souls and not in the first place on the Christ of God. This is why Scripture continually points out to us that the Savior of the world is also the Creator of the world—indeed, that the reason he could become its Savior is only *because* he was its Creator. Of course, it was not the Son of Man, the Incarnated Word, who created. Everything human in the Mediator himself was also created, just as creaturely as it is in us. But Scripture nevertheless points out again and again that this firstborn from the dead is also the firstborn of creation, and that the Incarnated Word always was and remained that same eternal Word who was with God and was God, and of whom it is written that apart from that Word nothing was made that has been made. So here we have the connection of Christ with nature, because he is its Creator, and also the connection of Christ with grace, because in re-creating he revealed the riches of grace in that nature.

# CHAPTER THIRTY-ONE

# DOOM AND GRACE

*The LORD God said to the serpent, "Because you have done this, cursed are you above all livestock and above all beasts of the field; on your belly you shall go, and dust you shall eat all the days of your life."*

GENESIS 3:14

§ 1    In the day when Adam and his wife ate of the forbidden tree, they did not die, which would have happened if no grace had been granted them. But that grace came, and through that grace, death in its all-destroying effect, both in the physical and in the spiritual realm, was preempted and arrested. We do not assert that death did not set in, nor that death did not seize man who had become a sinner, and in him, all creation. We are claiming only that on the day of the first sin, death, instead of unfolding to its consummate effect, had a bridle put on it. At the moment of sin itself Adam died in his soul and Eve died in her soul, and death crept into their inner existence. From the moment of their first sin, it was certain that sooner or later they would die temporal death, as indeed they have. Their physical existence also was no longer perfect. And thus anyone born of a woman will one day enter eternal death, unless the "seed of the woman," Christ, bore that eternal death for them and thus removed it from them. With Holy Scripture before us, there can be no dispute about this. But while we concede this, it does not weaken in any way the fact that the full effect of death, in body and soul, did not take place *in that day*, but that to the contrary, (1) the full effect of death was suspended and restrained, and (2) a way was opened for the escape from death.

Viewed in this light, the so-called judgment that came over Adam and Eve after the fall acquires something other than a purely condemning and avenging character. It is a lacuna in preaching and education that in the discussion of these sentences [Gen 3:14-19] the focus is only on the judgment they contain, and the grace shining through them has not been given equal emphasis at the same time. Had it involved only judgment without grace, then the sentence, both for Adam and for Eve, should simply have been, "You have eaten from the tree of which I commanded you not to eat, therefore you must now die the death you have willfully brought upon yourself, namely, eternal death." Immediately after this sentence had been pronounced they both would have fallen down dead, descended into hell, and by perishing in eternal doom would have brought an end to the human race.

We must agree that before the fall what God had told them would happen if they sinned would have come true only in this manner. In fact, we would go even further. If God had not intervened with grace, things with Adam and Eve would have come to this conclusion and none other, simply because the poison of sin would have killed them. If someone takes a dose of strong poison, he or she dies automatically and inevitably from it, unless helping love arrests the fatal effect of the poison by administering an antidote. Without further judgment or final sentence, therefore, Adam and Eve would have died the final death on that same day, if God the Lord had not taken action on their behalf against death. We therefore acknowledge that the judgment that came over them involves a punishment as well, but we also want to extol the love of God in this context and show that at the same time grace revealed itself in this judgment upon Adam and Eve.

A careful rereading of the judgment that was pronounced confirms this. Over against death stands life; and for life two things are necessary, namely, the emergence of life and the maintenance of life, as indicated in the sacrament of baptism and the sacrament of the Lord's Supper. Baptism is the sacrament of birth, and the Lord's Supper the sacrament of nourishment. §2

Read what is said to Eve, and we see life coming into being and being born. And then read what is said to Adam, and we see how the life that had come into being is maintained and nourished. Had death proceeded directly and absolutely, then Eve's sentence should have been: "You die, and the mother in you dies, and no child will ever be born of you." That would have been the mother curse; that would have been the sentence of death. But God does not say this. To the contrary, he says the exact opposite: You will bear children, and her name is not "mother of death" but mother of all living. So now she is called *Eve*, and this proclaims to all succeeding generations how already in paradise, immediately after the fall, death has been restrained and the fountain of human life is opened up again. Had absolute death set in, then the mother in Eve, from which our entire human race had to come, would be closed forever. And behold, the opposite happens: the womb of all human life is opened up. The Lord says, "You shall bring forth children." This, if you will, is the word of creation to which we and everyone called human owe our being. Here, therefore, life instead of death is at work.

And it is no different with Adam's sentence. Hunger brings death, but bread maintains life. To him who is about to die, it should be said, "Bread will be taken away from you and hunger shall become your death." But now the opposite is said: "You shall eat bread." And what does this say other than that life will not immediately drain away into death, but that it will be *nourished* and *maintained*. If we divert our attention for a moment from what is further said, if we let rest for a moment what the Lord still adds to this, and take from Genesis 3:16 only the words, "You shall bring forth children," and from Genesis 3:19 only the words, "You shall eat bread," then these words contain a double prophecy that, combined into one, says, "I, your God, restrain death and in spite of the fact that you invoked death and brought it upon yourself, I, your God, will to the contrary cause *life* to be born and *life* to be maintained."

§ 3      Certainly, pain is added, for Adam as well as for Eve. God says to Eve, "You will still bear children, but in pain"; and to Adam, "You shall eat bread from the earth, but in pain." Or as it says literally, to Eve: "in pain you shall bring forth children," and to Adam: "in pain you shall eat of it all the days of your life." Indeed, the pain that will henceforth accompany life at its birth and in its ongoing outworking is even placed in the foreground of the sentence. The character of the sentence even continues to dominate the statements, and we would not think of detracting from that character. In the sentence upon Eve, it says emphatically, "I will surely multiply your pain in childbearing; in pain you shall bring forth children" [Gen 3:16]. God speaks here as judge, something no less apparent from what follows:

"Your desire shall be for your husband, and he shall rule over you." This apparently harks back to the sin committed, in which Eve had exercised rule over Adam. She had drifted away from Adam. On her own initiative she had entered into spiritual contact with Satan. And it was she who had led Adam astray. Over against that drifting away, God now places the magnetic force with which she will be attracted to the man, and over against her leading of him now comes her being led by him. A strong desire shall draw you toward him, and you will not rule over him, but he over you, a sentence that directly referred to the nature of her sin. And, let us add, a sentence that has continued down through the ages and still continues essentially unchanged, neither by the snares in which so many a woman catches the man, nor by the emancipation fever that at present rages more and more among women.[1] Even in this imitating of man, woman still acknowledges his supremacy. That which one imitates one is acknowledging as being superior. Look at how young girls like to play like boys, but you don't find a boy who says, "I'd rather have been a girl," and if a boy does, you scorn him.

And so it is with Adam's sentence. In what God says to Adam, we notice even the form of the sentence. For it says, "Because you have listened to the voice of your wife and have eaten of the tree of which I commanded you, 'You shall not eat of it'..." What follows is thus directly introduced here as punishment. Note that this also happens in Satan's sentence, but not in Eve's. To the serpent God says, even as to Adam, "Because you have done this." In the serpent's case and in Adam's case, the naming of the crime precedes the sentence, and after the crime has been mentioned, the stipulation of the punishment follows in the sentence. Only in Eve's case this does not happen. God does not say to her, "Because you have listened to the serpent and led your husband astray, therefore..." To the contrary, any indication of her crime is missing. In Eve's sentence the only thing mentioned is the punishment that is imposed. And this is entirely in agreement with the fact that all humanity is pronounced guilty, not in the trespass of Eve but in the sin of Adam. Not she, but Adam was the head. Not she, but Adam was the responsible person. Humanity fell, not when

---

1. By the phrase "emancipation fever" Kuyper is referring to the late nineteenth-century phenomenon of increasingly popular women's rights movements in political, economic, and legal realms.

she trespassed but when Adam fell. She is the intermediary, not the person through whom the decision comes about.

The person through whom the fall came is and remains Adam, even though Adam was led astray. The state of rectitude was violated, not because Eve allowed herself to be led astray by Satan, but because Adam allowed himself to be led astray by Eve who had already been led astray. Eve's and Adam's spiritual life was joined in solidarity. And only because Adam fell did sin become a fact and get passed to all his descendants. It is not Eve who gets children in her image and likeness. The human being, the sinful human being of whom this is written, is not Eve, but Adam. From him, not from Eve per se, come original guilt and original sin. Correspondingly it is therefore said to him and not to her, "Cursed is the ground because of you … thorns and thistles it shall bring forth for you … till you return to the ground, for out of it you were taken; for you are dust, and to dust you shall return." This punishment also harks back to the crime. In paradise Adam was offered a garden of delight full of splendid fruit trees, a garden that offered all food to man without any effort or pain. But man was not satisfied with the situation God had provided for him. The tree of knowledge, which was of a higher order and whose enjoyment was denied him, had stirred him. God's ordained arrangement did not satisfy him. He wanted more than God had ordained for him, and therefore he ate of that forbidden tree. Accordingly he now descends below the condition of paradise. From the fruit of the tree he is now relegated to the plants of the field. That field will not yield its food automatically. To the contrary, what it will produce automatically are thorns and thistles. And he shall be able to eat bread, but only by the sweat of his face, when he himself battles the accursed nature of the soil and with great exertion forces that soil to produce its food for him.

In the second place, Adam's body was formed from the dust of the earth, but he was united with his God through spiritual inbreathing. Adam severed this bond, this spiritual bond, when he sinned. When faced with the choice between his God and God's command on the one hand, and the earth with that tempting tree on the other, he had said farewell to his God and chose for that tree. Correspondingly he is now told that he will indeed have what he himself chose. He chose for the tree that had come out of the earth, and therefore he shall return to the earth. Dust from dust, his body shall decompose into dust.

In this way, it is apparent that we are not detracting at all from the character of the sentence as punishment. We merely insist that we must not overlook the grace that so unmistakably shines in this sentence itself. Strange! In the other sentence, the one given to the serpent, everyone acknowledges and every commentator points out that in this judicial sentence nothing less than the gospel is expressed. In the sentence pronounced upon Adam and Eve, to the contrary, these people close their eyes to this mystery of saving grace. By contrast, our standpoint is that grace shines in all three of these judicial sentences—not only in the verdict on the serpent but also in the sentence pronounced upon Adam and Eve. In the serpent's sentence we see particular grace, while in the sentence pronounced upon Adam and Eve we see general grace or common grace.

§ 4

How are we to understand the sentence given to the serpent? Generally the serpent itself is glossed over and we think exclusively of Satan, who had used the serpent as an instrument. Not infrequently these words are understood as if the serpent refers to Satan himself, something we are tempted to do by what is stated in Revelation 12:9: "that ancient serpent, who is called the devil and Satan," as well as the designation "brood of vipers" that is applied to the hypocrites in the New Testament [Matt 23:33]. But this is not the right approach, because in this way we gloss over the words of the sentence. For the phrase "Cursed are you above all livestock and above all beasts of the field; on your belly you shall go, and dust you shall eat all the days of your life," cannot apply directly to the Devil but must be understood as applying to the serpent as an animal. It is not given to us to penetrate the enigma that lies behind this. The life of the animal world is a closed book to us, an unopened mystery. No one can determine how an animal can be guilty and be punished because Satan has used it as an instrument, and nothing remains for us but to accept the fact, as reported here, that the serpent as animal is also declared guilty and is punished. Calvin says that nothing changed in the situation of the serpent and that also before [the fall] it crawled on its belly and ate dust, but this explanation is in our opinion untenable.[2]

When God says, "Because you have done this the curse of going on your belly and eating dust will come to pass," then we have no right to say that this was not the reason and that it was the same way beforehand. When it says of Eve that she now will bear children in pain, everyone understands

---

2. See *CCS*, ad loc. Gen 3:14.

this to mean that apart from sin she would have given birth without pain. And when it says of Adam that he now shall eat bread by the sweat of his face, everyone understands this to mean that without sin he would have enjoyed his food without effort. And thus we must also understand the sentence upon the serpent. If the serpent had not become the instrument of Satan, the serpent would not have moved on its belly and would not have eaten dust. The clear text does not allow for any other interpretation.

This cannot be grasped if we live with the supposition that after the fall in fact nothing changed about or on this earth, and that the earth as we now know it in fact looks just as it looked, outside paradise, exactly as God created it. But it is precisely to this entire notion that we object. As the narrative of Genesis 3 indicates, the earth previously did not produce thistles and thorns, there were no carnivorous animals, and the situation must have been quite different. The curse that came over the earth is not fiction but full reality. And the earth under the curse, the ground, the plant kingdom and the animal kingdom, looks quite different and manifests itself entirely differently than when it was an earth under God's creation blessing. Of the earth it is said "And God saw everything that he had made, and behold, it was very good." [Gen 1:31]. But now, by contrast, the curse rested on the earth and its various realms of life.

If we keep this in mind, then it is obvious that significant changes must have taken place, in a manner that we cannot explain, in the condition and state of the ground as well as in the plant kingdom and the animal kingdom. One of those changes was in the appearance and manner of the serpent's existence. The sentence given the serpent was not a pseudo-sentence, but a real sentence. It is impossible to determine how such a change was possible. Nevertheless, think of the caterpillar and the butterfly. When a child hears for the first time that a caterpillar and a butterfly are the same animal, the child does not believe that either. This creepy, crawling animal is supposed to be the same animal as that beautiful butterfly? And yet it is true. Of course, we are absolutely not arguing that similarly the serpent was originally a beautiful animal like the butterfly and was subsequently reduced to a state comparable to that of the caterpillar. But we point out that an animal that does not crawl but flies, and an animal that does not fly but crawls, can organically be the same animal. And so there is no reason per se to reject the possibility that the serpent initially had another shape unknown to us, and now under the curse was reduced to that crawling shape that slithered in the dust.

If we are not to violate the narrative, the enmity between the serpent and man must be understood in the first place to refer to the actual serpent and only then can we penetrate the spiritual background. Throughout Scripture the serpent is depicted as the enemy of our human race. When someone calls a woman a serpent, he is expressing the harshest judgment that can be pronounced on a woman. And on the lips of Jesus, *serpent* is the terrible name the hypocrites receive. It is incredible how even today many thousands of human lives are destroyed in Asia and Africa by snakes. And also in snake charming through the sound of tones, man still celebrates his triumph over the world of snakes in rather remarkable fashion. There is no single wild animal that human beings can render so completely powerless as the snake. The snake charmer keeps ten or twelve snakes in a box, and in the East we can see young girls wrap big heavy snakes around their necks as if they were not living snakes but fur boas.[3] However unfathomable all these mysteries of the animal world may be to us, for our part we stay with the word of Scripture and understand therefore the sentence upon the serpent as applying in the first place to the serpent itself. The serpent continues to occupy an entirely unique place among all the animals.

But of course this is not the end of it. We encounter the serpent when it is first mentioned not merely as an animal, but as an instrument of Satan. It is declared guilty and punished, not because of any evil it did as an animal, but because it allowed itself to be used as instrument of Satan. It would therefore be quite superficial to understand the sentence pronounced on the serpent as a sentence restricted to the animal world. Behind the animal existence of the serpent lies a spiritual background. And though it has not been revealed to us what real connection exists between the serpent and Satan, the punishment goes via the serpent to Satan, and thus the sentence upon the serpent must also be understood with Satan in view.

---

3. Kuyper is relying here on popular accounts and imagery of the East. The farthest east he personally traveled was later in life to Romania, Asia Minor, Syria, and Israel. For Kuyper's travels around the Mediterranean recorded in his *Om de oude Wereldzee*, 2 vols. (Amsterdam: Van Holkema & Warendorf, 1907), see James D. Bratt, *Abraham Kuyper: Modern Calvinist, Christian Democrat* (Grand Rapids: Eerdmans, 2013), 322–35.

# CHAPTER THIRTY-TWO

# PLACING ENMITY

*He disarmed the rulers and authorities and put them to open shame, by triumphing over them in him.*

Colossians 2:15

§ 1     More than once the question has understandably been raised regarding what God's speaking to the serpent meant. After all, the serpent was an animal. An animal does not understand such words. The conclusion is then that such speaking to the serpent in the proper, natural sense is out of the question. Generally speaking, we concede this. But anyone who has delved more deeply into the animal world has noticed clearly that one animal differs greatly from another. You need only compare the dog with the cat, the horse with the cow. A dog and a horse certainly understand something, if not through understanding words, then most certainly through sound and tone, whereas the cat and cow are impervious to the same sounds. And when we look at what wild-animal trainers and those who formally train other animals have been able to accomplish with the most common animals, and what they can make such animals do on command, then it is difficult to come to any other conclusion than that we are generally very mistaken if we deny animals all sensitivity to our human utterances.

If this is true of us humans in general, and to an even greater extent of people who specialize in this, how much greater then must the receptivity have been to voice, sound, and tone when God the Lord spoke. In this context we must not forget that the snake is still extremely sensitive to tone changes in sounds, as evidenced by the paralyzing effect of snake charming. Nor must we forget that in Holy Scripture the serpent is always portrayed as being gifted with a special degree of skill and deliberation. This is so true that Jesus even holds up the snake as an example because it is "wise,"[1] that is, it never acts thoughtlessly; that "the way of a serpent on a rock" is recommended to us as a marvel of skill [Prov 30:19], and that the first time the serpent appears in Holy Scripture it is said in Hebrew to be very 'arum.

This 'arum is rendered "crafty," but two things must not be lost from view. First, this concerns the nature and the exceptional quality inherent in the serpent, apart from the effect Satan had on it. This 'arum was therefore a quality God himself had created in the serpent and can thus not be intended in any negative sense. God had looked upon the serpent and had seen that it too was very good (Gen 1:31). And second, this same word 'arum is translated elsewhere in Scripture not as crafty but "prudent" (Prov 12:16, 23; 13:16; 22:3; etc.). To take but one example: Proverbs 22:3 says, "The prudent sees danger and hides himself, but the simple go on and suffer for it." Here prudent is a translation of the same word 'arum that is used of the serpent in Genesis 3:1. If we connect this with what Jesus says of the serpent being "wise" in the sense of cautious and farsighted, then it seems to us that this word of Jesus refers back to Genesis 3:1, but also that in Genesis 3:1 'arum should not have been rendered "crafty" but "skillful, prudent, farsighted, cautious, clever," as exegetes of old also rendered it. This would at the same time eliminate the unsettling element in Jesus' recommending of an objectionable, disturbing quality of the serpent and making it an example, for his words then would refer not to the serpent in its evil practices, but to the serpent as God created it.

Similarly, among humans as among the animals, there are those who naïvely suspect no evil, who do not look two steps ahead, but there are also those who are more clever, who watch their step by noticing everything and being prepared for everything. Well, that being prepared for everything, that innate cleverness, would then have been originally created in the serpent by God. Satan had abused that quality in the serpent. Because of that quality in the serpent, more than any other animal the serpent was capable of discerning the wrath of God in the pronouncement of the curse.

---

1. Matthew 10:16; SV voorzichtig: "prudent, careful."

And this quality, one that in all respects is an excellent quality, was what Jesus recommended to his disciples. So we see that all the links fit together.

§ 2     Before we take leave of the serpent as serpent, we must still say something here about the enmity between this animal species and our human race. And though the meaning of this word of the Lord is quite definitely not exhausted by its significance for the animal world, we nevertheless do not understand Genesis 3:14–15 in a natural manner if we do not permit these verses to be applied to the animal world as well. It requires no elaboration if we say that today there definitely is enmity between humans and serpents. Anyone coming under the power of a somewhat alluring serpent is doomed, and year after year tens of thousands of people are killed by snake bites. This raises the question whether it was like this from the beginning. When God looked upon his creation and declared it to be very good, did the serpent already at that point have the capacity of spitting poison, and was it already at that point filled with enmity against humans? The reason we answer this question in the negative is not that the life of Adam and Eve then would have been in danger. This problem could have been solved by saying that Adam and Eve had sufficient sway over the animal world to restrain the serpent, even as today people still partially do this. The reason is that, in our opinion, it is not compatible with the perfection of God that he would have created the animal world in this way. The perfection of creation demands harmony, and here the terrible disharmony would have been introduced into his creation by God himself. And apart from man, the small, gentle animals would in an instant have become a prey of the snake and of other carnivores or poisonous animals. And even more significant are the words, "I will *put* [place, establish] enmity between you and the woman, and between your offspring and her offspring." These words show that something new enters here. An enmity that exists does not have to be placed, indeed it cannot be placed.

If this leads to the supposition that the harmful, poisonous, and carnivorous animals were originally not harmful, not poisonous when created, and not carnivorous when they first appeared in paradise, then this certainly provides a basis for the assumption that this placing of enmity, however much it is concentrated in the serpent, nevertheless had further implications and indicates how in the animal world a radical change must have taken place through which terrible murderous instincts broke out that at present still pits entire animal species against one another and against the human race. It is remarkable in this respect that from of old, prophecy paints for us a picture of the future in which animals that are now carnivorous will reveal another nature. Thus we read in Isaiah 65:25 (in connection with the serpent's eating dust) that "the lion shall eat straw like the ox," that all harmful and mauling elements shall disappear, because "they shall not hurt or destroy in all my holy mountain." And elsewhere (Isa 11:7–8) we read that "the cow and the bear shall graze; their young shall lie down together; and the lion shall eat straw like the ox. The nursing child shall play over the hole of the cobra, and the weaned child shall put his hand on the adder's den." These passages supply clear indications that the present nature of poisonous, harmful, or carnivorous animals is not constant, not original, not necessarily permanent, but that it came about as an intervening phase. The proclivity was not part of creation; one day it will disappear, but now it is present.

What then is more obvious than seeking the solution to this riddle in the telling word of the Lord: I will *place enmity* between you and this animal species. If it was the case that the animals that were once nonpoisonous and noncarnivorous now have been made poisonous and carnivorous, then therein lies a very clear and completely poignant explanation of the way in which this enmity has been *placed*. It then also explains to us how one and the same lion can alternately be a symbol of Satan and a symbol of Christ. For on the one hand we read that the Devil prowls around like a roaring lion [1 Pet 5:8], and on the other hand, that Christ is the Lion of the tribe of Judah [Rev 5:5]. Applied to the Devil, the lion refers to the animal that now exists, whereas the lion testifying to Christ is the lion that existed originally. Zoological anatomy cannot answer the question how such a tremendous change could take place in the mode of existence of these animals. The anatomical study of animals can only dissect the animals as they are found at present. What they were like originally falls outside its research. And even if it shows us very cleverly that the organs and parts of the body in the animal as it is found today are entirely suited for mauling and eating flesh, it proves virtually nothing against the possibility of the eternal Being omnipotently transforming that which he had formed with equal omnipotence.

On the basis of the preceding we conclude that this "placing of enmity" between the serpent and humanity refers to nothing less than the enormous change in the serpent's nature and way of life, transforming it from a gentle, harmless, and clever animal into a poisonous, harmful, and crafty animal. And if this is true, then it is obvious that the same also

§ 3

applied to the rest of the animals that are now harmful, poisonous, and destructive. Originally there was no enmity between these animals and humanity either, but it is God who, after the fall, has placed enmity between these animals and humanity. It was necessary to highlight a piece of the history of the fall rather elaborately because otherwise it is impossible to reconcile what nature shows us with the perfection of the Creator, which is something unbelief has so often capitalized on.

People talk about a deer in all its beauty and loveliness, which is attacked by a tiger that pounces on the defenseless animal and tears it to pieces; or a dove in its loveliness that encounters a hawk that plunges its talons and beak into the sweet bird and tears it apart. These people then ask you whether this is really the creation of a God of love. It is these common natural phenomena that gave rise among pagans to all kinds of notions about a destructive God who supposedly exists alongside the saving God. And we must concede that such terrible facts recurring day after day and night after night in all of nature are incompatible with the confession that God created everything according to its kind and that he saw it and found it very good. And this is why this *"placing* enmity" is so important to us, together with the prophecy of the lion eating straw like the ox and the child playing with the cobra and the adder, because they show us that in all these terrible things we do not see nature but antinature, an abomination that comes not from God but from sin. No, the animal world as it now exists was not conceived by God and not brought about in his work of creation. What manifests itself now is the curse in its dreadfulness. Originally that animal world was different, it was worthy of God, even to such a degree that the cherub of heaven can be symbolized to us in the lion, the eagle, and the ox.

The conclusion of God's sentence upon the serpent, that the serpent shall bruise man's heel but that man shall bruise the serpent's head, must in connection with the preceding of course be applied to the animal world as well. And then the general import of these words, as applied to the animal world, can be nothing other than that the harmful animal does endanger our life and will harass and harm our race, but in the great struggle between the harmful animals and our human race the victory remains ours. In the individual struggles between humans and animals, the animal may often win, but in general all wild animals will be defeated and Eve's race will be triumphant in the conflict between the "seed of the woman" and the "seed of the serpent," that is, between the human race and the animals. In populated civilized regions there are no longer wild animals, and no matter how fiercely a tiger or hyena may be armed, humanity already possesses so much superb weaponry that no leap of the tiger will outrun its shot.

If, with this explanation, justice has been done to the literal words of Genesis 3:14-15, then the entirely different question arises as to what deeper meaning lies behind these words. We fully acknowledge this deeper meaning as well; we wanted only to begin here as well by taking the words of God in their natural, most obvious sense. And we fail to do this if we immediately skip over the snake, giving no further thought to the snake and instantly shifting Satan ahead of the snake. This is considered spiritual, but it is a spirituality that goes against Holy Scripture. If therefore sound interpretation demands that we first do justice to what is stated literally, we are equally justified in investigating now, as a second step, the deeper or, if you will, the spiritual meaning residing in these same words. We are justified in doing this because of the connection in which the serpent appears here. For the serpent has harmed Eve not because it was a poisonous, harmful animal, but because it had become an instrument of Satan.

§ 4

The punishment meted out in the sentence must therefore not be considered apart from the evil spirit that hid behind this serpent. The serpent had been the passive instrument here. The serpent itself had not really done anything, but had allowed Satan to operate through it. Thus when it says in Genesis 3:14, "Because you have *done* this," these words establish a direct link between the evil spirit that made use of the serpent and the serpent who became its instrument. This connection, which leads us from the serpent as an animal to the ancient Serpent, the Devil, is therefore not prominent but implicit in the words themselves.

If we take this connection as real, then it must of course be understood to mean that the fallen angels or, if you will, the devils, possess the ability to make contact with the animal world and that there is also a certain connection given in creation between the demons and the animal world. You need think only of the cherubim, on the one hand, and of the demons on the other hand, who cry out that they want to enter into the pigs [see Mark 5:10-13]. And if our view is correct that the characteristics of being poisonous, harmful, carnivorous, rabid, and so on, were not originally created into the animal world but entered it through the curse, then something demonic lies hidden in the poisonous, carnivorous, and rabid aspects of the animals. This is manifested in a terrible way in a human who has been bitten by a rabid dog. The frenzy in which such an individual destroys himself or herself indeed possesses a demonic character, and anyone who has ever witnessed such a horrific scene must acknowledge that this simply cannot be in accordance with the requirement of God's original creation.

Thus we do not understand the connection between the serpent and Satan merely as being a manner of speaking, or in a purely metaphorical sense, but in the proper and real sense. Satan had come to humanity through the serpent, and conversely within the hearing of these human beings, the judgment upon Satan came through that same serpent to Satan. Understood in this way, "*placing* enmity" acquires a much broader meaning and further import. Eve had been amiable with the serpent, as we still deal amiably with a dog or horse—but we must keep in mind that Eve did not deal with the crawling serpent as it exists today, but with the serpent when it still possessed its form as created, which was apparently beautiful and alluring. But no person befriends an animal as creepy and repulsive as the snake is now, especially not a woman. Satan had made use of that amiability, that unguarded contact with the serpent, to get on a footing of intimacy with the woman, and he had succeeded.

In this way the spiritual poison entered the human soul, a poison that would merely be represented subsequently in the poison of the serpent. A bond was established between Satan and the human heart, and every child of God knows only too well what fearsome effects still frequently emanate from that bond with Satan in all kinds of stimuli toward evil and in all kinds of temptation. Since we were born in our original sin, we stand on a much more intimate footing with Satan than with God, and to some extent we can say that our depraved nature stands on a footing of friendship with Satan, on a footing of enmity with God. The sinner does not have it in his power to change this, because this cannot become different unless his nature is changed. And this change in nature is something no sinner can accomplish himself. Only God can bring about this change in the sinner. Only he can *place enmity* between Satan and our nature, by regenerating that nature and having us be born again.

§ 5    In fact, the words "I will place enmity" thus contain the entire revelation of particular grace. It is the proclamation that God the Lord will intervene and that within the same human heart in which Satan caused the turn from good to evil, God will now in turn accomplish the return from evil to good. This, and nothing less than this, is contained in those significant words.

In the second place, in the words that follow, "between your offspring and her offspring," lies the prophecy that death will enter, but not on that day in the absolute sense. Indeed, if that had been the case, there would have been no seed of the woman and our race would never have been born. So in the words "and her offspring" lies the decree of grace that humanity is not finished off, that there will appear an entire human race with a long history, and that the struggle between humanity and Satan will not remain the struggle between Satan and that one woman, but will become an age-long struggle between Satan and our human race.

And finally, the last addition, "he shall bruise your head, and you shall bruise his heel," contains the clear announcement that this struggle of our human race with Satan will not be an endless repetition of constantly the same thing, but that it will manifest a process, a history in the proper sense, and that this terrible history will lead to the final decision in which one day the fundamental victory of the Son of Man over Satan will be won. In that sense, therefore, we have every right to call Genesis 3:15 the first revelation of the gospel. The gospel is found here in two ways: subjectively in the announcement of the new birth—that is, after the placing of enmity; and objectively and finally in the prophecy of the final triumph that will lead to a son of man crushing Satan's head under his feet. Election is not mentioned. Both notions, on the one hand that our race will be victorious and will be saved, and on the other hand that only what is born again will participate in that salvation, are still intertwined. Nevertheless, the personal aspect is already present. It is stated in so many words that God regenerates Eve personally. For the enmity begins by being placed between *her* and the serpent. And it appears that Eve has also understood that the final triumph will come through one man. For after Cain's birth she says, "I have gotten a *man* with the help of the Lord," thinking that in this child, who would shed the blood of his brother, that man had already come who, by shedding his own blood, would obtain life for his brethren.

# CHAPTER THIRTY-THREE

# RE-CREATION

*And they heard the sound of the LORD God walking in the garden in the cool of the day, and the man and his wife hid themselves from the presence of the LORD God among the trees of the garden.*

GENESIS 3:8

§ 1    In that day Adam would fully die,[1] and behold, he lives nine times as long as the oldest one among us, and reaches an old age of almost one thousand years. In this telling fact lies the redemptive thought that the majesty of God's justice works against sin and reacts to it by shifting, postponing, and delaying its effects. Judgment is suspended for a time, the execution of the sentence is delayed, and the triumph of justice is postponed. It will not come to pass that the full punishment follows immediately after the sin, but a period of centuries is interpolated between the sin and the full and absolute execution of the sentence. This is the long-suffering of God, the first condition for every manifestation of grace. In God, long-suffering means that he *postpones* wrath, that he restrains the vengeance of his justice for a time, thereby creating room so that grace can become operative. Without this long-suffering, neither saving grace nor common

---

1.  *Note by the author*: The word *volsterven* (analogous to *volstaan, volharden, volkomen, volwassen*) best reflects the sense of the Hebrew. [Ed. note: Kuyper uses the word *volsterven* here, a neologism consisting of *vol* ("full" or "complete") and *sterven* ("to die"), hence "fully" or "completely die."]

grace would be conceivable. It is always that long-suffering that constitutes the indispensable background of all saving grace.

Thus what would have followed immediately in paradise is shifted forward many centuries to the last day; between paradise and the last day now comes room for a long-extended history of humanity, and saving grace extends over that humanity in its long history. Here is hidden, therefore, a mighty act of God that governs the entire life of the human race, an act to which attention certainly must be drawn. By virtue of the creation ordinance, our human race was destined to unfold gradually as an organism in all of its branches. But when sin entered, and like a quick-acting poison threatened to kill off the wellspring of this entire organism, the poison of sin did not lead to the killing off of this whole organism, but the effect of this poison of death was restrained in a miraculous way.

In view of God's omnipotence, no one will dispute the possibility that Adam and Eve could have immediately suffered eternal death and that the same God who created the first human pair could have created a second human pair in their place. Or, if we look only at the elect, and if we consider those elect as nothing but a collection of individuals, then it would as such be quite conceivable that God would have made all his elect enter life in the manner of Adam, through direct creation. Yes, we would go even further and not hesitate to say that, if an all-prevailing interest had not been at stake, then casting Adam and Eve into eternal death followed by the creation of new, individual elect persons would have had everything in its favor. You need think only of what horrors of sin would then have been cut off, what human suffering would have been prevented, and above all how with this approach the doomed, who now enter eternal death, would never have been born. God the Lord nonetheless did not choose this path of creating anew but rather maintained the organism of our human race, now poisoned by sin; he wrought within this race the miracles of his grace and from that organism he permitted his elect to emerge as the choice flowers of his power.

All of this shows obviously that all other considerations had to yield to a supremely holy concern that depended on the preservation of the human race, even though it was poisoned. This dominant concern could of course have its ground only in God, because for man as man it would have been much more preferable if the doomed had never come into being. The moving cause could therefore lie only in this, that such a re-creation would have constituted the failure of the first creation, a foiling of God's order and God's work by means of the order and work of Satan. Therefore, the honor, the majesty, and the prestige of our God required that Satan would be denied this triumph over the Lord our God, and that the end of all things could show how Satan's scheme ended up in mere vanity and God's order ultimately shone in the triumphant radiance of wisdom.

§ 2    Once we have grasped this, we sense something of holy indignation vibrate within us when we hear this grand distinction between *new* creation and *re*-creation being presented as something of secondary importance. Not, of course, that we would impute evil intentions to the Anabaptists, who traditionally taught this, as well as all manner of later groups who have come in their wake, as if they deliberately and intentionally wanted to rob God of his honor. But nevertheless it hurts to see how people in such circles are so minimally concerned with the honor of God. Note well that those who, like the Anabaptists, reject re-creation and choose for new creation foist upon God an entirely opprobrious absurdity.[2] Had new creation been chosen, then postponing the judgment would be senseless, allowing the continued existence of our race poisoned by sin would lack any purpose, and the circle of the elect could have come into being through new creations without adding the terrible multitude that ends in eternal damnation. The fact that these doomed individuals were and are nevertheless born then remains entirely without motivation and becomes a fact of repulsive arbitrariness.

If the re-creation of that which had been first created, rather than the creation of something new, is the rule God has chosen, then we understand why our race, no matter how much poisoned by sin, continued to exist and to develop into its generations, families, and individuals. We also understand how God's honor depended on the fact that his glorious work of creation would ultimately be shown not to have failed but to have served the glorification of his name. Then there is a foundation on which the whole development of this terrible history rests. Although we do not understand the fearful mystery of the doomed, we then nevertheless realize how the

---

2. Kuyper here means to contrast theological traditions that would emphasize greater or radical discontinuity between created nature and redemptive grace ("new creation") over against a more continuous and restorative relationship ("re-creation"). Kuyper's preference for the latter emphasis is apparent in his previous discussion of nature and grace, where we find such formulations as "We cannot grasp *grace* in all its richness if we do not notice that the fibers of its roots penetrate into the joints and cracks of the life of nature." See CG 1.30.4.

honor of God ultimately stands higher than the salvation of the creature. And though it remains unfathomable to us, we nonetheless receive the impression that it is reasonable, so that we do not simply remain silent and prostrate, but can kneel down in worship before the unsearchable riches of the wisdom and knowledge of God. But if we move away for a single moment from the governing notion of *re*-creation and slip into the false notion of a kind of creating *anew*, then any reasonable motive for all of this falls away; everything acquires an absurd character, and we get the impression of mere arbitrariness, so that any impulse to worship is transformed into a dull and meaningless dumbfoundedness.

Therefore, we cannot emphasize enough that the entrance of sin was followed by neither the full extent of death nor the new creation of God's elect, but to the contrary, judgment was postponed and eternal death was deferred. For this shows convincingly that the Lord our God wanted to allow our human race, after it had been poisoned by sin, to continue to exist and to develop as would have been the case apart from sin, and to show now, in full view of the whole universe, how his marvelous grace was able to carry out his divine ordinance against Satan's raging while nevertheless maintaining his holy justice unharmed and unimpaired. For this purpose, it was necessary first of all to shift and defer the ultimate decision, and second, to restrain the lethal effect of sin in the swiftness of its process. Only where both these conditions were fulfilled could a realm emerge where the saving grace for the redemption and sanctification of God's elect could be fully operative.

The facts are in full agreement with this. If in our foolishness we had §3 come to the aid of Adam and Eve after their fall, we would undoubtedly have spoken to them in great detail about the way of salvation and only very incidentally about their everyday earthly life. But this is not how God does it. He says not even a word to Adam and Eve about salvation in Christ. What he does say about the One who will come in the person of Christ to trample the serpent underfoot, he says not to Adam, nor to Eve, but to the serpent. This is a remarkable fact that clearly shows how the Lord places in the foreground of his redeeming work not our salvation, but the preservation of his honor over against Satan. Even in the announcement that Eve (the Lord is silent about Adam) will be regenerated because God will put enmity between this woman personally and Satan, he does not speak to her but to the serpent.

Only thereafter does the Lord turn to Adam and Eve, not to reveal the way of salvation to them but solely to speak to them about their earthly existence, and to show how his judgment on sin will affect this earthly existence while at the same time grace will rescue this earthly life and make it bearable. If what the Lord spoke to the serpent had not been included, then particular, saving grace would not have been mentioned at all. In what God says to Adam and Eve nothing but the provisional judgment of common grace is being sounded, and even in what the Lord says to the serpent, particular grace is found in only two words: "I shall *place* enmity" and "he shall bruise your *head*," while the rest of what is said to the serpent relates to common grace rather than to particular grace. It is therefore incomprehensible how the dreadful history of Genesis 3 can be discussed over and over again without paying attention to common grace, which is almost exclusively being sounded, while instead focusing virtually entirely on what God said to the serpent and on the punishment Adam and Eve received.

The restraining of sin and its consequences, which constitutes the real essence of common grace, is manifest immediately in what we read of Adam and Eve after their fall. For we read that in shame they tried to hide from each other with their body and from God with their whole being. Would this have happened if sin had had its full and final effect in them? Or to phrase the question differently: Do you think that after his fall Satan similarly tried to hide in shame? Of course not! And Satan is not ashamed of his audacious rebellion against God, but rather boasts in it and, defying God, proudly raises up his head before the thrice Holy One. Does not even our experience among sinful people teach us that reckless sinners whose conscience has been seared and whose heart is hardened, far from being ashamed of their sin, on the contrary angrily boast in their sinful daring and take pleasure in evil? And yet, sin has not yet reached its full scope even in such sinful people. They have not yet succumbed to eternal death. Individuals from such circles have at times come to eternal life.

Assume for a moment, therefore, that in Adam and Eve sin had had its ultimate effect all at once, as a quick-acting poison—then their repentance, their shame, and their hiding from each other and from God become entirely inexplicable. If it is nevertheless certain that sin, left alone and operating freely, is such a quick-acting poison, even to the extent that no one doubts whether spiritual death immediately began to operate within Adam and Eve, then it follows that this shame and their blushing before each other and before God can be explained only if restraining grace intervened immediately. Restraining grace therefore set in immediately after the fall, and what our churches teach about the "little sparks" or "small traces" of the image of God in the sinner is nothing but the confession of this sin-restraining grace that set in immediately after the fall, not only for the elect but for all people, that is, for our human race as a whole.[3] This did not arrest spiritual death. We are all born spiritually dead in "trespasses and sins" [Eph 2:1]. But death is followed by the decomposition of the corpse. And it is that spiritual decomposition of the corpse that could be restrained, not entirely but in part. Not entirely—so that the dreadful effect of sin would become evident to everyone, but *in* part—so that also in this way the riches of God's creation and of his re-creating grace would be glorified in our sinful race.

If we ask where in Genesis 3 we find the restraining of the power of sin in man, then we must point first of all to the fact that, far from placing himself over against God in reckless sinful pride after his fall, on the contrary, with fear in his soul Adam trembled before God and fled from him in anguish. Add to this that, far from reveling in their nakedness, as many sinners, men and women, do today, on the contrary, Adam and Eve were gripped by a painful feeling of shame and made a covering from vine leaves for what they felt had become their shame. But understand us clearly: we are not saying that this shame involved repentance toward God, a sorrow reaching out to the Eternal, or a saving stirring of the conscience. Nothing indicates this. Rather, their repentance reminds us of that of Esau. Do not forget, even in the repentance of someone like Esau or even of a Judas, common grace is speaking. Satan never repents and cannot repent. Had either Esau or Judas already been completely like a devil, they would have laughed in God's face and would have been proud of their dreadful deed. Thus even if we concede unreservedly that such a repentance cannot effect anything toward salvation, we nevertheless maintain that repentance as such never springs from sin but is a reaction

---

3. Kuyper's reference here to "little sparks" and "small traces" of the image of God picks up on common imagery in the Reformed teaching on the doctrine. Thus Calvin writes (*Inst.* 2.2.12) that even "in man's perverted and degenerate nature some sparks still gleam." See also *CCS*, ad loc. Rom. 10:18: "The Lord, even during the time in which he confined the favour of his covenant to Israel, did not yet so withdraw from the Gentiles the knowledge of himself, but that he ever kept alive some sparks of it among them."

against sin and therefore can and may be explained only on the basis of common grace.

§ 4       Almost, though not exactly, the same applies to the attempt made by Adam, as well as by Eve, to *excuse* themselves. When Adam says to God, "The woman whom you gave to be with me, she gave me fruit of the tree, and I ate," and when Eve says in the same spirit, "The serpent deceived me, and I ate," then something is expressed in the answer of both that cannot be explained apart from common grace, apart from the restraining of sin. Satan would never have excused himself, but rather would have been insolently proud of his evil. Satan with all his devils does tremble at the power of the Lord, but it is the trembling of combativeness that is ready to take a stand against the power of the Lord. But here we notice nothing of this devilish character of consummate evil. Every word makes it apparent that what they wanted most was *not* to have eaten of the tree.

We do not say that it was true repentance over their sin as such, but it is apparent that it was awe of God's majesty, whose wrath they feared, that made them cower in fear. Nor do they utter any untrue word. It was true— the serpent *had* deceived Eve, and she had eaten. And also, God had given Eve to Adam as helper, and instead of being a helper for Adam she *had* led him astray, and thus he too had eaten. There is no love in what Adam says. He does not spare his wife even at his own expense; rather, he accuses Eve so that he may escape. Indeed, he goes even further. He tries to diffuse God's right to be angry by adding, "The woman whom you gave to be with me." In his mortal terror he does not even spare God's ordained arrangement. In his daring plea we hear something of Job's overconfidence [see Job 32:1–4]. But even if this is the case, both their [Adam and Eve's] answers also imply an attempt to distance themselves from sin and to reach back to their original righteousness. They do not pride themselves in their evil deed but express that the deepest cause of their sin did not spring from themselves, but was like a drop of poison injected into their soul from the outside.

§ 5       We observe the same phenomenon in our children, about which unwise parents, as well as some teachers, so often mistakenly get angry. A child has done something wrong, and many people would like for that child immediately to own up to it, and without adding anything by way of excuse promptly confess his guilt and take all guilt upon himself. But this is not how our children are. They are like Adam, at least the better ones among our children, and like Adam they first try to hide the wrong, hoping that it will not come out. If it comes out anyway, they confess, but reluctantly. And when they confess they always try to add something by way of excuse. Many parents and teachers cannot stomach this addition; sometimes they get angry about it and call it inappropriate nonsense. And yet this is looking at it entirely the wrong way. No, in that attempt at self-justification, as in the case of Adam and Eve, we recognize their unconscious realization that the sin they committed did not really spring up altogether from within themselves, that an inexplicable power had exerted an effect upon them, and that in the depth of their soul they themselves did not really have peace with this wrong action. When we understand this well, we see something wonderful in it.

But on the other hand, when we encounter a lad who says, "I couldn't care less, yes I did it, but so what?" then the Christian with psychological insight recognizes that this boy is much farther gone. It becomes difficult, of course, if a lie is mixed in with that excuse and the child begins by denying that he has done it, although he knows that he definitely did it. But however painful and dangerous that attempt at denial may be, we nevertheless must guard against singing along in the choir with those who put a premium on the "righteousness" of those shameless individuals who brazenly admit their evil deed while at the same time looking you unabashedly in the eye.

So here we encounter profound mysteries of the soul that at this point pedagogy has very inadequately thought through and analyzed. But whatever we can say, it is certain that the very fact that Adam and Eve excused themselves shows clearly that sin had not done its full and final work in them as yet, but was restrained in their soul's awareness. Without common grace, when the last small spark in the soul has been extinguished and the last small trace of the image of God has disappeared, and the process of hardening has reached its final stage, then all excuse ceases and nothing remains but pride in the evil that has been committed, which is then no longer called evil but is believed to be good. In Adam and Eve we cannot discern any trace of this; rather, every trait in their attitude reveals the opposite and is therefore conclusive proof that the restraining of sin was already accomplished in them, and they were at that point already speaking by virtue of common grace.

This is entirely in accordance with the fact that when Adam had fallen, God the Lord sought the fallen sinner. Had sin immediately reached its final consummation in Adam and Eve, and had it not been restrained, then this searching would have been unthinkable. God never searches for Satan, but always repels Satan and makes him his opponent. The searching of gracious love is possible only vis-à-vis the creature who, however much that creature may be spiritually dead and depraved in his nature, nevertheless still possesses a point of contact for divine influence. The fact per se that the Lord does not reject Adam but turns toward him, calls him, and searches for him, proves therefore that already at that point sin had been restrained in him, and that after that hidden grace for the first time there now follows the revelation of grace through the word of the Lord.

Therefore, we must reject any notion suggesting that sin was fatal but not all that fatal, since there always remained a flicker of life in the sinner. No, in itself sin, if it is not restrained, is immediately, *absolutely* fatal, a poison that neither exempts nor spares *anything*. But this is the point: grace, common grace intervened, and through this common grace of God, sin was prevented from immediately bringing its poisonous, deadly work to full completion.

# CHAPTER THIRTY-FOUR

# DEPRAVITY RESTRAINED IN THE HEART

*Wretched man that I am! Who will deliver me from this body of death?*

ROMANS 7:24

Careful consideration of what took place in paradise after the fall of man showed, first, that the struggle against Satan was placed in the foreground, and that the ultimate victory over Satan was not promised to fallen humanity, but woven into the sentence given to the tempter. It also showed, secondly, that punishments were meted out to Adam and Eve that were in both cases related to the lengthening of their personal life and the lengthening of the life of the human race. Those punishments meant on the one hand that human beings would be born, and on the other hand that the accursed earth would produce food for their sustenance. And thirdly, it showed that a change took place in both the plant kingdom and the animal kingdom that related to the disappearance of paradise and the transfer of our fallen human race to an earth that under the curse acquired an entirely different existence and appearance.

§ 1

This shows that the common notion that the involvement of God's grace in this world after the fall had to do primarily and principally, as well as directly, with the salvation of sinners, does not correspond with what Holy Scripture reports. Nothing, not even the smallest thing, about this is promised to Adam and Eve. They learned that salvation would come, not from what God says to them but from what he says to Satan. And neither to Adam nor to Eve is a single word said about their eternal salvation. They are given notice only that distress and sorrow await them. And even the lengthening of the life of our human race is not expressed directly in so many words but is implicit in the sentence. This essentially confirms the Reformed confession that in this predominant moment, not the salvation of the sinner but the upholding of God's honor over against Satan weighed heaviest, and that the gracious decision with regard to the sinner was dominated entirely by divine concern for his own honor. For this reason, the Methodist perspective on the paradise narrative is upon closer examination utterly untenable.[1]

Satan acted as God's enemy in order to destroy God's work in his creation. Rather than "keeping" paradise, as he had been commanded, Adam has turned it over to Satan and has in fact made himself Satan's ally. And this is what God's omnipotent deed opposes. He breaks this alliance and puts enmity, and he prophesies to Satan that he will be crushed by the seed of the woman. And at the point where sin would immediately have brought the full extent of death on our race if it had not been restrained in its effect, God directs his omnipotence against that deadly effect of sin, restrains it, and thereby makes the continued existence of the human race possible. But he does so always in such a way that God's justice is maintained in the distress that comes over all souls, so that it shines for the future as well, in the bruising of the heel that will happen to the seed of the woman.

Thus the maintaining of God's honor remains entirely in the foreground, and belonging among the means that must serve this purpose are both saving grace, which is particular, as well as common grace, which extends over our entire race. And the relationship between the two is such

---

1. Kuyper may have in mind the idea of the *felix culpa*, or "happy fault," in which God is praised for allowing the fall into sin because it meant that Christ would come and redeem humanity. John Wesley himself believed that the fall opened the way for greater levels of human holiness and glory. This view of the fall is not merely Methodist, however, but has roots in patristic and medieval theology. See Barry E. Bryant, "Original Sin," in *The Oxford Handbook of Methodist Studies*, ed. William J. Abraham and James E. Kirby (New York: Oxford University Press, 2009), 535–36.

that common grace is revealed almost exclusively in what is said to Adam and Eve, and particular grace only in what Adam and Eve could deduce from the words spoken to the serpent and did indeed deduce, as we may infer from the name Eve gave Cain: "I have gotten a man with the help of the LORD" [Gen 4:1], a declaration showing that she already expected from Cain the fulfillment of what had been prophesied concerning Satan. And this also shows that already at this point, enmity against Satan had been put in Eve's heart, for she rejoiced in the defeat she thought Cain would bring upon Satan.

It is quite remarkable that we do not hear anything in paradise itself about the restraining of sin in the heart of man. From the narrative itself we can deduce the fact that this restraining did take place, but this spiritual fact is not mentioned explicitly. That the fact as such took place we notice from the shame that came over Adam and Eve, the vine leaf with which they covered their nakedness, and their fleeing from the face of the Lord. The hardened sinner does not flee but defies God to his face, as Satan does. We also discern that such a restraining would take place in a more effective way on the basis of what God says about placing enmity and the prophesied crushing of Satan by the seed of the woman. But God's act of grace in the heart of man is not specifically mentioned. What the church of Christ has taught and confessed about the still-glimmering little sparks and about the small traces has been drawn from the narrative by deduction but not taken from it in so many words. In the rest of Holy Scripture there are all kinds of indications that confirm this confession of the church, but even those indications do not speak of the restraining of sin in the form in which the church confesses it.

§ 2

Nevertheless, the truth thus confessed is for that reason no less firm, provided that we do not weaken the character of sin. If we see in sin a cause of spiritual and physical weakening, but not a deadly, quick-acting poison that if unrestrained immediately leads to spiritual, temporal, and eternal death, then there is certainly no restraining of sin—a conclusion to which Calvin was the first to point, and on which the entire doctrine of common grace is built.[2] This is why the Reformed confession has continually placed full emphasis on the deadly character of sin and has seriously

---

2. This conclusion follows from the general tenor of Calvin's discussion in his Genesis commentary at this point. See *CCS*, ad loc. Gen 3:19: "For God does not consider, in chastising the faithful, what they deserve; but what will be useful to them in future; and fulfils the office of a physician rather than of a judge."

combated any weakening of the concept of sin. "Completely incapable of any good and prone to all evil" was the formula in which the Heidelberg Catechism expressed this truth.[3] And when we stand immovable in this dreadful truth, then it is quite natural that we find traces—in the paradise narrative, in all the rest of Scripture, in human life around us, and in our own human heart—of a divine working through which the swift and absolutely fatal effect of sin has been and is still being restrained in many ways, even where there is no saving grace involved at all. Or do we not find among the pagan nations and unbelievers in our own surroundings many phenomena that show a certain inclination toward good things and a certain indignation about all kinds of crime? True, not an inclination toward anything that has to do with salvation, but an inclination toward what is virtuous and harmonious? Are there not acts of maliciousness and dishonesty, and violations of justice, against which the public conscience, also among nonbelievers, rebels? And are there not many deeds of neighborly love and mercy that can be mentioned that have been performed by unbelievers, sometimes putting believers to shame? When Pharaoh's daughter saved the infant Moses from the Nile, did she do evil or good? And is it therefore not clear that the absolute ruin of our nature by sin—a truth we wholeheartedly confess—is in many cases in conflict with reality? And do we then not see clearly how, in the face of such cases, we must do one of two things: either surrender our confession of the deadly character of sin, or hold on to that confession with all our might, but then also confess along with it that there is a common grace at work that in many cases restrains the full, deadly effect of sin?

§ 3 We reach the same conclusion via another route as well. The spiritual condition is always the basis for the external condition, at least when we look in general rather than at specific cases. A generation, a family, or a tribe in which sin operates recklessly and without restraint also comes to ruin externally. Even nations that are unsettled internally soon succumb externally. Think of Babel, Moab, Ammon, or imperial Rome. It appears that instead of succumbing soon after paradise, our human race has persisted all these centuries, such that, with ups and downs, a continual development of our human race has occurred whose result is that we now stand on a much higher plane than the human race in the days of Nebuchadnezzar or Cyrus. If this is so, then this is proof that humanity's

---

3. Heidelberg Catechism, Lord's Day 3, Q&A 8.

spiritual collapse cannot have proceeded unhindered and unrestrained. A humanity concerning which nothing else could be said than that under the curse it is "prone to all evil" and "completely incapable of any good" could not have had such a history. The history of our human race through all these many centuries is therefore proof that on the one hand the terrible law of sin did indeed rule, but on the other a law of grace broke that power of sin.

Let us picture clearly the interconnectedness of things. In the human soul lay the center of life for this entire earth. If life in Adam's soul succumbed, then the death of his soul would bring about the death of his body, followed by the death of our whole race and in its wake the curse upon this whole world. All this was tied together like links of a single chain. Thus, if the world were not to perish altogether under the curse, if our human race were not to be destroyed, and if Adam's body were to remain alive yet for nine centuries, then the absolute effect of death in his soul would have to be broken. Had it not been broken, then it would have meant the end of him, of his body, of our race, and of the whole world. That it did not end but that the world endured, and our race emerged on this earth, and Adam lived another nine centuries, was possible only because in his soul the last sparks were not extinguished but fanned to new life, and because, when the image of God in him was about to disappear entirely, divine grace intervened to rescue the last traces.

Let us be understood clearly: this does not apply exclusively to the §4 elect. Common grace does not treat them in a special way. What we expound here applies to our human race as such. Granted, the elect also benefit from it, and up to a point we can say that everything revolves around God's church. For should the elect come into being and should they be born, then the first requirement was that our race had to continue to exist. How else would the elect have been born? Also, particular grace is connected with common grace and makes use of it. Without common grace, the church of Christ would not find a place to stand among our human race. One day, when common grace departs and the rule of the Antichrist breaks out [see 2 Thess 2:3–7], the church will be taken up in the air [see 1 Thess 4:13–18]. But however close the connection between particular grace and common grace may be, we must nevertheless never lose sight of the fact that common grace has a purpose in itself. Common grace has operated for ages in China and India without there being any church of Christ in those countries. We still enjoy the fruits that have come from common grace in Greece and Rome in the days when even the name of Christ's church had never yet been mentioned. The fundamental issue in principle involves God and not man. Just as he lets his flowers bloom and spread their fragrance on mountains and in valleys where never a human foot has trod, and even as God has his cattle on a thousand hills where no human benefits from it, so too God has let the wonder of common grace operate among all peoples and in all nations, even where this had no direct connection with the salvation of the elect.

Common grace must therefore be viewed on its own. We must understand the wonder that God worked in the heart of man immediately after the fall by injecting an antidote into the heart against the poison of sin. We must understand that this miracle of grace had already been performed when Adam fled from God, before the seeking, rescuing grace reached out to call Adam forth from his hiding place. Had nothing been done to Adam's heart, death would immediately have effected complete destruction. That sin did not lead at once to the full implementation of eternal death was due only to the fact that God seized Adam by his heart and performed the miracle of common grace in it. This miracle was *not* regeneration. That miracle belongs to particular grace. Regeneration does not restrain sin, but conquers and destroys it. Regeneration transforms evil into good, unrighteousness into righteousness, death into life. It is an act that cuts out the cancer at the root itself and replaces it with the power of eternal life. But this is absolutely not what common grace is. It tempers but does not extinguish. It tames nature but does not transform it. It reins in and restrains, but in such a way that when the bridle ceases to function, evil automatically gallops ahead once again. It prunes the wild shoots but does not heal the root. It leaves the inner driving force of the self to its own evil, but prevents the full effect of that evil. It is a restraining, detaining, impeding force that curbs and brings to a halt.

This is precisely why common grace works in such a variety of ways. In general more strongly after the flood than before the flood; more strongly in Japheth than in Ham; and to varying degrees among all peoples and nations, among all tribes and races. Not only does this working of common grace vary from people to people, but it varies also from family to family, and in the same family between father and mother, between brother and brother, between sister and sister. Its restraining effect is, in fact, not the same in any two people. Beyond this, it differs throughout the course of history as well. There may be an era in which common grace seems increasingly to withhold its effect and sin can increasingly run its course, followed by periods that show such a marvelous working of common grace that an age of bliss seems to have dawned. Yes, even in our personal life (apart from our conversion and our particular grace) there will have been days and even years when it seemed as though common grace abandoned us, and then we could once again rejoice in a working of common grace that kept us on the path of virtue and honor.

So this common grace is an omnipresent working of God's forbearance §5 that reveals itself wherever human hearts beat and spreads its blessing upon those human hearts. For even though we sometimes hear of reprobates and scoundrels who have sunk so far and have become such brutes that we would almost doubt whether there can still be the faintest trace of this common grace in their heart, we Christians have nevertheless been taught that even the villain who has sunk to the lowest level can still become the object of common grace. How then could we ever posit that the last vestige of common grace could have departed from any human heart? Where the last small spark of common grace disappears, nothing remains but a devilish existence and the last possibility of salvation is cut off. It is precisely common grace that upholds the humanity of the sinner so that he might become an object of mercy. And even when we can no longer discern even the faintest glimmer of this common grace, we nevertheless continue to confess that, hidden under the ashes, such a spark still always glows. Certainly, some abominable people can fall incredibly low, yet their fall would be even deeper had they become totally devilish and had the last vestige of common grace disappeared from them. Even the fact that they are still alive and that they prolong their existence on this earth shows that there is still a force at work that upholds them. If they were abandoned completely, then their existence on this earth would be over and they would sink into eternal death.

By speaking of small sparks and tiny remnants, the church of Christ §6 has wanted to express that this common grace has established its foothold within the sinner himself. We can cage a wild animal behind bars, or we can tame it. If we do the former, then we find our fulcrum for rendering the animal harmless in its cage and bars, that is, in something *outside* the animal. But if we succeed in taming the wild animal completely, then we use neither cage nor bars, but we have found our fulcrum *within the animal itself*. This is virtually never possible with carnivores, but the once-wild elephant is tamed in this way. So the question arises here too whether common grace is nothing more than a force outside man that makes it impossible for him to break out into a complete abandonment to sin, or whether it seeks a fulcrum within fallen man himself and thus tames him from the inside. And then we must certainly acknowledge that common grace often works completely from the outside by removing the occasion for sin, by placing someone under discipline and custody, and so much more.

But this does not touch on common grace in its nature, that is, in its general import for our whole human race. If we investigate that nature of common grace, then the confession still speaks of glowing sparks and of the remnants that still manifest themselves, not of something external but of something that is found within man, within his inner being. The life that is in us arises from our personal self, and this also manifests itself in our inclinations and capabilities. After the fall, by reason of sin's nature, evil creeps into us, falsifies our life, and tries to penetrate into our inclinations and capacities in order hereby to lead us to sinful deeds. If the restraining of sin had taken place only at the point where without that restraining it would have come to the sinful deed, then common grace would be nothing but an external coercive force.

But that is not how common grace works. From within us it restrains the continued effect and the penetration of the poison of sin, so that it does not rob our whole life, all our inclinations, and all our capacities of all that God's image had imprinted on them. This does not excuse us, for if it were up to us, we would let the poison immediately work to its full effect. It does not take away the depravity of our nature, for if common grace were to disappear for just a moment, our nature would suddenly show itself in its absolute depravity. But common grace chose its base within our own heart for its outward working. Thus the small sparks still glow within us, small remnants are still noticeable there, and that is what common grace makes use of to restrain the madness of sin within us. It is not a new force that was created within us, but something of the original force that was still maintained. The flame smolders and simmers on the inside, but the all-destructive bursting out of that flame is prevented from the inside.

God has shown this grace to Adam and Eve immediately after their fall. Otherwise they would have reviled and cursed God after their fall. But now they trembled before his majesty and fled. And this grace is shown to them, not personally as in the case of particular grace, but as bearers of our human nature. It is our depraved human nature in which this restraining and taming power has glorified itself. And when fallen Adam begat sons "in his own likeness, after his image" [Gen 5:3], then he generated children who were depraved like him, but in whom that depraved human nature exhibited this same mark of common grace.

# CHAPTER THIRTY-FIVE

# DEPRAVITY RESTRAINED IN THE BODY

*For the creation was subjected to futility, not willingly, but because of him who subjected it.*

ROMANS 8:20

§ 1     The fixed starting point for the confession of common grace has now been identified. This means, negatively, that when man fell, he did not immediately fall utterly but saw the full extent of death postponed. This means, positively, that common grace entered immediately after sin crept into the human heart and thereby the direct and absolute effect of that sin in our human race was restrained. Or to put it more succinctly and in their mutual relationship, both sin and death as the fruit of sin gained dominion over man, his race, and the world, but this dominion was curbed by God, and such principally in the human heart itself. Small sparks, remnants that otherwise would have been extinguished and inexorably and immediately destroyed now continued to sparkle and glow, not because of any virtue that might be within us but thanks only to the common grace of God. The doctrine of original sin—of the *total* depravity of our human nature—is again and again in danger of being weakened in a semi-Pelagian sense whenever we attempt to explain these small traces on the basis of anything other than common grace.

But even if the fixed starting point for "common grace" lies in man himself, it does not confine itself to this restraining work in the human heart. Man is not only a spiritual being but exists at the same time physically, and there is also a world that belongs with this body. Soul, body, and world belong together.[1] The soul, still in its original righteousness, has a body in original perfection and a paradise as its world. One day, at the close of the age, the blessed soul shall possess a glorified body and the kingdom of glory as its world. The soul of a damned person, which has become devilish, will one day exist in an entirely unnatural body, with hell as its world.

A soul sunk into sin, in which the effects of sin have been restrained for a while, will thus also have to possess a body subject to sickness and death, but a body in which the full effect of death is restrained for a while yet, and he will have to live with that soul and that body in a world that lies under the curse, but without that curse being fully implemented as yet. We sense that only in this way and in no other way can justice be done to the constitution of soul, body, and world.

Luther and Calvin, but especially the latter, have therefore emphasized that all that is bothersome, disturbing, or dangerous from the perspective of our body or of the world in the presently existing order of things did not exist in paradise but came only when, because of sin, the curse spread across the earth and together with the visible world also affected man's body.[2] According to Calvin, the significance of the change that took place is that "all the evils of the present life, which experience proves to

---

1. See *Inst.* 1.15.3: "Although the primary seat of the divine image was in the mind and heart, or in the soul and its powers, yet there was no part of man, not even the body itself, in which some sparks did not glow. It is sure that even in the several parts of the world some traces of God's glory shine."

2. For Luther, see *LW* 1:204: "As Paul points out, the earth itself feels its [sin's] curse. In the first place, it does not bring forth the good things it would have produced if man had not fallen. In the second place, it produces many harmful plants, which it would not have produced, such as darnel, wild oats, weeds, nettles, thorns, thistles. Add to these the poisons, the injurious vermin, and whatever else there is of this kind. All these were brought in through sin." For Calvin, see *CCS*, ad loc. Gen 3:18: "He [God] more largely treats of what he had already alluded to, namely, the participation of the fruits of the earth with labour and trouble. And he assigns as the reason, that the earth will not be the same as it was before, producing perfect fruits; for he declares that the earth would degenerate from its fertility, and bring forth briers and noxious plants. Therefore, we may know, that whatsoever

be innumerable, have proceeded from the same fountain."[3] He mentions in this context even inclement weather, frost, hail, and so forth, to make us understand that nothing is excepted.

§ 2    We are told extremely little about the change that took place in man's physical condition. There are only three indications that can help us. In the first place, there is the sentence for Eve that she will bear children in pain, indeed, in multiplied pain. "I will surely multiply your pain in childbearing; in pain you shall bring forth children" [Gen 3:16]. It cannot be disputed that the emphasis here falls on the pain. The creation ordinance was "be fruitful and multiply" [Gen 1:28]. What is new is therefore not that the woman will bear children, but that she will bear them in pain. We will not entertain the question whether apart from sin the manner of bearing children would have been different. We limit ourselves to the fact that what should in itself have been a quite natural event now becomes highly painful, not only giving birth itself, but often the pregnancy as well. Knowing firsthand the cost to the woman of having a child, we do not get the impression at all that it would have been this way in the creation ordinance and that God would have said of this: "and God saw that it was good." We are faced here with something that in many ways violates nature and has necessitated the emergence of an entire field of science to avert the worst consequences. Help, preferably very skillful help, is needed. Nevertheless, again and again the mother succumbs in sacrifice for the life of her child. And more than one interpreter rightly points out that so many kinds of suffering happen to the woman, not only in and before the birth of a child but even if she remains childless, through all kinds of illness and affliction that accompany a woman's life. So Scripture and experience are in full agreement. And the terrible fact that this aspect of the woman's life is, as it were, overwhelmed in various ways by discomfort and pain, such that time and again she puts her life at risk, cannot be explained from creation, but can be explained only on the basis of sin. It shows us what remarkable changes must have taken place also in the physical condition of humankind as a consequence of the fall into sin.

It is not very wise to view this in a mechanical sense. The body has an organic connection with the soul, and it is therefore much more

---

unwholesome things may be produced, are not natural fruits of the earth, but are corruptions which originate from sin."

3.  CO 51:75: "Ex eodem prodiise fonte omnes praesentis vitae aerumnas, quas experientia innumeras esse ostendit." [Ed. note: For the English, see CCS, ad loc. Gen 3:19.]

understandable that so tremendous a change as that which came about in the soul through sin also had an impact on the condition of the body. We know from personal experience how strong the influence of our spirit on the condition and even on the appearance of our body is when we look at our face in the mirror as it reflects our various moods, and we also notice it around us daily. In the case of insane people it is often terrible to see. But even if we see the influence the soul exerts on the body, and although the artist can present this clearly to us, the matter itself remains a mystery and no one is able to explain clearly how the sin in Eve's heart had such an impact on her body that she could bear her children only in pain. Meanwhile the fact remains, even if insight into how it happened escapes us. What we know, therefore, is that sin attacked not only her soul but also her body, and caused such a weakening, deterioration, and upheaval in her body that this occurrence, most natural in itself, would now become, entirely unnaturally, a bloody operation, sometimes a semi-murder, or worse.

The second point, in which we encounter a similar indication, is what §3 God spoke to Adam. As such, it requires no further elucidation that the effect of sin on the body applied not only to the woman but also to the man. Both are equal with regard to the bond between soul and body. So if we know from what was said to Eve how Eve's female nature and the nature of all women is physically disturbed, then we know simultaneously that the same took place with Adam, and that his body also suffered the direct consequences of sin. And this is confirmed in what the Lord said directly to Adam himself, that henceforth he would work in the sweat of his face and would eat his bread in pain. Herein the fatigue of the body is expressed, the beading of the sweat on the face as a sign of that fatigue, and thus the need for more robust nourishment, formerly the fruit of the tree, now bread. Especially when there were still only two humans on earth, which was for the most part rather lush, providing nourishment for two mouths could not create a problem. The fact that now the emphasis falls so heavily on the pain and exertion can be explained only from the feeling of physical weakness that came over the first man as a consequence of sin. We are used to this from our youth and don't think anything of it, and we therefore find it so difficult to understand what kind of punishment lay in "working for his bread." But when we imagine Adam, who had first stood in the perfection of his body for which any kind of weakness or lethargy was totally foreign, then we can understand how this announcement of the "sweat of your face" contains an indication of the weakening that Adam's body had undergone.

A third indication, finally, lies in Genesis 3:21, which states, "And the LORD God made for Adam and for his wife garments of skins and clothed them." This is generally taken to refer only to the covering of their shame. But although we gladly acknowledge that this is also implied, we nevertheless cannot concede that this exhausts the meaning of these words. They contain much more, not only in connection with the idea of sacrifice, but also in relation to the body. Note two things. First, that Adam and Eve themselves had already made loincloths of vine leaves sewn together, and thus already had found a covering of their shame in the narrower sense. In the second place, we must note that what God made for Adam and Eve were garments. The word used here is used also for the *tunic*, the garment commonly worn in Israel, a close-fitting garment that covered the entire upper body and hung down below the hips. We must therefore think rather of a garment that was given to man and woman to let them go from the unclothed to the clothed state because of increased sensitivity of the weakened body to rain, wind, cold, and heat. And if we understand it in this way, we have indeed a third indication of the decline of the body. The body had acquired a need that it had not known before.

§ 4    If we conclude from this that immediately after the fall, not only the perfection of the soul but also the perfect strength of the body was broken, then this weakening of the body appears here as an effect of death. It is, as Augustine already noted, a process of death if, even without dying immediately, life gradually subsides because it bears the germ of its decay within itself.[4] Only in this way must the gradual devastation of the human body be understood. The resistance of the human body had been weakened, and the harmful influences that endangered it internally and externally appeared from all sides. We still speak today of healthy and sick, and each of us immediately knows whether we are well or unwell from how we feel, but only man in paradise has been healthy in the absolute sense, when he was still as God had created him, and we will be perfectly healthy again only when one day our body will be glorified. In this in-between state we all carry the germ of death within us, and the distinction

---

4.  See Augustine, *The Literal Meaning of Genesis*, in *On Genesis*, trans. Edmund Hill, ed. John E. Rotelle (Hyde Park, NY: New City Press, 2002), 11.42(32), p. 453.

between being healthy and being sick that we now observe is never anything but relative.

This becomes especially clear when we realize that this involves not only the personal physical existence of Adam and Eve, but the hygienic condition of our whole human race. That condition is such that among all peoples an army of physicians and surgeons has had to emerge to combat the myriad diseases and ailments, and all kinds of preventive measures must continually be taken in order to continue to enjoy a relative sense of well-being through caution, temperance, and moderation. Some people whose blossoming health impresses us are stronger by nature but do not realize what treasure they have received. Otherwise, when we look at our families one by one, and in those families at the individual members one by one, and we let them tell us about their complaints and ailments and illnesses and unpleasant experiences, then we notice all too quickly that in many ways suffering is virtually universal, and that a deathlike shadow, alas, hangs all too gloomily over our human existence.

Add to this the pestilence with its destructive force, which nowadays is largely restrained, thank God. Think of the mysterious germs of death that moved untraceably across almost all of Europe again in the influenza [pandemic].[5] Think of the hereditary causes of death in the dreadful diseases of tuberculosis and cancer that pursue so many generations as a fearful scourge. Think of the small ailments of headache, oral pain, nervous pain, and so forth, that sometimes destroy one's entire *joie de vivre*. Yes, ask yourself how it happens that each time when the season gets colder and the air more piercing, a whole cadre of otherwise strong men and women is afflicted in their respiratory organs and within a short time carried to their graves. And when we think of all this happening as though before our eyes, we see how death goes forth breathing destruction upon our entire human life, clearly showing us the dreadful consequences of sin also for our bodily existence.

It is an evil that becomes even worse, in that it does not work itself up merely from the root of our life, but it also repeatedly renews itself

---

5. See Burke A. Cunha, "Influenza: Historical Aspects of Epidemics and Pandemics," *Infectious Disease Clinics of North America* 18, no. 1 (2004): 148: "During the 19th century, three influenza pandemics occurred in 1830 to 1831, 1833 to 1834, and 1889 to 1890. As in the preceding century, major epidemics occurred between pandemics. ... The 1889 to 1890 pandemic originated in Russia and devastated Europe before reaching North America in December 1889."

incidentally. For it is not only *original* sin that has brought about this physical disruption in our nature as such, but the fearful law of death functions above and beyond this by continually and repeatedly drawing new corrupting strength from *actual sin*. Death not only threatens our body through the original sin in paradise, but again and again through new sins in generations and individuals. That Cain murders Abel is a force of death that comes over Abel through Cain's sin. Even if we don't think of direct murder and poisoning, how much weakening of the strength of the body is not due to all kinds of sins of intemperance, boisterous behavior, wanton living, not keeping God's ordinances. How many families and generations, even peoples and nations, have through all kinds of excesses of sin descended and sunk into a condition of physical weakness, so that in the end you could read the degeneration on the degraded visage and determine it by the distorted and bent shapes. How many evil illnesses do not exist that pursue some families like veritable plagues and appear to be virtually unavoidable. And seeing all these physical miseries, who will doubt for a moment the revelation of Scripture that sin has affected, weakened, and disrupted not only the life of man's soul, but most certainly also his physical existence, and has subjected it to death.

§ 5      But behold here as well common grace.

If common grace had not entered also in relation to the body, it is self-evident that this terrible power of sickness and death would, if not immediately then shortly thereafter, have made an end to man's physical existence, especially when humanity consisted of only very few individuals. But this is not what happens. On the contrary, grace intervenes and restrains the evil effect of the consequences of sin also with regard to the body. To the first man is given a lengthening of life, even a lengthening of centuries, and the fact that many have tried to discount those long lives of the ancient patriarchs is only because they did not understand the grace, not only for themselves but also for our entire race, implicit in the lengthening of the life of these ancient ancestors. In addition to this marvelous lengthening of the lives of the ancient forefathers, common grace as it relates to the body manifests itself even in the punishment imposed on Adam and Eve. True, she will bear children in pain, but she will nevertheless bear children. Children will be born. Death will not be able to prevent the emergence of the young, new life. And even though still today death claims its victims especially among the newborn, in his common grace

God nonetheless ordains the law of birth, which cries out against the law of death, and among all peoples supersedes the power of death.

Common grace speaks similarly in God's ordinance for work as the means for strengthening the body and for acquiring food to maintain that body. Humanity is not cut off—it will be born, and after having been born will be able to live on this earth. The shadow of death will cover our race, but with the seed of death in our blood it will, thanks to common grace, nevertheless be able to reveal its inner treasure of life, to achieve a history in which it manifests its meaning, and to glorify its Creator in its rich diversity in gifts and talents. History itself already points powerfully to this, in the fact that God himself indicates to man his need for clothing. For realizing what it means that a savage people walks around virtually naked, whereas a civilized people wear clothing, even under a hot sky, makes us sense how within this one fact of clothing lies embedded the opening up of a world of development that still continues to unveil to us its marvels (along with its sins, of course).

Indeed, common grace extends much further yet. For the fact mentioned above, that in our tattered condition we can still speak of prosperity and well-being and health, albeit only in a relative sense, is exclusively a fruit of this common grace of our God. If even for a moment we feel really good and robustly healthy, we owe it to this alone, that out of pure grace our God suppresses the working of death in us, and we must therefore praise our God for it. And if we read how God himself protects fallen man against the rawness of the atmosphere by clothing him in sheep's wool, are we not also being shown one of the most beautiful dimensions of common grace when we see how the earth, though it brings forth thorns and thistles, also brings forth healing herbs against all kinds of sickness? It is a dimension of miraculous common grace when the human mind is given the capacity for discovering the secondary causes of many kinds of pestilence and illness, thereby preventing their consequences. Yes, do we not taste the mercy and loving-kindness of our God when he elevates this common grace, also with regard to the body? And this to such an extent in our lives that in the end all kinds of suffering are mitigated, all kinds of calamity are prevented, and in case of illness or accident we have at our disposal so much skilled help that exerts a restraining impact on the deadly effect of sin? The fact that medical science has for many years turned itself against God's honor and has appointed itself to take God's place in having control over our lives must not cause us to overlook the marvelous love of our God that speaks so obviously also in this dimension of common grace. The point is not to oppose death forever, because all of us will descend into the grave, but to worship the loving-kindness of our God who, through the herb he permits to grow and through the skill he imparts to man, temporarily restrains the working of the poison of death.

# CHAPTER THIRTY-SIX

# DEPRAVITY RESTRAINED IN NATURE

*Cursed is the ground because of you.*

GENESIS 3:17B

This is how common grace began in the *soul* of man, by keeping the small sparks from being extinguished. Common grace found its second foothold in man's body by providing support for his physical life force, which temporarily postponed death. But now common grace had to bring about also a third effect, namely, in man's world. This chapter will deal with this third starting point of common grace.

§ 1

The facts communicated to us are (1) that the earth was cursed because of man; (2) that there was a change in the condition of the plant kingdom, so that the earth now produced thorns and thistles; (3) that a change came about in the state of the animal kingdom—think only of the serpent; and (4) that paradise disappeared.

These four related facts point therefore to a very important transformation of the appearance of this world. As became apparent in the early chapters on common grace, a second change in the condition of this world came about during the flood, which by itself already makes it impossible for us to draw conclusions from the present condition about the situation as it was before the flood. But we must never draw conclusions from that preflood condition regarding the condition that existed through and after creation, for an enormous change had already occurred within that original condition through what Holy Scripture calls *the curse*.

With respect to our planet we must distinguish four periods or conditions. First, the condition described in Genesis 1:2 with these words: "*The earth was without form and void, and darkness was over the face of the deep. And the Spirit of God was hovering over the face of the waters.*" Second, the condition that came about through the omnipotent deeds of God in the subsequent five days of creation, whose results were seen in paradise and of which we read in Genesis 1:31: "And God saw everything that he had made, and behold, it was very good." Third, the condition that came about through what we read in Genesis 3:17: "Cursed is the ground" because of man. And fourth, the condition that was brought forth when "all the fountains of the great deep burst forth" [Gen 7:11]. Only now have we come to the condition of the earth as it still exists for the most part at present and will continue to exist until the day comes when "once more I will shake … the earth" (Heb 12:26) and "the elements shall melt with fervent heat" (2 Pet 3:10 KJV).

This clear indication of Scripture that the condition of this world has already changed three times and will be changed once more does not in the least supply us with a scientific explanation of these changes. That remains the province of science, and we may say in general that the research into our earth and its inner reaches does indeed show that more than one such violent change in the earth's crust has taken place. It is quite remarkable in this context that the oldest books of Holy Scripture already speak of such violent upheavals occurring in a time when no one as yet thought of such scientific research and when as yet virtually nothing was known about it through direct research. It is therefore sufficient for us that Scripture and research into natural phenomena have already come to similar conclusions to the extent that both establish the fact of more than one such upheaval, even though in the nature of things each throws its own light on the matter. For the scientist draws all his knowledge from material phenomena and tries as much as he can to explain things on the basis of natural causes.

Conversely, forgoing such a scientific explanation entirely, Scripture points us exclusively to the spiritual cause of these violent upheavals and of the final violent upheaval that is yet to come. Scripture calls the change that took place after the fall the *coming of the curse* and it tells us that this curse has come over the earth *because of man*. Of course, science cannot judge this; it cannot tell us anything about it; it is stone-blind to that spiritual background and must limit itself to research into the lower, material effects that took place. It knows nothing of the spiritual unless it allows itself to be instructed by the Word of God. The crust and the bowels of the earth can tell science what upheavals have taken place, but the scientist cannot know anything about the deepest cause of this upheaval unless God, who brought it about, reveals it to us.

In itself, however, the thought that there is a definite connection between the spiritual and the material is not strange but rather attractive to us. The relationship within our own being between our soul and our body shows us this. Sin in the soul automatically brings a curse on the body, disrupts the body, and brings it to a lower level. Similarly, if it is true that there is a direct connection between man and the world he inhabits, then it is not the least bit strange that the change that came about in man, both in soul and in body, must also have had consequences for the condition of this earth. Even in ordinary history, where forces that maintain the world are still operative, but no forces that create, we see again and again how the arrival of man changes the appearance of the landscape. When we compare the condition of the land of our own country in the time of the Batavians[1] with the appearance of our country today, we scarcely recognize what existed at one time in what we see now. Yet all changes of that kind have come about very slowly and gradually, independent of man's doing, even if we take into account the change caused by the sinking or rising of the level of the soil along our sea coast. No matter how substantial these kinds of change in the condition of the land may have been over the course of history, they still offer merely a very weak analogy for the awesome changes that took place in what is called the prehistoric era. Scientific results also indicate that back then, forces were at work that, though having subsided for the most part at present, have brought about not merely small, gradual changes, but very violent and abrupt changes in the earth's crust.

For those of us who must explain these upheavals as students of Scripture rather than as scientists, it is certain that these very major

§ 2

---

1.  The Batavians were an ancient Germanic tribe native to the Netherlands.

changes in the condition of the earth are caused by divine actions that have struck our entire world as with a single, awesome agitation and have changed it in terms of its constitution and condition. In accordance with God's order, the condition of man's soul, of his body, and of his world advances and regresses together. As the one is, so is the other. Everything in this world is geared toward man, finds its end only in man, and the whole plan of creation and the condition of the earth and the world can be explained only from man as the linchpin. According to what divine ordinance and law the spiritual determines, the condition of the visible remains a mystery to us. We do not know, and any speculative twaddle about it is groundless chatter. The fact is certain, but the explanation is withheld from us. For that reason we will have to be content with the knowledge that the right or wrong relationship in which man, as the linchpin of the whole creation, stands toward God serves as the cause for God turning his face toward the world either in blessing and favor, or in wrath and curse. Whether man stands aright and for that reason God's favor turns toward the world, or man takes a wrong position and thereby draws God's wrath toward this earth, each is the cause for this same world being at one time a paradise blessed of God, and being at another time darkened under God's curse, bringing the elements into a harmful struggle, toning down or degrading the progress of life in all the kingdoms of nature.

§ 3     There is no question here of an external, mechanical punishment, as when a thief receiving lashes receives an external, mechanical punishment. We must not say that because man fell into sin, the beautiful and lovely paradise was taken from him. No, there was a connection between fall and curse. Just as in the case of a drunkard there is a connection between his sin and the destruction of his physical strength, his domestic happiness, and his social prosperity, so too there was a connection and relationship between the sin in paradise and the loss of that paradise. The earthly judge adds punishment to sin, and a father must act in the same way in raising his child. If, when the child does not want to work, the father punishes him by withholding food, then the punishment is added externally. But in the case of the Judge of heaven and earth, the punishment here stems from the sin itself. Sin itself brings its own punishment in its wake. Sin and punishment are not mechanically welded together but stand in an organic relationship to one another. And this is what Scripture expresses, first through the addition that the curse comes over the earth because of man, and second, by establishing a direct link between the disappearance of paradise and the sinful condition of Adam and Eve.

If we are to understand common grace on this point, then we must keep in mind that grace was also manifested amid the evil itself, through the restraining of its destructive effect. In this way, as we saw, common grace worked in man's spiritual nature. That nature became depraved, but grace restrained the corrupting effect at the point where it would have reached its full effect, and thus something of the original remained in the small sparks. Death was also at work in man's physical nature, but that death was restrained in its effect, and thus a measure of physical well-being was retained, herbs could resist illness, and temporal death was postponed. And now the same thing happened with regard to man's world, or if you will, to nature around him. Wrath had its effect, the curse came, but the effect did not run its full course. Here too a restraining took place, and in that restraining lay common grace here as well. Had that restraining not taken place, then the destruction would immediately have continued until it reached the "without form and void" state that characterized the earth before creation formed a world out of this earth. Death is decomposition, and if all strength and power had gone to decomposition, ultimately nothing would have remained but this "without form and void" condition. But this did not happen. The deadly effect began its work but at a certain point it was restrained by grace. Scripture expresses this with the simple contrast that the earth would indeed bring forth "thorns and thistles," but it would nevertheless still produce bread for man. The thistles and thorns show us the curse; the bread shows us common grace. From earliest times, the rose has appealed to man in a mysterious way: the stem of the rose yielding both its sharp thorns and its opening bud, fragrant and beguiling to the eye, speaks to us as a flower from paradise, which now can hurt with its thorns but presents us with a symbol of common grace in the rose itself.

For that reason, we are wrong to complain about the thorns rather than marveling at the allure that has remained in the fragrances and colors of the rosebud. If we have learned to measure the depth of sin in the light of God's Word, we realize and know that if we had received what we deserved, the whole world around us would be formless and void, no kernel of grain would ripen on the stalk to silence our hunger, indeed, no spring or stream would offer us water to quench our thirst. Immense wilderness regions are spread across every point of the compass, as if to call out to us

§ 4

how the world would be for us if no common grace had intervened. And in the portrayal Scripture gives us of the world of the doomed, all has been taken away, including the water, and the rich man in the place of pain cries out for someone to dip the tip of his finger in water to cool his burning lips [Luke 16:24]. So even water is grace, a marvelous gift of our God, left to us by common grace.

And when we remember what splendor for eye and mouth and ear and feeling this world can still offer us in spring, summer, and fall, then how can we not kneel in grateful worship before a God who is so merciful and gracious that he left all this to us, in spite of the fact that we called down the curse upon ourselves? When all of that disappears in winter, and the shroud is spread over the earth, and even the water freezes solid into ice, we behold in this winter scene a continual reminder from God of what our life would be like without common grace. And what so delights us in spring is precisely that it makes us drink in once again the luxuriance of common grace. Those who have no knowledge of sin consider that man cannot have fallen so deeply because he still has such a rich world around him. But anyone taught by God, likewise in the doctrine of sin, rejects such a vain self-exaltation, acknowledges that the arid desert should have been our world, and with praise exalts the common grace of our God, who still has his sun rise on the evil and on the good, clothes the lilies for us in beauty, and feeds the birds in the woods, so that they may sing for him, but yes, for us sinners as well.

§ 5    Thus we feel both the curse and common grace in the earth itself, in the animal kingdom, and in the plant kingdom. We see it in the condition of the earth itself, when we compare the desert with the oasis and wilderness with fertile plain, and when we consider winter alongside springtime. We see the same contrast before our eyes in the plant kingdom, where on the one hand we see the curse in thorns and thistles, in wild parasitic plants, in poisonous and harmful plants. But on the other hand we also see common grace in the bread that feeds us, in the luscious fruit that refreshes us, in the flower whose fragrance wafts toward us, and in the herb that heals us. And also in the animal kingdom we encounter on the one hand the curse in the animals that are now wild and carnivorous, in all kinds of poisonous insects, and in those tiny organisms that are visible only under the microscope and enter our body as microbes. But on the other hand we also encounter common grace in all kinds of useful animals that serve and help us, feed us with their meat and milk, give us their eggs, increase the sociability of our life as pets, or warble for us with their God-given song.

We can notice this same twofold effect everywhere in nature around us. Storms and hurricanes are forces that bring destruction and threaten life, but in a milder form wind is the force that serves us and purifies the atmosphere. The sun singes and nourishes at the same time. Frost lets life grow rigid, but it kills a host of vermin and benefits the fields. Thunder frightens and makes lightning strike, but it refreshes the air that has become too muggy. And so it is in fact with all phenomena in nature. On the one hand there is always the destroying, devastating effect that comes from the curse, and on the other hand the restraining of evil that places the forces of nature at our service and benefits us. This is a contrast that we must keep clearly in mind in order to understand the provident rule of our God, for today the providence of God no longer functions on the basis of the original creation but is governed by this duality of the curse and of the common grace that restrains this curse.

But keep in mind that this common grace is *not* particularized, and thus is not geared to someone's personal sin, but relates exclusively to the shared sin of our race in the fall. Common grace stands in direct contrast to particular grace. Particular grace is personal and is geared to the personal; common grace by contrast always follows the rule that God "makes his sun rise on the evil and on the good, and sends rain on the just and on the unjust" [Matt 5:45]. If we lose sight of this we continually stand before the despairing question why the boat of a decent fisherman perished in a storm at sea, while the ship of the godless pirate was spared in that same storm.

We have yet to say but a word about the disappearance of paradise. This is not told to us in so many words in Scripture; we are told only that man was expelled from paradise [see Gen 3:22-24]. However, the one does not conflict at all with the other. Rather, man first had to be led out of paradise before paradise could disappear. But let us not create any fantastic notion about this disappearing, and let us not think, as the Roman Catholics do, that paradise was picked up and taken elsewhere.[2] What was paradise

§ 6

---

2. Kuyper is referring to the belief that after the fall, paradise was transported to heaven and serves as a place where departed believers reside until they reach eternal blessedness. This notion of paradise as an intermediate location between earthly existence and final blessedness, however, was only one of several different Christian interpretations of the postfall location and function of paradise. See

except a wide portion of the same earth on which we live? But that same nature which we now see in its impoverished state then shone in higher splendor. This involves the same question we encountered in regard to the original righteousness of man. That original righteousness, our churches confess, was not something that was added to our nature, but a higher development of that same nature that at present is depraved within us. And in the same way, paradise was not something that was added to the nature of this world, but a development of that same nature on a higher level.

When we compare nature around us in winter, spring, summer, and fall, we see before our eyes what an all-encompassing change is brought about simply by a minor change in the relationship of a small portion of the earth to the sun. When it comes to paradise we therefore have to think of nothing else than the original glory and perfection of nature around us as belonging to and befitting the original righteousness within the human heart. The disappearance of paradise then follows automatically because God withdrew his blessing in part, even as the summer garment of nature subsides in fall and winter. Even if we were to rediscover in Kashmir, or wherever, the place where paradise once stood, we would not find paradise there again; in that spot we would now find an ordinary piece of the earth, depressed by the curse and upheld only by common grace.

But this does not in the least alter the fact that the disappearance of paradise may have been linked to the whole upheaval caused by the major changes in the earth's crust that occurred at that time, traces of which are still apparent all around us. For the curse was an all-encompassing and all-pervasive working that came from God Almighty and his holy wrath, and that assailed the nature of the earth itself and of the plant and animal kingdoms so momentously that they would henceforth display quite different phenomena. The curse and its restraining by common grace did not become noticeable on one specific point or another, not in this or that plant, not in this or that animal. The effect of the curse was general; it attacked all of nature. And there is literally no single thing of which we can say that it exists now in the same way that it existed at one time in paradise. What we see now and observe around us is nature, not as it was originally, but as it has become. And we cannot arrive at a clear worldview,

---

Jean Delumeau, *History of Paradise: The Garden of Eden in Myth and Tradition*, trans. Matthew O'Connell (New York: Continuum, 1995), 23–70, 155–74.

a clear vision of life and of nature, unless we remember at every point that the original perished in what at present bears the mark of the curse, and unless at the same time we discern the reining in of that curse in the work of common grace that calls for our adoration of God.

# CHAPTER THIRTY-SEVEN

# FROM PARADISE TO THE FLOOD (PART 1)

*Then the LORD said, "My Spirit shall not abide in man forever, for he is flesh."*

GENESIS 6:3A

§ 1      This brings us to the end of the careful rereading and reconsideration of the rather extremely important first three chapters of Genesis. These have led us to two conclusions: First, that man who fell took death into himself, became a prey of death, and now lies in the midst of death so that, were he left to his own devices for even one moment, man would immediately sink into eternal death by virtue of his depraved nature. But also, second, that as soon as this death and curse crept into man—into his soul and body, but also into his world—a working of God's grace intervened to partially restrain this death and this curse in his soul, in his body, and in his world. And because this grace did not confine itself to a few individuals but was directed at the human race as such, this gracious working of God rightly bears the name *general grace* or *common grace*.

We now return to the Noahic era, with which we opened our exposition of common grace. Meanwhile, more than sixteen centuries lie between paradise and God's covenant with Noah; the significance of these centuries for our human race requires a brief elucidation. If we stay for the time being with the commonly accepted data, then the genealogy from Adam to Noah leads us to the conclusion that the covenant with Noah was made in the year 2340 BC, that is, the year 1656 after the creation of Adam. About this period of more than sixteen centuries extraordinarily little has been revealed and handed down. But when, going back from our time into the past, we first take the eighteen centuries[1] that have now passed since the birth of Christ, and then the more than twenty-three centuries that, according to the commonly accepted chronology, have elapsed between the flood and the birth of Christ, and we then add to these the more than sixteen centuries that separate Noah from the creation of Adam, then it appears that this well-nigh entirely unknown first period covers about one-third of the history of humanity. For that reason, it is important for us to get at least some idea of the significance of this period. We can do this only by taking the small indications we find in Genesis 4:1–6:6 and relating them to each other, noting as well what new elements came in the Noahic period.

The condition of our human race was different in this first era of more §2 than sixteen centuries than it is now, as is immediately apparent from three indications that seem to identify a change in conditions.

To this belongs in the first place what we read in Genesis 6:3: "My spirit shall not always strive with man, for that he also is flesh."[2] These words give us to understand that before the flood the Holy Spirit contended in a different manner with man than thereafter. The reason for this change is given: man apparently was incapable of enduring this contending with the Holy Spirit because he is flesh. The tension, the battle, the struggle of the Spirit of God with the spirit of man exists now as well and cannot cease until after the judgment of the last day. But God can continue this contending of his Spirit with man's spirit in very different ways: stern and awesome, or with restrained wrath and sparing gravity. And full justice is done to Genesis 6:3 only when we consider that the contending of God's Spirit with man's spirit was much more awesome and much less sparing in the first sixteen centuries, while in the period after Noah it took on a much more moderate form and less vehement character. A father on earth can take two different approaches to disciplining a recalcitrant child, using either a very stern or a more moderate form of discipline, trying first with severity and then with more kindness. Similarly this word gives

---

1. Eighteen centuries at the time when Kuyper wrote these articles (in *De Heraut* in 1895–1901; published in book form in 1902–5).
2. KJV; ESV: "My Spirit shall not abide in man forever, for he is flesh."

us the impression that in the first period God the Lord dealt much more sharply and severely with humanity and in the second period much more graciously. The severe approach had hardened the sinner and had caused unrighteousness to overflow. This is why this first, unsalvageable generation is now eradicated in the flood, and after the flood a new era of more abundant common grace begins.

The second indication of this nature lies in Genesis 8:22, where we read that "While the earth remains, seedtime and harvest, cold and heat, summer and winter, day and night, shall not cease." This implies that the course of life became a regular, fixed order. We should not understand this to mean that before the flood *all* regularity, *all* order was absent. The order of day and night cannot have been interrupted (see Jer 33:20, 25). The influence of the revolutions of the heavenly bodies, and thus also the influence of the atmosphere, now follows a certain regularity but with great variations within that regularity, so that one winter is very severe, another one mild, one spring is balmy, the other inclement, and so too summer and winter manifest themselves in very different degrees of heat and cold. So we can understand very well that these differences were much greater in the past, so great that it often seemed as if the fixed order of nature was totally disturbed. The laws that govern these variations in the atmosphere are still to a large extent a mystery, even if some progress is made in solving them. But once those laws have been discovered, it would of course be apparent that, depending on whether the moving cause became stronger or weaker, these variations could themselves also be stronger or weaker. And Genesis 8:22 must be understood only in the sense that after the flood there came more permanence, steadiness, stability and thus also more consistency in the transitions, whereas before the flood those transitions sometimes had such an inconstancy that the regularity that of course continued to exist was almost hidden from observation. So human life in that period must of course have become extremely disturbed.

Finally, the third indication is found in Genesis 6:5 compared with Genesis 8:21. Both verses deal with the condition of man's inner life. Genesis 6:5 describes this condition before the flood in this manner: "Every intention of the thoughts of [man's] heart was only evil continually," whereas after the flood, Genesis 8:21 limits itself to the observation of the simple, much less sharply delineated fact that "the intention of man's heart is evil from his youth." We already noted the conspicuous difference between the two descriptions of the condition of the human heart in our discussion of the Noahic period.[3] Genesis 8:21 speaks neither of "every intention" nor of "continually" nor of "only evil." Apparently in Genesis 6:5 we have a description not of the normal spiritual condition of man under the rule of common grace, but of the condition as it had gradually become through a partial moving out of reach of common grace. For Genesis 6:5 explicitly adds, "The Lord saw that the wickedness of man was great in the earth," something which seems to indicate the deterioration and worsening, the degeneration and corruption, that had come since the line of Seth had mixed with the line of Cain. In connection with the first indication that we found in Genesis 6:3, this cannot be understood in any other way than that the severe contending of God's Spirit with man's spirit had hardened the spirit of man and thus the fruit of common grace had become almost entirely lost. In relation to this, it is striking that the word spoken in paradise, "in the day that you eat of it you shall surely die," had been fulfilled literally in the members of that generation. As soon as the degeneration had progressed to the extent that the effect of common grace on the heart had been reduced to virtually nothing, the whole mass of people perished in one day in their watery death.

If we take these three indications together, then they enable us to describe with a degree of accuracy the so-called signature of this era, or if you will, its spiritual significance. Of course the notion that would otherwise be the most natural one, namely, that this would reflect a mistake on God's part, is out of the question. It would then be as if, after first subjecting humanity to a severe test, the Lord realized after the fact that this could not continue and that humankind had become unmanageable under it, and that for this reason he then first eliminated the failed generation in order to try again in a more prudent and effective way with humanity after the flood. It does indeed seem as if Holy Scripture itself supports this notion, for example, by saying that "the Lord regretted that he had made man on the earth," and that "it grieved him to his heart" (Gen 6:6), but the sense and meaning of this human expression when transferred to God is so transparent that it would not be worth the effort to deliberately elucidate this whole topic once again. All that Holy Scripture reveals to us about God as a God whose works are known from eternity and "with whom there is no variation or shadow due to change" [Jas 1:17] definitely precludes any notion of a failed experiment on the part of the

§ 3

---

3. See *CG* 1.3, "The Noahic Covenant Was Not Particular."

Lord our God. In that sense "he is not a man, that he should have regret" (1 Sam 15:29).

Conversely, the entirely different situation that existed prior to the flood has a very serious significance for us sinners. If after the fall common grace immediately had been as strongly suppressing and restraining as it is now, then a true awareness of sin among the people would have been unthinkable. If we are born with a poison in us, but at the same time with the antidote in our heart that renders the effect of the poison largely harmless, we must end up deluding ourselves that we are in fact not poisoned, though there may be something wrong with us and that not everything is as it should be, but that there cannot be a deadly poison that we supposedly carry with us in our heart.

Today this is still the prevailing and common notion among people who are without a knowledge of the Word. They carry the deadly poison in their heart, but the goodness of God that restrains the deadly effect of sin in them through the antidote of common grace, and thus preserves them in conventional righteousness and uprightness among people, causes them not to believe the profound depravity of sin, so that they categorically deny it. Of course, they acknowledge that they slip up *occasionally*, they are not yet *perfect*, but for the rest they live in the conceit that they are fine, virtuous, good people, moving continually toward perfection.

So if common grace had functioned immediately after the fall in the same way in which it operates at present, then it would have been unthinkable that our generation would have acquired the knowledge of sin, and because the absorbing of saving grace depends on that knowledge of sin, common grace would not have enabled particular grace but would have worked against it. It was therefore in accordance with the requirement of psychology that common grace did not immediately begin to operate at the full strength with which it operates now. The decree of particular, saving grace required a different beginning. It was a beginning that consisted in this, that by letting common grace operate at first less strongly, God showed the human race what would become of it if grace operated less strongly and differently.

If we had asked Adam after his fall and before his conversion whether he was so bad that he could go only to perdition, and whether a race born from him would virtually destroy itself in degeneration and brutalization, Adam certainly would have answered *no* and would have considered himself to be very well capable of making it, assuming he did his best. This is the self-deception in which sin, strongly muzzled by common grace, necessarily traps the sinner. But look at the way out. As Scripture testifies, Adam's first child Cain, born in his image and likeness, already sinks so low that he commits fratricide, insolently denying any obligation to keep the law of love, and in his crime rashly opposing God. Yet for many centuries there stood over against this evil development of Cain and his line the more gentle development of Seth's line, under the influence of particular grace. So it seemed as though this evil turning adrift of Cain and his descendants depended more on the individual than on our human nature. And this is why it continues until at last both lines intermingle. And only then does it become very clear how truly depraved our human nature really is, how in that nature the deadly poison of sin increases hand over fist, and how in a short period it already had come to that disastrous point where man gradually became entirely brutalized, where all the higher aspects deteriorated and a life of murder, sensuality, and lasciviousness brought hell on earth.

In this way God the Lord has shown our human race in the facts of §4 history itself what the end result is if God the Lord leaves our race to its own devices, if he does save it by grace but does not intervene forcefully enough with his grace so that man's evil, bestial spirit, which immediately swings into rage, is entirely bridled and kept under control. Continuation of human life as it was then would have cut off all hope for the future. Our human race would have become utterly degraded. Atavistically—that is, through heredity—that degraded condition would have been transferred to human descendants and in them would merely have become still more severe. Upbringing, social interaction, and example would have caused the evil to break out in even more terrible forms. And in the midst of this kind of humanity, God would never have received the honor due him, and the church of the Son of God would never have found a place to stand.

It is obvious, then, that completely destroying the generation living at that time, followed by reviving the human race from the cut-off stump, from the one family that had remained faithful to God, was the only way that could lead to the fulfillment of God's decree. But if this is the case, then it follows also that after the flood common grace had to operate in a stronger and different way. Had the impact of common grace remained the same as before the flood, then a race would have developed that was precisely the same as that which had developed the first time from Adam.

Ham would have killed Shem, and all the terrible misery would have repeated itself in the same manner. For we cannot think of a single reason why it would have ended better with Shem, Ham, and Japheth than with Cain, Abel, and Seth.

We must place full emphasis on this if we are to sense clearly and powerfully the extremely important significance of that first failed development of our race, a development that perished in the flood. This significance pertains to our knowledge both of our human circumstances as they exist now and of the way of salvation. The apostle Peter compares the flood with holy baptism, and at every baptismal ceremony our Reformed churches call attention to the deep significance of the flood, of the perishing of the generation that lived then, and of the deliverance of Noah and his family. Superficial minds no longer understand this, and in the end most ministers of the Word have simply left out this element at baptism. They considered it a strange addition. And indeed, it had to be strange in the eyes of ministers of the church who had been alienated from Scripture in a completely absurd way. To anyone, by contrast, who views our human life in the light of the Word, it is clear that just as holy baptism bridges a realm that separates a holier generation, that is, a generation equipped with richer grace, from the generation of the heathen, so too during the Noahic generation, the flood separated a less deeply depraved generation [Noah and his family,] by means of more grace, from the preflood generation that had degenerated in its own evil.

So we can distinguish three stages of grace after the fall. First, we see the common grace that functioned immediately after the fall, a grace that spared mankind but in such a way that in a short time, from its own nature, humanity developed into doing all kinds of evil. Second, we observe common grace as we now know it and as it became operative for the first time after the flood, a grace that not only spared humanity but also made possible its development in terms of a higher degree of civic righteousness. And third, we recognize a particular grace that has functioned already ever since paradise and assumed a provisional form in Israel, but for the first time, thanks to the incarnation of the Word, under the dominion of holy baptism, has achieved the double effect of causing Christ's church on earth to flourish and, thanks to the functioning of that church, of causing the operation of common grace among the Christian nations to reach its full effect.

§ 5     Attention must be drawn to one more point here.

In its first period (from Adam to Noah), common grace had a strong impact on the physical existence of man, coupled with a less strong effect in the spiritual realm. This is apparent from the fact that the life span in the first generation was at least eight times longer than it is today. For the period before the flood, this points undoubtedly to a stronger countering of the effect of death in the human body, as Genesis 6:4 confirms, where we read that there were giants on the earth in those days, "the mighty men who were of old, the men of renown." This is no longer the case, and immediately after the flood we see the life span of our race reduced nearly to its present length. We shall return to this in another context.[4] But let us note here that the increase of our physical strength against the working of death is in inverse proportion to the increase of our spiritual strength against the working of spiritual death. The desires of the flesh and those of the spirit are, after all, opposed to one another [Gal 5:17]. This is why generally someone who is very strong and powerful physically knows stronger temptations to sensual sin than someone who is physically weaker and more gentle. A feeling of an excess of power elicits bullying, brutality, and lasciviousness.

Let us not say, therefore, that in this respect common grace was allotted less generously to the pre-Noahic generation. Rather the reverse is true. The shrinking of our life span is an *increased* grace. Old sinners are generally the most dangerous ones, and those who have centuries ahead of them to continue in their evil have every chance that they will break out in even more horrible unrighteousness. In this way everything is in harmony. The longer life span of the body is related to the lesser degree of common grace before the flood. And conversely, a greater degree of grace was evidenced by the fact that after the flood, this long life span was discontinued and excessive physical strength was reduced. Herein was a weakening of the flesh that, coupled with a strengthening of the spirit, steered toward the same goal from two sides. That goal was to create a condition of human life in which the dominion of the stronger spirit over the weaker flesh would call forth a less dissolute human life. Thus all conflict disappears, and if we pay attention to all the data of Scripture in their mutual interrelatedness, we succeed in clearly grasping the difference between the eras before and after the flood.

---

4. See also *CG* 1.4.4, and 1.16, "The Original Life Span."

# CHAPTER THIRTY-EIGHT

# FROM PARADISE TO THE FLOOD (PART 2)

*If you do well, will you not be accepted? And if you do not do well, sin is crouching at the door. Its desire is for you, but you must rule over it.*

GENESIS 4:7

§ 1    There is also no difference of opinion about the grave significance of the stretch of history between paradise and Ararat, or if you will, between Adam and Noah. In that long period of sixteen centuries our human race was granted a lesser portion of common grace than today. The consequence was that the development of sin progressed more unrestrainedly. Out of this, a condition was gradually born so dissolute that the only remaining solution was the extermination of this entire generation while saving the one and only family that still resisted this development. In this way we see demonstrated empirically what self-destruction the depravity of our nature yields if grace does not flow toward us from all sides to restrain depravity's deadly effect. And it is that greater grace, that gentler grace, that has come to us after the fall, and the seal of that greater grace is the hallmark of the Noahic covenant. This requires no additional words.

But what does require our attention yet is a more careful consideration of the situation of our race between paradise and Ararat, and what effect of common grace had become observable already under the continuation of that first situation. The reports we have in Genesis 4–6 may be sparse, but they do not leave us entirely without a clue, and what they tell us is highly important.

We cannot even begin to estimate the number of individuals to which the human race had increased at the time of the flood. Taking into consideration only a fertility rate that is empirically valid, then we certainly would not be exaggerating if we assumed a doubling of the number of persons every half-century. Sometimes the fertility rate appeared to be much higher yet, and there are abundant examples of families that began with a man and a woman, that then expanded in half a century from two to twelve persons or more, and that witnessed a further increase in the number of living persons in that extended circle due to the beginning of a third generation. If we assume that their original physical strength exceeded ours, that there were not many hereditary illnesses as yet, that there was plenty of living space on earth, and if we take into account the fact that the life span of humans covered centuries, then we might logically surmise that the increase in the earth's population will have been even much more rapid.

The much longer life span in those days especially plays a role here, in two respects. In our situation we must always subtract the number of deaths from the number of births in order to find the net increase. But if in those first centuries people generally reached an age of hundreds of years, then it would follow that in the first eight centuries there would be no deaths to subtract. And second, the question arises whether the period of fecundity, which after the flood was not even close to a century, as evidenced by the narrative of Abraham and Sarah, before the flood in fact lasted for several centuries. Note that Jared fathered Enoch when he had already reached the age of 162, that Methuselah was 187 when Lamech was born to him, and that Noah saw the light of life when his father Lamech was already 182. We leave undecided here whether in each case the first-born child is in view. It is not stated, and it is therefore possible that in this genealogy the one listed was not the firstborn but the child that did in fact inherit the patriarchal estate.

In any case, it seems that before the flood the patriarchs still fathered children at an age that already in the time of Abraham is put before us by Scripture itself as being entirely infertile (apart from a divine miracle). The possibility exists therefore that these patriarchs also fathered children afterward; the addition in Scripture, after the mention of Lamech's birth in Methuselah's 187th year, that Methuselah lived another 782 years and had other sons and daughters, raises this to the level of near certainty. Today the woman's fecundity continues for half of a long human life span, that of the man for three-fourths. By that measure, Methuselah could thus have fathered children during the sixth century of his life. As such it was therefore quite conceivable that a given patriarch in his old age could see children around him numbering in the dozens. If we combine the two—the centuries-long absence of deaths and the probable much larger number of births from a single human couple—then this strengthens our supposition that the doubling of the number of living people in half a century is likely far too low rather than too high.

§ 2 But if, to be on the safe side, we stay with doubling the number every half a century, then the human race could still have expanded to one million persons after ten centuries, not that long after Adam's death. And when we add another six centuries until Noah, then by quadrupling in each century, we obtain a total that far exceeds the present population of the earth.

Based on this, we would therefore reach the conclusion (even if we let the growth rate decline gradually) that in the days of the flood, the various parts of the earth must have been rather densely populated, and we certainly do not eliminate such a possibility in the least. But if, on the other hand, we pay rather close attention to what Scripture reports about the flood and about what preceded it, then the probable conclusion we reach is quite different. In those narratives we are very clearly given the impression that Noah was able to survey the human population living at that time. He warned that population in the name of the Lord. He preached the gospel of salvation to them, and the flood did not come until after the announcement of the coming judgment had reached those who were then alive. This does not give the impression of a situation in which every continent was populated, but rather of a society that did not move beyond the boundaries of what today we would call one people or one country, of very modest proportions.

Added to this is the fact that the line of Seth apparently did not make contact with the line of Cain until shortly before the flood. Then for the first time, we read, they began to intermarry. We can conceive of this only along these lines: that after Abel's death, Cain had traveled across a mountain range to an entirely different valley, settled and expanded his line there, so that both lines, each on their respective side of such a mountain range, could have continued to live separately for many centuries until finally, when both groups had expanded, the shepherds and shepherdesses of both sides made contact with one another and thus the relationship finally began. If this is the case, then we can also deduce that during the time preceding the flood the earth's population was still so small that it populated only a relatively small portion of central and western Asia. And we come to the same conclusion if we take note of the total lack of any distinction between one people and another before the flood, of any indication of kings or chieftains, even of any mention of wars fought, whereas such divisions, appointment of chiefs, and wars among groups could not have failed to occur if the population of the earth had reached hundreds of millions.

Instead we receive the overwhelming impression that the entire population still lived together as one big family, and that their patriarchs, one from the line of Seth, the other from the line of Cain, exercised patriarchal authority. We hear as yet nothing of mighty states or of world conquerors. Everything still moves along in a domestic fashion, entirely in accordance with family customs. On these grounds we believe we may assume that when the flood came, relatively speaking the world population was still very small and must be pictured, not as a sprawling mass, but as a group of neighboring families.

If we ask to what we must attribute the relatively limited increase in the earth's population, given such long life spans and such a favorable situation, then the beginning of Genesis 9 may give us an explanation. For there we see common grace intervene after the flood to safeguard the life of humanity in three ways. The promise is made that the course of nature will henceforth be regular and that thus the destructive force of the elements will be tempered. It is announced that the wild animals will not attack so ferociously to destroy man. And a decree of God is issued to more effectively protect man's life against man himself. Does not the supposition follow from this that before the flood the destruction of human life through unnatural death must have been very, very prevalent? And if we pursue this thought, such that we must imagine the fury of the elements being much greater then, that the wild animals raged terribly among our race, and that the murder inaugurated by Cain among our race continued in gruesome fashion, then all of this supplies the ready explanation as to why the race remained numerically far below the high number that it otherwise could have reached. The generation that perished in the flood

§ 3

was therefore small enough to be surveyed as a whole. The preaching of salvation could go out to that entire generation. And after the flood, it was a genuine relief and an uncommonly great grace that the fury of the elements was restrained under a fixed law, that the wild animals were kept more in check, and that murder was punished with death by humans in the name of God.

To a certain degree we may even say that by himself Noah could still reach the whole generation living at that time, but also that, however feebly his authority may have been acknowledged, he was the head, ruler, and king of the entire human race at that time. It is evident that before the flood the patriarchs exercised a certain authority. In every social circle there are always things that must be regulated, judged, and punished, and no one will call into question that the authority for this rested first with Adam as father over his children and then as patriarch over his descendants. He would have exercised this authority for the first nine centuries, after which it transferred to Seth when Adam died. After having thus been transmitted, it must ultimately have devolved to Lamech, Noah's father. Lamech died five years before the flood, and during those last five years Noah himself must have been invested with patriarchal authority, which is also likely because otherwise that evil generation might have prevented the building of the ark.

In addition to this patriarchal authority in Seth's line there must have been another patriarchal authority in Cain's family, so that for many centuries two groups of people must have existed side by side, each with its own head and each living according to its own customs. This led to a collision only when the two lines established relationships. In this connection we read that after this relationship was established there appeared "the mighty men who were of old, the men of renown" [Gen 6:4]. However nonspecific this expression may be, it clearly points to family heads who refused to accept any longer the authority of the patriarchs and, not caring about any higher authority, simply enforced with a strong arm whatever pleased them. Surely, then, already under Lamech patriarchal authority had declined considerably, and during the five years before the flood, when this authority rested with Noah, it certainly existed in large part only in name.

§ 4    Two other facts give us some insight into the progress of our race in terms of general human development during that time: first, the inventions of the three sons of Lamech, and second, the building of the ark. The first fact introduces us to three discoveries or inventions: the process of making iron, the production of musical instruments, and fashioning tents for dwellings. Of course, God taught humanity all of this. Each important invention that brings about a significant change in the life of humanity is an invention that God places within the human heart. A spark of genius kindled in the spirit of an individual aims at a goal willed by God. And the progress implicit in these three inventions was great indeed. From days of old it has been noted that God permitted these three inventions, which supply a strong proof of his common grace given to our race, to emerge not from men of Seth's line, but from men of Cain's line.

We would not have expected this. We would have assumed since it was under the Lord's curse that Cain's line would have been left to its own de- vices, and that the blessing that common grace contributes to our human race in all kinds of ways would have come via Seth's descendants. Yet the reverse is true. We don't read anything of such important and momen- tous inventions in connection with Seth's line, but by contrast, we find within one family in Cain's line three sons, each of whom has such an im- portant invention linked to his name. Jabal, Jubal, and Tubal-cain stand at the head of the list of men who have enriched our human life through their inventions.

When we connect this to the undeniable fact that in the subsequent history of humanity, the development of the natural side of human life has generally come not from pious people but rather from unbelievers, then this phenomenon seems to manifest an ordinance governing the en- tire course of common grace. It was not Israel who advanced the develop- ment of arts and sciences and business and trades; rather, what antiquity has bequeathed to Christian nations in this respect has come almost ex- clusively from the pagan peoples in Babylonia, Egypt, Persia, Greece, and Rome. And when later in Europe human life develops among baptized nations, we see that those who advanced life in the material realm were again generally not those who devoted their life to the Lord, but rather those who disregarded his service.

We saw that in Solomon's day the people who feared God wanted to build a temple for him, but an architect had to come from pagan Phoenicia to complete the work, and this appears to be the fixed rule and ordinance in the realm of common grace. It is the story of Moses over and over again. The man of God gets his schooling from the wise men of Egypt, and it is from Egypt that Israel brings with it the knowledge of many kinds of crafts. From these facts we can deduce that God the Lord, far from placing the pagan nations and unbelieving individuals outside his order and plan for the world, rather uses precisely the generation that wanders away from him, and thus cannot serve him in his temple and his sanctuary, to serve him and fulfill his counsel in the material and natural realm, so that later the generations that fear him may also profit from these discoveries in the natural realm.

§ 5     We see this in the building of the ark. We do not deny in the least that this required higher guidance. Building a ship of large dimensions was of course utterly unknown among a generation that lived in mountains and valleys and at most practiced river navigation. Building a colossal ship like the ark was therefore something exceptional and unusual, something for which there was no blueprint. To this extent we therefore also acknowledge that the architectural genius for building the ark must have been an exceptional gift of God. But while we acknowledge this, it shows as well that the ordinary crafts of that time must have reached remarkable heights, and that in this area our race must have made considerable progress already before the flood.

Think what skill and proficiency would have been needed for such a building project and to what relative level of perfection the instruments and tools for working with wood and iron must have come: we certainly get no mean impression of what common grace had at that time already contributed to development in our race. That knowledge was of course taken along in the ark and inherited by later generations, and to that extent we may maintain that the period before the flood was also of great significance for the development of humanity that came later.

§ 6     In addition to this, there is another ordinance of God that leads to Seth, Enosh, Enoch, and Noah. Under Enosh "people began to call upon the name of the Lord," which of course does not mean that Adam did not pray and Eve did not kneel before God, but it indicates that only under Enosh a kind of public worship of the Lord was established. This of course did not take place when Adam was still alive, but only much later, when Enosh had taken his place as patriarchal head of our race, around the tenth century. We do not know how this worship was organized, but we can deduce from the phraseology "*people* began to call upon the name of the Lord," that this refers to a worship in which the entire clan of Seth participated. The great importance of this public manifestation of religion for the development of our race stood perhaps on the same level as the importance of the inventions of Lamech's three sons. For it cannot be gainsaid that public worship has perhaps an equally strong impact on a nation as the most important invention in the material realm. And although by the nature of things, that establishment of public worship had a more direct purpose for particular grace, it must not be denied that it also contained an expression of common grace, to the extent that it was not intended for the elect only, but put a religious stamp on the whole of human life in Seth's generation.

Enoch's being taken away by God at 365 years of age remains a puzzling fact, which at the time must have made a strong impression since it is recorded as quite an exceptional event. His father and his son lived for eight centuries and more, but he was taken at an age less than half of that. It would have been understandable if this had happened to a godless man. But it is reported to us precisely about Enoch, of whom is said something that is not said of any of the other patriarchs: he walked with God, that is, he had entered into a hidden concourse with God and had seen the enigma of a sacred mysticism unveiled. And such a man is now taken in the middle of his years, in a manner that is not explained further to us, but must nevertheless have taken place in such a way that everyone knew: God has taken Enoch to himself. That bond with heaven, that initial appearance of the sacred mysticism, and that manifestation of the mystery that it is precisely the God-fearing person who departs—these features naturally contained a wealth of instruction that, because the fact was so impressive, could not be lost any more. Add to this how prophecy manifested itself in Noah and how God's revelation, which had been silent since paradise, sounded its voice again among our race, then it strikes us how particular grace joins together with common grace in order to merge completely for a moment in the ark.

In contrast to this, then, stands the moral and religious dissoluteness of Cain's line and, after the merging of the two lines, of the whole of renegade humanity. We see this in the wanton and lascivious Lamech, his glamorization of Cain, his unholy marriages, the mighty men of renown who arose, the mocking of Noah, the eating and drinking, marrying and giving into marriage up to the day that the flood came—in all of this we see how during those centuries, common grace had operated in the moral realm as well, but in such a limited measure that it involved an unleashing, a hardening and numbing, of the human heart.

# CHAPTER THIRTY-NINE

# THE FLOOD: JUDGMENT AND ACT OF GRACE

*In which a few, that is, eight persons, were brought safely through water.
Baptism, which corresponds to this, now saves you.*

1 PETER 3:20B–21A

§ 1    Thus the flood was undoubtedly a judgment, but nevertheless at the same
time, and perhaps equally, an act of grace, a demonstration of salvation,
and a very important element in the whole ordained arrangement of God's
common grace. In the preceding we have pointed out how the holy apostle
Peter, comparing the flood with holy baptism, sees in both of them an act
of God for salvation, and he characterizes the water of both the flood and
baptism as water of salvation. Although he does not deny that there was
also a judgment in the flood, it is for him in fact a judgment no different
than the judgment contained for us in baptism. For whoever descended
into the water of baptism thereby confessed his sin and accepted the sentence of death that he had to undergo because of that sin. Those who are
baptized are buried, and in that being buried lies the completion of death
and that completion of death is the judgment. Less attention is generally
paid to this significance of holy baptism, but Scripture speaks clearly on

this point, and the public language of the Reformed church also leaves no room for doubt, asking parents if "you acknowledge, that although our children are conceived and born in sin, and therefore are subject to all miseries, yea, to condemnation itself?"[1] Even as in the days of the flood the waters buried those then living, so also are we *buried* in baptism. But although we must strictly hold on to this judgmental significance of the flood, and although it would be beneficial if more emphasis were placed on this judgmental aspect of baptism, nevertheless in his well-known statement about flood and baptism the holy apostle Peter lets go of that judging significance and points exclusively to the saving import of both, in baptism by particular grace, in the flood by common grace.

In other words, he says this: "In the days of Noah, when the ark was prepared and the patience of God was not followed by conversion of the generation then living, a small number of people was nevertheless saved through the water, and in that water of the flood another water was foreshadowed as a counterpart, namely the water of holy baptism which is now offered to us as a means for salvation, even as in those days the water carried the ark and set it safely down on Mount Ararat." Let us note the curious quality of water; it can do two things simultaneously: both smother to death and save to life. All water has this dual property. In case of shipwreck it is the same water that seeks to fill our mouth to kill us, and yet also offers resistance under our arms to help us keep afloat. Nothing is therefore so well-suited to supply us an image of the nature of common grace, which virtually always consists in the fact that this grace enters where there is judgment and displays another side of that judgment. The judgment that overtook our human race was terrible when, except for eight persons, the whole bundle of branches and twigs that had sprouted from our trunk was cut off as with one slash and only those few twigs remained. But in this judgment lay simultaneously the moral salvation of our race.

Had evil continued to develop in the same horrible way as before the flood, then the more decent part of humanity—the part that had already dwindled to only eight persons—would soon have been swallowed up

---

1. See "The Form for the Administration of Baptism to Infants of Believers," in "Liturgy of the Reformed Dutch Church, or the Forms Used Therein," in *The Psalms and Hymns: With the Catechism, Confession of Faith, and Canons, of the Synod of Dort, and Liturgy of the Reformed Protestant Dutch Church in North America* (Philadelphia: Mentz & Rouvoudt, 1847), 60.

entirely by the godless majority, and any higher, more noble future for mankind would have been cut off. After Noah's death it was already Shem against Ham, with Japheth halfheartedly in between. What would it have been like if the flood had not come and Ham would have had the entire evil world behind him and Japheth would quickly have been led astray? Cutting off the godless majority in order to make a nobler development of our race possible was therefore an act of *salvation*. We can see this as long as we keep in mind that this salvation did not consist merely in the fact that Noah, his wife, and his three sons with their wives came away with their life, but rather in the fact that through sparing and saving that one family, the moral salvation of our entire race had become possible.

Peter himself points to the higher significance by what he says about baptism. For he cuts off any notion that we should limit ourselves to the external effect of baptism. Baptism, he says, must not be understood as washing away the uncleanness that clings to the body. Granted, whoever descended into the water of the bath of baptism and was completely immersed was cleansed physically. But that is incidental here. It is the means, not the goal. The actual goal lies in its spiritual import, and that spiritual import is intended for the preservation of the spiritual life, not a clean body but a good conscience. That and that alone is what we ask of baptism, or expect of baptism. And baptism brings this to us not through the water itself, but through the power that proceeds from Christ, thanks to his resurrection. Indeed, it happens in the very same way in the flood. For here too the ark that floated on the waters first of all saved physically by keeping Noah and his family alive. But this was not the main point for him, not the essential purpose. That essential goal was the preservation of the higher good known as humanity, the preservation of God's church, the safeguarding of the possibility that Christ would be born, and keeping the way open to a more holy development of the life of our human race. For a correct understanding of common grace, therefore, there is virtually no statement of Holy Scripture as important as this word of 1 Peter 3:18–22. Anyone who has properly understood this pithy, albeit somewhat tortuous, formulation, fully grasps the character of common grace.

§ 2    The right to speak of *grace* in the literal sense of the word when it comes to common grace, appears for the first time with the flood. That grace was indeed operative also after the fall in paradise, but it remained hidden. We hear the pronouncement of judgments, nothing but judgments; and other than this, only particular grace, which points to Christ, has its say. After the fall we therefore had to look behind the judgment to discover common grace and we discovered this common grace in the facts, in the arrangements, in the ordinances of God, but it was always viewed only from the perspective of judgment. It was grace that spared Eve's life so that she could become the mother of all living, but what she hears and understands is only that she will bear children in pain. But precisely this becomes different in and after the flood. For here there is indeed also the language of judgment, but the notion of salvation is expressed equally decisively from the start, and after the flood it is even as if judgment recedes into the shadows altogether, and only thoughts of grace find expression. Once Noah and his family have left the ark, we hear the language only of encouragement and reassurance. There was cause for this. The whole of human society existing at that time had been swallowed up and had disappeared, and Noah and his small family suddenly stood alone and forsaken on the desolated earth that still showed all the signs of destruction and bore the corpses of people and cattle in quite large numbers. For Noah and his family this must have been so unforgettably moving and heart-rending that we could imagine that it would have driven all of them insane. Thus, if they were to regain the courage and energy to continue living, to begin a new life as the human race after those horrible events, then it was necessary that God visited them in grace and supported their faltering steps on such a painful path. And the appearance of the Lord after the flood fully serves this purpose. The rescued human race receives virtually nothing but words of encouragement and comfort, and from that hour forward, common grace no longer functions as it had for centuries, but is now announced and revealed as grace.

This happened, of course, in the making of a covenant.

When God enters into a covenant with his creature, it is a gesture of favor, of condescending goodness, of grace. Grace for the sinner is in fact inconceivable without the making of a covenant, simply because any basic relationship, any fundamental relationship between God and man itself depends on the covenant of works, which is why all sin has the character of a breach of covenant. Hence no restoration of the relationship is possible if another covenant does not take the place of the covenant that was violated and breached. On these grounds our later theologians have placed the beginning of the covenant of grace in paradise, even though it is first mentioned in the Abraham narrative. Particular grace is inconceivable apart from a covenant of grace. And although even Calvin does not mention the covenant of grace before the history of Abraham, nevertheless he also teaches that the church has existed from paradise, and of course Calvin did not teach a church without the covenant of grace as foundation. In his theological dissertation, the still deeply lamented Dr. Van den Bergh has very correctly refuted the notion that according to Calvin and the Calvinists, the covenant of grace did not intervene, at any point, until Abraham.[2] On this matter our Reformed thinkers and commentators are indeed unanimous. It is only to be regretted that, while being open to the deep significance and the early origin of the covenant of grace, they have focused too exclusively on the covenant of saving grace, while paying too little attention to the covenant of common grace, even though the latter is mentioned first in Holy Scripture and operates very broadly even before the covenant of particular grace comes more clearly to the fore. Moreover, this covenant of common grace is even clearly delineated in Noah's history before the covenant of particular grace in Abraham's history.

§ 3    Making a covenant is an act of friendship. In its nature depraved through sin, our human race stood over against God in enmity, but it is striking how the making of the covenant after the flood does not take this enmity into account. This act treats man as if he were friend rather than foe, as though forming a relationship with man against a third party, namely, against the Evil One and against the ruin he has brought and still continues to bring on our race and our world. Let us stay with the simple, original meaning of the words and not allow a term like covenant to become a sound without meaning for us when it occurs in Holy Scripture. When Germany and Austria and Italy make a covenant or treaty or alliance, everyone understands what it means, realizing that the purpose of such a treaty or covenant is to avert the danger that might threaten from the side of France or Russia.[3] This is always the meaning and significance of a covenant. Parties join together to avert dangers that threaten, to resist a third, ominous power, and to establish a close relationship to achieve this purpose.

---

2. Willem van den Bergh (1850–90), *Calvijn over het genadeverbond* (The Hague: W. A. Beschoor, 1879).

3. Kuyper is referring to the Triple Alliance of 1882, the originally secret agreement made between Germany, Austria-Hungary, and Italy in defense against the Triple Entente of that same year between Britain, France, and Russia.

So when we see God the Lord enter into a covenant with humanity after the flood, then the notion of *covenant* must be understood here in the same sense, and we are given to know that humanity was in danger, that this threatened danger was coming from the side that was also inimical to God, and that God now enters into a covenant with humanity against the evil power of Satan and Death, the side from which that danger was threatening to come. We must not make the mistake of thinking of this covenant as being intended only for our salvation. Satan definitely did not threaten only our salvation, but also God's honor. By creating our human race in his image, God had linked the honor of his name to the perfection of our race. Our race could not perish in sin and death without God's honor suffering.

If we may express ourselves for a moment in human terms, we would say that not only man, but also God had a vested interest in not cutting off the future development of our race. That concern with God's honor could not be defended over against Satan except by humanity. And the covenant that God makes with humanity thus serves in fact to safeguard the dual interest: on the one hand God's honor, on the other hand, the salvation of our race. God therefore links himself to our race, and he links our race to himself. Not, of course, as if from his side man could contribute anything whatsoever to God, but precisely because he could be significant for the honor of God; God created him through his grace and by grace supplied him the weapons for waging battle for his honor. In fact, through the cloud of witnesses, the honor of God's name is therefore maintained and defended against Satan, even though it is self-evident that God must equip his witnesses for doing this.

In the Noahic covenant, therefore, God gathers together our entire race and with our race also this whole earth, all of nature, in order to prepare, out of the same thing that Satan had chosen as an instrument *against* God, an instrument now to be used *for himself* and to be turned against Satan. Therefore sin has not been eliminated, human nature remains, before and after, inherently depraved, and the working of sin and death continue unremittingly. But the coming, restraining, deferring, and postponing grace that had been at work since paradise and that had preserved our race, now becomes manifest to all in the form of the making of a covenant.

§ 4

From this moment forward, common grace is not only at work, but it is also proclaimed, and the rainbow stands in the clouds to show, as often as the light of the sun wrestles with the cloud of rain drops, how the light not only breaks through the clouds but even presses that cloud into its service to shine forth a beauty first hidden. Just as the covenant is the form in which common grace is manifested, so too the rainbow is its sacred symbol. If we think of the rain as the element that darkens, especially as it falls in the East for months on end, then in the rainbow we see the sun that, although it does not dispel the rain, instead chooses the falling rain as its instrument for reflecting its glow and causing that glow to enter the human eye with even richer beauty than does its regular light.

And this same is also the essence of common grace. The working of sin and death wrestle against the light. God does not cancel the working of sin and death. Rather, his judgments continue, but in those judgments themselves his common grace manifests itself. If death and sin ceased to operate, then no restraining force could work against them. But precisely because of their unremitting continuation, common grace works against them just as unremittingly and salvifically.

The whole notion that gained ground under the influence of the Roman Catholic Church—namely, that human life and the world outside the church stood outside all covenantal grace, and that only through the institutionalized church a certain sacred claim could be imposed on our human life—must therefore be rejected. Most certainly, "the whole world lies in the power of the evil one" [1 John 5:19], and the whole world is accountable to God [Rom 3:19], but this does not cancel out the definite fact that at the time of the flood, quite apart from the personal salvation of individuals, God made a covenant with this sinful race and with this depraved world in the person of Noah, and this covenant was and remains a covenant of grace.

Thus a salvific relationship between God and the world does not come into existence first through the church, but rather the reverse: already at the time of the flood God accepted in grace that world, along with our entire race, along with even all living animals, so that on this earth our race could offer an inheritance for the church of God. It is undeniable that particular grace, and thus the appearance of the church as well, contain an element that *strengthens* common grace. The simple comparison of countries like England and the United States with Borneo or New Guinea establish this beyond all doubt. Wherever the church of Christ takes hold of minds and controls public opinion, this is in every respect conducive to the development of common grace. But no one must therefore turn the order of things around. The covenant with Noah is not made with the church but with our human race and with the natural world, and this covenant continues to have its effect also in countries and among peoples where the church of Christ is not yet even known.

At the beginning of this study we have demonstrated extensively that this making of the covenant with Noah and this proclamation of common grace in the rainbow was also accompanied by an initial change in the actual living conditions of the generation living at that time.[4] We refer back to that discussion with a brief reminder that a threefold relationship was established. First, the appearance of this earth underwent significant changes through and during the flood and did not become what it is now until after the flood. Second, man underwent a change in physical strength as is apparent from the fact that his life span decreased drastically immediately afterward and soon reached a length that is still often reached today. And third, the moral deterioration before the flood was replaced by a more serious approach to life. Ham remains a harmful element, but for the rest a more elevated quality dominates in the now-renewed human race. Japheth still vacillates between good and evil, but when things come to a head he chooses for Shem and against Ham.

§ 5

In broad lines the period after Noah thus brings a recapitulation of what we found in paradise after the fall. For there also common grace has an impact first of all on nature, in the second place on man's physical life, and thirdly on his spiritual life. The flood therefore closes off the era in which a weaker effect of common grace had resulted precisely in the manifestation of the ruin brought about by evil at its most terrible. Now an entirely different period begins, in which common grace, expanding more strongly and powerfully, does not cut off the degeneration of various groups within humankind but nevertheless did make, God be praised, the nobler development of what was hidden in our human race possible, both in the natural and in the spiritual realm.

This does not mean that common grace from that moment on until now has remained what it was at the time of the flood. On the contrary, there is as we shall see a variety of new elements that changed the working of common grace, in the confusion of tongues at Babel as well as in so many other things. But the confusion of tongues at Babel as well as the calling of Abraham, and the turnabout that came with Jesus' coming on earth, not only in relation to the church but also in common grace, changes its

---

4. See *CG* 1.12, "A New Dispensation."

working but does not change for a third time the realm where common grace worked. The others, the physical condition of man and his spiritual condition, have been changed twice: the first time immediately after the fall, the second time through and after the flood, but since then these things have in the main remained as they have become after the flood. Shifts and changes have taken place in the earth's crust, but the entire appearance of the world has not changed again. Physically our race has become alternatingly stronger and weaker, but by and large our life span has remained less than a century. And also the spiritual disposition of human beings may have varied in different periods and regions, but we discern nevertheless through all of history, among the Assyrians and Persians, Egyptians and Phoenicians, Greeks and Romans, people of the same impulses and the same aspirations as we still find among us. And thus we may say that our human race has ascended along two stairways of common grace to the level where we still live at present and will live until the return of the Lord. There is a judgment in the flood, but there is also a resurrection of our human race in the flood.

# CHAPTER FORTY

# AFTER THE FLOOD

*These are the clans of the sons of Noah, according to their genealogies, in their nations, and from these the nations spread abroad on the earth after the flood.*

GENESIS 10:32

According to the most commonly accepted chronology, seventeen quarter-centuries elapsed between the flood and Abram's departure from Ur of the Chaldeans. The flood is then put at 2348 BC and Abraham appears on the scene at 1921 BC.[1] Unless an exceptional increase in fecundity took place in the generations of that era, the population of the entire earth in the days of Abraham can therefore not be put higher than somewhat over twenty million.[2] But before we get to the situation in Abraham's day, Holy Scripture draws our attention to three events: (1) Noah's prophecy concerning our human race; (2) the confusion of tongues in the valley of Shinar; and (3) the deeds of Nimrod, who is called "a mighty hunter before the LORD" [Gen 10:8].

These three events are also directly related to the development of common grace. It is not as if particular grace did not begin operating until Abram. To the contrary, as we saw, particular grace began to work immediately after the fall as well. When Eve received Cain she had already come

§ 1

---

1. The mid-twenty-fourth century date for the flood became part of the "commonly accepted chronology" especially after the famous work of James Ussher (1581–1656) to develop a chronology based on the biblical text.
2. See Kuyper's discussion in *CG* 1.38, "From paradise to the Flood."

to new life. But up to the history of Abraham, the working of particular grace does not as yet mesh with the wheel of history. Until Abram, church and world are intermixed, and only through his calling from Ur of the Chaldeans does the church get a separate realm, albeit for the time being still tied nationally to one particular people. But that is not how it was from the days of Noah until Terah. Then there were also children of God and children of the world, but they still lived mixed together. The children of God were not yet organized among themselves, either nationally or ecclesiastically.

All that lies between Noah and Abram, therefore, points indirectly but not directly to particular grace; it relates to our entire human race and belongs therefore to the realm of common grace. For this constitutes the permanent and decisive distinction, that common grace is the grace that is at work in our entire human race, with Adam as its covenant head and Noah as its second progenitor. Conversely, particular grace is at work only in the community of the elect, that is, in that restored and renewed humanity that received Christ as covenant head.

Considered superficially, the narrative of Noah's prophecy makes a strange and curious impression. A small, insignificant event takes place in Noah's family, and now it seems as if the fate of the world arranges itself according to the punishment and the reward that were ordained for the three sons of Noah in connection with this domestic incident. At this point we are not concerned with Shem and Japheth. But when we read concerning Ham that in an unguarded moment he forgot himself, and we then hear that this small offense is avenged so severely not only on him but also on all his descendants, so that still today entire peoples and nations are under a curse that was imposed on Ham because of that domestic transgression, then our sense of justice rebels and this story is distasteful to us.[3] The first thing we must do, therefore, is to strip this event of its seeming insignificance and shed light upon its historical significance.

§ 2 Imagine a railroad with a single set of tracks that at a given point split up in three directions. Then, as you have often seen with your own eyes, there is first a point where over a short distance the sets of tracks still run more or less parallel. But then the distance between the three sets of tracks begins to increase. It is not long before they veer farther away from each other, and gradually entire fields come to lie between them. And a

---

3. See CG 1.12.10n4.

few hundred meters farther on they have diverged so far that when we ride on one track we no longer think of the other ones. Nevertheless the point of divergence is decisive for the direction in which those tracks continue. That seemingly minor veering off at that first point leads, if it is to the right, the whole rest of the way to the right, or if to the left, the whole rest of the way to the left. This illustration from the material world shows us how a very small deviation at the starting point can determine the entire further development. It is as with a shot from a piece of artillery at five kilometers' distance. If such a shot is to hit its target, then the piece of artillery must be aimed with extreme accuracy. For if the trajectory of the ordnance deviates even a minute fraction when it leaves the cannon's mouth, then this seemingly insignificant deviation grows into a very noticeable distance at the end of five kilometers, and the whole shot has been in vain.

Well, things go the same way in the spiritual realm. In the life of a child there are sometimes seemingly very insignificant events that nevertheless in fact determine the entire future of the child. The question becomes whether such a seeming triviality—a dangerous word, a bad example, a wrong treatment, or whatever—makes an exceptionally profound impression on the child due to circumstances or as a result of the child's mood. Also, whether this impression has time to settle in without other, contrary impressions weakening the first wrong impression, or whether soon thereafter something happens again to reinforce that first impression. In this way if a seemingly most trivial matter finds us in a certain mood or in a certain mental condition, it can make an impression on us that stays with us, that does not go away, that ultimately settles in our character and thus determines our whole future development.

But it does not stop with this. Even though character as such is not hereditary, it cannot be denied that in certain families one character trait or another seems to be passed down. Some families even bear a reputation that continues from father to son, a name that by analogy with a particular animal or attribute rather accurately expresses the main trait of what everyone still always notices in the character of that family. Naming names here would be too hurtful and is not necessary. When we think of the cleverness or other traits of certain animal species, such commonly used family names automatically come to mind. When we consider how the most striking character trait of that family derives from the character of him who was the ancestor of this family, and also how perhaps one of the most trivial events in his early years had had a marked influence on the character of this ancestor, then we see immediately how the seemingly most trivial causes can in fact have the most far-reaching consequences. A family into which anger and quarrelsomeness have crept and become dominant may for centuries have to struggle with all kinds of bitter family misery that is causally related to the angry or quarrelsome character that developed in the founder of that family. And a quarrel during a child's game may have led to the sharply delineated development of that angry or quarrelsome character of the founder.

§ 3     This tragic chain of centuries of misery due to an originally insignificant incident also occurs in the physical realm. It may be that centuries ago a man who became the founder of a new family contracted tuberculosis through carelessness. This tuberculosis led to his death, was transmitted to his children and thus became hereditary in the family, and dominated the future of ten, even twenty generations in that family and has poured forth a stream of misery over it for centuries.

Even the facial features of the family are included in this. For the facial features, like the whole build and shape of the body, are related to the disposition of the spiritual being that lives inside such a body. A sharp head with prominent features betrays quite a different type of person than a round head with strong curvature. There are people who strike us as sympathetic because of their friendly face, and others who repel us with their sharp look. All this rests on the principle that what the face displays reflects the human being behind that face. If the facial features in a given family are clearly delineated and transmitted from father to son to grandson, then this also shows clearly how strong the influence is that an ancestor exercises, through his own inner mode of being, upon all his descendants down to distant generations.

Only when we keep this clearly and sharply in mind do we begin to realize something of the awesome responsibility under which our personal life stands. It would almost make us afraid, and it is indeed something to be afraid of for anyone who does not believe in an all-governing God. But the fact cannot therefore be ignored that if we must conclude anything from this, it is that every family stands under the obligation to note its sinful character traits, to combat them and change them with God's help, so that the hereditary misery that pursues it like a curse may initially be brought under control and ultimately disappear.

Not marrying and not begetting children therefore makes the life of a man or woman of character so unremarkable. Those who marry and get children build a railroad that stretches over an unforeseen distance, whereas the life of an unmarried individual is at most a railway of a few kilometers on which the rail car of his own personal life rides to and fro. But conversely, those who marry and have children are under a responsibility that is so much greater. For in one sense, in their own lives such individuals live already in advance a remarkably large portion of the life of all of their descendants.

Although little objection can be raised to the main import we have attributed to these undeniable facts, what happened with Shem, Ham, and Japheth then appears in an entirely different light than if we look at this event in an incidental, superficial, and ordinary way. For it is in the nature of things that the founder of a large family bears a greater responsibility than the founder of a small family. But the founder of an entire tribe still far exceeds the founder of a single clan in all this, just as those who, like Jacob, become the founder of a whole nation in turn far exceed the founder of a single tribe in power and controlling influence. Each nation also is different here by virtue of its numbers and the length of its existence. If the whole Chinese people has sprung from a single ancestor, then throughout the ages that one man naturally exercises a much more powerful influence than Moab, who was only the ancestor of a small nation that soon disappeared. And when we go on, we come from the founder of the nations to the founders of the races, and then we ascend from him to the founder of the whole population of the earth.

§ 4

At this point, it surely requires no argument to show that, through their personal existence and even apart from what they did, a man like Noah, together with his three sons, have, through body and appearance as well as soul and character, exercised an influence on the development of our race and on the entire history of humankind that dwarfs even the impact of an Alexander the Great or a Napoleon. And if we apply what we just developed—namely, how seemingly trivial events in someone's life can have a most significant influence on the formation of his personal character—then the result follows that in the case of the founders of races, and in the case of Adam and Noah as the founders of our entire race, the most trivial events in their lives could be of great significance for the entire history through which our human race would develop. And with this knowledge before us, if we now reread the narrative of Genesis 9:20-29, then our perspective on that narrative has indeed changed, so that we suddenly understand that this is in fact an extremely important piece of our human history that has been written down.

Men of importance who found the time to describe their own life and who had the courage to put the formation of their own character on display, have told us time and again how all kinds of trifling trivialities occurred in their early years that, according to the clear statement of their consciousness and memory, have had an uncommon impact on their whole subsequent development and the entire course of their life. What God the Lord presents to us here in his Word is the biography of our human race, and God knew how this small event in Noah's family would have an impact on the formation of their character and thus also on the formation of the character of the races and nations, indeed a greater impact than all kinds of great things that were later done by Noah's sons. This is why God does not tell us about the other deeds of Shem, Ham, and Japheth but does tell us about this insignificant domestic detail. If we were to have had to sketch Noah's history, we would certainly have omitted this story, and we would have told how Shem, Ham, and Japheth managed to protect themselves from wild animals, to build themselves homes, to cultivate the soil, and so forth. But God passes all this by. He knows how the actual cultural history of humanity is ruled much more by the inner motivations of the tribal character than through all external developments. And therefore all those other things are omitted from the divine narrative and only this story is included at some length, in nine verses.[4]

§ 5 But we must guard against one misconception. What we intend to say is absolutely not that until this incident Shem, Ham, and Japheth were like a blank piece of paper and that only through this incident the main feature of their character was drawn on this paper. Had they indeed been blank paper until that moment, then such a small and trivial incident could never have drawn such a deep furrow in their character. This is why we pointed out earlier how the question as to whether such incidents can make an indelible impression on us depends entirely on the mood and mental state in which we find ourselves. So we can say both things: namely, that on the one hand, there was already within Shem, Ham, and Japheth an

---

4. The range of verses in Gen 9:20–29 is actually ten verses, although Kuyper may be omitting here the final verse, "All the days of Noah were 950 years, and he died" (v. 29), from consideration as part of the actual story of Shem, Ham, and Japheth.

inner state that really came to outward expression now for the first time; and that on the other hand, this incident decided once and for all the main feature of their character and nature.

Unlike Adam, Noah was not a new human being. Adam was without father and mother and without genealogy. Not so Noah. Lamech was his father, and we are told his whole genealogy from Adam on. In him personally we therefore already are dealing with inherited and hereditary character. Psychological analysis would have shown how all kinds of features from the character of his ancestry were mixed together in Noah's character. And when now the trio of Shem, Ham, and Japheth split off from this one man Noah, then we have in them also not original characters, but three men in whom much of what preceded Noah and was transmitted from Noah to them had an aftereffect.

Even Noah's wife must not be forgotten here. For it is a fact that it is definitely not always the character of the father that works through in the children. Even we ourselves see all too often how entire branches of a family acquire a different face and a different character through marriage with a woman who imprints the children with her stamp. With Shem, Ham, and Japheth, therefore, we must certainly take into account not only Noah himself, but perhaps his wife equally so, something we cannot say with certainty because the rule does not always apply, but something we must admit as a possibility. Indeed, we cannot even stop here. The fact has been noted repeatedly that sometimes the characters of the father and of the grandfather differ markedly, and that nevertheless the child exhibits more the character of the grandfather than of the father. Thus it can and indeed does happen that when three sons are born into a family, one has the character of his father, the other the character of his mother, and the third more the character of one of the two grandfathers or grandmothers. There is an entirely unexplored field here to which science has paid little attention as yet, and where more than enough material for research is readily available, even if only in royal families. But although we might not yet be able to point to completely conclusive results in this area, the fact as such is not subject to any doubt.

Frequently things develop differently, and it seems as if one of the father's characteristics divides into three features, such that each of the three children seems to receive one aspect of his character, with that one part developing more independently in its own way as an individual character trait. But even if we assume this in Noah's case, so that his character would be a combination of what became divided among Shem, Ham, and Japheth, this does not cancel out the original connection with the grandfathers and grandmothers of Noah and his wife. For in this case, Noah had a mixed character, in which three basic traits converged, and what his wife possessed by way of inherited character from her ancestors had a separating impact on this mixture, so that in Shem, Ham, and Japheth the three traits that were still one in Noah manifested themselves separately.

In Adam alone there was nothing hereditary, nothing derivative, for within him was that single totality created by God himself from which all human character traits, in their holy and unholy features, have derived. But this is not how it was with Noah, and therefore our relationship to Noah is entirely different than our relationship to Adam: in Adam there was no ancestral effect; in Noah there was. For we must assume, though proof is lacking, that in the flood not a single basic trait of the human character was permanently lost, and that in Noah and his wife, in the larger context of their parents and ancestors, all rays of the human character converged as in one beam. For otherwise our human nature would have been mutilated by the flood, and it would not be comprehensible how in Shem, Ham, and Japheth the three basic types of our whole human race were fixed.

# CHAPTER FORTY-ONE

# THE TOWER OF BABEL

*So the* Lord *dispersed them from there over the face of all the earth, and they left off building the city.*

Genesis 11:8

The classification of humanity into three races, according to the three sons of Noah, ostensibly does not agree, at least not with the necessary accuracy, with the variety of races that are actually found on earth. We can say in general that the great group of Indo-Germanic peoples, the Semitic group of peoples, and the population of Africa represent to some degree the divisions that correspond to the sons of Japheth, the sons of Seth, and the sons of Ham. But this is not the end of the matter. For in addition to these three groups of peoples we encounter also the mighty group that encompasses Mongolia, China, Japan, Annam,[1] and Siam.[2] In addition, there is the great Malaysian race that we know from our Dutch East Indies and a part of Africa. Then we also have the race of the American Indians, to say nothing of the Aztecs and other smaller groups. We should also notice

§ 1

---

1.  The name of a French protectorate in the nineteenth century, part of modern-day Vietnam; strictly speaking, its central provinces (*An Nam* in Vietnamese).
2.  Modern-day Thailand.

that in Africa itself everyone who is black and dark-skinned cannot by any means be reduced to a single main type.

We will return to this division of the nations and peoples when we discuss the table of nations in Genesis 10. But already here we wish to state how, in connection with our previous chapter, the threefold division based on Shem, Ham, and Japheth does not lead with any kind of necessity to accepting only three races. Today when a Scot marries a Spanish woman, it is not uncommon to see three kinds of children born from such a marriage: the one blond with blue eyes, the next dark with dark eyes, the third with features from both. Thus it was also possible that Shem, Ham, and Japheth produced not three but nine very different types of people, as long as we assume, as *must* be assumed in light of the previous chapter, that the three wives of Shem, Ham, and Japheth were women of a distinct type, each of them markedly different from her husband. If we assume this, then there is nothing strange in the fact that among the children of Shem one strongly resembled Shem, while another looked like his wife, and a third one came somewhere in between. The same can be assumed of the sons of Japheth and the sons of Ham, and this alone would result in nine essentially different kinds of people.

We cannot even preclude the possibility that these differences diverged even more widely; even now we see not infrequently how sometimes the type of the grandfather or grandmother, which seemed to have disappeared, reemerges in their grandchildren, even when the father or mother did not in any way manifest this type. We sometimes observe the same phenomenon among birds, when a white duck and an equally white drake get ducklings with colored or black feathers. And thus we see that the fact that Noah had only three sons absolutely does not by itself preclude the possibility that the world of humanity became divided into nine or even more groups or races. It remains striking in this context that from of old the more direct descendants of Shem and Japheth have dominated the history of our human race, and that Ham's descendants never could achieve significance, whereas the other races outside the main groups, with the exception of the Mongols, either languish or disappear.[3] But more about this later.

---

3. Here, as elsewhere, Kuyper is speaking from a particularly Eurocentric perspective, rendering his judgment of the historical primacy of Caucasians and European civilization (often linked to the descendants of Japheth) relative to that of Middle Eastern, Asian, and African peoples.

What now calls for our attention is what happened at the building of    § 2
the tower at Babel, a fact of utmost significance that until now has received far too little attention.

For in Genesis 11:2 we read that the human race, after having already
strongly multiplied again, migrated to the East[4] and thus reached the
plain of Shinar. This narrative agrees with the flood narrative. According
to the latter, the new society began in the vicinity of Mount Ararat, that is,
in the highlands of Armenia, and this makes it eminently understandable
that when the people greatly multiplied they decided to move to the plain
because the mountain region no longer offered sufficient room to live.
Only relatively few people can live in a high mountain region, and migration is always from the mountainous country to the plain. The valley to
which they descended was the great plain that constituted the streambed
of the Tigris and Euphrates and thus lay in the direction of the former
paradise. Our race thus returned, through that migration, to its original
cradle. They traveled in a southeasterly direction and finally reached the
region where Babel later came to be situated.

It is striking that the people did not spread out from the highland to
that plain, but they traveled there all together.[5] It did not happen that
the settled families stayed where they were and only the younger people
traveled eastward, but they all set out together. It was, if you will, the first
migration of a whole nation, a resettlement of our entire race. No one remained in the Armenian highlands. "The whole earth," that is, our whole
human race, "used the same language and the same words. It came about
as they journeyed east, that they found a plain in the land of Shinar and
settled there."[6] This is a statement whose plain sense is that they went
there all together, without leaving family behind. We do not say that this
latter was precluded, but the narrative does not indicate it and rather
leads us to assume the opposite.

This great journey took place of course under a certain leadership.    § 3
In the mountains people lived together in small groups, as happens still
today in every mountainous region. These groups were separated by
mountain ridges, and each of these small groups most likely organized
patriarchally under a forefather. But now, as they traveled from the

---

4. Kuyper bases his argument on a reading from the SV, "to" (*tegen*) the East.
5. The SV states simply, "when they traveled toward the east," and the SV commentators note that this is often understood to refer particularly to Ham and his progeny.
6. Gen 11:1–2 NASB.

mountains to the plain, these separations and divisions fell away and they all came to live together. This required a measure of government, a measure of organization, certain regulations, a measure of leadership, first during the journey and later during the settlement in the plain of Shinar. This leadership was probably provided by the assembly of the forefathers, who together formed a kind of council. From what was decided by this council of elders we surmise that they were concerned lest they would be scattered. They feared that they would stray away from each other when the one went in one direction to graze and the other in another direction. To prevent this, the elders decided to build one great city, so that within its walls and within its immediate vicinity the population could keep living together as one. They also decided to build inside that city a very high tower whose top would reach up to the clouds, and whose high peak would always let the scattered and wandering groups know to which point they had to return.

In the mountains they had of course lived in wooden homes, like all mountain people still do today. In the mountains there is wood to be cut, whereas cut stone is usually lacking. Hence virtually all homes in the mountainous regions of Switzerland, Tyrol, Norway, etc., and even the churches and schools are built entirely of wood. We may therefore assume that the descendants of Noah also lived in such wooden homes in the Armenian highlands. But now that they had descended to the plain of Shinar, this abundant wood was lacking and so they had to look for other building materials. And from of old the plain of Shinar offered the best materials one could wish for. The soil consisted of rich clay from which excellent bricks could be made; we can still see such stones in large quantities in the museums at Leiden, London, Paris, and Berlin. And in addition to clay there was also an abundance of bitumen that could be used as mortar or cement. It was therefore quite natural that they immediately decided to build brick houses, to build a wall around this collection of houses, and to build a tower in the city they had created. Thus we read that they said, "'Come, let us make bricks, and burn them thoroughly.' And they had brick for stone, and bitumen for mortar. And they said, 'Come, let us build ourselves a city and a tower with its top in the heavens, and let us make a name for ourselves, lest we be dispersed over the face of the whole earth'" [Gen 11:3–4].

§ 4 Now in this there lay a profound sin, a direct resisting of God's ordinance. For already from the beginning of creation man had been commanded and instructed to multiply "and fill the earth" [Gen 1:28]. And after the flood the same ordinance was repeated once again: "And God blessed Noah and his sons and said to them, 'Be fruitful and multiply and fill the earth'" [Gen 9:1]. There can be no disagreement on this point. It was the burden God gave our race that we should not remain together in one place, but that we should spread out over the earth and thus fill the earth. And this plan at Shinar went directly against this mandate and against this definite ordinance of God, because it involved the intention not to spread out, not to disperse, but to remain in one small area, in one plain, in one giant city.

It is not easy to understand the operation of and the responsibility for such a sin. For we can ask ourselves: Were not a number of families allowed to remain in the plain of Shinar? And if so, how then was it decided who had to go and who had to stay? And if this cannot be decided, then who was to blame and how is that blame to be assessed? Taking into account only the personal sins of this or that person doesn't solve the problem. To the contrary, the sin committed here was an evil that sprang from the bosom of the entire generation living at that time. Their leaders had formulated it and the masses were willing to implement it. This was a case of stirring up the emotions, of an all-pervasive and stirring impulse.

When among the Boers of the Cape Colony in South Africa the so-called "trek" arose, this urge to migrate gradually gripped a multitude of people. The trek was sustained thereafter as well, and has not yet reached its end. In retrospect everyone senses how God has, without anyone suspecting it, awakened in that trek of the Boers of the Cape Colony a force that dominates the entire future of Africa and in part even the history of the world.[7]

Such a trek is the exact opposite of what manifested itself in the plain of Shinar. Then they also should have *trekked*, but they were unwilling to do so, instead opposing the notion of a trek in principle and on purpose. "No trekking but staying together" was the slogan. And even as people will now agree in retrospect that the Boers of the Cape Colony would have resisted God's divine plan if they had not left, so too the generation living at that time in the plain of Shinar resisted the will of the Lord by not wanting to spread out. Remaining in Shinar was a deliberate intention, a foundational notion for their whole society, a guideline for their actions.

---

7. Kuyper is referring here to a migration in the 1830s and 1840s away from the British-controlled Cape Colony, known as "The Great Trek." This migration led to the formation of a number of smaller Boer republics.

§ 5      Two remarkable expressions in the narrative of Genesis 11 indicate that this is how the narrative must be understood. First, what God says in verse 6: "This is only the beginning of what they will do," and second, what the people call out in verse 4: "Let us make a name for ourselves." They could of course not make a name for themselves among other people, since there were no other people. This making a name can therefore only refer to the future; it is as if they said, "Let us establish a name here that will endure through the centuries." This corresponds to the other expression: "This is only the beginning of what they will do." Both expressions thus distinctly articulate the notion of establishing a law for future generations of the human race by the plan they had conceived to build that tower at Babel and to indicate the goal that should be kept in view. Their speaking contained a plan for the world, and that plan for the world, which stood in diametric opposition to God's plan with the world, could be described as follows: "Let us not multiply too much, let us not spread out over the earth, let us not populate the whole earth, but let us limit ourselves to forming one single, relatively small people, leaving the rest of the earth unused."

If on the one side we take the history of the nations as it has actually developed on five continents, and place over against it the Shinar-plan of one small group of people, in and near one city, living together with one tower in view of all, then we immediately sense the mighty contrast between the great, rich, mighty thought of God and the petty, small-minded, and blinkered spirit that spoke in this plan of humanity. In God's plan all powers and gifts with which he had endowed our race would gradually be brought to light to the glory of his name. But according to this selfish plan for building the tower at Babel, all this would have been smothered and destroyed. According to the plan of God, the overflowing measure full of kernels of wheat is scattered over the wide field, and soon the fields will shimmer with the golden waves of grain. But according to the plan of Shinar, the seed grain would be locked up in a musty cellar to suffocate and molder there. God would make a name for himself according to the counsel and plan of the Lord of Hosts, and the entire history of our race would result in the glorification of that name of our God. But if things had gone according to the plan and counsel of Shinar, then the name of the Lord would have been overshadowed and crowded out by the name of this God-forsaken narrow-mindedness. Thus it was sufficiently demonstrated how the leitmotif in the heart of him who inspired such a plan, Satan, was nothing but a seeking of self and enmity against God. It was not a mistake, a wrongly conceived plan, but most definitely the expression of a mind hostile to God that, without being aware of all its aspects, would have ended up directly foiling God's counsel and obstructing his kingdom.

Although we concede that not every man, woman, and child would have remembered the command to "fill the earth," and although we consider it even less likely that every individual deliberately intended to go against this divine ordinance, it is nevertheless obvious that the heads and elders of the people knew very well what God had commanded, so that they could neither devise nor carry out their plan without deliberately and knowingly setting aside and thereby transgressing that divine mandate. It therefore involved not simply guilt, but definitely deliberate guilt as well. In the plain of Shinar they sinned against God with a high hand [see Num 15:30].

Only in this way do we obtain clarity on the importance and significance of this rebellion against God in the plain of Shinar. It was humanity being obstructive against its God, pitting our will and wisdom against the will and wisdom of our God. And thus it no longer sounds strange when we read further about the anger-filled majesty with which God thwarted this evil intent and this sinful venture. Of course, God's acting is presented in anthropomorphic garb. God does not actually descend to look at what humanity is doing, for all things lie naked and open before him with whom we have to do. And above all, let us not cling too closely to that descending of God, because artistic paintings and confusion with pagan stories have put us on a wrong track. For among the heathen there circulated, in more than one form, a story of giants or titans who had forged the rancorous and audacious plan to climb the highest mountains and from those high peaks to storm the heavens.[8] This story was then linked with the story of building the tower of Babel, because it speaks of a tower "with its top in

§ 6

---

8. Among the myths Kuyper refers to here may be the Gigantomachy, an ancient Greek tale of an attack on the Olympian gods by giants, who were defeated at the conclusion of the battle by thunderbolts from Zeus. Dante's *Inferno* connects the mythology of the Gigantomachy and the building of the Tower of Babel in canto 31, where Nimrod, "by whose evil thought / One language in the world is not still used" is depicted as a giant. See Dante Alighieri, *The Divine Comedy*, trans. Henry Wadsworth Longfellow (Boston: Fields, Osgood, & Co., 1871), 1:31.77–78, p. 194. In another tale the twin giants known as the Aloadae also schemed to lay siege to Olympus by standing atop a stack of mountains. A volley of arrows from Apollo ended the Aloadae's designs.

the heavens." And because the story of those giants or titans ends with the god of heaven descending with lightning and throwing the titans back, people have erroneously presented what happened in the plain of Shinar as if God had descended to throw down and shatter the sky-high tower with lightning and thunder.

But this depiction is radically and implacably at odds with the narrative of Genesis 11. An attentive reading of the narrative even makes us doubt whether the building of the tower had made much progress. Verse 4 clearly states that they first wanted to build a city, and only then a tower in that city. And then follows in verse 8 the statement, "they left off building the city." Therefore, the drastic action of God was not put off until the city and the tower were completed in due time, but to the contrary, God intervened when they had just begun building the city, when very likely the tower rose only just above its foundation. But what deserves more careful attention is that not a word is said to the effect that God destroyed the tower or the city. Nothing is mentioned of God throwing down even a single brick. All it says is that they were interrupted in their building and because of this interruption they quit building.

The majesty of God's action, therefore, is not depicted as an external display of power, but rather as the silent majesty that achieves the greatest goals with seemingly the most insignificant means. For it says, "Come, let us go down and there confuse their language, so that they may not understand one another's speech" (v. 7). So nothing was visible to the eye. At first they neither noticed nor understood what was happening, and suddenly they discovered that they had become strangers to one another in their language. They no longer understood one another. And no matter what they did to communicate their surprise to one another, and to remove the barrier that had descended among them, they suddenly stood over against one another as alien beings. We will deal with this fact itself in a subsequent chapter.[9] But let us note here how infinitely much more delicate and more divine this course of events is than having lightning or a tornado knock down the tower of Babel. God appears to do nothing. Only a small change occurs imperceptibly in the instrument of speech. And the immeasurable consequence of this seemingly insignificant change is that the whole history of humankind takes an entirely different course.

---

9. See the next chapter, CG 1.42, "The Confusion of Language."

# CHAPTER FORTY-TWO

# THE CONFUSION OF LANGUAGE

*Therefore its name was called Babel, because there the LORD confused the language of all the earth. And from there the LORD dispersed them over the face of all the earth.*

GENESIS 11:9

The confusion of language at Babel was not the result of the shattering and scattering of our human race; rather, our race scattered as a result of the confusion of languages. Because they no longer understood one another, the individuals, families, and groups living at that time parted ways. Every attempt to explain what happened at Babel in a natural way must therefore be rejected. The Holy Scriptures clearly tell us that here a mighty miracle took place that determined the whole future. It also tells us that implicit in this miracle was a judgment, and that this judgment was executed on the whole then-living generation. This miracle and this judgment are even tied to the name of the city of *Babel*: "Therefore its name was called Babel, because there the LORD confused the language of all the earth." [The Hebrew verb] *balal* means "to jumble up, to disturb." The stem of this word is *bal*; *bal-bel* was then likely derived through doubling of this stem and was later contracted to *Babel* through the omission of the first *l*. The emphasis in this word fell on the final rather than on the first syllable. It was pronounced Ba*bel*, not *Ba*bel. The Greeks pronounced

§ 1

this Babel as Babyl-on. And thus we find in the New Testament always *Babylon* and in the Old Testament *Babel*, a name that, according to the narrative in Genesis 11, came into being only after the dispersion of humankind, and since the Hebrews, or the descendants of Shem in general, remained here, it was automatically derived from the Semitic language group to which Hebrew also belongs.

It cannot be determined with certainty whether we actually still have remnants of the "tower of Babel" in the ruins of Babylon that still remain. In times past it was thought that we still have those remains in the ruin that bears the name *Birs Nimrud*. Today many are of the opinion that the ancient monument can still be found in the ruin called *Babil*, on the other side of the Euphrates. In any case, tradition maintains that the crumbled tower still exists, and scholars are generally of the opinion that much can be said in favor of the correctness of this tradition. If the notion is correct that the *Birs Nimrud* is a piece of the original tower, then it also appears that the "tower of Babel" was not a tower that went straight up, like our towers, but rather was a tower in the shape of our stepped gables: extremely wide at the bottom and then set back numerous times (as many as six) at right angles.[1] This would indeed agree with the plan for an enormously high building, although the narrative itself indicates that the tower had only been begun and was far from being completed. Only much later various rulers appear to have attempted to make the colossal structure higher, without any indication that completion according to the original plan was ever achieved.

§ 2 Returning from the "tower of Babel" to the "Babylonian confusion of language," we note first of all that in the sinful plan of the families gathered in the plain of Shinar we encounter the better element being subsumed under the evil element. Again, as happened in Genesis 6, we see how the "children of man" gained the upper hand over "the children of God." The contrast between Shem and Ham, which began with Noah's sons—while Japheth stood hesitatingly in between—was of course transmitted to their descendants. But already in the plain of Shinar the godless group had gained the upper hand over the God-fearing group to such an

---

1. Kuyper is describing a terraced-step structure, or ziggurat, which many biblical scholars believe is the intended meaning of the term "tower" (*migdal*) in the Babel account. See William Osborne, "Babel," in *Dictionary of the Old Testament: Pentateuch*, ed. T. Desmond Alexander and David W. Baker (Downers Grove, IL: InterVarsity, 2003), 74.

extent that the evil plan of the former is carried out and the latter joins in without resistance. At least we do not find any trace of protest against the audacious plan coming from the side of the God-fearing people living at that time. Apparently their voice had long since been drowned out, they could scarcely stir or move, and left the leadership entirely in the hands of the renegade people. In the end all participate, and this second apostasy of our race, the apostasy after the flood, has a universal character. Unanimously and with one voice they perpetrate the evil that provokes God's anger. Insufficient attention has been paid to this fact. The profound sin committed here by our entire race is inadequately grasped, and consequently the serious significance of what took place here is not understood.

In this context we must note that in the narrative of Genesis 11 the general name *God* is not used, as it was in Genesis 9, but the covenant name LORD. This shows that the miracle and the judgment of the confusion of languages served to safeguard against the thwarting of the grace of the covenant. The stream of sin had once again swallowed our entire race, and for that reason the purpose of the covenant of grace would have been thwarted unless, thanks to Abram's calling and segregation, a *particular* people would later have been set apart through *particular* grace. For the purpose of that setting apart and that segregation it was necessary that humanity, which was still one, be separated into parts, and thus as preparation for what was to come, the confusion of language at Babel is directly related to the separation of Abram and the particular calling of Israel. Immediately after the narrative of what happened in the plain of Shinar follows therefore the genealogy that goes from Shem to Abram, and already in the first verse of the next chapter comes the glorious revelation of Abram's calling that brightened the whole future. Note that the confusion of language at Babel lies behind us before the first revelation of the Word, or of Holy Scripture, in the narrower sense begins.

The confusion of language as such cannot be understood unless we take the trouble to think for a moment about the nature of *language*; conversely, every attempt to understand the nature and coherence of the various languages utterly fails if the fact of the "confusion of language" is insufficiently considered. For when we think with a measure of seriousness about our human languages in their essence and coherence, we always run into two contradictory phenomena. On the one hand, we discover in every language a certain fixed rule, a certain regularity, a certain fixity of

§ 3

forms. On the other hand, we equally find all manner of deviations from the rule, all kinds of exceptions, all kinds of irregularity.

The Greek philosophers were already puzzled by this conflicting element in language. Everything that went according to the rule they called *analogy* or correspondence, and everything that was an exception they called *anomaly* or irregularity. Depending on whether they took the one or the other phenomenon as their point of departure, they ended up with entirely divergent notions concerning the essence, origin, and nature of language. But it is precisely this contradiction between, on the one hand, a measure of regularity and, on the other hand, a measure of irregularity that is explained fully if we pay attention to the confusion of language. For it presupposes that at first there was only regularity, correspondence, and uniformity, and that later some kind of irregularity broke this regularity.

In addition, in the oldest languages we know, the regularity is much greater, and we see the decomposing effect of anomaly spread insidiously as an evil that has crept in at a given point. And the same applies to the coherence of languages among themselves. The conviction that existing languages cohere with one another and have not emerged independently has become increasingly common, especially thanks to the historical language study initiated by Lambert ten Kate.[2] While for a long time it was thought, for example, that Russian and Dutch had nothing in common, it has now been shown in detail how all Germanic, Romance, and Slavic languages are at their root related to one another. We are also able to trace the connection between the Indo-German and Semitic languages, thanks to the studies of Dr. Abel.[3] And there is no doubt that further study will lead to the insight how at bottom all human language is fundamentally one and through the various languages has merely been "particularized" into endless variegation.

2. Lambert ten Kate (1674–1731), *Aenleiding tot de kennisse van het verhevene deel der Nederduitsche sprake* [Introduction to the elevated portion of the Dutch language], 2 vols. (Amsterdam: Rudolph en Gerard Wetstein, 1723).
3. Carl (or Karl) Abel (1837–1906) was a German comparative philologist. He authored several works on the basic commonalities of languages, including an introductory lexicon of the common root words of Egyptian, Semitic, and Indo-European languages: *Einleitung in ein Aegyptisch-Semitisch-Indoeuropaeisches Wurzelwörterbuch* (Leipzig: Wilhelm Friedrich, 1886).

On the other hand we cannot disown the fact that the separating of the single human language into multiple languages has taken place so strangely, so mysteriously and curiously that we virtually despair of ever discovering anything more or different than very vague, floating, general indications about the connection between, for example, the African languages and our European languages. Well then, also this contradiction between the apparent unity of origin and the yet so curious divergence of languages can be explained only if we hold to the biblical narrative. If we hold to the twofold fact that all language was at one time one, and that this single language did not splinter gradually into many languages but was forcibly confused, then we have in hand the key that perfectly fits to open for us a clear picture of both that unmistakable unity of origin and simultaneously curious and otherwise inexplicable particularization of languages. If we perceive nothing but gradual development, there would be no room for the confusion of language at Babel. But since we continually lose track of that gradual development of the languages, it is precisely that Babylonian confusion of language that reconciles our conviction concerning the unity of origin with our incapacity to demonstrate its organic splintering.

Meanwhile we must clearly distinguish two things: (1) the disruption or confusion of languages; and (2) the principle of irregularity and of irregular "particularization" that penetrated into the essence of all human language. §4

To begin with the latter, everyone knows how our own Dutch language is not at all spoken in the same way in every region of the country. When we hear someone from the province of Zeeland and a Frisian, in each case we hear something quite different. In the same way, Flemish and the speech from the provinces of Brabant, Groningen, Gelderland, and so forth differs. This is the difference in dialect that we encounter not only in our own country but in all countries, such that each language splinters and "particularizes" into a number of dialects. We also know that our language strongly resembles German, so that we have here a transition from one language to another that is within reach of everyone. And finally, it is clear how quite different rules apply in the various dialects and cognate languages, and how those rules are continually violated within those dialects and those cognate languages themselves by all kinds of exceptions, which often cannot be explained on the basis of that dialect or language itself but ultimately on the basis of related dialects and cognate languages.

This shows, therefore, how even in those languages and dialects that acquired their present form centuries after the confusion of language at Babel, the principle of this confusion is still operative.

Had this not been the case, and had the confusion of language limited itself to the dividing of the one, single language of that time into, say, twelve separate languages, then we would have encountered neither more nor other than those twelve languages, and those languages would have remained the way they were originally, century after century. Because it appears that long after the confusion of language at Babel other languages have continually divided from the earlier languages, that each of these new languages diverged into dialects, and that each of these dialects steadily changed and absorbed all kinds of irregularities, the fact cannot be contradicted that ever since Babel there has crept into human language a principle of dividing and confusion that is still operative.

§ 5    We must, however, distinguish this principle of disruption from the actual disruption that took place in that one moment and that became the cause of a deep cleavage between one protolanguage and another, a cleavage that today is still the cause of our being virtually unable to trace the relationship between those various protolanguages. The result of this confusion that took place was that one person simply no longer understood the other. They spoke very differently, they had become strangers to one another. And no matter how hard they tried to reestablish a linguistic connection with one another, it proved to be impossible. This does not mean, of course, that if there were, say, three hundred thousand people together, that each of these three hundred thousand began to speak his or her own language, so that three hundred thousand languages sprang up and no one could find another person who spoke like himself or herself. This would be an absurd notion.

Apparently the intent of the narrative is that the generation that was together in the plain of Shinar broke up into certain groups, perhaps no more than ten or twelve in number, that spoke the same language among themselves but who as groups, each with their own language, faced each other as strangers. We may even assume, on the basis of what we still know about the coherence of the languages, that the descendants of Shem constituted a separate group alongside those of Japheth and Ham, and that the languages that split off within each of these three groups diverged less than the languages among the three main groups. Perhaps we would not be going too far if we claimed that the dividing up of the single language did not go beyond the difference that we can still point to in the linguistic groups that were divided at the root.

When we ask how this dividing up of the single language spoken at that time into ten or twelve separate languages came about, then we certainly miss the mark if we envision it as if God gave to each of these groups a language prepared beforehand by inserting it mechanically and externally into memory and that God thus taught them this language. This is a mechanical, external notion of the essence of language that someone unacquainted with the nature of language may form but that no expert can accept. Our human language is the clothing in terms of sounds of what inwardly stirs in our soul. Notions, inclinations, and thoughts arise in our inner being. Our soul receives sensations, emotions, impressions. It observes, it notices, it makes connections and distinctions. And all this together impels and compels our inner being to express outwardly what is going on inside us, to express it aloud for ourselves, for God, or for humans or animals. And the sounds, the tones, the words that serve us in this effort constitute, as soon as this expression comes under the firm control of our reason, our human language. The reality that one language is different from the other can also be explained from the fact that inwardly one group of people exists differently than another, that the other has different understandings, receives other experiences, feels differently, thinks in a different manner, and that therefore it expresses itself differently and speaks a different language.

§ 6

Thus while people still spoke the same language in the plain of Shinar and that one language separated there into a dozen languages, then it follows that, through an act of God's power, a change was brought about in the inner existence of the humanity that lived at that time. Someone still may have a poignant life experience about which he later says, "I became a *different person* then"; in the same way God Almighty must at that moment have worked in such a majestic and formidable way in the being of those groups of people that they stood over against one another as *different people* and consequently spoke a language that was mutually incomprehensible.

This is not to deny that this was accompanied by a change of their speech organs. Careful linguistic study has proven how the changes of one language into another are actually to no minor extent the result of changes that have come about in the relationship between throat, lip, palate, tongue, and teeth as a result of climate, way of life, condition of the land, and so forth. Our throat cannot produce the guttural sounds made by Arabs and Moors. While despite their best efforts, the French in turn cannot reproduce, for example, our Dutch *sch* sound and other sibilants. If we also take into account that the whole formation of the head differs greatly from race to race, as well as the speech organs, then it is logical to surmise that what happened at Babel not only explains the differences between the languages, but at the same time also the impressive difference between the races, mentally as well as physically, and specifically between the speech organs.

§ 7    Careful consideration of what happened in the plain of Shinar leads therefore to the conclusion that the miracle that took place there was of far greater import and much more formidable in its consequences than is generally thought. According to the common notion, nothing changed in or about people living at that time, and only the mechanical phenomenon took place that they began to speak strangely. They parted company. And that was all. But now that we know by contrast how language is directly related to a person's inner being, and one's manner of speech is related directly to the arrangement of throat, lip, and tongue, we see as through a veil how we stand here before a much more tremendous event that in fact dominates the entire subsequent history of our race.

Through a mighty miracle God suddenly breached the spiritual unity of our race and the unity of our physical formation. And as soon as that inner and external unity was broken, then, as a necessary consequence, the various groups spoke differently than before. A wedge was driven into the trunk of our race. That trunk split. And with the splitting of the trunk of humanity, human language also split into a multiplicity of languages. The original, single language was gone. It no longer existed, although each of the languages that had newly come into being sprouted as a separate shoot from that original language, so that the knowledge of that original language would suddenly uncover for us the relationships between all those different languages.

In this context the beautiful conjecture has been made that the speaking of the apostles on the day of Pentecost and in part the speaking in tongues (*glossolalia*) mentioned in 1 Corinthians 14 were probably more a speaking in the original language of paradise.[4] This would also explain

---

4.  *Note by the author*: We must not lose sight of the fact that although the speaking in *glōssai* or tongues mentioned in both Acts 2 and 1 Corinthians 14 is stated both times using the same expression, there is nevertheless a great difference between the two phenomena. Only on the day of Pentecost was the phenomenon original,

how the Parthians, Medes, and Elamites who were gathered in front of the upper room each thought to hear their own language, and this because that one original language, which was the mother of all their languages, reverberated in the languages of all. This surmise also appeals to us, as is known, because it is infinitely more elevated and spiritual than the much cruder mechanical notion as if each one began to speak, at the same time, languages they themselves did not know or understand. The pouring out of the Holy Spirit restored, in a spiritual manner, the unity of our race that had been broken in the plain of Shinar. And this corresponds so beautifully and in such a God-glorifying way to both the fact that the paradise language returned on the day of Pentecost and that the Parthians, Medes, and Elamites, no matter how far they had wandered away, still understood the paradise language, even though it could only sound to them as if it were their own Parthian, Median, or Elamite language [see Acts 2:1–11]. Only this notion restores the spiritual meaning to the language miracle and is directly related to the outpouring of the Holy Spirit. At the same time, the enormous development of linguistic studies in which our century may boast precludes any mechanical notion of such a linguistic phenomenon.

---

faultless, and perfect. The result was that at that time the paradise language was not only spoken, but what was spoken was also understood by each person as being his own language. The *glossolalia* described in 1 Corinthians 14, on the other hand, is a phenomenon that is weakened, an after-flowering that finally fades away. Here the soul does still speak to God in a holy language, but the understanding of this language is given only to those who can interpret it.

# CHAPTER FORTY-THREE

# ABRAHAM'S CALLING IS UNIVERSALISTIC

*I will bless those who bless you, and him who dishonors you I will curse, and in you all the families of the earth shall be blessed.*

GENESIS 12:3

§ 1      With the twelfth chapter of Genesis a new vista opens up in the scriptural narrative of revelation. Abraham now comes on the scene, and with the "father of all who believe" [Rom 4:11] the narrative suddenly switches from the track of common grace to that of particular grace.[1] The first eleven chapters deal with the world and the human race in general, but with chapter 12 the channel suddenly narrows; in the historical narrative the world stage now shrinks to Palestine and the human race to Israel. All that follows in Genesis, and then in Exodus, Leviticus, and everything else that has come to us under the name of Moses, also in the historical books, in the Psalms, in the Prophets, even into the Gospels, continually relates almost exclusively to Abraham's seed, until at last on the day of Pentecost the *nations* join in again, and finally in the apocalyptic vision on Patmos

---

1. For more on this basic distinction, see *CG* 1.1.1n2.

the great multitude that no one could number, "from every nation, from all tribes and peoples and languages" [Rev 7:9] are shouting with joy before him who sits on the throne and the Lamb. Only eleven chapters are devoted to what was common to our entire race, and the more than a thousand chapters that follow cover in the main only one region of the world and one nation and what pertains to it.

Due to lack of careful reflection, this seeming disproportionality has dangerously promoted particularism. It has allowed the false notion to enter that the fate of the nations and the importance of the world are of lesser concern to us, and as people had once locked the straying Jew within narrow confines, so too the Christian needed to scrupulously enclose himself within the narrow confines, first of the Jewish-particularistic hut, then within a church set up after the Jewish pattern, and for the coming centuries in a Jewish-tinged kingdom of heaven, with a rebuilt Jerusalem as its center. Even missions then do not rise to a higher vantage point than to save souls from the masses of the nations and to transfer them into the particularist sheep pen.

And ultimately missions, as well as the life of the church and the future of Christianity, are dominated by the question of the conversion of the Jews. As long as the Jews as a nation do not choose again for Israel's Messiah, the higher power that must bring about the breaking through of the kingdom of God is absent. A particularistic striving and driving that emerges from a false notion of Abraham's calling can only rest in the chiliasm that has been combated and rejected continually by all Reformed churches.

The issue of chiliasm, with its Jewish chimeras, is not, as people suppose, an issue of interpretation but an issue that determines the entire position we as people who confess the Christ take up vis-à-vis the revelation, and thus it determines our entire world- and lifeview.[2] The chimera of chili-

---

2. Kuyper is criticizing a literalistic expectation of an eschatological millennium, a belief found first among some Jewish sects during the Second Temple period, but also found among various Christian groups throughout church history. See Philip Schaff, *History of the Christian Church*, 8 vols. (New York: Charles Scribner's Sons, 1910), 2:614: "The Jewish chiliasm rested on a carnal misapprehension of the Messianic kingdom, a literal interpretation of prophetic figures, and an overestimate of the importance of the Jewish people and the holy city as the centre of that kingdom. It was developed shortly before and after Christ in the apocalyptic literature, as the Book of Enoch, the Apocalypse of Baruch, 4th Esdras, the Testaments of the Twelve Patriarchs, and the Sibylline Books. It was adopted by the heretical sect of the Ebionites, and the Gnostic Cerinthus." Schaff continues: "The Christian

asm and the Reformed perspective on faith and life stand in fundamental opposition to one another. Chiliasm is falsely Jewish-particularistic; the Reformed confession by contrast is universalistic, and a reconciliation of the two positions is inconceivable.[3] If chiliasm is true, then our Reformed confession is a lie. But if we embrace our Reformed confession, [based] on the witness of the Holy Spirit, then we must decidedly and squarely place ourselves in opposition to all this Jewish corruption of the truth.

We must, of course, not suspect evil intent on the part of those brethren among us who are still more or less cursed with this error. To the contrary, *their* straying is only the bitter fruit of the slackening in the Reformed confession that has taken place over the past two centuries. We are merely stating that for their sake we must not evade their false notions, and that especially the Reformed churches must never feed this evil through any statement for which they are responsible. This has been understood very clearly in the 1896 report of the Deputies for Mission among the Jews, and it demonstrated earnestness, courage of faith, and a sense of duty when they removed of their own accord one single sentence in which the old leaven was still at work.[4] We must clearly understand that the so-called fragmented interpretation of all kinds of prophetic statements that the chiliasts use to strengthen their position does not put any weight in the scales. Everything here depends on the correct perception of the relationship between particular grace and common grace or, if you will, of a correct understanding of the relationship between the original work of God that we admire in creation, and the other work for which we jubilantly give thanks after having drunk from the Fountain of salvation.

---

chiliasm is the Jewish chiliasm spiritualized and fixed upon the second, instead of the first, coming of Christ. It distinguishes, moreover, two resurrections, one before and another after the millennium, and makes the millennial reign of Christ only a prelude to his eternal reign in heaven, from which it is separated by a short interregnum of Satan. The millennium is expected to come not as the legitimate result of a historical process but as a sudden supernatural revelation."

3. Kuyper speaks of the universal scope of particular grace in terms of its relevance for all nations and peoples, not merely for a particular nation or people. This is an understanding of universalism distinct from other conceptions that would affirm the salvation of all creation. See also *CG* 1.29.5n6.

4. A briefing on the report, "Rapport van de deputaten voor de Zending onder de Joden," particularly as regards the sentence "The Jews will one day be a nation again" (*De Joden eens weer een volk zijn zullen*), appears under the title, "Zending onder de Joden," *De Heraut*, 957, April 26, 1896, 2.

Since we are dealing with common grace, it is of course not our task to §2 trace the course of particular grace as it begins in Genesis 12 and reaches its turning point in Acts 2. But it does belong to the doctrine of common grace to investigate in what relationship to common grace particular grace functions, and to what extent common grace continues under the work of particular grace, or whether common grace rather comes to a standstill and is restrained through particular grace. The latter notion was for many years the commonly accepted one among us, and in the practical realm it still is accepted to no small extent. If the orientation of the books discussing biblical history that have gained popularity do not present too distorted a view of the instruction given in our catechism classes for many years, then we may say without fear of exaggeration that after its cursory treatment of the first eleven chapters of Genesis, this instruction focuses mostly on particular grace and is generally silent about common grace. And if we listed with any kind of accuracy the texts that are preached for an entire year in all our churches, then a careful study of that list of texts would lead us to no other conclusion than that (apart from fortuitous exceptions) the preaching limits itself generally to particular grace.

This should not be understood to mean that we argue for catechism classes and preaching that would not make the introduction to particular grace its main task. Rather, the comment intends to say that particular grace is treated too much in isolation while neglecting its foundation in common grace and its ultimate goal: the salvation of the world that was created, maintained, and never abandoned by God. The sad consequence of this error is that particular grace floats in the air; the salvation of our soul is dissociated from our position and our life in the world; the floodgates open for the influx of Jewish particularism; and our Christian people are hindered from arriving at a thoroughly sound, truly Christian world- and lifeview that impassions their faith and steels their resilience.

The Methodism that has crept in reinforced this evil, which was inseparable from its earnest intent, and in order to cut off a variety of §3 misunderstandings, it may be useful to focus somewhat closer attention on that earnest intent—we almost wrote "on that earnest calling"—of Methodism.[5] In order to clearly distinguish the lighter and darker sides of Methodism, we must never lose sight of the fact that originally it absolutely did not emerge as a church-founding force but exclusively as

---

5. For Kuyper's understanding of and attitude toward Methodism, see *CG* 1.34.1n1.

a church-inspiring one. In the days of Wesley and Whitefield the state church in England had become fossilized in its hierarchical gentility. It was more reminiscent of a mausoleum than of a temple of the living God. The dry bones were many, the rustlings of the Holy Spirit few. The dead, dry state of the church gripped Wesley's heart and caused him to ask how life could be brought back to this valley of death. To this, Methodism was his mighty, overwhelming answer. It had to come to a revival; the deaf had to be shaken awake, and it was necessary to search practically for the best *method* to achieve this goal.[6] Over against the disgraceful condition of the church the actions of Methodism were therefore fully justified; and as often as any church, wherever it may be, threatens to sink into a similar sleep of death, the aftereffects of Wesley and Whitefield's attempt will always be justified. The Réveil that took place in the first half of the nineteenth century had a similar origin and is applauded by every child of God, albeit under the critique of the Spirit.[7] Thus shone its bright side from which we never should withhold our tribute of esteem and gratitude.

But this same Methodism veered off toward evil when, instead of letting the regained vitality serve the reformation of the church and considering its task to be finished as soon as this had been achieved, it came to disparage ecclesiastical life and finally substituted a "Methodist fellowship" for the church. Methodism, however excellent in shaking awake a church sunk into sleep, leaves the path of truth as soon as it begins to consider the church of Christ, with its offices and ministries, as secondary, as pointless, as superfluous, and thinks that it can put its own human action in the place of Christ's institution, and finally undertakes the bold venture of claiming for its inadequate society the title and rights of Christ's church. Methodism is not designed for this, is not suited to it, and lacks the data and the leading idea. We see this also in the Methodist phenomenon of the Salvation Army.[8] It says that it does not want to take people

---

6. *Note by the author*: The name *Methodists* was first applied in Oxford to a class of physicians who introduced a fixed method in healing. This name was later transferred to Wesley and his followers.

7. The Réveil ("revival") was an evangelical reform movement in the Netherlands with similarities and connections to the evangelical revival in England.

8. The Salvation Army is a denomination and charitable organization founded in London in 1865 that has Wesleyan doctrinal emphases and that focuses on evangelism. The group has membership and holds religious services but does not practice the sacraments. Today the group is well known for its social welfare services. See E. H. McKinley, "Salvation Army, The," in *Dictionary of Christianity in America*, ed.

out of their church, that it wants only to foster spiritual life, and yet the result is, in the thinking of the male and female soldiers of that sect, that the church is no longer anything, the Salvation Army everything, and as an entirely new manifestation of Christ's kingdom, this Salvation Army in fact inserts itself in the place of the church he has established.

The reason Methodism has fallen into this serious error, which ulti- §4 mately ends in sin and sacrilege, lies exclusively herein: in an evil moment the connection between nature and grace, and thus also between common grace and particular grace, was lost from view. The word *Methodist* itself proves this. For what does the name *Methodist* mean? The name is derived from the word *method* and refers to someone who brings a sinner to conversion by a fixed method. This is based on the notion that all sinners must come to life in the same manner; that the awakening from death to life is tied to a certain method; and that when we apply this method in the work of conversion, it will succeed, and when we do not apply this method, we plow on rocks; and thus also that those who walk the path of conversion in this way are truly included among the sheaves of the living, whereas the state of grace of those who have not trod this fixed path of conversion must always be in doubt.

This would indeed be perfectly correct if grace operated apart from nature, with particular grace detached from common grace. Then, even as in an army, the method of spiritual exercise and spiritual training should be one and the same for everyone. And it is indeed from this military notion of uniformity of exercise and training that the notion of the Salvation *Army* has come. But this is precisely how it is *not*. The single beam of light of grace breaks into greatly varied tints and colors, depending on how it falls on the prism of our natural life, and particular grace does not reveal to us the uniform but the variegated or multiform wisdom of God, precisely because common grace manifests itself in all kinds of different forms and shapes.

One's past before conversion can be very different for one person than for another. A person can have been born in a wild environment where neither God nor his command was taken into account, or into a quiet and God-fearing family in which the fear of the Lord was considered the beginning of all wisdom. One will, as a result of his sensual nature

---

Daniel G. Reid, Robert D. Linder, Bruce L. Shelley, and Harry S. Stout (Downers Grove, IL: InterVarsity, 1990), 1043–44.

and manifold temptations, have lapsed into flagrant sins, whereas another will have allowed evil to sprout more stealthily and quietly in his soul. Your lot may put you in a time of vigorous spiritual life or in years of deadness and withering. Your nature and disposition can be directed outward and pull you toward the world, or your temperament may make you withdraw into yourself. The seed of eternal life can have been placed in you before, during, or shortly after your birth, or it can be sown later in your dead soul, according to God's sovereign counsel. Thus there are all kinds of differences between people, and everyone's nature and disposition and past vary. And this is precisely the reason why the awakening to the blessed awareness of faith and the resulting conversion takes a very different form within one person than it does in another. In the one, the thunder of the Lord reverberates through the soul, while the other discerns nothing but the rustling of the soft coolness—not because the latter does not know the terror of the law, but because he already knew that law through a God-fearing upbringing, even if he did not yet understand it in its spiritual scope.

The truly Reformed individual has an eye for this rich and manifold variety, and this is why Calvin as a rule even admitted children of fourteen or fifteen years old to the Lord's Supper.[9] The Reformed person looks through grace to the nature behind and underneath it and therefore takes into account both common grace and particular grace. The Methodist, on the other hand, indeed prefers the worst and lowest-sunk sinners, because it is precisely in them that conversion most strongly demonstrates the character of the sudden and overwhelming [experience]. In them there is a transition from hell to heaven. The Salvation Army therefore also turns by preference to drunks, adulterers, thieves, and suchlike. In those people the *method* is vindicated in the best and fullest possible way.

But even though they also apply the same method to less egregious sinners and unbelievers, their rule always remains that conversion must

---

9. As outlined in Calvin's *Ordonnances Ecclésiastiques* (CO 10, part 1:28) of 1541 (available in English as "Draft Ecclesiastical Ordinances," in *Calvin: Theological Treatises*, trans. and ed. J. K. S. Reid [Philadelphia: Westminster, 1954], 56–72), children participated in Sunday catechism classes where they were taught the basics of the faith. Once a child was sufficiently instructed and could recite a summary of the catechism as a profession of faith, he or she was admitted to the Lord's Supper. The age at which children made this profession varied, but Kuyper's estimate here seems accurate. The summary that children were required to recite may be found in CO 6:147–60.

travel through stages that are the same for all, must generate the same sensations and experiences in all. Moreover, it is precisely this perfect regularity of the path of conversion that supposedly leads us to recognize the genuine children of God. It does make a difference whether we are dealing with a meddling Methodist or with a more mystically inclined one; for the former, focused on converting others, pays more attention to the method in order to know how he himself must convert another, whereas the mystical Methodist uses that method more as a criterion to test the genuineness of the conversion of others; but at bottom both errors are one. They think that grace is separate from nature and they therefore posit a fixed method of conversion for all who come to life.

They know nothing, therefore, of a work of God in the unconverted long before his conversion. For them all of this is and remains uniform. And this causes the Methodist to value almost exclusively the application of his method by people to people, and they cannot sufficiently open their eyes to the work of God that precedes and works in the work of man, and is the sole reason why it succeeds. As we know, it is precisely as a result of that uniformity that Wesley descended ever more stridently into Arminianism. Whitefield did protest against this, but the end result has shown that Methodism, viewed as a worldwide phenomenon, virtually everywhere has denied Whitefield and has chosen with Wesley for Arminianism.[10]

The Reformed confession, by contrast, maintains with determination §5
the connection between nature and grace, and thus also between common grace and particular grace, and it neither can nor may tolerate the Methodist view except in an emergency as a means to awaken out of its slumber a church temporarily sunken into sleep. But then it must always be on the condition that it never imposes the rule and the law of its extraordinary and helping character on the church of Christ and never substitutes it for the rule and the law of that church. And the Reformed are of the opinion that they alone follow the teaching of the Holy Scriptures

---

10. The two most prominent early Methodists, George Whitefield and John Wesley, while in agreement on most matters of doctrine and piety, were on different sides of the doctrinal debates that have traditionally divided the Reformed and Arminians. On the differences between Whitefield the Calvinist and Wesley the Arminian, as well as the subsequent theological trajectories within Methodism and evangelicalism, see Mark A. Noll, *The Rise of Evangelicalism: The Age of Edwards, Whitefield, and the Wesleys* (Downers Grove, IL: IVP Academic, 2003), 119–23, 266–73.

here and defend their only correct perspective over against those who think differently.

After all, at the intersection point where the line of particular grace chooses its own path with Abraham and diverges from that other path of common grace, which until Abraham was intertwined with particular grace, the Lord our God clearly and in so many words expresses that the setting apart of Abraham in particular grace finds its ultimate goal in the broad stream of the nations from which at this point this particular grace branched off. The final word of Abraham's call is not that a few of these nations will be incorporated into his family, but quite differently, that all "the families of the earth" (and all families of the earth together constitute our human race) "shall be blessed" in him [Gen 12:3]. It does not say all *individuals*, but all *families*, to indicate clearly that some individuals will be lost, but that the families will be saved. This certainly does not mean *all peoples*; the end result is quite different. Thus entire native African tribes, for example, were eradicated before the good news of the gospel ever penetrated into the heart of Africa. No, *all families* here means the human race in its broad segments.

The prophecy that he would be made into a great nation is further explained in Genesis 17: he would be "the father of a multitude of nations" [v. 4]. The notion that in Genesis 12:1–3 Abraham is appointed as father of only the Jewish nation cannot for a moment be maintained in light of the further explanation provided by Scripture itself. "Not the children of the flesh," says the holy apostle Paul in Romans 9:7–8, but "the children of the promise are counted as offspring." And in Galatians 3:28–29 he further explains that in Christ there is neither Jew nor Greek, but that all who believe in Jesus are "Abraham's offspring, heirs according to promise." Abraham is for him then "the father of all who believe," regardless of whether they were of the uncircumcision or the circumcision (Rom 4:11–12). On this point there can be no difference of opinion, at least not among those who bow before Holy Scripture. It is beyond a shadow of a doubt that the "seed of Abraham" viewed prophetically refers not to the Jews but to the "believers," and that he is the father of all who believe from all families of the earth. This also eliminates the notion that the Jews were "the children of Abraham" in the sense of the promise, and that from the rest of the nations only a few would be added to the Jewish nation after its salvation. No, the point of departure in Abraham's calling is immediately and in the exalted and full-orbed sense as universalistic as possible, and encompasses definitely not only Jews but all nations of the earth.

God therefore does not withdraw from the world when he calls Abraham, in order to consider henceforth the rest of the world as superfluous and only the Jewish people as humanity proper. From the beginning God is focused on the salvation of the world, and Abraham's call stands in the service of that salvation. The setting apart of Abraham and the emergence of the Jewish people take place only as an instrument toward the realization of that high goal. This cannot be understood in any other way than that during the centuries of preparation for our salvation that lay between Abraham and Bethlehem, God the Lord was definitely involved with the nations in order to put them in the position in which they had to be in order to be able to receive the Christ.

# CHAPTER FORTY-FOUR

# ABRAHAM'S HISTORY

*I will make you exceedingly fruitful, and I will make you into nations, and kings shall come from you.*

GENESIS 17:6

§ 1     The course of the history of Abraham and of the two patriarchs after him was quite different than would be expected on the basis of the usual understanding of his calling. According to that common notion, Abraham was called out of Ur of the Chaldeans in order to live on his own in Canaan, among tribes quite alien to him, in order to pass on to his descendants the remnants of the true knowledge of God as a holy inheritance pure and unadulterated by avoiding all contact with other tribes. Had it been up to us to determine the course of Abraham's life, we would have preferred to have him pitch his tent in a solitary region; we would have established the rule that he have as little contact as possible with the surrounding tribes; and only one avenue of contact would have remained open—namely, only those who wanted to come under Abraham and who wanted to be incorporated into his family would have been welcome in his tent. But for the rest, Abraham would have had to close himself off from those who lived around him. He would have to leave Ur in order not to be contaminated by the idolatry that was rampant in Chaldea. And thus in Canaan he would of course also have to be weaned away from everything that in Ur could have been the cause of his fall. In this perspective Abraham's life history should therefore have taken place in perfect isolation. He would have had to wander among the Canaanite tribes like a drop of oil floats up and down on the waters: Carried by the water, surrounded by water, but with only repelling contact.

But if we open the fourteen chapters in Genesis (12–26) in which we are briefly told Abraham's life history, then we find literally nothing of such a strict separation, of such a sharp isolation; rather, we are faced with the fact that this history, certainly not exclusively but to a remarkable extent, consists of stories about all kinds of encounters and involvements that Abraham had with persons outside his family.

It is therefore worthwhile to trace in somewhat more detail what is recorded in this regard, so that the wrong impression, caused by false dogmatism, may give way to the correct impression that the story wants to give us. And then it appears without any doubt that not only in the word of Abraham's calling did the emphasis fall on the blessing of "the nations" as God's ultimate goal, but that in fact his entire departure to Canaan, his actions in Canaan, and his life as shepherd-prince among the other princes of Palestine, involved seeking contact, establishing all kinds of connections, setting up of all kinds of relationships and associations, rather than withdrawing and isolating himself.

This is so true that even the entire notion that the move from Ur of the Chaldeans to Canaan was primarily aimed at that isolation will have to be modified, also in light of the written relics that have been found in Egypt and Babylonia. For we are even now in possession of very extensive fragmentary writings from the century in which Abraham lived.[1] Not writings on paper or parchment, for they would have perished long ago, but rather writings in stone, either inscriptions on monuments or records and letters on rectangular bricks of clay. Back then it was customary in Egypt as well as in Babylonia to write on unbaked clay tablets by means of symbols and letters that were pressed into this soft tablet with a metal stylus. These unbaked clay tablets were then exposed to the heat of the oven. In this way they became so hard and the writing was so firmly embedded that even today, after thousands of years, it is still perfectly legible to us.

---

1. It is not clear which writings Kuyper has in mind, but one possibility is the tablets of the Babylonian king Hammurabi (ca. eighteenth century BC), which had been discovered and translated into English during the time Kuyper was writing. See, e.g., *The Letters and Inscriptions of Hammurabi*, ed. and trans. L. W. King, 3 vols. (London: Luzac, 1898–1900).

From this rather extensive collection we now know with fairly great certainty that those who traveled in those days from Ur of the Chaldeans to Canaan definitely did not escape the influence of the idolatry that was rampant in Chaldea, because the prevailing way of life in Babylonia and its indigenous idolatry had been carried across to Canaan long before Abraham arrived at Mamre. There was indisputably very lively traffic with Egypt to the south as well as with Chaldea or Babylonia to the east. Virtually everything that Abraham left behind in Ur of the Chaldeans he found again in very similar fashion in Canaan. This definitely does not entail our denial that breaking with his family and going to live among nonrelated tribes exerted a separating influence. Looking for a wife for Isaac outside Canaan proves the contrary [see Genesis 24].

All we are contending against is the notion that having once arrived in Canaan, Abraham suddenly stood in the midst of an alien world and was cut off from all contact with this new world around him. Rather, the command to go out to "*the land* that the Lord would show him" [Gen 12:1] served to shift the territory of revelation (which first had to be sought in the heart of Asia, because the origin and cradle of our human race had lain in the heart of Asia) to the coast of the Mediterranean Sea, or to what is commonly called the Levant.[2] For God had planned and ordained Palestine, at the intersection of the dynamic of Levantine life, to serve the coming of his kingdom. Connected to Babylonia and Persia in the east, to Egypt in the south, to Greece in the north and to Rome in the west, Palestine constituted the center of what would be "the great world empire" in the days of Jesus. In God's speaking the emphasis falls much more on the land than on the people who lived there. Abraham had to go to "*the land* that God would show him," and later special revelation also speaks again and again of Mount Zion as the "*place* of rest" that God had chosen for himself.

§ 2

This already changes the common notion somewhat; moreover, such change is reinforced rather than weakened by what we are further told of Abraham's exploits. It immediately deserves notice that Abraham leaves Chaldea not alone, but accompanied by his nephew Lot. We leave aside the question whether this was so ordained of God or whether it was an

---

2. The Levant refers to a broad swath of land encompassing the western portion of the "fertile crescent" in Mesopotamia, including the coastal areas of Canaan and Israel, referred to here as Palestine.

indulgence on Abraham's part deserving of disapproval. In any case, the fact cannot be denied that Lot went along, and as a consequence, two new nations came into being in the vicinity of Palestine, the Moabites and the Ammonites, which would not belong to Israel and were entirely idolatrous nations and as such must be counted among "the nations." Furthermore, through these two nations Israel came into a familial relationship with the surrounding nations, the direct opposite, therefore, of a particularistic isolation. No one will want to place the emergence of these two nations outside God's direction; this already shows that Israel's isolation must on no account be taken to mean that the human bond—we do not say the religious or even the national bond—between Israel and the nations was cut off.

In this context the incident with Ishmael speaks even more strongly. Hagar was an Egyptian slave woman, and so probably not from the line of Shem but rather from that of Ham. Nevertheless Hagar is taken into Abraham's family. She is not a slave in the disdainful sense of the word; rather, she is Sarah's confidante. And when the son of the promise does not come, and Sarah remains barren, Sarah does not discuss with Abraham putting a woman from her own clan in her place, but she chooses this woman of foreign blood; nothing indicates that Abraham resists this idea, nor that he insisted on choosing another substitute. No, Abraham begets Ishmael with this foreign woman of Egyptian descent, and he gives the child the name "God has answered" as if to accept him as the son of the promise.

This action of Abraham undoubtedly expresses unbelief, and Abraham as well as Sarah suffered for this act of unbelief. It nevertheless shows that neither of them understood the separation of the nations at all in a particularistic sense. Their sin is commonly sought in that they resorted to an Egyptian woman, as if their sin would have been less serious had they taken a Semitic slave woman. No, their sin of unbelief consisted exclusively in this, that they took God's work out of his hands and did not leave the implementation of his promise to him. But the choice of an Egyptian woman as such is not in the least branded as sin. To the contrary, it is this Egyptian slave woman who in fact receives the first appearance of the Messiah. She experiences what every child of God would consider marvelous grace in the life story of one's own soul, not only in that she receives divine comfort, but also her descendants are promised blessing in the richest sense of the word. Even to Abraham God said concerning

Ishmael: "I have blessed him and will make him fruitful and multiply him greatly. He shall father twelve princes, and I will make him into a great nation" (Gen 17:20). Even more striking: Ishmael, the son of the Egyptian, receives not only the promise of marvelous blessing, but when God has established his covenant with Abraham and has instituted the sacramental sign of circumcision, Ishmael is the first one to receive this sign; he is considered by Abraham as one who is included in the covenant of God.

All this runs diametrically counter to the notion that the main purpose of God's leading of Abraham was to cut him off entirely from the nations and to confine him to his own family. The birth of Ishmael has established for a far distant future, whose completion has not yet been reached, a bond of physical tribal relation between the nation of Israel and the broadly expanded Arabian race. The whole Islamic world still looks back upon Ishmael as its progenitor. For many centuries the bitter struggle between crescent and cross has been nothing but the continuation of the struggle between Ishmael and Isaac in Abraham's tent. And the adversity with which missions have had to struggle to this day in the Islamic countries, even as the bloody tragedy that took place recently in Armenia and Constantinople,[3] is ultimately nothing but the aftereffect of the opposition inaugurated in Abraham's household.

§ 3    All this would have happened in just the opposite way, of course, if according to God's counsel and plan the calling of Abraham would have had as its goal the cutting off of his people from the rest of the human race. Then the existing, earlier ties had to be severed, and no new ties should be established. Instead we now find that those new ties have been very firmly established, because the Moabites as well as the Ammonites and also, much more significantly, the Muslims actually emerged from Abraham's circle as new nations, related to his own descendants. In the third place, the same also applies, but even more strongly, to the Edomites who came

---

3. Kuyper is likely referring to the Hamidian Massacres (or Armenian Massacres; 1894–1896) in which Abdul-Hamid II, the last sultan of the predominantly Islamic Ottoman Empire, instituted the brutal suppression of the Armenian minority throughout the empire. These massacres were widely reported in the European press and took on additional significance because most Armenians were Christians. Estimates of the death toll range from one hundred thousand to three hundred thousand. See Rouben Paul Adalian, "Armenian Massacres (1894–1896)," in *Historical Dictionary of Armenia*, 2nd ed. (Lanham, MD: Scarecrow Press, 2010), 152–54.

from the second patriarch through Esau, which is why we must pay attention to them here as well.

There is a striking difference between the emergence of the Moabites, Ammonites, and Ishmaelites on the one hand, and the Edomites on the other, a difference that is of extreme importance for us. Ammon and Moab came from *sinful* comingling, and Ishmael was born from *unbelief*. To that extent we could still maintain that these three nations are indeed physically related to Abraham but that this relatedness went against God's leading of Abraham. Therefore, even though the fact remains that the emergence of entire nations, especially of a nation like that which came from Ishmael, which still continues to play such an important role in history, cannot be placed outside God's divine plan, yet the sin of Lot's daughters and the unbelief of Abraham and Sarah forbid us to draw from these two facts as such a conclusion about God's revealed will.

It is entirely different with the birth of Esau. It is utterly indemonstrable that the simultaneous birth of Jacob and Esau from Rebecca involved a sin of their joint mother or an act of unbelief on the part of Isaac. To the contrary, when in the epistle to the Romans Paul comes to speak about the birth of both, he explicitly states that nothing was at work here except God's predestination, and before Jacob had done anything good or Esau anything evil their lot and course of life were fixed. The birth of Esau from Isaac, the emergence of the Edomites from Esau, and the fact that Israel is thus related to this idolatrous nation, are together explicitly presented as an act of God's absolute sovereignty. He, the creator of all children of humankind, has ordained it this way in Rebecca's womb, and through an act that was utterly independent of any choice of human will, he has established this remarkable tie between Israel and Edom, a tie whose effects we still see in Jesus' day, when Herod the Idumean places the Son of David before his judgment seat. If we take this fact as our point of departure and from this perspective view what happened with Ishmael, and move from there back to Moab and Ammon, then we are fully justified in our conclusion that it has been God's counsel and divine plan *not* to cut his people Israel off from the connection with the rest of our human race, but on the contrary, to weave intentional ties through which the nations would have relationships and human fellowship with Abraham.

But this is not all. In Abraham's history, ties are established not only  §4
between the nation that would come from his loins and other nations that would emerge as new nations from his own descendants, but Abraham

also continued to maintain friendly relations with the nations he encountered in Canaan and around Canaan as well. We read in Genesis 14:13 that Abraham had allies. This means, of course, that as shepherd-prince he had allied himself with other shepherd-princes of equal standing from among the Canaanites in order that they would assist him and he them. They are even mentioned by name. They were three brothers, Mamre, Eshcol, and Aner. With these allies he marched against Chedorlaomer, the king of Elam, who had advanced from the direction of Babylon against the Canaanite princes of the Valley of Siddim, taking with him Lot and his family. Abraham positioned 318 men in battle array. Mamre, Escol, and Aner each probably put up an equal number, so that the combined battle force consisted of some 1,300 men. And with these, Chedorlaomer, who today is known from the Babylonian records as a king of the east at that time, was defeated.

We are told this in passing, but it shows that Abraham did not isolate himself whatsoever. Someone who establishes an alliance seeks community, and community is the opposite of isolation. Moreover, this alliance had been established earlier, so that from the outset Abraham apparently chose a position in the midst of the political relationships of his day. In view of this, he had an army that to us may seem small but was quite considerable for that time, and so he definitely lived in his context as one of the powers in the Canaan of his time. This event, mentioned incidentally, provides us with a perspective on how Abraham conducted himself that is entirely different from what we would commonly have imagined. We are so easily inclined to think of Abraham and Sarah as two lonely wanderers who lived apart from all contact with the surrounding tribes, but the facts show us rather that Abraham represented a degree of power and with this power he entered into normal relationships with his neighbors.

§ 5      What we are told further about Abraham's actions in Egypt [Genesis 12], at Gerar, among the Hittites [Genesis 20], and especially at Salem [Genesis 14], confirms in every respect this revised perspective. He travels to Egypt because there is no grain in Palestine, and in Egypt he hardly stays in hiding but rather comes into contact with the court and the officials who went so far as to take Sarah, as a woman of princely descent, into the palace of Egypt's king, thinking that she was Abraham's sister. And when he leaves Egypt he does not shrink from accepting considerable gifts of cattle and livestock from the king of Egypt.

Even more remarkable is Abraham's experience at Gerar with Abimelech, a shepherd-prince like himself. The notion that already in that day, idolatry in Canaan had reached such proportions that all knowledge of the true God was totally absent, is flatly contradicted by the scriptural narrative about Abimelech. Matters go so far that it seems for a moment as though Abraham was less concerned than Abimelech with the revealed will of God. Abraham had tried to cover himself with a lie about Sarah, and it is Abimelech who points Abraham to the sin that this involved before God. God even appears to Abimelech in a dream, and Abimelech immediately obeys that revelation of God. Sarah is sent back to Abraham's tent, and ample gifts accompany her, not only cattle but even a thousand pieces of silver. Abraham acts before Abimelech as a prophet, and the two part company, not the one an idolater and the other a servant of God, but both of them people bowing before the God of heaven and earth.

The purchase of the cave of Machpelah gives a similar impression. §6 Abraham was of course a "stranger and sojourner" in Palestine—he did not own any land. When Abraham arrived, the land had already been taken into possession by others. These were, therefore, the established personages and he was a nomadic prince, a wandering patriarch who, due to the very sparse population in those days, always found pastureland in abundance for grazing his cattle. He had no fixed abode but lived in tents, like the Bedouins do still today. But for the rest he hardly lived in isolation, so little in fact that he enjoyed excellent relations with the native princes in the land. When he says, "I am a sojourner and foreigner among you," the prince of the Hittites answers, "You are a prince among us." Indeed, as proof that Ephron as well was not standing as a reckless idolater before Abraham, servant of the Most High, he adds: "You are a prince *of God* among us" [Gen 23:5-6]. Furthermore, the entire remainder of the encounter and the negotiations do not in the least bear the character of enmity or of a finicky tendency to keep himself apart, but Abraham speaks as to his equals, he is apparently known by them, he encounters compassion in his sorrow and a generous willingness to grant him his request in relinquishing the cave of Machpelah to him. They even want to give him the cave for nothing, and only when Abraham insists do they accept three hundred shekels for the purchase.

Even if we leave out of consideration for the time being the far more important meeting with Melchizedek, what we have advanced thus far shows in every way (1) that in God's plan Abraham's physical descendants were not limited to the nation of Israel but also wove ties between themselves and the nations; (2) that Abraham did not live in Canaan as an isolated wanderer, but was on a footing of familiar relations with the tribes among whom he lived; and (3) that Abraham did not live as the only servant of God among solely evil idolatry, but among those tribes he still found here and there some knowledge of the only true God—indeed, God even had a revelational relationship with Abimelech, for example.

The marriage with Keturah, which we mention only in passing, is of course entirely in line with this. For through this second marriage Scripture traces the bonds of descent between Abraham, on the one hand, and the Midianites and a whole series of other nations, on the other. Indeed, it is as though through this marriage to Keturah, Scripture wants to emphasize again, almost redundantly, the tie between Abraham and the nations outside Israel [see Gen 25:1-6].

# CHAPTER FORTY-FIVE

# ABRAHAM AND MELCHIZEDEK

*See how great this man was to whom Abraham the patriarch gave a tenth of the spoils!*

HEBREWS 7:4

The three patriarchs, Abraham, Isaac, and Jacob, and specifically the one who was first called, who himself had been born and married in Ur of the Chaldeans, were definitely not hermetically closed off from the life of the nations. They remained connected with the nations by all kinds of ties, and even established new ties with the life of the nations outside of Israel, ties they either entered into themselves or that were established for them through God's divine plan. This does not require further elaboration after what has been expounded in our previous chapter. But as that chapter already indicated, the main event that characterizes Abraham's relation to the nations is Abraham's encounter with Melchizedek. It is on this event that we now must focus more closely.

§ 1

It goes without saying that in our discussion we follow the exposition of this narrative that is presented to us in the letter to the Hebrews in connection with Psalm 110. As often as Scripture itself explains some other portion of the same Scripture, all difference of opinion about the correct meaning of such a portion of Scripture comes to an end. Since we have here the meaning of Genesis 14 elaborately explained in Hebrews 6 and 7 in connection with Psalm 110, any notion about Abraham's actions that is contrary to this interpretation must be rejected, and the key to the correct understanding of Abraham's separation must conversely be sought in Hebrews 6 and 7. Doubt is still possible concerning all other contacts of Abraham with the nations, and to some extent room can be allowed for dual meanings. But here that possibility is cut off. Here Scripture itself speaks, clearly and extensively, about the proper meaning and the true sense of what Scripture itself has told us, and on this point contradiction or even doubt would be equal to a rejection of scriptural authority. Since we are writing for those who with us hold this authority high, we therefore emphasize especially that we have come to a point here that provides us with a firm and sure point of departure for our entire view of the relationship between Israel and the nations, and also of the relationship between common grace and particular grace, and this in connection with both the original creation of God as well as with the glory to come.

§ 2    Hebrews 6 and following shows convincingly that the encounter of Abraham with Melchizedek does indeed have a lofty and important significance. There we read, "Therefore let us leave the elementary doctrine of Christ and go on to maturity." And what does the sacred author consider to be the "elementary doctrine" of our religion? He enumerates them himself as encompassing (1) the doctrine of God, (2) the doctrine of repentance, (3) the doctrine of baptism, (4) the doctrine of laying on of hands, (5) the doctrine of the resurrection of the dead, and (6) the doctrine of eternal judgment. All these things are to him nothing but the first principles of the Christian confession, which he described in Hebrews 5:12 as "milk for beginners." And over against this "milk for children" he now places the "solid food for the mature" and calls upon his readers to go with him "on to maturity" by joining him in looking at the history of Melchizedek.

Peculiar, you may say? Is this then the doctrine of higher maturity? And is it correct to declare in the church of Christ that the history of Melchizedek is more important and significant for us than the doctrine of God, of baptism, of repentance, of the resurrection of the dead, and of eternal judgment? You can scarcely believe it; and for many years it has not been believed. People read past it, and for the time being they still kept occupying themselves, even those among the more deeply taught brothers and sisters, with the "elementary doctrines," arguing and disputing about the doctrine of baptism and of repentance and of the resurrection and of the judgment, while quietly leaving aside this deeper doctrine of

Melchizedek to which Paul pointed.[1] *De Heraut* was the first to feel called on more than one occasion to focus the attention of Reformed Christianity on what Paul called a going on to maturity. It did so by stating that the concise content of this significant section is nothing less than that the doctrine that particular revelation, and therefore also particular grace, has only an interpolated significance. Thus not particular revelation but the creation ordinance is lasting and enduring.[2]

Thus as a result the naïve notion that Paul would have sought the idea of "going on to maturity" in the exposition of a somewhat knotty passage from the Old Testament came to an end. According to that notion, the progress of God's children to maturity would consist in a measure of exegetical skill. Being able to explain this or that difficult passage in the Old Testament then would have become the mark of purer grace and of a higher spiritual life, a backwards and absurd notion against which the common sense of the church fortunately forcefully rebelled. No, when the holy apostle, with such an impressive word by way of introduction, occupies our attention for two entire chapters with the encounter with Melchizedek, and says that in the correct understanding of that encounter lies the key to a deeper insight into the mystery of God, then it goes without saying that this event must have a much further-reaching import, and we do not understand the apostle if we fail to notice this further import of his word.

If by contrast we read and reread Genesis 14, Psalm 110, and Hebrews 6–7 with sufficient attention, then it soon becomes apparent that here indeed lies the main point for the whole connection between the ordinance of creation and the ordinance of special redemptive revelation, and that only on the basis of what is narrated we can cause the true and sweeping light to fall on the entire course of God's revelation.

There is a notion of God's revelation that makes it appear as if, after the fall into sin, the creation ordinance that lies behind this revelation

---

1. Kuyper assumes Pauline authorship of the epistle to the Hebrews, a view with precedent in the Reformed tradition. See, for instance, the Belgic Confession (1561), art. 4, which includes Hebrews among "the fourteen epistles of the Apostle Paul."

2. Kuyper may be referring to a series of articles focused on particular grace from *De Heraut* in 1879 and 1880 that subsequently appeared as a volume in a series of devotional Bible studies in 1884. See *AKB* 1884.09. See also Abraham Kuyper, *Particular Grace: A Defense of God's Sovereignty in Salvation*, trans. Marvin Kamps (Grandville, MI: Reformed Free Publishing Association, 2001).

becomes of secondary importance, and as if redemptive revelation now comes in order to bring about an entirely new situation. But what the apostle reveals to us here by contrast challenges this notion as untrue and incorrect, and in its place he puts the truth that redemptive revelation bears only a temporary character, that it comes only to disappear again and that, when one day redemptive revelation will have realized its full content, the original creation ordinance, now completed and made unassailable, will in the eternal kingdom of our God be made the everlasting mode of all things in heaven and on earth.

The two notions are of course irreconcilable. The one precludes the other. Since the latter notion is revealed to us by Scripture itself and the former is based only on human imagination, we and those who with us hold fast to Scripture do not doubt for a moment that we must reject the former and choose the latter, and thus also urge the church of God and all her theologians and ministers to decisively accept the latter. The extensive section from Prof. Steffens's speech that we recently translated fully deserved to be made known in a broader circle in our country, precisely because it moved along this same line.[3] The position we take up in this matter ultimately determines our entire view of the Christian religion and the church and of the relationship of both to natural life. And we consider it an honor and a rare privilege belonging to the Reformed confession that when it had not yet achieved full clarity on this point, nevertheless, it, as the only one among all the confessions, drew the main line soundly.

§ 3    When we examine the narrative further, then it immediately catches our attention that we still find knowledge of the only true God, not only at Gerar in Abimelech, but also in Melchizedek at Salem. For this king is expressly called a "priest of the Most High God." This alone would appear to make the common notion untenable that when he left Ur of the

---

3.  Nicholas M. Steffens (1839–1912) was a German theologian who studied at Kampen and immigrated to the United States in 1872, where he served at Western Theological Seminary in Holland, Michigan, as well as at the German Presbyterian Theological School in Dubuque, Iowa. He corresponded with Abraham Kuyper and was involved in translating some of Kuyper's work, including his Stone Lectures, into English. See AKB 1898.15 and 1903.16. Kuyper refers here to Steffens's inaugural address as Van Vliet Professor of Theology at the German Presbyterian Theological School, published as *Christianity as a Remedial Scheme* (Dubuque, IA: J. J. Reed, 1896). With a short introduction and under the headline "Calvinisme in Amerika," a portion of this speech appeared as "Het Christendom als herschepping," *De Heraut*, September 13, 1896, 1–3.

Chaldeans, Abraham went to live in Canaan in a land where idolatry had already smothered all true faith so that there remained for him no spiritual point of contact with the population of the land. It is certain that the Canaanite nations were exterminated four hundred years later because of their abominable idolatry. But we have no right to draw from this fact the conclusion that this wretched abomination had already poisoned all of Palestine in the days of Abraham. To the contrary, nothing appears in Abraham's history that points to an exceptionally abominable outbreak of idol worship, and conversely we find three shepherd-princes whom Abraham chooses as allies: a king at Gerar who still openly receives revelation from God, a king at Salem who is a priest of the Most High God, and even among the Hittites we hear Abraham being honored as "a prince of God." Only at the court of Egypt is there no comment of this nature. But for the rest, virtually every encounter with the native princes gives us the impression that the service of the true God still persisted alongside all kinds of idolatry that had crept in.

From this perspective, there appeared to have been little difference between the Ur of the Chaldeans whence he departed and the Canaan where he went. In the land Abraham left, the service of the teraphim[4] had even penetrated into his own family, and in the land where he arrived, traces of the worship of the true God could still be observed and are clearly mentioned. This is something that corresponds entirely to the reports that nowadays have come to us from the ancient Egyptian and Babylonian archives and monuments. Also according to those very extensive and unanimous reports, Canaan had at that time fallen completely under the influence of Chaldea, and the dominant forms of Babylonian idolatry had permeated Canaan.

The difference between the population of Ur of the Chaldeans and the population of Canaan seems to have involved much more their natural temperament and national inclination rather than an idolatry that by that time had already broken out in terrible form. This is why, when a wife had to be sought for Isaac, Abraham did not choose a wife for his son from among those families in Canaan where people still knew God, but

---

4. Teraphim were religious objects, possibly household idols, that were used in divination and spiritist practices and whose use is almost always condemned in the OT. See J. A. Motyer and M. J. Selman, "Teraphim," in I. Howard Marshall, Alan Millard, J. I. Packer, and Donald J. Wiseman, eds., *New Bible Dictionary*, 3rd ed. (Downers Grove, IL: IVP Academic, 1996), 1163–64.

mandated his servant to seek a wife for his son "*not … from the daughters of the Canaanites*" [Gen 24:3]; he refers here to her descent and family, but he does not make any mention of her idolatrous propensity. If the notion is correct that the population of Canaan had descended in large part from Ham, then the contrast in Abraham's day was not yet between the service of God and idolatry but, quite otherwise, between the blessing that was promised Shem and the curse that was laid on Ham.

§ 4      But however this may be, Abraham meets Melchizedek who had left Salem to honor Abraham as victor. Abraham had repulsed the invasion of the Elamites under Chedorlaomer, which is why the king of Salem went out to meet him to offer him bread and wine. It is quite remarkable that this was precisely the king of what later would be Jerusalem. What was not known in the past, but what is now known from Egyptian archives, is that even back then Jerusalem was a place of importance that had been occupied repeatedly by the Egyptians in order to ensure their rule over all of what later was called Judaea.[5] Jerusalem was by nature the important point that decided the possession of all of Canaan.

Here, under God's divine plan, a predecessor of David in the line of kings who established their throne in Jerusalem goes out to greet Abraham, from whose loins David would be born. Here one of those historic moments is occurring that under God's divine plan carry a glorious prophecy. David himself as king of Jerusalem has apparently thought of his predecessor on the throne, and from this it can be explained that as he was prophesying in the spirit of Christ, he portrayed him as a king who would no longer have a high priest beside him, but who himself would be both king and high priest. To express this thought, he sang about his great Son as "a priest forever after the order of Melchizedek" [Psa 110:4]. For Melchizedek, his predecessor on the throne of Jerusalem, had in fact been both king and priest of the Most High. It was therefore quite natural for David to mention Melchizedek in his song.

---

5.  Kuyper is probably referring to the Amarna tablets (fourteenth century BC), which were part of the archives of the Egyptian pharaohs Amenophis III and Akhenaten and include letters to the pharaoh from his vassal king in Jerusalem. Although these tablets testify to Egypt's rule over Palestine, they date from a period several centuries later than the period during which Abraham and Melchizedek probably lived. See Shlomo Izre'el, "Amarna Tablets," in *The Oxford Encyclopedia of Archaeology in the Near East*, ed. Eric M. Meyers (New York: Oxford University Press, 1997), 1:86–87.

David ruled there where before him a Melchizedek had ruled. He was the first king of Jerusalem whom Scripture mentions after Melchizedek. And it was precisely in this Melchizedek that he saw something that he himself lacked. David was king, but not high priest. Melchizedek had possessed that additional attribute, but David did not. But precisely that additional trait, that higher aspect, would one day return in Christ. And therefore the Messiah would not only be king like David but also, like Melchizedek, priest of the Most High [Heb 7:11].

Above all we must hold on to the fact that Melchizedek appears here as the superior one, not as the inferior one. "It is beyond dispute," the apostle says, "that the inferior is blessed by the superior" (Heb 7:7). Also, the inferior gives, the superior receives. If Melchizedek offered the blessing, and Abraham accepted it, and conversely, Melchizedek received the tithes and Abraham gave them, then we must conclude that Abraham appears in Genesis 14 as the inferior and that Melchizedek is acknowledged and rendered homage by him as the superior one.

The apostle invokes the full powers of language to accentuate this superiority, this exaltedness, this excellence of Melchizedek. He praises him as "priest of the Most High," as "king of peace," as "king of righteousness" [Heb 7:1-2]. He points out how both his kingship and his priesthood depended on neither his father nor his mother, nor on his genealogy; how it would have neither beginning nor end; how he, more than Abraham, Aaron, and David, resembled the Son of God and was therefore his example and his likeness; and that kingship and the priesthood, combined in him into one, arose therefore not from a particular redemptive act but from the original ordinance of God. If we understand this differently, then all these statements of Paul's are simply unintelligible, and this is why people have made Melchizedek an unreal person, not a historic king of Jerusalem but a kind of fleeting appearance of the Christ, something that directly contradicts the clear narrative of Genesis 14, is irreconcilable with Psalm 110, and is utterly incompatible with Hebrews 6-7.

If we are to understand both Genesis 14 and Hebrews 6-7, we must unwaveringly hold fast to the reality of the historical reports that there was at that time in Salem, later Jerusalem, a king who still feared God. He still combined in his person, in accordance with the original divine plan, the kingly and the priestly office. He possessed this priestly office, not by virtue of a special redemptive revelation, but by virtue of that original creation ordinance that called upon man as man, that as king he would rule over creation in the name of the Lord, as priest he would bring him the offering of love and praise, and as prophet he would proclaim his name. The blessing that Melchizedek pronounced over Abraham was therefore the priestly blessing, and by giving him the tithes Abraham honored him as priest.

§ 5     Over against that priesthood of Melchizedek, which stemmed from the creation ordinance, Paul now places another priesthood, named after Aaron, and his explicit statement is that in terms of its significance for God the priesthood of Aaron ranked far below the priesthood of Melchizedek. He proves this in four ways. In the first place by showing that Levi was still in the loins of Abraham, and with Levi also the priesthood of Aaron, and therefore in Abraham Levi and Aaron gave tithes to Melchizedek, thus acknowledging the superiority of his priesthood.

Second, by showing that Aaron's priesthood is tied to descent from a specific tribe and to birth from a specific father and mother, whereas the priesthood of Melchizedek, entirely independent of this, simply comes from human life according to God's creation ordinance—if you will, directly from man having been created in the image of God.

In the third place he proves Melchizedek's superiority and Aaron's inferiority by showing that Aaron's priesthood lasted only for a certain number of centuries, after which it ended and disappeared, whereas the priesthood of Melchizedek, grounded in our human nature itself, will last for eternity.

And finally, in the fourth place, from the fact that Aaron's priesthood depicted reconciliation but could not bestow it because it was merely symbolic, whereas the priesthood of Melchizedek, which was revived and brought to completion in Christ, produces with one sacrifice the reconciliation that remains forever and also bestows in actuality what was only depicted in Aaron's sacrifice.

From all this he finally draws the conclusion that therefore the Son of God, having become like man, has functioned not in the priesthood of Aaron but in the original priesthood of Melchizedek, and therefore in a priesthood that he did not inherit from Joseph or Mary but assumed by taking upon himself human nature according to the ordinance of God, expressed in Psalm 110. In a priesthood that ranked not below but above Abraham, Levi, and Aaron. In a priesthood that did not arise only for a time, simply to disappear again, but one that was destined to be in force forever. And finally, in a priesthood that did not merely depict the essence of the matter but possessed, bore within itself, and supplied the essence of the matter.

All of this is data we cannot rehearse without reaching the direct and immediate conclusion that in Christ, in his gospel, and in his kingdom we are not honoring a continuation of the preliminary, temporary, and transient redemptive revelation in Israel, but to the contrary, these are together making manifest in glory what was intended in the creation ordinance of God but was broken by sin. In the appearance of the Son of God, there speaks an eternal love that has loved, not Israel in a restricted sense, but the world. Not "Son of Israel," but *Son of Man* is the honorific title for the Messiah. Without particular grace both the world and human nature would have remained in death and destruction. But on the other hand, particular grace has no other purpose or calling than to save both that world and our human nature in the full universalistic sense. Israel serves the nations, and the fruit of Israel's suffering is that those nations enter the kingdom of God.

# CHAPTER FORTY-SIX

# ISOLATION MERELY AN INTERLUDE

*Then the LORD said to Abram, "Know for certain that your offspring will be so-*
*journers in a land that is not theirs and will be servants there, and they will be*
*afflicted for four hundred years."*

GENESIS 15:13

§ 1    The typically Jewish notion—which is unfortunately still current also
among some Christians—that with Abraham's call God the Lord for the
time being takes leave of the nations in order to occupy himself almost
exclusively with Israel for many centuries until on the day of Pentecost
the nations are called back again from obscurity, has been shown to be
untenable and false. In that perspective, everything in God's dealings with
Abraham should have served to isolate him from the nations, to separate
him from his environment, and close him off from the life of the nations.
But we just saw how, contrary to this, his calling is aimed directly toward
the nations; how a whole series of nations physically descends from him;
how his entire life history is full of encounters, of evidences of interaction and association, even to the extent of alliances with the surrounding
tribes—indeed, how the service of the only true God still had sporadic aftereffects among the peoples of Canaan, and how Melchizedek, the king of
Salem, was as priest of the Most High even superior to Abraham and was
honored by Abraham as his superior; and how, finally, in this Melchizedek

the life of the nations is shown to us as the proper realm in which the kingdom of God will reach its splendor and from which Christ will even derive his priesthood as Messiah.

Therefore the encounter between Abraham and Melchizedek cannot be emphasized enough. We would think that once Abraham makes his appearance in Canaan, all honor bestowed by God will be concentrated on Abraham, and all that Canaan itself produced would be contemptible and doomed in the eyes of the Lord. Abraham elected, all of Canaan rejected. In him the fear of God, while among the nations in whose midst he lived nothing but abominable idolatry. And behold, entirely in conflict with this thinking (which the Jew likes so much to embrace in order to elevate himself above the nations) we find the clearest traces of the knowledge of God not only in Hagar the Egyptian woman, in Ephron the Hittite, in Abimelech the Philistine, but in Melchizedek we even encounter a priest of the Most High who, long before Israel brought burnt offerings on Mount Zion, offered the sacrifice on behalf of the nations to God on that hilltop chosen by God: Melchizedek, before whom Abraham bows down as before his superior, from whose priesthood, in contrast to Aaron's priesthood, the psalmist derives the high-priesthood of our Savior, and to whose impressive appearance the sacred apostle draws our attention in order to make us understand very clearly the relationship between Israel and the nations, between nature and grace, between common and particular grace.

The children who still "live on milk" do not understand these things. They must remain stuck on the doctrine of baptism and of the repentance from dead works (see Heb 6:1–2). But one who is weaned off the milk and develops a desire for "solid food" in order thereby to progress toward more perfect knowledge and clearer insight, is called to see precisely in that encounter of Abraham and Melchizedek the key to the deep mystery to which Paul points us again and again: namely, the "the mystery of his will, according to his purpose, which he set forth in Christ as a plan for the fullness of time, to unite all things in him, things in heaven and things on earth" (Eph 1:9–10). For what we have said in this regard is not our view on the matter, but the plain, clear revelation concerning the relationship between Abraham and Melchizedek as the Holy Spirit himself has given it to us in Scripture. Whatever counterarguments the particularists and chiliasts may raise, the fact remains that Christ is not high priest after the order of Aaron, but after the order of Melchizedek, and that therefore

Abraham stood as the lesser in relation to Melchizedek as his superior, and the progenitor of Israel stood as the subordinate one before the priest-king from the nations.

§ 2    We must pay attention to three things if we are to acknowledge this without reservation but at the same time without underestimating Abraham's high and entirely unique calling.

In the first place, the true character of Abraham's calling and separation: We cannot doubt for a moment that a separation indeed took place. It is clearly stated: "Go from your country and your kindred and your father's house" [Gen 12:1]; and it also becomes clear in, among other things, the choice of a wife for Isaac, in the disapproval of Esau's marriage with Canaanite women, in Jacob's marriages, in the sin against Dinah by Shechem, in confining Israel within its own covenant, in isolating Israel as a nation among nations, and most strongly perhaps, in the question Jesus asks the Canaanite woman about whether it was permitted to take the bread of the children and give it to the dogs [see Matt 15:26].

Let no one therefore read into our exposition of the doctrine of common grace the least intent to weaken or deny in any way this separation willed by God. That separation comes to the fore clear as day in the Old and New Testaments. It is just that this separation does not bear an absolute character in Scripture but is very clearly indicated to be a relative one. It is temporary in nature, not enduring and permanent. Its goal is exclusively the bringing about of salvation, not its development. It creates the dispensation of the shadows, not the dispensation of the substance. Also, it is aimed at focusing the life of faith, not at developing the power God created within our human nature. Related to this is the fact that Holy Scripture distinguishes quite clearly between the Abrahamic and the Mosaic periods. The apostles rarely line up behind Moses but continually behind Abraham, precisely in order to bring into relief the unbreakable bond between the particular grace in Israel and the common grace among the nations by focusing on Abraham's calling, the character of his faith, and God's leading of him. "The law *came in*" (Rom 5:20), and the foundation on which Abraham's separation rests is not the law but the *promise* that Abraham would be "the father of many nations" (Rom 4:17) and definitely not the father of one nation.

§ 3    In the second place, attention must be paid to what we read in Genesis 15:16: "For the iniquity of the Amorites is not yet complete." God said this to Abraham four centuries before Canaan's sin would have fully matured, and precisely in this word lies the key to the riddle how on the one hand idolatry in Canaan was still so moderate in the days of Abraham, and how on the other hand this idolatry had become rampant so quickly and terribly in the days of Joshua that the sentence of extermination was carried out upon these nations. The contrast is striking. In Abraham's day there is scarcely a single mention of idolatry in Canaan, but to the contrary, repeated mention of aftereffects of the knowledge of the only true God among these nations. In Moses' and Joshua's day, by contrast, the cancer of idolatry had eaten its way into the life of these nations so terribly that rescue appears to be impossible. Attention has generally not been paid to this contrast, and the error has been made of imagining the nations of Canaan being equally as idolatrous and deeply degenerate already in Abraham's day as they acted in Joshua's day. And the four centuries that lie in between have then also been skipped. Yet this won't do.

If we go back four centuries in the life of our own nation, we arrive at about 1500, still before the Reformation, when the character, condition, and significance of the people in the Netherlands still differed entirely from what it is now. If this is enough to show how incredibly the state and situation of a nation can change over the course of four centuries, then it is conspicuous how much more pronounced that difference could be in the prevailing state of the nations back then. In the childhood years, transitions from one state to the next are much greater than in adulthood. A child changes strikingly between ages one and five, and so too a boy between fourteen and eighteen, whereas conversely a man sometimes changes so little between forty and forty-four that any effort to determine changes in his personal appearance or in the expressions of his spirit is in vain. Consequently, we may assume that the changes brought about in the condition of the Canaanite nations in the course of four centuries were so overwhelmingly great that, had we gotten to know these nations in the days of Abraham, we would barely have recognized them as the same nations in Moses' day.

The statement that the sin or the iniquity of the Amorites is not yet full, is not yet complete, must therefore not be understood as if it was already almost full, so that only very little had to be added. Rather it should be understood quite differently: "The cancer, the germ of destruction that is unmistakably present in the heart of these nations must yet ripen and bud forth and become complete." That it is precisely the Amorites that are mentioned here corresponds to the jubilation that went up in the days of

Moses at the destruction of the kingdom of Og, the king of Bashan, and also with the political influence attributed to the tribe of the Amorites in Egyptian antiquities. If we ask whether in those days Abraham himself could already see that such profound depravity and such an unspiritual cancer were hidden in the tribe of the Amorites, we would not like to answer the question in the affirmative. At least, there is no evidence for it. But do not forget that it is not Abraham but God himself who speaks here, and that God the Lord, who knew the Amorites and their heart and mind naturally knew, as God, what lethal poison had already permeated the national life of this nation at that time, and what the result would have to be of the continuing effect of this lethal poison after four centuries. Understood in this way there is no contradiction at all between the fact that in Abraham's day we still notice so little of the profound decay of these nations, and that nevertheless in Moses' day, four centuries later, the incurable iniquity of the people had become complete.

§ 4 Finally, in the third place, we draw attention to the Lord's prophecy to Abraham that "your offspring will be sojourners in a land that is not theirs and will be servants there, and they will be afflicted for four hundred years" (Gen 15:13). This shows us that in God's sovereign plan the separation and contrast between Israel and the nations arose not in Canaan but in Egypt. Abraham, Isaac, and Jacob moved freely and unhindered among the Canaanites. They made alliances, were respected and honored there, and even found spiritual affinity for the service of the only true God. But in Egypt they would dwell as in "a foreign land,"[1] and slavery would await them there, and they would be oppressed there, in order to be molded into a closely knit unit as a nation precisely through that oppression.

Note what God said not about the kings of the Canaanites, but about the pharaoh or king of Egypt: "For this very purpose I have raised you up, that [through your destruction] I might show my power in you, and that my name might be proclaimed in all the earth" (Rom 9:17; compare Exod 9:16). Actually, the contrast between idolatry and the service of God appears already in Abraham's day to have manifested itself much more sharply in Egypt than in Canaan. And it appears even more clearly—and this is something we must especially pay attention to—that the caste system, which breaks up the unity of our human nature and separates

---

1. See Acts 7:6 SV, "een vreemd land," a reference to God's prophecy to Abraham in Gen 15:13.

human being from human being, was already back then the foundation of Egypt's national existence.

When Joseph's sons come to Egypt to buy grain, there is a separate table set up for them in Joseph's palace because, so we read in Genesis 43:32, "the Egyptians could not eat with the Hebrews, for that is an abomination to the Egyptians." It was a matter of course that a nation that was divided into sharply separated castes and scarcely allowed human concourse between these various elements of their own populace had to cut off all closer contact with strangers. The aristocratic pride among themselves could not but foster national pride over against the foreigner. Thus Jacob's descendants lived in an isolated region in Goshen. The isolation that did not yet exist in Canaan and which they did not seek in Egypt was imposed on them by the particularistic spirit of the Egyptian court.

We must therefore surrender the notion that the separation, the isolation, of Abraham's family had been sought by the patriarchs and had come about by the contrast with the Canaanite nations. Instead, in agreement with the numerous and clear pronouncements of the Holy Scriptures, we must accept the unambiguous report that this separation, this segregation, this being detached, and this national isolation was automatically found by them in Egypt and was, by virtue of their being sent to Egypt, willed by God himself. If we had not received the report of Abraham's curious vision in the dream, we could still say that in order to escape from hunger, Jacob's sons had journeyed to Egypt of their own accord. But with the report of this meaningful dream before us, any such understanding of what happened dissolves. The transfer of Abraham's descendants to Egypt is merely the implementation of a design contained in God's plan of salvation, a design announced by God himself already in the early days of Abraham's stay in Canaan.

But precisely this is what gives this isolation, this particularism, the character of an inserted intermezzo and why it can no longer be the actual hallmark of Abraham's calling as such. Abraham's calling, Abraham's sending out, all his activity in Canaan, the promises given to him, his comings and goings among the nations, and the most noteworthy encounters of his life do not bear a particularistic character, but rather serve in every respect to identify his call spiritually and to strengthen, not weaken, the bond that connects him with the life of the nations and thus also keeps him connected to the life of humanity. If Abraham had stayed in Ur of the Chaldeans, he would have stayed in contact only with his own people.

§ 5

And precisely through his transfer to Palestine he is brought into contact with all leading nations of those days. Even though it is perfectly true that he entered into kinship with the foreign nations, and that such entering into kinship was disapproved of and regretted by Isaac in the case of Esau, it is equally unquestionable that by the transition from patriarchal to national life the separation between Israel and the nations was for a while made complete by erecting a high wall of separation, both through God's plan and through his giving of the law. Nevertheless, this entirely temporary national isolation does not begin until after, in the history of the patriarchs and especially in the life of Abraham, the broad foundations have been laid for a higher development that includes all nations and will encompass the entire life of the world.

If we mistakenly focus on only the interim period of national isolation, staring ourselves blind at it, and if as a result we do not have an eye for the entirely different basic character of the redemptive revelation received in Abraham's calling, his struggle of faith, and his actions among the nations, then we view the salvific mysteries with Jewish eyes and not with the eyes of the apostles, in a chiliastic half-light and not in the full daylight of the revelation in the old and new covenants. For Paul's whole battle against Jewish particularism always comes down again to not continuing to stare at that wall of separation that closed off the national life of Israel, but to direct the eyes of the believers behind that wall of Sinai's law to Abraham as the father of all believers, in whose whole appearance the basic character of the revelation is portrayed for us.

The Law, that is, the national arrangement of Israel as nation, is not the essential, not the original, not that which remains. This entire dispensation has come in between. It is an interlude—a link in the chain. And the scope and significance of the covenant of grace must be evaluated not according to this period of law for isolated Israel, but on the basis of the promise of God given to Abraham as the father of many nations. "For the promise to Abraham and his offspring that he would be heir of the world did not come through the law," the apostle declares. "For if it is the adherents of the law who are to be the heirs, faith is null and the promise is void." No, the promise rests on faith in order that it might be firm for "all his offspring—not only to the adherent of the law but also to the one who shares the faith of Abraham, who is the father of us all" (Rom 4:13–14, 16).

The trunk that stands between the root and the crown of the olive tree has, as it were, been inserted. That trunk is isolated through a thick bark and has contact with neither the soil nor the air. But the olive tree must be judged not by its isolated trunk but by its root and crown, for from the root comes its life and in the crown flourishes its fruit. Both root and crown are not isolated but have full communion, the root with the soil into which it extends its root system, and the crown with the sun and the air through its countless leaves. And thus it is also with the plant of salvation. In Abraham is the root, in Christ's church is the crown, and between those two lies the national dispensation of Israel, enclosed within a thick bark. But precisely for this reason the nature and character of the plant of salvation must not be measured by bark and trunk but by the root lying in Abraham and by the fruit sprouting as the crown in Christ's church.

Only in this way do we judge scripturally. Only in this way do we follow the apostolic distinction. And only in this way do we expel the Jewish leaven from our Christian confession. It is this truth that the prophecy of Israel continually maintained over against the scribes. It is this foundation of salvation to which Christ returns continually in his conflict with the Pharisees. It is this primordial revelation to which Paul continually appeals in his soul and life struggle with the Jewish Christians. It is this surety that our Reformed churches have defended tooth and nail over against all lovers of chiliastic chimeras. This is, therefore, not a side issue but nothing less than "the revelation of the mystery that was kept secret for long ages but has now been disclosed and through the prophetic writings has been made known to all nations, according to the command of the eternal God, to bring about the obedience of faith" (Rom 16:25–26).

# CHAPTER FORTY-SEVEN

# THE GREAT MYSTERY

*Making known to us the mystery of his will, according to his purpose, which he set forth in Christ.*

EPHESIANS 1:9

§ 1    The conclusion of our previous chapter already pointed to the "mystery" that was extolled particularly by the apostle Paul in the calling of the nations. We now must go into more detail about what the apostle says in this regard. For apparently more lies behind his speaking about this mystery than we would suspect on the basis of superficial reading. When Paul speaks not once but again and again in such solemn language and with such an impassioned tone about a "mystery that was kept secret for long ages but has now been disclosed ... according to the command of the eternal God," are we then right to think here of nothing but the possibility that a non-Jew who repents will also be saved? Assume that Paul had not mentioned this mystery at all, would anyone at all have thought that only someone of Jewish descent could be saved? Or didn't even the most rigid particularist among the sect of the Pharisees teach that a non-Jew could also participate in Israel's salvation? Indeed, did they not zealously pursue missionary work and did they not travel across land and sea to make proselytes of non-Jews [see Matt 25:15]?

The fact that someone of non-Jewish descent could also be saved was a mystery to no one. Everyone knew this and everyone agreed. Nor can the deep mystery lie herein, that a non-Jew can now be saved without circumcision. Neither Abel, or Enoch, or Noah, or Shem were circumcised, yet no one claims that they were therefore lost. And even if we assume that salvation for the non-Jew in fact still depended on his letting himself be incorporated into the Jewish nation, what difference would it make as such for this individual? Incorporated or not into the Jewish nation, as long as he was saved [it would make no difference]. It is therefore safe to say that if we read what Paul says about this mystery and we merely understand him to say that those of non-Jewish descent can also be saved without incorporation in Israel and that we therefore must do missionary work, we do not do justice to the apostolic word and would gloss over its profound meaning, although the involuntary impression must arise that Paul can at times express himself in such high-flown terms.

The intent of the apostolic testimony here is so little understood that we don't even think of teaching this mystery in the Christian church. We do teach the mystery of the incarnation of the Word, and also the great mystery that marriage is a reflection of the bond between Jesus and his church, but this mystery to which Paul points not once but again and again is barely mentioned at all. It has not been absorbed into our Christian consciousness. It is not counted among the mysteries of the Christian religion. We read past it. And in reading past it, Paul's statement about this is taken in such a flat, bland sense that if taken in this way, we would not have lost anything had Paul remained completely silent about this mystery.

We therefore begin by bringing together what the sacred apostle has in fact said on this topic.

In the first place we read in the letter to the church of Rome this in chapter 16:25–27:  § 2

> Now to him who is able to strengthen you according to my gospel and the preaching of Jesus Christ, according to the revelation of the mystery that was kept secret for long ages but has now been disclosed and through the prophetic writings has been made known to all nations, according to the command of the eternal God, to bring about the obedience of faith—to the only wise God be glory forevermore through Jesus Christ! Amen.

Second, he writes in the letter to the church at Ephesus, chapter 1:9–11:

> Making known to us the mystery of his will, according to his purpose, which he set forth in Christ as a plan for the fullness of time, to unite all things in him, things in heaven and things on earth.
>
> In him we have obtained an inheritance, having been predestined according to the purpose of him who works all things according to the counsel of his will.

Third, we read in this same letter, chapter 3:9–11:

> To bring to light for everyone what is the plan of the mystery hidden for ages in God who created all things, so that through the church the manifold wisdom of God might now be made known to the rulers and authorities in the heavenly places. This was according to the eternal purpose that he has realized in Christ Jesus our Lord.

Fourth, we read in Colossians 1:26–27:

> The mystery hidden for ages and generations but now revealed to his saints. To them God chose to make known how great among the Gentiles are the riches of the glory of this mystery, which is Christ in you, the hope of glory

Fifth, Paul writes to Timothy, more briefly because Timothy already knew the mystery (2 Tim 1:9–10):

> Who saved us and called us to a holy calling, not because of our works but because of his own purpose and grace, which he gave us in Christ Jesus before the ages began, and which now has been manifested through the appearing of our Savior Christ Jesus, who abolished death and brought life and immortality to light through the gospel.

And likewise, even more briefly, to Titus (Titus 1:1–2):

> Paul, a servant of God and an apostle of Jesus Christ, for the sake of the faith of God's elect and their knowledge of the truth, which accords with godliness, in hope of eternal life, which God, who never lies, promised before the ages began.

And finally, the holy apostle Peter expresses himself in a somewhat similar style, albeit less elaborately, in this manner (1 Pet 1:20–21):

> He was foreknown before the foundation of the world but was made manifest in the last times for the sake of you who through him are believers in God, who raised him from the dead and gave him glory, so that your faith and hope are in God.

Simply putting together these seven remarkable statements shows sufficiently that we are not dealing here with a secondary issue, but with an important part of revelation. At the same time, the expression "mystery" that is continually used, and the lofty language in which the thought is expressed, prove that this is about a truth that is not only important but also sublime. This is also apparent in another word of Paul's that has a somewhat modified aim but nevertheless points in fact to the same mystery. In Romans 9:25–26 we read:

As indeed he says in Hosea,

> "Those who were not my people I will call 'my people,'
> and her who was not beloved I will call 'beloved.'"
> "And in the very place where it was said to them, 'You are
> not my people,'
> there they will be called 'sons of the living God.'"

In the meantime, during the centuries before the Reformation, the §3 Christian church had done so little justice to this doctrine that Calvin still had to write, "It is not agreed among the learned in what sense he calls the gospel a hidden mystery in this place."[1] And then he concedes that those who acknowledge that it refers to the call of the Gentiles are on the right track. But he nevertheless adds that this superficial solution does not satisfy him, and that he is not far from surmising that the whole difference between the old and new covenant is to be found in it. Yet Calvin has definitely not succeeded in bringing this matter to clarity. The extensive insertions he wove into his later edition show that he struggled with

---

1. *CCS*, ad loc. Rom 16:25.

the issue.[2] And it is in fact at the end of his last insertion that the light briefly dawned on him (but without further elaboration) when he sought the mystery herein, that God wanted to subject the whole world, our entire human race, or as he expresses it, "all the nations to the obedience of faith."[3] So this doctrine awaited further elaboration after Calvin. Even with what Calvin wrote, the doctrine had hardly received proper treatment yet, and after him it has been all too painfully neglected by our theologians.

The key to understanding this whole series of statements correctly lies herein, that the mystery appears to be sought on the one hand simply in the incarnation of the Word, and on the other hand in the inclusion of the nations. These two are continually intertwined. The calling of the nations is not added to the incarnation, nor is it sufficient to say that we acknowledge it as flowing from the incarnation, but we fathom what Paul says only when we understand that he lets both of these—on the one hand the incarnation or the coming of Christ, and on the other hand the calling of the Gentiles—appear in our conception as one and the same mystery.

The meaning then is this: We do not understand the incarnation if we stop at the fact that Jesus was born a Jew. This fact is incontrovertible. For he himself said, "Salvation is from the Jews" [John 4:22], and this definite fact had to be maintained over against the heretical sentiments of the Samaritan woman. But if we do not go any further, we do not understand the incarnation. The Word became not Jew, but *flesh*. That is, even as children partake of flesh and blood, so too the Son of God has taken on *our human nature*. He took on that human nature, not from the air, nor through new creation. No, he took it from the human race that already existed, from the actual flesh and blood that had been propagated, beginning with Adam, from generation to generation until the days of the manger in Bethlehem. He thus took upon himself that human nature in a specific form, in a specific nation, in a specific tribe, from a designated woman; and when we come to these further specifics, then he is Mary's son, from Judah's tribe, the son of David, from the seed of Abraham (Heb 2:16).

But all of this concerns and touches on only the further particulars. When we baptize, we sprinkle *particular* water on the forehead of the

2. Calvin published three editions of his Romans commentary. These appeared in 1540, 1551, and 1556, respectively. Kuyper may have in mind the changes that Calvin made between the 1551 and 1556 editions. The variants between these two editions are presented in the text in CO 49:1–292.

3. CCS, ad loc. Rom 16:25.

one being baptized. We have no other option. It is water from this or that stream, from this or that well, from that particular pump or that designated water supply. But all these further details are secondary. Granted, we cannot get around this, but the main point in baptism remains, not that the water comes from this or that source, but that it be water. It is not immaterial which water it is. We will not take murky, smelly water but preferably clear and pure water. Yet in baptism it is the water as such that is what truly matters. The liquid must not be oil, not wine, not blood, but water, even as in the sacrament of the Lord's Supper it must not be water, nor blood, nor oil, but wine, and specifically wine that is red. And in the case of that wine we also always use a *particular* wine, from this or that country, pressed from grapes from this or that vine, but these particulars are also secondary in the wine of the Lord's Supper, and the main point remains that it be wine.

And this is how it is in this case. The Word becomes flesh. The Son of God takes on our human nature. This he can do only by being born into a particular nation, from a designated tribe, through a family mentioned by name, from one woman ordained for this purpose, who carries him in her womb and shares her flesh and blood with him; and that nation is of course Israel, the tribe is Judah, the family is David, and the woman is Mary. Yet here too these further specifics are secondary; they are the means, not the goal; and the main point and goal remain, namely, that he took upon himself human nature, the flesh and blood of Adam, the nature of our human race, that which over the whole world distinguishes the human being as human being from all other creatures. The Christian church has therefore continually confessed, and our Reformed churches still confess as well, that our salvation in principle depends on the fact that he has taken upon himself true human nature, even though in God's sovereign plan he could do this only through Mary. To put it succinctly: theoretically Jesus' birth from another virgin would have been thinkable, but it is *unthinkable* that he would have taken on a nature other than human nature. Then he would not be our Savior, and he could not have atoned for our sins.

If this has made clear that the main point of the "mystery of godliness" lies herein, that the Word became flesh and that the Son of God took upon himself our human nature, then we can also understand how this fact is directly related to the salvation, not of Israel but of the world, of our race, of humanity as humanity. If being born as Jew were the main point or the essence, and if the Son of God had taken on Jewish nature but not human

§ 4

nature, then he would of course be the Savior of the Jews, but not the Savior of humanity as such, and he would have atoned for the sin of the Jews but not for human sin. But if conversely, it is the case that he took on not the specifically Jewish but universal human nature, that nature that is the nature of all of us, in which all that is called human lives and exists, so that the Jewish aspect was merely the point of departure for taking on the essence of our universal human nature, then it follows also from this that he is not the Savior of the Jews but the Savior of the *world*, and that through him not merely the sin of the Jews but human sin, the sin of our human nature, has been atoned. This approximates what Paul extols to us as the *deep* mystery, namely, that the coming of Christ does not at all involve an exclusively Jewish salvation, but to the contrary, a grace of God that extends to all that is called human, to all nations. For God so loved not the Jews but the *world*, that he gave his only Son, that *whoever*—that is, whoever is a human being—believes in him should not perish but have eternal life [see John 3:16].

§ 5     When after this brief exposition and explanation we reread the statements of Scripture quoted earlier, we will see that what at first appeared as confusion now disappears immediately, and everything fits when the mystery is sought, one time in the incarnation and another time in the calling of the nations. Both express the same thing. Incarnation means taking on human nature and not merely Jewish nature. And that the nations are called also indicates precisely that the Son of God comes to save not only the Jews, but also the world. Once we clearly understand this, then it appears in retrospect that this entire hidden mystery is taught not only in the passages we have quoted, but elsewhere as well. For example, when 1 Timothy 3:16 states, "great … is the mystery," then this mystery is sought on the one hand in the fact that God is manifested in the flesh, on the other hand that he is preached, not among the Jews but among the Gentiles, and that he is believed, not in Israel but in the world. We read there: "Great indeed, we confess, is the mystery of godliness: He was manifested in the flesh, vindicated by the Spirit, seen by angels, proclaimed among the nations, believed on in the world, taken up in glory." Yes, then it becomes even more apparent that this same mystery is not by any means taught only by Paul, but that the holy apostle John proclaims the same truth to us when he, scarcely mentioning the birth of Jesus from Mary, indeed, even keeping Mary as the mother of Jesus in the background, places all emphasis on the fact that the Word has become flesh, and that the Christ as such saves the world [John 1:14, 29].

And we beg those brethren who still cannot fathom these riches of the gospel to surrender all suspicion that we are referring here either to a salvation of *all persons*, or to a *universal atonement*. This whole heresy has absolutely nothing to do with the piece of truth that we are defending and expounding and enjoining upon the church of God, and those who think otherwise should not blame us but their own ignorance of Holy Scripture. It is as clear and plain as anything can be clear and plain that the Holy Scriptures teach a *particular* atonement, not a universal one, not the salvation of all persons but solely of the elect. And that yet those same Scriptures teach as distinctly and decisively as possible that the *world* is saved and that the Son of God has taken on our *human nature*. For it stands written, and we must not overlook this, that the Son of God has taken on the likeness, not of the Jew but "the likeness *of men*" (Phil 2:7), that he took on *human form* (Phil 2:8), and that the mediator between God and *men* is the *man* Jesus Christ (1 Tim 2:5), not that the *Jew* Christ Jesus is the mediator between God and the *Jews*. And thus it states equally distinctly that Christ is the *Savior of the world* (John 4:42), that he "gives life to the *world*" (John 6:33), and that he will give his life "for the life of the *world*" (John 6:51). He does not say, "I am the light of the Jews," but "I am the light of the *world*" (John 8:12). And it is not the Jews but the *world* that God has so loved that he gave his only Son (John 3:16).

These are such strong statements and are intended so earnestly by John, that he, as we will explain in more detail, does not wait to let the eternal Word come to the fore in Abraham's calling, but rather in the act of creation; he does not depict this Word to us first as the source of revelation to Israel, but immediately as the light and life of the world. And let us not say that we find this in John but not in the other Gospels; for in the first place, we do not understand the objection, as if what the apostles Paul, Peter, and John tell us would be less the truth than what the apostle Matthew reports to us, or Luke the physician. But this also misrepresents the facts. For it is not in John or Paul but in Luke that we read that the angels in the fields of Ephratha sang, not "good will toward Jews" but "good will toward *men*," and not peace in Palestine but *peace on earth*. The question is not what a Jew but what a *human being* shall give for his soul. The disciples receive the promise, not that they will be fishers of *Jews* but that they will be fishers of *men*. Above all, Christ is certainly the Son of David and from

Abraham's seed, but he nevertheless calls himself generally and almost always not Son of David, nor Son of Abraham, but *Son of Man*. This name *Son of Man* occurs some eighty-eight times in the Gospels, over against very rare occurrences of Son of David, and then never as a proper name with which he refers to himself.

Thus it is undeniable that the coming of Christ into this world means automatically that he has come to all of humanity, to all that bears the name human, not to Israel but to the nations, and this is so because he has taken on our human nature and our human flesh. And when Paul calls this the great mystery, the mystery proper of the gospel, then this shows that anyone who defends the universalism of the gospel and opposes particularism, whether in its Anabaptist or in its chiliastic form, truly is not tilting at windmills or splitting hairs but mounting a guard at the main gate of the stronghold of the gospel, and would therefore be a coward and commit treason to the cause of their Lord if he let himself be deterred by anyone from doing this. That Paul calls this a "mystery" that was "hidden for ages and generations" can be explained by the fact that indeed from Abraham's calling on, for a period of almost two thousand years, the divine revelation had receded from the broad universalistic stream that watered the whole world into the very narrow, strictly particularistic streambed of Israel. But although this had naturally created the impression that this withdrawal into the narrow streambed of the Jewish people meant an abandoning, a surrendering, a leaving of the world and humanity and the nations to their own devices, the glorious point is that it appears in retrospect how this concentration of the revelation in Israel, far from abandoning the world, had in God's sovereign plan and purpose the precise goal of later finding the world again and in this way of saving the world.

# CHAPTER FORTY-EIGHT

# NO OASIS IN THE WILDERNESS

*But the Jerusalem above is free, and she is our mother.*

GALATIANS 4:26

We may dare assume that we have succeeded in our attempt to make our readers grasp clearly and unmistakably at least the importance and seriousness of the point we are dealing with. For we have shown how the apostle brings the section about Melchizedek to the fore as one of those points by which we can recognize the person who has advanced toward maturity. And we have also made clear how the great mystery that Paul emphasizes again and again must be sought in nothing else than this, that the Son of God took on not Jewish nature but human nature, and as such is the Savior not of the Jews but of humankind—the Jews of course being included in humankind.

§ 1

If this is therefore the doctrine with which one moves on from the "milk of infants" to "the solid food of the mature," and at the same time is the great mystery that was hidden for many centuries but came to light in the manger at Bethlehem, then it is a lacuna, a deficiency in our Christian perspective, if such an extremely important doctrine has not been incorporated into it. This deficiency is caused primarily by paying insufficient attention to the doctrine of common grace, that is, to God's involvement with humanity *as humanity*, also outside the path of conversion proper.

The further we develop this doctrine of common grace, the more clearly we shall discover the far-reaching significance of this doctrine, not only for dogmatics, but also for our entire world- and lifeview, and for the praxis of life.

Two fundamental notions stand here in conflict.

The first is that by catching man in the snare of sin, Satan thwarted the glorious work of God in creation. As a consequence of the fall, human nature is now entirely depraved, human life one continuous horror, this world one great arena of sin and misery. Nothing further can be done to this human nature, this human life, and the eternal wonder of God's grace is that a few souls are saved. For those souls, salvation is set apart and prepared in a separate sphere. God lets go of all the rest of humanity. Everything else that was at work on and in the world was from the Evil One, and God works only in that sphere that is his own. In that sphere, salvation has been achieved through the work of God, and all conditions have been fulfilled that had to be satisfied to save the few souls that are saved, who must then be incorporated within this narrow sphere. And thus it goes until the end. Then comes the judgment, a judgment in which our human nature, our race, our entire human life goes under with the whole world. The kingdom of God then will consist herein, that those few saved souls will shine around God's throne as glorious spiritual beings.

Over against this false foundational notion, in the meantime, stands an entirely different foundational notion based on Holy Scripture. And this true, foundational scriptural notion teaches us that Satan has not thwarted God's work but has only temporarily darkened its splendor, that far from surrendering our human race and our human life to Satan, God has indeed continued to contend with Satan for this his abundant creation and will ultimately wrest it away from him. It teaches that to this end God has done two things. First, his common grace has restrained the full effect of sin and destruction in our nature, in our race, and in our human life. And second, he has prepared, worked out, and completed his particular grace within a separate sphere. When this separation had served his purpose, he went out to the world with this achieved salvation that was intended for the world, for our race, for each human being who would believe. And he brought the mainstream of human life under the influence and dominion of that salvation to claim his elect from all nations, and to claim for the benefit of those elect and to his own glory all human life for Christ. From this a crisis is born that extends from the leaven of the gospel over the satanic impulse in that world. This crisis will not come to an end until the final judgment. And then it will become apparent that our nature, our humanness, our human life, is saved in body and soul, along with the renewed earth. Thus after the damnation of the unbelievers, the original work of God will gloriously bloom before his throne for all eternity.

These are the two foundational notions that govern the entire perspective on the kingdom of heaven, on the gospel, on Christianity, and on human life.

In the meantime the first, false foundational notion appears in three very modified, partly mixed forms. It is important to focus attention on these three forms. We prefer to distinguish them as the *chiliastic*, the *Roman Catholic*, and the *spiritualistic*.

The chiliastic or narrow Jewish perspective tells us that when the world fell away from him, God selected the man Abraham, and from that man prepared himself a people that would be the bearer of salvation, not merely temporarily and as a foreshadowing in symbols, but a people that would in fact determine the primary group from which those to be saved would come. Not that every Jew would be saved, but rather that all those who would be saved had to come from the Jews or be incorporated into the Jews. Everything outside that sphere was given over to perdition and served only to give life to those who would come from the nations to the Jews. In Paul's day this was applied on principle and in an absolute sense. Anyone could come to Christ, but access to Christ was open only via circumcision. One who was born a Gentile had to become a Jew in order in this way to be a Christian. It is this slogan that John the Baptist and Paul opposed most vehemently. God is able, the herald of Christ proclaimed, to raise up children for Abraham from these stones [see Matt 3:9; Luke 3:8]. And Paul did not cease to affirm that in Christ there is neither Jew nor Greek, Scythian nor barbarian, and that those who let themselves be circumcised from the aforementioned motivation did not gain Christ, but lost Christ [see Gal 3:28; Col 3:11; Gal 5:2–6].

But since then this Jewish sentiment has appeared in modified form as a consequence of circumstances. This foundational notion was changed when Jerusalem was destroyed, the Jewish national state was obliterated, and everyone saw before their eyes that the Christian church was recruiting from the Gentiles. Because of their guilt, the Jews were pushed to the background, but only for a time; later the Jews will reclaim their old, original position; Jerusalem then will be rebuilt and the Jewish nation state will be restored; as king of the Jews Christ will rule once again on this earth; and those saved from the nations will be blessed once again under the shadow of Israel.

The *Roman Catholic* notion differs from this, but its formal point of departure is the same, except that the Roman Catholic Church here takes the place of the Jewish nation. For also in the Roman Catholic perspective, all that lies outside the church has been abandoned; salvation is contained within the circle of the saving church. Therefore, only that portion of human life succeeds that is taken up into the sphere of that church. The whole of human life, to the extent that it undergoes this holy influence, must receive its rule of life from that church and be placed in service to the flourishing and splendor of that church. And the end will be that all who belonged to that church and stood under the wings of that church will one day shine before God's throne, whereas everything that stands outside that church will perish.

The third, or *spiritualistic* form of this foundational perspective, found among the Anabaptists and the mystics, seeks the circle of the separated neither in the Jewish nation, nor in the institutionalized church, but in the spiritual company of the enlightened and the born again. Human life outside that spiritual circle is, also in this perspective, worthless and destined only to perish. All that matters is that spiritual circle. Only with this circle does God occupy himself in the narrower sense. This circle renews itself in every century by the bringing in of the elect. This circle of the elect separates itself from the world and avoids it. And thus it continues until the end, until the last judgment, when God will eradicate all that is outside that circle and will gather everything included in that circle—which actually means only the *souls* of the elect—around his throne. The world then disappears, our human life disappears, and the body also disappears. Satan gets all those things, and only the souls of the justified remain with God eternally.

§ 2     We see that these three perspectives differ very widely. But each of these three nevertheless shares this common foundation: all three make a separation between our human life and our human world on the one hand, and a separate circle within that life and that world on the other hand. For the chiliasts, even as for the Jewish Christians in the past, that circle is what they call *Israel*. For the Roman Catholics it is the institutional Roman Catholic Church. And for the spiritualists of all stripes, it is the community of the enlightened. Over against that separate circle the rest of human life, as all agree, has only transitory significance. It continues to exist only until judgment day. Then it perishes forever, falls prey to destruction, and becomes plunder for Satan. And what then will remain forever and constitute the kingdom of heaven is either Israel, together with what was incorporated into Israel or overshadowed by it; or what is within the church triumphant and lives under its shadow; or what was by rebirth transferred from the world into the communion of saints.

Our eyes are open to the very considerable difference in the elaborations of the foundational notion among these three varying perspectives. We fully acknowledge this and know very well that the chiliasts present the matter differently from the Jewish Christians in Paul's day; that the Roman Catholic Church interprets the matter very differently than do the chiliasts; and that the spiritualists in many ways stand directly over against the chiliasts and the Roman Catholics. We certainly will have the opportunity to point to that variety of distinctions a number of times. But all three agree in the main that they are not concerned about the salvation of the world but only about the exaltation of their own separatist circle, so that all that lies outside that circle serves in fact only to glorify that group.

Over against this foundational notion stands the foundational understanding that we confess. We say that God has not surrendered his work of creation to Satan to save out of it only one single circle, but that God loved the world; that he reached out in mercy to our human race; that he therefore has turned away the effects of sin and destruction through common grace; that he has continued to work throughout the centuries in the world of humanity, also outside of particular grace, and that he separated out of this world a circle for preparing the balm of Gilead; but he has also prepared that balm, not in order that the world would exist merely for the sake of that balm, but that that balm might serve and save that world. Therefore the work of God in common and particular grace is aimed at re-creating this earth into a new earth, this world into a new world, humanity into a new humanity, and to that end the sinner into a child of God. This implies of course that only the elect will be saved, and only those who believe in the Son of Man will escape destruction. But in, with, and for those blessed elect who will one day constitute the new humanity, everything (other than the persons loyal to him) that Satan once seized will once again be wrested away from him, and the whole original creation will be brought to the final goal for which God Almighty called it into being.

§ 3      Faced with the choice between these two foundational conceptions, everything we have brought up from Holy Scripture thus far impels us to reject the first and accept the second foundational conception. We have been insisting that each of the following is true: Melchizedek stands above Abraham; the order of Melchizedek returns in Christ, while the order of Aaron vanishes and disappears; the gospel states that God so loved not the Jews but the world that he gave the world his Son; Jesus' name is not Son of the Jews but Son of Man; this is the great mystery, that salvation in Israel is prepared for the nations, that is, for our human race; and the prophecy says that one day our body will also be glorified and this earth, after having melted, will be restored in new splendor. Now if, as we have been arguing, all this is true, then the conclusion is that God did not leave the world and our human life in the hands of Satan to save only a certain circle of individuals but to the contrary, that segregated circle is, first in Israel and now in the institutional church, only the means and instrument in God's hand for contending against Satan for *all* his plunder and for restoring to God's glory that which God once created but that fell away from him.

This argument must of course be decided primarily in the arena of Holy Scripture by making clear how Holy Scripture views the position of Israel. For in Israel the notion arises of the segregated sphere according to God's plan, and all ecclesiastical or spiritual particularism never has anything in view but being the continuation or imitation of that segregated circle of Israel. The Roman Catholics see the Zion of God in their institutionalized church; the spiritualists look for that same Zion of God in the society of saints. To some extent nothing can be said against this. There remains a segregated circle that exists until the end, and that segregated circle will always bear the image of the Zion of God in Israel, whether it is sought in the church or in the society of saints. But if this is true, then it depends entirely on the correctness or incorrectness of our perspective on Israel's segregation, whether we understand the meaning of the segregation of the church or of the segregation of the God-fearing incorrectly or in accordance with the demands of Scripture. For the argument is not about whether or not such a segregated circle must exist. Between us and those whose ideas we challenge, no difference of opinion exists as to whether such a segregated circle will exist and must exist until the last judgment. We mutually accept this requirement and that fact. The whole dispute involves only this question: How does and how must that segregated circle relate to our human living outside that circle? Therefore, it is of such paramount importance that we form for ourselves correct and clear notions from the Holy Scriptures concerning that relationship willed by God.

In this context, we saw that the first patriarchs did not yet segregate themselves from the life of the nations in the sense that the life of people outside their tents was no longer of concern to them. That segregation in a strict sense arose only after Israel's passage through the Red Sea. We also saw that in Abraham's day there was still a knowledge of God in Abimelech, in Ephron, and in the king of Salem, as well as an involvement of God with these princes. We saw as well that Melchizedek is not a secondary figure but is placed above Abraham as a model of Christ. After Golgotha and the day of Pentecost it became apparent that the segregation of Israel had served simply to prepare the balm of Gilead for the world, something Israel had not understood.

§ 4

Entirely in line with this is the equally undeniable truth that in Israel lay only the shadow, not the essence of the matter; this was the symbolic expression of the true religion, not our "reasonable" religion (that is, not the religion that realizes its essential nature [see Rom 12:1]). The Holy Scriptures express this most clearly in what they say about the two Jerusalems. It is written, says Paul in Galatians 4:22–31, that Abraham had two sons. The one was born according to the flesh, the other through promise. And thus the one was born by a slave woman, the other from the free woman Sarah. These things, he says, have a different meaning than would appear on the surface. For it implies that the covenant of Sinai was unto slavery, and that the Jews were children of this covenant of servitude, and conversely, that the covenant of the New Testament is a covenant of freedom, resulting in the children of promise. And in order to shed full light on this far-reaching notion, he goes to the earthly Jerusalem as the city on the mountain chosen by God, to which the Jewish Christians in the church of Galatia still continued to look forward, and then with a poignant word he suddenly points the religious conscience away from that earthly Jerusalem to an entirely different Jerusalem that lay not on Mount Moriah, but the Jerusalem in heaven. Your Jerusalem, O children of the Jews, that lies on Zion, is in servitude, but the true "Jerusalem above is free, and she is our mother" [Gal 4:26].

Two Jerusalems are therefore placed over against one another. In the first place is the earthly Jerusalem, which bore only a reflection of the true one and was therefore itself nonessential. In the second place is the true, essential Jerusalem that is with God, and therefore free. There is still more. For this remarkable statement, which in itself would already decide the matter, does not stand alone. In Revelation 21:2 we also read, "And I saw the holy city, new Jerusalem, coming down out of heaven from God"; and again in verse 10: "And he [one of the seven angels that came to John in verse 9] carried me away in the Spirit to a great, high mountain, and showed me the holy city Jerusalem coming down out of heaven from God." In Revelation 3:12 Christ writes to the church at Philadelphia: "The one who conquers, I will make him a pillar in the temple of my God. Never shall he go out of it, and I will write on him the name of my God, and the name of the city of my God, the new Jerusalem, which comes down from my God out of heaven." And in Hebrews 12:22 God's people are told that under the New Testament they have come "to the city of the living God, the heavenly Jerusalem."

Clearly and explicitly the earthly Jerusalem, with its temple on Zion, is being placed over against another Jerusalem, and this other Jerusalem is distinguished from the earthly one herein, that it is called the new Jerusalem, the holy Jerusalem, the heavenly Jerusalem, the Jerusalem that comes down from God out of heaven. This is therefore the perspective from which everything we know of the earthly Canaan, of the earthly Zion, and of the earthly Jerusalem must be judged and understood. In that earthly Canaan, in that earthly Zion, in that earthly Jerusalem, there is never the essence, that divinely willed and enduring reality. The earthly one contains nothing but the representation, the symbolization, the example, or the type. And all those who understand or interpret the prophecy differently end up taking the wrong path.

# CHAPTER FORTY-NINE

# SYMBOL AND TYPE

*Now this may be interpreted allegorically.*

GALATIANS 4:24

After Golgotha and the Mount of Olives, the holy, the heavenly Jerusalem, the "Jerusalem that is above and comes from God out of heaven" has taken the place of the Jerusalem of Melchizedek, of David, and of Herod. Holy Scripture states this clearly, not once but repeatedly, and whoever puts or presents the matter differently in order to maintain his Jewish and particularistic notions, contradicts in an unforgivable manner what the apostles, led by the Spirit, have revealed to us in the name of the Lord; even more, what Christ himself showed to John on Patmos.

§ 1

Without paying further attention to this objection, we continue our argument assuming the indisputable facts that the Jerusalem of David has not been of permanent but only of transitory significance for the kingdom of God, and that Christ would lead us from the Jerusalem of that day, which was a shadow, into the true, real, and permanent Jerusalem.

In the meantime we must at this point preempt an obvious misunderstanding that can easily creep in. For many who hear about this heavenly Jerusalem take it entirely metaphorically in a spiritualized sense. For them Jerusalem was the place where God revealed his presence, so that we now should understand Jerusalem as the holy mystery in which our soul may sometimes experience how good it is for us to be near unto God. And whereas this communion of ours with the eternal Being is still always defective and imperfect on earth, Jerusalem was then viewed in a still higher way, in the full sense, as the nearness of the Lord enjoyed by the blessed spirits in heaven.

If understood in this way, Jerusalem is taken in a figurative sense as a name for all that lies hidden in spiritual mysticism. But this is not how we intend it when we say on the basis of the Holy Scriptures that the Jerusalem of David has now come to naught, to be replaced by the heavenly Jerusalem and not again by the former Jerusalem. What John saw on Patmos was not a spiritual event but the image of a future reality. What he saw shows us in broad lines the rebirth, not of the soul, but of "heaven and earth." It shows us how all that exists melts and dissipates, and how a new order comes in the place of this "old" state of affairs. He sees as in a panoramic vista the glory of the new earth and of the new heaven, and he sees the new Jerusalem descend on that new earth from that new heaven. And this city of the living God with its gates of pearl is described for us.

Succinctly we can therefore say that also on that new earth, under that new heaven, there will be a center of the revelation and worship of God, and it is this center that is presented to us as the Jerusalem that descends from God out of heaven. We will not offer any further explanation except to say that, of course, this must not be taken in a coarse, sensual sense nor according to the limitations of our present condition; but any notion that this should be understood in a purely spiritual sense is excluded. The earth is present once more, but renewed. The blessed have been raised in the glorified body and are present on the renewed earth. And the heavenly Jerusalem is uncovered, not for the soul's eye but for their heightened sensual perception.

§ 2    Once this point of departure has been settled, we point out as well that in the New Testament not only the name Jerusalem but also other names from the old covenant are divorced from the specific places and cities and mountains they referred to in ancient times. Take, for example, the name Zion, which is most closely related to the name of Jerusalem. It is patently obvious that Hebrews 12:22 and Revelation 14:1 are two passages in which the name Zion occurs, not as a reference to the hilltop where the temple of Solomon once stood, but with an entirely different meaning. We read in Hebrews 12:18, 22-24, "For you have not come to what may be touched. ... But you have come to Mount Zion and to the city of the living God, the heavenly Jerusalem, and to innumerable angels in festal gathering, and to the assembly of the firstborn who are enrolled in heaven, and to God, the judge of all, and to the spirits of the righteous made perfect, and to Jesus, the mediator of a new covenant, and to the sprinkled blood that speaks a better word than the blood of Abel." It simply would not make sense to think here of a rebuilding of the ancient Zion. For clearly the New Testament is here being contrasted with the Old Testament, the blood of Christ contrasted with the blood of the martyrs and of the offerings, the universal church contrasted with the particularistic church in Israel, the heavenly Jerusalem contrasted with the old earthly one, and so too the new Zion contrasted with the Zion that was situated next to David's palace. Just as the heavenly Jerusalem replaces the earthly Jerusalem, making the latter antiquated and obsolete, so here too the heavenly Zion, the Zion that will one day be the center of the church triumphant, will make the ancient, earthly Zion superfluous and abrogate it.

Revelation 14:1 leads to exactly the same result. There we read, "Then I looked, and behold, on Mount Zion stood the Lamb, and with him 144,000 who had his name and his Father's name written on their foreheads." This also does not refer to the hilltop in Palestine, but to a glorified Zion upon which the Christ appears in his glory. The mere fact that the 144,000 saints appear there with him shows this. For this number is not intended in a numerical but a symbolic sense. All saints together comprise infinitely more than 144,000. No, this number is obtained by multiplying 12 by 12 and then by 1,000, and serves to indicate symbolically the fullness and completeness of the abundantly immense number. *Three* is the number of the divine, derived from the divine Trinity. *Four* is the number that indicates the earth, derived from the four points of the compass. Therefore, 3 × 4, or 12, indicates that the divine has fully permeated the human. This number 12 is multiplied by 12 to indicate the fullness of the dispensation. There are two dispensations, that of Israel and that of the nations, which merge. And that number 12 × 12, or 144, is multiplied again by 1,000 to indicate the fullness of the number of individuals. Therefore, 144,000 is a symbolic number, meaning the fullness of saved humanity in its entirety as it already then stood in God's vision. There simply would not have been room for this innumerable multitude on the relatively small hilltop of the ancient, earthly Zion. And this, therefore, already decides the claim that in view here is not the ancient Zion but the heavenly one.

What applies to the name "Jerusalem" and the name "Zion" applies equally to the name "Israel." When it says in Galatians 6:16, "And as for all who walk by this rule, peace and mercy be upon them, and upon the Israel of God," then those who would take this "Israel" as referring to the Jewish people would understand nothing of Paul's letter to the churches of Galatia. Every knowledgeable person knows that here "the Israel of God" refers not to the Jewish people, but to the church of the new covenant. It is entirely in the same sense in which Paul wrote to the church of Rome that "a Jew is one inwardly, and circumcision is a matter of the heart, by the Spirit, not by the letter" (2:29), or in Romans 9:8, "It is not the children of the flesh who are the children of God, but the children of the promise are counted as offspring"; or finally, in Galatians 3:7, "Know then that it is those of faith who are the sons of Abraham."

§ 3      This entire understanding of Scripture has pervaded the life of the church to such an extent that we speak of Canaan in the sense of the heavenly Canaan; of the Jordan River in the sense of the stream of death through which we must wade to enter the heavenly Canaan. In addition, phrases like the Valley of Achor, the balm of Gilead, and so many more have well nigh become fixed expressions for what is not intended in a temporal Jewish sense, but in a universal-spiritual sense. We have here a use of language in the church that, far from being arbitrary, is generally directly in line with what Paul declares, that these things "may be interpreted allegorically," and with his constant habit of applying the things of the old covenant in a spiritual sense to the things of the new covenant.

In Holy Scripture this transfer even extends not only to names of the sacred, but also to what is branded as unholy. When it says in the hymn of the angels of the Apocalypse, "Fallen, fallen is Babylon the great, she who made all nations drink the wine of the passion of her sexual immorality" (see Rev 14:8), then no one would think of the ancient Babylon of Nebuchadnezzar that perished long since, nor of a restoration of the ancient Babylon in its former glory, which is directly precluded by the prophecy; but everyone understands that here the name Babylon points to the consolidated world powers inimical to God. Even as it says in Revelation 16:19, "God remembered Babylon the great, to make her drain the cup of the wine of the fury of his wrath." It is nothing but what the woman from Revelation 17:5 has written on her forehead: "A name of mystery: 'Babylon the great, mother of prostitutes and of earth's abominations.'" Christian poetry has given that name Babylon alternately to all kinds of cities that were for a time the center and seat of the unholy world power. Da Costa did it in his poignant poem about Paris.[1] This metaphorical use of such names is so common in Holy Scripture that we read in Revelation 11:8 something similar with regard to the names Sodom and Egypt. Sodom was the city in Canaan where the abomination of sexual sin manifested itself for the first time in its most heinous form, and Egypt was the land that under the Pharaohs of Moses' day was the first to engage in direct battle against God. And it is in memory of this that Revelation 11:8 states, "Their dead bodies will lie in the street of the great city that symbolically is called Sodom and Egypt, where their Lord was crucified." This spiritual application of names occurring in the Old Testament has made an impression on the world, and the expression "the language of Canaan" was derived especially from this use of proper names.[2]

With these facts before us, we now ask how must we judge the interpreters of Old Testament prophecy who in all seriousness want to interpret all that has been written about the future glory of Israel, of Jerusalem, of Zion, and of David's house as if it referred to the old, earthly, Jewish Jerusalem, and deduce from this that when Christ returns, he will begin by restoring his kingdom locally in Canaan and specifically in what is at present Islamic Jerusalem? The panoramic character of prophecy alone already precludes this. *Panoramic* is understood to mean that the prophetic vista telescopes the various stages of the development of the church under the old and new covenants and even into the kingdom of glory, so that these stages overlap and simultaneously provide a single continuous

§ 4

---

1. Isaäc da Costa (1798–1860) was a Dutch poet and a leader of the Réveil. Kuyper is referring to Da Costa's poem "Paris," which contains the following lines as rendered in English: "[Paris] is the Babel of our time / Like Babel she will one day collapse in ruins / ... / That city is modern-day Gomorrah / The bestialized Sodom of Europe." See Isaäc da Costa, *Da Costa's kompleete dichtwerken*, ed. J. P. Hasebroek (The Hague: D. A. Thieme, 1876), 320.

2. Taken from Isaiah 19:18, "'language of Canaan' is a phrase that refers to the prophetic and metaphorical language used by God's chosen people when they talk of the kingdom of God and its realization in the last days. It was employed by the Puritans in the sixteenth and seventeenth centuries to describe the language the saints will use when the kingdom has been established. The phrase thus refers at once to a prophetic vocabulary available to contemporary saints as they speak of the future and to the mode of discourse to be enjoyed by those saints when the Scripture promises are fulfilled." See Mason I. Lowance Jr., *The Language of Canaan: Metaphor and Symbol in New England from the Puritans to the Transcendentalists* (Cambridge, MA: Harvard University Press, 1980), vii.

perspective from Jerusalem in the days of the prophecy to the heavenly
Jerusalem that is to come. Take, for example, Isaiah 60:13–22, which reads,

> The glory of Lebanon shall come to you,
>     the cypress, the plane, and the pine,
> to beautify the place of my sanctuary,
>     and I will make the place of my feet glorious.
> The sons of those who afflicted you
>     shall come bending low to you,
> and all who despised you
>     shall bow down at your feet;
> they shall call you the City of the Lord,
>     the Zion of the Holy One of Israel.
> Whereas you have been forsaken and hated,
>     with no one passing through,
> I will make you majestic forever,
>     a joy from age to age.
> You shall suck the milk of nations;
>     you shall nurse at the breast of kings;
> and you shall know that I, the Lord, am your Savior
>     and your Redeemer, the Mighty One of Jacob.
> Instead of bronze I will bring gold,
>     and instead of iron I will bring silver;
> instead of wood, bronze,
>     instead of stones, iron.
> I will make your overseers peace
>     and your taskmasters righteousness.
> Violence shall no more be heard in your land,
>     devastation or destruction within your borders;
> you shall call your walls Salvation,
>     and your gates Praise.
> The sun shall be no more
>     your light by day,
> nor for brightness shall the moon
>     give you light;
> but the Lord will be your everlasting light,
>     and your God will be your glory.
> Your sun shall no more go down,
>     nor your moon withdraw itself;

for the Lord will be your everlasting light,
    and your days of mourning shall be ended.
Your people shall all be righteous;
    they shall possess the land forever,
the branch of my planting, the work of my hands,
    that I might be glorified.
The least one shall become a clan,
    and the smallest one a mighty nation;
I am the Lord;
    in its time I will hasten it.

Here is a panorama that immediately in the opening sentences refers to Jerusalem and the altar of burnt offering, for Isaiah 60:7 speaks of the rams of Nebaioth that will be accepted on the altar of Zion. But it does not stop there. The panorama soon becomes a perspective on eternity, and ends with showing us the new situation, the new order of things as it will be on the new earth, under a new heaven, as is apparent from the statement that there will no longer be a sun or a moon, that all suffering has been done away with, and that the human beings that are still there "shall all be righteous," and that the righteous "shall possess the land forever" [v. 21].

This occurs continually in prophecy, again and again: the perspective almost always starts from the existing Jerusalem, from the local Zion, from the actual suffering of the Jewish people. But from there it moves through all the stages of revelation, finally coming to rest in the vision of the eternal glory that comes on the new earth, under the new heaven. All these prophecies take the church of God in the Israel of their day, that is, Jerusalem, as their point of departure. But those who imagine that because of this, all that comes later remains tied to that early Jewish element and refers back to it, misunderstand the spirit of prophecy. They prove that they do not understand the panoramic character of these visions and come into open contradiction with the interpretation the Holy Spirit has given us through the apostles in the New Testament. In the New Testament lies the key that for us is the "key of knowledge" [Luke 11:52] to the Old Testament, and whoever does not use or know that "key of knowledge" remains standing before the Old Testament as before a closed gate.

Later we may have the opportunity to maintain the ancient confession of the truth in more detail over against the chiliastic tendencies among

§ 5

many in our century. Now we limit ourselves to making clear to our readers how this involves in fact not a secondary, but a primary issue of the greatest consequence. Christ himself has said as emphatically as possible, "See, your house is left to you desolate" [Matt 23:38]. This is not said for merely a period of time, or conditionally, but absolutely. From the hour of Golgotha, the former Jerusalem is finished. It is rejected. It is waiting only for its terrible destruction. And from this hour onward, the prophetic eye of the people of God is no longer focused on the Jerusalem that awaits its destruction, but on the Jerusalem that comes from God out of heaven, the Jerusalem that is above.

This, however, does not stand in isolation but is directly related to the doctrine of the atonement. For the old Jerusalem had its center in Zion, and derived its significance from the temple; that temple was great, not because of its wood and stone, its gold and copper, but through the presence of the Lord of lords behind the curtain and through the atonement offering on the altar of burnt offering. That offering and that presence of God were the soul of the temple, that temple was the soul of Zion, and Zion was the soul of Jerusalem. No more than you can keep a human being alive merely by subjecting the corpse to electric shocks if the soul does not reenter it, can Jerusalem be restored without Zion, Zion without its temple, and that temple without the offering and the presence of God behind the curtain. Jerusalem is not that mountain, not that stream, not those buildings, not that gate. Jerusalem's external appearance was merely the body in which the sacred lived.

Assume that Palestine were artificially taken away from the Turks, the Muslims were expelled from Palestine, and the entire country were inhabited by Jews, under a Jewish government: then the Jews could build a temple again, and they could bring offerings again, but they could never again bring back the presence of God behind the curtain. It would be and remain a temple without God and a mockery of the majesty of the Lord. For Christ himself has said that now the temple is no longer on Zion, but in his body. The curtain in the temple was torn, from top to bottom. God has moved out of his temple on Zion. And on the day of Pentecost God, the Holy Spirit, entered into his real temple—the church of the elect—into the true, mystical body of Christ. After his essential sacrifice on Golgotha all Jewish sacrifices are null and void, without purpose and vain. And any attempt to restore either that offering or that temple or the earthly Jerusalem signifies nothing less than the denial of the true sacrifice Christ has brought and of the mighty fact that God's temple is now in the body of Christ, or, viewed more broadly, that the dispensation of the shadows that gave Jerusalem its radiance has once and for all been replaced by the dispensation of fulfillment, which is not connected with the earthly Jerusalem but with the heavenly Jerusalem. It is ipso facto an impossibility to want to cling to both the fulfillment in Christ and the dispensation of the shadows. The one precludes the other. And Paul calls any attempt to do so "foolish" on the part of the foolish Galatians [Gal 3:1]. Reaching back to the shadows means letting go of the Savior.

The fact that people nevertheless continually fall into this extremely questionable and highly dangerous error, that otherwise excellent men like Darby[3] and Da Costa have more or less fallen into it, and that all kinds of otherwise God-fearing Christians have followed in their footsteps, must be explained only from this, that Israel had not only a metaphorical but also an exemplary significance, that it was not only symbolic but also typical. The difference between a mere allegory or symbol and a type or example can be made clear by comparing the Passover lamb and David. The Passover lamb, of course, symbolized Christ. As the Passover lamb was slaughtered for Israel, so has our Passover Lamb, namely, Christ, been slaughtered for us. David, on the other hand, was not symbol but a type of Christ. In connection with David, it must be said not only that in his kingship he symbolized the kingship of Christ, but also that in fact the Christ has come from the loins of David as concerns the flesh. In the symbol there is only equality of traits. In the type or example there is, in addition to the equality of traits, a connection in reality. Christ was the son of David. And the same is true, to a certain extent, of Israel. Israel not only symbolized the people of God, it *was* the people of God for a time, and when Israel ceased to exist as a national state, the people of God was generated from Israel. Salvation is from the Jews. And thus our confession must be that salvation was not merely symbolized upon Zion, but that the salvation of the world has actually come from Zion.

These two then, the symbolic and the typical significance of Israel, of Zion, of Jerusalem, have raised confusion in the minds of many, in the sense that the symbolic was abandoned as having been absorbed in Christ,

§ 6

---

3. John Nelson Darby (1800–82), an early leader of the Plymouth Brethren, was the father of dispensationalism and one of the most influential proponents of premillennialism.

but the typical was retained; even today, especially with regard to the end times, people still want to cling to this external reality. It is not adequately thought through how Israel, because it was also typical, in reality takes its own place among the nations. Throughout eternity Israel will be numbered among the nations, and will retain a typical place among those nations, without therefore seeing the former relationship restored that has now come to an end and passed away. Even if we wanted to assume that the place on earth where Zion stands will regain a special significance on the new earth, that new significance of Zion would occur under such entirely different relations and in such a radically different order of things, that we simply cannot guess, surmise, or state anything about it. We are not even permitted to stammer here. However, what is not merely permitted to us but has been given us as an imperative duty is that, in obedience to the Word of God and taking captive all our thoughts and notions to the truth of Scripture, we will understand that when the reality has come the shadow is past. We are forbidden to fall back into the errors and delusions that Paul has opposed with such earnestness and severity in the epistle to the Romans, as well as in Galatians and in the epistle to the Hebrews. And banning all Jewish particularism from our Christian, our Reformed confession, we repeat after the apostle, "In speaking of a new covenant, he makes the first one *obsolete*. And what is becoming obsolete and *growing old* is ready *to vanish away*" (Heb 8:13).

# CHAPTER FIFTY

# ISRAEL FOR THE SAKE OF THE NATIONS

*Truly, I say to you, among those born of women there has arisen no one greater than John the Baptist. Yet the one who is least in the kingdom of heaven is greater than he.*

MATTHEW 11:11

When the substance comes, the shadow that it had cast automatically disappears. A sacrifice of rams or bulls on the altar of the Lord is unthinkable after Golgotha. Now that Christ, who himself is our high priest, and in whose mystical body God the Holy Spirit makes his dwelling, ministers at the altar in the sanctuary above, no temple and no holy of holies can exist on Zion any longer. The curtain has been rent from top to bottom with a tear that never can, nor ever may, be repaired. Every attempt to restore any ministry of shadows after Christ has come is the same as denying Christ and denying the value of his unique sacrifice. As long as her husband is at sea, the fisherman's wife may point her child to the portrait of father, but when the husband has returned to shore, she points her child to father himself. To then bypass him by pointing to his shadow image would be an affront to love or an act of insanity. And therefore our

§ 1

forefathers have always pointed out that those who, after the appearing of Christ, continue to hang on to the shadows and ceremonies, to times and places, not only err but violate the honor of the Christ. Even as the apostle combated this evil sharply and unsparingly in the shadow-worshippers of his day, so too our ancestors attacked this same evil in the ministers of ceremony of their day. And we also hope to be found faithful to the end in combating this evil.

The nations do not exist for the sake of Israel, but Israel has been as it were inserted for a long time into the great drama of world history *for the sake of the nations*. Israel has and maintains its significance until the kingdom of heaven comes. But no sooner was the arrival of that kingdom of heaven announced than the task entrusted to Israel came to an end. Jesus expressed this most pointedly when he called John the Baptist "more than a prophet" and even called him the greatest born from women in Israel but [then] immediately followed this by saying that this greatest among the greats in Israel was still less than the least and lowest in the kingdom of heaven [see Matt 11:9–11].

Israel did not grasp and understand this. Israel dreamed that she herself was God's kingdom, and therefore fantasized that the Gentiles had to enter Israel via proselyte baptism. Even the disciples initially could not think otherwise than that Jesus had come to restore the kingdom *to* Israel. For Jesus, it was a source of suffering in itself to hear the disciples come back again and again to that kingdom of Israel understood in the Jewish sense. But John the Baptist attacked that Jewish illusion from the very beginning. It was not the case that the Gentiles had to enter Israel through a spurious baptism, but Israel itself had to enter the kingdom of heaven, together with the Gentiles, through the *true* baptism. It was not the case that Israel was already in the place where it had to be, and that the nations had to convert to Israel. No, Israel itself had to repent, Israel itself had to be baptized, Israel itself had to cease being exclusively Jewish and enter into the kingdom of heaven. The best ones among the Jews had to do the same thing as the Gentile soldiers: repent and let themselves be baptized in order to pass over from the kingdom of shadows into the real kingdom, the kingdom of heaven. There was no preferential status attached to physical descent from Abraham. God is no respecter of persons. God could raise up children of Abraham also from these stones. And the result was that in that day hundreds and thousands of Jews from all cities and townships in Palestine as well as in the Diaspora converted to Christ; that great mass of converted Jews was then taken up into the Christian church; but in sub-sequent generations these converts so completely forgot their Jewish descent that after the passing of a few centuries no one could tell whether someone originally belonged to the Jewish nation or whether his ancestor had belonged to the Gentiles.

It is high time that the Christian church see this clearly once again. §2 The resurgence of chiliasm is not merely an exegetical error but assails the entire divine plan of salvation in Christ; it closes its eyes to the connection between the work of creation and of re-creation; puts particularism on the throne again where only universalism may reign; once again threatens to nationalize the Christian religion as a sect instead of welcoming its emphasis on the salvation of the world. Chiliasm, more than anything else, obstructs the true conversion of the Jews to the extent that it disproportionally stimulates their national sentiment and prevents converted Jews among us from reaching full conversion. It applies also to the Jew that he has "arrived" only when he can boast, "It is no longer the Jew who lives, but Christ who lives in me. And the life I now live in the flesh I no longer live as Jew but through him who purchased me with his blood" [see Gal 2:20].

The only realistic point in all these chimeras lies exclusively in this, that Israel has really achieved a place among the nations and maintains this position. This point we discuss in somewhat more detail later, but we want to say here that this reality must lead to the realization that the purpose is not to let the nations be absorbed into Israel, but to let Israel, as one of the nations, be absorbed into the nations.[1] And in accordance with Jesus' demand every converted Jew must say in this regard, "Lord, give us among the nations the lowest, the least, the last place, for my nation, more than any nation, has assaulted your dear Son and persecuted your church to the point of bloodshed." This, so that the Lord may then answer that, not for the sake of the Jew's merit but because of the irrevocability of his election, Israel will no longer stand apart but be counted among the nations, and will one day forever possess the place it has forfeited a thousand times but that through electing grace, already demonstrated in the miraculous birth of Isaac, had been established from all eternity.

The nations do not exist for the sake of Israel, but Israel exists for the §3 sake of the nations. Never depart from this foundational truth. If it had

---

1. See, for instance, Kuyper's discussion in *CG* 1.51, "Jehovah and the Nations."

been the Lord's design and intent to seek the isolation of Israel before all else and to keep Israel out of contact with the nations, would it even have been thinkable that the Lord, to whom the whole world belongs, would have chosen the region of Palestine for Israel and would have sought Zion as the place of his rest? If you want to isolate a tribe, a nation, a people, then you must let it dwell on a remote island, in an elevated mountainous region, or in a remote corner of the earth. On this earth God possesses islands in abundance large enough to accommodate the whole nation of Israel, islands that could have completely isolated Israel, especially in those days when maritime navigation was as yet virtually nonexistent. Also on elevated mountain plateaus, like Pamir or Kashmir, Israel could have developed entirely segregated from the other nations, even as there are still today nations in these highlands of Asia that over the centuries have had virtually no contact with the rest of the nations. And even if the Lord had wanted to choose for this isolation neither an island nor a mountain plateau, he only had to let Abraham move from Ur of the Chaldeans eastward instead of westward to let the Jewish people propagate for centuries apart from all contact with the rest of the nations, in the land where since then the Chinese have settled.

But we find in fact the exact opposite. And we may say without exaggeration that God the Lord showed Abraham precisely that region that was least isolated and most in contact with the nations of the earth. Indeed, when you ask an authority on history the question, "Which location on this earth was at that time the point where the lifelines of most nations intersected?"—then not a single location could be pointed to that definitely fulfilled these requirements more completely than Palestine. As long as America and Australia were not yet in the picture, the known and inhabited world involved only three continents, namely, Asia, Africa, and Europe. Of each of these three only a relatively small portion was of importance: western central Asia, southeastern Europe, and northeastern Africa. These three sections of the only three then-known continents lay facing each other along the Mediterranean Sea. What was then considered the known world was formed by one large body of water, the Mediterranean Sea, in the center and around it three large land areas: western Asia, southern Europe, and northern Africa. There were also people living elsewhere, but within these boundaries moved the great, mighty stream of life of our human race: the Arameans, Arabs, and Persians in Asia; the Egyptians in Africa; the Romans and Greeks in Europe. The rest of the tribes and nations did exist, but had no influence and were of no account. Should you ask at what point amid that limited world of those days, these three main currents—the Asiatic, the African, and the European—met and intersected, not simply for one moment in time but during the almost twenty centuries that would elapse between Abraham's calling and the birth of Christ at Bethlehem, then we seriously ask whether any other answer is possible than *Palestine*. The great caravan routes that connected Asia with Africa ran through Palestine, and the great powers of Asia and Africa fought each other over the possession of this land; and it was across the sea that defined Palestine's coast that both continents had contact with what the Scriptures call "the islands" [or "coastlands"] and what history knows as Greece and Rome.

No one who wants to hide and isolate himself goes to sit in the marketplace where all main streets lead, and anyone who wants to go boating far from the busy boat traffic does not drift around in the shipping channel. Therefore it is natural that Israel's location can never have had isolation as its goal. It was not a forgotten island, not an isolated mountain plateau, and not a remote corner of the earth; rather, it lay precisely in the center of the world of that time, at the intersection of the strategic caravan routes, at the point where all the noisy life of the nations of the time came together. It shows rather the opposite purpose and definite intent: Israel was placed there where it had to dwell to be able to minister for the salvation of the nations.

§ 4

Today the stream of the nations has been completely rechanneled. The Fellahin in Egypt are England's plunder.[2] Babylon and Nineveh lie in ruins. The Greeks have been reduced to nothing. What once was the land of Rome is now the least among the nations of Europe. For Europe, the south is now insignificant and its life force lies in the north. In Asia, Turkey is a land that is sinking, and the key lies now in China and Japan instead. In Africa, Transvaal and the entire south are now of much greater interest than the land of the pyramids. America has been added as a new world. Australia is seeking and pursuing a future. If today a place had to be found for the nation of Israel that corresponded in nature to the place it received back then from God, it would of course not be in the present cul-de-sac of Cyprus and Palestine, but in the heart of Europe.

---

2. At the time of Kuyper's writing, Egypt was under British control. "Fellahin" (or, "peasants") made up the majority of the Egyptian population.

Get this firmly in your mind, and don't, like an unthinking youngster, keep sticking unhistorically to the old names, and you will be able to understand how absurd it is, how contrary to all reason and all historical sense, to keep dreaming of Palestine as if today it could still be the heart, the center, the world market of the nations. Those who make propaganda in England for the notion that the English people are actually the lost tribe of Simeon, and that therefore the Jewish glory of ancient Israel is revived in the English people, show at least that they have a somewhat better notion of the political relationships and the historical changes.[3]

§ 5     Well, whatever the case may be, the fact remains that Israel was placed by God precisely there where it had to live under the conditions of that time, to exist for the nations and to be able to serve the nations. Even as the angels are ministering spirits sent by God for the sake of those who will inherit salvation, so also is Abraham, and in him his descendants, sent out to mount at this important place the spiritual guard on behalf of the people of that day, in order to serve those nations and in those nations to the world. Shem had to pitch his tents here and nowhere else in order to be able to bless Japheth.

Corresponding with Israel's calling as a nation understood in this way were the starting point, the course, and the outcome of Israel's history. Israel was called when God said to Abraham, "In you all the families of the earth shall be blessed" [Gen 12:3]. In the course of its history, Israel came into constant contact with all prominent nations in succession: with the Assyrians, the Babylonians, the Persians, the Egyptians, the Greeks, and the Romans. And in the outcome of Israel's history, we see the blessing of Israel transfer to the nations, whereas Israel itself disappears almost suddenly and forever, not as a nation but as a people. It comes on the scene with the mission to bless the nations, it lives in steady and constant contact with all nations of any significance, and once it had borne its fruit and brought forth its Messiah, the curtain is torn, the temple is demolished, Jerusalem is laid waste, and Israel's national state is abrogated forever.

---

3.  British Israelism—the myth that the English people were descendants of one or more of the Lost Tribes of Israel—dated back to at least the seventeenth century. Books espousing versions of this myth were especially popular in the nineteenth and early twentieth centuries, particularly those by Richard Brothers (1757-1824), John Wilson (1799-1870), and Edward Hine (1825-91). See Tudor Parfitt, *The Lost Tribes of Israel: The History of a Myth* (London: Weidenfeld & Nicolson, 2002), 36-57.

Israel exists *for the sake of* the nations, it lives *with* the nations, and it disappears *for the sake of* the nations.

As for the middle one of these three—its living in contact with the nations—we already have provided the proof for this from the lives of the patriarchs and from the formation of the nation under Moses. Let us now focus on history and prophecy. People often picture the situation that obtained during Israel's history as though from ancient times and in every age Israel was a nation like it appeared to be in the days of John the Baptist and Jesus: a nation that stood completely loyal to the service of Jehovah and was separated from the other nations. But that entire notion is in conflict with the data of history. To the contrary: until the Babylonian captivity the number of the faithful among the Jewish people was mostly small, sometimes reduced to seven thousand individuals, and in the days of Isaiah it had shrunk to a small group of God-fearing people. The vast majority on the other hand was involved in all kinds of idolatry. Ten of the twelve tribes fell into public image-worship, even into Baal worship. And in Judah and Benjamin things went so badly that Solomon already permitted holy places and shrines to be built for a variety of idols. Only a single king had the courage to go after idolatry publicly; and Jerusalem knew a period when virtually every idol had its altar within the walls of the holy city and the land was covered with idolatrous shrines and idolatrous altars on the high places.

Only when we take this abominable fact into account do we understand the mournful cry from the souls of God's saints who in the psalms searched for relief. Only then can you understand the suffering of the prophets, and can you obtain a genuinely realistic impression of the struggle of those in Israel who were faithful to God. When Isaiah received the command, "Bind up the testimony; seal the teaching among my disciples" (Isa 8:16), the separation between the idolatrous people and the small group of the godly was prophetically accomplished. Only then did the purification come in the Babylonian captivity; and what returned from that captivity was definitely not the entire Jewish nation. That nation never did return, but continued living in the eastern regions. No, what did return was a relatively small number of Jews who had renounced all idolatry and now clung unwaveringly to the worship of Jehovah; from this small number was born the new nation-state that we find in Jesus' day in Jerusalem.

This evil fact of the prevalence of idolatry in Israel for ten centuries is simply inexplicable under the old notion that Israel lived all those §6 centuries in segregation and isolation. Conversely, if we see that Israel was placed by God at the intersection of the main caravan routes of the nations and therefore came into continuous and steady contact with the nations, and that the threads of its own national existence were continuously interwoven with those of the nations, then we understand how we must view Israel's struggle of faith precisely in terms of whether, despite being in continual contact with the nations, it would be able to preserve spiritually the sacred path in purity, and thus one day be a blessing to those nations. Then we understand the extraordinarily strong temptation to which Israel was exposed. Then we understand how even a person like Solomon succumbed. Then we can appreciate how if we had been placed before the same temptations, we would have succumbed like Israel. And when we look across all those wide streams of Israel's sins, in the end seeing the blessing for the world flowing from that same Israel, then we worship God all the more profoundly from our heart because of the marvelous and omnipotent power of God's electing grace that despite everything ultimately causes Israel to fulfill its mission.

All of Israel's history is in fact one continuous coming into contact with the nations around it, and this in three spheres. In the first place their contact with the forbidden sphere of the Gentiles whom they had left in their own land, in direct contravention of God's explicit command. Second, the sphere of the Moabites, Edomites, Philistines, and so forth, located in their immediate vicinity. And third, the sphere of the world powers that successively emerged in the eastern part of Asia in Nineveh, Babylon, and Persia, that emerged in Egypt, or those that later swooped down on Asia and Africa from Greece and Rome. Trade demonstrates the same level of contact. The caravans traveled across the region of Palestine from the east to the west and south, and Solomon himself carried on shipping across long distances. The temple was built by Hiram from Tyre. The queen of Sheba comes with royal splendor to Jerusalem to admire Solomon. There is no hermetic seclusion anywhere, but rather contact and traffic everywhere.

§ 7 And when we turn from these facts of history to the more idealistic tone that still speaks to us so inspiringly and comfortingly from the consciousness of Israel in the prophecies of psalmist and seer, then there too we find the nations and Israel combined under one single perspective. Granted, a separating feature runs through psalm and prophecy as well. The truth repels the lie, the fear of the only true God repels the worship of the creature. And in the image of Israel the separation between the kingdom of Christ and the kingdoms of this world is foreshadowed. This separating feature even continues as sharply as possible, so sharp and dividing that it could not be any sharper. But meanwhile we never find Israel alone, but always Israel gathered with the nations under one perspective. When God begins his judgment, the whole earth, all the nations, are called to listen. Concerning each nation it is prophesied that one day it will sing God's praise. "The nations, the nations all together will praise you, O Lord" is the main theme that will never be silent. And what comes so clearly to the fore in the psalms speaks even more strongly in prophecy proper. Jonah's entire prophecy is directed toward Nineveh. Nahum's burden also is aimed at Nineveh. And virtually all great prophets see in their visions definitely not only Israel and Judah come on stage, but sometimes even more the nations of the east and south and west.

That does not satisfy the particularistic mind. People would prefer to read only about Israel, in order to then apply it to themselves. One wonders how the church of Christ benefits from the ancient oracles about the Ethiopians and Moab, about Babylon, Egypt, about Syria and Greece. But the Lord has nevertheless willed it so. And still now, and until the end of ages, he wants to show us through these prophecies how his involvement for judgment and for salvation is not at all limited to that small piece of the world of which Jerusalem was the capital, but is extended and still extends and will always extend to the whole world, to all its nations, because that whole world is of his making and all these many nations are his creation.

The gaze of the Lord is neither limited nor narrow, but always large and wide, and even as he still summons the church of Christ to Christianize the whole world and all its nations in its missionary work, so too he shows us from of old how he himself seeks the world through Israel, even when Israel was segregated as shadow and type of what was to come, how he goes out to that whole world in love, and summons all nations to enter the kingdom of heaven. Of course, we are faced with the same danger as that to which Israel succumbed. Within the walls of the monastery there is relative safety; when it was completely isolated in the Babylonian captivity Israel did not succumb to idolatry, and when we close ourselves in and close ourselves off in a sectarian way, we are formally less susceptible to danger. We know very well the enchantment of every kind of particularism. But even that inviting appeal must never cause us to stray from the path of God's holy ordinances. And those ordinances, including those that involve Israel, tell us clearly and plainly that our God claims nothing less than the world, and that the voice of him who calls goes out to all the nations.

CHAPTER FIFTY-ONE

# JEHOVAH AND THE NATIONS

*His lightnings light up the world; the earth sees and trembles.*

PSALM 97:4

The notion that God's work of grace was withdrawn entirely from the na-   §1
tions, from the calling of Abraham until the day of Pentecost, in order to
focus it entirely on Israel, has been shown to be incompatible with the
clear revelation of Scripture. All other nations were *not* a mass of humanity, forgotten by God, which procreated aimlessly and pointlessly while
only Israel had significance. We must not even say that Israel was the
pearl and all that lay outside it the shell, or that Israel was the wheat and
all nations together the chaff. These two images do contain the acknowledgment that the nations did have importance for Israel, since the pearl
does not develop without the shell, and the wheat does not ripen without
the chaff. But these images carry too much the secondary notion that all
that really mattered was Israel and the whole world existed only for the
sake of Israel. The one wearing the pearl is not interested in the shell; the
one baking bread does not give a thought to the chaff. And this would in
fact be an inversion: the sick person does not exist for the sake of the medicine, but the medicine for the sake of the sick person. And so too Israel
was created by God to save the nations. Had Adam not fallen, there would

never have been an Israel. And therefore we turn history and the plan of God around when we suggest that the nations existed for the sake of Israel.

At this point we encounter an understandable objection that we must not gloss over. Is it then no longer true, we are asked, that the universe exists for this earth, this earth for humanity, humanity for the church, and the church for Christ? And we unhesitatingly answer this question in the affirmative, provided that we do not take the church as institution but as the body of God's elect, that is, the mystical body of Christ. In that sense, on the basis of God's Word we consider it to be definitely true that all things revolve around Christ as the Center, that the elect have been given him by the Father, and that consequently our entire human race with its history revolves around the church of God. And without waiting for the counter-objection that may be deduced from this, we want to fill in the name "Israel" here for "the church of God" and thus concede that the whole history of the world is dominated by "Israel."

With this, however, you make no headway for your Jewish particularism. When it says in Jeremiah 33:22, "As the host of heaven cannot be numbered and the sands of the sea cannot be measured, so I will multiply the offspring of David my servant, and the Levitical priests who minister to me," then it cannot and must not be understood in a dynastic or hierarchical sense. It does not mean that the royal house of David, as a historical dynasty, would burst forth into millions and millions of princes and princesses, nor that the tribe of Levi would populate half the world. Clearly the meaning of this prophecy is that Christ would be born from David and that all the elect are incorporated in Christ and, as his brothers, would be the eternal seed of David. Similarly the Levites had been few in number among physical Israel, but under the spiritual Israel the ministers of Christ would burst forth into an innumerable multitude.

Here we also sense the typical bond. Christ came in fact from the loins of David as concerns the flesh. It is, to put it a bit strongly, David's flesh and blood that the Son of God took on from Mary, that went to the grave after the cross, that was raised from the dead, and that now will be his human nature forever in heaven. When Christ returns on the clouds, he will return in the Davidic flesh, and every eye shall see him that way. Through regeneration and incorporation into the mystical body of the Lord all the elect actually share in this. We can say that by not merely calling us his brothers but making us his brothers, David's great Son also makes us more than adopted "sons of David." This in fact is how the prophecy is fulfilled that the offspring of David will be multiplied like the host of heaven and the sands of the sea [see Jer 33:22]. And in this sense it is undeniable that the whole mystical church of Christ is in its essence Israel, not in a metaphorical sense but in an antitypical sense, and around this "Israel" all of humanity and the whole history of the nations revolve.

But then the name "Israel" does not occur here in its typical but its antitypical meaning. That name then does not refer to one single small nation that lived in Palestine, but to the "body of the elect from all generations of the earth, from the beginning of the world till the end, gathered under Christ as its head, incorporated in him, deriving this antitypical name of *Israel* from him as David's Son after the flesh."[1] This then is an extension of the rule that the nation of Jacob was created and enriched by God in order to prepare the medicine of eternal life for other nations, i.e., for the nations of the world. And the mystical element lies only herein, that this "balm of Gilead" that was prepared in Palestine for the whole world is not a medicine that is applied externally but a medicine that penetrates to the root of life and is effective only through regeneration and faith.

We also sense how totally *non*particularistic but divine-universal revelation is when we turn, for example, to Psalm 97: "The LORD" it reads there—Jehovah, our covenant God—"The LORD reigns," and then: "Let the *earth* rejoice; let the many *coastlands* [the nations west of Palestine] be glad" [v. 1]. "His lightnings light up the *world*; the *earth* sees and trembles. The mountains melt like wax before the LORD, before the Lord *of all the earth*. The heavens proclaim his righteousness, and *all the peoples* see his glory. ... Worship him, *all you gods!*" [vv. 4–7]. "For you, O LORD, are most high *over all the earth*" [v. 9].

§ 2

Preceding this is Psalm 96: "Sing to the LORD, *all the earth!* ... Declare his glory among *the nations*, his marvelous works among *all the peoples!* ... Ascribe to the LORD, O *families of the peoples*, ascribe to the LORD glory and

---

1.  The language here closely resembles that of the text of the Heidelberg Catechism Lord's Day 21, Q&A 54, as well as the Canons of Dort II.9. See also Abraham Kuyper, *E Voto Dordraceno: Toelichting op den Heidelbergschen Catechismus*, 4 vols. (Amsterdam: Wormser, 1892–95), 2:130–34. Kuyper may also be relying on the typological arguments associated with Patrick Fairbairn, as in his *The Typology of Scripture*, 2 vols. (Philadelphia: Daniels & Smith, 1852); and *Hermeneutical Manual* (Philadelphia: Smith, English & Co., 1859), 468: "Christ is at once the antitypical or the true Israel, and the antitypical or true Son of David; since in Him all the promises made concerning these were to stand fast, and the high calling of God was to find its proper realization."

strength! Ascribe to the LORD the glory due his name; bring an offering, and come into his courts! Worship the LORD in the splendor of holiness; tremble before him, *all the earth*! Say among *the nations*, 'The LORD reigns! Yes, *the world* is established; it shall never be moved. He will judge *the peoples* with equity.' ... He will judge *the world* in righteousness, and *the peoples* in his faithfulness" [vv. 1, 3, 7–10, 13].

And when we look at the psalm that comes after Psalm 97, it says there also, "He has revealed his righteousness in the sight of *the nations*. ... All *the ends of the earth* have seen the salvation of our God. ... Let the sea roar, and all that fills it; *the world* and those who dwell in it! ... For he comes to judge *the earth*. He will judge *the world* with righteousness, and *the peoples* with equity" [Psa 98:2, 3, 7, 9]. So throughout the book of Psalms the constant leitmotif is that "there is no place where his voice is not heard." The tabernacle of the LORD is erected in Shem, but in order that Japheth would dwell in it.

§ 3     So we do not in the least receive the impression of a world that doesn't matter, that the Lord's involvement in the world would be limited to only that one small nation, but quite otherwise, of a God who seeks his world, whose glory covers the entire earth, who on this earth leads the nations, all tribes of the nations, and the Gentiles or, if you will, "islands" [or "coastlands"] with his providential sovereignty, in order to shepherd them with his truth and his judgments and to summon everything he created in this human life to bring the offering of praise and worship.

On further reflection everyone will immediately and without reservation agree that it would be unthinkable to limit the providence of God through all those centuries to Israel. The providence of God covers all things. And if Jesus teaches us that even the sparrow that is sold for two pennies [see Matt 10:29–31] and the flower of the field that soon withers are included in that providential sovereignty of God [see Matt 6:28–30], then it is a matter of course that no people is too small and no nation, in whatever century it has existed on this earth, is too inconsequential for God the Lord to have ruled over that people and that nation and to have maintained them. Yes, even when considering the peoples and the nations, we must not stop at this general level. For among those peoples there is no family, and in such a family no husband or child, that has not been the object of God's providential sovereignty and care. Whether they are called Scythians or Barbarians, Elam or Joktan, among all those groups throughout those centuries there was not a single slave or child that has lain at its mother's breast who was not led by God in his providence, given life by God, and all the hairs on his head, including the head of that small infant in Elam, were numbered.

Every suggestion automatically disappears, then, which supposes that God the Lord had indeed taken those nations into account in broad lines, as we do in a historical survey, but that the deep and all-penetrating aspect of God's sovereign plan could be glorified only in Israel. No, throughout those centuries when, from the days of Moses until the day of Pentecost, Israel was segregated from the Gentiles, God's work among the Gentiles continued from day to day and night to night among every nation, in every town and village, in all their families, in every individual, down to the slave and the infant. His involvement with the nations was therefore not a superficial one, but a great and mighty work that calls for adoration, one that penetrated down to the smallest and most insignificant details.

Moreover, this was true not only because God cannot leave any part of his creation to its own devices, but it was thus determined from eternity past in the counsel of his pleasure, and in the eternal decree of his divine will. In that decree each people, each nation, and each generation and each individual in that nation and in that people was included in that decree—including the entire course of their life and all that such life would bring them. In executing his decree, God cannot turn his back on the nations to focus his involvement solely on Israel. His decree included the fate of the entire human race, not only in broad lines, but down to the smallest details and particulars. This is so even if our mind gets dizzy at the thought that throughout all those centuries, among all those nations, not a swallow built its nest in the barn, not a lily bloomed in the field, without God pointing the swallow to its place or God clothing that lily. This is how far removed the truth is from the notion that the nations through all those centuries were merely human filler, chaff, in order that Israel might bloom.

Of course, we must make a distinction here between God's general providence, his special providence, and his most special providence. But that distinction does not affect the extent of his involvement, but only the degree of closeness of the connection that exists between the creature and his God. God's providential sovereignty over an animal is equally as broad in its extent as his sovereignty over a human being. The fish does not ever breathe through its gills without God providing oxygen for those gills. The young lion goes out to seek its nourishment from God

§ 4

[see Psa 104:21]. And no matter how incredibly swiftly vermin, especially bacilli, reproduce, never a single insect or a single bacillus is called into being without God doing it and God knowing it. God's providence is the same over all creatures in its extent, because for all creatures it is absolute, all-encompassing, and perfect. And so there can be no question of less or more, large or small, simply because God's power and omnipresence carry and preserve everything, and nothing on the earth, in the sea, or in the air would be able to stir or move apart from his will. This is true of human beings and angels, of animals and plants, of liquids and solids. God maintains it all.

But there is a distinction in the degree of closeness in the relationship in which God has placed the various creatures to himself, and in this respect a star stands above a barren wilderness, the lily above the grass of the field, the lion above the jackal—and the smallest human infant above the king of the desert in the animal kingdom. So too does the least in the kingdom of heaven stand above the best in Israel, and Israel in the centuries of its segregation above the rest of the nations of that time. Our Reformed confession, therefore, calls "most special care" the care of God for his elect. Under this most special care for his elect, the confession honors and praises in a still higher and ultimate sense the care of the Father for his only Son, when he gave him to the world in order to save the world.[2] This very special care is not wider in extent, but deeper, more intimate, more tender because here its encompasses the spiritual life, goes from heart to heart, and reaches forward to eternal salvation. Understood in this way, God's care for Israel was indeed different from his care for the nations: not a wider but a warmer care, not a greater but a richer care that did not extend further but was more intense, more full, more penetrating.

In that sense, as we shall see, Paul can therefore say that God had abandoned the Gentiles and given them up whereas he had married Israel.

§ 5     In the meantime, the Scriptures definitely do not show us the whole sphere of God's providential sovereignty. The goal of Scripture is to show us how God created Adam, how Adam fell, how then from that fallen Adam the Christ was born, and how God through this Christ regained his humanity in "the congregation of the perfectly justified" [see Heb 12:23].

---

2. See also the Belgic Confession, Art. 13, which teaches that the doctrine of divine providence "affords us unspeakable consolation, since we are taught thereby that nothing can befall us by chance, but by the direction of our most gracious and heavenly Father; who watches over us with a paternal care."

That, and that alone, is the correct thread that runs through the whole of Scripture, and because that thread from Abraham to Christ does not run through the nations but through Israel, for that reason and that reason alone does Scripture narrow its focus during those centuries to Israel. But it does this not so absolutely that there is not again and again, as it were, a beam of blinding light cast also upon those nations, and we see how in the meantime the life of the nations continues and moves along as a stream that one day will end up at the point willed by God, where it will absorb into itself from Israel the stream of the higher life.

We already saw this with regard to the peoples in Canaan in the days of the patriarchs. For in that history the focus of the scriptural narrative is Abraham and the Israel that was to come and the Christ who was to be born. But in the meantime, it is again and again apparent how God continues his work among the nations. We see how he adds one nation after the other, descended from Abraham and Isaac, to the nations that are already present. We hear of the peoples in the Valley of Siddim, put under severe pressure by Chedorlaomer and his Elamites and then delivered and liberated by Abraham. We hear of Abimelech who still knows God and to whom God even reveals himself in a dream. Especially in Melchizedek, the prince and priest appears before us who, coming from the Gentiles, nevertheless was destined to be image-bearer of the Christ in Jerusalem, long before David sat on the throne there. Then that shaft of the intense white light suddenly focuses on Egypt, and we notice how in that land a highly developed people lives, skilled more than any people of that time in all arts and wisdom, developing more richly what had originated in Babylon and ready to transmit to Moses "the wisdom of the Egyptians" [Acts 7:22] and thus transmitting the information to Israel as a people. We see how God the Lord is at work through Joseph his servant to save the people of Egypt from death by starvation. We hear of the strange dreams God gave the king of Egypt, and of the interpretive light that he ordained for Pharaoh for a correct understanding of those dreams.

And thus it goes throughout history. Again and again we are shifted from Israel to the nations, and we discern in the midst of those nations abundant activity and a God who is involved with these nations and uses them as his instrument or casts them down in his judgments. This is apparent most clearly in God's sending Jonah to Nineveh. Jonah is the prophet of whom we hear nothing in Israel. We rather get the impression that God raised him up specifically with Nineveh in view. He was destined and

§ 6

ordained to go to that pagan city to bring the call to repentance to that city of the nations. And where Israel again and again killed and stoned its prophets, lo and behold, all of Nineveh, led by its ruler, repents at the call of Jonah. Here is a fact so remarkable that Jesus himself draws attention to it, to Israel's shame [Matt 12:41-42]. It is not, of course, as if Nineveh was saved unto eternal life. Involved here was merely desisting from sins that called and cried out to heaven, and returning to the sobriety of life. But the fact remains that a messenger from Jehovah gets a hearing in pagan Nineveh, which would be unthinkable if God the Lord had not worked in the hearts of its ruler and people.

Alongside Nineveh the Lord places the Queen of Sheba, a princess from Arabia, who traveled to Jerusalem to hear the wisdom of Solomon. Here we suddenly see how in the heart of Arabia, where initially everything appeared to be dark, a kingdom exists that had achieved a rich development, and how a woman ruled over this kingdom who, far from being immersed in lust for power and sensuality, had received a heart from God for the higher things of life. God gave it in her heart to travel to Jerusalem from afar and to put treasure upon treasure at the feet of Solomon for what wisdom from Jehovah she might receive from Solomon's mouth. It also shows how God the Lord had promulgated the knowledge, or at least the rumor, of his truth among the nations, and how even in faraway Sheba people knew of the light God had given Solomon.

Cyrus is an equally striking example. Many years before Cyrus would become king over Persia, God had already revealed to his prophet, and through this prophet to the nation of Israel, the name he would bear, the kingdom he would rule, and the great act he would accomplish during his regency. Connected with the prophecy about Cyrus is the great fact that the mighty nation of Babylon would one day be attacked and destroyed by the mountain peoples from the southeast. And when the day set by God has come, then Cyrus is present, he rules over Persia, he destroys the kingdom of Babylon, and God inspires his heart to let Israel go in freedom. And under all of this and because of all of this, God calls this pagan king "my anointed" and says to him, "I will go before you and level the exalted places, I will break in pieces the doors of bronze and cut through the bars of iron, I will give you the treasures of darkness and the hoards in secret places, that you may know that it is I, the Lord, the God of Israel, who call you by your name" [Isa 45:2-3].

Not quite as sharply delineated but equally transparent is what the Scriptures tell us about Damascus and Naaman the Syrian; about Tyre whence Hiram came with the skills to build the temple of the Lord; about the widow in whose house God performed miracles; of the kingdom of Belshazzar about which Daniel prophesied; about the kingdom of Ahasuerus about which Esther's history tells us; not to mention the smaller nations that Israel swallowed. Thus throughout Israel's history we find one continuous involvement of the God of Israel with the nations outside Israel. The mention of this involvement serves primarily to illuminate the fortunes of Israel, but it is continually apparent how those nations, far from having sunk into insignificance, instead play a very remarkable role, having achieved an all-around rich development of power and insight, and how the word is continually confirmed that God held the heart of all these kings and nations in his hand like "a stream of water" [Prov 21:1]. And when at last the hour finally arrives when Israel will fulfill its sacred calling in the Christ, then we find at that point the Romans ordained of God to rule over Israel. We hear of an emperor at Rome whom God inspired to call for a census, which caused Mary to journey to Bethlehem. And when Christ has been born, then through the stars of the firmament God has already proclaimed the birth of the Wonder of the world to the wise men in the east. And these wise men come from the land of the sun to Bethlehem in Judea to place gold and incense and myrrh at the feet of the Infant. God had taught the wise men from the east to understand his stars, he taught them through these stars, and that instruction of God among the nations serves as instrument for the God of Israel to glorify his dear Son at his coming into the world.

CHAPTER FIFTY-TWO

# THE MESSIAH AND ISRAEL

*As regards the gospel, they are enemies for your sake. But as regards election, they are beloved for the sake of their forefathers.*

ROMANS 11:28

§ 1 Therefore any notion that Palestine was the Lord's pleasure resort, and all the Gentile land outside it merely wild heather, irrevocably falls away. The world does not exist for the sake of Israel, but Israel for the sake of the world. If that world had not sunk into sin and death, the whole nation of Israel would never have existed. Through the miraculous birth of Isaac, God the Lord called the nation of Israel into being exclusively to fulfill his counsel of salvation and restore forever what seemed to have been lost forever in Eden.

This entirely unique and singular position of Israel explains the attitude Jesus adopted vis-à-vis Israel: on the one hand the most strict respect for the difficult privilege of the Jews, on the other hand the severest judgment upon that same Israel to the extent that it went against its calling.

Jesus' respect for the sacred privilege given by God to Israel goes so far that the Canaanite woman from the region of Sidon must hear the almost taunting words, "It is not right to take the children's bread and throw it to the dogs." Without qualification Jesus states that he "was sent only to the lost sheep of the house of Israel" [Matt 15:24]. When the disciples are sent out they are even forbidden to preach the gospel either to the Gentiles or to the Samaritans. With a narrow, exclusivistic sense they are charged, "but go rather to the lost sheep of the house of Israel" [Matt 10:6]. And lest anyone make it appear as if only the first three Gospels speak in this tone, let us remember that also John, in whose Gospel Jesus announces himself so clearly and as inclusively as possible as "the Savior of the world," reports how Jesus says to the Samaritan woman that "salvation is from the Jews" [John 4:42, 22].

Jesus, who appeared as the Savior of the world, spent his time almost exclusively among Israel during the years of his earthly existence. As an infant he was brought to Egypt at the behest of the angels, but as a youth and as a man Jesus did not make any propaganda tour to Greece, Rome, or Egypt. He barely crossed the borders of the Jewish territory. He did not even try to recruit noble young men for his apostolate from among the Greeks. All of his disciples came from Israel and were chosen according to the number of Israel's tribes. And when finally the "apostle to the Gentiles" was called, the man from Tarsus was again a Jew. The sacred boundary is thus strictly observed. In Israel the salvation of the world must be prepared, and only when that salvation is complete and Christ has ascended to heaven, the wall of separation falls and grace flows over the field of the world.

But over against this stands just as definitely that Jesus announces their judgment to the Jews, to the extent that, being dissatisfied with this their calling to serve the salvation of the world, they elevated themselves in their pride. There is no people on which as terrible a judgment rests as on the Jewish people. To the degree that more was given to them, more would be demanded from them. And squarely against this rule stands the fact that there is no people that fell into deeper sin than Israel. Theirs was the light while the rest of the nations still walked in darkness, and the grace given to Israel is beyond comparison with the favor of God the other nations enjoyed. And yet that richly gifted, marvelously blessed people has more than any nation become stiff-necked, brought grief to its God, kicked against the goads, and whored away from its God, until finally they pressured the imperial judge who wanted to spare the life of Jesus and wildly urged his violent death. The ultimate end of their corrupted development was, as Paul says, that they "killed both the Lord Jesus and the prophets, and drove us out, and displease God and oppose all mankind

§ 2

by hindering us from speaking to the Gentiles that they might be saved" [1 Thess 2:15–16].

On this one point Israel's entire judgment is concentrated. Israel existed only to bring forth the Messiah, so that the world might be given back to God by Christ. And when finally, after a preparation of two thousand years, this Christ was born from Israel, Israel did not worship that Christ but killed the Son of God "so that the inheritance may be [theirs]" [Luke 20:14]. It is exactly what Paul says: they killed the Lord Jesus and tried to prevent that this salvation would go out to the world [see 1 Thess 2:16]. They were called to bear fruit to the honor of God in the midst of the world, and instead of answering to that glorious calling they have wanted to steal the balm of Gilead for themselves. The bee gathers honey that others may delight in its sweetness, and this is how Israel should have been. But instead of delighting in that splendid task, Israel hung like a spider in its web in order to keep everything for itself.

Israel's calling was based on the principle of love. It had to want to be there to serve the world. And behold, it manifested itself in the most rigid egoism. It wanted to exist, not for God nor for the world, but for itself.

Those from whose lips we never hear a single word in our day that reflects a holy anger about "this decay of the best"[1] that God had prepared in Israel, but who to the contrary continually raise a cheer for the Jews, might ask themselves whether their love for God's honor and for the Christ of God whom the Jews nailed to the cross and killed, is not damaged by their disproportionate national sympathy. Jesus at any rate took a very different position vis-à-vis the Jews. To Jerusalem Jesus said, "See, your house is left to you desolate" [Matt 23:38]. And over the Israel that stoned and killed the prophets and would also vent the vengeance of its pride, he pronounced the terrible judgment that God would bring an evil death on the evildoers and give their vineyard to others. "Therefore," he continued, "I tell you, the kingdom of God will be taken away from you and given to a people producing its fruits. And the one who falls on this stone will be broken to pieces; and when it falls on anyone, it will crush him" [Matt 21:43–44]. "But I tell you that it will be more tolerable on the day of judgment for the land of Sodom than for you" [Matt 11:24].

---

1. This reflects a Dutch proverb, "Het bederf van het beste is het slechtste" (The decay of the best is the worst).

God's calling nevertheless remains firm, but it is precisely the firm-  §3
ness of God's calling that shames Israel's obstinacy and unfaithfulness all
the more profoundly. In the twenty centuries that preceded Bethlehem, a
large multitude of God's elect from Israel were saved, virtually solely from
Israel. And also after Bethlehem, thousands upon thousands from Israel
entered the kingdom of heaven before as yet a single individual from the
nations had been baptized in the name of the triune God. Israel has abandoned its God, but God has not abandoned his people. Israel still walks
among the nations as a miraculous sign of God's omnipotent sovereignty,
and whereas Moab and Edom have long since perished, and Babylon fell
into ruins, and Egypt was handed over to the Islamic crescent, the nation
of the Jews lives on, and is a force in this world, no longer through Jehovah
but through Mammon. And there is still no stronger enmity against the
church of Christ than that which comes from Israel, now empowered
through Mammon.[2] At no single point in history do we see the contemptible unfaithfulness of humanity manifested so vexingly and palpably as
in the persistent fierceness with which the nation of Israel arrays itself
in opposition to the Anointed of God and the faithfulness of the Lord. It is
one continuous, poignant struggle, in which the honor of God's faithfulness rises ever more highly, and the faithlessness of the people once chosen by God manifests itself ever more exasperatingly. It even happens
that those few Jews who, when they are saved as a brand from the fire and
brought to Christ, once they are converted, are with very few exceptions
only very rarely crushed under the terrible guilt of the Jews but appear
rather more or less still to pride themselves on their Jewish ancestry. This
is something through which, sad to say, so incredibly much of the blessing
they could bring and should have brought to Christ's church is lost.

We can understand very well that someone who is born of the Jewish
nation and has through wondrous grace nevertheless found Christ, feels
that he stands in a somewhat different relationship to Christ than we,

---

2. The historic association rooted in specific social contexts of Jews with money has
   been occasion for anti-Semitic discrimination. The origins of this phenomenon
   and the stereotypically negative assessment of Jews by many Christians are to be
   found in the long history of Christian Europe. When combined with the legal prohibition against Jewish participation in many other professions, "the economic
   forces pushing Jews out of other occupations were matched by others pulling them
   into the money trade." See Derek J. Penslar, *Shylock's Children: Economics and Jewish
   Identity in Modern Europe* (Berkeley: University of California Press, 2001), 17.

children of the Gentiles. The Jewish nation is and remains exceptional. But the right to boast in this belongs only to that son of Abraham who first, more deeply than any child of God from the Gentiles, crumbles under the terrible guilt of his forefathers and his race, yes, scarcely comprehends that divine grace has been shown to one born of a nation so profoundly guilty, grace that had been forfeited a thousandfold. That tone we hear very seldom, indeed, almost never. In the absence of that tone of deepest self-abasement and most fearful self-humiliation about Israel's disgraceful unfaithfulness and crushing guilt, we witness the sin of ancient Israel still at work in the present-day converts from the people of the Jews.

§ 4     Nevertheless, God's counsel will stand. The Jews are not a vanishing people. Israel remains. And when one day the number of the elect approaches its fullness, and the end of the world is near, the firm election of God will break out again gloriously among those same Jews, in order to make full the number of the called and the elect from Israel, in order that the whole of predestined Israel will be saved. This new multitude from Israel, together with the tens of thousands who were saved from Israel before Bethlehem and the tens of thousands who assented to the Hosanna of the Son of God after the day of Pentecost, will come to God and his Anointed, and this whole large multitude of Israel from the ancient covenant people will enter into the coming glory of the Christ, together with the whole host of those who were added from the rest of the nations. This is not because all differences between one nation and another will dissipate in that kingdom. The differences between nations, even as the differences between individuals, are based on the predestination and sovereignty of our God.

And therefore, even as the blessed will retain their own character and distinct place as individuals in the kingdom of glory, so that each one will receive the white stone of approval with a name written on it that no one knows but God and the person himself [see Rev 2:17], so too each people and tongue and nation will bear the imprint of its own character, purified of all impure admixture. The same will be true of Israel. Israel will continue to bear its own type in the kingdom of glory, its own stamp, its own character among the multitude no one can number, not as the Jew spoiled and ruined it, but as God had gloriously envisioned it for Israel one day. But there will be nothing of preferential treatment or of elevation above the nations because, contrary to what the Jew has in view, the true Israel of God will be gloriously conspicuous precisely in that it will have unlearned forever all Jewish questions as to who is the greatest [see Matt 18:1].

We therefore occupy the true position vis-à-vis the Jews only when we recover what is written on the front and back of the apostolic commemorative coin.³ On the front: "As regards the gospel, they are enemies for your sake." And on the back: "But as regards election, they are beloved for the sake of their forefathers."

Anything that goes beyond this does not serve to make the Jews Christians but has as necessary consequence that the Christians become more Jewish again.

Thus the conclusion is easily reached.                              §5

After the fall in paradise, the world does not sink, as Satan had intended, into eternal damnation. To the contrary, from the outset saving grace begins to operate in general by means of common grace in the restraining of sin and depravity, in particular through particular grace in the bringing about of life and the springing up of salvation that will flow from Golgotha into the stream of the life of the nations.

When sin and depravity nevertheless seethe wildly, recklessly, and tempestuously against grace and threaten to overwhelm it, then God the Lord purifies our human race by letting the poisonous dregs perish in the flood and setting our race on a new course. If we think of our human race as a plant that grows tall, then this plant was cut down to the root in the flood, not that it might die but that it might sprout again from the Noahic root.

But also in that renewed human race salvation could not break through unless strength were sought in isolation. The stream of grace had to become narrower. The mystery of the concentration was effective, and that concentration took place in Abraham's line, called into existence from Abraham through a miracle of God's omnipotence.

---

3. It is unknown what coin Kuyper is referring to here. In the background may be an allusion to the so-called Judaea Capta coins, which were issued by the Roman emperor Vespasian and his sons for a quarter-century after the capture of Jerusalem and the destruction of the second temple in AD 70. The most famous of these coins include the caption "Judaea Capta," Latin for "Judaea conquered," a phrase that Kuyper may also be alluding to in the following section ("Jerusalem is captured"). But there were a great variety of these commemorative coins, along with many others inspired by them, minted throughout the empire. The practice is common up through to the present day. The text Kuyper attributes to the front and back of this particular coin is derived from Rom 11:28.

That isolation, that concentration is not the goal but the means so that Christ might be born. Only through this will the goal of this concentration have been achieved. With the appearance of Christ, Israel has forever lost its reason for existence. The fullness of salvation has arrived. The sluices are opened again, the dams are broken through, salvation flows again over our entire human race, and the world church is born in the heart of the nations.

§ 6    If after this salvation had still been tied to the Jewish land, to the Jewish nation, to the Jewish name, then Christ would not have been hated but would have been seated on David's throne in the city of David. That was the dream of the Jews, a dream that occupied the disciples as well for a long time.

But as high as the heavens are above the earth, so high are God's thoughts above the thoughts of the children of man [see Isa 55:9]. No, the Anointed One of God should not be King over one nation but King over all nations, and King not over the Jewish land but King in the whole world created by God. He could not be this by having his seat in the capital of one single nation. Ruling the whole world from the capital city of a single nation was the sinful, imperious notion of imperial Rome, but not the intent of the kingdom of heaven. To rule the world, all of humanity, Christ had to be exalted at the right hand of God in heaven. His ascension was a necessity, and it is only the ascension that inaugurates the kingdom of Christ over the whole world.

And now comes the day of Pentecost. People from all nations stand around and near the upper room: the Parthians with the Elamites and the Cretensians with the Arabs, men from Cappadocia and Pontus and all of Asia Minor, from Egypt, from Libya and from the Romans, Jews and proselytes, no longer separated but mixed together. And with this whole multitude a great crowd soon breaks into a song of praise to Jesus, for the Holy Spirit has descended, and in that Holy Spirit God himself has returned to the world, to our race, and soon the voice of the one who is calling, the bringer of good news, goes out to all regions [see Acts 2:1–12].

Initially we still see, for year after year, people from the Jews and people from the Gentiles, men and women with their God-given offspring, enter the church of God separately. Both streams, from Israel and from the nations, separated for so long, now flow together, and for a moment wildly mix together like foaming waves. Those from the Jews yet once more make the sinful, reckless attempt to keep the church Jewish and to keep it from becoming organizationally catholic. But that attempt, cursed by God, is like the hand of a child who wants to hold back the current of a stream. It is not long before the Jewish element abandons its goal. It blends with those from the Gentiles who have been converted to God, and in the world church of Christ, which soon takes up position over against Rome's world empire, both elements are finally completely merged. Jerusalem is captured.[4] The Jewish nation as an entity disappears from the earth and Palestine loses its significance. It is "the islands," ["the coastlands"] of southern Europe where Christ causes his rule to break out. The mystery is unfolded and all nations see the outcome of God's sovereignty. The salvation prepared in Israel, for the world. And now that this salvation has been prepared, the Jewish nation recedes completely into the background. The old has passed away, behold, all has become new. The baptism of the nations has replaced the circumcision of the Jews, and when no Passover lamb is slaughtered anymore, they gather from all nations and tongues at the Lord's Supper, in remembrance of the blood of the new covenant.

This sketch of the basic outline of the Israelite dispensation has only §7 seemingly diverted us from the topic under discussion in these chapters.

That topic is and remains common grace, the common grace shown to our human race. Now we will turn to an investigation of God's sovereignty over the nations.

But the most wide-ranging and clearest discussion of that common grace would not be able to penetrate our understanding if the false particularistic tendency that crept from Judaism into Christ's church had not first been restrained and driven back.

For many people, the distinction between the dispensation of the old covenant and that of the new covenant is still so indistinct that, without even suspecting into what kind of error they lapse, they continually present you with all kinds of quotations from the old covenant in order to defend their view on the things of Christ's church in the present. This brings with it the danger that the old Jewish leaven creeps in again. Simply because our heart is equally as evil as that of the Jews of ancient times, consequently the same abuse of God's revelation in the old covenant lies in wait at the door of our heart as well.

This unnuanced opening of the Bible to confirm truth and to find the rule of life is truly Jewish-legalistic and goes directly against the rich

---

4. See previous note on "Judaea Capta" coins.

historical and organic character of the revelation of God. Indeed, the old covenant still pertains to us, and it is a deficiency in the confession of our Lutheran brethren that they neglect the old covenant too much, as if they could understand the New Testament apart from the old covenant.[5] On this point as well, Reformed theologians grasped the correct insight, and it is they who, more than all other Protestants, have maintained the high value and significance of the Old Testament. But a spiritual sluggishness has come over the Reformed churches as well. From sluggishness they forgot to consistently apply to the things of the old covenant the category of the shadows in contrast to the category of fulfillment. And thus in a noticeable way, within our circles the false particularism, the false exclusivism, the spirit of conceit and of self-elevation and bigotry—in short, the sectarian demon—has crept in.

Therefore that evil spirit had to be hunted down first in its hideaway, and this could not be done successfully without opposing, from Abraham to Golgotha, the confusion that still spreads insidiously over all of Israel's role in history. We don't flatter ourselves that this will have banished the error. In Sunday schools and in catechism books and in all kinds of sectarian circles, that false Old Testament spirit will persist for many years to come. But precisely because of the force and the toughness with which that spirit maintains itself, we could not avoid taking the trouble of placing the revelation of God, beginning with Abraham's history, in the right light: in that light that the Reformed confession always sheds upon it.

With this last comment we have not said too much. When we go with a measure of carefulness through the marginal notes in our Reformed SV[6] as well as the headings of the Psalms and Prophets, we would flatly contradict the truth if we did not concede without further ado that all these explanations of our forefathers always maintain the broad, spacious perspective that encompasses the whole world church. There is no hint or trace of a particularistic, sectarian tendency in which a Jewish leaven is still at work. The question could rather arise whether, in many of the comments on Holy Scripture, the world church does not stand too prominently in the foreground, and whether the historical reality from which

---

5. Kuyper likely has in mind here the distinction between law and gospel that characterizes much Lutheran theological reflection. See "Law and Gospel," Art. 5 in the Formula of Concord (1577), in *The Book of Concord: The Confessions of the Evangelical Lutheran Church*, ed. Theodore G. Tappert (Philadelphia: Fortress, 1959), 447–79.

6. *Statenvertaling*. See also *CG* 1.7.5n3.

the revelation came is not too much kept in the shadows. This was not true of Calvin. For him the universal perspective always arises out of history itself. And it is in that spirit that we also have elucidated Israel's role.

# CHAPTER FIFTY-THREE

# THE LIGHT IN THE DARKNESS

*The light shines in the darkness, and the darkness has not overcome it.*

JOHN 1:5

§ 1  The result of our investigation thus far is that the nations did not exist for the sake of Israel, but that Israel was called into existence by God for the sake of the nations. God sought his honor, the honor of his name, and he did not seek it in what was added to the nations through Isaac's birth, but in humanity itself, which he created in Adam and which since then had expanded into the nations. The world has definitely not been abandoned in order to insert Israel in its place; but both before and after the flood, before as well as after the time of Israel, it remains: "for God so loved *the world*." Out of love for the world, as his creation, he has given Israel to this world, not for the sake of Israel but in order to give his only begotten Son through and from Israel to that world, which he loved and continued to love immutably.

If this is so, then it follows that God has been at work in this world through all those centuries, has guided this world, and has prepared this world for the reception of what would come out of Israel for this world. This would not have had to be the case if Christ were not only *from* the Jews, but in that sense also primarily *for* the Jews, if converted Gentiles were merely added to Israel as an appendix, as an addition and appendage.

Anyone building a cottage retreat in the woods first finishes the cottage and then looks how he will lay out the paths through the woods, and how he will use the fortuitous position of some groups of trees to the benefit of his retreat. By contrast, anyone wanting to use a kind of exotic plants for decorating his yard, knowing that those foreign plants will require special preparation of the soil, does not wait with preparing the soil until the exotic plantings arrive, but takes care that the soil is ready when they arrive.

Similarly, if we were to understand God's sovereign plan in such a way that he, despairing of the salvation of the world and as if to compensate for the loss of the world, would have created Israel as a kind of especially holy people to whom would later be added at most a fragment of the nations, then there could certainly not have been a prior activity of God among the nations. Then in Israel God would have had the actual nation he was after, and all the rest would have been of minor importance.

If, on the other hand, Israel served merely to cultivate that wondrous Shoot that, as an exotic heavenly vine would be planted in the soil of this world, then of course two kinds of activities on God's part had to take place from the beginning and in mutual connection: (1) the preparation of the Vine in Israel, and (2) the preparation of the world to be able to receive that Vine.

Even among people, anyone who took a different approach would be showing a lack of wisdom. And here we are dealing not with human wisdom but with the wisdom of our God.

This can be demonstrated in two ways.

First, by checking how, when the gospel went out into the world, the path for the gospel in and through the world had been made completely level. And second, by asking what God himself says about it in his Word.

Starting with the latter, we must pay attention to the mysterious beginning of the Gospel of John.   § 2

John does not proceed like Mark, who, after first mentioning the Baptist, suddenly introduces the Christ. Nor does John proceed like Luke, who takes as his point of departure the expectation that lived among the God-fearing Jews. And John proceeds unlike Matthew, who goes back to Abraham, and then from Abraham via David to Mary and then to the Christ. No, John does not speak about Abraham at all; he has John the Baptist going ahead of Christ as the ringing of the bells precedes the coming of the king, but he urges us to learn to understand Christ's identity beyond the Baptist in Israel, and beyond Israel in the world, and beyond the world in terms of the ground of life, and beyond that ground of life of the world in the eternal Word, and thus all the way back to God's being.

He begins, neither with the Baptist, nor with Abraham, nor even with the beginning of creation, but far beyond that beginning of things created: he begins in eternity, before the foundation of the world, and because there was nothing then but God, he takes his beginning in God himself.

John discloses to us a world of rich and glorious life within that eternal being of God, even when as yet no created world existed. This is the God expressing himself from eternity within himself, in his Word, or as stated in Proverbs 8:[25-26,]30, "Before the mountains had been shaped, before ... the first of the dust of the world," says the eternal Word, "then I was beside him, like a master workman, and I was daily his delight, rejoicing before him always." This is the portrayal full of majesty of the perfect life of love in God, even before a world existed to which his love could go out. For us this is a mystery, because we lack any capacity to conceptualize that divine household in the inner being of God, but it is a mystery that nevertheless really exists. A rich and glorious life did not come into being for God for the first time when the world came into being. Then God would have been from all eternity a dead or a slumbering God who did nothing. He would have been as though in need of the world, and that world would have made God's life delightful for the first time. This is turning things upside down.

No, if we are to think of the life of our God with appropriate dignity, we must instead imagine that if this world had never come into being, there would have been from eternity nothing, absolutely nothing, except God and God alone. We must think that had he existed without creation, being eternally alone, our God would have been entirely satisfied and beatific within himself, in such a way that the creation of the world neither could nor did add anything to that beatific state.

We cannot understand this, of course, if we think of God as a rigid unity of persons, for how could one single person, eternally alone, enjoy a beatific state? But we do understand it if we confess more than nominally the holy triunity of our God. Then we do not see the personality of God as deficient and in need of help, but as three persons, so that God possesses within himself the full life of personality. And if we can then raise ourselves up to the point where if necessary we would give the whole world in order to gain Christ, and if we confess with Augustine, "My heart remains restless in me till it finds rest in God," then we understand how perfectly glorious and perfectly blessed that divine life within God himself must have been from all eternity, that holy interaction of God with God in the triunity of the persons.[1]

Of this the holy apostle writes, "In the beginning was the Word, and the Word was with God, and the Word was God. He was in the beginning with God" [John 1:1–2]. In three mighty strokes, therefore, he depicts the full blessedness of the divine Being, as a blessed, holy interaction of God with God in God himself, an interaction that transcends all understanding.

Only then can all that is created be addressed: the creation, the world, §3 the universe, things visible and invisible, angels and humans, body and soul in the human being, and in that soul thinking and willing, praising and loving. All this is creaturely. It is not eternal. It comes into being after God had been self-sufficient and blessed within himself from all eternity. It is not what is real and essential. That which is essential is only in God. What we call the world, the universe, or the cosmos is added from the overabundance of God. If it had never come into existence, God would have lacked nothing. But it comes into being because it pleases the rich and blessed God to make the reflection of his own glory radiate in this overwhelming abundance of his own creative power.

*Reflection*—that's what it is.

It is not a creation of newly invented things, as when among humans the man of wealth decorates his salons with pieces of furniture and wall decorations and precious objects that have nothing to do with his own being. No, all that God creates is organically related to his own being. This organic relationship reaches its pinnacle in man, who is created in the full sense "in the image of God." But this organic relationship is not limited to this either. It permeates everything, because everything is created through the Word, and there is absolutely nothing among what has been created that is not related in its origin to that Word that was from eternity with God and that was God.

All that has been created is not out of the Word. In that case it could be a product merely of divine power, but still consist of invented, thought-up things with no relationship to God's being.

---

1. See Augustine, *The Confessions*, trans. Maria Boulding (Hyde Park, NY: New City Press, 1997), 1.1.1: "You stir us so that praising you may bring us joy, because you have made us and drawn us to yourself, and our heart is unquiet until it rests in you."

But this is not how it is. All that has been created is created out of the Father and absolutely not out of the Son. "Yet for us there is one God, the Father, from whom are all things" [1 Cor 8:6a]. And the Son is not the Word *out of which* but the Word *through which* all things have come into being. "And one Lord, Jesus Christ, through whom are all things and through whom we exist" [v. 6b].

The imprint of the Creator is therefore impressed upon all that has been created. The world contains nothing, not a single thought, that has not been taken from the divine Being and brought about by the Word who himself is God. Therefore all that has been created corresponds to the being of God. It stands in indissoluble organic relationship with the being of God through the Word. In man God created his image; in the entire creation, at a further remove, he created a reflection of what in him is hidden in thought, will, and power. All things have been made through the Word, and apart from that Word not anything was made that has been made [see John 1:3].

§ 4    After having pointed to the exalted God in his self-sufficient and blessed God-ness, and then to the divine abundance of creation as a reflection of himself, John the evangelist now proceeds to seek in this world, in this created realm, the center in man. First God within himself. Then God in his creation. Now within that creation the image of God: *man.* "In [the Word] was life, and the life was the light *of men*" [John 1:4].

What is "light" here? Light is the light in our spirit. Light is our consciousness. Life is in all things that have been created, but gold, the sun, the palm tree or cedar know not of their own life, and the lion or the horse barely do. In all the rest of what God created there is no consciousness, no self-discovery. Animals, as preformation of what would be in man, have sensations. But only man received the Word, and therefore creation through the Word becomes apparent in man.

In that creation there was life. The created realm was not a dead mass. It had life, and the life that was and is in it, is the Word itself. "In him was life," that is, "In the Word was life." So the fact that the world possesses life is not due to itself. It does not have that life from itself nor in itself. It has life only because the Word is in that creation. The Word does not shine into the world, as if the world existed of itself and only now and then the radiance of the Word would shine into it. This is how the sun is for the earth. The sun stands outside our earth, but beams its radiance into it. But then, our earth was not created by the sun. It stands outside the sun. With the Word it is entirely different.

In Colossians 1:16–17 Paul tells us three things: (1) that Christ existed before all things; (2) that all things were created by the Word; but then also (3) that in him all things together exist through him. In Greek, Paul expresses the notion of holding together in one word: *synestēken*, which means that all things exist now and eternally by the Word *as a single entity*, taken in their organic interconnection. Were the Word to withdraw from it, the universe would fly apart like dust. Only the eternal Word in the creation makes it the bearer of the thoughts of God and thereby makes it into a cosmos. Thus the eternal Word is in all things, in stars and in suns, in stones and in metal, in flower and branch and root, in the birds of the heavens and the fish in the sea. All that is and lives came into being through him and exists through him. He is the supporting and animating force that upholds it all so that it remains standing. And even as the most beautiful hot air balloon collapses into a flat heap of cloth as soon as the hot air escapes, so too would this whole divine work of art, the universe, collapse into a flat and shapeless nothingness if the eternal Word would withdraw from it for even one moment.

But this life that is in the world descends and ascends by the Word. §5 In the Word, that life is as transparent as crystal, as shiny as gold, as holy as the holy things of God. But in each creature this "eternal life" penetrates differently. It is not equally clear in every creature. Thus the life of the eternal Word descends very deeply, in order to create first a merely material, though still glorious, abundance that chemistry can disclose to us in the realm of the minerals. Within that broad field of chemistry there is an unfathomable wisdom. We can gaze at it for centuries, and we can sense worship overtaking our soul, yet entirely bypassing our higher, our personal, our inner life. Even the exalted glory of the organic is still entirely absent in that substratum of creation. The life of the eternal Word therefore had to descend very deeply to utter speech also in that lowly sphere, to be *the Word* in it.

But from that lowly sphere that life of the eternal Word ascends to ever higher glory.

First toward organic life. Then from the sponge to the cedar and the palm tree. From the fungus to the rose and the lily. From the grain to the grape. Soon still higher into the organic world that is not limited to one place but freely moves around. There first crawls the worm, the horse runs, the tiger makes its jump, the eagle flaps its wings through the clouds. And finally comes the human being.

In this ascending series of creatures, the eternal Word reveals itself each time more richly and fully. Not that each time still more is added, because the eternal Word is undivided and unbroken and is glorious in every creature. But one creature is more transparent, less opaque than the other. It is always the voice of the eternal Word that vibrates in and through everything, but not every creature conducts that sound equally purely. And thus the eternal Word speaks in the ascending series of creatures ever more fully, richly, clearly, and purely. Until the final transition comes in man. The highest. In man the eternal Word speaks to the point even of speaking through a creaturely word.

§ 6     It is not as if that speaking of the eternal Word restricted itself to the things of the created realm in their essence and existence. On the contrary. That eternal Word is and speaks also in all that happens in and with the created things. In Psalm 29 we read of that voice of the Lord: "The voice of the Lord is over the waters; the God of glory thunders, the Lord, over many waters. The voice of the Lord is powerful; the voice of the Lord is full of majesty. The voice of the Lord breaks the cedars; the Lord breaks the cedars of Lebanon. He makes Lebanon to skip like a calf, and Sirion like a young wild ox. The voice of the Lord flashes forth flames of fire. The voice of the Lord shakes the wilderness; the Lord shakes the wilderness of Kadesh. The voice of the Lord makes the deer give birth" [vv. 3–9]. A poignant display of God's omnipotence is in the storm and in the thunder. Yet the richest, fullest speaking of the voice of the Lord is in the human voice. "In his temple a son of man gives him honor" [see v. 9].

The apostle John expresses it in this way, that life becomes light for the first time in man; and what does this mean but that only in man does life brighten and light up into consciousness of self and consciousness of the creation around him, a consciousness of his God through the eternal Word that works in him and by which he exists.

Pure olive oil is nothing but liquid light because the very best oil of the olives burns completely, without leaving behind any residue. Kerosene also yields light, but it is mixed with other substances and ignites at a higher temperature.

So too life does not yield equal light in the life of all people. Among people as well there are those who can emit only partial light and an impure light at that. There are those who, like olive oil, can become altogether light, if someone else ignites it for them and in them. And there are also intellectual and spiritual virtuosi who, like kerosene, ignite spontaneously and give light, if the temperature of life rises sufficiently.

But however different the degree may be, the life in all people is light-bearing, because no matter how great the difference in intensity, every human being has a consciousness of self, of the world, and of God. In all human beings reason speaks. All humans express that reason in human language. In all humans the eternal Word speaks in the creaturely word, in language, in the voice.

This threefold consciousness belonging to a man is not something new §7 that is added to his life. When the olive oil gives light, that light comes out of the oil, coming into contact, of course, with the air (even as our human consciousness is unthinkable without that which surrounds us), yet in such a way that the light is not added to the oil as a second ingredient, but flames up out of the oil. The oil becomes light. And in the same way the light of our consciousness is not added as a second ingredient, but it is our life, it is the life of creation, it is the life of the eternal Word in creation that becomes light in us, that brightens into light and shines as light. Even as in God his life and his divine consciousness are not two but one, so too in us life entails light, and the light unfurls life.

This is what John says: "In the Word was life, and the life was the light of men" [see John 1:4].

Man neither derives his light from elsewhere, nor from himself, nor did he create it. He lives by the eternal Word. The eternal Word that causes him to exist is his life. And that life expands within his consciousness to light. To light in all directions. Light in the intellect, light in the choosing activity of his will, light in his social existence, light in his moral existence, light in his art and scholarship, light in the eye of the soul with which he sees God.

But now that mirror in which the eternal Word was reflected breaks. Sin enters. And that sin causes the mirror to crack and fracture—a thousand cracks across the surface of the mirror that was at first so clear and smooth.

What now?

With and through sin, has the revelation of the eternal Word now departed from the world that bears the curse, and from man who comes under doom?

Never.

After all, hell also exists only through the eternal Word. "All things"—and after all is said and done, that includes the place where there is weeping and gnashing of teeth—"hold together in him" [see Col 1:17]. In the outermost darkness as well, just as in the pitch-dark night, the majesty of the Lord of lords is hidden.

Except everything has now become darkness.

§ 8    But behold—common grace; the eternal Light has not allowed the darkness on earth to become "outermost darkness" [see 2 Pet 2:17; Jude 6, 13]. Had there not been a separating, restraining grace, nothing would have been able to fend off the ever-increasing blackness of the darkness expanding into pitch-black night.

But that restraining of common grace has come.

"The light shines in the darkness, and the darkness has not overcome it" [John 1:5].

There was no darkness in paradise. As soon as there is mention of darkness, at this moment the world appears before our eyes as having sunk in sin.

And also in that darkness there *was* of course the eternal Word, even as the eternal Word is in the outermost darkness of hell.

But this is not what the evangelist is referring to.

He is speaking of an intentional act of the eternal Word. He does not say that the eternal Word was also in the darkness. That is true, of course. But he does say that the Word shone into the darkness—shone into the darkness in such a way that the darkening could not progress further. So that a twilight remained in the midst of darkness.

And that twilight in the midst of the darkness, those rays of light shining through the mists into the darkness—that is common grace.

Therefore it is grace in a deeper sense, pitying grace, because although the darkness strengthened itself against this shining light, it did not capture the light, did not ingest or absorb the light, but rather tried to the extent it was able to banish the light through its own self-darkening.

# CHAPTER FIFTY-FOUR

# THE BAPTIST

*He was in the world, and the world was made through him, yet the world did not know him.*

JOHN 1:10

In the so-called prologue of John (John 1:1–14), five different things are said about the eternal Word: (1) that the eternal Word *was*; (2) that it *shines* as light; (3) that this light *has come*; (4) that John the Baptist *witnesses* about the Word; and (5) that the eternal Word *has become flesh*. This eternal Word *is* from all eternity with God; it *shines* in the world; it has *come* to Israel; it is *witnessed* about by the Baptist; and it has *become flesh* and has *dwelt* among us, in Mary's Son.

§ 1

We must pay close attention to the distinction between the being, shining, coming, and dwelling among us of the eternal Word if we are to understand the prologue of John.

Beginning at the end, verse 14 tells us, "And the Word became flesh and dwelt among us, and we have seen his glory, glory as of the only Son from the Father, full of grace and truth."

This is the completion of this glorious revelation. Immanuel, God with us. God himself, in human nature, not merely approaching and coming to man, but dwelling among men, never again to be separated from our humanity. For now also, in heaven, the eternal Word has remained in our human nature, Christ remained the Head of reborn humanity, and the blessed humanity is in part already around and with him.

Thus it was not in Israel, and this is why between Israel and the incarnation stands the testimony of John the Baptist. First in verse 6 and then in verse 15, the figure of John the Baptist is placed life-size between the Israelite dispensation and the coming of the Light in Bethlehem. John the Baptist is neither a product of Israel, nor a continuation of what existed or happened in Israel. The Baptist stands above everything that arose from Israel or was sent to Israel.

With a solemn "Truly I say to you," Jesus himself testified: "Among those born of women there has arisen no one greater than John the Baptist" [Matt 11:11]. Thus the Baptist stands above Isaiah and David, above Elijah and above Moses, above Abraham and Noah. No one is his equal. He is greater than all. It must be acknowledged only in this manner, or we diminish the mighty intent of Jesus' words. For all of these were born of women before John, and Jesus emphatically states that all these stood below the Baptist.

§ 2 Until now little attention has been paid to this. People have read past this word of Jesus too quickly, which is precisely why it has remained so enigmatic that the prologue speaks first of John the Baptist and only then of Israel. Look at verse 6, where it says, "There was a man sent from God, whose name was John"; and only then follows in verse 11: "He came to his own [Israel], and his own people did not receive him." We would be inclined to say that this is the inverse order. "He came to Israel" should have come first, and only then, "There was a man sent from God, whose name was John." Not much attention has been paid to this seemingly inverse order in the past, today somewhat more. And the most recent interpreters have been led astray into taking "coming to his own" as referring not to his revelation in the Israelite dispensation but to his being born in Bethlehem. In doing so they confuse the whole prologue and take it out of its context, as Dr. Bernhard Weiss did recently in the latest edition of Meyer's commentary series.[1] We are not in the habit of referring to the writings of contemporary scholars by name in our Bible studies for the church, but here it was necessary because Meyer's is still the most widely used

---

1. Bernhard Weiss (1827–1918) was a renowned German NT exegete. He was also the reviser of commentaries on the NT in the series of Heinrich August Wilhelm Meyer (1800–1873), including the commentaries on Matthew (9th ed., 1897), Mark and Luke (9th ed., 1901), John (9th ed., 1902), Romans (9th ed., 1899), the Epistles to Timothy and Titus (7th ed., 1902), Hebrews (6th ed., 1897), and the Epistles of John (6th ed., 1900).

commentary series. But its most recent interpretation of the prologue would lead to the loss of the entire rich revelation concerning common grace, which our forefathers as well as the authors of the annotations to the Dutch Bible confessed to being contained in that prologue.[2]

We may not give even the appearance of not wanting to take note of this most recent interpretation and of simply wanting to cling to the older interpretation.

We took our firm point of departure, therefore, in Jesus' word that places the whole Israelite dispensation, including Moses and Isaiah, below John. And this point must therefore be further elucidated before we continue. By itself it sounds strange. We know so little about John. What we know of his preaching is brief and extremely simple. No miracles are reported of him. And the most characteristic saying we have of him is that he was not worthy to untie the strap of Jesus' sandal. And it is this declaration that superficially leaves an impression of insignificance rather than of a person of significance who is supposed to be greater than even a Moses, a David, and an Isaiah.

We therefore acknowledge unreservedly that the personal significance of Moses or Isaiah certainly was not less than that of John the Baptist, but rather exceeded it by far, in fact. It is not the person of this envoy, but rather the nature of his mission that puts him at such an elevated level. At the court, the ranking of the envoys is determined not by their personal significance but by the nature of their mission. §3

And if in that sense we do not look at the person but at the nature and character of his mission, then we must immediately note, first, that the coming and mission of John the Baptist, not that of Moses or Isaiah, was announced centuries ahead of time. Shortly after his coming on the scene, the Sanhedrin, the official representative body of Israel, had dispatched a commission of inquiry to the Baptist to investigate who he was and what his mission meant. In [chapter 1,] verse 19 it says that "the Jews sent priests and Levites from Jerusalem to ask him, 'Who are you?'" and that these emissaries, these deputies, these commission members kept insisting, saying, "Who are you? We need to give an answer to those who sent us. What do

---

2. The SV annotations observe at John 1:11 that "his own" refers to the Israelite people, to whom Jesus "came particularly not only after his incarnation through the preaching of the gospel, but also before his incarnation through various appearances, manifestations, and deliverances."

you say about yourself?" [v. 22]. And to that question the Baptist answered literally, "I am the voice of one crying out in the wilderness" [v. 23].

This clearly referred to Isaiah 40:3, as other evangelists also note. It is thus certain that the coming, not of Moses nor of Isaiah, but of John the Baptist had been announced centuries before as a coming of entirely unique importance.

But there is more, and therefore we point out, secondly, that his birth is also announced by an angel, and that he received the Holy Spirit before he was born. Certainly, the birth of Isaac was also announced by an appearance of angels. But when we look at two facts—first, the announcement by the angel, accompanied by the miracle of Zechariah's becoming mute and later his inspiration and prophecy; and second, the rather unique fact that he received the Holy Spirit already in his mother's womb and leaped within Elisabeth to greet Mary's infant Jesus—then in these two facts, even as in the prophecy of Isaiah 40:3, lies a quite unique honor and grace that was bestowed only on John and no one else.

Third, a very exceptional revelation was given to John that allowed him to decide without hesitation or doubt that indeed Jesus was the Christ; to introduce the Son of God to the disciples, and through this to the world; and to lead Christ through baptism from a private Jewish life into his world calling as Messiah.

§ 4    The impression John's appearance made was so overwhelming that all Israel went out to him; the rulers of the land had to reckon with him; even the unbelieving Pharisees, out of fear of the people, did not dare repudiate his holy mission; and the crowned murderer who had him beheaded still trembled on his throne years later, terrified that the risen Jesus might be John resurrected.

And if this already shows that his mission was graced with quite unique distinctions, it is also not difficult to realize how his mission itself stood above all missions in Israel and occupies a position between the Israelite dispensation and Jesus' own appearance. For until John the Baptist it was generally assumed that Israel was the blessed people and that every non-Jew, in order to find salvation, had to become a proselyte. Among the Gentiles there was death, among the Jews, life, and through proselyte baptism a Gentile went from death into life. That was the Israelite dispensation, its character, its national personality. As long as that dispensation continued, this could not be changed. Baptism was not for the Jews, but baptism was only for the Gentiles, a baptism for transferring the Gentile people into Israel.

But this Israelite position is decidedly not the position John the Baptist takes. To the contrary, he repudiates this standpoint, he destroys it, and over against it he posits the claims that the pious Jew as well as the Gentile soldier and tax collector both need his baptism, and that the baptism of the Jew serves to transfer him from the Israelite dispensation into the new dispensation of the kingdom of God.

Thus it is clear and plain that the Baptist occupies a place between Israel and the Christ; that he does not call people *to* Israel, but calls people from Israel and invites them to Jesus; and that his baptism is not intended to affirm Israel, but on the contrary to bring an end to Israel's dispensation. Baptizing was not a secondary aspect of his preaching; it was its main point. He is not John the Preacher but John the Baptizer, and his principal mission thus transcends Israel by far. Thus we understand what Jesus meant when he said that the Baptist stood above Abraham, Moses, and Isaiah. But thus we also understand why John the evangelist, when he introduces Jesus' coming into the world, in his prologue immediately goes to John the Baptist, because he and not Israel was Jesus' forerunner, his herald, the one who announced him. And only then he inserts the Israelite dispensation between the two as a transient dispensation that has passed. §5

A rereading of John 1:1–10 confirms this interpretation. After all, in the first part of the prologue we are first told who the Word was from eternity; then how the Christ is the Light that shines in the world; further, that the world did not know what to do with this Light; and finally, that precisely because of this, the Light sought and found access to the world via a different route, in order to bless it. The latter is introduced in verses 6–7 by referring to John the Baptist, and only now, after John the evangelist has pointed to John the Baptist, the eternal Light is put in the context, not of Israel but of the world in general, for whom the incarnation of that eternal Light was intended. For it says that John himself was not the Light, but that he came to bear witness about the Light, and this Light about which he witnessed "gives light to everyone ... [It] was coming into the world ... the world was made through him, yet the world did not know him" [John 1:8–10]. This then is the reason he now sought the world in a different way, through the incarnation, and had it announced through John the Baptist.

This [coming into the world] has also been robbed of its significance through a wrong interpretation, which takes it to mean that after having §6 been born in Bethlehem, the eternal Word was now in the world by virtue of that birth, and thus, through his coming into the world, illuminated everyone. This is a quite untenable interpretation that must be rejected decisively. Coming into the world he did not become the Light that enlightens everyone but was the Light that enlightens everyone. It never could be said of the manger in Bethlehem that it immediately enlightened everyone. Jesus even intentionally confined this light to Israel until his death. The disciples were not allowed to go to anyone but the lost sheep of the house of Israel. If it said that this Light enlightened "the world," then we could concede this interpretation. But now it says everyone, and this cannot nor may be understood in any sense other than that such an activity that proceeded from the Christ proceeded to every human being individually. And such an effect does not lie in the realm of particular grace but can lie only in the realm of common grace. That which affects everyone is not particular but general. And thus the words "coming into the world" must not be understood as referring to the Light but to every human being. Each individual human is, from the moment of entering the world, shone upon by that Light. The authors of the annotations to the Dutch Bible very correctly explain this as the light of reason "that still remains in fallen man, to bring him some knowledge of God's nature and service, yet not leading to salvation."[3]

Thus common grace manifests itself in the fact that the eternal Word did not leave the world but continued to shine in it with his Light. He had made that world, and because it was his handiwork he stayed in it. "He was in the world, and the world was made through him, yet the world did not know him" [John 1:10]. But now this eternal Word begins to dwell among us, and in that new revelation of particular grace he will now enlighten and save not Israel, but that world that did not know him. Not, of course, everything that is in that world, but that world taken as a whole, the world as his creation.

Meanwhile there is yet a third item between this shining upon and dwelling in the world. The eternal Light shines in the world without end, from the hour of creation into all eternity. But the Word has made his dwelling among men only through his incarnation. And this dwelling is, of course, a much stronger, much more intimate, much richer and mightier form of revelation than merely shining. Already implicit in this

---

3. See SV notes at John 1:5, 10.

is the difference that distinguishes re-creation from creation. In the creation the eternal Light shines; in that which is re-created the eternal Word dwells. "[I and the Father] will come to him and make our home with him" [John 14:23].

But there is yet a fourth item that stands between shining on and dwelling, namely, the coming of the Light. "He came to his own," which means something else than that he "shines in the world" or "dwells among us." Coming is more than shining and less than dwelling, and this coming is what is said of the eternal Word among ancient Israel. "He came to [what was] his own, and his own people did not receive him."

§ 7

It does not say he came to his own persons, nor to his nation, but to what was his own, which apparently refers to what John writes in chapter 4: "Salvation is from the Jews." He took on flesh from Mary and thus became the Son of David. He therefore stood in a very different relationship to the Jews than to the world in general. The whole coming on the scene of Israel and the Israelite dispensation stood separately and were in that sense what was his. And he has come to what was his, that is, among Israel he revealed himself now and then through theophany or prophecy, not regularly but rather at intervals, with a coming and going that as such stands in direct contrast to his dwelling permanently. We have only to remember how four hundred years had passed since Malachi without the Messiah having visited his people, and think as well of the four centuries in Egypt that were without any revelation: together already eight centuries. And thus we may say that the character of the revelation to Israel lay precisely in that coming and going, a coming that stands in contrast to the dwelling.

Consequently this Israelite dispensation did not lead to salvation. To that extent, his coming to Israel lies on one line with his shining in the world. He shone into the world and the world did not know him. And thus also: He came to Israel, but his own people did not receive him. Only when we come to the fourth point, the dwelling among *us* thanks to the incarnation, the goal is reached. But not before. Both the common grace in the world and the more restricted grace among Israel have led to nothing other than that both the world and his own people rejected him. The eternal Word has not been rejected in the world and accepted in Israel; no, he was let down and repudiated by both. In this respect Israel and the world stand altogether on one line. The world has not known him, and his own people have not received him. Both Jews and

§ 8

Greeks are equal in their guilt; the Jews bear an even heavier guilt to the degree that more light was given to them.

This is established historically. For centuries, one idol after the other was worshipped on the heights and even in Jerusalem. The twelve tribes were finally cast out many centuries before the birth of Christ. And the group that returned under Cyrus was definitely no longer the nation but a weak remnant from very few tribes. Already four centuries before Christ we must seek the mass of the Jewish people not in Palestine but in the Diaspora or dispersion. And what returned, that handful of Jews from the great mass, did recover through ecclesiastical and political organization. But when Christ appeared, as a nation they cast him out by means of their representatives in the Sanhedrin, nailed him to the cross, and killed him. When Christ came to dwell among us, Israel gave him no hosanna, but only a curse.

In ancient times and over the past nineteen centuries, there have been thousands from Israel who came to life, but they did not owe this to the Israelite dispensation of the Law, but to the election and regenerating grace of God, even as now. "But to all who did receive him, who believed in his name, he gave the right to become children of God" [John 1:12]. They are not saved as children of Abraham, but God has given them the right to relinquish that birth from the flesh and from the will of a man, to receive the eternal Light and thus to become children of God, born not of Abraham, but of God. Only thus, on the basis of the preceding, do we understand what being born not from flesh but by spiritual birth means. Otherwise, if we do *not* think of the contrast with the birth from Abraham, this does not make sense here. But if we take it as the Baptist put it: "God is able from these stones to raise up children for Abraham," the connection remains crystal clear [Matt 3:9; Luke 3:8]. He has come to what was his own, but his own people have not accepted him, and those individuals from Israel who did receive him have done this not by virtue of their birth from Abraham, but by virtue of their birth from the Spirit of God.

§ 9 Thus "coming to his own" merely constitutes an intermediate link, and the main point is and remains that the eternal Word stands in twofold relationship or connection to the world. The first is that as Creator of that world he is its Life and its Light, and that he has remained the Light of the world even after the darkness of sin had come over that world. This is common grace. And in the second place, as mediator of God and man he has entered this world now to dwell among us, which means particular grace.

The world sunk in sin, meanwhile, in both instances opposes the eternal Word. It is blind, and it therefore does not understand the Light of common grace. It is obstinate and therefore resists particular grace. Jerusalem has killed and stoned the prophets and crucified Christ. Thus no salvation would be possible. Everything would come to naught because of the unremorseful and unrepentant, sinful human heart. And there is therefore only one way out. The very birth of the human being must be done over again. He must be changed down to the root of his being. And when this occurs, whether before or after the birth of Christ, sinners are changed into children of God, and those who are then changed, yes, they receive the Christ, they comprehend the Light, and they acclaim the Mediator.

The eyes have then been opened, and those whose eyes were opened "have seen his glory, glory as of the only Son from the Father, full of grace and truth" [John 1:14].

And from their lips it then resounds, "Behold the Lamb of God that takes away the sin of the world" [John 1:29].

# CHAPTER FIFTY-FIVE

# THE TINY SPARKS IN THE GENTILE WORLD

*Though they know God's righteous decree.*

ROMANS 1:32

§ 1    From the inspiring opening words of the Gospel of John we saw three things concerning common grace. First, that in "the light of men," that is, in his consciousness, or, if you will, in his existence as thinking and willing being, the very life of the eternal Word reveals itself. For it says, "In him," in the Word "was life, and the life was the light of men" [John 1:4]. With this we definitely do not intend to say that the life of the eternal Word would manifest itself only in the fact that we do not lead a nonconscious life like plants do. With the eye goes the light, even as the light goes with the eye, and with both eye and light goes a world on which the eye can gaze and on which the light can shine. It is also this way in a spiritual sense. The soul of man, that is, his inner life, has an eye to see, but that eye would not be able to see and not be capable of observation if there were not a world that could be observed spiritually, and if no spiritual light shone into this spiritually observable world. Thus here too, eye, light, and world belong together as three connected elements, and only in their combination and unity do they constitute our intellectual and delibera-tive existence. And now the apostle teaches us that this capacity of our spiritual eye for sight, this enabling us to see by the spiritual light, and the object that our soul's eye observes by seeing, come neither from us nor from the creature. Rather, both in us and in the world, it is the eternal Word himself, by which all things have been made [see John 1:3] and by which, as the epistle to the Colossians tells us, all things hold together [see Col 1:16–17].

Second, we found that as the result of sin, darkness has come over that whole world of our conscious human life: darkness, obscuration, and darkening, both in our soul's eye and in the object to which the soul's eye directs its gaze. We have only to compare a youthful eye that still has its full sharpness and that peers at a newly minted ten-guilder coin that still shines in full purity, with what an old man with poor vision observes when he looks at a ten-guilder coin that has lost virtually all its golden sheen after having been in circulation for years. Then you have a clear idea of the difference between what man observed spiritually before, and still briefly after, the entrance of sin.

And finally, third, it became apparent that the light of the eternal Word nevertheless continued to shine over that darkened world. Not, of course, as if the clarity of the light remained equal to what it was originally. Light that breaks through clouds and mist does not give nearly the same glow as the light of the sun in a totally clear sky. But this does not take away the fact that even now the light still shines into the darkness, even if the eye of the soul of the human being wrapped in his own darkness is too weak-ened to recognize the radiance of the eternal Word in the light that breaks through the mists [see John 1:5].

This threefold result of our investigation shows, therefore, that the world of the children of man, also outside Israel, continued to be borne by the eternal Word, and that the light of that eternal Word continued to shine in the life of man, after as well as before the fall. Satan and sin have not succeeded in making the darkening and obscuration complete. We have received this grace: that what otherwise would have been an Egyptian darkness is tempered to a darkening in heavy mists, but mists that allow a half-light to come through [see Exod 10:21–29]. It also appears that the grace extended to our race that had fallen into sin consists not in the gift of something new, nor in the regiving of something we had lost, but exclusively in the continuation of something that lay at the foundation of our creation. The light that shines now shone equally before the fall. It has not been absent only to shine again, but it continued to shine in spite of the mists that enveloped our human life. But even as the sunlight sometimes struggles with the clouds in order to prevent the mists from becoming too heavy in order still to be able to shine through, so too this eternal Light has, for our benefit, prevented and averted the solidifying of our darkness into pitch-black night, and in this way continued to enrich us, even if only with a half-light.

§ 2   Now we must investigate how this testimony of the apostle John agrees with the testimony of the apostle Paul in the first chapter of the epistle to the Romans. It is clear that both apostles, the one in John 1, the other in Romans 1, deal with the same matter. For both clearly speak first of humanity in general and then separately about the Jews. John makes this distinction by first speaking of "men" in general and "the world" in verses 4 and 10, and then about "what was his," referring to Israel, in verse 11. And in quite the same manner the apostle Paul speaks first of the "unrighteousness of men" in general (Rom 1:18), and then separately about the guilt of the Jews (Rom 2), finally presenting in chapter 3 both Gentiles and Jews—that is, the whole world—as condemned before God, concluding that "no flesh" can justify itself before God.

And although both apostles speak of the same matter, nevertheless each sees it from his own perspective, which causes an apparent contradiction that on closer inspection is no more than appearance. The difference in viewpoint lies herein that John, who wants to discuss the mystery of the incarnation of the Word, begins with the Second Person of the Trinity, proceeds from there to creation, from creation to the fall, and finally from the fall to common and particular grace. The apostle Paul, on the other hand, who wants to discuss quite a different mystery, namely, justification by faith, begins with the relationship in which God had placed man to himself, in order then to show how man has falsified and spoiled that relationship and is now utterly powerless in himself to make that relationship again into a spiritually pure relationship.

We can clarify the difference between the two if we first imagine a young mother, in the joy of motherhood, with her infant, and then imagine that same mother standing before her adult son who touches her soul through his misconduct. When we first pay attention to the mother with her child, we start from the mother and think how that mother gave life to her child and despite the pains of giving birth, reaches for that child in tender love. But if we take the same mother with respect to the adult son, who consumes her tender heart with sorrow, then we start from the misconduct of the son, to show how he repudiates and denies all right relationship with his mother, yet can be brought to a halt only by the love of that repudiated mother. Well then, what John presents us is that mother with her infant; what Paul attests to is that same mother, but then in relation to her lost son. And when we clearly keep in mind this difference in the starting point on the part of the apostles in their respective discussions, then we discover that between their respective testimonies there is nothing but undisturbed harmony.

What then is the apostle Paul affirming for us? §3

His starting point is the undeniable fact that there is manifested under heaven an "ungodliness and unrighteousness of men," which gives no other impression than of people "who by their unrighteousness suppress the truth" [Rom 1:18]. He even depicts the ungodliness and unrighteousness in broad strokes: the ungodliness in terms of idolatry, the unrighteousness in terms of extreme immorality. Throughout all the centuries and in all the regions of the world, our human race has manifested itself as idolatrous and inclined to breaking out into all kinds of immorality. The more that human life gradually reached a fuller development of its powers through prosperity and maturation, the more strongly both that idolatrous and that immoral tendency manifested themselves. In remote, rural areas there may still be a certain simplicity, and through that simplicity a certain staidness may still be maintained, but this is not how human life celebrates its great triumphs in the founding of a mighty metropolis: then, whether in the Babylon of the east or in the Rome of the west, idolatry and immorality break out in their most heinous forms to finally combine in idolatrous immorality.

Against that actual condition, the apostle says, "the wrath of God is revealed from heaven" (v. 18). After all, that world sunk into idolatry and immorality does not exist out of itself nor for itself, but it exists through God and for God. And because both that idolatry and that immorality place the world in a position before God that is the exact opposite of what it should be, the relationship is unrighteous, the opposite of righteous. The judgment of unrighteousness rests upon the world, and through this it calls down upon itself the wrath of God.

This now prompts the question whether that world of humanity, which has manifested itself in this and in no other manner throughout every century and at every point of the compass, sank into this deplorable condition in spite of itself, or knowingly. Imagine for a moment that after the fall, the darkening of man's religious, moral, and intellectual consciousness had continued until the end, so that man had immediately sunk utterly into the depths of complete ruin; then there could not be anything surprising in this brutalized and devilish condition of the world. The world would immediately have become hell itself, and in such a hellish condition humanity's world could, of course, not have shown anything but death, depravity, and unrighteousness. Who expects the tiger not to kill, or the wolf not to plunder, or the hawk not to lie in wait for the dove?

§ 4    Precisely with this in view, the apostle now tells us that this is most definitely not the condition of humanity fallen in sin. He expresses this most strongly in verse 32 with these words: "Though they knew God's righteous decree." And he describes it even more broadly in Romans 2:14–15, where he says that when the Gentiles "are a law to themselves. ... They show that the work of the law is written on their hearts, while their conscience also bears witness, and their conflicting thoughts accuse or even excuse them."

Therefore the situation after the fall, also according to the testimony of the apostle, is not that this darkening changed all at once into pitch-black night, and all religious and moral awareness was totally deadened in sin, but to the contrary, that this otherwise necessary final impact of sin has been restrained, and thanks to that restraining there remains in people a consciousness of good and evil, an awareness of justice and injustice, a certain knowledge of what God wants and does not want. However dense and heavy the mists may be in which people are enveloped as sinners, the light did not abandon the struggle but continued to penetrate those mists. But even as John says that the darkness has not overcome the light, so Paul declares that the truth continues to shine into this unrighteous situation, but we by our unrighteousness suppress that truth [see Rom 1:18]. Our eye may be extremely weakened, but we can nevertheless with some effort discern some half-light of the truth. But we don't want to do this, and we deliberately close our eyes in order not to see. However heavy the mist, the light still breaks through, but we deliberately stir up clouds of dust in front of us in order to make the mists even thicker and impenetrable. And thus it is that we do not enlist or welcome or draw toward us the light that is seeking us, the truth that is pressing upon us. Instead, we banish and exclude and suppress it in our unrighteousness. Here as well, the doctrine of common grace is speaking clearly. The mutilating has not persisted but has been restrained. The light of truth has definitely not retreated altogether but has *continued* to shine. It is strictly due to us that the light does not penetrate to our soul's eye.

Common grace is present, but we have rejected it.

Paul demonstrates this not only in the moral realm, but he takes it to a higher plane by demonstrating it equally in the religious realm. In fact, this is even his starting point. Idolatry is not the consequence of immorality, but immorality results from idolatry. Even as the fear of the Lord is the beginning of all wisdom, so also leaving the Lord is the beginning or starting point of all folly. For that reason, he places in the foreground that man has exchanged the glory of the immortal God for images resembling a mortal creature and knelt down before them [see Rom 1:23].

§ 5

This fact is of especially great importance for the initial insight into common grace.

Two items must be clearly perceived here. First, idolatry itself proves the existence of common grace after the fall. All idolatry attests to a need to worship. An animal does not worship God, but neither does it commit idolatry. It lives and exists outside of any notion about or impulse toward religion. And the lost in hell do not worship the Eternal, but neither do they commit idolatry. So it is with the devils as well. For the devils know the inclination to let themselves be worshipped, but they themselves cannot worship any other object. If we assume that without being bridled or restrained, sin could have reduced our human race immediately to total and final confusion and brutalization, then idolatry could never have arisen. The mere fact that wherever people have lived idolatry has arisen is proof that the urge to worship has remained in man. This could not have been the case if common grace had not restrained and curbed the total degradation of sin.

Second, we must note that this urge to worship is not an invention of people, but a work of God in the heart of people and the world of people. The apostle expresses it clearly: "Although they knew God, they did not honor him as God" [Rom 1:21]. He does not say, "because they do not know God, they have worshiped the creature." No, he says the exact opposite: "Although they know God they refuse to worship him, the Eternal, and instead bow down before the creature."

The apostle supports with twofold evidence the pervasively dominant fact that even the sinner who has fallen deepest still has a certain knowledge of God but goes against it. The first is that God is still manifest even in the sinner, the second, that God is still manifest in the world. The first he expresses in these words: "For what can be known about God is plain to them, because God has shown it to them" (v. 19). The second he describes in this way in verse 20: "His invisible attributes, namely, his eternal power and divine nature, have been clearly perceived, ever since the creation of the world, in the things that have been made." Thus, thanks to common grace, the spiritual light has not totally departed from the soul's eye of the sinner. And also, notwithstanding the curse that spread throughout creation, a speaking of God has survived within that creation, thanks to common grace. This is entirely in line with Psalm 19[:1–3], which says that "the heavens [still] declare the glory of God, and the sky above [still] proclaims his handiwork. Day to day pours out [abundant] speech, and night to night reveals knowledge. There is no speech, nor are there words, whose voice [that is, that there is no people or nation where the voice that proclaims from the heavens the majesty of God] is not heard."[1]

§ 6    Thus even after the flood there has still remained in the sinner, internally and externally, some possibility of knowing God. Not sufficient for salvation; this scarcely needs to be added. Besides, we are not dealing here with particular grace. Yet it is a real possibility to know God to an extent that would definitely have been cut off if sin and curse had continued unabated. This is thus a knowledge of God and of his justice that persisted in spite of our sin, and that was and is still maintained, due not to our efforts but despite our unrighteousness, by the common grace of God.

Idolatry is therefore not an ignoring of God, and it is not something new, an inventing of something entirely different in the worship of the creature. No, under the impulse that God still exercises in the sinner's heart, idolatry is the sinner turning that urge around, wanting to worship God in the idol. Even as Jeroboam, the son of Nebat, sought to worship the God of Israel in the calf statues at Dan and Bethel, this is and remains the deepest essence of all idolatry [see 1 Kgs 12:25–33]. The impulse of God's majesty works within the soul, and from the world of his works it operated within the human heart, and it is this divine impulse within the heart that people throw away in sin and falsify into an idolatrous inclination. "For although they knew God, they did not honor him as God or give thanks to him, but they became futile in their thinking ... and exchanged

---

1. Kuyper's own interpolations to the biblical text are indicated here by brackets which do not appear in the original Dutch.

the glory of the immortal God for images resembling mortal [creatures]" [Rom 1:21, 23]. Idolatry thus does not argue against common grace, but is its clear proof.

As for the nature of common grace, Paul, like John, teaches that it is nothing new that descended into the world, but it is something that has existed for ages, and still exists, in God's preserving from destruction what he himself had put into creation. This he expresses by emphasizing that "his invisible attributes, namely, his eternal power and divine nature, have been clearly perceived, ever since the creation of the world, in the things that have been made" [Rom 1:20]. So a new revelation has not come, but the revelation that shone through in creation has been sustained, has been continued over against the destruction of curse and sin, and has been maintained through common grace. The revelation would have been lost and would have disappeared if sin could have continued its decay unhindered. But precisely *this* God has prevented, precisely this has been thwarted by common grace. And thanks to this common grace, the result has been achieved that the sinner still knows the justice of God, and the revelation of God in the human heart and in creation still continues to function even after the fall.

# CHAPTER FIFTY-SIX

# THE TINY SPARKS EXTINGUISHED

*And since they did not see fit to acknowledge God, God gave them up to a debased mind to do what ought not to be done.*

ROMANS 1:28

§ 1    If, therefore, thanks to common grace, the knowledge of God still continued to reach humanity even after the fall, no spiritual fruit was born from the natural knowledge of God. Although we must confess with Romans 1:19 that "what can be known about God is plain to sinners" to the extent even that "the work of the law is written on their hearts" [2:15], and although we must also acknowledge that, as Romans 1:20 teaches us, "his invisible attributes ... have been clearly perceived, ever since the creation of the world, in the things that have been made," nevertheless after the flood our human race has not persevered in the service of God and in the fear of the Lord. On the contrary, almost immediately the straying away from the God who had saved our race in the ark entered the bosom of the race that had been saved, and ever more heinously did the old sin break out again among the nations, leading the nations astray from bad to worse.

The apostle Paul explains this from the fact that it pleased God to gradually *scale down* his common grace. This common grace had broadened after the flood, but now it shrank again, and the apostle sketches for us this shrinking of common grace in these words, that God gave up our human race to a debased mind.

Three times Paul emphasizes this fact.

First, he writes in verse 24:

> "*Therefore God gave them up* in the lusts of their hearts to im-
> purity, to the dishonoring of their bodies among themselves."

Then in verse 26:

> "*For this reason God gave them up* to dishonorable passions. For
> their women exchanged natural relations for those that are
> contrary to nature."

And a third time in verse 28:

> "And since they did not see fit to acknowledge God, *God gave
> them up* to a debased mind to do what ought not to be done."

We must therefore not read past this act of God. This is an act of God of great importance that we must take into account if we are to understand the historical development, degeneration, and decline of the nations before the coming of the Christ. It is not putting it too strongly to speak of an act of God in this context. Three times it says, not without a certain emphasis, that God has *given up* the nations. Any giving up of a nation's direction is a definite act. Thanks to common grace, God had begun to take the guidance of the nations into his own hands after the flood. But when a general apostasy emanated once again from the root of sin, God gave up the guidance and replaced it with another guidance, namely, that of their own debased heart, thereby giving it in fact to the guidance of Satan.

This giving up of the nations by God must therefore not be understood in the sense of common *hardening*. Hardening of the heart as such stirs up resistance and enmity against God, whereas being given up as such means only that the evil of sin is not restrained as strongly by God as in the past and consequently continued its corrosive process in a very dangerous manner. What is pointed to three times as the result of this giving up of the nations is not an audacious, God-provoking pride like that of Pharaoh, but always moral decay, the sinking of the human into the animal sphere. Paul establishes an undeniable connection between the brutalization of human life and idolatry, but always in such a way that idolatry comes first, that this idolatry stirs God's anger, that this anger of God leads to the giving up of the nations to a debased mind, and that the degeneration and refined brutalization sets in as the result of this having been given up.

To put it succinctly, the deterioration begins with the sin against the first table of the Law, and the consequence of that sin against the first table of the Law is that by way of punishment God lets the nations decay in their sin against the second table of the Law. First they have "exchanged the glory of the immortal God for images resembling mortal man and birds and animals and creeping things" (v. 23). Then and for that reason, "God gave them up in the lusts of their hearts" (see v. 24). After God let them go, they have come "to impurity, to the dishonoring of their bodies among themselves" [v. 24] and they have "exchanged natural relations for those that are contrary to nature" (see v. 26). And finally they have lapsed not only into committing bestiality but even into giving approval to those who in this manner threw away their human honor (see v. 32).

§ 2    This piece of history, seemingly so simple as it stands written here, requires further explication on more than one point.

In the first place, we must point out that this is a matter not of what happened with each individual human being, but of what happened with our human race outside Israel, generally referred to as "the nations." It is important to make this distinction here in order to be safeguarded against entirely false notions. It is completely true as such that in Romans 1, not one single sin is mentioned that did not occur also in Israel and that did not desecrate the covenant of God in Christian countries as well. And although we do not know any details of human life in this regard before the flood, even so nobody will doubt that in those days of general moral collapse similar sins would have called out to the Most High for vengeance. But if this is true, if all sins and abominations mentioned here occurred before the flood as well, and among Israel and the baptized nations, in short, in all centuries and among all nations, how then, we ask ourselves, must we understand that Paul presents this brutalization to us as if it resulted only from God's later abandoning of the nations? After all, we do not read anything about idolatry before the flood. So everything Paul is saying in Romans 1 cannot refer to the period before the flood, but must refer to the course of human life after the flood.

This seeming contradiction is resolved if an adequate distinction is made between the life of *individual human beings* as such and the communal life they led as *nations*. Even the best of families and lineages occasionally includes a prodigal son who remains lost. Examples of individual degeneration and brutalization are found in the highest as well as the lowest classes of society. There have always been moral monsters. But of course it is something quite different to see a single bad person come from a noble line, the line itself remaining noble, than to see an entire line degenerate and watch the nobility that once characterized it lapse into worldliness, avarice, fraud, and immorality. In the former case, God maintains the line through his common grace, despite one evil member; in the other case, the entire line is abandoned. It is quite different whether a single wild shoot sprouts from an otherwise healthy tree, or that the tree itself grows wild. This same distinction applies to the nations. Corporal punishment cannot be eliminated from the administration of justice of any nation, no matter how eminent it may be, for among all nations a murderer will arise now and then.[1] But this fact in itself does not prove that the nation as such is depraved. To the contrary, precisely the fact that the nation punishes the murderer with death shows that it does not want to have any truck with his actions but rather condemns them. On the other hand, if a situation arises where robbing and murdering become daily occurrences and the whole population takes the side of the murderer, such that not the murderer but the judge who sentences him receives threatening letters, then the evil has crept into the nation itself and that nation has deteriorated into lawlessness.

Therefore, what Paul tells us in Romans 1 does not in the least deny that all the sins and abominations he mentions there were also known before, nor that those same sins and abominations had also occurred frequently in Israel. But it states that in the past all these sins occurred only sporadically—now and then, here and there, in the case of a few individuals—but were still denounced and condemned by the law, by public opinion, and by the national conscience; but from the moment that God let go of those nations and gave them up, these sins captured the very heart of these nations and eroded the vitality of these nations. §3

This is true to such an extent that, when in the days of Isaiah the same turnaround crept into public opinion, so that even in the taverns in Jerusalem the moral order was turned around and they began calling evil good and good evil. This scandalous behavior resulted in the rejection of Israel and in the Babylonian captivity. Through this evil turnaround in the national consciousness of Israel, Israel put itself on a par

---

1. Kuyper treats the topic of capital punishment more fully in *CG* 1.8–10.

with the Gentiles; it came therefore under the same judgment as the Gentiles and could now only be healed homeopathically. Israel did not unlearn its hankering after the Gentiles' way of life until God forced it to see from close by and to experience directly in a Gentile country all the misery attached to the Gentile way of life. That and only that cured Israel permanently of the abomination of idolatry, not the whole of Israel but the "holy seed" that remained in Israel (see Isa 6:12–13), and made possible the sprouting anew of the stump of the felled tree of the people of Israel.

There can also be no doubt about the correct interpretation of the "giving up of the nations" [see Rom 1:24, 26]. It does not mean that there were not all kinds of personal examples of brutalization and degeneration in the past, but rather that after the flood there was first a period in which the nations as such still denounced, punished, and spoke out against such abominations; thereafter began a second period in which God let them go, so that the nations temporarily reconciled themselves to the evil, the poison dripped into the blood of the members of the nations, and ultimately the nations as a whole degenerated and became ripe for perdition.

§ 4     A second explication that cannot be omitted here is of an entirely different nature.

It involves the question whether this letting go of the nations, this decreasing and limiting of common grace, took place suddenly or gradually, so that the decrease progressed from less to more. There is then no doubt that this question must be answered in the latter sense. Common grace did not withdraw all at once completely from the life of the nations. The withdrawal took place gradually, and we must even add that this happened more prominently in one nation than in the other. We know this already from the history of the nations. In Sodom and Gomorrah the evil had progressed to such an extent in the days of Abraham already that only the Dead Sea reminds us of the location where these cities once flourished. And whereas in Sodom and Gomorrah the evil had broken out to an extreme, we find in the same time, near the Dead Sea, a man like Melchizedek, who as priest-king still serves the Lord and blesses the patriarch of God. When we compare on the one hand the condition of the African nations, of the cannibals and of so many more with the situation in Persia, with Greece in the era of the heroes, with the early times of the Roman republic on the other hand, then we see clearly how the degeneration among the nations breaks through at very different times among various nations. We must not lump the life of the nations after the flood all together as if they were all the same.

A distinction must therefore be made between tribe and tribe, between nation and nation, between one state and another, in two ways.

There are tribes and nations who because of their weak disposition always remain on a lower level, and there are other nations who were from the beginning given a high calling among the nations. The Canaanite nations and the indigenous races in Africa stood on a low level and remained there; the Egyptians, the Persians, the Greeks, the Romans stood on a high level and were destined for great things.[2] Hence evil developed much more rapidly among the people of a lower level, much more slowly among the people who stood on a higher plane. The people on a lower plane are already morally leprous and cancerous when the higher nations still show by and large a noble face thanks to common grace.

But also, second, in each nation a distinction must be made between the various periods it went through in its national existence. First a period of naïve, patriarchal life, then a longer or shorter period of relative flourishing, and finally a period of weakening and exhaustion, until the nation plummets and fades, sometimes even to be overtaken by other nations, and then disappears. There is a distinction in starting points among the various nations. The descendants of Shem and Japheth begin with receiving a larger portion of common grace than the descendants of Ham. But on the other hand, there is also a distinction within the same nation between its rise, its flowering, and its demise. And it is in this historical progression that the withdrawal of common grace and the giving up of such a nation to a debased mind successively occurs in the various nations.

Our third explication of Romans 1 touches on the distinction between the various aspects of common grace.

§ 5

Common grace extends over our entire human life, in all its manifestations. There is a common grace that manifests itself in order and law; there is a common grace that manifests itself in prosperity and affluence; there is a common grace that becomes visible in the healthy development of strength and heroic courage of a nation; there is a common grace that shines in the development of science and art; there is a common grace that enriches a nation through inventiveness in enterprise and commerce;

---

2. For more on Kuyper's racial judgments from his Eurocentric perspective, see *CG* 1.12.10n4; 1.41.1n3. See similar instances in *CG* 1.61 and 1.62.

there is a common grace that strengthens the domestic and moral life; and finally there is a common grace that protects the religious life against an excessive degeneration. As for the latter, we only have to compare Islam with the service of Baal Peor [see Numbers 25] to sense immediately what a powerful functioning of common grace is active in the religious realm in Islamic countries. And if we want to get a clear picture of the difference in the effect of common grace in another area, compare then, for example, what we are told of the Egyptians in the days of Moses and the Batavians in the days of Claudius Civilis.[3] Among the Egyptians we see a high development of wisdom and skill in various areas of art and business enterprise; but social life existed on a low level, as demonstrated by the division into castes, as well as the moral life, as demonstrated by the wife of Potiphar. Conversely, among the Batavians we see an absence of all development in business, art, or science, but a social and moral life that is still relatively healthy.

This shows that the various levels and components of common grace do not always rise and descend together. Common grace can still function very powerfully in the intellectual development of a nation, while common grace may have withdrawn almost completely from that same nation in the moral realm. What is reported to us from the circle of Socrates, how even in that circle of the wise men of that time all kinds of unnatural sin had crept in, while at the same time a depth of insight survived that can refresh us still today, shows sufficiently how common grace can work in segmented ways. It withdraws one ray of light at a point where another ray of light may shine all the more powerfully. The common proverb, "The greater the genius, the greater the ass,"[4] expresses the same truth applied to individuals; but the same is true of nations and peoples. They can stand

---

3. Gaius (or Claudius) Julius Civilis was a Batavian prince who led a revolt against the Romans in AD 69–70. See Simon Hornblower, Antony Spawforth, and Esther Eidinow, eds., *The Oxford Classical Dictionary*, 4th ed. (New York: Oxford University Press, 2012), s.vv. "Batavi"; "Iulius Civilis, Gaius."

4. An earlier rendering of the Dutch "Hoe grooter geest, hoe grooter beest" as equivalent to the English proverb "The better work-man, the worse husband" does not seem to exhaust Kuyper's meaning here. See Rudolph van der Pijl, *English Phraseology; or Dictionary of English Phrases and Proverbs* (The Hague: Johannes Allart, 1816), 508. For this particular rendering, compare Edgar Allan Poe, "Peter Pendulum, The Business Man," *Burton's Gentleman's Magazine and American Monthly Review*, February 1840, 87.

on a high plane in intellectual development while having sunk morally to a very low level.

We must remember that Paul—from whose hand we have the report concerning God's giving up of the nations and the depiction of their deterioration—knew Asia Minor, Greece, and Rome. So he had witnessed both the good political structure and the orderly administration of justice that was maintained, as well as the prosperity and the affluence people enjoyed at that time, together with the high development of trade and commerce, of science and art, which constituted the glory of the time of the emperors. It is obvious that in speaking of the withdrawal of common grace, he cannot have meant a withdrawing of common grace in every area and in every aspect of its functioning. To the contrary, he saw before his own eyes how common grace worked even more powerfully than ever before. And thus his intent cannot have been anything other than that the giving up of the nations "to a debased mind" [Rom 1:28] referred exclusively to the withdrawal of common grace from the nations in the religious and moral realm. In this realm God gave up the nations to a debased mind, and in this realm only, while in many other areas his common grace may never have shone as brightly as back then. §6

The contents of Romans 1 confirm this.

Where Paul describes in detail the disastrous results of this giving up of the nations—that is, of this withdrawal of common grace—he points exclusively to the manifestations of moral decay, unnatural sins, fornication, avarice, injustice, envy, murder, deceit, maliciousness, gossip, hatred toward God, pride, insolence, disobedience to parents, foolishness, faithlessness, lack of natural love, implacability, ruthlessness, doing things against their better knowledge, violating their conscience, and having a desire for evil. These are phenomena that lie altogether in the moral realm and contain nothing that could makes us think of withholding common grace in a variety of other areas. The sin of the nations was their apostasy from God and their falling into idolatry, and for that sin of idolatry God has punished them with the sin of immorality.

But this must not be understood in the sense that these various aspects of common grace functioned separately and without connection to one another. There is most certainly a connection between common grace in the religious and moral realm; but equally a connection between common grace in the moral realm and common grace in the other realms of life. Even after moral deterioration has set in, a nation can continue to flourish for a period of time through the order of the state and the judicial structure, through commerce and trade, art and science. Nevertheless, the moral decay has an unavoidable consequence that finally the body also weakens, health dissipates, the more noble senses in the areas of science and art become dormant, the order is shattered, justice becomes bent, and finally the state itself falters and collapses.

That is what we have seen in the Greece and Rome of that time. The mighty Roman Empire that flourished outwardly still in Paul's day but was inwardly already disintegrating and morally degenerate, ultimately collapsed in every domain and finally perished ignominiously. Therefore, although Paul sees as yet the withdrawal of common grace only in the moral realm, this moral decay also contains a prophecy of a complete giving up of the then-prominent nations. As apostle of the Lord he discusses only the root of all higher human life. But of course, as soon as deterioration in the root of the life of those nations could no longer be denied, it implied that the trunk with its branches was also doomed. And in that sense God withdrew from the nations as such.

# CHAPTER FIFTY-SEVEN

# THE PREFERENCE OF THE GENTILES

*For the sons of this world are more shrewd in dealing with their own generation than the sons of light.*

LUKE 16:8

Reading and rereading Romans 1 indeed confirms the impression that Paul sees a withdrawal of common grace in three distinct stages, a point which now needs to be elucidated further. §1

As we have already noted, the apostle mentions not once but three times, in verses 24, 26, and 28, the fact that God has given up the nations, or, if you will, the Gentiles. This alone most definitely contradicts the notion that has come into vogue especially in our time that the Gentiles gradually climbed from very coarse to less coarse to a more refined idolatry, and thus to a somewhat purer form of religion. According to Holy Scripture, it was not progress but always decline that occurred. In terms of its most profound functioning, common grace has not gradually expanded, but shrunk. God did not draw the Gentile nations closer to himself and join them more intimately to himself, but has gradually given them up to their own debased mind. And this "giving up" of the nations to their own debased mind, which now must be explicated, appears to have gone through three steps: (1) the falsifying of their relationship to God; (2) the falsifying of their relationship to one another; and (3) the falsifying of their relationship to themselves.

Paul identifies idolatry as the cause of God's curtailing his common grace and giving up the nations. They have exchanged the "glory of the immortal God" for the image of a mortal man, of a bird, or of another animal [see Rom 1:23].

That was the root of every evil. The transgression of the first commandment led, as we saw earlier, to the transgression of the other nine.

Even though this idolatry originally had no other purpose than to worship the true God in an image or symbol, as in the case of the calves at Dan and Bethel, all worship of God through an image actually led to making the worship of God unspiritual, and ultimately to transferring the worship of the living God to the mute image.

This then led, under the righteous judgment of God, to the first restricting of common grace, because the relationship in which man stood to his God was first of all falsified in the very worship of that God. Paul shows this in the fact that they then began "dishonoring of their bodies among themselves" [Rom 1:24], which apparently points to the shameful wantonness that was introduced in the worship of the idols, especially in Asia. For the leading thought in all worship is that we must devote our best to our God and must give up to him what is most precious to us. This cannot lead to going astray as long as the worship remains spiritual. But once we move away from this spiritual standpoint, then it is entirely understandable that people begin to say, "The most precious thing I have is my child, so I must devote my child to god." In this way, led astray by this thought, they offer their child to Moloch and let it be burned in the copper stomach of Moloch. Similarly it is equally understandable that a young woman says, "The most valuable thing I have is my virginal honor," and led by this thought she sacrifices her virginal honor in the temple of her idol. This is what happened, and in worship ceremonies such as those of Baal Peor it had become law that young women in that manner, through such an immoral act, demonstrated their veneration for their idol. A mixing of spirit and flesh—that necessarily had to falsify the relationship in which the Gentiles still wanted to place themselves vis-à-vis God. This was a total obliteration of the boundaries that separate the sacred from the profane. Even worse is that this evil, alas, has been seen among Christians for three centuries, as it was repeated in Anabaptism,[1] something lamentably encountered even now, here and there in our country as well, though fortunately only in very isolated cases.

From this first falsification flowed a second falsification, namely the falsification among these nations of the mutual relationship between persons, specifically, the gender distinction. This relationship is anchored in the creation ordinance that humanity shall be *man* and *woman*. True, we stand in all kinds of other relationships to one another, but the splitting of our species into two genders is and remains the fundamental distinction on which our entire society is based. There is therefore no more profound decay of our entire society than when this original distinction and relationship, established by God as foundational, is repudiated and falsified. And yet, once idolatry and unbelief crowd out the worship of and belief in the true God, the necessary punishment follows: a falsification of this *mutual* relationship between persons. Paul indicates this in verse 26, when he says, "For this reason God gave them up to dishonorable passions. For their women exchanged natural relations for those that are contrary to nature," and their men did the same. We must keep in mind here that in those days, this terrible evil had spread insidiously throughout the most developed nations, and especially among their most cultured circles, to such an extent that nobody was ashamed of it but everyone publicly defended it. This abomination certainly has occurred in all ages, also in Christian countries, but then at least it was denounced so sharply by the public conscience that the guilty one had to flee or else took his own life when it became public. But in Paul's day by contrast it had become a fashion that no one any longer considered evil. And how this evil is also fundamentally related to unbelief is best shown by the fact that even today a book coming out of unbelieving circles saw the light of day in which this abomination is again being advocated and recommended.[2] Once again it

§ 2

---

1. Kuyper may have in mind teachings and practices associated with the Münster Rebellion (1534–35), an attempt to set up a "New Jerusalem" in the German city. See also *CG* 1.61.7.
2. There were a number of prominent campaigns for decriminalization of homosexual acts as well as social acceptance of homosexuality throughout the nineteenth century. Perhaps the most famous advocate on the European continent was the German lawyer and author Karl Heinrich Ulrichs (1825–95), who published numerous books and tracts pseudonymously as well as under his own name.

follows the rule of Romans 1:26: When the people leave God, then God also gives them up to this abomination.

§ 3    And then follows lastly the third stage where common grace contracts, indicated in verse 28, that is finally characterized by the falsification of the relationship in which the individual stands to himself, that is, in the falsification of the conscience, described in these words: "they not only do them but give approval to those who practice them."

Between this and the preceding stage there is also a transition, albeit not a fundamental one. Paul does not point out until verses 29–31 that the falsification of sexual life brings with it a total destruction of the moral fabric of society: breach of justice, breach of marriage, breach of temper, covetousness, malice, envy, murder, strife, deceit, maliciousness, slander, gossip, mocking of what is holy, defamation, haughtiness and pride, inventing evil, disobedience, foolishness, breach of promises, absence of the kind of love that even the animals still know, stubborn implacability, and an absence of any compassion—a list of sins that we can hardly hold before the nations sufficiently enough. But in all of this what is being stated is nothing else than that the fabric of society is necessarily wrenched loose from all its moorings once the foundation of the sexual life is falsified. In all this it is the same evil, only manifesting itself differently in its consequences. But the decay reaches a new development through this, whereby ultimately not only does shame disappear but the conscience is so completely falsified that people begin to take pride in evil and to rejoice when they see evil. This is the devilish feature: Not falling and succumbing out of weakness, but from lust in evil, even where people themselves do not seek enjoyment or profit in the evil. It is purely rejoicing in the fact that evil occurs.

These are the three stages in which the curtailment of common grace occurs. Then it cannot withdraw any further until it suddenly vanishes altogether and the man of sin, the son of perdition, is revealed, who will worship the evil within himself as a divine good. He is the instrument of Satan, personally putting himself on the throne as God. But we will elaborate further on this in the next three chapters. At this point we only remind how this withdrawal of common grace does not take place in the same way at the same time among all nations, but in each nation differently and at different times. In the days when Paul depicted for us this withdrawal of common grace in the Roman Empire, the moral life of our Germanic ancestors stood, as we already mentioned, on an incomparably higher level, and the peoples of northern Europe have later for the most part been preserved from sliding into these depths of evil through their transition to Christianity. But it is certain that the nations of Europe north of the Alps are moving toward the same abhorrent stages of moral deterioration and decay if the leading classes persist in their apostasy from the living God and do not desist from their efforts to replace the Christian spirit with the pagan spirit of the Roman Empire in the development of philosophy, in art, and in the general view of life. The evolutionary theory as recently applied to the nations, a perspective coming from Berlin, is already the prelude to such a sad outcome of history. If the dechristianization is not halted, then the same causes must again lead to the same consequences, and God will ultimately give up the Germanic peoples to their own debased mind, leading to their falsifying each of the three fundamental relationships of life. The portents are already announcing their presence.

Meanwhile we must note that common grace definitely does not function only where particular grace is absent, but it also encompasses that part of human life where particular grace exalts itself. To keep the contrast clear, let us contrast Israel with the world of the Gentiles. Applying it to Christian nations today would be too complicated at the moment. The contrast between Israel and the nations is sharply delineated, known to everyone, and of fundamental importance. In Israel particular grace was functioning; in the nations it was not. But this must never be understood as if common grace at that time was extended only to the nations, whereas in Israel nothing but particular grace was functioning. If we view it in this way, we show that we understand nothing of Israel's history, nor of the work of the revelation of God in Israel. We must understand well that in one era after another, the larger portion of the Jews stood spiritually outside particular grace, drifted into idolatry, and died with an uncircumcised heart. But apart from this, it is thoroughly wrong to imagine particular grace as something that stood alongside common grace or replaced it. To the contrary, particular grace always presupposes common grace, and the presence of common grace is the necessary precondition for any functioning of particular grace. Without common grace any functioning of particular grace would be unthinkable. So we must also definitely consider common grace within Israel as one of the foundations of its national life. Particular grace could not be grafted onto the wild trunk of the sinful human life unless that wild trunk was first pruned by common grace.

§ 4

In this connection there is only an apparent contradiction between the notion presented above and the saying in Luke 16:8 that we put at the beginning of this chapter: "The sons of this world are more shrewd in dealing with their own generation than the sons of light." For there is no doubt that the shrewdness of the children of the world is also a fruit of common grace. What is being said here is that common grace is in fact functioning much more strongly among the children of the world than among the children of God. This being the case, we might get the impression that in Israel—they are after all "children of light"—if common grace was not absent, it was still of lesser importance. This would be all the more contrary to our view, since we just stated that common grace is the necessary presupposition preceding all particular grace.

We must therefore not ignore this seeming contradiction. The correct situation must be elucidated.

§ 5 The solution of this apparent contradiction lies in the distinction between the twofold functioning of common grace we pointed to earlier: on the one hand the moral-religious, on the other hand the intellectual-artistic area of our human life. Our soul is one, and all manifestations of life together constitute our human life in its fullness. But we see again and again how every manifestation of life hardly achieves the same development in all human beings. God has created in each human being an artistic sense, but it is undeniable that many people who are otherwise commendable and sometimes even cultured have dulled rather than developed that artistic sense. On the other hand, some art lovers have been so almost totally absorbed in artistic sensibility that they are virtually colorblind in every other area of life, even in the moral area. The same can be said of theoretical and practical intelligence. Individuals who can think profoundly and clearly, in whom theoretical intelligence is highly developed, will often be blind in the religious area, lax in the moral realm, insensitive in the artistic area. Similarly a man of practical intellect, that is, someone who is handy and cunning in business matters, will have smothered all other forms of higher development under this one trait of his development.

So in itself it is not difficult to understand that common grace can function in various ways in these various branches, as long as we don't lose sight of the fact that these various functions are not equal either in value or in significance. For a nation's flourishing, artistic development, no matter how highly valued, is not comparable to the gift of intellectual development. And intellectual development in turn lags far behind the moral-religious force that manifests itself in a nation. The functioning of common grace will be comparatively strongest and most fundamental where the moral-religious life in the fallen sinner is most powerfully protected from total collapse; this functioning will be richest where artistic and intellectual life flourish simultaneously. The functioning of common grace will be weakest where intellectual or artistic life flourishes whereas moral-religious life suffers damage.

If we keep this in mind, then the varied functioning of common grace and the superior shrewdness of the children of the world over that of the children of light immediately becomes clear. The functioning of common grace in the intellectual and artistic realm has undoubtedly been much more pronounced among the nations than among Israel. In Israel art is scarcely worth mentioning when we compare it with the artistic development in Greece. The ancient Egyptians demonstrated practical intelligence, as did the Romans in the period of their flowering, in a much higher sense than the Israelites. And where theoretical intelligence is concerned, the best thinkers in Israel cannot even be compared with the most excellent of the Greek thinkers. Throughout history it remains as it was in the days of Tubal-cain and Hiram. The descendants of Seth lag behind those of Cain in intellectual-practical development, and when Solomon wants to build a temple for God, the master builder for that temple must come from pagan Phoenicia. It is always Moses who would lead God's people, but he is nourished intellectually by the wisdom of the Egyptians.

We must therefore abandon any attempt to elevate Israel above the nations with respect to the artistic or intellectual realm. In this respect common grace functions much more weakly in Israel. The children of the world were more capable and inventive than the children of light. But this lack did not preclude the functioning of common grace among these children of light as well, in that the most noble functioning of common grace, namely, in the moral-religious area, has manifested itself in no nation as strongly as in Israel, as well as in those individuals in whom *no* particular grace had renewed their heart. We can go even further and say that the nonmanifestation among Israel of human development in the intellectual and artistic areas was God's sovereign plan that would allow for a consolidation of common grace in the one moral-religious area. The result shows again and again how a very high development in the areas of art and intellect rather detracts from the pure moral development. Our conclusion is therefore that Israel certainly did lag behind the nations in many areas, but it lacked so little in common grace that Israel alone among all nations rather experienced for many centuries the highest functioning of common grace, namely, in the moral-religious area.

# CHAPTER FIFTY-EIGHT

# THE CONTINUED EFFECT OF DECAY

*Let no one deceive you in any way. For that day will not come, unless the rebellion comes first, and the man of lawlessness is revealed, the son of destruction.*

2 THESSALONIANS 2:3

Must we understand the fact that God has given up the nations, that is, as punishment for their idolatrous disposition has he withdrawn his common grace from them, in the sense that the nations thus punished were in the end deprived of all common grace? Is there no longer any common grace at work at all among the Chinese and Japanese, in our Dutch East Indies among the Javanese and Bataks, or in Africa among the Zulus and the people of Bechuanaland?[1] A fire once lit but no longer contained keeps burning until all its fuel is consumed. So it is with the fire of sin in the nations. If God no longer contains the burning of the fire of sin, then it must continue to spread like wildfire and must end in the destruction of all human life.

§ 1

---

1. Javanese: native people of Java, an island of Indonesia; Bataks: native people of northern Sumatra, an island of Indonesia; Zulus: native peoples of the southern portions of Africa, particularly the nation of South Africa; Bechuanaland: modern-day Botswana in Africa.

On a small scale this is in fact what has happened with numerous native tribes in Africa, who systematically murdered among each other until finally entire tribes vanished from the earth forever. In America almost the entire native population has disappeared and it remains to be seen whether the copper-colored race will not cease to exist altogether. And when we compare the remaining tribes and nations in Asia with the groups that lived there in ancient times and throughout the course of history, then there are not a few that at one time flourished and since have perished. To stay within the boundaries of scriptural history, who knows today what happened to Moab and Ammon, to Amalek and the Philistines? In fact, we can observe that even on a large scale, entire tribes and even entire nations can disappear; in part they have been literally massacred and in part they have been absorbed into other nations, so that it is no longer possible to speak of an independent existence nor of the propagation of the unique character of these former nations. To this extent, therefore, we can say that idolatry leads to moral decay, and that moral decay can lead to total social disintegration, and that when God totally gives up a nation, such a nation perishes and disappears.

Meanwhile it does not in the least follow from this that common grace as such finally withdrew completely and entirely from the nations who as a group had descended into idolatry, had fallen into immorality, and were socially ruined. The resilience that almost suddenly manifested itself in the people of Japan after a sleep of centuries rather gave the impression of the opposite.[2] No matter how great a flood of barbarians and Saracens successively overran ancient Greece and Rome and destroyed existing institutions, these regions are nevertheless still inhabited and bustle with life that is still connected with their ancestry. In Africa, even after all that mutual massacring, there are still millions and millions of native Africans who continue their ancient traditions. Thus it cannot be denied that many perished and disappeared, but it is equally certain that most nations, viewed as a whole, have continued their existence throughout the centuries, albeit in other configurations and in modified mutual relationships, and that the population of the earth, including those who were not baptized, increased rather than decreased.

If it is certain that the complete withdrawal of common grace would in a short time have brought in its train the utter self-destruction of our

---

2. Japan was largely isolated and closed to the West from 1639 until 1868.

human race, then this is sufficient to show how God, even after giving up these nations to a debased heart, nevertheless preserves them from total destruction by means of a much weaker but still very real functioning of his common grace. Even among the most degenerate nations, among the peoples that have gone farthest astray, even among the cannibals, we must therefore never speak of a total absence of common grace. What still maintains them, even in the midst of their degeneration and brutalization, is not their own native strength but exclusively the grace of God.

When Jesus said before his ascension, "Go therefore and make disciples of *all nations*, baptizing them in the name of the Father and of the Son and of the Holy Spirit" [Matt 28:19], this ordinance of the kingdom was based on the assumption that among all nations there still was a measure of common grace at work. In a nation that had been entirely devoid of common grace or had fallen away, any point of contact for the gospel would be lacking, and any mission among such a nation would be unthinkable. To such a nation would be applicable what Jesus said in another context about not casting pearls before swine [see Matt 7:6]. Throughout the centuries, the Christian church, in its sense of duty to carry out missions among all nations without distinction, therefore expressed its conviction that there is still a portion of common grace, no matter how little, even in the nations that have morally strayed farthest. The results have shown that susceptibility to the gospel among some nations is very small, but also that never has a nation been found without a few of its individual members capable of bowing the knee before Jesus and of joining with people of all tongues in confessing his holy name.

§ 2

Moreover, the fact that common grace never withdraws altogether follows immediately from the law and rule of the Noahic covenant, under which since Noah's day all people live and all nations will live until the return of Christ. As we have seen, God made a covenant of grace with our whole human race, and with this entire earthly realm, including the animals. And even though this *common* covenant of grace must be very sharply distinguished from the *particular* covenant of grace unto salvation, the covenant character of this general covenant of grace that encompasses all peoples and nations must not be weakened or misunderstood. It is and remains a covenant, made with solemn vow and firm promise and made forever, for as long as this world in its present dispensation continues. "While the earth remains," as Genesis 8:22 says, this covenant of God with the world and its inhabitants will remain.

Although it appears convincingly, therefore, from Romans 1 that common grace can decrease in degree and effect, nevertheless Genesis 8 and 9 forbid us ever to think of any complete disappearance of common grace before the final judgment. That grace continues throughout all ages and among all nations, and beyond that, in every age and for every nation common grace is the only force that upholds human life in the non-Christianized part of the world. Human life before the flood did not have this guarantee of the covenant of grace. Therefore the human life of that time perished in the flood, and the flood itself was the factual proof that at that time common grace withdrew entirely. But it is the covenant of grace that followed that ensures and affirms to us that this will not happen in the same way a second time, that such a terrible judgment will not repeat itself during this dispensation. It also means that we would literally and audaciously contradict God's witness if we were to speak of the nations that exist now as if they are beyond all grace. That grace is still present. That grace is still functioning. And all involvement of the Christian nations with these declining nations, whether in the political or in the missionary arena, that fails to take into account this functioning of common grace in these nations weakens the work of God and thereby weakens its own efforts.

§ 3    But if on this basis it is certain that the "giving up of the nations" of which the apostle speaks must never be understood as a total withdrawal of common grace, it nevertheless does not follow that this total withdrawing of common grace will not one day take place. The present dispensation of life in this world will not last forever. The history of this world will come to an end at the time ordained by God. Christ shall then return, enter into judgment, and then the hour will also come when the era of common grace, as distinct from particular grace, will be closed off permanently. At that point the Noahic covenant expires and the kingdom of heaven begins.

On the new earth, under the new heaven, there will not be a single knee that does not bow before him nor a single tongue that does not confess his name. Any human life like what now exists and even flourishes somewhat apart from Christ and closed off from particular grace will then be impossible. Naturally it is not the case that what common grace now upholds will then perish. On the contrary, the upholding of what is human will then even pass over into the glorification of all of human life. But after the judgment common grace will no longer function separately from particular grace. Common grace and particular grace will then completely merge, and both will be swallowed up in the revelation of the glory of the freedom of the children of God. Everything that bears within it the life-principle of Christ will then shine in glory, but everything that lacks this life-principle will be given up to its own self-destruction. The only thing necessary for the transition from this earthly existence to the hellish one will be that God withdraws *all* common grace. The only thing remaining to the sinful creature is then his own sinful nature. That sinful nature will then develop in accordance with its nature to the bitter end. And that development of the sinful nature in accordance with its own sinful drive, what else will it be but the life of hell? A night that will never again be interrupted by a dawn.

In this context we must now point to what is revealed to us through Paul about the man of lawlessness, the son of destruction. He tells us in the second epistle to the church of Thessalonica that the return of the Lord will be preceded by the rebellion, and when the rebellion has come, the mystery of lawlessness will be revealed [see 2 Thess 2:1-12]. This revelation of the apostle cannot be understood except in connection with the doctrine of common grace. In the days of our forefathers it was understandable that this statement of the apostle Paul was turned against the Roman Catholic hierarchy. In those days almost every commentary, including the annotations to our Dutch Bible, held to this notion. In those days people wrote that the man of lawlessness, the son of destruction should not be understood as referring to a single, specific individual but to a series of persons who succeeded one another in office.[3] These office-bearers will take their seat "in the temple of God," that is, they will lodge themselves in the church of Christ, in the church of the living God. They will present themselves there as "a god" and will let themselves be honored as a God, showing themselves as being God. Their power will continue until the Lord will destroy them with the breath of his mouth, which was understood to be the pure preaching of the gospel. And thus the way was paved for seeing the fulfillment of this prophecy in the rise of the papacy that assigned itself divine infallibility,[4] let itself be honored with great ceremony, persecuted the church of God to the point of bloodshed,

§ 4

---

3. See SV notes at 1 Thess. 2:3 on the "man of sin" (*mens der zonde*) or "lawlessness" (ESV).
4. The dogma of papal infallibility was formalized during the First Vatican Council (1869-1870), but the backgrounds of the dogma stretch into the medieval period,

and was crippled and broken in its power when finally, in God's sovereign plan, the pure preaching of the gospel went forth again in the days of the Reformation.

It is quite understandable that this interpretation was reached in the sixteenth century. We who are allowed to confess the gospel in more tranquil times hardly comprehend anymore what kind of tyrannical power had been exercised among the nations by the Roman Curia. It was not a struggle merely about certain rights and liberties, but in the fullest sense of the word, a struggle for life. And it is not difficult to imagine what kind of nervous exhaustion befalls a person whose own life and the life of one's wife and children are threatened daily. When the stake is smoldering, every interpretation of Scripture becomes automatically relevant to one's life. Indeed, we would go still further. There was a partial truth in this interpretation. For the apostle himself says in verse 7 that while "the mystery of lawlessness" will be revealed in its fullness at the end of time, "it is already at work"! The full revelation of lawlessness takes place only at the end of this dispensation, but the rule is that its early labor pains will constantly occur in the course of the centuries, so that there is every reason to see also in the Roman Curia, as it manifested itself in that time in dominating the nations, the manifestation of an unspiritual power.

Imagine for a moment the situation that would have occurred if back then the Roman Curia had succeeded in suppressing the Reformation altogether, so that all nations would have suffered the same fate as that suffered at present in Spain, Portugal, Italy, and the South American republics[5]; it is clear that our human life would have collapsed altogether. At present the influence of the northern and western portions of Europe has still had an impact on Spain and other Roman Catholic countries, and this has still kept alive much that would otherwise have perished completely. Even the Roman Curia was forced, through the persistence of the Reformation, to reform itself to no small extent at the Council of Trent. The Roman Catholic Church today is no longer the Roman Catholic Church it was then; in fact, they can scarcely be compared. The evil that was at work back then has been restrained to no small extent.

---

and according to Roman Catholic arguments, to Scripture and tradition in the apostolic age.

5. These are countries where Roman Catholicism remained dominant after the Reformation.

But if we imagine that this restraining had not taken place, and that the Roman Curia, after violently suppressing the Reformation in all countries as it has succeeded in doing in Poland, Spain, and Portugal, could have expanded its power over human souls undisturbed and unhindered and could have reached unprecedented dominance, then it does not take a great deal of imaginative power to visualize the extinguishing of the human spirit and human life that would have resulted in both Europe and America. Imagine North America as a second South America, England as a second Portugal, Prussia as a second Poland, France as a second Spain, and the entire national life in those countries deprived of the influence that even Spain, Italy, and Portugal experienced from the north. Powerful progress within the history of humanity would barely have been possible.

Back then, the evil, the raging of unrighteousness, had definitely come to nest within the Roman Curia. Its triumph at that moment would have been the ruin of Europe and with it the demise of our human life. It is clear that this same evil, that same raging, withdrew from Rome after this and has now come to nest within other powers. To such an extent even that at present the Roman Curia cooperates to no small extent in opposing the ragings of this same evil that have now arisen. But as anachronistic as it is to judge the present Curia on the basis of the Curia as it was back then, as still happens frequently in our circles, it violates historical sense just as strongly when many contemporary Roman Catholics want to prove on the basis of Rome's current behavior that the Curia of the sixteenth century was without blame. This is incorrect to such an extent that the fear cannot be suppressed that, were Rome to lose its counterbalance and succeed in reestablishing absolute power, the same causes would lead again to the same consequences, albeit not in the form of the past, but with a comparable effect.

But even if we concede on this basis that the "mystery of lawlessness" §5 was active throughout the course of history as early birth pangs, and that in the sixteenth century one of those stirrings manifested itself in the tyranny of the Roman Curia, the thesis is definitely untenable that 2 Thessalonians 2:1–12 found its ultimate fulfillment in the Curia. This confuses the birth pangs of evil with the birth itself.

The text itself also contradicts such an interpretation. For the context shows clearly that, according to the apostle, the revelation of the "man of lawlessness" immediately precedes the return of the Lord. The church at Thessalonica lived with a measure of fear that the coming of the Lord lay in the immediate future. People were afraid that the end of the world stood at the door. This confused people's spirits and disturbed the tranquil course of domestic, social, and ecclesiastical life. This is why the apostle writes to this church, "We ask you, brothers, not to be quickly shaken in mind or alarmed, either by [...] a spoken word, or a letter[. ...] For that day of the Lord will not come unless the rebellion comes first, and the man of lawlessness is revealed" [2 Thess 2:1-3]. This permits no other interpretation than that the rebellion and the revelation of the man of lawlessness will occur immediately prior to the return of the Lord. The church at Thessalonica did not have to be alarmed "that the day of the Lord has come" [v. 2]. First the rebellion has to come, and that had not yet happened. This implies, of course, that when the rebellion would be present, and the son of destruction would be revealed, the day of the Lord would be imminent, and then there would indeed be cause for such distress in spirit.

This is a certainty that is made still greater by what is added: You know what is restraining him now. Thus Christ cannot come unless the rebellion comes first. The fact that the rebellion has not yet come "restrains" the coming of Christ. But then it is also certain that once the rebellion has come and the son of destruction has been revealed, nothing stands in the way and the return of the Lord is to be expected immediately thereafter. Saying that in the Roman Curia "the man of lawlessness" appeared already in the seventh century, despite the fact that this condition has already persisted for more than ten centuries, while the return of Christ is still delayed, cannot be squared with Paul's testimony.

Neither must we understand the words "whom the Lord Jesus will kill with the breath of his mouth" [2 Thess 2:8] as applying to the breaking of papal power through the Reformation. Bruising and crippling are not the same as killing. A man of lawlessness who is killed ceases from any activity, power, and influence. Furthermore, the expression will kill by the breath of his mouth indicates a punishing and destroying act of God's power, who will break into the existing order of things in miraculous judgment, even as is added that this man of lawlessness will be killed by the appearance of his coming.

Nor can we concede in this connection, finally, that "the man of lawlessness" should be understood not as a distinct individual, but as a hierarchical series of persons over a period of more than a thousand years. We gladly acknowledge that the Antichrist will have predecessors; neither do we contest that the spirit of the Antichrist is at work long before he appears. But the expressions "man of lawlessness" and "son of destruction" are delineated so sharply and defined so narrowly that we denigrate the clear wording of Paul's testimony if we do *not* think here of a single individual. Thus we consider the interpretation of our forefathers entirely understandable in light of the storm that swirled around their heads, and we also maintain that there were definitely early labor pains of the "mystery of lawlessness" throughout history and specifically back then in the Curia of Rome. Most certainly one of those early labor pains manifested itself in the spiritual tyranny that the Roman Church tried to assert over humanity in the sixteenth century, but the concrete prophecy of 2 Thessalonians 2:1–2 nevertheless refers to an entirely different event, to an event which does not lie in the midst of history, but which will conclude the history of our race and will be followed immediately by the appearance in the clouds of the sign of the Son of Man.

# CHAPTER FIFTY-NINE

# THE FIXED PATTERN OF THE PROGRESSION OF EVIL

*But concerning that day or that hour, no one knows, not even the angels in heaven, nor the Son, but only the Father.*

MARK 13:32

§ 1      The insight Holy Scripture grants us into the things to come does not serve to satisfy our curiosity, at least not primarily. Prophecy is too high and too sacred to be reduced to a kind of predictive skill. When Jesus himself explains the purpose for which the things to come are foretold, then he posits the purpose after rather than before the fulfillment of what has been announced. For he said, "Now I have told you before it takes place, so that when it does take place you may believe." This is a principle that, in addition to John 14:29, we encounter twice more, first in John 13:19 and then in John 16:4. John 13:19 is almost verbatim the same: "I am telling you this now, before it takes place, that when it does take place you may believe that I am he." And in John 16:4 in these words: "I have said these things to you, that when their hour comes you may remember that I told them to you." It certainly does not follow from this that the prophecy about things to come does not have a certain meaning for the present as well. Ancient Israel most certainly derived comfort and strength from the messianic prophecy, and the Israel of the new covenant receives inspiration and hope from the prophecy of the Maranatha.[1] But the significance for the present disappears almost completely, especially with respect to more specific predictions.

No matter how often and repeatedly Jesus pointed out to his closest disciples that, according to the Scriptures, he "must suffer many things and be rejected by the elders and the chief priests and the scribes and be killed, and after three days rise again" [Mark 8:31; see Matt 16:21; 17:12, 22–23], his disciples did not understand, they did not comprehend the prophecy, and it had no effect on them [see Luke 24:1–9]. Even the rather personal prophecy to Peter about his denial before the crowing of the rooster was not grasped by Peter in its prophetic power. Only after the denial had become a fact, and Jesus had been handed over, and it was finished on Golgotha, did the disciples remember that Jesus had foretold all of this to them. And even this remembering happened so falteringly that Jesus himself first had to show the disciples on the road to Emmaus, word for word, how all this had been predicted, and how Moses and all the prophets had announced a Messiah who had to suffer all these things in order to enter his glory [see Luke 24:13–27]. The very specific prophecies about the betrayal and the thirty pieces of silver, the thirst, the purchase of the field of blood, and so much more were even couched in terms that precluded any understanding of these passages beforehand. Nevertheless the evangelist points out again and again that all these things had to happen so that the Scriptures might be fulfilled.

So this is not an incidental comment but a fixed rule of prophetic interpretation. We must not lose sight of this rule when we come to the predictions of the apocalyptic, that is, of the predictions that point to what precedes Jesus' second coming, to the difference that the return of the Lord will make, and to what will follow after the parousia of the Christ. Some pretend that they have the key in hand to interpret those predictions and apocalyptic visions down to the minutest detail and lay bare their meaning so clearly in every aspect that it seems that they could

---

1. *Maranatha* is used here as a synonym for the parousia, or the second coming of Christ. See also *CG* 1.1.1n3.

already now write the history of what will happen only then. This in irreconcilable contradiction to what we have just read coming from Jesus' own lips. The meaning of what Jesus himself has predicted about this, the actual meaning of what both Paul and Peter declare about this, and especially the actual meaning of what is held before us about this in the Revelation of John, will become transparent and clear only when those times will have come. Then, in retrospect, it will appear how that down to its smallest details, the program of what was to come had been outlined beforehand. Not now but only then, in that hour, it will be the sign and proof for God's church that it will not fall prey to powers that annihilate one another, but that it is led by her Lord and King, first in the thunderstorm, then in the storm, and only then in the gentle coolness. And then, in the midst of its suffering, the church will glorify the Holy Spirit who had predicted the course of all these things for centuries. But as long as the hour is still far away and the events do not delineate themselves more clearly, the church of Christ is in the same situation as that in which the disciples found themselves before Golgotha: it must enter into the general scope of things to come, but it must forgo digging deeply into the explanation of the details.

§ 2   This had to be said first also because, in the interpretation of 2 Thessalonians 2:1–12, a curiosity has repeatedly been aroused that seeks to know and search for precise indications where we have been granted only a general perspective on the course of things to come. What this and other apocalyptic revelations contain tells us only that: (1) after Jesus' ascension a spiritual struggle will ensue between the powers of the kingdom and the powers of darkness; (2) this struggle will go through a necessary process; (3) this process will ultimately lead to a great rebellion; (4) that rebellion will end in a terrible manifestation of lawlessness, finishing with the rule of a tyrant; (5) lawlessness will have become incarnate as it were in the appearance of that catastrophic individual, and at the point, when the process cannot go further, Christ will return to settle by his judgment the terrible struggle of heaven and earth.

Add to this that this process will go through many stages, and in each of these many stages "the mystery of lawlessness" will manifest itself in the interim in an analogous manner, so that the church will repeatedly face, in succession, a significant forsaking, an apparent breaking out of rebellion, and a more intimate manifestation of God to his people. This exhausts the primary content of all these apocalyptic revelations. All preaching is erroneous that subordinates these main features to the background in order to divert the church with more specious interpretations that never go beyond guesswork and therefore never can have the effect of strengthening, comforting, and inspiring the church of God.

Understood in this way we must now show the connection between common grace on the one hand, and the course of this spiritual struggle on the other. In itself there is something enigmatic in the fact that after Jesus' ascension this fearful process still had to be endured, by now for more than nineteen centuries already. Apparently the early Christian church was not prepared for this, and the disciples' question about the day and hour when the Messiah would establish his kingdom remained suspended on the lips of many.

From the very beginning, two directions arose in the church. On the one hand there were those who, satisfied with the present, did not feel a need for the return of Christ and who, like so many thousands and tens of thousands of believers today, thought it the most natural thing in the world that the church remained on earth and Christ in heaven. Death took the entire multitude of believers to glory, one after the other, without their crippled faith ever thirsting for the revelation of glory; they envisioned rather the revelation of Jesus' glory in an infinite future, without the cry "Amen, come Lord Jesus, yes, come soon!" ever arising from their soul. These people are reproved by the apostolic word whenever it points to the return of the Lord as the indispensable supplement, the necessary complement of all that preceded. It is over against the spiritual aridity of these complacent people that the words sounded, and still must always be sounded: "The Lord is near, behold, he comes quickly, and his coming will be like a thief in the night."

But alongside and in contrast to this group of satisfied and complacent people who were devoid of any thirst for the return of Jesus, stood quite a different kind of Christian, especially those Christians from among the Jews who feverishly and almost tempestuously pressed toward the parousia of the Lord. For these people, what would happen in the churches on earth was as yet of minor importance. These Christians were heedless of a spiritual struggle that was still to come, that would run its necessary course in fixed stages. They imagined that every struggle had been finished and decided at Golgotha. They knew only one contrast, the one between Israel and the Gentiles.

§ 3

Well then, the coming of the Christ of God had abolished that contrast, which formerly had been to the disadvantage of the Gentiles and to the advantage of Israel. Israel's King had triumphed, and the converts from the Gentiles were kneeling in silent worship before the Messiah of the Jews. What else needed to be done, other than that the King of Israel would descend again from the same heaven to which he had ascended? With the power given to him he would destroy all the raging of the nations, in order that the kingdom of heaven might triumph across all the earth.

The apostolic word had to address them in an entirely different way. It had to be made clear to them that the spiritual struggle was definitely not over, and that all kinds of significant activity of spiritual struggle had to precede the final scene of Jesus' return. They also needed to see how, with the triumph of Israel over the Gentile world, the process planned by God was still so far from being finished that only now for the first time that process could begin to take place in the life of the nations, and in this way only after a hard and bitter struggle in the life of humanity could this process be resolved. While the first group was addressed by the apostolic exhortation, "The Lord is near, behold, he comes soon," the admonition to second group was the reverse: "The Lord is *not yet* coming." It says clearly, "Be not alarmed, as if the day of the Lord has come. For that day will not come unless the rebellion comes first and the man of lawlessness is revealed" [see 2 Thess 2:1–3]. This is a twofold apostolic admonition that gives the superficial impression of contradiction but which is resolved in perfect harmony if we see clearly the two distinct mindsets manifested among the Christians of that time and since then throughout the ages.

Now, even as then, we encounter among believers in the Lord two mindsets. On the one hand, people who scarcely think about the Lord's return, who neither focus on it nor reflect on it, who are quite alien to the Maranatha. As long as they personally die saved, they would think it neither unusual nor unnatural if, after their death, the life of the church on earth would continue quietly century after century. But on the other side we encounter time and again Christians in the church who press toward the return of the Lord with the same feverishness as some Christians in the early church, who would prefer to interpret the signs of his coming in such a way that they could expect the Lord to return still before their death, or at least very shortly after their death, and who remove the struggle of the church entirely outside any connection with history and with the course of human life, and see no reason why the Lord has not come long ago and why he should not come tomorrow.

Well then, the ministry of the Word must speak out just as clearly against both of these tendencies as did the apostolic word in the first centuries of Christianity. To the first must be preached that the coming of the Lord is an indispensable, necessary, concluding act of God's entire revelation, and that the Lord is always near. But the other, more feverish brethren must be healed of their one-sided spiritualism, and they must be told that the Lord is not yet coming unless first the great rebellion has come and the man of lawlessness has been be revealed. They must also be explicitly warned not to see in each temporary apostasy the great apostasy, nor to see in the preliminary activity of the mystery of lawlessness the manifestation of the man of lawlessness and the son of destruction.

Out of a one-sided reaction against chiliasm, the Reformed persuasion had reached the point of permitting the Maranatha on our banner of faith to fade in a culpable manner. And therefore we must praise and thank divine sovereignty that chiliasm has directed us Reformed Christians again forcefully and passionately to that Maranatha. But on the other hand, we must take care that we do not allow this movement to tempt us to fall into the other extreme. Precisely as Reformed Christians we must hold fast to both elements of the confession: on the one hand, that the Lord is coming, and for the eye of faith, that coming is very near; but on the other hand, that the Lord does not come before the process ordained of God finally ends in the great rebellion and in the gigantic manifestation of the mystery of lawlessness that will incarnate itself in the appearance of the terrible man of sin.

What is the cause, what is the reason that first such an intense process must be endured, and that this process must lead to such a dreadful manifestation of sin before Jesus returns? For those who are Pelagian at heart, this is not a question at all. For them, after all, each decision depends on the free will of human beings. If people only willed differently, then tomorrow the whole world would be saved. It is due only to man's unwillingness that it continues to be an uphill struggle for Jesus' church on earth. There is nothing firm here.[2] There can be no question of necessity.

§ 4

---

2. Dutch: *Pijl is hierop niet te trekken.* Kuyper uses *pijl* ("arrow") instead of *peil* ("level," esp. "water level"), a common confusion in Dutch. The image is derived from seafaring, where *peil* refers to the point used to determine the course of the ship. The confusion with *pijl* may come from the image one can associate with it, namely,

A regular and necessary process of things is simply unthinkable. Things proceed as they proceed because the free will of man, which most often ends with his unwillingness, constantly destroys every hope that arises. But there is no single conceivable reason why it would change. God the Lord can cut short the course of world history as easily tomorrow as two hundred years from now. That history is nothing more than the constant monotonous repetition of the same things. The only motive for a delay of the Lord's return can be so that out of future generations some will perhaps convert to Christ.

But this is not the view of those who hold fast to Scripture, including the Reformed Christian. To them God's counsel is revealed. They know that not the imaginary free will of man but the "counsel of [God's] will" [Eph 1:11] determines the course of things. For them it is certain that the end of all things, including the goal of all existence, is fixed in God's pleasure. All that precedes that end can be nothing else than the totality of the means determined by God, which, within the nexus of cause and effect ordained by him, will lead to the final outcome. Just as humanity is by no means equal to the grains in a pile of sand in the eyes of God, but rather constitutes one body, an organism comprised under one head, so too the history of the world is for them by no means a disjointed collection of discrete events. It is rather a well-connected chain, a stream that moves through a streambed determined by God, propelled by the breath of his Spirit.

The biblical Christian sees in the history of the world all kinds of forces, all kinds of spirits, and all kinds of elements that, at the God-appointed time, forge all kinds of connections, collide in all kinds of ways, do battle for supremacy according to a fixed spiritual law, and make their appearance successively in all those forms that their nature and capacity allow, resuming that gigantic struggle each time in a new form. And therefore they understand that a necessary process definitely continues here, one that cannot come to rest before each of these powers and spirits has exhausted the full content invested in them and each has come to full development. And before God is vindicated in that complete development—demonstrating in the result itself what the final end will be of that full development of the powers inimical to God—only when they have

that of drawing back an arrow to shoot at a target. Elsewhere Kuyper uses the phrase with *peil* rather than *pijl*. See Abraham Kuyper, *Om de oude Wereldzee*, 2 vols. (Amsterdam: Van Holkema & Warendorf, 1908), 2:398.

come to full development, will he annihilate those powers of evil and those spirits of lawlessness. "Zion shall be redeemed by justice" [Isa 1:27] and also Satan's fortress will fall with justice, and when at one time it will sound from the lips of angels: *Fallen is Babylon, fallen is Babylon!* then the result itself must constitute proof that God did not cut off Babylon before it could prove its full power, but he destroyed it only when the results had demonstrated that nothing could be hoped from Babylon, that Babylon could not be saved, when at the full-blown height of its development it collapsed as dust and rubble before the majesty of God.

On one of the last days before his death, Jesus spoke the remarkable words to his disciples indicating that of that day or that hour, the hour of the end, "no one knows, not even the angels in heaven, nor the Son, but only the Father," for the Father has fixed the determination of that hour by his own authority (Mark 13:32) [see also Acts 1:7]. The spiritualist and the Methodist do not understand this saying. How can this be? The Father has given all things to Christ, and does he then not know the day and the hour when these things will happen? After all, can he not come when he wants to? The Father has kept this within his own authority?

§ 5

Nevertheless, Jesus says that he does not know that day and that hour, but in this he is dependent on the Father. But Reformed believers do understand this saying. For they have learned to distinguish between the sphere of the Father and our creation, the sphere of the Son and our redemption, and the sphere of the Holy Spirit and our sanctification. For them a light has dawned on how the end of the ages is not determined according to the rule of the work of redemption, but lies determined in the creation ordinance. In that creation ordinance lie the origin and development of all powers and spirits of the human life that set themselves in opposition to God and that in the history of the world will churn against God. And precisely because the end comes only when the struggle between the Spirit of Christ and the spirit of the world will have been fully waged to the end and will have been exhausted, and the complete process of that struggle will have been finished, therefore the foundational determination for that day and for that hour lies not in the sphere of redemption but in the sphere of creation, and consequently the Father has the determination fixed by his own authority. Once we are certain of this, then it strikes us how here, common grace not only has a voice but even takes the lead. For it is only thanks to common grace that those forces and powers of our human life were not smothered in their germ form, but instead saw the possibility of full flowering opened up to them.

# CHAPTER SIXTY

# THE PROCESS OF SIN

*And then the lawless one will be revealed, whom the Lord Jesus will kill with the breath of his mouth and bring to nothing by the appearance of his coming.*

2 Thessalonians 2:8

§ 1     We can speak of both a doctrine and a history of common grace. The doctrine determines what must be understood and confessed with respect to common grace; the history shows us how the functioning of common grace has proceeded until now, how it proceeds, and how one day it will end. Here again history includes prophecy, and prophecy includes history. We must be able to survey in one glance not a portion of the course of history, but the whole course, from the first paradise that once was until the second paradise that is coming. Only then does our spirit find rest when thinking about common grace.

After having traced the historical course of common grace from paradise to Noah, from Noah to Abraham, from Abraham to Christ, and from Christ to the church of the new covenant, we now had to ask ourselves what connection the apostles establish between common grace and the end of all things. And here we found that the apostles on the one hand continually maintain over against the complacent and contented believers the truth of the return of the Lord as the indispensable final act that for the eye of faith always stands directly in the foreground as if it were certain that the Christ would yet appear that very day before the setting of the sun. But on the other hand, the Scriptures equally firmly insert a broad and long history between the ascension and the return by telling us that there is something that restrains the return of Christ; for that reason Christ cannot come as yet; his return is not imminent. First the mystery of lawlessness must have finished fomenting and must have spent its force; and this full development of the mystery of lawlessness will be complete only when the great apostasy will be manifested, and when finally out of this great rebellion the man of lawlessness and the son of destruction will have come. For this is how we find it predicted and presented, not only in the writings of Paul, but also in the Revelation of John. In this final book of the Bible a whole series of events is inserted between the Mount of Olives and the new Jerusalem, and in this book of visions we find the announcement of beginning birth pangs that precede the final manifestation of evil when finally a terrible rebellion and the appearance of the monster who, because he is inhuman, is characterized as beast. It concludes with annihilating that monster and breaking forever the power of Satan who is at work in this monster, by an act of the Lord's power.

There is a direct connection between common grace and this insertion of a long, necessary, and indispensable piece of history between ascension and return, springing from God's counsel. The connection is so close, in fact, that we can say that if no common grace had been functioning, then that piece of history would have been inconceivable, and this broad historical development finds its propellant and motivation only in the existence of common grace. The reason why we have elucidated this point in somewhat more detail and with more emphasis is that until now that connection between common grace and the end of things has been given only very incidental attention.

In order to see clearly the need for this connection, imagine for a moment that no common grace had gone forth and the mercy of our God had manifested itself only in particular grace. What would the situation have become? We can measure this by way of comparison in terms of the condition of our race when the flood came. Not that all functioning and aftereffects of common grace had ceased altogether, but at that time the functioning of common grace had been weakened to such an extent that we can clearly see the direction it would have gone if common grace had finally ceased altogether.

Ultimately, had there been no flood and after that flood no new, powerful emanation of common grace, it would have become a hell on earth, one big insane asylum, a general dulling and brutalization, one great

§ 2

physical and spiritual degeneration into the most hideous diseases and inhuman cruelties, one great universal, mutual self-destruction of humanity. Assume for a moment that even in the midst of such a situation, the function of particular grace had continued. Then that function would had to have consisted in this, that in such a dishonored and self-consuming generation children would have been born here and there who were destined for eternal salvation. But these elect would, of course, not have been able to come to any society of saints, to any worship of God, to any training in godliness, to any manifestation of the church. Their life would have been cut off before they reached the age of discernment, and the entire functioning of particular grace would have remained a hidden work of the Spirit in the heart.

The activities of Israel over many centuries, continuing prophecy, the fruit of the incarnation of the Word—none of this could have happened. The pharaohs would have massacred Israel, the Jeremiahs would have suffocated in the pit, the infant Jesus would have fallen under the sword of Herod's soldiers. Nowhere would a historical development have been thinkable. Neither the people of God nor the church of the Lord would have found a place anywhere to stand. If anything sprouted as a fruit of particular grace and showed itself above ground, it would immediately have been trampled and annihilated as soon as it appeared.

Of course, the hidden power of the Holy Spirit could have regenerated and sanctified internally, and the number of the elect would not necessarily have been reduced, but all this would have been without significance for life on earth. It would altogether have been suffocated by death before it could manifest itself and develop here. If in that situation God the Lord had decided to hasten the conception and birth of his elect, and had regenerated all of these, then there would have been no conceivable reason why the history of the world would have gone on any longer. There would be no single purpose for the continued existence of the world. The end could occur at any moment. The sooner it came, the less shame and self-debasement, and the less scorn for God's holy name.

§ 3     And even this is conceding too much. It hardly needs to be pointed out that in the total absence of common grace—even if we take into consideration only the time since just before the flood—Israel as a nation would never have come into existence, there would not have come a shoot from the trunk of Jesse, and Christ would never have been born of Mary. The entire development of the history of particular grace, to the extent that it would have come to external manifestation, would immediately have been curtailed, and nothing, absolutely *nothing*, would have been conceivable other than the internal working of the Holy Spirit.

On this assumption, not only would no segment of history have been inserted between the ascension and the return, but no ascension and no return could have taken place. All this has become possible only through common grace. It leveled an area of human life of which a sacred portion could be set apart. It produced a place of rest for the Zion of God. It made possible, no less, the appearing and dwelling among men of the Son of God. But even if we do not go this far and assume for a moment that Israel nevertheless would have existed and Christ would have come, and that his ascension would have taken place so that the return was still ahead, then the fact remains that in the total absence of common grace, the mere notion of a history of the church of Christ in its struggle with the world would simply have been absurd. The church would have been massacred in persecution as soon as it began to blossom. The Christian religion would have lacked any point of contact with the life of the world. Any delay in the return of Christ would have been nothing but a pointless prolonging of wretchedness and misery. The long-suffering of God would have found no sphere to manifest itself. And the only conceivable mercy would have consisted in allowing, the sooner the better, the elect to be conceived and born, to regenerate them, to cut them off from all sin through death, and at that point to have the sign of the Son of Man appear in the clouds.

But apart from the indispensability of common grace for all external manifestations of particular grace, we must pay attention to how common grace explains why lawlessness will ultimately manifest itself in such a terrible way in the "man of sin" or the "son of destruction." For even if we assume that without common grace it would also have come to a monstrous manifestation of lawlessness, this fearsome mystery would never have manifested itself in this particular form. For the form of that manifestation in one great apostasy and the appearance of the man of sin will be caused precisely by the functioning of common grace. The lawlessness would in any case have manifested itself terribly, both with and without common grace, but only common grace gives it this refined form.

§ 4

We see this phenomenon already in preliminary indications. By virtue of his animal instinct, Cain understood quite well how to kill Abel, even when common grace had not yet led to a higher development of human skill and to a richer development of human knowledge. Even as the tiger knows quite well in which spot he has to strike his claw to hit the heart of the buffalo, so Cain knew how to hit Abel so that he collapsed in death. But how entirely different murder has now become, when the poacher can shoot the game warden with a shot from a double-barreled carbine at a distance of hundreds of yards. There has been war on earth as long as groups of people with conflicting interests opposed each other. But how significant is the battle of Abraham with Aner, Mamre, and Eshcol against Chedorlaomer compared with a war tragedy like what took place between France and Germany in 1870?[1] Do we need further indication that on the one hand only common grace has brought about this finer human development in knowledge and skill, but that, even as it has blessed, it has also increased a hundredfold the means of annihilation and destruction in crime as well as war? Thus it has already lent, and will increasingly lend, to the manifestation of lawlessness an entirely different, much more highly developed form.

§ 5        In the middle of [the nineteenth] century the leading spirits (within our country a man like Opzoomer[2] foremost) deluded, entirely in good faith, the children of our nation into believing that a better development of schools would automatically turn the tide of crime. For every new school that sprang up we could close a cell in the prisons. In itself this contained a measure of truth. Illumination through knowledge, if applied appropriately, can restrain the degeneration of a nation. Such is the salutary power of every development in the sphere of common grace. But what these otherwise such bright minds forgot is that that same common grace, because it operates in a sinful world, and thus also impacts unsaved persons, places its weapons at the disposal of evil as well as of virtue. This is why the results were so disappointing.

Christians in their sphere did benefit from it, but in the hideouts of crime, in the circles of reckless dissipation, and in the marketplace of chicanery, that high development in knowledge and skill has led to—could only lead to—nothing but refined abomination, more skillful fraud, more poisonous ideas, and more cunning sin. The law is beginning to realize

---

1. Kuyper refers here to Franco-Prussian War (1870-71). On the French side, over 17,000 men were killed or wounded; on the Prussian side, 8,300.
2. Cornelis Willem Opzoomer (1821-92) was a Dutch jurist, philosopher, and theologian. He was a professor at Utrecht University from 1846 to 1889. Among other things, Opzoomer advocated for universal public education and was a proponent of positivist philosophy.

its increasing powerlessness over against this more skillful, better armed, shrewder evil. Superior power can be placed over against raw violence, but what can be erected against an ingenuity and a cunning, against a skill and a wiliness, that simply laugh at the naïveté of the law? Recently a nobleman, dressed in the latest fashion and wearing kid gloves, in broad daylight rang the doorbell at the house of a wealthy widow in a busy neighborhood in Paris, a highly civilized city. He entered the house, rendered her insensible with the contents of a flask, strangled her, took her goods and her money, and quietly disappeared. This type of murderer would be entirely inconceivable apart from common grace. The development and refinement must, thanks to common grace, first have reached a very high level to make such a type possible.

We observe the same phenomenon in every sphere. It remains the same sin, century after century, in its essence always equally inimical to God and devilish in origin, but its development and the forms in which this sin manifests itself keep pace with the general development of life. Murders are different today than they were in the past; but we also swindle one another in a more refined manner today. Robbing and stealing occur more covertly and unnoticed; people go on a spree with tons of gold belonging to someone else and "disappear" at the right moment with a first-class ticket in the most sumptuous cabin of a floating palace. In the past a thief stole a hundred, sometimes a purse of a thousand guilders. These days people are barely satisfied with a systematic swindle that has its eye on tons of gold at a time.

In the realm of divorce, fornication, immorality, all kinds of natural and deviant sins, the most outrageous theories are presented in the most attractive, love-breathing form, and refined sins are made possible by means of publicly displayed artificial devices. False witness is no longer, as it was in the past, merely a calling of names or jeering after someone on the street or in alleys, or pasting a libelous rumor on a wall; today it is a far-flung system of mocking and scoffing journalism, and we even see a woman's hand lend itself to promoting the evil rumors of others in smart, seductive book form. Covetousness has been developed into a system that dominates all of life, fed and stimulated by advertising without parallel and by displays in shop windows as if the shop had become more than a palace. We see ostentation and pomp everywhere; and under that constant stimulus, cupidity is extolled as the passion of energy and as the means to advancement.

COMMON GRACE • VOLUME 1

And so it goes in the most literal sense in every area. Common grace always continues raising the standard of our social life, enriching our knowledge, multiplying our human skill, refining our way of life, making life easier, more enjoyable, freer, and through all of this our power and dominion over nature ever keeps increasing. But also, by the same measure, common grace better arms sin, making it more ingenious in its devising, more multifaceted in its manifestation; the mystery of lawlessness has ever more means at its disposal in every realm of life, cloaking itself in forms that increase the power and allure of sin immensely.

§ 6    This same phenomenon manifests itself equally in that elevated realm where the thoughts of man concentrate in the great center from where life is explained and life must be governed. For also in this realm sin is as old as the world. The sin against the first table of the law was born even before the sin against the second table of the law. But also that sin was in the past more powerless, precisely because of its uncivilized and superficial form. It resulted in a curse, in blasphemy, in idolatry. But since common grace increased man's intellect a hundredfold, and also in this area the means at man's disposal kept multiplying, the curse changed into an atheistic system, blasphemy into a godless theory of life, idolatry into a lifeview that glorifies man and bans all faith. The most capable thinkers, the best intellects are the ones who today ponder and reflect on the sin against the first table of the law, who peddle the fruit of their godless chase in beautiful tomes, and who are as a result honored, feted, believed, and extolled even after their death.

This then is the manifestation of the "mystery of lawlessness" at the center of life from which the whole will be viewed and then dominated. It is not the least unpleasant fruit of the misuse of common grace that it sharpens the resistance against God and his Word, and strengthens the enmity against Christ and his church. And all this proceeds along the lines of a fixed process, following a line that was determined beforehand, obeying laws that, though we know them less, are equally as firm as the laws of chemistry that show us the combinations and transformations of substances. The one necessarily gives birth to the other. One consequence stimulates and pushes toward the other. We can show this process from the past; demonstrate how today it follows a similar path; and prophesy on the basis of this the path it will follow in the future; only, each time it is refined, in a more powerful form, better integrated, but dominating the whole of our human thinking. In our human self-awareness it becomes ever more the dethroning of the living God, feeling first like God, omnipotent, ruling everything, constraining everything, until finally mysticism also begins to merge into this self-awareness in order to arrange also a new, ordered worship for the newborn god of our human self. First the worship of the genius, then the praise of the virtuosi, and later the offerings brought to him who is mighty and great.

And this continues until the end, until finally it cannot go further. All human thought has then exhausted itself on this long road, so that the self-deification of man has become absolute; and in the end the fruit of this refined sinful development is ripe, and only then can it happen that the full-blown result of this process will ultimately be embodied in the person of one all-powerful human being, and that mighty, all-dominant man will be the man of sin, the son of destruction.

And then it is finished.

Then sin, which falsifies everything, spoils everything, turns all that comes from God ultimately against God, has misused the full harvest that was gathered in the field of common grace as a treasure with which it has strengthened itself against God. Then the mystery of lawlessness will reach its end in that one terrible man, it will be completed, and will have come to its full manifestation, and therefore it will ultimately not be able to do anything else than turn the whole power of the world against Christ and his people and his church. Days of trouble for God's church on earth, which, if these days were not shortened, would even draw the elect along into the apostasy [see Matt 24:22, 24].

But those days will be shortened.

It is then between that all-powerful man of sin who rules the whole world and Christ, to whom the Father has given all power in heaven and on earth. And because it cannot go any further, and a further delay of the final judgment would therefore be meaningless, the Christ of God will then end the drama of world history, destroy the man of sin by the Spirit of his mouth, and appear himself gloriously in all his saints.

# CHAPTER SIXTY-ONE

# THE FINAL JUDGMENT

*Fallen, fallen is Babylon the great! She has become a dwelling place for demons.*

REVELATION 18:2

§ 1     The "*man* of sin" is someone other than the devil in person. With the appearing of Satan the insulting drama of unrighteousness *begins*, but the *man* of sin appears for the first time in the concluding scene [see 2 Thess 2:1–12]. Even Judas is not yet "the son of perdition" [John 17:12]. His abomination was followed by throwing down the pieces of silver as an acknowledgement of betrayal, by fleeing, and by suicide, whereas the man of sin will be a being that defies and withstands God, a man who sinks away into the lake with scorn for God on his lips. Of course, his inspiration for that will come from the Evil One, but that inspiration from Satan will nonetheless come to expression in human shape, in human form, with human powers. It will be a phenomenon that Satan cannot produce apart from our human race. Even where the book of Revelation mentions the beast and the image of the beast, this doesn't eliminate the human character of this abominable phenomenon. The terms "animalistic" and "bestial" refer here not to a kind of animal, but to humanity in its deepest degradation, that moves beyond the bestial in its animosity. Now, that man of sin was unimaginable in paradise, shortly after the fall. That man of sin could not appear in the days before the flood. Nor yet in Pharaoh's time. Nor yet when Judas betrayed his Lord. Nor yet when ancient Rome vanished. Nor yet when the September massacre defiled Paris.[1] Nor yet now, and not yet soon. That man of sin cannot come before the development of the powers embedded in our human race, these hidden gifts and talents, will have ascended to their highest level.

Mere wicked intention, pure enmity against God, does not suffice here. The powers, the means, the instruments for waging battle must be readied in order to make possible the influence of this wicked intention. And this was not the case in paradise, or in Noah's day. That development of human power can occur only gradually, and can arrive in its fullness only at the end. How could human power of more than three centuries ago compare with the power of our human life at the end of the nineteenth century? In our day the spirit of science predicts the rise of altogether different powers and capacities before the new century dawns. That's how it continues to progress, and will continue to progress until the end, until that last point is reached beyond which it cannot go, when *every* hidden power is discovered, released, regulated, and fully harnessed. Only then will that terrible man be able to rise up, who, as though uniting in one hand all the threads of these various capacities, will wield them apart from God, will direct them against God, and will harness them as if he were God. If we were to take common grace out of play, that development of human power would never arrive, the arena for that development would be missing, and everything would return to chaos. Therefore it is the case that only in the appearing of the man of sin, the final scene of the drama of common grace will be played out.

Were we to ask whether the phrase common grace is not self-contradictory in being called "grace," ending as it will by leading to the strongest manifestation of sin, then we will need to distinguish astutely at this point. The cross of Golgotha is and remains the highest point of particular grace, and nevertheless it was on Golgotha that human wickedness was

§ 2

---

1.  The September massacres of 1792 were "violent and murderous attacks on prisoners in Paris by Revolutionaries fearing an allied invasion of Paris combined with a counterrevolutionary inspired insurrection." The massacres spread to areas outside of Paris as well. "At Paris, of a total of 2,600 prisoners, between 1,100 and 1,400 died, among them 82 Swiss and Royal Guards, 223 priests, and somewhere between 49 and 87 other political prisoners." See S. Lytle, "September 1792 Massacres," in *Historical Dictionary of the French Revolution, 1789–1799,* ed. Samuel F. Scott and Barry Rothaus, 2 vols. (Westport, CT: Greenwood, 1985), 2:891–97.

manifest most atrociously. Is this a contradiction? We know better. Well then, there is nothing different here. In the complete development toward which our human life and human power over nature gradually advance under the protection of common grace, God is glorified. It is his divine plan, his work, that comes to expression. *He* is the One who sowed all these capacities in the field of human nature. Apart from common grace, the seed buried in that field would never have come to the surface, would never have flowered. Thanks to common grace that seed germinated, emerged, grew tall with its stalks, and will one day stand in full bloom, to the praise not of man but of God, the heavenly Husbandman. The artistic work of God that Satan wanted to destroy will then be complete after all, and will finish its completion. When it is finished, the world will glorify God as Builder and Chief Architect. What in paradise was a mere bulb will then be in full blossom. Except that just as through sin man abused paradise and therefore had to be driven out, so too the man of sin will one day attempt to turn this entire system against God, and hence be consumed by God through the Spirit of his mouth.

§ 3     This leads us naturally to discuss the judgment, and we must examine common grace in connection with that. Here we will not consider a portrait of this judgment like the one Jesus provides us in Matthew 25. That prophecy sketches for us with two broad strokes simply the fate of those who have lived before the Christ of God in a genuinely spiritual relationship, or in a false pretended relationship. That prophecy pertains to the judgment at its midpoint, related to belief or unbelief in Christ, and in that context there is naturally no talk of common grace. In Matthew 25 it is only love shown toward the saints for the sake of Christ that forms the test for eternal weal or woe. But things are different in the book of Revelation. There we find not only prophetic indication of what lies in the foreground of the judgment, but also apocalyptic identification of what will constitute the background of the judgment, and it is precisely this that touches upon common grace.

In that context Babylon is the chief focus. Not the Babylon where Israel went into captivity, but the Babylon that is always relocating, always surviving, always changing its appearance. The Babylon of Isaiah's day represented world power, and was the chief city of the great world empire that constituted at that time the consolidation of everything belonging to human art, human power, human wisdom, human wealth, that had been invented by means of human ingenuity and combined in one concentrate.

For that reason Babylon became the figurative name referring to that consolidated world power itself. For that reason as well, in Jesus' day the real, essential Babylon was no longer the ancient city of Nebuchadnezzar, but the city on the seven hills, the great world city of Rome's emperors. That is why later, singer after singer applied the name of Babylon to Paris. And that is also why it can be claimed as a generalization that now, with the faster concourse between countries and the increasing universalizing of global living, that name of Babylon no longer refers strictly to one particular city but to world power in its universal expansion. Just as in Isaiah's time the features for the image of Babylon were derived from the city of Nebuchadnezzar, so too in the book of Revelation those features were drawn from imperial Rome; these features nevertheless serve, both with Isaiah as with John, to portray the same image that this world power as such both displays throughout the ages and will again display at its consummation in the last day.

The question in this context is: Which image will it be? Will the Babylon involved in the last judgment display the features of an untamed barbarity, as when sin manifests itself in its lower stages of development, whether in our back alleys or among the uncivilized tribes of Africa? Or will that latest Babylon in the day of judgment have led human development to the apex of refinement and well-rounded unfolding? If the former, this would then mean that common grace had extinguished its glow. If the latter, that would then be the proof that common grace will advance until the end, spreading splendor throughout our human life, making that life radiate from the inside out. What do you think? §4

Open your Bible to Revelation 18, where Babylon's fall is prophesied for us. Already back in Revelation 14 the prophecy of the approaching end went forth when the angel sang and called out: "Babylon is falling." But here in chapter 18 that fall has happened. God's messenger who will accomplish the judgment descends from heaven; the splendor of his appearance radiates throughout the earth, or as it literally says: "the earth was made bright with his glory" [v. 1]. He begins to call out: "Fallen, fallen is Babylon the Great! She has become a dwelling place for demons" [v. 2]. The separation now takes place. The complete division between church and world is accomplished. "Come out of her, my people, lest you take part in her sins, lest you share in her plagues; for her sins are heaped high as heaven, and God has remembered her iniquities" [vv. 4–5]. Arrogantly, in self-sufficient pride, that world power still rages against God: "In her heart she says, 'I sit as a queen, I am no widow, and mourning I shall never see'" [v. 7b]. Precisely then her doom "will come in a single day, death and mourning and famine, and she will be burned up with fire; for mighty is the Lord God who has judged her" [v. 8].

Here we truly have the portrayal of this consolidated world power at the very moment of its final defeat. And what kind of portrait is spread out before you? This is no wild power, but a "mighty city," the image of a well-ordered and tightly integrated power. "Alas! Alas! *You great city, you mighty city*, Babylon! For in a single hour your judgment has come" [v. 10]. In that city there glistens all the grandeur "of gold, silver, jewels, pearls, fine linen, purple cloth, silk, scarlet cloth, all kinds of scented wood, all kinds of articles of ivory, all kinds of articles of costly wood, bronze, iron and marble" [v. 12]. In that city everything will carry the scent of "cinnamon, spice, incense, myrrh, frankincense," there will be abundant stores of "wine, oil, fine flour, wheat," filled with "cattle and sheep, horses and chariots," and its residents walking around as those whose bodies are clothed in finery and whose minds are richly developed ("full of bodies and souls of people") [see v. 13]. There is in rich abundance "the fruit for which your soul longed," "all your delicacies and your splendors" [v. 14]. "Seafaring and business" [see v. 17] will flourish and blossom into a prosperity never known before. Wealth will predominate, the kind that dazzles everybody, and costly riches will set the tone. With hypnotic melodies the purest and finest music will drown out every complaint. There will be "the sound of harpists and musicians, of flute players and trumpeters" [v. 22]. Practitioners of every art will glorify human life. Especially in the evening hours, when the lights have been lit, the glory of this Babylon will shine forth. Witchcraft will supply life with a mystical glow. It will be one great banquet and one great feast. The voice of the bridegroom and of the bride will sound without stopping. That is how this great Babylon will radiate upon the earth, and thus this great Babylon "is laid waste in a single hour" [see v. 17].

§ 5    As a way of foreshadowing, such judgment was repeatedly executed upon every consolidation of world power that might for a time have been called Babylon, but then failed. That's what we see with Nebuchadnezzar's Babylon, that's how Pharaoh's empire failed, as well as the Rome of Caesar Augustus. People sensed something of this when part of Paris went up in petroleum fires some twenty-five years ago, and the residents of that city fed on rat flesh.[2] But still, all of this was merely the *foreshadowing*, fore-shadowing that would recur, but all of this was not yet the destruction of Babylon as such. In that foreshadowing one sees Babylon falling, only to rise again somewhere else, and to regain her power.

By contrast, what the Revelation of John prophesies to us is not a *temporary* vanishing of that world power, nor its defeat in a particular locale. No, rather its entire, final defeat, such a defeat that it would no longer exist afterward. For "so will Babylon the great city be thrown down with violence, and will be found no more" [Rev 18:21]. Here judgment will come in a single hour. All those who loved her will mourn, but a cry of jubilation will sound forth from God's angels and from the saints upon earth, for God's judgment will be evident in that event. For when Babylon is laid waste, then under her foundations, deep in the earth, will be found "the blood of prophets and of saints, and of all who have been slain on earth" in their fight and struggle against the ungodly world power [Rev 18:24].

With this we have answered the question put earlier. At the moment of her defeat, Babylon, that is, the world power that has developed on the basis of human life, will display not the image of a raging horde, of bestial barbarity, but on the contrary, the image of the highest development of which human life is capable. The finest forms. The richest blossoming of wealth and glamor. The fullest effulgence of everything that makes life radiant and resplendent. From this we know that common grace will endure until the end, and only when that common grace will have made every power embedded in human life to flourish, then the man of sin will find the sleek arena of his cultivated power, and then the end will be near, then the judgment will come, not gradually but suddenly, in a single day, in a single hour.

Naturally in this context one must distinguish between the two very different operations of common grace. Common grace operates in the entirety of our human life, but not in an identical way in every part of this life. There is a common grace directed to the internal part of our life and another part of common grace is directed to the external dimension of our human life. The former operates everywhere that civic righteousness, family loyalty, natural love, human virtue, the development of public conscience, integrity, fidelity among people, and an inclination toward piety

§ 6

---

2. Kuyper refers here to the fires and petroleum scares of the Paris Commune conflicts with the French Army (1870–71).

permeates life. The other part of common grace manifests its operation when human power over nature increases, when invention after invention enriches life, faster concourse between countries arises, the arts flourish, the sciences enrich our knowledge, the enjoyments and delights of life multiply, when a glow comes upon every expression of life, its forms become refined, and life's common features grow in their attractiveness.

But at the end of history both of those operations will not come to complete flourishing in the "great Babylon." The glory of the world power that will be defeated in the judgment will exist only in that second kind of development. The enriching of life's external features will go hand in hand with the impoverishing of life's internal qualities. The common grace that is at work in the human heart, human relationships, and in public customs will gradually shrink and become less, and only that other operation of common grace, the one that enriches and expands the human mind and human senses, will find consummation. It will be a most beautiful and white painted sepulcher, but for the one who opens it, full of dried and stinking bones of the dead. The most splendorous life on the outside, with death in the heart. That is the Babylon that will ripen unto judgment. Everyone who compares the effulgence of human life now with the dullness of life in the preceding century knows where things are heading, and what kind of judgment he needs to register about that hitherto unknown rich development of our external human life.

§ 7  Actually it must be admitted consequently that the common grace of the one side assists the development of the world's sinful power, and thus also the power of Satan. Among the wild uncivilized tribes, sin is terrible, but their barbaric unrighteousness still displays a far more limited power of sin than our civilized society. At its root sin is equally wicked in both spheres, but in the atmosphere of barbarity, sin cannot grow as fully from this root. Knowledge increases power, and therefore the power of evil as well. Wealth as such contains a magnification of sin's power, one that undermines whatever has remained solid within humanity and predisposes humanity for moral turpitude and degeneration. Satan knew this, and so when he tempted Christ in the wilderness of the Transjordan, he pointed the Son of Man not only to the kingdoms of the world, but also to "all their glory," and added, "for it has been delivered to me, and I give it to whom I will" [Luke 4:6]. Jesus even called Satan "the prince of the world." For that reason, our fathers from of old continually insisted that those confessing the Lord should keep themselves far from the maelstrom of wealth, knowing that Satan's poison swirls in wealth and whoever dabbles in it will be infected with that poison. Theirs was a summons to seriousness and sobriety that in our day cannot be repeated loudly enough. In his kingdom Satan has indeed been enriched by common grace.

Had common grace not intervened between both of these in paradise after the fall, then the development of our human life would have been as good as finished. Over against nature, the human person who had been completely ruined inwardly would have been as good as powerless, and sin would have broken out only in lunacy, murderous inclinations, and barbaric, bestial impulses. Only common grace has enabled sin's development at a higher rate, in more refined form, in an abundance of ramifications, in breathtaking forms of power. The Evil One sneaks into everything human, in order to steal it for himself and to rob it from God. He tastes this already with particular grace. The question, "Are we to continue in sin so that grace may abound?" [Rom 6:1], together with the entire antinomian movement, especially the abominations seen and experienced among the Anabaptists of Münster, are and were neutralized through nothing else than the opposition of the Holy Spirit.[3] Theirs was therefore an attempt that never succeeded any more than partially and temporarily, one that is arrested repeatedly and therefore cannot lead to any culmination.

But this is entirely different in the arena of common grace. In this arena that attempt must succeed and persevere and lead to a final outcome, precisely so that it may be evident that common grace impedes but does not extinguish evil, that common grace offers us a crutch in order to hobble along, but does not repair the ankles and knees—in short, that common grace can be of help for this life but is never saving, nor does it make the transition into eternal life. It is precisely that sneaking of Satan into the work of common grace that seals the indispensability of particular grace for the believing heart.

---

3.  The apocalyptic Anabaptist community of Münster, Germany, was formed in 1533 and soon took control of the city. The community rejected existing secular and ecclesiastical authorities, practiced polygamy and the community of goods, and crowned their leader, John of Leiden, as king on the throne of David. In 1535, the city was retaken by military force and the leaders of the movement were later executed. See Karl-Heinz Kirchhoff, "Münster," in *The Oxford Encyclopedia of the Reformation*, ed. Hans J. Hillerbrand, 4 vols. (New York: Oxford University Press, 1996), 3:97–98.

The world always opposes the church with its claim that if the cultivation, civilizing, and refining of life simply continues, then the end must come, our incompleteness is overcome, and the perfect man triumphs at last over sin and misery. If the opportunity to achieve such a cultivation, civilizing, and refinement of life had been cut off for our human race, humanity suffocated by sin could cry out: "Were our time and strength permitted us to evolve and be civilized, we would have arrived apart from the grace of God and would have needed no Savior." But now they cannot. They were given time; they were afforded the opportunity. Their evolution had already made giant strides; their civilizing eliminated all barbarity; their refinement astonishes the imagination. And if the outcome of this century is nothing else than that despite all this rich evolution, the old sinner remains a sinner and the human heart regresses instead of becoming more pure, then we sense that there is no salvation to be found along this route and on this path. And if things continue this way until the end, and evolution and civilizing have reached their zenith, so that thereby opposition against God will ascend and increase in equal measure, until one day God himself causes it to dissipate with the breath of his mouth, then when all is said and done, the end will consist of having the outcome of world history provide a single testimony for the indispensability of particular grace, and the culmination of things will glorify the Christ of God as the only true Savior of the world.

# CHAPTER SIXTY-TWO

# THE ABIDING PROFIT

*They will bring into it the glory and the honor of the nations.*

REVELATION 21:26

A final question arising in this context is this: With the destruction of this present form of the world, will the fruit of common grace be destroyed forever, or will that rich and multiform development for which common grace has equipped and will yet equip our human race also bear fruit for the kingdom of glory as that will one day exist as the new earth, under the new heaven, overflowing with righteousness?

As everyone immediately realizes, this question is not without importance. If nothing of all that developed in this temporal life passes over into eternity, then this temporal existence leaves us cold and indifferent. Everyone without an appetite for eternal life will then advance in terms of that existence, but everyone seeking a better fatherland will be unable to feel any affinity for it. After all, one day everything will be gone, unlike the caterpillar that is wrapped like a chrysalis in order later to appear in more exquisite form as a butterfly, but instead like a stage on which a series of performances were exhibited but after which nothing remains but an empty floor and unsightly walls. By contrast, if that rich and variegated development of our human life contains something that passes over into eternity, then the temporal obtains abiding significance, and everyone seeking a better fatherland will feel entitled and compelled to set a portion of his heart upon it.

In this connection immediately we place in the foreground our denial, in the nature of the case, of any gradual process whereby what came into our possession by science, technology, inventions, and so on, would transfer automatically and in their current form into the kingdom of glory. Holy Scripture firmly teaches us that the present form of this earth will perish, that the elements will be found to have burned, and that the existing arrangement of the cosmos will be broken "with a great roar" [see 2 Pet 3:10]. "The form of this world passes away along with its desires" [see 1 John 2:17]. So we readily admit that a gradual transition, a genuine development, whereby the new order of things would emerge out of what exists now, is unthinkable. One day there will be an unspeakable catastrophe that will consume the entire cosmos, and along with it there will be an immense change in the arrangement of sun, moon, and stars. Not a single human writing, not a single human work of art, will transfer from the existing situation into the new one. First everything that exists will perish, and only then the new order will emerge out of that apparent chaos. There can be no difference of opinion about this among those who bow before the authority of Holy Scripture. "But the day of the Lord will come like a thief, and then the heavens will pass away with a roar, and the heavenly bodies will be burned up and dissolved, and the earth and the works that are done on it will be exposed" [2 Pet 3:10]. All these things will perish.

No, if anything transfers from the one to the other situation, this can be nothing else than the hidden life germ, the foundational significance of things; and on the new earth something akin will need to emerge from that germ, but something of a higher order and with richer glory. We know what happens with dahlias, tulips, fern bulbs, and the like. First they had spread out, sprouted stems, and produced blossoms; but then came the cold of winter, and the farmer cut them off one by one at the root, removed the bulbs from the ground, and stored them. Once the longer days of springtime arrived, the same farmer brings those bulbs out again and entrusts them once more to the ground, bulb after bulb, and soon a plant appears that was even more beautiful than the one last year. Here, then, we see the return of the same life, a richer life than the previous one; for as the fruit of earlier life, the fern plant grows up more powerful and thick. We see the same thing with young fruit trees. Every winter the tree is stripped of its leaves and flowers, so that nothing but bare wood remains; but every spring the wood grows luxuriantly once again, and the onset of its fruit is more plentiful than last year.

In this way it is very conceivable that with the perishing of this world, the entire foliage of common grace, if we may put it this way, will be stripped and removed, and nevertheless with the flourishing again of the new earth, the germ of this common grace will bud luxuriantly, the better to flourish precisely as the fruit of earlier development. Or if you would like another metaphor, recall your childhood games and their relationship to your life as an adult. Of course those games were play, and nothing more. At one point all that playful living goes away and all the toys are put in the corner, until no eye sees them anymore. But still anyone familiar with this realizes that one's character comes out in that playing, and how that childhood playing helps shape and nurture us, so that later when the adult man or adult woman labor in their larger life calling, the fruit of their childhood games, if these were guided properly, also comes to expression. So too, one could say that here on earth we did little else than play, but nevertheless, when our toys are one day destroyed, the fruit of this playing whereby we developed will be seen in eternity.

To prevent misunderstanding, let us distinguish in this context between the constituent parts of our human life and the development to which those constituent parts succumb or will gradually succumb in this earthly dispensation. For those constituent parts of our human life do not arise from common grace, but from creation. Together they constitute everything for which God supplied human nature when he created it. In themselves they constitute not the life of common grace, but natural life. After all, we must recall that had sin not entered the world, all these constituent parts of our human life would have continued, with even more beauty and abundance. It is altogether obvious that these inalienable and inseparable constituent parts of our human endowment, of our human nature, and of our human existence, transfer together into eternity. Were this not the case, then in eternity we would simply cease being human. If we will be human beings there, just like here we were born and exist as human beings, then it is absolutely necessary that these various constituent parts of our human life transfer together into eternity. §2

Our churches confess this in the doctrine of the resurrection of the flesh. The human being consists of soul and body. At death a person leaves his body; but at the resurrection of the dead a person's soul is reunited with his body, and Christ will transform the body of his redeemed child "to be like his glorious body, by the power that enables him to subject all things to himself" [Phil 3:21]. So first the body departs. It is dissolved.

It decays. But the invisible germ thereof continues to exist, and we receive our body again as a more glorious body. The description in 1 Corinthians 15 is sufficient and decisive here. In that sense, it must be said that in the same way, all the factors, all the powers, all the elements belonging to our human nature or to our human essence by virtue of creation, will emerge the second time, although with more abundance, versatility, and glory.

This is certain, even apart from thinking of common grace. Take, for example, a human baby who died at birth, and who happened to be elect. That human child experienced no contact with common grace in its broad development, and still that infant will also one day experience the return of his body lost so early, and will appear one day much more gloriously in this renewed body. Entirely apart from any operation of common grace, this fixed axiom continues to operate, whereby everything that constituted what was human according to creation will belong to the essence of humanity also on the new earth, though in more luxuriant form and in a situation of more exalted glory. We are not discussing that at this moment. But we are discussing the claim that thanks to common grace, this arrangement of our human powers and capacities reaches a certain level of development here on earth, in order then to pose the question whether this development that has been attained already nevertheless vanishes without leaving a trace, or whether a certain fruit of this prior development will be carried into eternal life.

§ 3    Even if this were not the case, then it would in no sense follow that this preceding development was purposeless. Even if we were to eliminate all the fruit that common grace would produce for eternal life, the fact still remains that common grace retarded Satan's vandalism, made human life possible on earth during all these centuries, provided the church on earth a place to stand, and disclosed the beauty of the work of creation, regardless of Satan. Personally it should be added that God is powerful to cause his elect who died in infancy entirely separated from common grace to come to fruition perfectly in eternal life. Among those elect who died early, there is undoubtedly a number of richly gifted geniuses, being of the highest order, who are capable of the highest and richest flourishing. One day our eye will be surprised that the multitude of the perfectly righteous on the new earth will be so enriched with such exceptional persons, drawn in large number from those who died early.

Even among those who came to fruition on earth and were then taken away, we have known so many of whom we wondered why God took them away; but if we could have seen or guessed what lay within those young toddlers, our surprise would have been even greater. This must be added with emphasis, so that any presumption might be cut off of attempting to bind the possibility of a rich future development to the preceding development on this earth. We absolutely refuse to do that. Rather we heartily acknowledge that much of what did not come to fruition here could emerge there in great abundance. This is something that we confess as a possibility for those afflicted with diseases that are not their fault, for the mentally handicapped or people with other physical deformities, people who in this life were arrested in their development by physical defects, like deaf mutes, and in part also the blind.

No, the issue currently under discussion involves primarily and principally the question of our communal human development, as that came about already here on earth thanks to common grace. Two otherwise equal people, the one living in this country in the tenth century, the other in the nineteenth century, were quite different and divergent in their development, simply because the communal environment in which they grew up was so entirely different. The same difference between two otherwise equal persons must be admitted even when both live in our century, but the one in Tehran in Persia, and the other in a richly developed city like London. Even in the single city of London and in the same time period, the difference between two otherwise equal people is still surprisingly great, depending on, for example, whether the one became a lamplighter and the other grew up in the family of a rich and influential statesman.

This is sufficient to make clear that the personal and the communal development within our human race are two different things. Personal development, involving nature and character, has been rather uniform throughout the centuries; but that communal development, which is the fruit of common grace, progresses steadily. [This progression is] by no means always holy. [Rather it is] often very unholy. True enough, but it progresses nevertheless in this sense, that in our nineteenth century in every arena of life the power of man over nature, the knowledge of situations, the means of community, the enjoyments of life, and so much more, have advanced so incomparably further from the preceding century. Whether that progress will continue, no one knows, but neither can anyone prove the opposite, and everyone must admit the possibility that before the Lord's return, that is, before the end of the world, a still far more rich development of the communal life of humanity than we now experience will be realized. Precisely this development would have been absolutely inconceivable apart from common grace, and is due to common grace alone. With an eye to this, the question arises whether this perpetually advancing development of humanity's communal condition will simply collapse and disappear and vanish in the culmination of the ages, or whether a fruit will emerge from this as well for the kingdom of glory.

§ 4    In connection with this, attention needs to be focused on what we read twice in Revelation 21, in these words: "and the kings of the earth will bring their glory into it" (v. 24, repeated in v. 26). Twice this is brought to our attention. The entire thought contains this: "I John, saw the holy city, the new Jerusalem, descending from God out of heaven; and the city does not need the sun and the moon to shine in it, for the glory of God illuminates it; and the peoples who are saved will walk in its light; and the kings of the earth bring their glory and their honor into it; and its gates will not be closed by day, for there will be no night there; and they will bring the glory and the honor of the nations in; and nothing will enter it that is impure or commits abomination and speaks lies, but those who are written in the book of life belonging to the Lamb" [see Rev 21:2, 23–27].

It is not talking here about any period preceding the end, but of the final outcome itself, as will be displayed after the conclusion of the judgment, as an abiding new situation. Following immediately after these words is the last chapter of Revelation, and the ceasing of every vision. Concerning this new, abiding situation it is said that all who sin or are impure, or speak lies, will be locked outside [see Rev 21:27]. As Revelation 22:15 repeats the idea, on that new earth there will be no place for "sorcerers and the sexually immoral and murderers and idolaters, and everyone who loves and practices falsehood" [see Rev 21:8]. To the extent that sin was interwoven and embedded in common human development, all of that is destroyed and perishes. But nonetheless it is added just as clearly that in this new situation will enter something of great importance from the life of the nations, that is, from the former life of humanity. And what is carried in from that preceding development of our human race into that kingdom of glory is called the glory and the honor of the nations.

What we should understand by this is not doubtful. Even now there are nations on this earth who bathe in honor and glory, while other nations are virtually devoid of honor and glory. Nations like England and Germany, to mention only two, are just as high in honor and glory among the nations as the nations of Afghanistan and Sudan are devoid and almost entirely bereft of honor and glory. In general one can say that with respect to honor and glory, the Christian nations far surpass the pagan and Islamic nations; even among the Christian nations it may be considered as established that the nations lying in the northern part of Europe and America surpass the more southern nations in honor and glory. England surpasses Spain. The United States far outpaces Venezuela or Argentina. Even as in our century such variety is obvious to everybody, so historically it may be established that ancient Egypt and Babylonia surpassed the Moabites and Elamites, and that the Greeks and Romans outshone the Persians and Carthaginians in honor and glory.

In this way we see that honor and glory indicate the degree of general development achieved by the nations in the course of history. Nothing need be exempted from this. It pertains as much to their development in the field of familial and social life as it does to political organization and jurisprudence, to science and art, to heroic courage and leadership, to economic activity and business, in short: to everything that taken together constitutes the power and the honor of a nation, and indicates its place among the most developed nations. As long as we understand, as the statement itself requires, that honor and glory are not intended to refer to an individual nation or to a single period, but that honor and glory are mentioned here as the possession of the nations, throughout the entire course of their history, then we may interpret this to mean nothing other than the progressive communal development that our entire human life achieved and will achieve in the history of the nations. And we are told that this profit, which of course is nothing else than the fruit of common grace, does not simply perish and is not simply destroyed in the universal cosmic conflagration, but such profit will have an abiding significance for the new Jerusalem, that is, for the new earth, for this honor and glory attained by our human race will be carried into this new Jerusalem.

Now we understand, as we used the word a moment ago, that carrying §5 in is not meant literally. No book, no work of art, no product as such will be transferred. "All these things will perish" [see 2 Pet 3:11], just as the corpse is entrusted to the earth, and the entire body becomes the prey of maggots and worms. But, says Paul, even though all things pertaining to our body will perish, nevertheless our body is like a grain of wheat. Something from it will germinate, and God will supply that germ with a new body [see 1 Cor 15:42–44, 53]. Entirely in the same way we have to imagine that all the forms in which the fruit of common grace blossoms now will one day perish, but the powerful germ that lies at the foundation of all of these things will not perish but abides, and one day will be carried into the new kingdom of glory, and God will supply this all with a new form that is in sacred harmony with the glory of his kingdom.

The outcome is that the centuries-long life of humanity, quite aside from bringing the elect into existence, will not pass away with no purpose. Apart from common grace our human life on this earth would never have attained any development. Now, under the dominion of this common grace, such human life has developed its significance not only for our present existence, but leads as well to an unfolding of human power and of capacities God created within humanity, which have importance also for eternity and have their significance for the kingdom of glory on the new earth.

This agrees entirely with what Paul says to the church of Christ: "All things are yours" [1 Cor 3:21], not only the messengers of God like a Paul or Peter, but also the world, also life, and not only the future but also the present things. For the fruit of the honor and the glory of the nations that will be carried into the new Jerusalem will exist not for those of the world, but only for Christ's redeemed, since they alone will appear on the new earth. What Jesus declares in the beatitudes, that the meek are blessed for they will inherit the earth [see Matt 5:5; compare Psa 37:11], is to be understood in no other way. It cannot mean that God's children will one day possess a naked earth, that is, merely fields, vines, and orchards. Those who inherit the earth must receive that earth into their possession together with everything that came into existence upon that earth to enrich it and increase its value. So then, in this life God's children must watch while those whom Scripture calls "the nations" steal for themselves that earth with its treasures belonging to the development of human life, and God's children, who are "the meek," have to tolerate this and acquiesce to this. But one day things will be reversed, and on the day of days it will be clear that the nations have done nothing else than work for God's children, since all the fruit of the labor of the nations will be thrown into the lap of the redeemed. What Scripture says about the property of the pagans being ours [see Exod 12:33–36; 2 Kgs 7; compare Matt 12:29], and about "the glory of the nations like an overflowing stream" (Isa 66:12), is misused by sinful greed in defending slavery, or in approving a budget surplus political policy for the sake of maintaining a colonial power like ours.[1] But anyone reading Scripture by the light of the Spirit understands this differently and understands it better. It is rather the case that all the nations together will lead the development of humanity to its highest point, and one day that honor and that glory of the nations will be carried into the new Jerusalem unto the glory of God and for the redemption of God's children.

---

1. The Dutch were one of the great colonial powers of the modern era, with interests ranging from the Americas to Indonesia. Typically these colonies were viewed as sources of prestige and profit for the colonizing powers, and the "colonial budget surplus policy" referred to an attitude in which the interests and well-being of the colonies were made "entirely subordinate" to the interests of the Netherlands. See Cornelis Fasseur, *The Politics of Colonial Exploitation: Java, the Dutch, and the Cultivation System*, trans. R. E. Elson and Ary Kraal, ed. R. E. Elson (Ithaca, NY: Southeast Asia Program Publications, 1994), 56. For an example of Kuyper's specific critical engagement with Dutch colonial policy, see the chapter on "Overseas Possessions" in *Our Program: A Christian Political Manifesto*, trans. and ed. Harry Van Dyke (Bellingham, WA: Lexham Press, 2015), 293–330.

# CHAPTER SIXTY-THREE

# FRUIT FOR
# ETERNITY

*For their deeds follow them.*

REVELATION 14:13

§ 1    The human development as fruit of common grace in the life of the nations taken in general has this deep significance for the "end of the ages," that "the honor and the glory of the nations will one day be carried into the new Jerusalem" [see Rev 21:26]. This conclusion automatically leads, however, to the next question, whether the *personal* development that each of God's children on earth individually owes to common grace accompanies them into eternal life, or disappears forever in the grave. In brief we respond to this second question with a testimony from the same book of Revelation: "Their deeds follow them" [Rev 14:13]. The fruit of common grace divides naturally into two parts. On the one hand, a universal fruit that emerges in the life of the entire human race and thus within the nations, concerning which it is said: "This honor and glory of the nations is carried into the coming Jerusalem." On the other hand, a special, particular, personal fruit that emerges in the life of the individual children of God, concerning which it is said: "Their deeds follow them." No other interpretation is possible than that the personal profit acquired for the formation and development of persons and characters here upon earth, also in civic life, is not simply lost and does not simply die off, but transfers into eternal life.

The entire sentence in which this testimony appears proves that this is the only possible interpretation of these words. A voice from heaven was heard. We read: "And I heard a voice from heaven saying, 'Write this: Blessed are the dead who die in the Lord from now on'" [Rev 14:13a]. It doesn't say, and we are unable to determine, whether this voice came from an angel, from Christ, or from one of the redeemed. It is sufficient that this voice contains a revelation from God to his people. That revelation includes two things. First, those who die in the Lord, that is to say, who die in living faith-communion with Christ, will from now on enjoy a blessed situation. The question whether this phrase, "from now on," refers generally to the time after Jesus' ascension or is to be understood in a narrower sense regarding those who die when the end is near, need not be discussed any further, and would distract us. Suffice to say that in our opinion, these words are to be understood to mean that after death, time ceases to afflict us, so that in this way the end of the ages would have occurred just as quickly and immediately for Stephen, one of the first to die after Jesus' ascension, as for those who will die in the last days. In the existence of eternity, a thousand years are as one day.

Meanwhile the main point relating to our subject lies in the second part of the testimony quoted above. We read, secondly: "'Blessed indeed,' says the Spirit, 'that they may rest from their labors, for their deeds [works] follow them!' " [Rev 14:13b]. Two things are being said here. There was labor for them on earth, and as fruit of that labor they obtained a work. This is just like a pupil who first devotes his exertion and effort to finishing his task, but then comes that culmination: when his task is finished and his labor is completed, then he takes his work along to school, his work follows him, and when he enters the classroom, his teacher says: "Let me see your work." Labor and work are related to one another just like the effort that one expended and the fruit that this effort and exertion produced. Expanding on this expression, the Spirit is saying, first, that the effort is ended at death, for they will rest from their labor. The eternal Sabbath dawns for them. But second, that their work, that is, the fruit of their labor, the profit obtained, does not remain behind, but goes with them and follows them. Any other interpretation is to be rejected. This verse especially cannot mean "the *reward* for their work follows them." Not only would this interpretation incorporate a doctrine of merit, which all of Scripture contradicts, but it means this as well: When one acknowledges, along with Scripture, that God does give a reward, not on the basis of merit but on the basis of grace, then it is obvious that the reward awaits them in heaven and comes to them from heaven. One cannot say of the reward that it enters heaven with them, or follows them as they enter into heaven. What follows them is the result obtained on earth, the profit obtained on earth by means of their effort, the fruit obtained on earth thanks to their effort. That result, that profit, that fruit goes with them into heaven, and for that they receive God's gracious reward in heaven.

§ 2    There remains only the question whether this profit, this fruit, this result has in view only their spiritual growth in a more narrow sense, or their common personal formation. Revelation 14:13 surely tells us nothing in answer to this question. The answer depends exclusively on another question, whether our spiritual and our common human development are two outcomes existing alongside each other or whether they are interwoven and have grown together. If they exist alongside each other, if the monastery idea were correct, and if piety consisted in becoming separate from common human life in order to seek redemption in a separate, intentional, one-sided, and exclusively spiritual formation, then this twofold result would be the answer. This position renders common human development worthless, and invests value only in what bears a specifically spiritual character. In large measure this is the same position taken by the Anabaptists, and following them, in part by the Methodists.

By contrast, one who confesses what the Reformed have confessed throughout every age—that our life is one, that the leaven must not remain lying alongside the dough but must be hidden within it in order to permeate and saturate it, and in this way true piety resolves our living before God and our living in the world into a higher unity—such a person cannot permit any separation to intrude here. No division may be permitted here. Our personal formation and development are the fruit of the entirety of our lives in our occupation, in our family, in our neighborhood, in the house of prayer, and in the prayer closet. Our effort and our labor in serving God extend across our entire lives. Our business is a divine calling just as much as our inner life follows a divine calling. The works that result at the end of our lives from this effort and from this labor proceed from the entirety of our earthly existence, both to the extent that this fruit arises from common grace and to the extent that it was animated by particular grace. If, therefore, the words, "and their works follow them," are to be understood to refer to the profit of our lives that enters with us into eternity, then this cannot but include the fruit of common grace for our personal life.

Meanwhile the objection deserves to be considered that arises from §3 the case of babies dying in infancy who could not share in the spiritual struggle within history. After all, this phenomenon is indisputable. Young children die by the thousands and tens of thousands, who faded early before they could experience the struggle of life. Too little attention is paid in Christ's church to this inestimable multitude of young children who received baptism after being born in the covenant, and then closed their eyes forever. People are gradually beginning to see that this innumerable multitude will constitute an important element in the eternal kingdom; firm hope may be nurtured especially for the salvation of these little ones. The number of the elect that we surmise, on the basis of our impression of things among adults, to appear to be so small could one day expand very remarkably precisely with the number of those children of the covenant who passed away early. Well then, those thousands and tens of thousands neither performed any labor nor expended any effort on earth. So for them there exist no works that would be able to enter with them into eternity as the result and fruit of that exertion and effort. It is not true of them that they rest in their labor, nor is it true that their works follow them into the glorious kingdom of God. How then, so people ask us, can you account for a personal fruit of development among those who died as adults, if this numerous multitude of children who died early and were saved early will be entirely devoid of this fruit and would thereby forever lag behind the others?

Our reply to this objection lies near at hand. Admittedly, if these children who died young cannot carry into heaven any fruit of their earthly development, then it follows that they similarly lack the spiritual development of adults. An infant who dies in the cradle dies without ever hearing God's Word, ever having stammered the name of Jesus, ever having known his atonement, ever having prayed a prayer, or ever having raised one song of praise in honor of God and his Anointed. If we want to conclude on the basis of their lack of development arising from common grace that therefore they will eternally lag behind, then we must conclude simultaneously that they will also eternally lag behind when it comes to spiritual delight. Yet we do not claim that. On the contrary, we admit that with the Lord our God there are other ways to introduce these children who have died young into the knowledge of Christ and into his redemptive work, and to supply their spiritual formation that they need for taking delight in their eternal salvation.

Therefore we acknowledge that with God there are *two* ways to bring his elect to this delight: the one that lies open for those who endure the effort of living upon earth, and the other that lies open for those who have never known this effort of living upon earth. If this is so, then pray tell, what is left of this objection? If the Lord our God has his own way to supply in these children who died young the deficit resulting from the lack of spiritual development upon earth, why wouldn't this same God have his own way to supply these children who died young with a personal formation equivalent to what we adults can acquire here on earth along the route of effort and struggle? The fate of those who die young and of those who live long on earth is certainly completely different, and the path of their contribution diverges entirely, but nothing prevents there being one and the same end, and that our God caused them to travel along two different paths both of which nevertheless end at the same point.

This claim can be fortified further by the obvious consideration that an unusually sizeable difference exists among those who wrestle on earth for a time with the struggle and effort of life. The one comes to conversion in his youth and afterward lives for more than fifty years, while another comes to conversion at a much later age and in such cases is often called out of this life shortly after his conversion. The difference consists in this, namely, that the first had fifty years for his personal formation, whereas the other had perhaps only a few months, barely a few weeks for walking the path of sanctification. Would that second person for that reason actually have to lag behind the first one? Would the inference be that an early death necessarily included an eternal attenuation of salvation? We think that no one would accept this vicious conclusion.

Consider a moment the difference presented by the opportunity to exercise oneself in struggle and effort that exists among various people. Compare a martyr with an ordinary church member who in a remote village throughout years of peace and tranquility quietly minds his business. What a training school for the one, and what absence of training for the other. Compare a man gifted with deep knowledge and having much time at his disposal for digging deeply into the mysteries of the kingdom, with a poor widow who, in order to obtain bread for her children, slaves and toils from early morning until late at night, happy enough simply to read a portion of God's Word before falling exhausted to sleep. Infinite variety. Variety in everyone's effort and labor, and connected to this are completely divergent "works" for everybody. Completely divergent as well, therefore, with regard to what enters into eternity with the one and with the other.

Must we infer from this that as a result, the least fortunate on earth will in eternity perpetually lag behind? One would argue that the parable of the rich man and Lazarus leads us to presume the opposite, and if we may also apply to this discussion the parable of the laborers in the vineyard, then the axiom also applies that many who are first will be last and many who are last will be first. Everyone entering the kingdom will receive payment of a full day's wage [see Luke 16:19–31; Matt. 20:1–16].

The conviction that God is able to have those who lagged behind social- §4 ly or spiritually here on earth nonetheless share in the full enjoyment of salvation, was so firmly held by our Reformed ancestors that they were instead seduced into claiming that life here on earth was indifferent, and thereby they defaulted from giving full play to the firm declaration of the Word that our Father who is in heaven would reward openly those who gave alms in secret [see Matt 6:3–4], and that those disciples who for Christ's sake had forsaken everything precious and valuable that they possessed on earth would receive it back a hundredfold on the day of glory, and would sit on thrones and judge the twelve tribes of Israel [see Matt 19:28–29]. Of course, this oversight is mistaken. For the sake of one truth of Holy Scripture we may never set aside another portion of its revealed truth. We must incorporate within our confession the *entire* truth of Holy Scripture. If we do this, then Scripture compels us to acknowledge both of these: (1) that on the one hand, the fruit and profit of what is obtained in terms of common human and spiritual development enters into eternity along with us; and (2) that on the other hand, God the Lord is able to supply the deficit for those who missed the opportunity on earth, due to early death or a more sedate course of life, to bring the sheaves into the barn, and is able to enrich them like the others.

An indication of this twofold route is not lacking in this life. To men- §5 tion but one concrete example immediately: Our churches have legislated that two kinds of people will serve as leaders in the church. On the one hand are those who have devoted themselves to the ministry by means of extensive exertion and effort, the fruit of which effort they demonstrate in their examinations. But on the other hand are those who give evidence of possessing singular gifts, quite apart from that exertion and apart from that effort. That regulation of our churches was very wise, and the outcome has demonstrated that along this second route the church is often blessed with men who, in terms of profitable fruit for the churches, surpass those traveling the first route. And what is the difference? On the one hand, long years of effort, an immense amount of time, very high costs, and on the other hand, neither effort not time nor financial cost. What they possess they received directly, and its fruit is occasionally excellent. Here we have a distinction that we prefer to use because it corresponds in so many respects to the difference between those who die as adults, having devoted all the exertion and effort of earthly life, and those who died young who were spared all of that, concerning whom we nevertheless confess that God will perfect them along an entirely different route and in an entirely different manner.

This difference cuts across all of life. It is the difference between those who achieve through much effort and study and practice, and those others who received talents and genius apart from devoting any effort, who nevertheless occasionally outperform those who put forth concentrated effort. The contrast between wisdom and prophecy, on the one hand, and erudition and science, on the other hand, rests upon no other distinction. Solomon had never crammed nor studied nor taken exams, and he was wiser than everyone else in the East, and Isaiah provided godly insights and perspectives that went far beyond the study of every school that existed in his day. Indeed, one can observe this twofold path of God among adults already. God permits the one to sweat and work, and he supplies the other already in the cradle or as though while asleep. Certainly we are not going too far if we use the standard of this very difference to explain the distinct development and formation of those who died as adults and of those who died already in the cradle, with an eye to their significance for the kingdom of heaven. If we assume that those who died young belonged to that second group to whom God gave singular gifts and in whom he created talents and genius, then there is nothing at all strange in our thinking that they were spared the exertion and effort of training, and that they will still be able to shine like the stars in the heavens.

§ 6    In this way we maintain the rule of Revelation 14:13, that when we die in Christ, although at death our effort and our labor cease, our works, that is, the fruit, the profit, the result of our labor enters eternity along with us. In addition, since our effort and our labor involved both the arena of common grace and the arena of particular grace, not only our spiritual but also our common human profit survives our death and grave. Moreover, the doctrine of the resurrection of the flesh prevents every kind of assumption that in this life, only salvation would possess special spiritual significance. The life of our body definitely does not belong to the arena of particular grace, but most certainly to that of common grace, and yet we all confess together on the basis of God's Word that the body too will be restored to us in eternity. Along this route as well, it is established in this manner that we neither can nor may permit any excluding of what belongs to common grace.

Indeed, we would go still further, and would never dare to argue that §7 those who had borne the daily grind on earth would for that reason have a certain privilege above the others who had been spared that heat of the day. Most assuredly their works follow them, and from those works flows a gracious reward. But this hardly excludes the possibility that in his sovereignty God the Lord can bestow, in a different way and along a different path, upon those who did not bear this heat of the day, a salvation that is just as closely connected to a personally complete formation that is applied to them in another way.

In this context pay close attention to the act of sanctification in death. Our churches confess that "our death is not a payment for our sins, but it puts an end to sin and is an entrance into eternal life."[1] This contains an act of sanctification. Until our death we have to run the course, and train ourselves through struggle and wrestling, to sanctify both our character and our person. But it is likewise true that even the holiest in this life will never possess anything but a small beginning of this perfect holiness. Therefore Paul longs to be redeemed "from this body of death" [Rom 7:24].

From God's side, this is how sanctification is perfected in two stages. First, he has us walk in the works that he has prepared for us [see Eph 2:10], and in this way through struggle and wrestling he enhances the sacred dominant tone of our character already here on earth. But the first act of sanctification forever remains merely partial. Then follows in death this second act of divine sanctification, that at death he cuts away sin from our heart once and for all and in this way completes our sanctification. Those who die later in life would still be completely unsuited for entering heaven if that entrance into heaven depended exclusively on the fruit of one's development obtained upon earth, and would have to be the exclusive privilege of those who had undergone persecution. On the contrary, the result obtained on earth attains power only if and because God functions as an intermediary in the hour of death with a miraculous act of

---

1. Heidelberg Catechism, Lord's Day 16, A 42.

sanctification, and perfects at once what in them until now had reached only a small beginning.

The fact that by dying too soon many missed the opportunity before their death to attain this small beginning, makes no principled difference between them and those who died as adults. The sanctification of both comes from God, and in such a way that the one receives here already a small beginning in this sanctification and the completion thereof only at death, while the other who misses that small beginning receives everything at once at the time of death. For us who look at the matter from this side of things, this makes a very big difference. An infant who dies without ever having known sorrow, trouble, and disappointment, and a graybeard who after a painful and troublesome wrestling for three-quarters of a century finally lays his weary head to rest, to our way of thinking are not to be seen as belonging in the same category. But seen from God's side, from the position of eternity, this matter looks entirely different. What are seventy or eighty years, when they pass by like a watch in the night, compared to the eternity of our God? And what is the small beginning of sanctification that is achieved by the best of believers here on earth, compared to the infinite perfection that is weighed in the scale of the sanctuary?

So there is nothing of privilege involved here. Upon both those who have borne the daily grind here on earth and upon those who merely budded only to fade, God in his sovereign plan can bestow through a miraculous act of his Spirit perfect sanctification at death. Only do not permit that equality to cause us to lose sight of the difference between the paths. Those who did not endure the daily grind have no works to follow them. Those who have borne the daily grind most definitely have works that follow them.

# CHAPTER SIXTY-FOUR

# THE COHERENCE BETWEEN THIS LIFE AND THE FUTURE LIFE

*When I was a child, I spoke like a child, I thought like a child, I reasoned like a child. When I became a man, I gave up childish ways.*

1 CORINTHIANS 13:11

The idea that the fruit that common grace bore for the entire life of the nations comes along into eternity, is taught by the testimony from heaven, "that the kings will bring the honor and the glory of the nations into the new Jerusalem that descends from heaven" (see Rev 21:26). The same is taught by another testimony, which tells us that "the works of the redeemed will follow with them" to the other side of the grave (see Rev 14:13), that the fruit of common grace is not lost for the individual person, but abides eternally. At this point we need to examine one final question in this context, namely, whether and to what extent Holy Scripture illuminates for us the connection that will exist between the operation of common grace in this dispensation and its fruit in future eternity. Naturally we know nothing about this by ourselves. Experience cannot assist us in

§ 1

this regard. Pure guesswork provides no certainty. If Holy Scripture tells us nothing about this, then we know nothing about it. In any case, it is only Scripture's revelation that can lift a corner of the veil, at least for one who believes Scripture.

Now there is one declaration by the apostle Paul that sheds light at this point. We are referring to what he says in 1 Corinthians 13 about the passing away of present knowledge, and our receiving an entirely different kind of knowledge in eternity [see 1 Cor 13:8–12]. Suppose that as the fruit of common grace, a child of God attained on this side of the grave such exceedingly broad knowledge, such clear insight, and such sharply tuned judgment. Thanks to that knowledge, on this side of the grave he attained a far higher position of personal development than the mariner tending the mast, a servant walking behind a plow in the field, or a weaver running the bobbin through the threads in a loom. Now suppose the thinker, sailor, farmhand, and weaver die. Here's the question: On the other side of the grave will that proficient, expert, refined thinker have any advantage beyond the other three, or will they all be equally perfect in eternity?

This is a deeply penetrating question that can be replicated in various forms. One person hardly knew any trouble and struggle, the other knew nothing but trouble and struggle and through them developed strength of will and patience. Over here a simple person dies, whose path was lined with roses; over there a soul wastes away in death as though persecuted by grief and sorrow and pain, but who was trained through such suffering. And we can expand this list. At every point, differences in life's fate, in aptitude, and in course of life, and the different life histories resulting from these, yield differences in the development of person and character, of will and intellect, of feeling and perception, among virtually everybody who has died. If at death we could weigh the spirits spiritually, we would see variation among them all, aside from their position in grace and development through grace, in terms of their personal value that was governed in part by common grace. No two would be equal.

And this leads to the question whether death equalizes that difference, or whether on the other side of the grave, just as here, a certain difference in wingspan will emerge. Note well, we are not asking whether this difference will continue perpetually in eternity. This would lead us to entirely different considerations. What we are investigating at the moment is only this: if two people die on the same day, whose relationship as far as their personal development is concerned we could assign a number from one to ten, whether both of those persons will stand at the same point on that scale of one to ten when they open their eyes in eternity, or whether in eternity they will both be equal, not with respect to their salvation, for we are not discussing that now, but with respect to the wingspan of their personal development.

If we peruse what Paul says in 1 Corinthians 13 about knowledge pass- §2 ing away, then at first glance it seems as though the question we are asking is to be answered in the negative. For we read: "For we know in part and we prophesy in part, but when the perfect comes, the partial will pass away" [1 Cor 13:9–10]. Earlier he had said, "As for prophecies, they will pass away; as for tongues, they will cease; as for knowledge, it will pass away" [1 Cor 13:8]. Viewed superficially, the issue appears resolved. If prophecy, tongues, and knowledge pass away, then they profit us nothing with a view to eternity, whether on this side of the grave we benefit others with prophecy, tongues, and knowledge, and are completely equal to another person who possesses neither tongues nor prophecy nor knowledge. Compare this to having money. One person dies rich, another dies poor, but since the rich person must leave his money behind and exit the world naked, in eternity the multimillionaire is completely equal, as far as money is concerned, to the man clothed in rags. If the principle that at death property and the possession of money and goods pass away applies to the possession of tongues and prophecy and knowledge, all of which also pass away, then the principle also obtains here that one who is rich in knowledge will, on the other side of the grave, be completely equal to the one who died as someone impoverished in knowledge.

It is not relevant that 1 Corinthians 13 is talking about spiritual knowledge belonging to the arena of particular grace, and not about common human knowledge and development that arises from common grace. Formally one and the same law obtains for that spiritual and that human knowledge. If spiritual knowledge that we acquire here passes away in the grave, then it follows a fortiori that our human knowledge will not survive the grave. Then it would appear that at death, our spirit will undergo such a sudden change that what lies behind us will have evaporated in the mist and an entirely new horizon will open before us; and this will occur in such a manner that between the horizon of this life and that of eternity, there exists no connection that we can observe. If the apostle had declared the opposite, that spiritual knowledge accompanied us into eternity, even then it still would not follow that common human knowledge slipped through the grave into eternity. But when he declares that spiritual knowledge passes away, then it does follow logically that nonspiritual, worldly knowledge, if we may express it this way, also produces no profit for eternity.

If the apostle's formulation that our spiritual knowledge *passes away and ceases* was supposed to be understood to mean that, just like our goods and money, it was entirely cut off from us at death, then no other conclusion would be possible than that nothing whatsoever of our common, human knowledge would be transferred along with us into eternity. Then at death our consciousness would be entirely erased; we would awaken in eternity with an entirely blank, untutored, uninformed consciousness, and in eternity our consciousness would receive entirely new content.

§ 3    Further investigation shows most clearly, however, that we neither may nor can interpret this "ceasing" and this "passing away" in this manner. After all, the apostle himself explains his intention in these words: "When I was a child, I spoke like a child, I thought like a child, I reasoned like a child. When I became a man, I gave up childish ways" [1 Cor 13:11]. The apostle is comparing the transition from this life to the next life to the transition from childhood to adulthood. The transition in our knowledge when we moved from childhood to adulthood is largely similar to the transition from the knowledge we possessed as adults and the knowledge that eternity will bestow upon us. In both instances, prior knowledge passed away. If you could claim that one who moved from childhood to adulthood took nothing from his childhood knowledge along with him in his knowledge as an adult, then you would have to conclude similarly that in eternity we would take *nothing* whatsoever from our earthly knowledge along with us. But if we know exactly the opposite to be the case, that the knowledge of the adult developed and matured from the knowledge of the child, then the apostle's comparison tells us that in terms of Paul's intention, our knowledge we possessed here on earth will exert great influence on the knowledge we will possess in eternity.

Does it still require explaining how the entire system of our nurture rests squarely on the assumption that as a child we need to lay the foundation in our younger years for the development of knowledge for which we will be capable as an adult? Can the fact be denied that a nurture entirely neglected in youth has disastrous effects in adulthood? Is it not firmly established that the impressions we receive as children exert an unusually powerful influence on our formation and development as adults? We know for certain that a child knows only in part, just as while on earth we know only in part; we readily admit that the knowledge of a child passes away, and that an adult talks differently, is oriented differently, and thinks differently than a child, just like while on earth we acquire knowledge that passes away, so that here we talk, are oriented, and think altogether differently than will be the case in eternity. But at the same time we may certainly infer from Paul's statement that a similar connection as what exists between the development of the child and the maturity of the adult will continue to exist between the knowledge we possessed here on earth and the knowledge we will share in eternity. The question before us must consequently be answered in the affirmative. At death, what occurs is not the eradicating, but the elucidating of our consciousness. Ours will not be an awakening in an entirely different, totally brand new world, but an awakening as though coming out of the fog into the noonday light, as though coming out of a blurry view from a distance into a clear, perfectly lucid view from nearby.

That we have to understand our transition from earthly life into eter- §4
nity in this and in no other way is confirmed by what the apostle writes after his comparison between the child and the adult. Immediately thereafter he writes: "For now we see in a mirror dimly, but then face to face. Now I know in part; then I shall know fully, even as I have been fully known" [1 Cor 13:12]. That formulation contains a Hebrew manner of speaking that for most people hinders the proper understanding of these words. For that reason we will explain this verse. This would be unnecessary if we could assume that everyone knew the annotations to the Dutch Bible, but since we cannot, such explanation is needed.[1] Paul is speaking here about *beclouded reason*; and this expression confuses most people. By the phrase *beclouded reason*, we understand a less clear expression that people often read but fail to understand correctly. Nevertheless, what we read in 1 Corinthians 13:12 has absolutely nothing to do with the phrase beclouded reason as we often employ that expression. That this is the case can be discerned already from the addition, "in a mirror." How in the world can we see a less clear manner of speech in a mirror? This problem

---

1. The Greek words rendered in English as "dimly" in 1 Cor. 13:12 are translated in the SV as "duistere rede," which means literally "beclouded reason," the reading that Kuyper aims to correct here. The SV notes at this point make the connection to a "mystery" or "enigma" (*een raadsel*), which is more closely related to the Greek *ainigma*.

is removed immediately when we realize that in Hebrew the same word is used to refer to thing or word. With the Hebrew word *dabar*, the Jew can be referring to either a *statement* or a *thing*. Paul the Jew transferred this same usage into Greek, and our translators would certainly have done better by translating it this way: "But now we look through a mirror at a beclouded something."

In a mirror we cannot see any *reason*, but we can certainly see *something* in a mirror. The mirror reflects everything standing or passing in front of it. So we can observe all of this in a mirror. Except that we observe all of this in the mirror as blurry shapes, especially if the mirror is not clear. In Paul's day people were hardly familiar with our huge, wide, crystal clear mirrors. The mirrors used in those days were not made of glass, but of metal, somewhat misshapen. Most were round and small in shape. As a result, the object reflected in such mirrors was usually defined very obscurely, dull in tint, and less sharply. In royal palaces this could be remedied somewhat by using extraordinarily fine steel for constantly polishing the mirror, but the mirrors generally used in those days were extremely fragile and could provide little more than a relatively beclouded image of the thing or the person it was reflecting.

§ 5    Paul talks about such a mirror in 2 Corinthians 3:18 as well, and tells us: "But we all, with unveiled face, beholding as in a mirror the glory of the Lord, are being transformed into the same image from glory to glory, just as from the Lord, the Spirit" [NASB]. The mirror Paul is referring to there is Holy Scripture. In that Holy Scripture we see portrayed for us an image of the glory of God in the image of Christ. But, the apostle is saying, that is not the clear, full, lucid image as the glory of God radiates essentially; no, it is like a reflection in a mirror—indeed comparable and completely reliable, but as though the mirror were fogged over with steam. The same distinction in clarity and lucidity that exists between the living person and his reflection in the mirror, exists between the essential glory of God in his majesty and the image of that glory presented to us in Holy Scripture. Nevertheless, this image of that glory has sufficient power to transform us according to it, and that this is possible is due to the working of the Holy Spirit.

This statement in 2 Corinthians 3:18 explains perfectly the apostle's other statement in 1 Corinthians 13:12. Here as well we learn about a mirror that reflects the image of God. What we observe here on earth is not God himself in his very person, but his image in the mirror. As a result, our knowledge of God is very incomplete, for the image of God that we see in the mirror is beclouded, that is to say, it is not the essence itself, but merely a beclouded image, since that image is blurred and less clear. So now we see in the mirror nothing other than a beclouded something, a less clear image of our God. But in eternity this will be different. Then that mirror will be gone. Then we no longer come, as we do now, with our back toward God and with our face toward the mirror; but then we will turn our back to the mirror and will be facing God himself. As a result, we will then no longer be seeing his beclouded image in the mirror, but God himself, face to face, and in this way we will know him even as we are known by him, the One who sees and fathoms us in our essence itself.

If with this 1 Corinthians 13:11 has become completely clear, then we cannot be adequately amazed by the rich imagery Paul is using to clarify such a complicated matter for us. There simply is no metaphor as clear as the transition from the consciousness of childhood to that of adulthood for helping us sense these two realities. For it explains the highly expressive distinction between the knowledge we possess here on earth and the knowledge we will have in eternity. And at the same time, it indicates the inner connection and close relationship that will exist between both sorts of knowledge. He clarifies these same things with the second metaphor, whereby he portrays the difference between seeing a living person face to face, and seeing his obscured reflection in a mirror. Here as well two realities come to light: on the one hand, the sharp difference between both, and on the other hand, the inner connection between them. Seeing a person's reflection, at a certain distance, captured by a tiny metal mirror, is something entirely different than beholding his actual living person. And still, even with this huge difference, it is and remains the person himself who casts his reflection in the mirror; anyone who never saw the person but only his reflection in the mirror recognizes the person based on his knowledge of the reflection.

§ 6

If it appeared initially that the forceful expression, *knowledge passes away*, eliminated all connection and relationship between our earthly knowledge and our knowledge in eternity, it has become axiomatically certain from our further explanation of the apostle's intention that we may not interpret his statement in that way; but rather he means that, since the one knowledge changes into the other, between both there exists a firm connection, and the relationship between both is not broken by death.

If this conclusion is solid, then we see with simultaneous hindsight how the expression, *We know in part*, completely confirms this interpretation. Anyone who speaks about a *knowing in part* thereby admits that he is imagining complete knowledge to be divided into discrete parts. If you have erected a wall only in part, then you complete the wall not by smashing that existing part of the wall and putting another wall in its place, but you would complete the wall by allowing to stand what had been finished and by adding the part lacking. The part belongs with the whole, and in order to possess the whole you cannot lack any of its parts.

If in the same way our knowledge on earth constitutes a part, albeit as yet merely a small part, of the completed knowledge, then we may infer that the knowledge and development acquired here on earth are not eliminated or removed, but in eternity the larger part is added to this smaller part, in order only in this way to attain unto perfection. In this way all doubt or uncertainty is removed once and for all. In this apostolic instruction it is clearly stated that at death earthly knowledge survives in eternal knowledge, with such a huge difference that compared to that eternal knowledge, the knowledge that we had here appears to have passed away, but in such a way that in fact what we possessed here remains one part of the whole, and as with the knowledge of the adult compared to the knowledge of the child, in the same way as well, in that eternal knowledge our earthly knowledge will continue to function and continue to matter.

§ 7    Those people are mistaken, therefore, who imagine that the formation and development of our spirit and the formation of our person and our character are incidental, matters to which a child of God hardly need pay attention, because they don't matter for eternity. These *do* matter somewhat for eternity; in fact, they matter *a lot*. Nothing is lost. Everything that was essential profit here remains profit for eternity. And anyone who continues training himself until he dies, who continues enriching and developing himself, will one day awaken from being that richer child on earth as a richer adult in eternity.

Agreeing completely with this is what the Lord Christ teaches us in his parable of the talents [see Matt 25:14–30]. Talents are a metaphor of the treasure entrusted to us; in ordinary life we talk about someone being a person of talent, in order thereby to indicate his lavish aptitude and the heightened development he has attained. Those talents are distributed unequally according to God's sovereign plan. But the Lord teaches us in his parable that in eternity, the man with five talents and the man with two talents are absolutely not equal to the man with one talent; nor is he teaching that it is insignificant for eternity whether one simply preserved his talent or developed it. Those five talents earned another five. That represented development. The fellow who received one talent earned nothing with it. This represents deficit and lack of development. It is so far from the case that Jesus would call this a matter of indifference for eternity, that it was precisely the man who did not develop his talent who entered eternity dirt poor, bereft of even that one talent, whereas the man with the five talents brought into eternity those five together with the other five he had earned. Even though we admit that both Paul in 1 Corinthians 13 and Jesus in this parable were referring in the first place to spiritual knowledge and spiritual talents, it is evident nonetheless that an enriched consciousness enters heaven rich, and a poor, or worse, impoverished consciousness enters eternity empty and poor.

In this way, then, there is transition, coupling, connection, and relationship. Insofar as common grace was the God-ordained means for forming our human person here on earth, and for enriching our spirit, and for developing our character, it may be established on the basis of Holy Scripture that the fruit of common grace, as far as individual persons are concerned, and as far as the enriching of the life of their consciousness is concerned, absolutely does not perish forever in the grave, but after having descended into the grave will again blossom eternally in that supreme, lavish, and completed knowledge that only eternity can provide us.

# CHAPTER SIXTY-FIVE

# THE CONNECTION BETWEEN THIS LIFE AND ETERNAL LIFE

*As a plan for the fullness of time, to unite all things in him, things in heaven and things on earth.*

EPHESIANS 1:10

§ 1   If it is true that "they will bring into [the new Jerusalem] the glory and the honor of the nations" (Rev 21:26), and if the fruit of his works will accompany everyone who is saved when they enter eternal salvation (Rev 14:13), and if finally the transfer of the fruit of his life into the next life will be like the transition from child to adult (1 Cor 13:11), then we have only to seek to answer the question concerning what conceivable connection exists between the nature of this temporal life and the character of eternal life. Apart from such a connection a transfer of the fruit of the one into the other could not be understood.

Nevertheless, both arenas of life appear to lie so far apart that we get the overriding impression as though life in the kingdom of glory would be so entirely different from life here on earth that hardly any feature of identity or correspondence between both of them is conceivable. Spiritual imbalance leads people simply to dismiss everything earthly as entirely lacking any further existence in eternity, and further to imagine life in heaven as consisting merely in spiritual activity and spiritual delight of an entirely religious nature. That spiritual imbalance is pressed so far that the resurrection of the flesh hardly counts for anything anymore, and every expectation of the Lord's return and of the manifestation of his glorious kingdom gets lost in the foggy mist. People suppose that everything that exists will have passed away for eternity, and regarding what is coming people form hardly any conception except that it would be entirely brand new, something entirely different, and thus emptied for us of every point of analogy.

In opposition to this, the testimony of Holy Scripture must again be honored. Apart from Holy Scripture we know absolutely nothing about what lies on the other side of the grave. In this connection, anyone who values the possession of any knowledge and any conception about this has no other approach open than to turn one's ear toward Scripture to listen and to receive instruction through the revelation of Scripture.

If we follow that rule, then we reach an entirely different outcome. §2 For in Holy Scripture, the new Jerusalem and the kingdom of glory are portrayed for us with pictures derived entirely from this life. We read of a new earth under a new heaven [see 2 Pet 3:13; Rev 21:1; compare Isa 65:17; 66:22]. The meek are given to see that they will inherit this earth, this globe [see Matt 5:5; compare Psa 37:11]. Mention is made of a city with foundations and gates [see Heb 11:10; Rev 21:12-14; compare Psa 87:1-2]. Flowing through the new paradise is a river of life, on both of whose banks trees are flourishing, bearing fruit twelve times each year [see Rev 22:1-2, 14; compare Gen 2:9-10; Psa 46:4]. The exalted tone of the future life is represented in terms of a meal, enriched with fat filled with marrow and with pure wine.

Although we readily admit that one cannot form conclusions about the shape of reality simply on the basis of figurative language in itself, nevertheless one may not forget that this figurative speech applies to a future life where those saved will exist not only as *souls* but also as *bodies*. From this future life Christ appeared to Stephen, Paul, and John in a form that fully confirms the notion "that we have our flesh in heaven as a sure pledge."[1] If one adds these two realities together—on the one hand, the fact that in the kingdom of glory we will have a physical existence, and on

---

1. Heidelberg Catechism, Lord's Day 18, A 49.

the other hand, the fact that the forms and appearances of eternal life are portrayed for us in images derived from presently existing reality—then it follows that we have to understand these images not as referring to a spiritual entity, but as images of a corresponding external reality. The name of paradise used for that future reality corresponds with this. After all, paradise existed not merely spiritually, but visibly and externally.

In thinking of a future paradise, one may therefore think of nothing other than a future real existence and visibly corresponding world. When Jesus says that anyone who has forsaken fields and houses here for his sake will receive them back in multiple form in eternal life [see Mark 10:29-30], this leads us to the same conclusion; whereas the prophets of the old covenant escape the chiliast interpretation only if one understands them in a way that corresponds to the Revelation of John, as referring directly to the external condition of blessedness belonging to the coming eternal world.

§ 3     From this no other conclusion is possible than that the dying of a grain of wheat for the purpose of that deceased kernel of grain later coming alive and adopting new forms in the stalk and the head, is the pregnant metaphor not only for our personal dying and later coming again to life in our glorified body, but at the same time we have the indication as to how one day this entire world will die and perish, but in order to bring forth out of its germ a similar, much more glorious world—except that it is purified from all curse and pain. There is no doubt that what exists now will one day perish and disappear, except that what will perish will be not the essence but only the form, and the essence itself will emerge in new and more glorious forms. Like the stalk grows out of the kernel of grain, while being so essentially unified with that kernel and related in kind to the kernel, and like our glorified body, no matter how different from our present body, will nevertheless remain one in kind with that old body, so too it must then be argued and accepted that the present world which one day will perish before the coming new world, will continue its essence in that new world. That new world will be of the same kind as this old world, and will be able to be explained in terms of it.

Once the new arrives, everything mechanical or artificial will be dismantled and replaced by something entirely different. An old church building that is dilapidated is demolished, the ground is cleared, and an entirely new building is erected on that spot, one that has nothing in common with the old building. But in organic life that is not how things go. Even though the caterpillar disappears in order to permit the butterfly to emerge from the chrysalis, the butterfly and caterpillar are nevertheless the same being, related in kind, and in terms of form and shape the one proceeding and derived from the other. So too, this year's foliage dies out, and next year new foliage arrives, but the one came forth from the other. Similarly, the generation of the previous century dies out, and now a new generation of people arises, but the generation that lives now proceeded from the one that died off, and in both of them, the life of the same human race continues. That is *not* the way it happens with what a person makes. All of that is mechanical. But it is indeed the way it happens with everything that God creates, because in its exalted form of life this exists organically, and therefore in its development its thread is never broken off but the one continually sprouts forth from the other. Proceeding on that basis, one may and must insist that this entire world, as one organic creation of God, will perish in terms of its form and shape, but will nevertheless retain its essence, and will cause this to emerge later in new forms that are related organically to the old forms.

If we believe and confess that Christ is and remains the center of §4 the kingdom of glory, and if we simultaneously confess that our Savior went to heaven with his body, and lives even now in this body, and in the kingdom of glory will triumph in our human flesh, then this requires that this kingdom of glory has an external form that does justice to this bodily existence of our Savior. A bodily existence has neither sense nor significance unless a world exists wherein that bodily existence can function. Otherwise it is neither serviceable nor satisfying. Otherwise what end would be served by this bodily existence of our Savior if he would be dwelling in nothing else but a sphere of invisible spirits? If we add to this the confidently prophesied fact that the elect will receive such a bodily existence for eternity, and that the kingdom of Christ must consist in his possessing as his subjects the elect who are living in this bodily existence, then we see how along this line of thinking it becomes clear that a purely spiritual kingdom could fit neither with our confession of Christ nor with our confession regarding our own future.

In this way the following claims are established: first, the kingdom of glory, the new earth, or whatever you wish to call it, will possess an external, sentient, visible reality; and second, this new form or shape of the visible world will be developed out of the now existing world, and will correspond to it in kind. For that similarity in kind and correspondence, together with a very meaningful difference, Holy Scripture even provides us a solid standard when it describes for us the material from which the walls of the new Jerusalem will be built. On this earth we have various kinds of metal, various sorts of stone. But even though both copper and gold are metals, and even though both metals are similar in numerous features, nevertheless gold far surpasses copper in glory. So too we find various kinds of stone, granite and marble, ruby and sapphire. But although all of these have the character of stone, nevertheless they diverge entirely in their inherent value, so that neither marble nor granite is hardly in the same class as the jewels. We express the difference between coarse and exquisite with regard to metals and stones by speaking of *precious* metals and of *precious* gems. What is remarkable is that Holy Scripture portrays as very common in the new Jerusalem what are known on earth as precious metals and precious gems, which appear on earth as rare and exceptional. What is the exception here and now will be the rule then and there, and what is here very common will pass away and vanish there. There will be walls of pure gold, and there even the foundations of the city will consist of emerald and topaz.

If it is certain that gold and copper, marble and sapphire, distinct and different as they are, nevertheless belong to the same creation, to one and the same world, to the same cosmic structure, and they constitute the component parts of the same unified organic entity, then we see along this line how the new earth will emerge out of the old one, will continue to be related inwardly to it, and will be united with it.

§ 5    This being the case, we now see the bridge that opens for us the passage from this dispensation to the future dispensation. Were it simply a breaking off, a breaking down, a destruction of what now exists, and the creation of something brand new, it would be inexplicable how the human development, for which common grace equipped us in this world, could have any significance and fruit for that entirely different and brand new manner of existence. But if it is certain that the coming new earth will be one in essence with the world existing now, and that we will live on that earth clothed with a glorious body that emerges out of our present body, then there is communion, then there is relatedness, then there is correspondence and agreement, and we can understand how what was achieved during the first dispensation can live on in the second dispensation.

Ice, water, fog, moisture, and steam are quite divergent forms manifesting the same essence, even though that essence emerges with a majesty and power in the form of steam that could not be guessed by looking at the ice. But knowing these various forms of the same essence, if we compare them with each other, we understand very well how our knowledge of flowing water helps us understand both solidified and evaporated moisture. If here already an incomprehensible range of our human knowledge and our human capacity is being formed by everything belonging to that visible earth, in order to subject that sensory nature to ourselves, and if we know that this our dominion over nature will be entirely perfected in eternity, then from this we understand how the knowledge and dominion over nature that was acquired here can and will have continuing significance for the kingdom of glory as well. Of course, it's not as though the algebraic formulas we invented here will be preserved in our memory for use in that new world.

Already in paradise Adam in his interaction with the animals shows us an entirely different sort of dominion over nature, a dominion whose effects we detect in Daniel's dominion over the lions in the den, and in the entire array of miracles by Christ and his emissaries that have been reported to us. Now as well the power of genius originates differently than the skill acquired by the pupil. But although both originate in different ways, and although they are of different sorts in that respect, nevertheless the genius works alongside the common man, who must become accustomed to each other; the efforts of both intersect, and we see before our eyes that a connection exists between both of them. The power that the animal tamer exercises over the wild animal without equipment, and the power that the Indian exercises through his tools, certainly differ in a very striking way, and yet both lead to the same goal. Although we accept that the dominion over nature, that the redeemed will one day possess, will correspond more with the capacity at work in Adam, Daniel, and Christ, and thus will bear the character of genius more than of study, nevertheless this does not contradict the fact that the result of the development of both can merge, even as this is seen already in our dispensation.

We are confirmed in this by what Paul tells us in Ephesians 1:10, in a §6 statement whose translation into our own language leaves nothing to guesswork as to the lavish notion it contains. We read: "as a plan for the fullness of time, to unite all things in him, things in heaven and things on earth." The correct understanding of this statement depends entirely on the proper notion attached to the Greek word translated here as "unite." The Greek word is *anakephalaiōsasthai*, which literally means "to take up under one head." To see what this means, we must open the Bible at Romans 13:9, where the same word appears in an entirely different context. There we read about various commandments that stand alongside one another like loose imperatives: You shall not steal, you shall not murder, you shall not commit adultery. And then Paul says that we can *take up under one head* all of these commands when we ascend to the principle: You shall love your neighbor as yourself.

Our translation renders this: All of these "are summed up in this word: 'You shall love your neighbor as yourself.' " In itself this is a fine translation, because we recognized the verb summed up to be equivalent to take up under one head. Nevertheless, we must realize that a sum in its proper sense tells us nothing, since it makes us think of a mathematical sum. We have five commandments in the second table.[2] We can count them. The total or sum is the command of love. The meaning of this word goes much deeper. Only what is organically connected and belongs to the entire organism has one head. The plant does not yet have that, though the animal does, and especially a human being does. It is the head that holds together the various members and parts of our organism. In the head, the various parts of our organic existence as a human being possess their unity. Remove this head, and the organism falls apart into its pieces. The organism no longer exists.

In this way the various commandments of God constitute one interdependent organic entity. They constitute one organic entity, because they arise from one principle. What we are here calling a *principle* is called in Hebrew *a head*. When we read, "In the beginning God created heaven and

---

2. The Heidelberg Catechism LD 34, Q&A 93, teaches that the Decalogue is to be divided into two tables. Although the earliest editions of the catechism in Latin, German, and Dutch associated four commandments with the first table and six commandments with the second, many modern Dutch versions of the catechism, as well as the text Kuyper used in *E Voto Dordraceno*, omit specific reference to the number of commandments in each table. Kuyper discusses the question of numbering and dividing the commandments in *E Voto Dordraceno* at some length. He observes that the fifth commandment has a kind of "dual character" (*tweeslachtig karakter*), and argues for grouping the commandments according to the internal structure of the Decalogue, particularly on the basis of his comparisons and analysis of parallels between the tables. Kuyper concludes that the fifth commandment is like the fourth and should be included in the first table. See *E Voto Dordraceno: Toelichting op den Heidelbergschen Catechismus*, 4 vols. (Amsterdam: Wormser, 1892–95), 3:483–90.

earth" [see Gen 1:1], we find a word that is derived from the word for *head*.[3] In Romans 13:9 Paul states, (1) that there are various commandments; (2) that these commandments sprouted like so many stalks from one root, from one principle; (3) that in order to grasp them in their unity, we must return to that root, to that principle, to that head; and (4) that this principle, this root, that head of the commandments of the second table is: You shall love your neighbor as yourself. Bringing all of these commandments under their head, gathering them together under their head, we arrive at this one universal principle.

So too here.                                                                                           §7

The entire world constitutes an organic whole. Meanwhile this organic unity broke apart through the curse and through the fall. As a result, earth and heaven, which belonged together as one organism under one head, have been torn apart from each other, and now lie as two great fragments of this originally unified entity that have been broken from each other. Christ will end this by means of his return. He will once again organically reconnect those disconnected members and parts of the one great organism; and he will do this by taking up all those organic parts once again under one head, gather them together once again under one head, and it is precisely this that is being expressed with the Greek word *anakephalaioō*.

The meaning is nothing less than this. Originally God created his universe as one connected organic whole. This artwork of the supreme Artist was ripped apart and wrecked by sin. As a result, it appeared as though the creation had been a mistake and God's purpose with that creation was thwarted, and this is what people thought for many centuries. But there was a mystery, a secret with God. Formerly people did not understand that secret, but it is revealed in Christ. And this secret consists in this, that the original plan of God was not neutralized, but continues full of majesty, and that God will thereby realize his world plan, that one day in Christ he will once again connect those parts and pieces of his creation, taken here as heaven and earth, under one head, that is, once again into one entirely organic, integrated, and connected entity. In his excellent lexicon, Cremer correctly indicates how the middle form of the verb used here expresses that God will do this for his own sake, that he will show "for himself" (for this is what the middle voice expresses), that is, for his honor,

---

3. The word translated as "the beginning" is the Hebrew *re'shiyth*, related to *ro'sh*, which can also mean "chief," "first," or "head."

for maintaining his honor as Creator, how his work of creation was not a flop, but continues gloriously and will be perfected.[4] It is in the re-creation of all things that the original creation triumphs. As a result, one senses that the rendering of "gathering together all things again into one" [see Col 1:20] is completely correct, but without further explanation comes nowhere near rendering the profound thought of the original.

Gathering all of that under one head again most definitely does not start for the first time with the parousia. On the contrary, God began this work already in paradise through the promise and through the regeneration of Adam, Eve, and Abel. That work continued through all the centuries in all of God's revelation and redemptive acts. That work was manifested principally in the incarnation of the Word, in the cross, and in the resurrection. The entire existence of the Christian church on earth still serves in large part to continue that grand plan of our God. Wherever the break originated within the human heart, and from the human heart extended to his body, and from his body passed through the curse to nature, there the restoration cannot occur in any other way than through the reversing of guilt and sin, and through the resurrection of the body of Christ. What will arrive at the parousia is not the beginning but the completion of this restoration.

All of this together is aimed at saving the honor of what God created, and one day making his entire creation excel again in organic unity. Since, however, common grace has been incorporated in this grand restoration plan, and constitutes part of that plan, and has made the continuation thereof possible, it is obvious that the fruit borne by this common grace must have a significance that is not passing, but permanent. After all, it was precisely that common grace that functioned to maintain the connection of God's people with the world. It focused on the life of this world. It upheld in that world the honor of God's creational work. And it worked together with particular grace in order along this route to make possible the permeation of the powers of the kingdom in that world. To that extent, therefore, it can be said that already in common grace we can see the preliminary signs of that powerful work of restoration whereby God the Lord saves not only the souls of people, but also their body, and not only the bodies of people, but also nature, and in that nature, the external life of humanity.

---

4. Hermann Cremer (1834–1903), *Biblico-theological Lexicon of New Testament Greek*, trans. William Urwick, 4th ed. (Edinburgh: T&T Clark, 1895), 748.

# CHAPTER SIXTY-SIX

# THE CONGRUENCE BETWEEN THE LIFE HERE AND THE LIFE HEREAFTER

*I tell you I will not drink again of this fruit of the vine until that day when I drink it new with you in my Father's kingdom.*

MATTHEW 26:29

With regard to the overflowing of life under common grace into the life of glory, we must supplement the *special* features discussed thus far with a *general* perspective. Those special features involved exclusively the fruit of common grace that pass over into eternity both from the life of the nations and from the life of individual persons. "The honor and the glory of the nations" are borne into the new Jerusalem, and the works of those who enter this new Jerusalem follow after them. This is something with regard to which we have shown the connection to be seen with the light of Scripture in this twofold respect between life here and life hereafter. The child becomes an adult; what is seen here as a mirrored reflection is seen there in its essence. Nevertheless, apart from these special features, which refer more specifically to the fruit of common grace for life

§ 1

in eternity, we need now to discuss the issue of how common grace, if it finally ceases and comes to an end, connects with the situation that emerges in the hereafter. In order that here as well, we may take our starting point from a clear statement of Holy Scripture, we begin our discussion with a somewhat puzzling statement of Jesus at the institution of the Lord's Supper: "I tell you I will not drink again of this fruit of the vine until that day when I drink it new with you in my Father's kingdom" [Matt 26:29]. These are words people usually read past, and words to whose broader application the church to this point has not attached all that serious a significance.

People have tried to explain these puzzling words in three ways that we deem inadequate. The simplest way is to suggest that Jesus is announcing that before his death and until his resurrection he would not be drinking wine with his disciples any more. After his resurrection he would have resumed doing so. Others have claimed that the vine is to be understood in a figurative rather than a literal sense. The coming glory is often represented as a meal with wine and abundance. Jesus would then have been saying: This Passover meal is our last feast on earth. What comes next is our feast in eternity. Finally, a third explanation has thought it necessary to view the entire statement to represent a spiritual drinking, and has connected it with our coming to the Lord's Table. Occasionally one encounters a fourth interpretation, one we think is more correct, namely, that the words are to be taken literally, such that here Jesus is declaring how the fruit of the vine will be known also on the new earth, but then in a higher glory, and how in moving so suddenly from the Holy Supper to his return, Jesus is prefiguring for his disciples the continuation in that future glory of earthly life enjoyed up to this point.

§ 2     That this is an important statement may be inferred from the fact that it appears in Matthew, Mark, and Luke. In Mark it is strengthened by the introductory word "*Truly*, I say to you" [Mark 14:25]. In Luke it appears in a somewhat modified form this way: "For I tell you that from now on I will not drink of the fruit of the vine until the kingdom of God comes" [Luke 22:18], which makes no difference for the meaning. What is more interesting is that in Luke's account this statement about "the fruit of the vine" is preceded by a similar statement of Jesus about the Passover. We read in Luke 22:15-16: "And he said to them, 'I have earnestly desired to eat this Passover with you before I suffer. For I tell you I will not eat it until it is fulfilled in the kingdom of God." We draw attention to this still more puzzling statement only in passing, since from it we see that Jesus did not restrict his prophetic word to talking about the vine, but connected wine and bread together.

It cannot be denied that here we find a prediction of what Paul expressed in this sense: "Remember the death of the Lord *until he comes*" [see 1 Cor 11:26]. Jesus will die and after his resurrection, ascend to heaven. This threatens to entirely spiritualize both Christ and his kingdom in the apostles' understanding, so that from now on they would lose sight of every connection between Christ and this earthly creation. Going out of the world to Jesus, to enjoy nothing but Jesus and to possess Jesus only spiritually, having to think no more about God's visible creation, about this artistic work of his creative power. This would be to divide Christ, removing all significance from his incarnation, despising his resurrection, rendering his existence in our flesh in heaven as worthless, in order to have left nothing more than a spiritual Jesus. This terrible heresy, "that denies that Jesus has come in the flesh," proceeding from the Antichrist, according to John's testimony [see 1 John 4:2–3], could creep in among the Lord's flock in this way.

Against this danger of spiritualizing Christ, the sacrament of the Lord's Supper functions to direct us tangibly to bread, where bread is broken and eaten, and wine is poured into the cup and people drink from the cup; both of these visual signs direct us to Christ's incarnation, suffering, death, and resurrection. For that bread is his body, and that wine is his blood.

That symbolic communion of bread and wine would possess a spiritual reality through the work of the Holy Spirit, and when one day this dispensation came to an end, and the Lord returned, the sacrament would fall away and the fleshly relationship between Jesus and his own would be restored. So the Lord's Supper functions as a helping instrument between Golgotha and the parousia, in order during this interim period, when Jesus is in heaven, to join the tangible with the spiritual. Naturally that lasts only until he comes. At that point the symbolic has served its purpose, and the real returns. As he surveys this interim period and ties the Passover meal directly to his return, Jesus says: I will eat this Passover with you again and drink this cup with you again only when the kingdom of glory will have come on the renewed earth under the renewed heaven. This is how we need to understand the impetus leading to these remarkable words spoken precisely at that moment. No longer do they seem to have been inserted strangely, loosely, unrelatedly into what Jesus said at the Lord's Supper. Only if we understand the meaning of Paul's addition, *until he comes*, in precisely the same way, do we understand the meaning of what Jesus was saying here about the new vine.

§ 3    We maintain the material significance of Jesus' words over against their spiritual or sacramental meaning because the assertive formulations with which Jesus spoke permit no other interpretation. Jesus was sitting with his disciples at the meal. The pitcher of wine was at hand, and the cup had been poured. Jesus raised that cup containing real wine, and passed it around among the disciples, and they drank. As this real wine was going around and was being drunk, Jesus said: "I will not drink again of this fruit of the vine." To understand such clear, assertive words spiritually or sacramentally does not work. The fruit of the vine can refer to nothing other than real wine. Concerning this real wine Jesus is saying that he will not drink it again with his disciples; the not-drinking of this wine will come to an end, on a particular day. For we read: "*until that day when I drink it new with you in my Father's kingdom*" [Matt 26:29].

On and after that day, the use of the wine returns, though in another form. It will be the same fruit of the vine, but *new*. The fruit of the vine will therefore receive a new higher form of existence on the new earth, and in that new form Jesus will one day drink the wine with his disciples in that kingdom of glory, when the kingdom of his Father will have appeared. One cannot imagine a resumed drinking of wine after the resurrection of Jesus from the dead, for after the resurrection of the Lord it was still the same old wine from before his death. Even today still, it is the old wine that we use for the Lord's Supper. The wine can become new only on the new earth under the new heaven. From this it follows that with the Lord's Supper the wine is still old and not yet new.

The claim of some people, that the kingdom of his Father appeared immediately after Christ's ascension, on the day of Pentecost, so that this would not have been referring to the kingdom of glory but simply to the church of the new covenant, is not acceptable, since Jesus had shortly before (see Matt 25:34) declared that for the first time in the judgment it would be said to the redeemed: "Come, you who are blessed by my Father, *inherit the kingdom prepared for you from the foundation of the world.*" Even though one can say that, in a certain sense, the kingdom has already come, in no case may one argue that it came on the day of Pentecost. If we see the kingdom as purely spiritual, then it was there already before Jesus' death, for Jesus himself said: "the kingdom of God is in the midst of you" [Luke 17:21]. If on the contrary, we take the kingdom to be both spiritual and external, then that kingdom comes in a heavenly manner with Jesus' ascension, in that Jesus is now seated at God's right hand, but it can come externally and in an earthly manner only with his return on the clouds, when the last enemy will be subjugated under Jesus' feet, and the kingdom will be given to the Father so that now for the first time it is called in the fullest sense, "the kingdom of the Father." Every other interpretation is excluded, because Jesus does not say: "Until my kingdom will have come," but "until the day that we will drink this new wine in the kingdom of my Father."

If this view is certain, then it follows that Jesus is portraying for us life on the new earth not merely as spiritual life but also as an outward life in rich creational abundance. He is also teaching that this abundance will emerge out of the old creation that now lies under the curse, by God renewing the appearance, the form, of this earth, and in this way making the vine to emerge in an upgraded, changed form. Therefore the fundamental idea is that the creation that God once called into existence by his word of power is destined to abide eternally; currently it has collapsed and has been robbed of its paradise luster; but by an act of God's power that will occur at the return of Christ, it will be raised out of its collapse in order to shine eternally with *more* than its paradise luster. §4

If we must avoid and flee the world that now lies in wickedness, to the extent that it lies in wickedness, then for God's sake we must love and honor this very same world in its core and essence, as the artistic work of the almighty power of our God. We must not want it to go away and be destroyed so that our spiritual one-sidedness can be satisfied, but we must long for the moment when it will cast off its blemishes and will radiate in new form as the perfected artistic work of our God. So the world will not be lost. What will pass away is the present form of the world; but what remains is God's creation, and that creation of God will ascend to still higher glory than it displayed at the time of its creation. As it was created, it was destined to develop to a still richer splendor. This was impeded by the curse. Rather than becoming richer, it became impoverished and parched. But this diminishing of the gold's luster is curbed, and then all the beauty hidden in it comes out again, even as it is simultaneously guided to its ultimate climax. Jesus himself calls this the regeneration of the creation (Matt 19:28). With the Passover meal he explained this saying to mean that the fruit of the vine passes over into the kingdom of glory, albeit ennobled. This may be something we dislike. In our dying we prefer to surrender that world and want to possess only heaven. But the ordinances of God do not follow this path. One day the earth will become new, one day we will be given a new body, and we will possess eternally an appearance that is not merely spiritual but also physical, not merely invisible but also among what will be visible, enjoying various luxuries, including drinking from the fruit of the new vine.

§ 5    When we connect this with common grace, then we perceive immediately how common grace, which is related not only to the life of our souls but also to our bodily existence and to the maintenance of this world, has maintained that world so that on "the great and awesome day" [Mal 4:5; Joel 2:31] it could be renewed. Had common grace not functioned, then immediately after the fall, sin, the curse, and death would have resulted in this entire world becoming entirely depraved, and nothing but one overpowering wilderness would have survived. This is what common grace averted. It curbed the advance of this cancer. It retarded the pervasive impact of death and decay. Though bleary and beclouded, the world as such continued to exist. The sun continued to shine on the wicked and the good. God had sworn to Noah in his universal covenant of grace that no flood would ever again engulf the earth.

In this way the world did continue to exist, and thanks to the continuing development of common grace in human life, the form of the earth has been gradually enriched. If we compare the heart of Africa with our landscape, we notice the difference. How many deserts have been transformed into beautifully constructed places! How many rivers have been dammed in their flow! How many wetlands have been pumped dry and turned into fields! How many regions that once were wild have been tamed and turned into delightful residential areas! What treasures have been brought up from the depths of the earth; what natural forces that lay dormant have been awakened; in how many ways has the human hand brought the form and value of the ground to a higher level! So we see how common grace includes far more than simply bringing about civic righteousness, but one of its fruits was to transform the earth that once produced thorns and thistles into a beautiful, luxuriant, profitable nature. This the world has continued to exist, its collapse has been arrested, and when Jesus returns, common grace will equip the earth completely in order as such to be renewed by Christ and disclosed in its most luxuriant development. Instead of saying that the visible world vanishes eternally and what remains is only the invisible church, we must far rather confess the opposite, that the visible church vanishes forever and what will one day continue in renewed form is this earth, and with it our human race, albeit with everything renewed, a human race consisting of none but the elect under the Son of Man as the Head of all.

If someone wishes to place the kingdom of nature and the kingdom of grace over against one another, then it must be confessed that common grace functions to save nature and to contribute to its glorification; but when this work of grace is finished, the ministry of grace will end, and the kingdom of glory will be the kingdom of saved, glorified nature, the display of God's original creation in perfect splendor. If we take grace in the sense of a divine power that resists sin and saves from decay, what activity could still proceed from this grace on that day when all the elect will have entered into salvation, every stain of sin will have been removed from every heart, and when the last trace or remnant of the curse, of our soul, of our body, and of our world will be taken away? Where everything is sanctified and glorified, the possibility of an additional functioning of saving grace falls away.

§ 6

Naturally Christ's atoning merit is and remains for eternity the foundation upon which the building of everyone's salvation will rest, and it is obvious that the redeemed will thank God eternally for his "inexpressible gift" [2 Cor 9:15], knowing how they are saved through grace alone, and delight in glory out of sheer grace; but a saving, an atoning, a regenerating operation of grace has at that point become completely inconceivable. Where no sinner exists and no sin exists in the heart of anyone, nothing remains to be saved because everything is saved that was to be saved, and no one will be able to be lost. Salvation in its perfected condition excludes every notion of ongoing saving grace. Every fruit of grace, both common grace and particular grace, will therefore be included in the glorification of the original plan of creation, that is, in the kingdom of nature; and Christ will also hand over the kingdom to God the Father, because the great work of salvation will then be completed and finished, and God the Father will be triumphant in his saved and restored creation that has been renewed in exalted glory. Then the earth will be full of the glory of the Lord, and God will cause his victory over Satan to be manifest throughout the whole universe. Then it will be clear how common grace has cooperated with particular grace in amazing harmony, to direct God's work, albeit along two different paths, to this one beautiful destination.

§ 7        Of the renewal that this world will undergo we can form only an approximate and analogous idea, because Scripture itself instructs us about it exclusively in this way. Like the silversmith melts gold in order to forge sparkling new ornaments from the melted gold, so too God the Lord will melt this antiquated and decrepit world, and all the elements will be found burning, in order out of that molten mass through a cooling process to bring forth the life germs preserved within it in more beautiful form. For this cosmic conflagration the immeasurable burning masses already lie ready in the earth's core, and the mountains that spew forth fire continually remind us how the intense cosmic fire lies hidden beneath the crust of the earth on which we dwell. That coal and diamonds are simply other forms of one and the same basic material displays the alchemy, and Scripture invokes the notion of how one day what is now just a common stone will be an altogether precious stone, to show us the much higher degree of perfection that all life will possess then. Already here God shows us the scale in terms of which we ascend from the lower to the higher.

The butterfly emerging from the caterpillar remains the most powerful example to guide us in imagining going through the transition from ugliness to resplendence in form; but here we must allow the process to continue one stage further, such that we imagine the butterfly making yet another transition into a still higher form, in turn excelling just as far above the butterfly form as the butterfly with its golden covered wings excelled above the crawling caterpillar. Imagine, according to that measure and method, the form of existence of all things on earth or of human life exalted, renewed, and glorified; gone are all plagues that tormented, all insects that destroyed, all poisons that killed, all germs that bred disease. There is no exhaustion and no loss of personal vital energy; no numbing cold or oppressive heat; nothing withered by the light of the sun or the glow of the moon, but bathed in original light; all that is lower developed into the higher; indeed, the entire creation of our God radiating nobly, luxuriantly, and divinely. If we can imagine all of this, then we will no longer consider it a contradiction to imagine in such a creation our Jesus, as he governs in that new world, leading an entirely renewed human race into the glory of God.

Well then, in that coming of Jesus to the restored world, in that gathering of the exalted Christ before whom every knee will bow, together with the creation redeemed from the curse and renewed, therein lies the connection of the endpoint of common grace with the situation that abides for eternity. At that point all common grace comes to an end. It can restrain nothing anymore, because there is nothing to restrain. It will disappear. It will cease. It will have served God's counsel. There will be no place for it to exist. But even so, it will not have been pointless. Through common grace alone it was possible for what existed to continue existing, and the manifold wisdom of God came forth in the fruit of its activity as well.

In summary, one can say that common grace produces three kinds of fruit for the kingdom of glory. First, we find such fruit in the development of our human race and of the gifts God embedded within this human race (the honor and glory of the nations). Second, we find such fruit in the development of character and personality among the individual elect (their works that follow them). And third, we find such fruit in the continued existence of this world so that it could be renewed (the new vine in the kingdom of the Father).

# CHAPTER SIXTY-SEVEN

# REVIEW

*Yes, the world is established; it shall never be moved.*

PSALM 93:1

§ 1    Now that we have followed the course of common grace from paradise to the parousia, and have reached our second milestone, it might be helpful to cast a quick glance back to the path we have opened, so that amid the multiplicity of perspectives we not lose the unity of purpose.

The psalmist sings: "Yes, the world is established; it shall never be moved" (Psa 93:1b). This is a song of praise to God, who alone has meaning and significance. So we acknowledge that there was every reason for instability; that had it been left to itself, the world would certainly have faltered; and that only the intervening grace of God preserved it from faltering.

A comparison with Psalm 46, where the same thing is said not about the world but about Jerusalem, supports this understanding. There we read in verse 6: "The nations rage, the kingdoms totter; he utters his voice, the earth melts"—namely, to save Jerusalem. This salvation is portrayed for us with the metaphor of waters raging and rivers overflowing, which would almost have engulfed Jerusalem. "But fear not, O city of God, the supreme King, you will not be moved, for God has been found to be a powerful Help in distress." Beyond all doubt that *not being moved* in Psalm 46 refers to preserving Jerusalem through God's special grace, when otherwise it would surely have been overcome and destroyed.

What Psalm 46 celebrates about Jerusalem in the arena of particular grace, Psalm 93 sings about the world in the arena of common grace. In Psalm 93 we find the same imagery of "rivers [or floods] that are lifted up," of "rivers that rage," of "the rivers that thunder," and here as well both the power and the majesty of the Lord are placed over against that raging of the rivers that threatens to engulf the world. "But the LORD on high is mightier than the raging of the great waters, than the mighty waves of the sea." On this, and this alone, rests the testimony that even so, the world will not be moved. It would have faltered, it would have been engulfed, but "the LORD has girded and robed himself with strength, he has established it, and this is why it will not be moved." In this way, Psalm 46 and Psalm 93 run parallel. Each speaks of a faltering that is threatening and appears unstoppable. In each, God is the one who intervenes and prevents the faltering by his almighty grace. But each is distinguished from the other, in that Psalm 46 is talking about Zion, the church, the people of the Lord, the body of Christ, and has particular grace in view; whereas Psalm 93 is looking at the world, the earth, our human life, our human race, and is talking about the domain of common grace.

But what is remarkable is the apparently contradictory use of the name with which the eternal Being is called by the psalmist. As people know, in the arena of particular grace that name is LORD or JEHOVAH, and in the arena of common grace the name usually is simply God. Correspondingly we would have expected that in Psalm 46 the name LORD would be used, and in Psalm 93 we would read: God reigns, the earth will not be moved. Nevertheless, we find just the opposite. In Psalm 46, where the psalmist confesses that Jerusalem will not be moved, we read: "God is in the midst of her" [v. 5], and in Psalm 93, where we read the promise that the world will not be moved, the psalm begins: "The LORD reigns" [v. 1]. When Jerusalem is mentioned, attention is drawn to the Creator of heaven and earth; and conversely, when it is confessed that the world will not be moved, attention is drawn to Israel's covenant God. This apparent contradiction is to be explained from the fact that continually in Holy Scripture attention is drawn to the close connection between common grace and particular grace. Each does not stand loosely alongside the other, but together they constitute a unity, together they serve the sovereign plan for the salvation of what God created, together they maintain his honor as Creator. Apart from particular grace, common grace would have had no goal. And similarly, apart from common grace, the divine intention for particular grace would not have been capable of being implemented. The shared starting point, as much for the line of common grace as for that of particular grace, is that in opposition to Satan, who wants to destroy his creation, God maintains his honor as Creator of that world. This is the same connection Jeremiah is speaking about when he says that if God's covenant with day and night, with sun and moon, could be broken, then his covenant with Israel would also be broken [see Jer 33:20–21].

§ 2     The facts are these:

God creates a world for his honor, and he creates and ordains that world in such a way that humanity will be the center of that world, and that the habitude of the human heart will decide concerning the habitude and the fate of the world. He created that human heart in a state of rectitude. In connection with the spiritual state of man's inner life, his body flourished as well, the world prospered, and everything within and around human living sparkled with glory.

The change in the human heart, when humanity fell, necessarily caused a complete change in humanity's external life, and thereby in the habitude and fate of the world. Sin introduced death into his heart, and from that heart brought death into his body. From the whole man death and curse flowed throughout all of nature. In this way a toxic principle of decay was unleashed that, had it been given free reign to perform its full work, would have eaten away man's heart entirely, ravaged his body completely, destroyed his race, and corrupted all of nature by means of its growth. This toxic cancer entered this world from Satan. His goal was to destroy the great artistic work of the Supreme Artist. So the world stood before this huge problem: Would Satan succeed? Would he succeed in causing this corruption to continue working in the human person, in our race, in this world, in the entire created universe? Or would a power arise to block this corrupting work, ultimately eliminating this cancer, overcoming death and the curse, and in the end cause God Almighty and his divine work to triumph over Satan?

The answer to that question was supplied immediately in paradise, partly in what God spoke, partly in what God did. The two factors of common grace and particular grace served to block corruption in its path, and assured the regeneration of man and creation.

§ 3     The toxin of sin was blocked within the human heart and in the heart of our human race. Original righteousness was lost, but through common grace some embers continued to glow, and small remnants of that original goodness were spared. Similarly the influence of the toxin of corruption was impeded within the human body. Man did not die on the very day that he sinned, but saw his life spared, to a span of some nine centuries. The curse fell upon nature, but that curse did not reach its full capacity. Although paradise disappeared and thorns and thistles now grew, nevertheless bread would still come from the field through human work; and amid the limitless destruction, human life on this earth nevertheless remained possible.

These are the three powerful dimensions of common grace that occurred. Absolute sin was curbed in *the human heart*. Complete death was curbed in *the human body*. The universal curse was curbed in *nature*.

When an arena for human life had been provided to our race, and a flourishing development of our human race had become possible, at that point particular grace appeared. This is a grace of an entirely different nature, with entirely different purposes, a grace that brought eternal life into the heart of Eve through regeneration, eventually in the heart of Abel as well, presumably also in Adam's heart. Already in paradise the great divine plan was unfolded for raising up from the seed of the woman the hero of God, whose heel Satan would bruise but who would crush Satan's head.

Those activities run through both dispensations of grace unmixed, §4 alongside and through each other, with the result that the portion of our race that lived from common grace alone steadily declines in moral power, and sees its small "remnants" of goodness decrease; whereas a small group, separated from that wild crowd, firmly maintains the fear of God thanks to particular grace. In Genesis 6 we see each of them split apart, after the contrast became manifest in Cain and Abel, later in Cain and Seth. Thereafter the dissoluteness increases, and the God-fearing group appears to be shrinking. In Genesis 9 it consists at most of one small family still holding on to God, while the rest of humanity has fallen prey to self-destruction. The uncommon powers of the original creation supplied such a gigantic scope to this dissoluteness. In this way God allows people to see how the human race, left to itself, despite partial grace, could do nothing but destroy itself morally and physically; and finally in the time of the flood, the moral self-destruction had progressed so far that it would have taken merely one surge to annihilate the last God-fearing family and thereby cut off the entire future of this world.

At this point God Almighty's hand intervenes and that entire race living at the time is handed over to death. It had placed itself outside of grace. It had manifested its satanic nature more and more. Everything that remained would be annihilated. So the flood comes. The end of this unspeakable judgment and of this immense catastrophe is that only one single family survives, with a husband, a wife, and three children to continue the entire human race. Our entire race was eliminated from the earth. Everything that remained was floating in the ark on the water. And when Noah left the ark, God gave the earth anew to our renewed human race, so that now our human race would shape that world for God and recover it for him.

§ 5     From this moment on, common grace took a fixed form for the first time. God established with Noah a covenant, not a covenant of saving grace, but a covenant of common grace. But this was nonetheless the kind of covenant of grace that was established through Noah not with the church but with the entire human race. This much is certain, that in the flood what perished was the living generation of that time, but not the human race. In that dark night thousands and tens of thousands of people drowned, but God did not hand over the human race to Satan. That was preserved in the ark, and from the ark spread again across the earth. For—and with this all will agree—the human race still exists on earth; and if it still exists, as all agree, then it follows that it must have been contained in Noah's family, that in and with Noah it was in the ark, and in and with Noah it left the ark. The covenant of common grace, with the rainbow as the sign of God's faithfulness, was truly established with our entire human race, and because nature around us must serve humanity and belongs to humanity, the covenant was made with nature itself. Consequently, the animals as well are included in that covenant of common grace, as we are explicitly told. This covenant of common grace entails that the existence of this world, unlike the destructive capacity such as the flood, will continue, but will do so within the parameters of God's creation ordinances, and will continue to exist that way until the Lord's return. The waters will not annihilate the earth again, and sowing and harvest will not cease again.

For a short time, the life of particular grace is again one with that of common grace. For the ark held, on the one hand, our entire human race, but on the other hand, also the church with its seed. But this intermingled situation didn't last long. We see the separation coming already with Ham. Shem opposes Ham, and Japheth intervenes between them. This accounts for why the moment has arrived for segregating a distinct arena for the activity of particular grace, and this happens with Abraham's call and in granting the land of Canaan to Abraham and his descendants.

From this time on there is a dual development. On the one hand, common human development of our race was borne only by common grace, resulting in the history of the nations, first in Babylonia, then in Egypt, later in Greece and Rome. In many respects this was a glamorous development that led successively to the sparkling use of the talents God had placed within our race, to the enriching of human life, to the refining of human consciousness, and to the elevation of human self-understanding. It led as well to the application in amazing ways of the human power given us by God, for great inventions, founding kingdoms, producing art, scientific reflection, refining form, and so much more. Even though sin continues to rage throughout all of this and weakens what was thought to be strong, yet when, due to sin, this development reaches a dead end with one nation, God shifts the arena to another nation that is less depraved, so that in this way that immense development can continue for century after century.

But together with this an entirely different development occurs in Israel, not as though no common grace was at work in Israel, but because in Israel particular grace came alongside common grace. Both were wed within Israel. Common grace is the foundation upon which the building of particular grace is erected, and it is particular grace that preserves individual elements of common grace among Israel from eroding. This is how it goes from Moses to Christ. And then Israel finally bears its fruit when the Savior of the world is born. No sooner is he born than the segregation of Israel comes to an end. The power of the nations had seized the holy territory. Rome occupied Jerusalem, and in the name of Rome's emperor, sentence will be pronounced in Jerusalem upon the Messiah. This explains his demise. But he rises from the dead and that resurrection constitutes the breaking of the bonds, the liberating of the people, the opening of the sluices that had separated the stream of Israel's national life from that of the nations. After his ascension the waters of particular grace soon stream in every direction across the fields of human life. §6

And what is happening now?

Is the stream of human life that springs from common grace simply dammed up and replaced by the stream of particular grace? We know better. One stream does not dam up the other, but both flow together, and in the Christian church both are gratefully honored—both the fruit of particular grace and the fruit of common grace. The separation is lifted, and in the Christian church (taken now not as institute but as organism) human life encounters a new future.[1] The nations that remain Jewish or Gentile, or later become Islamic, may exercise influence temporarily, but later they lose virtually all significance, and ultimately it is only Christian nations that bear within themselves the real development of our human race. They dominate the world. Theirs is the power over that world. They stand along with God as being responsible for that world. This explains that in the bosom of Christian nations is to be seen the richest fare that has ever been spied out: a rich development of the life of the soul arising from regeneration joined with a rich development proceeding from the life of common grace. The highest development in the arena of trade and business, of science and art, blended together with the richest demonstration of the power of grace proceeding from the eternal kingdom. The life of common grace never achieved such rich progress as it has especially among Christian nations.

§ 7     But unregenerate life in the bosom of these Christian nations has latched on to that rich development of the life of common grace, to misuse it as a power for unrighteousness, directing it against God. That has happened in the market, in the house of ill-repute, in science, in art, in the ordinary concourse of convivial life, extending into Christ's church, through heresy and apostasy.

The mystery of unrighteousness is at work in this.

The more that apostasy increases, the more power this mystery exercises. Gradually it organizes. It tries to become master of human life, to dominate that life, and to dechristianize that life once again. In 1789 this attempt was principially and publicly manifested.[2] From that time it has continued, seeking to push back the church, to unravel the Scripture, to obscure any vision for eternity, to distract people away from the spirit to

---

1. For a seminal exposition of this distinction between the church as institute and organism, see Abraham Kuyper, *Rooted and Grounded: The Church as Organism and Institution*, trans. Nelson D. Kloosterman (Bellingham, WA: Lexham Press, 2015).

2. That is, in the French Revolution (1789–99) there was a conscious attempt to dechristianize French society. The political party with which Kuyper was affiliated, the Anti-Revolutionary Party, took its name in opposition to the French Revolution. On the self-identification of this movement, see Abraham Kuyper, *Our Program: A Christian Political Manifesto*, trans. and ed. Harry Van Dyke (Bellingham, WA: Lexham Press, 2015), 1–15.

the flesh, and instead of every knee bowing before the Christ of God, it makes every knee bow before the glorification of man *as man*.

Whether this anti-Christian development of common grace will yet be restrained for a time we cannot determine. But even if it is restrained yet for a certain period, God's Word tells us that it will definitely continue until the end, and then it must eventuate in a universal oppression of the Lord's people, and in the consolidation of all power on earth in the hand of a terrible man, the man of sin, the son of corruption. God will wipe out that abysmal person by the Spirit of his mouth. Christ will appear on the clouds. The judgment will commence. The earth will be annihilated not by water, but this entire earth will be melted by fire. Then out of that cosmic conflagration the new earth will arise that under the new heaven will flourish to God's honor, the new earth upon which all God's redeemed will triumph endlessly in their glorious body with Christ.

This will be the outcome: not that what lay behind all this will simply have passed away and perished, but that the honor and the glory of the nations will be carried into that new Jerusalem, and that the fruit of common grace, both in terms of our human race as well as individual elect persons, will continue to be active in God's glorious kingdom. Both particular grace and common grace will then have completed their course. As the dispensation of grace for the purpose of saving and redeeming, it will necessarily reach its end when everything to be saved will have been saved. God's original creation will again rise in its purity and perfection from the mists generated by sin, death, and curse. Indeed, what was embedded in germ form in the original creation will be developed to its full glory. No new falling away will be conceivable. Satan will have been cast away forever. All his raging will have been destroyed. And in the eternal future that will dawn, God alone will be great. He who conceived this world in his eternal wisdom, who created it by his almighty power, and who, when that world failed and challenged him, saved it from faltering by his multiform wisdom, and re-created it after having once created it, in order then to make it eternally to be a theater of his grace and his glory.

# WHY THE TERM "COMMON" GRACE?

Before continuing, we need to insert at this point a brief response to an entirely different question repeatedly addressed to us, one that seems to require clarification.[1] Why is it, people have asked us more than once by letter, that you always speak about "common," and not about "universal," favor or grace?

The answer to this question is simple: our fathers spoke of "gratia *communis*," and in our language the word *communis* means not "universal" but "common." In Latin the word does mean "universal," equivalent to *universalis*, from which we get our word *universal*. We are not contesting the fact that both of these concepts often mean practically the same thing, but nevertheless a distinction does exist between them that we would do well not to neglect. That distinction consists in this, that *universal* refers to something that is found everywhere, something that is valid everywhere, and by the nature of the case is applicable to everyone. Whereas by contrast, the word *communis* or *common* refers to something that is shared in common among a particular group.

Here we have that group known as humanity, our human race, and this divine favor is shared in common among this group. The word *universal* views the persons or things to which it refers as existing on their own,

---

1. The text for this appendix is taken from *CG* 3.20.8. Kuyper interrupts his discussion of church and state to insert this explanation of the title of his entire project.

apart from any connection or relationship, and it expresses that the same feature is valid for or is found with each of these members. Legal prescriptions are universal, since they apply to all individual objects without distinction. A theorem is universal, in that it is valid in every given situation. A preamble is universal, because it does not descend into particularities but is limited to what applies to all the particularities.

By contrast, people speak of a *communis opinio*, something we call a "common judgment," because that opinion has arisen within a particular group and has gained common currency among that group. In this manner people used to speak of a "commonwealth" to describe a group in which everyone together pursued their life's happiness. In the same way we speak about "by common consent," referring to something agreed upon within a particular group. The phrase "common purse" refers to sharing costs within a particular group. A "common pasture" means the pasture in which all the farmers belonging to a particular group are allowed to have their animals graze. To "provide common access" is to bring an issue within reach of the circle in which our language is understood. Here, then, when talking not about something belonging to everyone by nature, but about a good given from someone to the group known as humanity, our fathers spoke very correctly not about "gratia *universalis*" but about "gratia *communis*." "Universal favor" was a phrase preferred by their opponents. Given our intention to discuss this doctrine thoroughly, we had to investigate which title would be most proper, and at that point we thought we needed to adopt the title, *Common Grace*.

True enough, the word *common* may not be used as much any longer, but from the phrases mentioned above, it seems evident that our language today retains an understanding of the word *common* in the sense we have explained. If this is so, then it enhances language when in connection with such discussions that involve very refined distinctions, we resuscitate moribund expressions. One would have no right to do this if this meaning of the word *common* had fallen entirely into disuse. But that is not the case here, as a glance in the most authoritative dictionary will confirm.[2] Though we would not think to malign someone who chooses differently,

---

2. See, for instance, J. H. Van Dale, *Nieuw Woordenboek der Nederlandsche Taal* (The Hague: Nijhoff, Wijthoff, Thieme, 1872), 275, which provides a primary definition of "gemeen" as referring to something "belonging to more than one person."

we firmly think we have sound reasons for preferring the phrase common grace or "common favor."

We will continue using the word *grace* [*gratie*] in the sense of *favor*, despite the fact that in popular usage, grace [*genade*] is identified so exclusively as saving grace.[3] The word *grace* [or *reprieve*] is still the word used universally to describe a stay of execution. And since our expanded argument is discussing precisely that grace which stays the execution of Genesis 2:17, the phrase *common grace* seemed not improperly to express the very character of our topic.

Undoubtedly it would have been better to place this explanation at the beginning of our discussion, but at that point it seemed unnecessary for us to explain our choice of title. Now, however, since objections have arisen, we thought we should insert our added explanation here.

---

3. Kuyper's original sentence contrasted two Dutch words, *gratie* and *genade*, whose technical rendering should perhaps be "favor" (*gratie*) and "grace" (*genade*). His title for this series is *De Gemeene Gratie*, and would then need to be *Common Favor*, but that would in turn generate misunderstanding for English language readers. The point to remember throughout this series is that for Kuyper, common grace was never *saving* grace.

# BIBLIOGRAPHY

Abel, Carl. *Einleitung in ein Aegyptisch-Semitisch-Indoeuropaeisches Wurzelwörterbuch.* Leipzig: Wilhelm Friedrich, 1886.

Adalian, Rouben Paul. *Historical Dictionary of Armenia.* 2nd ed. Lanham, MD: Scarecrow, 2010.

Alighieri, Dante. *The Divine Comedy.* Translated by Henry Wadsworth Longfellow. Boston: Fields, Osgood, & Co., 1871.

Ames, William. *The Marrow of Sacred Divinity.* London: Griffin, 1639.

———. *Medulla Sacrae Theologiae.* Franeker: Balk, 1623.

Augustine. *The Confessions.* Translated by Maria Boulding. Hyde Park, NY: New City Press, 1997.

———. *On Genesis.* Translated by Edmund Hill. Edited by John E. Rotelle. Hyde Park, NY: New City Press, 2002.

Avramescu, Cătălin. *An Intellectual History of Cannibalism.* Translated by Alistair Ian Blyth. Princeton: Princeton University Press, 2011.

Ballor, Jordan J. *Covenant, Causality, and Law: A Study in the Theology of Wolfgang Musculus.* Göttingen: Vandenhoeck & Ruprecht, 2012.

Bavinck, Herman. *Reformed Dogmatics.* Translated by John Vriend. Edited by John Bolt. 4 vols. Grand Rapids: Baker, 2003–2008. Originally published as *Gereformeerde dogmatiek.* 4 vols. Kampen: J. H. Bos, 1895–1901.

———. *De Algemeene Genade, Rede bij de overdracht van het rectoraat aan de Theologische School te Kampen op 6 December 1894.* Kampen: Zalsman, 1894.

———. "Herman Bavinck's 'Common Grace.'" Translated by R. C. van Leeuwen. *Calvin Theological Journal* 24, no. 1 (1989): 35–65.

Bellarmine, Robert. *Opera omnia.* Vol. 4, *De gratia primi hominis.* Naples: Josephum Guiliano, 1858.

Benedetto, Robert, and Donald K. McKim, eds. *Historical Dictionary of the Reformed Churches*. 2nd ed. Lanham, MD: Scarecrow, 2010.

Bente, Friedrich. *Historical Introductions to the Symbolical Books of the Evangelical Lutheran Church*. St. Louis: Concordia, 1921.

Berkouwer, G. C. *Man: The Image of God*. Translated by Dirk W. Jellema. Grand Rapids: Eerdmans, 1962.

Blackburn, Simon. *The Oxford Dictionary of Philosophy*. 2nd rev. ed. New York: Oxford University Press, 2008.

*The Book of Concord: The Confessions of the Evangelical Lutheran Church*. Edited by Theodore G. Tappert. Philadelphia: Fortress, 1959.

à Brakel, Wilhelmus. *The Christian's Reasonable Service*. Translated by Bartel Elshout. Edited by Joel R. Beeke. Vol. 2. Grand Rapids: Reformation Heritage Books, 1992.

——. *Logikē latreia, dat is Redelijke godsdienst*. Vol. 1. Leiden: D. Donner, 1893.

Bratt, James D. *Abraham Kuyper: Modern Calvinist, Christian Democrat*. Grand Rapids: Eerdmans, 2013.

Bryant, Barry E. "Original Sin." In *The Oxford Handbook of Methodist Studies*, edited by William J. Abraham and James E. Kirby, 535–36. New York: Oxford University Press, 2009.

Calvin, John. *Calvin's Commentaries Series*. 45 vols. Edinburgh: Calvin Translation Society, 1844–56.

——. "Draft Ecclesiastical Ordinances." In *Calvin: Theological Treatises*. Translated and edited by J. K. S. Reid, 56–72. Philadelphia: Westminster, 1954.

——. *Institutes of the Christian Religion* (1559). Edited by John T. McNeill. Translated by Ford Lewis Battles. 2 vols. Philadelphia: Westminster, 1960.

——. *Ioannis Calvini Opera Quae Supersunt Omnia*. Edited by Guilielmus Baum, Eduardus Cunitz, and Eduardus Reuss. 59 vols. Corpus Reformatorum, 2nd ser., 29–87. Brunswick: Schwetschke, 1863–1900.

——. *Ordonnances Ecclésiastiques* (1541). In *Ioannis Calvini Opera Quae Supersunt Omnia*, vol. 10, no. 1. Edited by Guilielmus Baum, Eduardus Cunitz, and Eduardus Reuss, 15–30. Corpus Reformatorum, 2nd ser., 38, no. 1. Brunswick: Schwetschke, 1871.

Cremer, Hermann. *Biblico-theological Lexicon of New Testament Greek*. Translated by William Urwick. 4th ed. Edinburgh: T&T Clark, 1895.

Cunha, Burke A. "Influenza: Historical Aspects of Epidemics and Pandemics." *Infectious Disease Clinics of North America* 18, no. 1 (2004): 141–55.

Da Costa, Isaäc. *Da Costa's kompleete dichtwerken*. Edited by J. P. Hasebroek. The Hague: D. A. Thieme, 1876.

De Beer, Taco H., and Eliza Laurillard, eds. *Woordenschat, verklaring van woorden en uitdrukkingen*. The Hague: Haagsche Boekhandel, 1899.

Delitzsch, Franz. *System der biblischen Psychologie*. 2nd ed. Leipzig: Dörffling und Franke, 1861.

————. *A System of Biblical Psychology*. Translated by Robert Ernest Wallis. 1869. Repr., Grand Rapids: Baker, 1966.

Delumeau, Jean. *History of Paradise: The Garden of Eden in Myth and Tradition*. Translated by Matthew O'Connell. New York: Continuum, 1995.

Fairbairn, Patrick. *Hermeneutical Manual*. Philadelphia: Smith, English & Co., 1859.

————. *The Typology of Scripture*. 2 vols. Philadelphia: Daniels & Smith, 1852.

Fasseur, Cornelis. *The Politics of Colonial Exploitation: Java, the Dutch, and the Cultivation System*. Translated by R. E. Elson and Ary Kraal. Edited by R. E. Elson. Ithaca, NY: Southeast Asia Program Publications, 1994.

Garner, R. L. *Apes and Monkeys: Their Life and Language*. London: Ginn & Co., 1900.

Hadsund, Per. "The Tin-Mercury Mirror: Its Manufacturing Technique and Deterioration Process." *Studies in Conservation* 38, no. 1 (Feb 1993): 3–16.

Heppe, Heinrich. *Geschichte des Pietismus und der Mystik in der reformirten Kirche, namentlich der Niederlande*. Leiden: Brill, 1879.

*Het Boek der Psalmen, nevens de Gezangen bij de Hervormde Kerk van Nederland in Gebruik*. The Hague: Hendrik Christoffel Gutteling, 1773.

Herbermann, Charles G., Edward A. Pace, Condé B. Pallen, Thomas J. Shahan, and John J. Wynne, *eds. The Catholic Encyclopedia*. 15 vols. New York: Robert Appleton, 1907–12.

Hillerbrand, Hans J., ed. *The Oxford Encyclopedia of the Reformation*. 4 vols. New York: Oxford University Press, 1996.

Hoeksema, Herman. *The Protestant Reformed Churches in America: Their Origin, Early History and Doctrine*. Grand Rapids: First Protestant Reformed Church, 1936.

Hornblower, Simon, Antony Spawforth, and Esther Eidinow, eds. *The Oxford Classical Dictionary*. 4th ed. New York: Oxford University Press, 2012.

Hunter, David G. "Sexual Ethics." In *Augustine through the Ages: An Encyclopedia*, edited by Allan D. Fitzgerald, 327–28. Grand Rapids: Eerdmans, 1999.

Hulbert, Charles. "Instances of Human Longevity in Europe." In *Museum Europæum; or, Select Antiquities, Curiosities, Beauties, and Varieties, of Nature and Art in Europe*. Shrewsbury: C. Hulbert, 1825.

Izre'el, Shlomo. "Amarna Tablets." In *The Oxford Encyclopedia of Archaeology in the Near East*, edited by Eric M. Meyers, 1:86–87. New York: Oxford University Press, 1997.

*The Jewish Study Bible*. New York: Oxford University Press, 2004.

Jones, William. "Discourse III. Delivered February 2, 1786." In *Discourses Delivered before the Asiatic Society: And Miscellaneous Papers, on the Religion, Poetry, Literature, etc. of the Nations of India*, 1:20–37. 2 vols. London: Charles S. Arnold, 1824.

Junius, Franciscus. *The Mosaic Polity*. Translated by Todd M. Rester. Edited by Andrew M. McGinnis. Grand Rapids: CLP Academic, 2015.

———. *De Politae Mosis Observatione*. In *Opuscula Theologica Selecta,*, edited by Abraham Kuyper, 329–92. Amsterdam: Muller, 1882.

Keil, Johann Friedrich Karl, and Hebraist Franz Delitzsch. *Biblical Commentary on the Old Testament*. Translated by James Martin. Vol. 1. Edinburgh: T&T Clark, 1866.

King, L. W., ed. and trans. *The Letters and Inscriptions of Hammurabi*. 3 vols. London: Luzac, 1898–1900.

Kirchhoff, Karl-Heinz. "Münster." In *The Oxford Encyclopedia of the Reformation*, edited by Hans J. Hillerbrand, 3:97–98. New York: Oxford University Press, 1996.

Kuipers, Tjitze. *Abraham Kuyper: An Annotated Bibliography 1857–2010*. Translated by Clifford Anderson and Dagmare Houniet. Brill's Series in Church History 55. Leiden: Brill, 2011.

Kuyper, Abraham. *Abraham Kuyper: A Centennial Reader*. Edited by James D. Bratt. Grand Rapids: Eerdmans, 1998.

———. *De Engelen Gods*. Amsterdam: Höveker & Wormser, 1902.

———. *E Voto Dordraceno: Toelichting op den Heidelbergschen Catechismus*. 4 vols. Amsterdam: Wormser, 1892–95.

———. *Encyclopedia of Sacred Theology: Its Principles*. Translated by J. Hendrik de Vries. New York: Scribner's, 1898.

———. *Lectures on Calvinism*. Grand Rapids: Eerdmans, 1931.

———. *Om de oude Wereldzee*. 2 vols. Amsterdam: Van Holkema & Warendorf, 1907–8.

———. *Our Program: A Christian Political Manifesto*. Translated and edited by Harry Van Dyke. Bellingham, WA: Lexham Press, 2015.

———. "Pantheism's Destruction of Boundaries—Part I." Translated by J. Hendrik de Vries. *Methodist Review* 75 (July 1893).

———. *Particular Grace: A Defense of God's Sovereignty in Salvation*. Translated by Marvin Kamps. Grandville, MI: Reformed Free Publishing Association, 2001.

———. *The Revelation of St. John*. Translated by J. Hendrik De Vries. Grand Rapids: Eerdmans, 1935.

———. *Rooted and Grounded: The Church as Organism and Institution*. Translated by Nelson D. Kloosterman. Bellingham, WA: Lexham Press, 2015.

———. "Sphere Sovereignty." In *Abraham Kuyper: A Centennial Reader,* edited by James D. Bratt, 461–90. Grand Rapids: Eerdmans, 1998. Inaugural address at the founding of the Free University of Amsterdam, October 20, 1880.

———. *Wisdom & Wonder: Common Grace in Science and Art*. Edited by Jordan J. Ballor and Stephen J. Grabill. Translated by Nelson D. Kloosterman. Bellingham, WA: Lexham Press, 2015.

———. *The Work of the Holy Spirit*. Translated by Henri de Vries. Grand Rapids: Eerdmans, 1946.

Laudan, Rachel. "Neptunism and Plutonism." In *The Oxford Companion to the History of Modern Science*, edited by J. L. Heilbron, 571–72. New York: Oxford University Press, 2003.

Lee, Brian J. *Johannes Cocceius and the Exegetical Roots of Federal Theology: Reformation Developments in the Interpretation of Hebrews 7–10*. Göttingen: Vandenhoeck & Ruprecht, 2009.

Lombard, Peter. *The Sentences*. Translated by Giulio Silano. Vol. 2. Toronto: Pontifical Institute for Mediaeval Studies, 2008.

Lowance, Mason I., Jr. *The Language of Canaan: Metaphor and Symbol in New England from the Puritans to the Transcendentalists*. Cambridge, MA: Harvard University Press, 1980.

Luther, Martin. *Luther's Works*. 55 vols. American ed. Edited by Jaroslav Pelikan and Helmut T. Lehmann. Saint Louis: Concordia; Philadelphia: Fortress, 1955–86.

Lytle, S. "September 1792 Massacres." In *Historical Dictionary of the French Revolution, 1789–1799*, edited by Samuel F. Scott and Barry Rothaus, 2:891–97. Westport, CT: Greenwood, 1985.

Macauley Jackson, Samuel, ed. *The New Schaff-Herzog Encyclopedia of Religious Knowledge*. 13 vols. Grand Rapids: Baker, 1949–50. Originally published in 12 vols., 1908–12.

à Marck, Johannes. *Christianæ theologiæ medulla didactico-elenctica*. Amsterdam: Borstius, 1690.

Marshall, I. Howard, Alan Millard, J. I. Packer, and Donald J. Wiseman, eds. *New Bible Dictionary*. 3rd ed. Downers Grove, IL: IVP Academic, 1996.

McKinley, E. H. "Salvation Army, The." In *Dictionary of Christianity in America*, edited by Daniel G. Reid, Robert D. Linder, Bruce L. Shelley, and Harry S. Stout, 1043–44. Downers Grove, IL: InterVarsity, 1990.

Meyers, Eric M., ed. *The Oxford Encyclopedia of Archaeology in the Near East*. 5 vols. New York: Oxford University Press, 1997.

Motyer, J. A., and M. J. Selman, "Teraphim." In *New Bible Dictionary*, edited by I. Howard Marshall, Alan Millard, J. I. Packer, and Donald J. Wiseman, 1163–64. 3rd ed. Downers Grove, IL: IVP Academic, 1996.

Muller, Richard A. *Dictionary of Latin and Greek Theological Terms*. Grand Rapids: Baker, 1996.

———. *Post-Reformation Reformed Dogmatics*. 4 vols. Grand Rapids: Baker, 2003.

Newbigin, Lesslie. *Foolishness to the Greeks: The Gospel and Western Culture*. Grand Rapids: Eerdmans, 1986.

Newton, Michael. *Savage Girls and Wild Boys: A History of Feral Children*. New York: St. Martin's, 2003.

Noll, Mark A. *The Rise of Evangelicalism: The Age of Edwards, Whitefield, and the Wesleys*. Downers Grove, IL: IVP Academic, 2003.

Osborne, William. "Babel." In *Dictionary of the Old Testament: Pentateuch*, edited by T. Desmond Alexander and David W. Baker, 73–75. Downers Grove, IL: InterVarsity, 2003.

Osterhaven, M. Eugene. "Covenant." In *Encyclopedia of the Reformed Faith*, edited by Donald K. McKim, 84–87. Louisville: Westminster John Knox, 1992.

Parfitt, Tudor. *The Lost Tribes of Israel: The History of a Myth.* London: Weidenfeld & Nicolson, 2002.

Penslar, Derek J. *Shylock's Children: Economics and Jewish Identity in Modern Europe.* Berkeley: University of California Press, 2001.

Poe, Edgar Allan. "Peter Pendulum, The Business Man." *Burton's Gentleman's Magazine and American Monthly Review*, February 1840, 87–89.

Praamsma, Louis. *Let Christ Be King: Reflections on the Life and Times of Abraham Kuyper.* Jordan Station, ON: Paideia, 1985.

*The Psalms and Hymns: With the Catechism, Confession of Faith, and Canons, of the Synod of Dort, and Liturgy of the Reformed Protestant Dutch Church in North America.* Philadelphia: Mentz & Rouvoudt, 1847.

*Reformed Confessions of the 16th and 17th Centuries in English Translation.* Compiled by James T. Dennison Jr. 4 vols. Grand Rapids: Reformation Heritage Books, 2008–2014.

Reid, Daniel G., Robert D. Linder, Bruce L. Shelley, and Harry S. Stout, eds. *Dictionary of Christianity in America.* Downers Grove, IL: InterVarsity, 1990.

Rivet, André. *Opera theologica.* 3 vols. Rotterdam: Leers, 1651–1660.

Rutgers, F. L., ed. *Het Boek der Psalmen, nevens de Gezangen bij de Hervormed Kerk van Nederland.* Amsterdam: J. Brandt, 1865.

Schaff, Philip. *History of the Christian Church.* 3rd rev. ed. 8 vols. New York: Charles Scribner's Sons, 1910.

Scott, Samuel F., and Barry Rothaus, eds. *Historical Dictionary of the French Revolution, 1789–1799.* 2 vols. Westport, CT: Greenwood Press, 1985.

Steffens, Nicholas M. *Christianity as a Remedial Scheme.* Dubuque, IA: J. J. Reed, 1896.

———. "Het Christendom als herschepping." *De Heraut* 977, September 13, 1896, 1–3.

Ten Kate, Lambert. *Aenleiding tot de kennisse van het verhevene deel der Nederduitsche sprake.* 2 vols. Amsterdam: Rudolph en Gerard Wetstein, 1723.

Tuke, D. Hack. *A Dictionary of Psychological Medicine.* Philadelphia: P. Blakiston, 1892.

Ueberweg, Friedrich. *System of Logic and Logical Doctrines.* Translated by Thomas M. Lindsay. London: Longmans, Green, and Co., 1871

Van Asselt, Willem J. "Cocceius, Johannes." In *Dictionary of Major Biblical Interpreters*, edited by Donald K. McKim, 316–17. Downers Grove, IL: InterVarsity, 2007.

————. *The Federal Theology of Johannes Cocceius (1603-1669)*. Leiden: Brill, 2001.

Van Dale, J. H. *Nieuw Woordenboek der Nederlandsche Taal*. The Hague: Nijhoff, Wijthoff, Thieme, 1872.

Van den Bergh, Willem. *Calvijn over het genadeverbond*. The Hague: W. A. Beschoor, 1879.

Van der Pijl, Rudolph. *English Phraseology; or Dictionary of English Phrases and Proverbs*. The Hague: Johannes Allart, 1816.

Van Mastricht, Petrus. *Theoretico-practica Theologia*. Vol. 8. Amsterdam: Societatis, 1715.

Vos, Geerhardus. "The Doctrine of the Covenant in Reformed Theology." In *Redemptive History and Biblical Interpretation: The Shorter Writings of Geerhardus Vos*, edited by Richard B. Gaffin Jr., 234-67. Phillipsburg, NJ: Presbyterian and Reformed, 1980.

"Zending onder de Joden." *De Heraut* 957, April 26, 1896, 2.

Zuidema, S. U. "Common Grace and Christian Action in Abraham Kuyper." In *Communication and Confrontation: A Philosophical Appraisal and Critique of Modern Society and Contemporary Thought*, 52-105. Kampen: Kok, 1972.

# ABOUT ABRAHAM KUYPER (1837–1920)

Abraham Kuyper's life began in the small Dutch village of Maassluis on October 29, 1837. During his first pastorate, he developed a deep devotion to Jesus Christ and a strong commitment to Reformed theology that profoundly influenced his later careers. He labored tirelessly, publishing two newspapers, leading a reform movement out of the state church, founding the Free University of Amsterdam, and serving as prime minister of the Netherlands. He died on November 8, 1920, after relentlessly endeavoring to integrate his faith and life. Kuyper's emphasis on worldview formation has had a transforming influence upon evangelicalism, both through the diaspora of the Dutch Reformed churches, and those they have inspired.

In the mid-nineteenth-century Dutch political arena, the increasing sympathy for the "No God, no master!" dictum of the French Revolution greatly concerned Kuyper. To desire freedom from an oppressive government or heretical religion was one thing, but to eradicate religion from politics as spheres of mutual influence was, for Kuyper, unthinkable. Because man is sinful, he reasoned, a state that derives its power from men cannot avoid the vices of fallen human impulses. True limited government flourishes best when people recognize their sinful condition and acknowledge God's divine authority. In Kuyper's words, "The sovereignty of the state as the power that protects the individual and that defines the mutual relationships among the visible spheres, rises high above them by its right to command and compel. But within these spheres ... another authority rules, an authority that descends directly from God apart from the state. This authority the state does not confer but acknowledges."

# ABOUT THE CONTRIBUTORS

**Jordan J. Ballor** (Dr. theol., University of Zurich; Ph.D. Calvin Theological Seminary) is a research fellow at the Acton Institute for the Study of Religion & Liberty, where he also serves as executive editor of the *Journal of Markets & Morality*. He is the author of books including *Covenant, Causality, and Law: A Study in the Theology of Wolfgang Musculus* (Vandenhoeck & Ruprecht) and *Ecumenical Babel: Confusing Economic Ideology and the Church's Social Witness* (Christian's Library Press), as well as editor or co-editor of numerous works, including *Church and School in Early Modern Protestantism* (Brill) and *Law and Religion: The Legal Teachings of the Catholic and Protestant Reformations* (Vandenhoeck & Ruprecht). In addition to working as a volume editor on *Common Grace*, he is also a general editor of the Abraham Kuyper Collected Works in Public Theology.

**Stephen J. Grabill** (Ph.D., Calvin Theological Seminary) is director of programs as well as senior research scholar in theology at Acton Institute for the Study of Religion & Liberty. He is author of *Rediscovering the Natural Law in Reformed Theological Ethics* (Eerdmans) and general editor of the *NIV Stewardship Study Bible* (Zondervan).

**Nelson D. Kloosterman** (Th.D., Theological University of the Reformed Churches [Liberated], Kampen, the Netherlands) is ethics consultant and executive director of Worldview Resources International, a service organization whose mission is to produce and provide resources designed to assist in understanding and applying a Christian worldview to responsible living in a global culture. He has served as minister and professor for more than thirty years and has translated dozens of works on Reformed theology and ethics.

**Ed M. van der Maas** (Th.M., Dallas Theological Seminary) is an editor and translator. Among his translations are several volumes of the *Korte Verklaring* (*Bible Student's Commentary*) and *Concise Reformed Dogmatics* (Van Genderen and Velema). Ed has worked for several Dutch publishers and was also the associate editor for the *New International Dictionary of Pentecostal and Charismatic Movements*. Until his retirement he was senior editor at HarperCollins Christian Publishers/Zondervan in Grand Rapids, MI. A native of the Netherlands, Ed lived in the United States for more than forty years before returning to his European base.

**Richard J. Mouw** (Ph.D., University of Chicago) currently serves as president emeritus and professor of faith and public life at Fuller Theological Seminary. A philosopher, scholar, and author, prior to his two decades as president he served as provost, senior vice president, and professor of Christian philosophy and ethics at Fuller Theological Seminary. He has also served as professor of philosophy at Calvin College in Grand Rapids, MI, in addition to his work as a visiting professor at the VU University Amsterdam.

# SUBJECT/AUTHOR INDEX

# SCRIPTURE INDEX

## Old Testament

## New Testament